Public Finance
and the American Economy

Second Edition

The Addison-Wesley Series in Economics

Public Finance and the American Economy

SECOND EDITION

NEIL BRUCE

University of Washington

Addison
Wesley

Boston San Francisco New York
London Toronto Sydney Tokyo Singapore Madrid
Mexico City Munich Paris Cape Town Hong Kong Montreal

Publisher: Frank Ruggirello
Executive Editor: Denise Clinton
Acquisitions Editor: Victoria Warneck
Senior Project Manager: Mary Clare McEwing
Supplements Editor: Meredith Gertz
Assistant Editor: Roxanne Hoch
Media Producer: Melissa Honig
Marketing Manager: Adrienne D'Ambrosio
Managing Editor: James Rigney
Production Supervisor: Katherine Watson
Project Coordination and Composition: Electronic Publishing Services Inc, N.Y.C.
Production Assistant: Andrea Basso
Manufacturing Buyer: Hugh Crawford
Design/Art Direction: Regina Hagen
Text Designer: Electronic Publishing Services Inc, N.Y.C.
Cover Designer: Joyce Cosentino
Cover Photo: © 2001 PhotoDisc, Inc., and AWL

Library of Congress Cataloging-in-Publication Data
Bruce, Neil.
    Public finance and the American economy / Neil Bruce.—2nd ed.
        p.   cm.
    Includes bibliographical references and index.
    ISBN 0-321-07815-2
      1. Finance, Public—United States. 2. Local finance—United States. 3. Government
spending policy—United States. 4. Fiscal policy—United States. 5. Entitlement
spending—United States. 6. Debts, Public—United States. 7. United States—Economic
policy—1993- I. Title.
HJ257.2 .B78 2001
336.73—dc21   00-059402

ISBN 0-321- 07815-2

  4 5 6 7 8 9 10—CRW—05

BRIEF CONTENTS

CONTENTS

PART FOUR   Government Transfer Programs   193

CHAPTER 7   Government and the Distribution of Income   195

CHAPTER 8   Spending on Programs to Alleviate Poverty   224

PART SEVEN   **State and Local Public Finance   547**

CHAPTER 18   **Spending by State and Local Governments   549**

PREFACE

Revising a textbook is not unlike renovating your home. Certainly, the motives are the same. You want to bring it up to date and add new features, remove things you don't like, develop a new appearance and impression, and improve functionality, flow, and continuity. Of course, you also want to make the final product more attractive to potential buyers. Added to this is a conflicting desire to maintain the integrity of the original structure as well as to preserve the tried, true, and familiar. The main difference, at least in the case of a public finance textbook, is sheer necessity. People can choose whether or not to renovate their homes, but in the fast-changing world of public finance, textbook material becomes obsolete in short order. It is a matter of revise or demise. One example is the federal budget. When I wrote the first edition, unified budget deficits of over $100 billion had been the norm for 20 years. In the second edition, it was necessary to address the issue of actual and projected surpluses large enough to pay off the entire national debt within a decade.

Revision and renovation have some other things in common. At the planning stage, ambition runs wild and no change seems too big. Later, reality sets in and you begin to wonder if, perhaps, a certain room (or chapter) does not need a complete makeover. Midway through the renovation, you are overwhelmed by the disarray and wish you had left things the way they were, or could start afresh with a whole new blueprint. You have nagging doubts about whether the object of your attention will ever be whole again, and, if it is, whether the patchwork will show. I hope that all traces of construction are gone and that instructors familiar with the first edition will find this not just a different book, but a better one.

NEW FEATURES IN THE SECOND EDITION

Authors sometimes experience a flicker of guilt in preparing a new edition. Was this new edition really needed, or is it just a marketing ploy? I have no such feelings. As a remodel, the second edition of *Public Finance and the American Economy* is an ambitious undertaking. The changes are too many to enumerate, so I will simply highlight the main ones.

Brand New Chapters

In addition to other changes, there are two whole new chapters. A new Chapter 7 contains a systematic description of the theory of government redistribution and a complete analysis of the different reasons for government transfer programs. There is also new information on the existing distribution of income and wealth, including comparisons across countries. The chapter explains in more detail than most the benefits and costs of redistribution and the equity-efficiency trade-off.

Chapter 17, another new chapter, outlines the main options for federal tax reform, including the national retail sales tax and other reform proposals in the news, such as the flat tax and the consumed-income tax. In each case, the efficiency, equity, and administrative implications of the reforms are identified and analyzed. The cases for and against taxing consumption rather than income are fully discussed, along with the different methods of taxing consumption. Reforms that would shift the tax system toward taxing wealth or taxing pollution are also described and analyzed.

New Material Added in Many Chapters

Many chapters have been changed and rewritten to make them more interesting and exciting for students to learn and instructors to teach. For example, Chapter 3 on public goods now includes the theory of privately-provided public goods and a discussion of the use of electronic tolls to reduce road congestion. Chapter 4 on externalities looks at the U.S. experience with tradeable permits in sulfur dioxide and other pollutants. Chapter 8 on the antipoverty programs describes the recent welfare reforms in depth and has an expanded section on new methods of measuring poverty. Chapter 9 on Social Security and Medicare has extensive coverage of the potential reforms to these programs, including privatization. The chapter also describes the experience of other countries that have tried different reforms.

Chapter 10 uses the topical issue of tobacco taxes to explain the basic theory of an excise tax, and Chapter 11 contains a diagrammatic explication of Harberger's general equilibrium model of tax incidence. Chapter 12 features a new treatment of the issue of tax fairness and also uses the methods of tax policy analysis to explain the double dividend of environmental taxes. In Chapter 13, the "marriage tax" debate receives additional coverage. The chapter also includes new material on the problems of measuring income for tax purposes. A summary of new methods and research on the effects of income taxes on the labor supply is found in Chapter 14. The difficult material on business income taxation in Chapter 15 has been revised extensively to make it more interesting for students to read and easier for them to understand. The chapter also has a new section on "corporate welfare."

Economic events forced me to make extensive changes to Chapter 16 on federal budget surpluses and deficits. The causes and effects of current and projected federal budget surpluses are explained in detail, and the chapter examines the relationship between the surplus and the problem of "saving" the Social Security program. The chapters on state and local public finance have been consolidated into a single section for greater continuity. Chapter 18 on state and local expenditures has expanded coverage of spending on education, including research on school voucher experiments. Chapter 19 discusses the latest developments in state and local taxation, with new material on the hot topic of Internet taxation.

New Internet Sources and Exercises

What a difference three years make; for the first edition, I spent countless hours in the basement of the library, looking up data in obscure and hard-to-find documents. In preparing the second edition, I spent numerous hours surfing the Internet for the most current data and interesting issues to include. In the process, I discovered that the internet is a terrific research tool for students of public finance. At many sites, data on government spending and taxes are readily and freely available, sometimes in spreadsheet form. To name a few, at different sites can be found the entire Federal Budget, the *Statistical Abstract of the United States,* the *Green Book on Entitlements,* and the statistical appendix to the *Economic Report of the President.* The Internet is also a great place to find government policy documents and studies, as well as analysis by many "think tanks" with an interest in government policy.

Because I want to share with my readers the dozens of useful sites I located, I have added copious references to Internet sites within each chapter. Also, to give students practice in using the Internet as a research tool, I have designed *Internet Exercises* for each chapter. Each exercise directs the student to an interesting and useful site, and asks him or her to answer questions or analyze a policy issue based on the information found there. In some cases, the student can actually perform government policy simulations, such as changing the tax system from an income tax to a sales tax.

New Case Studies

Engaging the student in learning was a major goal of the first edition. I have tried to enhance participatory learning in this edition by adding case studies to each chapter. In each chapter, two sections titled "A Case in Point" apply the material learned in the chapter to a real-world problem. Each case is followed by questions designed to provoke students into thinking more deeply about the issue and to generate informed classroom discussion. Many cases are based on all-new material. In Chapter 1, a case examines the government's balance sheet and the question of government solvency, and in Chapter 2 a case on the deadweight loss of Christmas illustrates the concept of deadweight loss. Chapter 4 presents a case study on tradable pollution permits so the student can learn how these markets work in practice. Coalition busting is the subject of a case in Chapter 6, which explores the implications of nontransitive majority voting for legislative decision making. In Chapter 7, a case on measuring the marginal cost of redistribution is used to explain the equity-efficiency trade-off. A case in Chapter 8 requires the student to estimate the cost of expanding Medicaid to cover everyone without health insurance, and Chile's privatized social security system and Canada's single-payer health system are the subjects of cases in Chapter 9. The "case of the double dividend" helps students understand the material they learned in Chapter 12, and a case in Chapter 17 estimates the rate of tax needed if the federal government were to adopt a national retail sales tax. In other cases, I have expanded on examples used successfully in the first edition.

CONTENT AND ORGANIZATION

Despite the many changes in the second edition, I have endeavored to preserve the main content and organization of the first edition. The book is organized traditionally, with the chapters divided equally between spending programs and revenue policies. Although I have followed the usual approach of presenting the spending topics before the tax topics, the chapters are written so that instructors who prefer to cover taxation first can do so without loss in continuity. As in the first edition, Part One provides an overview of the basic facts about government spending and revenue, and Part Two covers the theory of market failure, public goods, and externalities. One pedagogical change is that Part Two now focuses exclusively on government policies that change the allocation of resources and the impact of these policies on economic efficiency. As in the first edition, Part Three covers two aspects of the government decision-making process—public choice and benefit-cost analysis. Issues and policies concerning equity and the distribution of income have been consolidated in Part Four to provide a more coherent treatment. Of course, efficiency and equity concerns are typically entwined in the real world of policy, but my experience has been that the systematic treatment of these different issues aids student learning and understanding. I have taken special effort, however, to explain and illustrate that efficiency and equity are often in conflict, which often causes disagreement about the best policies to choose.

Part Five introduces the basic theory of taxation, including the effects of taxes on markets, the incidence of the tax burden, and the methods for evaluating different tax systems. Part Six provides a comprehensive and completely up-to-date examination of the federal income tax system and its effects on the economy. In another organizational change, I bowed to convention and collected chapters on state and local public finance in Part Seven. In the first edition, the spending policies of state and local governments were covered in the first half of the book along with the other spending topics. This arrangement emphasized my belief that the important subject of state and local government should not be relegated to the "back of the book." I hope that I have maintained my commitment to a greater emphasis on the state and local sector with two strong chapters, as compared with the single chapter devoted to the topic in other public finance textbooks.

In writing the first edition, I was guided by my belief that the subject of public finance is essential for interpreting and understanding the parade of fiscal events and proposals we encounter in the news practically every day. This is no less true in the second edition. For this reason, *Public Finance and the American Economy* stresses policy issues more emphatically than do many other public finance textbooks. At the same time, understanding these issues requires the appropriate background in economic methods. This text is written for students who have taken intermediate microeconomics, or at least a solid principles course that equips them with the requisite analytical tools, such as the indifference curve diagram. Nonetheless, the book should be accessible to students who have more limited backgrounds, provided that they are willing to do some preparation. I have used intuitive and diagrammatic explanations wherever possible, often coupled with numerical examples. More technically demanding topics, such as the private provision of public goods and the Harberger model of tax incidence, can be skipped without loss in continuity. The main Appendix can be used to review microeconomic theory, as deemed necessary.

I have attempted to write a book that students will enjoy and have taken every opportunity to pique their interest. The "Case in Point" sections are good starting points for generating classroom discussion on current policy questions, something that I have found highly productive in teaching public finance. The Instructor's Manual provides further help in using the case studies in a classroom context. Many of the problems at the end of the chapters are also designed with classroom discussion in mind, and the Instructor's Manual is again useful in developing these questions for classroom discussion.

Two problems that all public finance instructors face are the provisional nature of the results of empirical research and the highly politicized nature of many of the topics we teach. Policy advocates, of course, seem far more confident than economists in their knowledge of the way things are. In discussing the debatable empirical research in public finance, I attempt to make judgments without being dogmatic. I present empirical results that I believe to be relatively robust as if they are facts, but point out the uncertainties and defects in research that I find more problematic. Similarly, I avoid promoting my own political viewpoint, but I have not avoided presenting the political arguments of others. I try to present the best arguments the two sides have to offer in any debate and leave it to instructors and students to decide which argument has greater merit.

SUPPLEMENTARY MATERIALS

An Instructor's Manual is available to adopters of the text. It contains chapter summaries, suggestions for organizing lectures and classroom discussions based on examples from the book, answers to the end-of-chapter discussion questions, and questions and problems suitable for problem sets, quizzes, and tests. The material in the Instructor's Manual draws on my experience in teaching public finance for more than 20 years and is designed to be helpful to both more and less experienced instructors. This manual is available on the text's Web site.

The companion web site features content keyed to chapters in the text. The site contains new questions and answers, discussion of public finance issues in the news, suggestions for reading, and links to data and information sites relevant to public finance. Visit the site at http://www.awl.com/bruce.

ACKNOWLEDGMENTS

Once again, I have been fortunate to receive comments, suggestions, and help from several sources. I would like to thank the reviewers of the second edition, who made wonderful suggestions that improved the book immeasurably. They were particularly adept at picking up errors, omissions, and inconsistencies. Perhaps their biggest help was in keeping me honest when I was tempted to take shortcuts. I appreciate it now much more than I did at the time!

Barbara Burnell, The College of Wooster
Ismail Ghazalah, Ohio University
Jonathan Hamilton, University of Florida
Randall Holcombe, Florida State University
Renee Irvin, University of Nebraska, Omaha
Kate Krause, University of New Mexico
Genevieve Peters, University of California, San Diego
Todd Sandler, Iowa State University
Benjamin Scafidi, Georgia State University
Catherine Schneider, Boston College
Michael Wolkoff, University of Rochester

I would also like to thank the reviewers of the first edition. Without their earlier input, there probably would never have been a second edition.

Jim Alm, University of Colorado, Boulder
Gary Anderson, California State University, Northridge
John H. Beck, Gonzaga University
Robert A. Blewett, St. Lawrence University
Robert T. Bray, California State Polytechnical University, Pomona
Paul Farnham, Georgia State University
Robert Fischer, California State University, Chico
Mary N. Gade, Oklahoma State University
Gary M. Galles, Pepperdine University
Fred Giertz, University of Illinois, Urbana
Timothy Gronberg, Texas A&M
Jonathan Hamilton, University of Florida
Charles Hawkins, Lamar University
Thomas Ireland, University of Missouri, St. Louis
Alan Kessler, Providence College
David Kiefer, University of Utah
Bruce R. Kingma, State University of New York, Albany
Gary D. Lemon, De Pauw University
Stephen E. Lile, Western Kentucky University
Jerry Miner, Syracuse University
Susan Parks, University of Wisconsin, Whitewater
George Plesko, Northeastern University
Thomas Pogue, University of Iowa
Esther Redmount, Colorado College

Paul Rothstein, Washington University
Jeffrey Rubin, Rutgers University
Daniel G. Rupp, Fort Hays State University
Bernard Saffran, Swarthmore College
Kathleen Segerson, University of Connecticut
Wendell Sweetser, Marshall University
David Terkla, University of Massachusetts, Boston
Richard Tresch, Boston College
Nancy White, Bucknell University
Nancy Williams, Loyola College

As always, my colleagues at the University of Washington were helpful and supportive. Laurent Martin, in particular, read several of the revised chapters and made many excellent suggestions. Thanks also to Robert Halvorsen, Shelly Lundberg, and Cindy Madden, who gave suggestions for the first edition, and Gregory Ellis of Seattle University who did the same for the second edition. Thanks to my students who were not shy about letting me know what they liked and didn't like in the first edition.

I would like to take this opportunity to rave about the folks I worked with at Addison Wesley Longman. Whenever authors complain about their publishers, I suggest they publish with Addison Wesley. It is a pleasure to work with their helpful and friendly staff including Joyce Cosentino, who developed the eye-catching cover for this edition, and Jim Rigney and Katy Watson, the in-house production representatives. Thanks are also due to Scott Hitchcock and the production staff at Electronic Publishing Services, Inc. I want to express a special debt of gratitude to Mary Clare McEwing at Addison Wesley for her advice, suggestions, and, most of all, her timely encouragement when I most needed it. I would also like to acknowledge her amazing patience, which I am sure I tried severely as I missed deadline after deadline. Mary Clare, you are the best.

Finally, as always, none of the aforementioned people is responsible for any errors, omissions, and shortcomings that remain.

PART ONE

Introduction

Chapter 1 provides an overview of how governments in the United States spend the taxpayer's money and how they collect the revenue they need to carry out these functions. Our objective in this chapter is to establish a mental "picture" of the government sector: what government is, how big the different levels of government are, how much they spend and collect in taxes overall, the composition of government spending, and the composition of tax revenue. Such a picture cannot be established by simply memorizing the dollar numbers. Billions of dollars are not amounts that most of us have everyday experience with, and the numbers change every year anyway. For this reason we focus on *comparative* amounts, usually expressed as percentages. That is, we seek to answer questions such as: How much is government spending compared with (as a percentage of) Gross Domestic Product, the standard measure of the size of the economy? What percentage of total government spending is spent by the federal government versus the state and local governments? What percentage of federal spending is for Social Security? What percentage of total tax revenue is collected in the form of income taxes?

How do these percentages compare with those of other countries or the United States in the past?

Chapter 1 also explains the government budget process. Some types of government spending, called discretionary spending, require annual appropriation bills. Other types, called entitlement spending, do not. In addition the government can "spend" money in ways that are not transparent in the budget, including guaranteed loans, tax expenditures, and regulations and mandates. If the government spends less than it collects in revenue, the government has a budget surplus. The chapter explains how the government surplus is measured and how the excess funds are used.

1 | Sizing Up the Government

Consider just part of a day in the life of a typical American family. The family awakens at 6:30 A.M. and showers with water provided by the city utility and heated by electricity from a government-built hydroelectric facility. Breakfast includes food products inspected by the Department of Agriculture and cooked on a stove meeting standards set by the Consumer Product Safety Commission. While eating breakfast, one of the parents scans the reports from the stock markets, regulated by the Securities and Exchange Commission. The children go to a public school where, if the family were poor enough, they would get breakfast and lunch courtesy of the National School Lunch and Breakfast Programs. Fortunately, our typical family is not poor. Both parents have good jobs, thanks in part to their college degrees from the state university.

One parent is late for the city bus today, so she drives to work on the city streets. Her car satisfies government fleet mileage standards and has government-mandated seat belts required by the National Highway Traffic Safety Administration and emissions controls required by the Clean Air Act. On the way to the expressway, she tunes in National Public Radio for the news. But first she must stop for gas, which is reformulated to reduce pollution by government fiat, and then at the bank to withdraw money from her federally insured bank account.

The other parent arrives at his place of employment, inspected for safety by the Occupational Safety and Health Administration, just in time for another meeting on the new pharmaceutical product developed by the company. The firm has been waiting over a year for approval by the Food and Drug Administration. After lunch, he is scheduled to fly to Washington, on a plane inspected according to standards set by the Federal Aviation Authority. On the way to the government-run airport, he glances at the clock on the city hall. He has worked nearly three hours and has just started to work for himself today. Three hours of his earnings are needed just to pay the taxes on his daily income. The sight of city hall reminds him that he must see about a permit for that new addition to his home....

As this vignette indicates, the impact of government on the life of a typical family is both pervasive and important. Although we take many government functions and services for granted, our lives would be much different if the government were suddenly to shut down. In fact, when the federal government shut down for a few weeks in 1996 because of the budget impasse, relatively few services were stopped because "essential" services were continued. Still, the inconvenience of the stoppage was enough that voters' anger soon caused the politicians to find a solution to the budget impasse.

Public finance, also known as **public economics,** is the study of how the government carries out its functions through spending and regulatory programs, and the tax policies the government uses to raise the revenue it needs to finance its programs. Because it is a field of economics, public finance utilizes the theories and methods of this discipline to examine and explain the effects of government programs and policies on the national economy. These include the effects of government-provided goods and services, such as national defense and schools; government transfer programs, such as Social Security and welfare; government regulations, such as environmental and safety regulation; and government revenue policies, such as the income tax and sales tax systems.

WHAT IS THE GOVERNMENT?

Like every major industrial country, the United States has a **mixed economy.** In a mixed economy, decisions about which goods and services are produced, and how the income needed to purchase them is distributed across the population, are made by both the private (market) sector and the public (government) sector. For example, consumers in the private sector decide how to spend their incomes on goods like cars, food, and clothing, whereas private businesses determine the amounts of different goods and services to produce and how to produce them. Governments decide how to spend public funds on goods like national defense, schools, and space stations and how to collect the tax revenue needed to finance government spending.

Like the national economy, the government economy is complex, multifaceted, and pluralistic. In addition to the federal government and the 50 state governments, there are more than 87,500 city, county, and district governments. There are also scores of government agencies, commissions, and corporations with alphabet soup names like NASA, FTC, and FDIC. In 1999, all governments combined employed over 20 million people (not counting 1.4 million military personnel), or about 15% of the employed nonfarm, civilian labor force. The occupations of government employees range from air traffic controllers at the nation's airports to zoologists at the nation's zoos.

What distinguishes government institutions from private ones? In some cases, such as a state-run research university and a private university, public and private institutions seem scarcely different. In general, government differs from private institutions in the following ways:

> ■ *Government has coercive power.* Governments can force people to do things, unlike private institutions that must rely on voluntary arrangements. The most important exercise of the government's coercive power is its power to tax the population to finance its programs. Unlike a private company, which can only entice us to buy its products, the government can force us to pay for schools, roads, and national defense. The government's coercive power is also apparent in its regulatory activities. Because of the dangers of coercive power, the government is subject to constitutional and electoral constraints.

▓ ***The main decision makers in government are popularly elected.*** Government decisions on spending, regulating, and taxing are made by politicians who are elected by the adult population or by government officials who are appointed by the politicians. By contrast, the chief executive officer of a private company is typically chosen by its board of directors. Even where decision makers are elected in the private sector, the voters are from a relatively small interest group.

▓ ***Government is not run for profit.*** Although some private firms are not for profit, the objective of most private businesses is to maximize profit. Profit, which is the surplus of revenue over cost, is not the objective of government. One difficulty in analyzing government is identifying exactly what its objective is. Also, government may not have a single objective. In some cases we will find it useful to assume that the objective of government is the welfare of the society, or *social welfare*. In many cases, we assume that the objectives of government are the private objectives of the politicians or the voters who elect them.

▓ ***Government has an obligation to serve all members of society.*** Since government is of the people and for the people, it has an obligation to serve everyone in its jurisdiction. Government must be impartial. One reason the government often involves so much red tape is to ensure that it does not treat certain groups better than others. Although private firms cannot overtly discriminate against certain groups, they are under less obligation to be impartial. Private firms care mostly about their shareholders. For instance, if they do not find it profitable to serve consumers in a particular community or region, they will not do it. In contrast, the U.S. Postal Service has an obligation to deliver mail everywhere in the country.

THE SIZE AND GROWTH OF GOVERNMENT

In 1999, the combined spending of the federal, state, and local levels of government in the United States amounted to $2620 billion on the National Income and Product Accounts (NIPA) basis.[1] The NIPA basis zeros out all intergovernmental financial flows because they simply move cash from one pocket of the government to another. The NIPA also measures government spending on an accrual rather than a cash flow basis, although this has a relatively minor impact on the amount recorded at the present time.

"Big government" is a common enough expression, but most of us find it difficult to imagine how big government is because "billions of dollars," the units in which government spending is measured, are not units that we encounter in our own lives. One way to appreciate the size of the U.S. government is to compare it with something else. For one thing, the $2620 billion spent by governments in the United States in 1999 is more than the entire gross domestic product (GDP) of

---

[1]This number is somewhat smaller than the dollar amount spent according to government financial records, because the financial records include amounts spent by one government that are received by another level of government or by a government agency or trust fund like the Social Security trust fund.

Germany, the world's third-largest national economy. GDP is the total value of final goods and services produced in an economy. In other words, governments in the United States spend enough to purchase the entire output of final goods and services produced by 40 million German workers.

Of course, one reason government spending in the United States is so large is the colossal size of the economy, so government spending is best compared with the nation's GDP. The GDP of the United States in 1999 was $9250 billion; thus government spending amounted to 28 percent of this GDP.[2]

While governments spending is about 28% of the country's GDP, this does *not* mean that they produce 28% of the GDP. In fact, the GDP of the government sector in the United States is quite small—less than 11 percent of the total GDP, or about $1020 billion. This amount includes goods and services produced by the government such as education, police and fire protection, and national defense. Even then, many of the goods and services purchased by the government are produced by private commercial firms. For example, the government provides national defense, but most defense hardware, such as Seawolf submarines and B2 bombers, is produced for the government by private firms.

Most government spending, about $1600 billion, is transfer spending. With transfer spending, the government gives money, like Social Security benefits, to people who then spend it on their own consumption. With transfer spending, the government does not control the use of economic resources. Control remains in the private sector, and the government simply redistributes the command over purchasing power from one group of people to another.

In other words, the statement that governments in the United States spend an amount equal to one-third of the GDP is simply a ratio that measures the size of one thing in terms of another. It is a crude but readily obtained measure of the importance of government in the economy. Measuring government spending relative to GDP is not fully informative, however. What we'd really like to know is whether a government that spends such an amount is considered big or small. To do this, we can compare the ratio of government spending to GDP in the United States with that in other countries and with the United States in other years.

Government Spending in Other Countries

Given the size of government spending in the United States, it is surprising to discover that some people think of the United States as a "small-government" economy. The reason is shown in Figure 1.1, which shows government spending as a percentage of GDP for the world's seven largest economies. Among these, the United States has the lowest ratio of government spending to GDP. The average for all seven countries is about 43.5 percent of GDP, which is nearly 12 percentage points greater than that of the United States. Relative to GDP, spending by government in the United States is among the lowest in the industrialized world. When we broaden our scope beyond the "big seven" economies, we find even

---

[2]GDP is now the preferred measure of the size of the economy. Earlier, a slightly different measure, gross national product—which subtracts from GDP incomes paid to foreigners and includes incomes of Americans earned abroad—was commonly used. In the United States, GDP and GNP are almost the same.

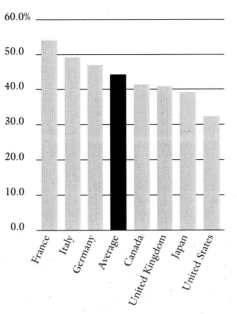

Figure 1.1
Government Spending as Percent of GDP in Selected Countries, 1999 (est.)
Compared with most other industrial countries, government spending as a percentage of GDP is lower in the United States.
Source: OECD, 1999. *Economic Outlook* #65, June 1998.

greater variation in the ratio of government spending to GDP. In Sweden, government spending is over 60% of GDP; in Turkey, government spending is only about 24% of GDP.

Although Figure 1.1 suggests the relative importance of government in different countries, we must be careful in interpreting it. For one thing, as mentioned, there are different types of government spending, and they are not comparable in terms of the extent of government intervention in the economy. For instance, suppose that government spending is a third of GDP in two countries, but in one country the government spends everything on transfer payments to persons, while in the other the government spends everything on military goods. In the first country, the government redistributes purchasing power but leaves decisions about the allocation of resources in the hands of private individuals; all of GDP is used for private consumption and investment. In the second country, the government reallocates a sizable fraction of the economy's resources away from satisfying private needs and uses them to purchase goods and services that individuals would not purchase for themselves.

Another reason the ratio of government spending to GDP is an inadequate measure of government intervention in an economy is that the government can interfere in an economy in ways that do not show up as budgeted spending. We discuss some of these ways later in this chapter.

The Growth of Government

As a percentage of GDP, spending by all governments in the United States was relatively stable—between 32 and 34%—between 1975 and 1995. Since 1995, it has declined to 28%. Over the twentieth century as a whole, government spending has grown more rapidly than the economy, and similar trends are found in all of the major industrial economies. Figure 1.2 plots government spending in the United

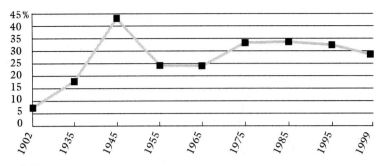

Figure 1.2

Government Spending (All Levels) as Percent of GDP
Over the twentieth century, combined government spending in the United States has risen as a percentage of GDP. Since 1975, government spending as a percentage of GDP has remained relatively constant, although it has declined in the past five years.
Source: Economic Report of the President, various years.

States as a percentage of GDP. At the beginning of this century, government spending was only about 7% of the country's national product; it grew to one-third of GDP by the early 1970s. During World War II, the most expensive conflict in American history, government spending temporarily approached half of GDP.

Several points about the growth in government are shown in Figure 1.2. First, the most rapid growth in the federal government occurred between 1935 and 1945, largely because of military spending during World War II. Second, from 1945 to 1955, government spending fell as a percentage of GDP, but it did not fall to prewar levels. After 1960, government again grew relative to GDP. This time both the federal and the state governments grew.

Why did government grow so much in the last century? Economists, other social scientists, and historians have been asking this question for years and will ask it for many more. It is an especially interesting question because growth in government happened in all major industrial countries, so the causes are not restricted to the United States. People who study this question cannot agree on a single cause.

One possible cause is growth in income. For this to explain growth in government relative to GDP, we must assume that the things government provides with its spending are highly income-elastic; that is, as people's incomes grow, their demand for the things that governments provide grows even faster. A second possible cause is the extension of voting rights to nearly all people. At the beginning of the century, many people—for example, women—could not vote, and low-income people were precluded by poll taxes. By the end of the century, everyone age 18 and older could vote. Extending suffrage may have created increased demands for government spending, in particular for transfer spending such as welfare and Social Security, because low-income people pay a small fraction of the taxes that finance the spending. A third possibility is the great improvement in the government's ability to tax the population. To spend an amount equal to a large fraction of GDP, the government must be able to tax very effectively. The ability to tax has grown over the century because of increases in information processing and, in the United States, changes in the law. The modern income tax was not levied until 1913, and it is hard to imagine how the government could raise large sums of money without it.

THE COMPOSITION OF GOVERNMENT SPENDING

Not only has the size of government changed over time, but so has the composition of government spending. *Composition of spending* means relative spending on different functions performed by government, such as defense and income security.

Government Spending by Function

To understand what government does in the economy, we must know what the government spends money on as well as how much it spends. Table 1.1 shows percentage shares of spending on different functions *for all levels of government combined* for the years 1952 and 1993. The function of government spending is defined by the purpose or principal need that the spending serves. The functional classifications in Table 1.1 are those used by John E. Dawson and Peter J. E. Stan of the RAND Institution, from whose study this table is taken.[3]

From Table 1.1, we see that how government spends has changed remarkably between 1952 and 1993. In 1993, the last year in Dawson and Stan's study, the largest fraction of government spending was on programs that provide income support for individuals. These programs, which account for 21% of government spending, include Social Security and federal, state, and local welfare programs. By comparison, in 1952 half of government spending was for national defense. In 1952, the Cold War had begun and the Korean conflict was still under way, so the largest part of spending by the federal government was military spending. The share of government spending on national defense declined steadily after 1952, while the share of "social spending" rose.

Table 1.1   Government Spending (All Levels Combined) by Function

Function	Percent of Total Spending	
	1952	1993
National defense	50.0%	14.5%
Other international	2.5	1.0
Education	9.8	15.9
Health	3.5	16.4
Transportation	5.8	4.5
Civilian safety	2.3	4.4
Support of individuals	10.4	21.2
Support of the economy	3.8	5.3
Support of the labor force	1.7	3.2
Utilities and commercial activities	1.8	0.2
Net interest	4.9	5.7
Other	3.8	7.8

Source: John E. Dawson and Peter J. E. Stan, *Public Expenditures in the United States: 1952–1993,* 1995, Table B.2.

---

[3]Elsewhere in this chapter, we make use of the functional classifications in the NIPA. Dawson and Stan (1995) explain the shortcomings of the NIPA classifications in their study.

By 1993, national defense accounted for only 14.5%, the fourth-largest share after support for individuals, health, and education. The shift of government spending from defense to social programs is sometimes called the "peace dividend."

Among social programs, the fraction spent on health by government grew the most over the four-decade interval. In 1993, spending on health was more than 16% of total government spending, the second-largest share; in 1952 it had been less than 4%. Table 1.1 shows that the things government spent revenue on were very different in 1952 than they were in 1993. Since 1993, the last year of the Dawson and Stan study, national defense has continued to decline as a percentage of total spending, and health has continued to increase.

Government Spending by Jurisdiction

The United States does not have a single (or unified) system of government but is a federal system that has many governments, including those at the state and local levels. In 1999, 67% of all government spending was done by the federal government. We include in federal spending the $224 billion the federal government gives to state and local governments as grants-in-aid. **Grants-in-aid** are transfers by the federal government to states and localities to help them fund shared spending on programs such as highways, education, and health.

The growth of government spending relative to national product and the division of spending among federal, state, and local governments are shown in Figure 1.3. This figure omits the years of World War II, when federal government spending increased drastically to fight the war. As the figure indicates, spending by all levels of government increased as a percentage of GDP, but federal and state spending grew more rapidly than local spending. In 1902, federal spending accounted for only about a third of total government spending. At that time, more than half of government spending was done by local governments such as cities, counties, and districts. Over

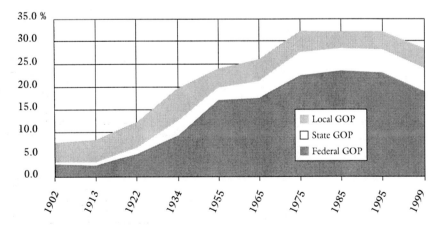

Figure 1.3

Growth in Federal, State, and Local Government Spending as Percent of GDP

Excluding the years of World War II, the steady rise in government spending over time is more apparent. We also see that the growth in government spending as a percentage of GDP has come mainly at the federal and state level. At the local level, government spending as a percentage of GDP has declined slightly.
Source: Statistical Abstracts of the United States, various years.

the century, spending by federal and state governments grew more rapidly than spending by local governments, so the relative size of local government decreased. We also see that the most rapid growth in the size of the federal government relative to GDP occurred before 1955, and that the most rapid growth in the size of the state governments occurred after that.

The change in the composition of spending by level of government reflects mainly changes in the things government does. At the turn of the century, the main functions of government were to meet local needs such as schools and police and fire protection. While local governments still perform these functions, relative demand for them has not grown appreciably over the twentieth century. Rather, it is the demand for government spending on health care, Social Security, and national defense that has grown, and since these functions are in the realm of the federal government, it has grown accordingly.

Different levels of government spend on different things. As Figure 1.4 shows, federal spending is concentrated on national defense, international affairs,

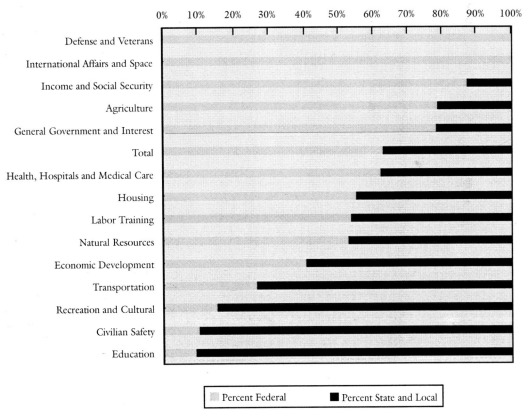

Figure 1.4

Spending by Level of Government and Function, 1996
The composition of government spending varies between the federal and state and local governments. Spending on national defense is solely by the federal government, whereas spending on education is mainly by the state and local government.
Source: U.S. Department of Commerce. Bureau of Economic Analysis, *Survey of Current Business,* October 1997.

1.1 Shrinking the Government

Many a politician has been elected by promising "to get government off the people's back." But through most of the twentieth century, government spending as a percentage of GDP grew or remained the same. Between 1992 and 1999, however, government spending as a percentage of GDP fell sharply from 32.9% of GDP in 1992 to 28.7% in 1999. This is nearly a 13% drop, which is large by historical standards. The following table shows the changes in state and local government spending and federal government spending and its major components, all as a percentage of GDP.

Critically analyze the following:

- Which level of government has shrunk the most? Which component is the biggest contributor to the fall in government spending?
- How do you think the following factors contributed to the fall in government spending as a percentage of GDP?
  - The world situation
  - The state of the U.S. economy (strong growth)
  - The political situation (a Republican-controlled Congress)

	1992	1999	Difference	Percent Change
State and Local	10.7%	10.1%	−.6%	−6%
Federal Total	22.2	18.7	−3.5	−16
Defense	4.8	3.0	−1.8	−37
Health and Medicare	3.4	3.6	+.2	+8.5
Income and Social Security	7.8	6.9	−.9	−11.6
Net Interest and Other	6	5	−1	−17.2

Source: The Economic Report of the President, 2000.

- They say the only thing certain about predicting the future is that you will be wrong. Nonetheless, make some guesses about how this table will look eight years from now.

agriculture, and social and income security, whereas state and local spending is concentrated on education, civilian safety, and transportation. In part this reflects the division of powers between the federal government and the states under the U.S. Constitution, although federal government spending accounts for part of total spending in all the major functional classifications. In Figure 1.3, federal grants-in-aid to state and local governments are counted as spending by the federal government, not as state and local spending.

FINANCING GOVERNMENT SPENDING

Governments obtain the funds they need by levying taxes, charging user fees for government goods and services, and borrowing in financial markets. Figure 1.5 shows sources of finance for various years. Three sources of government funds are indicated: receipts of the federal government, receipts of state and local governments, and net borrowing by combined governments. Receipts of state and local governments are from their own sources only and exclude funds they receive from the federal government. In 1999, about 69% of total government spending was financed by receipts of the federal government and 34% by receipts of state and local gov-

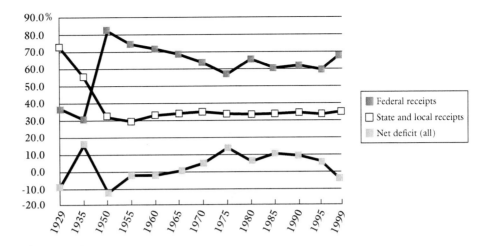

Figure 1.5

Sources of Government Finance, 1929–1999

The sources of government finance have also varied over time. Federal taxes are the most important but have declined slightly since 1950, replaced mainly by an increase in federal borrowing. The share of taxes and other receipts by state and local governments has remained relatively constant over the postwar period. *Source: Economic Report of the President, various years.*

ernments from their own sources. Unlike in past years, governments did not finance any spending by borrowing. In 1999, governments ran surpluses of about 3% of total spending. This surplus is shown as a negative source of funds in Figure 1.5.

As you can see from Figure 1.5, the share of receipts of state and local governments has remained relatively constant over the postwar period, at around a third of combined government spending. Before World War II, receipts by state and local government financed over half of government spending. During the postwar period, the share of federal receipts declined from a high of more than 80% in 1950, while the share of borrowed funds increased until the late 1990s. The rise in borrowed funds was due mainly to the increased use of deficit financing by the federal government between 1965 and 1995.

Nearly 90% of the current receipts of the government are obtained from taxes. Current charges (user fees), such as post office revenue, university tuition, charges for utilities, and fees for airports and parks, account for the balance. State and local governments rely on current charges more than the federal government does, but they too derive most of their revenues from taxes.

Many different types of taxes are levied, but most can be classified as taxes on incomes, taxes on goods, and taxes on wealth and property. The term **tax structure** means the shares of total tax revenue collected by the different types of taxes. Tax structures for different levels of government are shown in Table 1.2 for 1996. This table shows that income taxes are by far the most important element of the overall tax structure, accounting for 70% of all tax revenue. Note that the federal government relies almost entirely on income taxes, collecting 92% of its tax revenue

Table 1.2   **Percentage of Tax Revenue by Type (1996)**

	Federal	State	Local	All Levels
Personal Income	45.2%	23.8%	5.8%	35.4%
Social Insurance (Payroll)	35.1	14.4	0.0	25.9
Corporate Income	11.8	5.2	2.0	9.1
Total Income and Payroll	92.1	43.5	7.7	70.3
General Sales	0.0	24.8	11.7	7.5
Excises and Duties	3.7	11.8	5.2	5.9
Total Goods Tax	3.7	36.6	16.8	13.3
Property	0.0	1.8	72.9	8.9
Other	4.2	18.2	2.6	7.5
Total Own-Source Tax Revenue	100.0	100.0	100.0	100.0

Source: U.S. Bureau of the Census, *Statistical Abstract of the United States, 1998,* Tables 507, 514, 539.

from them. Federal income taxes include the familiar personal income tax (which makes April such a busy month for accountants), the Social Security and Medicare taxes on payrolls, and the corporate income tax.

State and local governments rely less on income taxes as a source of revenue than the federal government does. A significant share of state revenue is obtained from taxes on goods and services, such as the retail sales tax levied in most states. While most states levy both a sales and an income tax, there is much variation in the relative importance of the two from state to state. For instance, seven states have no personal income tax, and five have no sales tax.

Taxes on property and wealth are relatively unimportant in the United States, except at the local level. Local governments obtain 70% of their revenue from property taxes, mainly from real estate taxes. This reliance reflects the fact that real property is immobile and cannot move from local jurisdiction to local jurisdiction in response to differences in local tax rates.

The tax structure, like spending, has not remained static over time. Figure 1.6 shows shares of federal tax revenue collected from personal incomes, corporate incomes, and excises and duties, for selected years since 1955. The most notable change is the large increase in the share from insurance trust, which comes mainly from payroll taxes. In 1955, payroll taxes accounted for less than 12% of federal revenue, but by 2000 they accounted for nearly 34%. This rapid growth in payroll taxes occurred because they are used to fund the rapidly growing Social Security and Medicare programs. The share of personal income taxes has remained relatively constant, at around 48%, while the share of corporate income taxes has declined from 26.5% in 1955 to 10.1% in 2000.

Government in the United States relies less than governments in other countries on taxes on the consumption of goods and services, and more on taxes on income and payrolls. As shown in Figure 1.7, taxes on goods and services account for over 32% of government revenue averaged over all members of the Organization for Economic Cooperation and Development (OECD), but for only about

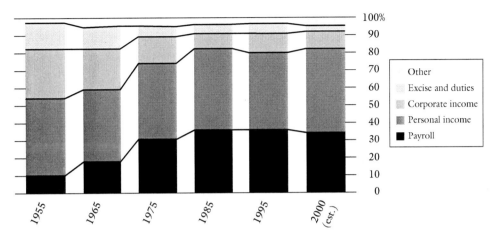

Figure 1.6

The Changing Federal Tax Structure, 1955–2000

The federal tax structure has changed over time. Notable is the rise in the importance of payroll taxes and the decline in the importance of corporate income taxes since 1955.

Source: Office of Management and Budget, *The Federal Budget 2000,* Historical Tables.

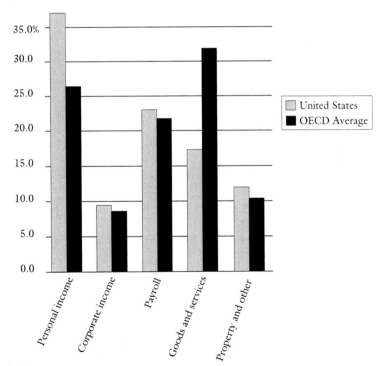

Figure 1.7

Tax Revenue Shares by Type of Tax, 1996

The tax structure in the United States differs from that of other industrial countries. Notable is the greater reliance on income and payroll taxes and the lesser reliance on goods and services taxes.

Source: OECD, *Revenue Statistics 1965–1997,* 1998.

17% in the United States. On the other hand, taxes on personal incomes collect a larger share of revenue in the United States than in the other countries.

ACCOUNTING FOR GOVERNMENT

Section 9 of Article I of the U.S. Constitution requires that money drawn from the Treasury be a "consequence of Appropriations made by Law," and that a "regular Statement and Account of the Receipts and Expenditures … be published from time to time." It is hard to believe that such a simple, direct constitutional requirement lies behind the massive, detailed federal budget that appears each year, not to mention the fierce and protracted negotiations between the administration and Congress that bring forth the budget.

Understanding the budget is important for two reasons. First, the budget is the means by which the government sets its priorities. In this regard, the government budget is similar to a household's budget. Each year, a prudent household examines how much it expects to earn and decides how much it can spend on different goods and services like food, shelter, clothing, and entertainment. Similarly, each year the government determines how much it will receive in revenue and decides how much to spend on different government functions like defense, Social Security, and education. Second, the information in government budgets is an important source of data for public finance economists and other analysts who study government. Understanding what the budget reports and does not report about government activities is essential for understanding and evaluating the impact of government on the economy. As we shall see, the government can achieve its objectives in ways that may not even appear in the budget, such as through regulation and "hidden" spending (sometimes called "backdoor spending").

The Unified Budget

The budget transactions of the federal government are reported in the **unified budget,** published annually by the Office of Management and Budget (OMB) as the *Budget of the United States Government.* The unified budget reports the cash outlays, receipts, and borrowing of the federal government, including federal **trust funds.** A government trust fund is a separate account for funds collected and disbursed for certain programs, like Social Security, Medicare, and unemployment insurance. The trust funds must be kept separate from general funds, and the revenue collected must be used for the designated purpose. The receipts of these funds are *not* part of the federal funds, for which other, nontrust programs can compete under the appropriations process.

Although the unified budget includes outlays and receipts of the government trust funds, when the budget total is calculated a trust fund can be excluded by designating it "off budget." In other words, a receipt or outlay of the federal government can be counted in the unified budget and designated off budget at the same time. In fiscal year 2000, $336 billion of federal outlays were designated off budget, as were $465 billion of receipts. The most important off-budget item in the

"Who do I see to get big government off my back?"

unified budget is Social Security. Spending on this program, and the receipts from the Social Security payroll tax, is almost entirely off budget. Only the administrative costs of the program are on budget. The budget of the U.S. Post Office is also off budget.

There is no unambiguous rule of accounting that determines whether a program is designated on or off budget. Ultimately, whether an item is put on or off budget is a political decision and reflects an agreement as to whether to count it when determining the official **budget surplus** or **deficit,** which is the difference between on-budget outlays and on-budget receipts.

The Budget Enforcement Act

An important part of the law controlling the budget process is the *Budget Enforcement Act* (BEA) of 1990, which was amended and extended in 1993 and 1995. The BEA divides federal spending into a *discretionary* type and a *mandatory* type (also called "direct spending"). Discretionary spending requires Congress to enact and the president to sign an appropriations bill authorizing the spending. In other words, the Congress and the president must take actions each year for the government to spend money on discretionary spending programs. These programs include national defense, foreign aid, highway construction, housing, and science. Permanent laws authorize mandatory spending. Such spending includes entitlements such as Social Security, Medicare, and Veterans' benefits. An entitlement is a program that requires the government to pay benefits to all persons who satisfy the eligibility requirements specified in the program legislation. It is sometimes called "uncontrollable spending," although it is not strictly uncontrolled because Congress and the President *can* change the amount spent by changing the law. The point is that they don't have to act. Failure to act means that the amount spent is determined by the existing legislation.

One type of mandatory spending is practically uncontrollable—interest on the national debt. If the government failed to pay interest on the national debt, it would be in default. This is such a serious breach of government trust that it is considered unthinkable except in a dire national emergency.

Since 1965, mandatory spending as a percentage of total federal spending has risen steadily. In 1965, 45% of federal spending was mandatory. In 1999, mandatory spending accounted for more than 70% of federal spending. In part, this is because of the declining percentage of defense spending, which is discretionary and was by far a much larger fraction of federal spending in 1965.

The BEA imposed a cap or upper limit on annual discretionary spending through fiscal year 2002. The Federal Budget for 2001 recommends revising and extending the caps until 2010. The purpose of the cap was to limit spending to reduce the deficit and to prevent the surplus from being reduced. The BEA also requires that *changes* in legislation that increase mandatory spending be offset by cuts in other spending or by raising additional taxes. This requirement is called PAYGO, for "pay-as-you-go." Like the cap on discretionary spending, PAYGO is intended to prevent new spending that would increase the deficit or reduce the surplus. Such spending would increase taxes on future generations, hence the term "pay-as-you-go." Together these requirements form a "Social Security solvency lockbox" to protect the surplus of Social Security taxes over benefits from being spent on other spending programs. Diverting the Social Security surplus to other spending implies higher taxes in the future when the baby boomers retire. (These issues are discussed at greater length in Chapters 9 and 16.)

Budget Surpluses and the Solvency of Social Security

If government receipts (revenue) exceed its outlays (spending), the government has a budget surplus. If outlays are greater than receipts, it has a budget deficit. The unified budget surplus in 1999 was $124 billion, which is equal to $1827 billion in receipts less $1703 billion in outlays. The entire surplus in 1999 is off budget because it is equal to the excess of Social Security taxes over Social Security spending. The on-budget receipts and outlays of the federal government were in balance (equal to each other) in 1999. For the 30 years before 1998, the federal government had budget deficits.

The unified budget surplus is approximately equal to the amount of the net national debt that the government retires (or pays down) in the year. The net national debt is the outstanding value of Treasury securities (government bonds) held outside the federal government. It is roughly equal to the accumulated unified budget deficits less surpluses over the country's history. At $3600 billion (end of 1999), the net national debt is somewhat less than the gross national debt, which is equal to $5606 billion. The difference is the amount of Treasury securities held by the federal government itself. The bulk of this government-owned debt is in the Social Security Trust Fund, which by law must invest its accumulated surplus in government securities. Analysts focus on the net national debt because the rest is owed by one pocket of government to another pocket of government. In 1999, the net national debt was equal to about 40% of GDP, which is down from a high of 49% in the mid-1990s but up from a post–World War II low of 24% in the mid-1970s.

The Office of Management and Budget projects unified budget surpluses to continue over the next decade. This means that the net national debt falls in dollar terms and falls sharply as a percentage of GDP as GDP continues to grow. Since the unified budget surpluses are off budget, the securities purchased back from the private sector will end up in the Social Security Trust Fund, which will increase by about the same amount that the net national debt declines. If the on-budget receipts and outlays remain in balance, the gross national debt will remain roughly constant. The interest payments on the Treasury securities in trust fund will also accumulate, pushing the trust fund balance to over $3000 billion by 2015. This "nest egg" will finance the Social Security deficit that will emerge when the baby boomers retire and the trust fund sells the bonds back to the private sector.

Governing Without Spending

Spending money is the most visible way the government carries out its functions, whether it is writing Social Security checks to retirees or purchasing a new aircraft carrier. Indeed, the entire budget process that controls what the government spends and ensures accountability for what is spent is based on the assumption that the implementation of government programs requires the appropriation and outlay of funds. However, the government can carry on some functions and achieve some objectives in ways that do not show up as budget spending. We will discuss three such methods: (1) tax expenditures, (2) loans and guarantees, and (3) regulations and mandates.

TAX EXPENDITURES. The main way the government "spends without spending" is by giving special tax breaks and preferences to persons, firms, and other governments. Such tax breaks are called **tax expenditures.** The term is meant to indicate that the government can make "expenditures" by using the tax system to give special tax breaks for certain economic activities or to certain taxpayers.

To illustrate, suppose that the federal government finds it difficult to attract a sufficient number of men and women into the armed forces. One way to solve this problem is to raise military pay to make enlisting more attractive. This solution means that more funds must be obtained for defense through the appropriations process, resulting in a bigger defense budget and higher government spending overall if other programs are maintained. The population must pay more taxes to achieve the government's objective.

Another way to accomplish the same objective, however, is to exempt military pay from the income tax. This raises the take-home pay of military personnel and makes enlisting more attractive. But this solution does not show up as increased government spending. Instead, it shows up as reduced government revenue. If the government maintains expenditures on other programs, it must raise taxes on everyone else to make up for the tax relief given to armed forces personnel. Again, the population pays more taxes to achieve the government's objective even though the government achieves its objective without increasing budgeted spending.

The functional equivalence of using budgetary expenditures and tax expenditures to achieve government objectives suggests they should be treated equivalently. However, the two methods are dealt with quite differently in the budget process. Budgetary expenditures involve appropriations and oversight, and the amounts are reported in the budget. Tax expenditures are forgone tax revenue and are neither reported in the budget nor subject to the appropriations process. Tax expenditures are reported in a separate **tax expenditure budget** that documents government functions carried out through the special provisions in the tax code and reports the revenue lost.

The dollar value of a tax expenditure is estimated by finding the revenue lost as a result of it. In 2000, the total of all tax expenditures in the federal income tax system amounted to over $600 billion. This included revenue losses of $56 billion for the mortgage interest deduction, which is a subsidy for home ownership; $81 billion for exempting employer-paid health insurance from income tax, which is a subsidy for health insurance; and $26 billion for the charitable gifts deduction, which is a subsidy for private philanthropy. We discuss these and other tax expenditures in more detail in Chapters 13 and 14.

LOANS AND LOAN GUARANTEES. By the end of fiscal year 1999, the outstanding direct and guaranteed loans of the federal government amounted to $1210 billion. This does not include the larger amount of guaranteed loans issued by government-sponsored enterprises (GSEs) like the Federal National Mortgage Association (Fannie Mae) and the Federal Home Loan Mortgage Corporation (Freddie Mac). Each year the government makes or guarantees billions of dollars in new loans to private individuals and firms.

Some direct government loan programs are like government spending because the money is lent at below-market interest rates. Parents often help their adult children by lending money to them without interest, or at a low interest rate. Most people would consider this act partly a form of "spending money on their children." In the same way, the government can spend money on agriculture by extending loans to farmers at interest rates below market rates through the Rural Electrification Agency or the Farmers Home Administration. The government also makes hidden expenditures on defense and commerce by extending low-interest loans to foreign governments to help them purchase exports of American military and nonmilitary goods.

Loan guarantees are another indirect form of government spending, and the implicit spending component is difficult to quantify. Consider a commercial firm that is having trouble borrowing money on its own account, perhaps because it is very risky or verging on bankruptcy. If private lenders are willing to lend to the firm at all, they would demand a very high interest rate. Suppose the government wants to give the firm aid. One way is simply to give the firm a grant or subsidy. This requires appropriating the necessary funds and writing a check to the firm. The resulting outlay is recorded as a government expenditure in the unified budget. Another way to help the firm is for the government to guarantee its loan. Since the loan is backed by the government, the firm can borrow at a lower interest rate. The lenders no longer view the loan to the firm as risky, because the default risk has been transferred from them to the nation's taxpayers. If the firm fails, it won't be the lender that loses—it will be the taxpayers.

Sometimes you hear that a loan guarantee does not cost the taxpayer a cent. A good example is the $1.5 billion loan guarantee given to the Chrysler Corporation in 1979. This guarantee allowed the company to borrow enough to retool its product line, restore its profitability, and repay its debt. Had Chrysler fallen into bankruptcy, the taxpayers would have had to come up with $1.5 billion. In the end, the federal government did not have to make good, so no cash expenditure was needed. Nevertheless, there was an indirect government expenditure because the taxpayers, through the government, underwrote the risk. This example points out the difficulty of quantifying the amount of indirect government spending associated with a loan guarantee. It is difficult to agree on the cost of this bailout to the taxpayers. Was it the difference between the interest cost Chrysler would have had to pay without the guarantee and what it did pay, or the expected cost to the government if Chrysler had defaulted?

Since 1992, the Federal Credit Reform Act has required that the costs of federal credit programs be estimated and budgeted. Specifically, the full cost of the subsidy associated with the loan or guarantee must be recorded as an obligation when the government makes the loan or commits to the guarantee. In 1999, the cost of federal direct and guaranteed loans was estimated at $80 billion.[4] This does not include the subsidy cost of guaranteed loans issued by GSEs.

REGULATIONS AND MANDATES.   Regulation is one way the government can achieve objectives such as improving environmental quality, protecting consumers, ensuring workplace safety, and providing accessibility in public places for the disabled, to mention only a few. In general, regulations and mandates are described as the **command and control** policies of the government, in contrast to taxing and spending. Just as tax expenditures and government lending can be considered hidden forms of government spending, command and control policies can be considered a hidden form of taxing *and* spending. Rather than taxing the population to purchase the resources needed for its objectives, the government forces firms and individuals to provide them directly.

---

[4]The cost of the subsidy implicit in federal loans is calculated as the "present value of the expected cash outflows for the government and the present value of the expected cash inflows" (see Office of Management and Budget, *The Budget of the United States Government, 2000. Analytic Perspectives*). The concept of present value is discussed in Chapter 6; for now, just think of it as the sum of present and future costs associated with the loan.

Government regulation in the American economy is pervasive and costly. In 1998, the federal government alone had over 128,000 full-time positions and spent $17.9 billion on administering regulatory programs. The budgetary cost of regulation is just the tip of the iceberg. Regulations impose costs on private individuals who must comply with them and can also cause inefficiency costs if they lead to a misallocation of the economy's resources. The Office of Management and Budget (OMB) estimates that the monetized costs of major federal social regulations as of 1999 are between $185 billion and $250 billion.[5] Some nongovernment analysts argue the cost is much higher. One study claims that the cost of federal regulation in 1998 was $737 billion![6]

To illustrate the hidden cost of regulation, consider the Americans with Disabilities Act (ADA), signed into law by President Bush on July 26, 1990. Title I of the ADA requires that employers make the workplace accessible to employees with disabilities. Title III requires that owners of places of public accommodation, such as hotels, office buildings, restaurants, and buses, provide accessibility to the disabled by installing ramps, widened aisles, restroom facilities, automatic doors, elevators, and Braille signs. Across the nation, the cost of such facilities amounts to billions of dollars.

Although the government requires firms to provide the resources needed for accessibility, the objectives of the ADA could have been attained through taxing and spending. The government could tax the population (or the firms) and appropriate the funds needed to provide accessibility. Either way, the objective—accessibility—is achieved, and the costs are borne by private individuals. But with a tax and spending policy, the government's activity is measured and reported in the budget as tax receipts and spending on publicly provided goods. With the ADA, no government tax or spending is recorded, except the budget of the regulatory agency.

Again, the point is not that the ADA and other forms of regulation are good or bad; it is that the government can achieve objectives through regulation *or* through tax and spending policies. If, as studies indicate, federal regulations impose hundreds of billions of dollars in costs on the private sector, the effect of the federal government on the economy is larger than the measured government spending. The fact that reported government spending is less when it resorts to regulation does not mean that the government is any less intrusive in the economy. It is just less visible.

Note that, ultimately, both spending and regulation rely on the government's power to coerce the private sector. In the ADA, the power to coerce is direct. The government makes it compulsory for private firms to provide the resources needed for accessibility, or face punishment (usually fines). In a government spending program, the resources needed to provide accessibility are acquired through voluntary exchange, but the money needed to buy them is coerced from the taxpayers. People must pay their taxes, or the government can seize their assets or garnish their wages. In extreme cases, it can send them to jail.

---

[5]Office of Management and Budget, "Draft Report to Congress on the Costs and Benefits of Federal Regulations," January 2000.

[6]Clyde W. Crews, *Ten Thousand Commandments: An Annual Policymaker's Snapshot of the Federal Regulatory State* (1999 Edition), Competitive Enterprise Institute Monograph, March 1999.

1.2   Is the Government "Insolvent"?

Most analysts agree that the government budget presents only a partial picture of government activity. One reason is that it does not report hidden taxes and spending in the same way as conventional receipts and outlays. Another reason is that it fails to account for the accruing assets and liabilities of the government, like government investment and federal employee pension and Social Security obligations.

A proposed solution is to report a government balance sheet, similar to that reported by businesses to shareholders. In addition to an income statement that reports receipts and outlays over its fiscal year, businesses also report the level and composition of their assets and liabilities at the end of each year in a balance sheet. The purpose is to provide shareholders with more information about the firm's operations so they can evaluate the firm's asset management (stewardship and efficiency) and solvency (ability to meet present and future payment obligations). Although the government does not have shareholders, the citizens can be considered "stakeholders" who have an interest in its operations. The Treasury Department and the Office of Budget and Management (OMB) both produce rudimentary federal balance sheets. The assets and liabilities on the federal government's balance sheet (in trillions of dollars) are shown in the table below. Also shown are the assets and liabilities calculated by the Citizens for Budget Reform (CBR), a public interest group.

	Treasury (1996)	OMB (1997)	CBR (1996)
Assets	$.1	$2.3	$22
Liabilities	3.8	5.7	44
Assets Less Liabilities	(3.7)	(3.4)	(22)

Sources: Statistical Abstract of the United States, 1999. Budget of the United States, Fiscal Year 2001, Citizens for Budget Reform, 1997 (http://www.budget.org/USABIS/balancesheet.html).

As we can see, the government's liabilities exceed its assets on all three balance sheets. The Treasury includes only the financial assets and liabilities of the government, such as cash on hand and the net national debt. The OMB also includes the physical assets of the government such as its land, inventories and structures, and nondebt liabilities like insurance and employee pension obligations. The CBR goes further and includes the value of future taxes as asset (although it seriously underestimates it) and obligations to pay future Social Security and Medicare benefits as liabilities.

Most economists are skeptical about the usefulness of a government balance sheet. Some suggest an alternative method of judging the government's ability to fulfill future obligations, called *generational accounting* (this is explained in Chapters 11 and 16). With this in mind, critically analyze and discuss the following list.[1]

- A business balance sheet, along with the income statement, is used by shareholders to evaluate the profitability of business investments. Given that the government investments are not based on profit, but presumably on the public good or interest, would a government balance sheet be useful for the purpose of judging government asset management?

- The government's main source of revenue is taxes, not income-earning assets. Given this fact, which of the balance sheets in the previous list item is best in principle (disregard accuracy) for determining whether the government can fulfill future spending obligations like Social Security?

- The OMB argues that the government is not insolvent (unable to fulfill future spending obligations) despite the fact that liabilities exceed assets by any measure. It offers as proof the fact that the government can borrow at a low, risk-free interest rate, which would not be the case if it were insolvent. Do you think this means that the government will have sufficient revenue to pay future Social Security obligations at current tax rates? Why or why not?

[1] It may help you to read "Stewardship: Toward a Federal Balance Sheet" in *The Budget of the United States for Fiscal Year 2001,* which you can get at http://frwebgate. access.gpo.gov/usbudget/index.html.

CONCLUSION AND SUMMARY

This chapter has introduced various facts about government spending and tax policies to show how government intervenes in the American economy and by how much. We have seen that measured government spending is just one way the government achieves its objectives. In Chapter 2 we turn to a more abstract question: What functions *should* government perform in an economy? What determines whether a particular activity is best performed by private firms or the government?

- The United States has a mixed economy in which the allocation of resources is determined both by decisions made by private households and firms and by decisions made by governments.

- The combined government spending in the United States was about 28% the gross domestic product (GDP), or about $2620 billion in 1999. As a percentage of GDP, government spending is smaller in the United States than in many other industrialized countries.

- The absolute and relative size of government grew rapidly during the twentieth century. Most of the growth relative to GDP occurred before 1970.

- The composition of government spending has changed markedly over the last four decades. In particular, national defense has shrunk in importance, while Social Security, health, and education have increased.

- The government obtains most of its revenue from taxes. The federal government relies heavily on income taxes, whereas state and local governments rely more heavily on sales and property taxes, respectively.

- The amounts collected and spent by the federal government and its trust funds are reported in the unified budget. However, the government can implement its policies and affect the economy in ways that do not show up as budgeted spending. These include hidden spending, such as tax expenditures and loan guarantees, and regulations.

QUESTIONS FOR DISCUSSION AND REVIEW

1. Often, government provides goods and services also provided by private businesses. For example, many communities have both for-profit hospitals and state hospitals. In this chapter we considered four different ways in which government differs from private business enterprises. How are the differences between government and business likely to be reflected in the service provided? For example: fees charged, access, waiting time, and number of patients per doctor?

2. Do you favor increasing or decreasing government spending relative to GDP? What types of spending would you change? How would your answer affect the relative size of federal and state and local governments?

3. Fees charged by the federal government for goods and services the consumer can choose to buy (like national park fees) are not counted as government revenue in the budget. Rather, they are subtracted from the outlays of the department or agency collecting the fee. Nonetheless, the revenue is deposited in federal funds and can be appropriated as Congress sees fit. With this in mind, do you think that

budget outlays on National Parks accurately reports the amount government spends for this purpose?

4. In the United States, government increases the availability of health insurance to households by exempting employer-paid insurance from income taxation (a tax expenditure), whereas most other countries have government-financed health insurance. How does this bias the measures of the size of government relative to GDP reported in Figure 1.1?

5. The term "peace dividend" refers to the hope that the government can spend more on social programs as world tensions subside and defense becomes a less pressing need. Some people argue that the peace dividend has mostly been spent. Explain this argument, using Table 1.1.

6. Governments help finance college education in at least three ways: (a) funding public universities, (b) making loans to students, and (c) not taxing "qualified" scholarships as income. Match these three to the following categories of government spending: (i) tax expenditures, (ii) budgeted spending, (iii) off-budget (or hidden) spending.

7. Evaluate: "One way to reduce the size of government is to reduce defense spending by reintroducing the military draft (which would allow reduced military pay)."

8. Internet Exercise. Although it is common to measure government spending relative to GDP, it is also useful to know what has happened to the level of *real* government spending (that is, government spending measured in dollars of constant purchasing power). Use the statistical tables from latest version of *The Economic Report of the President* to calculate a series on the level of spending in constant dollars by the federal and state and local governments from 1965 to the latest year available. Chart these series using the chart function on your spreadsheet. Currently (March 2000), the 2000 edition of the ERP is available at http://w3.access.gpo.gov/eop/. The tables in spreadsheet format are at http://w3.access.gpo.gov/usbudget/fy2001/maindown.html. You will need tables B-58 for consumer prices and tables B-82 and B-83 for federal and state and local government spending.

9. Internet Exercise. Although it is somewhat dated, try the budget simulation site provided by Berkeley's Center for Community Economic Research at http://garnet.berkeley.edu:3333/budget/budget.html. This site allows you to vary different categories of federal spending and tax expenditures and then calculates the impact on total government spending, tax expenditures, and the budget surplus or deficit. Using the long version, increase outlays in a way you think appropriate while keeping the budget deficit unchanged by decreasing tax expenditures. How do total budget outlays change? Can you conclude that government is bigger?

SELECTED REFERENCES

The federal budget is explained in some detail in Stanley E. Collender, *Guide to the Federal Budget: Fiscal 2001*. Also useful is the OMB's *A Citizen's Guide to the Federal Budget*, which is available free at http://w3.access.gpo.gov/usbudget/. Two books on "hidden" government spending are *Hidden Spending* by D. S. Ippolito and *Checks Unbalanced* by B. Leonard. The benefits and costs of government regulation are discussed in Robert W. Hahn, "Government Analysis of the Benefits and Costs of Regulation," *Journal of Economic Perspectives*, Fall 1998.

USEFUL INTERNET SITES

Analysis of the federal budget policy is available at numerous sites. Start with the Office of Management and Budget at http://www.whitehouse.gov/OMB/ and the Congressional Budget Office at http://www.cbo.gov/. A good site providing links to all types of budget analysis is http://www.policy.com/. Click in budget policy under Economics in their Issues Library. Also excellent is the Center on Budget and Policy Priorities at http://www.cbpp.org/ and the Economic Studies division of the Brookings Institute at http://www.brook.edu/es/es_hp.htm. Information on state budgets can be found at http://www.piperinfo.com/state/states.html by selecting the state and finding its budget management department.

Good sites for U.S. data include the Federal Budget documents at http://w3.access.gpo.gov/usbudget/fy2001/maindown.html, Statistical Appendix to the *Economic Report of the President, 2000,* found at http://w3.access.gpo.gov/usbudget/fy2000/erp.html, Secs. 9 and 10 of the *Statistical Abstract of the United States, 1999* at http://w3.access.gpo.gov/usbudget/fy2000/erp.html, and the governments survey of the U.S. Census at http://www.census.gov/govs/www/index.html.

International government statistics are available from the Organization for Economic Cooperation and Development (OECD) at http://www.oecd.org/statlist.htm#ecostat, The World Bank Group at http://www.worldbank.org/data/, and the International Monetary Fund at http://www.imf.org/external/pubs/ft/gfs/manual/index.htm.

PART TWO

Government

and the

Allocation

of Resources

In every economy, people must choose how to use their scarce resources. As individuals, we decide how much we would like spend on goods and services that we consume privately, such as food, clothing, and housing. As voters, we decide how much we would like to spend on goods and services that we consume collectively through the government, such as education, national defense, and highways.

In Part II, we learn about the factors that determine how an economy should and does allocate its resources between competing private and public uses. Chapter 2 begins by examining the workings of a market system, and develops the concept of economic efficiency and its relationship to the welfare of the people in the economy. Markets do not always allocate resources efficiently. Such "market failures" provide a potential role for government to increase economic efficiency. An important cause of market failure is the fact that private firms have little incentive to provide certain types of goods, called public goods. Chapter 3 explains the idea of public goods in detail and derives the necessary conditions for such goods to be provided efficiently. The chapter also describes government public good spending programs like national defense and highways.

Externalities are a type of market failure that occurs when market decisions affect third parties in certain ways. For instance, private decisions to consume and produce gasoline create air pollution that imposes costs on everyone. Because people disregard the pollution costs of their market decisions, the market allocation of resources is not efficient. Chapter 4 catalogues the different types of externalities and discusses the policies and programs that governments adopt to rectify the inefficiencies they create.

2 Markets, Efficiency, and Government

Foreign visitors to Tokyo, Japan, are surprised to see farmers tending crops of broccoli and radishes amid high-rise office and apartment buildings. Entire city blocks are devoted to truck farming, just minutes from Tokyo's bustling Ikebukoro subway station. With land prices in urban Tokyo reaching as high as 7 million yen (about US$70,000) per square meter, these are possibly the most expensive fruits and vegetables in the world. Tokyo's urban farms, which produce about 10% of the produce consumed by the city's 12 million residents, survive because of government subsidies, tax breaks, and strict land use rules that reserve the land for farming as part of the Japanese government's policy of encouraging self-sufficiency in food production. Whatever the merits of such policies, economists see the farms as an extreme example of economic inefficiency.

For **economic efficiency,** a scarce resource should be employed in the use that has the highest economic value. Although economic value is not always equal to commercial value, it is all but certain that the land used for these urban farms has greater economic value when used for residential and office buildings. By using the land for farming, the economy loses the higher value of these alternative uses and creates an **efficiency cost** or **deadweight loss.**

One need not travel to Tokyo to find examples of economic inefficiency. To promote greater self-sufficiency in energy production, the U.S. government spends over $7 billion annually to give farmers and agribusiness subsidies and tax credits to grow corn for the purpose of producing ethanol. In 1995, about 500 million bushels of corn, or about 6% of the total crop, was used to produce automotive fuel, which is used mostly in the Midwest. Studies have found that producing ethanol actually uses more energy than it provides, and ethanol fuel contributes to smog as well. The main impact of the program is to keep corn prices nearly 10% higher than they would be otherwise. The ethanol program creates economic inefficiency because the scarce resources used in producing ethanol have higher economic value in producing other crops, such as soybeans or wheat.

Government programs are not the only source of economic inefficiency. Market incentives direct resources to uses that have the highest commercial value, and in some cases, the commercial value is different from economic value. Commercial value depends on the prices at which goods and production factors are bought and sold. Economic value is the price people are actually willing to pay. Willingness to pay and market prices may diverge when buyers or sellers do not reap all of the benefits or bear all of the costs of the activities in which they are occupied. By allocating resources according to commercial value rather than economic value, market incentives can create an efficiency cost. Economists call this **market failure.**

In this chapter, we develop the idea that many of the economic functions of government can be justified as a means of achieving a more efficient use of the economy's scarce resources. We begin by considering how economic efficiency is related to the level of well-being or social welfare in an economy. We then address the question of how to measure the cost of economic inefficiency. With these concepts in mind, we examine the conditions needed for market allocations to be efficient, and we identify categories of market failure where market allocations are not efficient. Where markets fail, we consider the types of government programs and policies that can be adopted to improve economic efficiency. We also briefly consider the relationship between economic efficiency and the equity or fairness criteria of social welfare.

THE PURPOSE OF NORMATIVE ECONOMICS

Economists make a distinction between positive and normative economics. **Positive economics** describes and explains how an economy functions. When doing positive economics, an economist makes simplifying assumptions, constructs theories and models to identify cause and effect, proposes hypotheses about economic behavior, and tests the hypotheses by observing economic variables. **Normative economics**, also called **welfare economics**, seeks to identify what is desirable for the economy. In public finance, we use welfare economics to identify the economic functions that the government can perform to the betterment of society and to evaluate the programs and policies the government implements.

In principle, positive economics, unlike welfare economics, does not require the economist to make explicit *value judgments* about what is good or bad for the economy. Value judgments are assumptions about worth that cannot be confirmed as true or false by observing and measuring economic variables. For example, the assumption of consumer sovereignty—that consumers are the best judges of what makes them happy—is a value judgment. Welfare economics is based on the value judgments of economic efficiency, which is whether economic resources are used where they have highest value, and distributional equity, which is whether the distribution of incomes conforms to some standards of fairness.

To clarify, suppose we wish to analyze a program like food stamps, which gives coupons exchangeable for food to poor families. A positive economic analysis might study how the program affects the level of food consumption by recipients and how the availability of food stamps affects their decision to work. It could also examine the *incidence* of the food stamp program—that is, who receives the benefits and who pays the cost of the program. A normative or welfare economics analysis would use the concepts of economic efficiency and equity to evaluate whether the food stamp program is a good way to help the poor. For instance, a normative analysis might conclude that the food stamp program is an inefficient way to help the poor because it distorts their consumption and labor supply decisions, and that an alternative program, say a tax credit, is preferable.

THE EFFICIENT ECONOMY

When evaluating government policies, it is sometimes difficult to untangle the many concerns different people may have about them. Likewise, it is difficult to untangle the efficiency and equity considerations of the policies. This can be compared to the problem of choosing a cake and dividing it among several people. Increasing economy efficiency is getting the largest cake that can be divided among the consumers. Increasing economic equity is dividing the cake more fairly. Combining the decisions of choosing the size of a cake and how it is to be divided can be perplexing, because in some cases needy people may get a smaller slice of a larger cake. Efficiency requires the government to choose the larger cake, but equity requires the government not to reduce the consumption of the poor.

Economists follow the approach of separating the efficiency and equity by assuming that the government can redistribute income (divide the cake) to achieve whatever distribution is deemed fair once the economy is as efficient as possible (once we have the largest cake). This allows us to focus on whether a policy or government program increases or decreases economic efficiency without worrying about equity. Later, in Chapter 7, we will see that economic and political realities mean that separating efficiency and equity is easier in theory than in practice. Nonetheless, it is a useful approach for organizing our thinking on such problems. For this reason we focus on economic efficiency in this chapter and those that follow, deferring the discussion of equity to Chapter 7.

Economic Efficiency and Pareto's Criterion

The practical definition of economic efficiency is that all resources are employed in the uses where they have highest economic value. Pareto's criterion, named after Vilfredo Pareto (1848–1923), relates the concept of economic efficiency to the levels of satisfaction (utility) that households in the economy enjoy. Pareto argued that if resources can be reallocated so that some or all households enjoy higher utility and none has lower utility, then social welfare in the economy is higher. This is called a **Pareto improvement** in social welfare. If an allocation of resources is attained for which it is *not* possible to make a Pareto improvement, the economy is described as **Pareto optimal.**

The advantage of Pareto's definitions is that they do not require us to make interpersonal comparisons of people's utilities. Since there are winners but no losers if resources can be allocated to achieve a Pareto improvement, we can argue that social welfare must be higher. In practice, however, most reallocations create winners and losers. We can still avoid the need to make interpersonal comparisons of utility by assuming lump-sum redistribution. That is, income can be reshuffled without any loss in economic efficiency. The assumption that lump-sum redistribution can be used to ensure that no one loses from a Pareto improving reallocation is called the **compensation principle.**

Pareto optimality and economic efficiency are equivalent concepts. Suppose the economic value of an acre of land is higher growing wheat rather than growing corn and that, for whatever reason, farmers currently use it to grow corn. If farmers shift the land into producing wheat, they gain because wheat has higher value. Of course, some households may lose from the reallocation, say because they must pay a slightly higher price for corn. However, because the value of wheat is higher, the winners (farmers) can, *in principle,* transfer a fraction of their gain to the losers (corn consumers) so that no one is made worse off. Since the winners have something left over, a Pareto improvement is achieved.

Marginal and Total Willingness to Pay

To make this discussion more concrete, we will analyze economic efficiency in terms of people's willingness to pay for certain goods. For simplicity, we assume just two people live in the economy, George (G) and Martha (M), and they consume just two goods, apples (A) and biscuits (B). George and Martha's preferences for these two goods can be represented by indifference curve maps. Figure 2.1 shows the indifference curve map of Martha, with her consumption of apples measured on the vertical axis and her consumption of biscuits on the horizontal axis. Along an indifference curve Martha gets the same level of utility from all consumption bundles, and indifference curves further from the origin correspond to higher levels of utility. George has an indifference curve map that is similar in its general properties, although the details about the shape of his indifference curves might be slightly different because he has different preferences.

Suppose Martha consumes the consumption bundle labeled z in Figure 2.1. We can measure the slope of Martha's indifference curve at this point by drawing a tangent. The magnitude of the slope (that is, disregarding the negative sign) of the tangent line has an important meaning. It is Martha's **marginal willingness to pay (MWTP)** for the good on the horizontal axis (biscuits), measured in units of the good on the vertical axis (apples).[1] Since no monetary unit exists at this level of abstraction, we must measure value in terms of the good on the vertical axis, which is called the **numeraire** good. The MWTP for biscuits indicates how much *value,* measured as a *quantity* of the numeraire good, Martha is willing to give up in order to consume one more biscuit. Note that as we move down the indifference curve, Martha consumes more biscuits and her indifference curve becomes flatter. That is, Martha's MWTP for biscuits decreases as she consumes more of them. Economists have observed that this is generally true for all goods and services. The more of a good is consumed, the lower the consumer's MWTP for it. This also applies to goods provided by the government, such as national defense, and environmental goods such as clean air.

In Figure 2.2, we plot the MWTP for biscuits by Martha. The quantity of biscuits Martha consumes is measured on the horizontal axis; her MWTP (the quan-

---

[1]The slope of an indifference curve is also called the *marginal rate of substitution.*

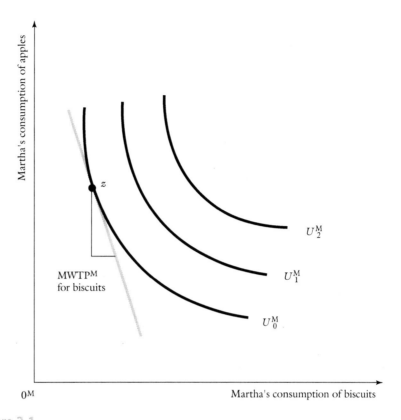

Figure 2.1

Indifference Curves and the Marginal Willingness to Pay

An indifference curve shows the combinations of two different goods that give the consumer the same level of utility. Its slope (ignoring the negative sign) at a point is equal to the consumer's marginal willingness to pay (MWTP) for the good on the horizontal axis (here, biscuits). That is, the slope shows the amount of the other good (apples) the consumer is willing to give up to get one more biscuit.

tity of the numeraire good, apples, she is willing to give up for one more biscuit) is plotted on the vertical axis. The MWTP is downward-sloping; to simplify, we assume it is linear as well. This MWTP curve is also the demand curve for biscuits by Martha, although it is not an ordinary type of demand curve.[2]

Suppose Martha consumes B_1 biscuits. What is the maximum she would be willing to pay to consume this quantity of biscuits rather than none at all? This payment, called her **total willingness to pay (TWTP)** for biscuits, is equal to the area under her MWTP curve. The height of the MWTP curve at each quantity is the amount she will pay to consume the next biscuit. Summing these amounts from the first to the last biscuit (B_1) gives her TWTP. Now suppose Martha pays P for every biscuit

---

[2]The MWTP curve is a Hicksian or "compensated" demand curve, since Martha is held on a particular indifference curve. An ordinary demand curve holds Martha at a certain level of money income. The difference between these two types of demand curves is explained more fully in the Appendix to Chapter 12 and in the main Appendix.

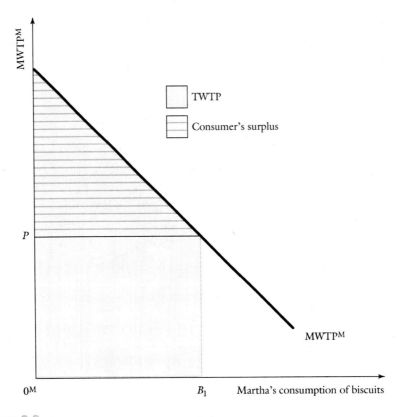

Figure 2.2

Total Willingness to Pay and Consumer's Surplus

We can plot the consumer's MWTP for different amounts of the good. The area under the marginal will-ingness to pay (MWTP) curve up to a given quantity is the consumer's total willingness to pay (TWTP) for that quantity. The TWTP is the amount the consumer would pay rather than go without. The excess of the TWTP above what the consumer does pay is called *consumer's surplus*.

she consumes. In this case, the total amount she pays is P times B_1, or the area of the rectangle in Figure 2.2. The excess of Martha's TWTP over what she pays is called her **consumer's surplus.** Martha's consumer's surplus is shown in Figure 2.2 as the area of the triangle below her MWTP curve and above P.

Conditions for Economic Efficiency

We can now illustrate what it means for an economy to be efficient, and the condi-tions that an efficient economy must satisfy. First, suppose the economy has a given endowment of biscuits and the numeraire good apples. Such an economy has no production, so it is called an *endowment* economy. The only issue of efficiency is the distribution of biscuits between the people in the economy, George and Martha. The efficient allocation of biscuits is that which maximizes the combined TWTPs of George and Martha. (An alternative, but more complicated, explanation using

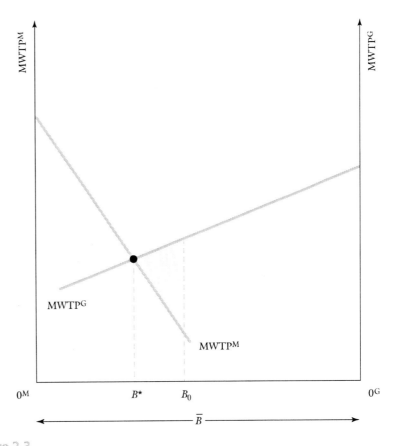

Figure 2.3

The Inefficiency Cost of Misallocated Consumption
An efficient allocation of consumption requires that a good be allocated among consumers so that all have the same MWTP for it. If a good is allocated so that one consumer has a greater MWTP than another, an inefficiency cost equal to the area of the shaded triangle is caused because the good is not used where it has highest value.

indifference curves is possible with a diagram known as the Edgeworth Box, explained in the Appendix to this chapter.)

Figure 2.3 shows both George's and Martha's MWTP curves. The length of the horizontal axis is equal to the total amount of biscuits available in the economy, $\bar{B}$. We measure the quantity of biscuits consumed by Martha to the right of the origin 0^M and measure her MWTP for biscuits on the left-hand vertical axis. We measure George's consumption of biscuits to the left of the origin 0^G and measure his MWTP on the right-hand vertical axis. To maximize the combined TWTP of George and Martha for the biscuit endowment, we must maximize the area under the two MWTP curves. This is done where Martha consumes $0^M B^\star$ biscuits and George consumes $0^G B^\star$ (or $\bar{B}$ minus $0^M B^\star$) biscuits. This is the allocation where George and Martha have the same MWTP for biscuits.

For any allocation of the biscuits between George and Martha other than $B^\star$, the combined TWTP for the biscuits is smaller. For example, when Martha consumes

B_0 biscuits and George consumes the rest, Martha's MWTP is much less than George's. Consumption by Martha is not the highest-valued use for biscuits in this economy—George places a higher value on them. Martha can trade biscuits with George in exchange for apples so that the combined TWTP for biscuits is increased by the area of the shaded triangle in the figure. By doing this, George and Martha are both better off, so there is a Pareto improvement. At B^*, this is no longer possible, so the economy is Pareto optional.

When an economy has a fixed endowment of goods, economic efficiency simply requires that the endowment of a good be allocated among those consuming it so that everyone has the same MWTP for it. What if the good has to be produced? To produce a good—say, biscuits—an economy must use factors of production that could have been used to produce apples. In Figure 2.4 we measure the total consumption of biscuits by George and Martha on the horizontal axis. Assuming that the biscuits are allocated efficiently between George and Martha, they have the same MWTP for biscuits. The curve labeled MWTP in Figure 2.4 is derived by adding the quantities of biscuits consumed by George and Martha at each level of the common MWTP. Geometrically, this is done by horizontally summing the MWTP curves of George and Martha. (To keep the figure simple, we do not show the individual MWTP curves.) Also shown is the marginal cost curve of producing biscuits, MC. The marginal cost of producing biscuits is the quantity of apples that the economy could have produced with the resources used to produce the last biscuit.[3] Typically, as more biscuits are produced, the marginal cost of producing biscuits increases, so the MC curve is upward-sloping.

The efficient level of production is B^* biscuits. At this quantity the consumers' MWTP for biscuits is equal to the MC of biscuits. At other quantities, the economy is not efficient. For instance, at output B_0, too few biscuits are produced, because the consumers' MWTP for biscuits (the amount of apples they are willing to give up for another biscuit) is greater than the marginal cost of producing biscuits (the amount of apples that must be given up to produce another biscuit).

At the efficient output of biscuits B^*, the area under the MWTP curve and above the MC curve is made as large as possible. This area is the sum of the surpluses to producers and consumers. It is equal to the TWTP for biscuits by the consumers (the area under the MWTP curve) minus the total cost of producing biscuits (the area under the MC curve). Assuming no fixed costs, the area under the MC curve is the total cost of producing biscuits because it is the sum of the marginal costs of producing each biscuit.

Measuring the Cost of Inefficiency

A T-shirt for sale at the Henry Art Gallery on the University of Washington campus reads "Any Surplus Is Immoral." Economists are not likely to agree, although they would grant that *marginal* surplus (the surplus associated with a change in

---

[3]Remember that because apples are the numeraire good, we can measure *values*, such as marginal costs, in *quantities* of apples.

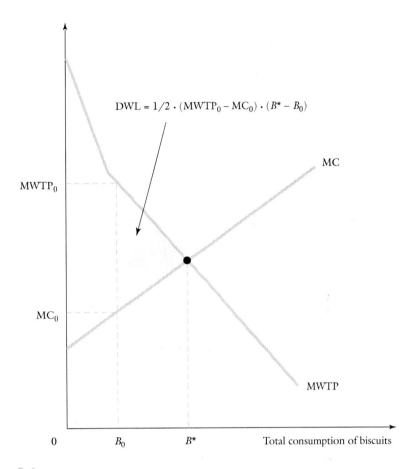

$$DWL = 1/2 \cdot (MWTP_0 - MC_0) \cdot (B^\star - B_0)$$

Figure 2.4

Measuring the Cost of an Inefficient Output

Efficiency requires that the output produced of a good be that for which the MWTP by consumers is equal to the marginal cost (MC) of producing it. If an inefficient quantity is produced, an inefficiency cost, or deadweight loss, equal to the area of the shaded triangle is caused. This can be measured as one-half the difference between the efficient (B^*) and actual (B_0) quantities of biscuits multiplied by the difference between the MWTP and the MC of biscuits at the actual output.

consumption) is inefficient. In fact, for economic efficiency, total surplus (for consumers and producers) should be maximized. If total surplus is not maximized, the economy is not efficient and a cost is imposed on the economy.

The cost of inefficiency, also called the deadweight loss (DWL), is measured as value lost to the economy when output is inefficient. Conversely, DWL measures the gain to the economy if resources are allocated more efficiently. The cost of the inefficiency (or DWL) of producing B_0 biscuits rather than B^* is equal to the area of the shaded triangle in Figure 2.4. When B_0 is produced, the economy loses the excess of the consumers' MWTP over the marginal cost of B^* minus B_0

biscuits. The area under the MWTP curve between B_0 and B^* is the consumers' willingness to pay for the extra biscuits, and the area under the MC curve is the cost of the extra biscuits to the economy.

When the MWTP and MC curves are linear, a quantitative expression for DWL is derived using the formula for the area of a triangle: one-half the height times the base. The height of the shaded triangle is the difference between $MWTP_0$ and MC_0. The base of the shaded triangle is $B^* - B_0$. Therefore, DWL is found as follows:

$$DWL = \frac{1}{2}(MCTP_0 - MC_0) \cdot (B^* - B_0).$$

For example, suppose a market failure causes a shortage of 100 biscuits relative to the efficient quantity. At this inefficient quantity, suppose the consumers' MWTP is 2 apples per biscuit and the marginal cost is 1 apple per biscuit. Using the triangle formula, the deadweight loss is equal to ½ times 1 apple per biscuit times 100 biscuits, or 50 apples. Here we measure DWL in terms of the numeraire good, apples. In practice DWL is measured in monetary units.

To summarize, economic efficiency requires certain equalities, all of which ensure that an economic resource is used where it has the highest value. In the two-person, two-good economy, economic efficiency requires the following equalities:

$$MWTP^G = MWTP^M = MC.$$

That is, George's marginal willingness to pay for biscuits is equal to Martha's marginal willingness to pay for biscuits, and both in turn are equal to the marginal cost of biscuits. When these conditions are met, the economy is Pareto optimal, and it is not possible to make either George or Martha better off without reducing the utility of the other.[4] When the conditions are not met, the economy is not efficient, and more value can be wrung from its resources. The lost value is measured by the deadweight loss.

MARKET SUCCESS AND MARKET FAILURE

This discussion helps us understand economic efficiency, but how does it help us understand the economic functions of government? We approach this question by considering a market economy where efficiency is achieved without governmental help.

Adam Smith's Invisible Hand

In a market economy, commercial value determined by prices and profits guides the allocation of resources. Market prices adjust to bring about a balance between the demands for different goods (by consumers who want to buy them) and the supplies available (from firms who want to sell them). Ever since Adam Smith,

---

[4]The conditions for economic efficiency are equalities because we are assuming that every factor is employed in producing every good, and every person consumes every good. More generally, inequality conditions occur when specialization occurs in the economy. These have been ignored in the interest of simplicity.

2.1   The Deadweight Loss of Christmas

Economists have long been puzzled by traditions of reciprocal gift giving, such as occurs at Christmas. In most cases, the gifts are in kind (goods and services); gifts of money, though perhaps not wholly unacceptable, are frowned upon. Some economists argue that reciprocal gift giving must impose a deadweight loss on the economy. The reason is that, ignoring sentimental value, gift receivers must value the gift at less than its monetary cost to the donor. If they valued it as much or more than its cost, they would have bought it for themselves. Professor Joel Waldfogel of Yale University asked a sample of Yale economics students to estimate the amount of cash that they would treat as equivalent in value to gifts they have received, ignoring sentimental value.[1] He found that, on average, respondents had an equivalent cash value (a marginal willingness to pay) equal to between 66% and 87% of the cost of the gift. Because the marginal willingness to pay for gifts received is less than the marginal cost of giving the gifts, Waldfogel argued that such gift giving imposes a deadweight loss on the economy. Based on Christmas gift spending of nearly $40 billion a year, he estimates the deadweight loss of Christmas to be equal to between $4 and $13 billion.

Critically analyze the following:

▪ Suppose Martha can buy flowers for $20 a bunch and buys ten bunches a year. George surprises her with two bunches of flowers a year. Show the deadweight loss in a diagram, assuming Martha has a downward-sloping MWTP curve for flowers.

▪ Waldfogel asked his students to value the gifts only as an object. Other researchers asked a sample of recipients the total value (including the value of sentiment) they place on gifts. In this case, they found that, on average, people value gifts at over 200% of their monetary cost.[2] If true, is the level of gift giving efficient or should there be more of it? If sentimental value is important, is it more efficient to give durable (keepsake) gifts like jewelry or spoilable gifts like flowers?

▪ Professor James Andreoni of the University of Wisconsin has shown that a donor gets a "warm glow" (of utility) by giving gifts, which is in addition to the utility of the recipient. How would such a warm glow affect the efficiency of reciprocal gift giving?

[1] Joel Waldfogel, "The Deadweight Loss of Christmas," 1993.
[2] Sara Solnick and David Hemenway, "The Deadweight Loss of Christmas: Comment," 1996.

economists have studied the role that market forces play in promoting the interest of the society.

In the *Wealth of Nations* Smith observes, "It is not from the benevolence of the butcher, the brewer, or the baker, that we expect our dinner, but from their regard for their own interest." Later, he argues that the individual merchant "intends only his own gain, and he is, in this and in many other cases, led by an invisible hand to promote an end which was no part of his intention. By pursuing his own interest he frequently promotes that of the society more effectually than when he really intends to promote it."

The modern version of Adam Smith's insight is called the **fundamental theorem of welfare economics**.[5] This theorem goes beyond Adam Smith's invisible

[5] There are actually two fundamental theorems of welfare economics. The one described here is called the *first fundamental theorem*.

hand by defining exactly the interest of society (efficiency) that is promoted by individual self-interest. It also describes the market conditions needed for the invisible
hand to lead to this result. The theorem is stated as follows:

> *Fundamental theorem of welfare economics: The market equilibrium of an ideal,
> well-functioning market system yields an efficient (Pareto optimal) allocation of the
> available economic resources.*

The theorem says that in a perfectly functioning—sometimes called **perfectly
competitive**—market system, the *independent* decisions made by consumers and
firms bring about an efficient allocation of resources without any need for coordination through government intervention. In this perfectly competitive market, consumers and firms pursue their self-interest and maximize their utilities and profits
respectively. All market participants must be *price takers,* so they cannot manipulate
market prices to increase their utilities at the expense of other parties.

It is useful to explain the logic of the fundamental theorem. Recall that a condition for efficiency is that Martha's MWTP for biscuits must equal George's.
How does the "invisible hand" bring that about? To answer this, suppose George
and Martha shop at the Mount Vernon market, where they buy apples and biscuits at posted money prices. Martha maximizes her utility by buying apples and
biscuits so that her MWTP for each good (in money) is equal the price posted in
the market.[6] In this case, her MWTP for biscuits in terms of apples (the slope of
her indifference curve) is equal to the *relative* price of the goods in the market.[7]
Shopping at the same market, George maximizes his utility in the same way. As
they leave the market, George and Martha have the same MWTP for the goods
because they maximized utilities by equating their respective MWTPs to the relative prices at the market. They did not need to coordinate their decisions to
achieve this. They maximized their utilities independently, and the "invisible
hand" did the rest.

How does the invisible hand ensure that George and Martha's MWTP for biscuits is equal to the MC of biscuits? The answer lies in the profit-maximizing decisions made by the producers. Perfectly competitive producers maximize their profit
by supplying an amount of each good so that the marginal cost (MC) is equal to
the market price. The ratio of the dollar marginal cost of biscuits to the dollar marginal cost of apples is the marginal cost of biscuits in terms of apples. Since the
profit-maximizing firms produce where price equals marginal cost, the MC of biscuits (in apples) is equal to the relative price of the two goods.

Market Failure and the Function of Government

When markets function well, as in the case of perfect competition, government policies are not needed to improve economic efficiency because the market allocation

---

[6] If Martha buys a combination of goods such that her MWTP for biscuits is greater than the market price
of biscuits and her MWTP for apples is less than the market price of apples, she is not maximizing her utility. She should return some of the apples to the shelf and use the extra money to buy more biscuits.
[7] The relative price is the ratio of the money prices, with the price of apples in the denominator.

is already efficient. At most, the government provides the institutions needed for the market system to function, such as a system of contract law and property rights enforcement. When markets depart from the perfectly competitive ideal, commercial incentives are no longer sufficient to direct resources to the uses that have the highest economic value. This is described as market failure. Market failure causes economic inefficiency, and the government can increase efficiency by choosing the appropriate policies to reallocate resources. We now briefly consider some important types of market failure and the government functions and policies they imply. Specifically, we examine four types of market failures: natural monopoly, public goods, externalities, and insurance market failure. As the last three are discussed in subsequent chapters, only natural monopoly is described in detail here.

NATURAL MONOPOLY. **Natural monopoly** describes a situation where a single producer can produce the entire output of a good at lower cost than can several producers. "Natural" means that, unlike in a contrived monopoly, a single producer is the most efficient way to produce market output. The main cause of natural monopoly is **economies of scale,** which means that as output increases fewer productive resources are required per unit of output. Examples of this occur in the distribution of water, natural gas, and electricity and in the telecommunications industries. It would be inordinately costly for several firms to provide these goods and services because it would require duplication of water and gas pipelines, and electricity and telephone wires.

The problem of natural monopoly is illustrated in Figure 2.5. In this case the quantity of a good, say electricity, is measured on the horizontal axis. The marginal cost (the incremental cost of producing an extra unit) is assumed constant, as shown by the horizontal line labeled MC, but average cost (total cost divided by output), shown by the curve labeled AC, declines steadily as output increases. Average cost declines because the large fixed costs are spread over more units of output. When average cost declines, marginal cost is necessarily less than average cost, as shown. The height of the demand curve, labeled D, indicates the consumers' MWTP for electricity. Because of natural monopoly, a single producer will occupy the market and, if uncontrolled, will seek to maximize profit by producing Q_M and charging a price P_M at which marginal revenue (shown by the curve labeled MR) is equal to MC. (See the main Appendix for a discussion of marginal revenue and profit maximization.)

The efficient output is Q^*, where MWTP is equal to MC. By charging a price equal to marginal cost P_{MC}, however, the producer would lose money because price is less than average cost. Without government intervention, the natural monopolist would earn a profit but produce much less than the efficient output. The efficiency cost of the uncontrolled natural monopolist is equal to the area of the triangle efg.

What sort of government intervention is needed in the case of natural monopoly? In many countries, the government owns public utilities including nationalized electric and telephone companies. In principle, a government-owned utility could charge P_{MC} and sell the efficient quantity of the good or service. Their losses are financed with government tax revenue. (In fact, many government utilities charge a high price and raise revenue for the government.) In the United States, government

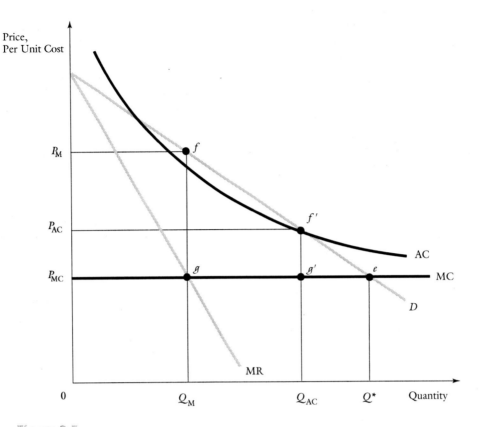

Figure 2.5
Natural Monopoly
In a natural monopoly, marginal cost (MC) is less than average cost (AC), which declines steadily as output rises. At the efficient output Q^*, where price equals marginal cost, the firm has negative economic profit. At the profit-maximizing output Q_M, a deadweight loss equal to the area of triangle *efg* is incurred. Typically, natural monopolies are regulated to set price equal to average cost, which occurs at output Q_{AC}. The firm breaks even, and a smaller deadweight loss equal to the area of the triangle *ef'g'* is incurred.

ownership is less common, although municipal governments own some local public utilities. Instead, the government regulates the rates set by investor-owned public utilities. Regulation is done by state governments and, in the case of interstate commerce of energy, the Federal Energy Regulation Commission (FERC).

In regulating rates, the government usually requires the public utilities to set rates no higher than average cost. In this case, the utilities set price P_{AC} and produce output Q_{AC}. Public utilities break even (earn a normal rate of return on their assets) and impose a smaller efficiency cost, equal to the area of the triangle *ef'g'*. Regulators could achieve full efficiency by requiring the utility to set its rates at marginal cost (P_{MC}), but in this case the government would have to subsidize the utility to cover its losses. Taxes, which typically impose efficiency costs of their own (discussed in Chapter 12), would have to be levied to finance the subsidy. This is an example of the theory of the second-best, discussed later in this chapter.

Under average-cost rate regulation, utilities have little incentive to minimize costs, so another type of efficiency cost (not shown) may arise. Also, rate-regulated public utilities may overinvest in capital facilities. For this reason, *deregulation* has become widespread in the United States. Under deregulation, the government maintains regulation or ownership of the *common carriers* (the distribution network of wires, pipelines, and microwave networks) and allows private companies to compete to provide service to consumers using these facilities.

PUBLIC GOODS.   In the natural monopoly discussion above, the good produced is an ordinary market good in the sense that it is a **rival good.** Only one consumer can consume a unit of rival good, like a kilowatt-hour of electricity or a gallon of water. If more people consume a rival good, more must be produced. A **public good** can be consumed by everyone for the same cost as providing it for one person. A lighthouse is a classic example of a public good. The lighthouse signal that warns one ship away from a dangerous reef warns all. Whether the lighthouse warns a single ship or a thousand, the cost is the same. For this reason, a public good is called **nonrival.**

In addition to being nonrival, many public goods are also **nonexcludable.** A good is nonexcludable if there is no practical way of denying it to people who will not pay for it. A lighthouse is also nonexcludable, because it would be difficult or impossible for a private firm to charge a fee to a ship for the benefit of seeing the warning signal from the lighthouse.[8]

MARKET EXTERNALITIES.   At the efficient output, the marginal cost of a good to the producing firm must equal the marginal cost to the economy. Similarly, the MWTP of the buyer must equal the MWTP for the economy. The marginal cost to the economy may be different from the marginal cost to the firm if production imposes costs on parties not involved in the market transaction. Similarly, the MWTP for the economy may differ from the MWTP of the individual consumer. These are called external costs and benefits, respectively.

An example of an external cost is a firm that causes pollution by reducing the quality of air or water. The external cost, imposed on people living and working around the firm who have a lower-quality environment, is part of the economy's marginal cost of the good, but it is not part of the marginal cost to the firm. The firm ignores the external cost, because it does not have to pay the people who are adversely affected.[9] Thus the external pollution cost is not incorporated in the market price of the good, making it appear less costly to consumers than it really is. For this reason, they consume an excessive quantity of the good from the standpoint of economic efficiency.

Since market output is inefficient with externalities, government allocative policies can be used to increase economic efficiency. For example, the government can

---

[8]Private lighthouses did exist at one time. These lighthouses warned ships of hazards entering a port to use facilities that were also owned by the lighthouse owner. The cost of the lighthouse was included in the port fees charged to the ship owners.

[9]That is, unless the firm is forced to compensate the people hurt by the pollution. In fact, this is one approach that government policy might take as a remedy to market failure.

regulate the amount of pollutants that firms discharge, or it can force firms to purchase pollution-reducing equipment. These are the types of policies administered through the Environmental Protection Agency in the United States.

INSURANCE MARKET FAILURE.   Insurance is a service that is widely sold by private insurance firms. But some types of risk are not insured completely, or at all, by private companies. For example, it is difficult or impossible to buy from private companies insurance against being laid off from your job. People want to insure against this risk, just as they want to insure against the risk that their house will burn down, so why don't insurance companies sell such policies?[10]

One reason for insurance market failure is that private insurance companies cannot distinguish between consumers who are a "good risk" and those who are a "bad risk" when selling insurance. They must set insurance premiums high enough to cover a mixture of good- and bad-risk consumers. But at such high premiums, only the bad-risk consumers want to buy insurance. The good-risk people don't buy insurance, because they'd be subsiding the bad-risk people. For instance, few university professors with tenure would buy private unemployment insurance because they know they have a low risk of losing their jobs. If the good risks drop out of the risk pool, the private insurance companies are left insuring only the bad risks. This prevents them from providing insurance at reasonable rates to all persons who need it.

ADVANCED ISSUES IN ECONOMIC EFFICIENCY

The analysis of economic efficiency considered so far is highly simplified. Two main issues complicate the application of the conditions of economic efficiency to real-world policy problems. The first is the possible impact of policies on the distribution of income, which raises concerns about equity. The second is the existence of distortions that prevent full efficiency and cannot be removed. In this case, the economists must search for "second-best" levels of economic efficiency.

Illustrating Efficiency and Equity Choices

An economy can be efficient but have a highly unequal, or inequitable, distribution of income. Using an earlier analogy, economic efficiency concerns the overall size of the cake; it says nothing about equity, which is about how the cake is divided among many consumers. If we want to consider equity in the distribution of income, it is necessary to make stronger value judgments than those proposed by Pareto.

Efficiency and equity choices are illustrated in Figure 2.6. We again simplify by considering an economy with just two people, George and Martha. We measure the utility of George on the horizontal axis and the utility of Martha on the vertical axis. Given the scarcity of the economy's resources, a limited set of utilities distributions

---

[10]Insurance that replaces your salary if you are injured and unable to work is available from private companies. This type of insurance is not subject to the market failure described in this section.

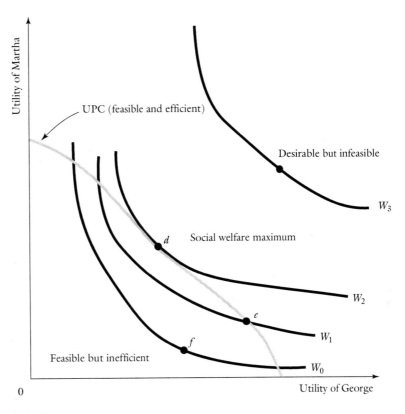

Figure 2.6
Maximizing Social Welfare
The utilities possibilities curve (UPC) separates the feasible and unfeasible distributions of utilities in an economy. An efficient allocation of resources allows a distribution of utilities on the UPC. At point *d*, the economy maximizes social welfare where the UPC is tangent to the highest social welfare indifference curve.

is possible. The **utilities possibilities curve (UPC)** is derived by finding the maximum utility of one person—say, George—for a given level of utility for the other. Every distribution of utilities on or inside the UPC is feasible in this economy. Points on the UPC are efficient or Pareto optimal; points inside the curve are inefficient. Points outside the UPC are desirable but are not feasible.

Figure 2.6 can help us think more clearly about government policies. A policy that promises to deliver a distribution of utilities lying outside the UPC would be popular, but it is not feasible.[11] A politician who advocates such a policy is preaching "pie in the sky." More realistically, government policies can achieve three things. First, if the economy is inside the UPC to begin with, the government can choose policies that make the economy more efficient by allocating resources to more highly valued uses. Such allocative policies can be used to achieve a distribution of

---

[11]A policy that promises more government spending and lower taxes at the same time would be an example.

2.2   Market Failure and Orphan Drugs

Orphan drugs are pharmaceutical products that are beneficial to people with rare health conditions. Because demand for the products is limited and the fixed costs of developing them are high, private pharmaceutical companies have no commercial incentive to develop and market orphan drugs. The argument is illustrated in the figure below. The demand curve, showing the consumers' MWTP, is very steep but only small quantities of the drug are demanded because the condition it treats is rare. The marginal (incremental) cost of producing the drug (once developed) is low, shown by the curve labeled MC, but the average cost (AC) is high. Average cost includes the high fixed costs of development. Once developed, the fixed costs are "sunk" costs and are irrelevant

for efficiency. The efficient quantity is Q^*, where MWTP is equal to MC.

The orphan drug problem bears similarity to the natural monopoly discussed earlier. Unlike the earlier case, there is no level of output at which the firm can earn a profit because the MWTP curve lies everywhere below the AC curve. The question is whether it is efficient to develop the drugs. It is efficient to develop a drug if its economic value is high enough to justify total cost. If Q^* is produced, the economic value is equal to the TWTP of consumers, which is equal to the area under the demand curve up to Q^*. The total cost is average cost times quantity, which is equal to the area of the rectangle labeled $0Q^*B(AC^*)$. The economic value of the drug exceeds total cost if the light shaded tri-

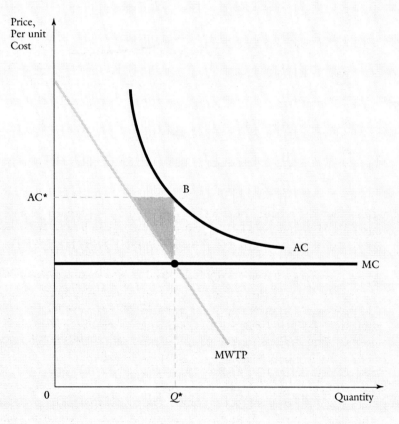

angle in the figure is larger than the dark shaded triangle, as shown. Nonetheless, the commercial value of the drug might not be high enough to warrant development, so the failure to develop is a market failure. The source of the market failure is nonappropriability—most of the economic value of the drug is in the form of consumers' surplus.

Critically analyze the following questions:

▪ Is there a commercial incentive to develop the drug shown in the figure? Would your answer be different if the company could perfectly price discriminate—that is, charge the highest price a consumer is willing to pay at each quantity?

▪ In 1983, Congress passed the *Orphan Drug Act,* which relaxes the testing requirements of the

Food and Drug Administration for new drugs developed for diseases affecting fewer than 200,000 persons in the United States. Such testing constitutes a significant fraction of the fixed costs of developing a drug. Explain, using the figure, how this Act would affect the decision to develop the drug.

▪ Other products, such as computer software, have low marginal cost of production and high fixed costs of development. As yet, Congress has not passed an "Orphan Software Act." Is it likely that such an Act would increase economic efficiency? (Hint: A necessary condition for market failure in this example is a very inelastic demand curve.)

utilities on the UPC. Second, if the economy is already on the UPC, the government can use tax and transfer policies to achieve a different distribution of utilities. These are described as distributional policies. Finally, the government may be able to shift the UPC to the right by increasing the total amounts of goods and services in the economy—say, by encouraging technological improvements. These growth and technology policies are used to augment the economy's productive resources or improve its technology.

When the economy is inside the UPC, the desirability of a policy that moves it to the UPC is clear enough. Such a policy can make everyone better off. For instance, both George and Martha are better off at the efficient utilities distribution *e* than at the inefficient distribution *f*. Suppose now that we are already on the UPC. How can we compare one efficient distribution of utilities with another and declare that one is better? To do this we must be able to weigh the gain in one person's utility against the loss to another, a comparison Pareto was not prepared to do.

In modern welfare economics, comparison of utilities is done using a **social welfare function.** This is simply a mathematical way of expressing the level of social welfare in the society as a function of (i.e., depending on) the distribution of utilities of the people in the economy. The social welfare function can take different forms to represent assumptions about distributional equity.

The social welfare function is discussed later in Chapter 7. For now, the idea of a social welfare function is shown in Figure 2.6 by an indifference curve map. Usually we think of indifference curves as consumption bundles that give a certain consumer a fixed level of utility (see the main Appendix at the end of the book for a discussion of consumer indifference curves). In Figure 2.6, the social welfare indifference curves consist of distributions of utilities that give society an equal level of social welfare. For instance, the social welfare indifference curve labeled W_0 represents all of the utilities distributions that give the society (consisting only of George and Martha) the same level of social welfare as the utilities distribution labeled *f*.

The assumptions about distributional equity embodied in the social welfare function allow the government to choose among different utilities distributions on the UPC. All distributions on the UPC are efficient, but the one labeled d gives a higher level of social welfare than any other. This distribution is the one where the UPC is tangent to the highest possible social welfare indifference curve W_2. To find such an optimal distribution of utilities would require the government to have an agreed-upon social welfare function. This does not seem likely in practice. Nevertheless, the idea of maximizing a social welfare function can sometimes be a useful way of thinking about policy issues in public finance.

In Search of the "Second-Best"

So far, we have idealized the role of government policy, in a certain sense. Welfare economics as it is described above is a search for the **first-best.** The first-best is an economic optimum that is constrained only by scarcity of the resources available to the economy. Sometimes, however, the best the government can achieve is a more modest outcome. In 1956, Professors Richard Lipsey and Kelvin Lancaster described a type of optimality they call **second-best.** They looked at the problem of choosing more desirable policy when some constraint prevents some of the conditions of efficiency from being satisfied. For example, efficiency requires that MWTP equal marginal cost for each good, but what if this condition is not satisfied for some good? What is the second-best that can be achieved? Is it desirable that MWTP equal marginal cost for the rest of the goods?

The answer is, "Not necessarily." Lipsey and Lancaster showed that a constraint that prevents one condition of efficiency from being satisfied may make it desirable to violate the others. The reason is that departing from the efficiency condition in one market can "cancel out" inefficiency existing in another market. In other words, in welfare economics "two wrongs can make a right."

An example is setting the fare for a public transit system. The efficiency condition for a first-best optimum is to set the fare equal to the marginal cost of the ride. People will ride the transit system only if their MWTP is as high as the fare, and this ensures that MWTP equals MC. But what if the alternative to public transit is commuting by car? Commuting by car has an external cost on the economy because additional drivers add to road congestion and air pollution. The price for using the road (zero) is not equal to the marginal cost of using it, so the MWTP to commute by car is not equal to MC. This is the second-best constraint. Given that the condition for efficiency is not satisfied in the use of public roads, it may be desirable to set fares on a public transit system below the marginal cost of the ride. This way commuters are encouraged not to drive, and the economy is made better off because road congestion and air pollution from commuting by automobiles are reduced.

The world of the second-best is a messier place than the world of the first-best, so economists enter it reluctantly. Why should constraints of the type introduced by Lipsey and Lancaster be irremovable? Resource constraints are understandable enough—there are only so many resources available in the economy—but what sort of constraint prevents a condition of efficiency, like setting price equal to marginal cost, from being satisfied?

Generally, the theory of the second-best reflects three types of constraints: political, property rights, and informational. The first two are relatively easy to understand. One reason for a second-best constraint is the existence of political "sacred cows," such as a subsidy for an industry located in the district of an influential member of Congress. This subsidy means that price is not equal to marginal cost in this industry, but it cannot be removed, for political reasons.

The absence of private property rights on public roads explains the second-best constraint in the example of public transit. If property rights for the use of a road can be established and enforced, users would be charged a toll for the congestion and pollution they create. In this case, price is set equal to marginal cost for the use of the road, and the most efficient fare for the public transit system is the marginal cost of the ride.

Constraints arising from limits on the information available to the government are subtler. The distribution of incomes realized in an economy depends on people's efforts, as well as their abilities and ownership of productive resources. People may be poor through no fault of their own, and equity requires the government to redistribute income to them. However, people who shirk on effort may also be poor. For example, a distribution like the one labeled point f in Figure 2.6, where Martha is far less well off than George, could arise because Martha puts in little effort whereas George works hard.

Martha might expend little effort because she expects the government to transfer income to her in the interest of greater equity. If the government had full information and knew that Martha's ability to earn income was no less than George's, it would judge them equally worthy and find no need to redistribute. In this case, Martha would also have no incentive to shirk on effort. But the government has limited ability to determine a household's effort, so as a practical matter it must base its redistribution decisions on observed economic circumstances. In this case, redistribution necessarily distorts household effort decisions. In other words, "first-best" redistribution, the type assumed in the compensation principle, is infeasible and the government must choose "second-best" policies that impose a trade-off between efficiency and equity. The **efficiency-equity trade-off** is considered further in Chapter 7.

CONCLUSION AND SUMMARY

In this chapter we have focused on economic efficiency as a justification for the economic policies of government. Economists stress economic efficiency because it is their specialty. However, in actual policy making, considerations of equity and political feasibility also play important roles in determining government decisions. We discuss these considerations in later chapters. In the next two chapters we expand on two important causes of market failure—public goods and market externalities—and discuss some of the programs governments enact in response to them.

- Normative economics (also called welfare economics) is a method for evaluating the worth of government policies. The main welfare criteria in normative economics are economic efficiency and distributional equity or fairness. In this chapter, we focused on economic efficiency as a justification for various economic roles of government.

- An economy is efficient if productive resources are employed in uses that have the highest economic value. Economic value is measured by the marginal willingness to pay (MWTP) for goods and services by consumers and the marginal opportunity cost of those goods or services to producers.

- An economy that is efficient is also Pareto optimal, which means that it is not possible to make one group of people in the economy better off without harming the welfare of others.

- Pareto optimality requires that consumers have the same marginal willingness to pay for a good if they both consume it. In turn, this common marginal willingness to pay should be equal to the marginal opportunity cost of producing the good. These are known as the efficiency conditions.

- The allocation of resources determined by an ideal market system, called perfectly competitive, is efficient because commercial values are equal to economic values. This result is known as the fundamental theorem of welfare economics. An efficient economy, however, need not be equitable.

- Real-world market economies are generally not efficient in the absence of government policies because of market failures. Causes of market failure include natural monopoly, public goods, externalities, and imperfect information in insurance markets.

- Where markets fail, resources are not employed in uses that have the highest economic value. Government can make the economy more efficient with programs and policies that reallocate economic resources, such as spending on defense and education. Governments may also subsidize or regulate private economic activity and offer social insurance programs.

- The cost of inefficiency can be measured as a deadweight loss on the economy. The deadweight loss is equivalent to the economy having fewer economic resources.

- In determining efficient policies, equity issues are avoided by assuming that the government can carry out lump-sum redistribution so that the gainers from the policies compensate any losers. This is called the compensation principle.

- In real-world policy making, the government typically has to settle for the second-best. The theory of the second-best analyzes how economic efficiency can be increased when certain constraints prevent the efficiency conditions from being fully satisfied.

- In a second-best economy, the government often faces a trade-off between greater efficiency and greater equity. This is because the government's attempts to redistribute income affect economic incentives and create inefficiency.

QUESTIONS FOR DISCUSSION AND REVIEW

1. Sometimes it is argued that a Pareto improvement may not be an improvement at all, because someone's utility could be reduced simply from being made *relatively* worse off. For example, suppose the poor *feel* worse off when they see someone else being made better off, even if their own consumption is unchanged. Is there a Pareto improvement?

2. A production process is inefficient from an engineering perspective if you can get the same physical quantity of a given output (say, tons of steel) by using less of some factors (labor, capital, raw materials, etc.). Can an economy be engineering-inefficient and Pareto optimal? Can it be engineering-efficient and not Pareto optimal?

3. Suppose Martha is allergic to apples and George cannot eat biscuits because of his false teeth. Is there a Pareto optimal allocation of a fixed endowment of apples and biscuits? Is it unique?

4. Does your total willingness to pay for water per month exceed your monthly water bill? Does it make a difference whether your water bill contains a fixed charge (an amount you must pay regardless of how much or how little water you consume)?

5. Figure 2.4 illustrates the deadweight loss caused when less than the efficient quantity of biscuits is produced. Is there a deadweight loss if too much is produced (that is, the quantity produced is greater than $B^\star$)? Illustrate with a diagram.

6. Internet Exercise. The government's agriculture policy often causes economic inefficiency. For example, the government may set floors on certain crop prices. A price floor is a minimum price that farmers must receive for certain crops and obligates the government to buy any surplus that the government cannot sell in private markets. In a diagram, show how such price floors would cause a deadweight loss. If you have any trouble, click on to the "Hands on" economics site provided by Purdue University's agricultural economics department at http://www.agecon.purdue.edu/academic/handson/theproduct/html/policymenu.html and click on the "welfare economics" module. This site provides a lively graphical illustration of the deadweight loss of different agricultural policies.

7. Many economists argue that deadweight losses cannot occur unless there is a market failure or the government interferes with voluntary exchange with regulations or taxes. If so, can you identify any reasons that there should be a deadweight loss to Christmas as described in A Case in Point 2.1?

8. In a recent antitrust trial, the Department of Justice (DOJ) contends that Microsoft's Windows® constitutes a form of natural monopoly. Because there are costs to having different users use different computer operating systems, it is more efficient for everyone to adopt the same software, in this case Microsoft's product. Suppose, for the sake of argument, this is indeed the case. What kind of cost of inefficiency would Microsoft impose if it prices Windows® to maximize profit? How would the DOJ want Microsoft to price its product if its goal is to eliminate inefficiency? Given that Windows® has high development costs but low marginal cost of production, what would be the difficulty in the DOJ's solution?

9. Suppose one presidential candidate promises to end government waste by eliminating programs such as the ethanol

subsidy. Another promises to make the economy more fair by raising taxes on the rich to increase welfare spending for the poor. Yet another promises to help every-body by reducing all taxes without cutting back any government programs. Illustrate these political promises using Figure 2.6.

SELECTED REFERENCES

The classic work on utilitarianism is *Principles of Morals and Legislation* by Jeremy Bentham (1791). A classical perspective on welfare economics is found in *Economics of Welfare* by A. C. Pigou; a "modern" treatment is found in *Welfare Economics* by Robin Boadway and Neil Bruce (1984).

Harold Hotelling proposed the method for measuring deadweight loss outlined in this chapter in "The General Welfare in Relation to Problems of Taxation and of Railway and Utility Rates" in *Econometrica* (1938). The meth-odology was developed further by Arnold C. Harberger; see Chapters 1 to 4 in his book *Taxation and Welfare* (1971).

The concept of the social welfare function was introduced by A. Bergson in "A Reformulation of Certain Aspects of Welfare Economics" in *Quarterly Journal of Economics* (1938).

"The General Theory of Second Best" by Richard G. Lipsey and Kevin Lancaster in the *Review of Economic Studies* (1956) formalizes the theory of second-best.

A P P E N D I X   T O   C H A P T E R   2

Illustrating Economic Efficiency with the Box Diagram

An economy consists of two people, George and Martha, and two goods, apples and biscuits. The total apples and biscuits in the economy are fixed at $\bar{A}$ and $\bar{B}$, respectively. Figure A.2.1 is a box with vertical and horizontal dimensions equal to $\bar{A}$ and $\bar{B}$. We can use the lower left-hand corner as the origin for Martha's consumption diagram, so her consumption of apples is measured along the left-hand side of the box above the lower left corner and her consumption of biscuits is measured to the right along the bottom of the box. We can use the upper right-hand corner for the origin of George's consumption diagram. This is a little confusing because George's consumption diagram is drawn upside down, but turning the book upside down puts George's diagram in its usual orientation. We measure George's consumption of apples down the right-hand side of the box from the upper right-hand corner and his consumption of biscuits to the left along the top of the box.

Using these axes, any point within the box or on its edges represents an allocation of the endowment of apples and biscuits between George and Martha. For example, at the lower right-hand corner, Martha consumes all of the biscuits and George consumes all of the apples. At the midpoint of the box, George and Martha consume equal quantities of both goods. The consumption of apples and biscuits by George and Martha for an arbitrary allocation f is also shown.

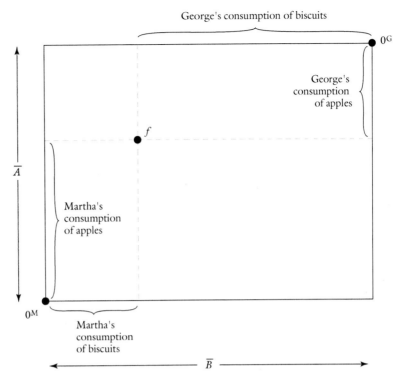

George's consumption of biscuits

0^G

George's
consumption
of apples

f

Martha's
consumption
of apples

$\overline{A}$

0^M

Martha's
consumption
of biscuits

$\overline{B}$

Figure A.2.1

Constructing the Edgeworth Box

The dimensions of the box are equal to the endowment of two goods for the economy as a whole. Measured from the origin 0^M, a point in the box shows Martha's consumption of the two goods. Measured from the origin 0^G, the same point shows George's consumption. Every point in the box and on the edges represents an allocation of the two goods across the two consumers.

We complete the diagram by drawing some of the indifference curves for George and Martha. Remember that George's indifference curve map is upside down. The completed diagram, shown in Figure A.2.2, is the **Edgeworth box diagram.** We can use the Edgeworth box diagram to show how a Pareto improvement can be achieved by reallocating resources toward their most highly valued uses. In this simple economy, our resources are the endowments of the two goods. At allocation f, George gets utility level U_f^G and Martha gets utility level U_f^M. George gets high utility for allocations to the left of this indifference curve (away from his origin) and Martha gets higher utility for allocations to the right of hers (away from her origin). Thus, at all of the allocations inside the lens-shaped area formed by the indifference curves U_f^G and U_f^M to the southeast of point f, George and Martha have higher utility, or one has higher utility and the other has no less. These allocations represent Pareto improvements. Note that both George and Martha can be made better off even though there are no more apples or biscuits in the economy. The apples and biscuits are simply reallocated between them. Where does the Pareto improvement come from?

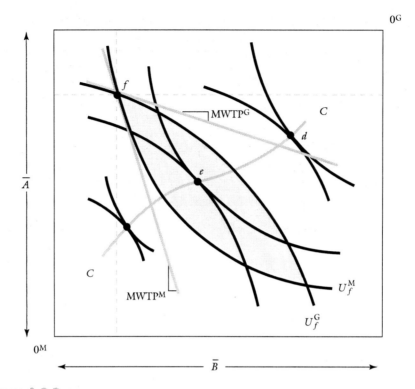

Figure A.2.2
Illustrating a Pareto Improvement in the Edgeworth Box
Drawing in Martha's and George's indifference curves relative to origins 0^M and 0^G respectively, we see that a reallocation of goods can yield a Pareto improvement when the MWTPs of the consumers are not equal. At allocation f, Martha's MWTP for biscuits is greater than George's MWTP for biscuits. Allocations where Martha consumes more biscuits and George consumes more apples, shown by the shaded lens-shaped area, give both consumers higher utility. Along the contract curve CC, the MWTPs of the consumers are equal, so one consumer gets higher utility only if the other gets less.

Looking at the slopes of the indifference curves of George and Martha at point f, we see that Martha's indifference curve is much steeper than George's. In other words, Martha has a higher MWTP for biscuits (in terms of giving up apples) than George does. Alternatively, George has a higher MWTP for apples, since his MWTP for biscuits in apples is very low. Thus at f Martha's consumption is the more highly valued use for biscuits and George's consumption is the more highly valued use for apples. When we reallocate resources into the lens-shaped shaded area, Martha consumes more biscuits and George consumes more apples, so we are reallocating our resources to where they have higher value.

Common sense tells us that such Pareto improvements cannot continue indefinitely. At some point, we can no longer reallocate consumption between George and Martha so that both of them get higher utility. At allocation e Martha's indifference curve is tangent to George's. In other words, Martha and George have the same MWTP for biscuits (and apples) at point e. Since it is not possible to achieve a Pareto improvement at allocation e, this allocation is a Pareto optimum.

The fact that an allocation is a Pareto optimum does not mean it is unique in this respect. There are infinitely many Pareto optimal allocations, even in this simple economy. Every point in the box diagram where the indifference curves of George and Martha are tangent is Pareto optimal. Pareto optimal allocations are shown in the box diagram by the curve CC. Economists call this line the **contract curve.** The contract curve illustrates an important point about the Pareto criterion: It is neutral about distributional equity. There are allocations on the contract curve where George and Martha get very different levels of utility, and allocations where they both enjoy roughly the same level of utility. Every allocation on CC is efficient, but society may not find them all equitable.

In Figure A.2.2, both consumers are made better off by switching from the inefficient allocation f to the efficient allocation e. However, it is possible to move from an inefficient allocation to an efficient allocation without a Pareto improvement in welfare. For example, allocation d on the contract curve is efficient, but George gets less utility at d than he does at the inefficient allocation f. If someone is made worse of by a switch from an inefficient to an efficient allocation, how can we say that an increase in efficiency is desirable?

The answer is based on the compensation principle developed by the British economists Sir John Hicks, Nobel Laureate 1972, and Nicholas Kaldor. According to the compensation principle, switching from inefficient allocation f to efficient allocation d is desirable because Martha, who gains from the switch, can make a payment to George, who initially loses, so that he too is better off. The side payment can be made by Martha voluntarily, or implemented through government tax and transfer policies. A side payment, by whatever method, allows the economy to reach an efficient allocation like e where everyone has higher utility. Thus an increase in efficiency makes possible a **potential Pareto improvement** in welfare, but not necessarily an actual Pareto improvement. It is this logic that supports the belief that efficiency is desirable, even if someone is made worse off in the process.

3 Public Goods in Theory and Practice

Although economists often use consumables such as food and clothing as examples of goods, the concept also encompasses less tangible things like the degree of safety we feel when walking down a city street, the cleanliness of the air we breathe, a lighthouse signal on a dangerous reef, and viewing a Vermeer collection at the National Gallery. These goods and services have some special properties, which lead economists to call them *public goods*. In this chapter we see why the government can play an important role in allocating resources more efficiently by producing and providing public goods.

NONRIVAL AND NONEXCLUDABLE GOODS

A good or service is **nonrival** if it can be consumed and enjoyed by everyone in the community at no greater cost than that of providing it for one person. That is, the cost of providing a nonrival good or service to an extra consumer is zero once it has been produced. (From this point on, we will use the word *good* to include both goods and services.) A broadcast TV program is a classic case of a completely nonrival good. Although the program is costly to produce, the production cost is the same whether one viewer or a million viewers watch the program.

In contrast, a good is **rival** if the marginal cost of providing a unit to a consumer is equal to the marginal cost of producing the good. A pizza is a rival good. The more people share a pizza, the less pizza each person can consume, so consumers are *rivals* for pizza.

A good is **nonexcludable** if there is no practical way of stopping people from consuming it (excluding them) if they refuse to pay. A broadcast TV program is not only nonrival; it is also nonexcludable, because it is not practical to stop people who refuse to pay from watching the program.[1] Although nonrivalry and nonexcludability are often combined in a good, they are distinct properties. Nonpaying consumers can be excluded from some nonrival goods. For example, a pay-per-view TV program is nonrival because the cost of an extra viewer is negligible. However, nonpaying viewers can easily be excluded by scrambling the signal.

---

[1]Strictly speaking, this is not quite true. In Britain, people must pay a fee to use a TV set to watch broadcast TV. The government equips a truck with a special antenna that can detect an operating TV set from the street. People found with operating TVs who have not paid the license fee are fined, or even imprisoned.

The "public" nature of a good defines the extent to which it possesses nonrivalry and nonexcludability. A **pure public good** is one that is completely nonrival, so the marginal cost of an extra user is zero, and completely nonexcludable, so that it is impossible to exclude nonpaying consumers at any cost. National defense is a good example of a pure public good. The cost of deterring war or preventing an invasion of the nation's territory by an enemy is the same regardless of size of the population, so national defense is nonrival. Nor is it possible to deny anyone living in the country the feeling of safety from aggression that national defense provides, so national defense is nonexcludable.

A **pure private good** is completely rival, and it is easy to exclude any consumer who refuses to pay. For example, pizza is rival, as explained earlier. It is also easy to exclude nonpaying consumers. If we refuse to pay the delivery person, we will not get the pizza. Most, but not all, market goods are pure private goods.

Generally, we refer to any good that is nonrival, nonexcludable, or both as a public good. Although public goods are often provided by the government, we should not assume that every good provided by the government is a public good. Nor are all public goods provided by the government. Garbage collection, say, is often provided by the city government, but it is both a rival and (potentially) an excludable good. In other words, garbage collection is a private good that happens to be provided by the government. On the other hand, most TV programs, even those on broadcast TV, are provided by private firms. Nonetheless, television programs have the properties of public goods. Private firms are able to provide broadcast TV programs, even though consumers cannot be excluded, because the programs can be "packaged" with advertising messages for which other firms are willing to pay the broadcaster. To keep the distinctions between the nature of the goods and the nature of the providers clear, we will describe all goods provided by the government as *government-provided* (rather than public) goods, and we will describe all goods sold by commercial firms as *privately provided*.

EFFICIENT OUTPUT OF A PUBLIC GOOD

An important question facing every economy is how much of the different public goods to produce. As always, the economy has resource constraints. Enjoying more of a public good like national defense means enjoying less of private goods like food and clothing because economic resources used to produce public goods are not available to produce private goods. In this section, we derive the conditions that describe the efficient quantity of a public good. In Chapter 2 we saw that the quantity of a good is efficient if the resources are employed in their highest-valued use. When is the public good the highest-valued use for our scarce economic resources? How does the nonrival nature of a public good affect the conditions needed for economic efficiency? To answer these questions, we start by planning a party.

An Illustration: Planning a Party

The difference between the conditions for an efficient quantity of a public good and those for a private good can be illustrated with a commonplace example. Suppose we want to plan a party. To make it simple, we will have a small party with only four people. We want to have a good time, but we don't want to waste our money. That is, we don't want to spend our money unless it gives a greater or equal value of enjoyment to the party guests. At the party we will have two goods—wine and songs. Our problem is how much to buy of each.[2]

The people at the party are George and Martha and John and Abigail. Their marginal willingness to pay (MWTP) schedules for the private good wine are shown in Table 3.1. For instance, George is willing to pay $2 for his first glass of wine, $1.75 for his second, and so on, down to $0.25 for the eighth. The MWTP schedules for wine by the other guests are shown in the other columns. The guests have different tastes, so their MWTP schedules are different.

If the marginal cost of wine is $1 (that is, each glass costs $1), how much wine should we order for the party? The answer to this question is straightforward. We should order a glass of wine for a guest as long as his or her MWTP is more than (or equal to) $1. Thus, we order five glasses for George because his MWTP for each of the five glasses is more than $1. We order no more than five for George because his MWTP for the sixth glass is only $0.75. Similarly, we order three glasses for Martha, six glasses for John, and two glasses for Abigail. The fact that the guests have *different tastes* for the rival good means that they consume *different quantities* of wine. Note that all guests have the same MWTP for the last glass of wine they consume ($1). Furthermore, because wine is a rival good (each glass can be drunk by only one guest), we must add the quantities consumed by each guest to find the total quantity of wine to order (16 glasses).

The problem is different when we are ordering songs. To simplify, we assume that the band knows only one song, "Hail to the Chief," and the question is how many times we should ask the musicians to play it. The MWTP schedules for the song for each guest are shown in Table 3.2, and we assume that each guest's MWTP decreases the more times the song is played. The guests have different tastes in music, so they have different MWTP schedules. To determine the number of times the song should be played, we must recognize that playing a song is a nonrival good.

Table 3.1 **MWTP for Wine: George and Martha and John and Abigail**

Glasses of wine per guest	MWTP (in dollars)			
	George	Martha	John	Abigail
1	$2.00	$1.50	$1.50	$1.20
2	1.75	1.25	1.40	**1.00**
3	1.50	**1.00**	1.30	0.80
4	1.25	0.75	1.20	0.60
5	**1.00**	0.50	1.10	0.40
6	0.75	0.25	**1.00**	0.20
7	0.50	0	0.90	0
8	0.25	0	0.80	0

---

[2]We are not actually going to charge the guests, because this is a party; but that fact is not important.

Table 3.2   **MWTP for a Song: George and Martha and John and Abigail**

Number of times song is played	MWTP (in dollars)				Sum of MWTPs for song
	George	Martha	John	Abigail	
1	$4	$2	$5	$1	$12
2	3	1.50	4	0.50	9
3	2	1	3	0	6
4	1	0.50	2	(0.50)	3
5	0	0	1	(1)	0

All four guests can enjoy the song when the band plays it, so the MWTP of the party for a rendition of the song is the sum of the MWTPs of the guests. For instance, the sum of the MWTPs for the first rendition is $12 ($4 + $2 + $5 + $1). The right-hand column shows the sum of the guests' MWTPs to hear the song for each number of times the song is played. Note that it is possible for the MWTP of a guest to be negative (a negative MWTP is shown in parentheses). Abigail doesn't like the song very much, so by the fourth time, she has a negative MWTP for it. This means she would have to be paid $0.50 to listen to the song a fourth time.[3]

Suppose the band charges $6 each time it plays the song, so the marginal cost of song is $6. In this case, we should order the musicians to play the song three times. We do not want them to play the song a fourth time because the sum of the guests' MWTPs to hear it again is only $3. Together George and Martha and John have a combined MWTP of $3.50, but Abigail has to be paid $0.50 to hear the song again. Note that different guests have different MWTPs for the third rendition of the song. Since all guests must hear the song the same number of times, *different tastes* are reflected in *different MWTPs*.

The difference between ordering efficient quantities of wine and songs is also shown in Figure 3.1. Figure 3.1A shows the party's MWTP schedule for wine, $MWTP^{ALL}_{WINE}$ by *horizontally summing* the individual MWTP schedules for wine. At each price for a glass of wine, we add together the quantities "demanded" by the guests according to their MWTP schedules. The total quantity of wine to order is found where the horizontally summed demand curve intersects the marginal cost curve of wine at $1 per glass.

Figure 3.1B shows the party's MWTP schedule for the song, $MWTP^{ALL}_{SONG}$ by *vertically summing* the MWTP schedules of the guests. The number of times the song should be played is found where the vertically summed demand curve intersects the marginal cost curve of song at $6 per playing.

Comparing Efficiency Conditions for Public and Private Goods

The party illustrates that the efficiency conditions for nonrival and rival goods are different. Indeed, they are reversed, in a sense. Consider an economy consisting of

---

[3]This assumes that Abigail must stay at the party and listen to it. If Abigail can simply leave the party, she can avoid listening to the song when she doesn't want to.

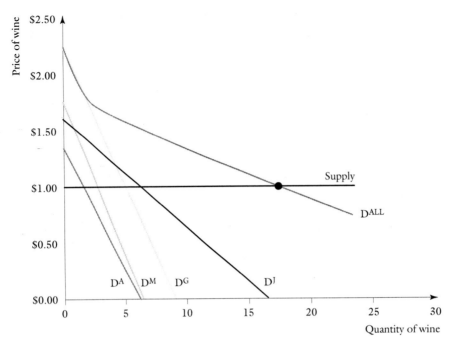

Figure 3.1A

Efficient Quantity of a Private Good

The MWTP schedules of individual consumers for wine are summed *horizontally* in order to find the MWTP$_{WINE}^{ALL}$ schedule. Wine is a rival good and a glass drunk by one partygoer is not available for others, so we need to sum quantities to find the amount to buy. That is, at each price of wine we add the quantities demanded by consumers and find the efficient quantity as the sum of the individual demands at the going price of wine.

many individuals identified as *a, b, c,* etc. that produces both rival and nonrival goods. To efficiently produce a rival good *R*, the total quantity produced must satisfy the condition that the marginal cost is equal to the consumers' marginal willingness to pay. Marginal willingness to pay is the same for every consumer, since they all vary their consumption until this is true. The total quantity of the rival good produced and consumed is equal to the sum of the individual quantities consumed:

$$MC_R = MWTP_R^a = MWTP_R^b = MWTP_R^c = \dots$$

and

$$Q_R = Q_R^a + Q_R^b + Q_R^c + \dots$$

In these equations, MWTI$_R{}^i$ is the marginal willingness to pay for the rival good by person *i*, MC$_R$ is the marginal cost of the rival good, and Q_R^i is the quantity consumed by person *i*.

By contrast, every person consumes the total quantity of the nonrival good *N*, so the quantity consumed is the same for everybody. To efficiently produce the nonrival good, the quantity produced must satisfy the condition that the marginal

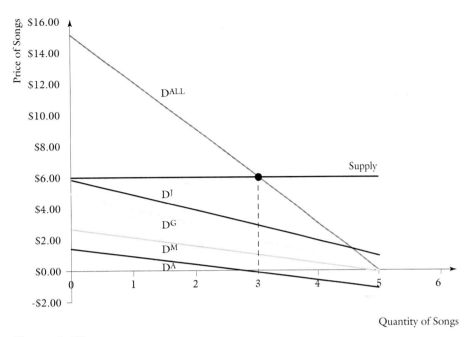

Efficient Quantity of a Public Good
The MWTP schedules of individual guests for song are summed *vertically* in order to find the MWTP$_{SONG}^{ALL}$ schedule. Song is nonrival and enjoyed by everyone at the party, so we sum the MWTPs of all guests to find the party's MWTP for song. The efficient quantity of song is found where the sum of everyone's MWTP is equal to its price.

cost of production is equal to the sum of the marginal willingnesses to pay for it by all consumers:

$$Q_N = Q_N^a = Q_N^b = Q_N^c = \ldots$$

and

$$MC_N = MWTP_N^a + MWTP_N^b + MWTP_N^c + \ldots \, .$$

In other words, efficiency for rival goods requires that the MWTPs are the same for everyone, and the individual quantities are summed. For nonrival goods, the quantity is the same for everyone, and the individual MWTPs are summed. For rival goods, people with different tastes consume different quantities. For nonrival goods, people with different tastes have different MWTPs.

The fact that people can have different MWTPs for a public good is worth stressing. People may (and, generally, will) disagree about the benefit of more or less national defense, even if it is provided at the efficient level. Ms. Hawk may think that more defense spending is very worthwhile, while Mr. Dove may think that such spending has very low value. In fact, some people may have negative MWTPs for defense, perhaps because they fear it poses a threat of war. The point is that different values are possible, even likely. Efficiency requires only that the sum of the different MWTPs equal the marginal cost of defense. A person's negative MWTP for defense simply diminishes the sum.

MARKET FAILURE WITH PUBLIC GOODS

Although we have seen that the condition for the efficient quantity of a public good is different from that for a private good, we have not yet explained why the existence of public goods leads to market failure. Why can Adam Smith's "invisible hand," described in Chapter 2, lead private decision makers to produce efficient quantities of private goods but not public goods? In other words, in what ways do the properties of a public good limit the ability of market forces to bring forth an efficient quantity?

Here is the short answer: The efficient quantity of a private good can be achieved by charging a price to ration the quantity available. Consumers are willing to buy the private good only if their MWTP is at least as high as the price. Furthermore, producers of a private good find it profitable to produce if they can sell it for a price that is at least as high as its marginal cost. In contrast, it is either *impractical* or *inefficient* to ration a public good by charging a price for it. It is impractical to charge a price when the public good has the property of nonexcludability, and it is inefficient to charge a price when the public good has the property of nonrivalry. Given that it is impractical or inefficient to finance a public good by charging for it, a nonmarket method of provision is needed. We begin by discussing the implications of nonexcludability.

Nonexcludability and the Free-Rider Problem

If people can enjoy a public good without paying for it, the **free-rider problem** arises. Free riders are people who are willing to pay for the public good (i.e., have a positive MWTP) but won't pay because the producer cannot force them to pay by excluding them from the good. The free-rider problem implies that private firms have little or no commercial incentive to provide a public good even though it may be the highest-valued use for some of society's scarce resources.

But even if firms have no commercial incentive to produce nonexcludable public goods, might not the consumers themselves provide such a good, since they directly benefit? After all, everyone can be made better off with a more efficient allocation of resources. Why don't we simply agree to do our part by providing the public good? To answer to this question, we consider the paradox called the **prisoner's dilemma** by economists. The prisoner's dilemma is an imaginary experiment that explains why no one in a group has an incentive to take actions that make everyone in the group better off (a Pareto improvement).

To understand the prisoner's dilemma, we return to a simple economy with two people, George and Martha, and two goods: biscuits and defense. Assume that George and Martha each have two hours of time to devote to production. Each can devote time to producing the private good biscuits (by baking) or the public good defense (by standing guard). One hour spent baking biscuits provides three biscuits for the producer and nothing for anyone else because biscuits are a private good. One hour spent standing guard provides one unit of security, which is a public good enjoyed by both George and Martha. In other words, when George stands guard, not only does he feel more secure, but so does Martha, and vice versa. We assume that the MWTP of each person for a unit of security is equal to two biscuits (we are using biscuits as the numeraire good).

Everyone has to eat, so we assume that George and Martha each must devote an hour of time to producing biscuits. We now examine the question whether they devote, or should devote, their second hour to producing biscuits or to standing guard. The four outcomes of the decisions made by George and Martha are shown in Table 3.3. Game theorists call such a table a **payoff matrix.**[4]

The left-hand top cell of the payoff matrix shows the outcome when neither George nor Martha stands guard and both spend all of their time baking biscuits. The payoff to each person is six biscuits (three biscuits per hour times two hours). In the left-hand lower cell we find the payoffs when George spends two hours baking biscuits and Martha devotes one hour to standing guard. In this case, George gets eight biscuits' worth of value—the six biscuits he bakes for himself and the two biscuits' worth of value he gets from Martha's standing guard. Martha gets only five biscuits' worth of value—the 3 biscuits she bakes in the first hour and the two biscuits' worth of security she gets from standing guard. She is worse off because she loses three biscuits by standing guard and gets only two biscuits' worth of security for herself. From Martha's perspective, standing guard is a bad deal. In the right-hand top cell we have the opposite case, where Martha spends two hours baking biscuits and George spends one hour standing guard. In this case, the payoffs are reversed: Martha gets eight biscuits of value, and George gets five. George will not want to stand guard either. For this reason, the outcome in the left-hand top cell, where neither person stands guard, is called the **noncooperative equilibrium.** Noncooperative means that individuals make decisions independently out of their own self-interest.[5] In the noncooperative equilibrium, everyone rides free and no one provides the public good.

Table 3.3   Payoff Matrix for George and Martha

	George uses both hours to bake biscuits	George stands guard for an hour
Martha uses both hours to bake biscuits	George and Martha each get 6 biscuits of utility.	George gets 5 biscuits of utility. Martha gets 8 biscuits of utility.
Martha stands guard for an hour	George gets 8 biscuits of utility. Martha gets 5 biscuits of utility.	George and Martha each get 7 biscuits of utility.

---

[4]Game theory is a branch of economic theory that explains how people or firms choose actions when the rewards they receive depend on the actions of others as well as their own. Thus, each person chooses actions strategically, taking into account how his or her actions affect the actions of others.

[5]This noncooperative equilibrium is also called a *Nash equilibrium* in honor of John Nash, a pioneer game theorist who received the Nobel Prize for economics in 1994.

Is it efficient for George and Martha each to spend an hour of time standing guard? The answer is yes, because the sum of the MWTPs of George and Martha for one hour of security is four biscuits whereas the marginal cost is only three biscuits. Standing guard is the highest-valued use of the second hour. The case where George and Martha both stand guard is shown in the right-hand lower cell. In this case, each person bakes three biscuits and stands guard for one hour. Since they both stand guard for one hour, each gets two units of security (one unit from his or her own hour and one unit from the other person's). These two units provide four biscuits' value to each person (two biscuits per hour times two hours). The total value to each person in the right-hand bottom cell is seven biscuits, which is a Pareto improvement over the noncooperative equilibrium in the left-hand top cell.

Table 3.3 illustrates clearly the paradox of the prisoner's dilemma. Both persons are made better off when they provide national defense by standing guard for an hour, but neither person finds it in his or her interest to do so. The reason for the market failure in this example is nonexcludability: the inability of the person standing guard to charge for the benefit he or she provides to the other person.

In a small group like this, we'd expect George and Martha to strike an agreement in which each would stand guard for an hour on the condition that the other person do the same. This **cooperative equilibrium** is a possibility in a small group in which each party can determine whether the other is honoring the agreement and not riding free. But in a large group, such as a country consisting of millions of people, a private agreement is impractical to negotiate and enforce. Everyone would have to spend too much time watching to be sure that others are not riding free, so the economy would wind up at the inefficient noncooperative equilibrium.

This example helps us understand why the government can improve economic efficiency by providing the public good. Unlike individuals, the government has the power to tax, or compel payments from the population. The tax revenue can be used to purchase the public good (i.e., to pay people to stand guard). The compulsory nature of taxes prevents people from free riding. The paradox of the prisoner's dilemma explains why the government's power to compel payments from people can make everyone better off even though no one would make the payments voluntarily. An individual is happier being compelled to make a payment for national defense because of the benefit he or she gets from that fact that everyone else is compelled to make payments.

The Private Provision of Public Goods

In the preceding example of free riding, George and Martha face a choice of either producing or not producing a public good. More generally, people face the choice of how much to produce or purchase of a public good. In this case, it is possible that the public good will be provided privately, although, as we will see, the quantity provided is less than the efficient quantity unless people act cooperatively. If each person decides separately how much to provide of the public good, the possibility of free riding will lead people to provide too little.

Suppose George and Martha can purchase different quantities of a public good—say litter pickup around Mount Vernon. As before, when a person provides a unit of the public good, he or she cannot charge the other person for the benefit that others enjoy from it. Assume the cost of picking up a unit of litter is $1 to each person. George's demand curve for litter pickup good is labeled D^G in Figure 3.2. The total quantity of litter picked up is measured on the horizontal axis, and George's marginal willingness to pay for picking up litter is measured on the vertical axis. As usual, we assume that George's MWTP declines as more litter is picked up. The position of George's demand curve depends on his *effective* income, which is equal to his money income plus Martha's expenditure on litter pickup. Martha's expenditure on litter pickup is equivalent to additional income to George because litter is a public good. If Martha spends $100 on litter pickup, George can spend that much less himself and buy other goods.

To be more specific, we assume George's demand curve for litter pickup is given by

$$P^G = a(Y^G + q^M) - q.$$

In this equation P^G is George's MWTP for litter pickup, Y^G is an index of George's income, q^M is the quantity of litter pickup purchased by Martha, q is the total

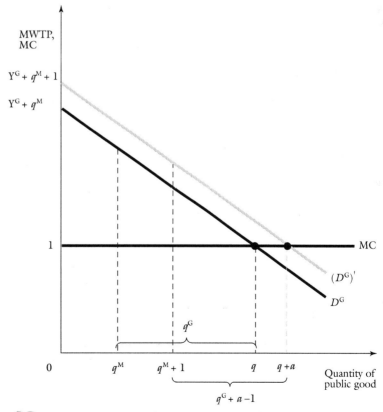

Figure 3.2

The Private Provision of a Public Good
When Martha provides an extra unit of the public good, the quantity provided by George falls by a fraction of a unit.

amount of litter pickup purchased by George and Martha together, and a is the fraction of an extra income that George is willing to spend on litter pickup.

George's demand curve is shown in Figure 3.2 for the case where Martha purchases q^M units of litter pickup. The quantity of litter pickup desired by George is q where his MWTP is equal to the marginal cost of litter pickup. Since Martha provides q^M units, George needs to buy only $q^G = q - q^M$ units. In making this decision, George assumes that the quantity provided by Martha is fixed and not affected by his decision.

We can now show that when Martha provides more litter pickup, George provides less because of free riding. For instance, if Martha provides an extra unit of litter pickup, George's effective income rises by one unit, and his demand curve shifts to the right by a units. This demand curve is labeled $(D_G)'$ in the figure. The total quantity of litter pickup desired by George rises by a units, so George reduces his own purchases by $1 - a$ units. This way, he enjoys exactly a more units of litter pickup (the extra unit provided by Martha minus his reduction).

More generally, we can set P^G equal to 1 (the marginal cost of litter pickup) and use the equation above to solve for the quantity of litter pickup purchased by George for quantity provided by Martha. It is $q^G = a \cdot Y^G - 1 - (1 - a) \cdot q^M$. Hence, if Martha purchased no litter pickup, George would purchase $a \cdot Y^G - 1$ units, while if Martha purchased $\dfrac{a \cdot Y^G - 1}{1 - a}$ units, George would not purchase any.

In Figure 3.3, we plot the quantity of litter pickup purchased by George on the vertical axis for each quantity purchased by Martha measured on the horizontal axis. The resulting line, labeled $R^G R^G$, is George's **best response curve.**

Clearly, George's behavior by itself cannot determine the quantity of the public good privately provided because his decision depends on Martha's. Of course, Martha's decision is determined in the same way—her decision depends on the quantity chosen by George. Martha's best response curve, derived the same way we derived George's, is labeled $R^M_R{}^M$ in Figure 3.3. The equilibrium quantities of the public good provided by George and Martha are found at the intersection of the two reaction curves. At this point, George is purchasing the quantity of the public good that he desires given the quantity purchased by Martha, and vice versa. Although the algebra is a bit tedious, we can establish that the equilibrium quantity of the public good purchased by George is equal to $q^G = \dfrac{a \cdot Y^G + (1 - a) \cdot (Y^G - Y^M) - 1}{2 - a}$.

This assumes that Martha has the same demand curve as George but has a different level of income Y^M. If George and Martha have the same income, the total quantity of the public good (the sum of George's and Martha's purchases) is simply $\dfrac{a \cdot Y - 2}{2 - a}$ where Y is George and Martha's combined income. For instance, if $Y = 9$ and $a = \frac{1}{3}$, George and Martha will together provide 1.5 units of the public good.

To find the efficient quantity of the public good, we need to sum the MWTP of George and Martha and set this sum equal to 1, the marginal cost of the public good. The algebraic details need not detain us, but the efficient quantity of the pub-

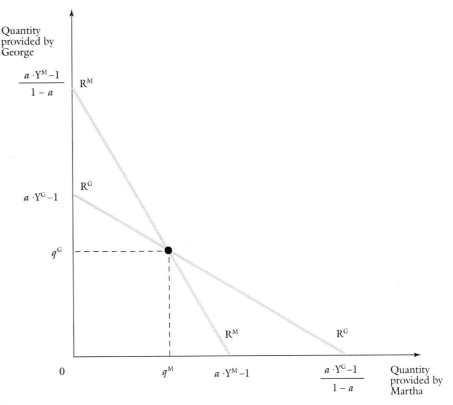

Figure 3.3

The Equilibrium Quantities of a Privately Provided Public Good
The equilibrium quantity of a privately provided public good is determined at the intersection of the providers' best response curves.

lic good in this case is $\dfrac{a \cdot Y - 2}{2 - a}$, which is three units in the example.[6] Thus by act-

ing noncooperatively in deciding the quantity of the public good, George and Martha systematically underprovide it.

Although this example is very artificial, the theory can be applied to real cases where a public good is "privately" provided. Later in this chapter, we will outline an application to the problem of national defense provided by countries in an alliance, and in Chapter 8 we apply the theory to charitable donations.

Problems in Providing Public Goods

To provide an efficient level of a public good, the government must first determine the population's MWTP for it. Recall that, in contrast to a private good, the

---

[6]You can derive the efficient quantity by solving the model assuming that George and Martha share the cost of every unit of the public good provided, so the cost to each is ½ rather than 1.

population's MWTP schedule for a public good is found by *vertically* summing the individual MWTP schedules. Although vertical summing is easy enough to describe and understand, the difficult problem for the government is to learn the individual demand curves. People do not automatically reveal their MWTP schedules for a public good to the government or anyone else. In fact, they may have an incentive to misrepresent their MWTP schedules to the government.

For example, if George thinks that the amount of tax he pays is fixed and is not affected by what he tells the government, while the amount of the public good he receives is affected, he has an incentive to overstate his MWTP for the public good. Since he believes that his marginal cost of the public good is zero, he prefers the quantity at which his MWTP is zero. To persuade the government to produce more of the public good, he exaggerates his MWTP for it. On the other hand, if Martha thinks that the amount of tax she pays depends on the MWTP schedule she reveals, but that the quantity of public good she receives is the same in any event, she has an incentive to understate her MWTP. This is just the free-rider problem. By understating her MWTP, Martha thinks that she will get the public good but that the taxes will be paid by someone else.

The problem of learning the public's demand for public goods is called the preference revelation problem. The methods available to the government for learning the preferences of the public, such as voting, are discussed at length in Chapter 5.

A second problem the government faces is deciding how the burden should be shared. **Burden sharing** describes the rules that determine how the cost of the public good is apportioned across the population. With a private good, determining burden sharing is not a problem—each consumer pays according to his or her MWTP. In other words, burden sharing for private goods is automatically determined according to the *benefit* principle of equity, which states that the cost of the good is borne by those who benefit from it. With a tax-financed public good, the method of financing the good is separated from the need to finance it by charging prices. The government could apportion the burden of the cost of the public good according to the benefit principle if it knew the public's MWTP schedules, but it doesn't have to. Instead, it can use another criterion, such as *ability to pay* for the public good. Ability to pay is the most common way of sharing the burden of a public good, both because it satisfies a basic notion of equity and because it does not require the government to know the MWTP schedules of different people in the economy. The government simply observes different people's ability to pay in terms of their income or wealth.

MIXED PUBLIC GOODS

A pure public good is completely nonrival and nonexcludable. All consumers in the economy benefit, and it is not possible to exclude anyone who does not pay. In contrast, a private good is completely rival, and consumers who do not pay are easily excluded. We also encounter goods that have various mixtures of these properties.

We consider three cases: (1) a nonrival good that is excludable so a price can be charged, (2) a congestible public good that is excludable, and (3) local public goods.

Excludable Public Goods

Producers of nonexcludable public goods cannot charge a price for them, so private firms and individuals find no profit in producing them. But what about a nonrival good that is excludable, such as a cable television program? The cost of allowing an extra person to view a pay-per-view program on cable television is negligible, so the good is nonrival; but nonpaying viewers are easily excluded because the firm will not unscramble the signal unless paid. Are market forces enough to encourage private firms to produce an efficient quantity of an excludable nonrival good?

The answer is usually no. The reason is that if a good is nonrival, it is not efficient to exclude anyone with a positive MWTP from consuming it. The cost to society of the extra consumer is zero, so excluding anyone means the loss of the benefits that person would have enjoyed. But a private producer must charge a price to cover costs and turn a profit. Lowering the price so as not to exclude people with low but positive MWTPs is not a profitable decision, even if it is an efficient one.

Suppose a pay-per-view program can be produced at a cost of just under $1 million, and that 1 million viewers have a positive MWTP for the program. We can order the viewers from those with the highest MWTP ($4) to those with the lowest (1 cent). In Figure 3.4, the viewers' MWTP for the program is plotted as a demand curve. For simplicity, we assume that the MWTP of the different viewers declines linearly. There are 500,000 viewers who have a MWTP of $2 or more, so the firm can cover the costs of producing the program and make a small profit by charging a pay-per-view price of $2. In fact, given the linearity of the demand curve, this price maximizes the revenue to the firm. Charging either a higher or lower price would not allow the producer to earn enough to cover the cost.[7]

Although commercial incentives are enough to get the program produced, the outcome is nonetheless inefficient. The reason for the inefficiency is that the excluded viewers do not impose a cost on the economy—the $1 million cost of the program is the same whether 500,000 or 1 million viewers see it. Excluding the viewers who have MWTPs of less than $2 makes the economy worse off by the total MWTP of the excluded group. In this example, that is about $500,000 (the average of $2 and 1 cent, times the 500,000 excluded viewers), which is shown in Figure 3.4 by the shaded triangle.

In this example, we assume that the producer must charge the same price to every viewer. If the firm can practice "perfect" price discrimination, and if it knows everyone's MWTP, it can charge each viewer a "personal" price equal to his or her MWTP. In this case the firm charges the first consumer $4, the second viewer a little bit less, and so on. The viewer with the lowest MWTP pays just 1 cent, so no one is excluded. The total revenue collected when each viewer is charged a price equal to his or her MWTP is $2 million, so the firm will produce any program that has a cost less than the viewers' TWTP. However, this efficient outcome requires the firm to have some method for establishing each viewer's MWTP for the program. This is

---

[7]For example, charging $3 per view would mean only 250,000 viewers, so total revenue is $750,000. Charging a lower price—say, $1—brings in more viewers (750,000) but again results in a lower revenue.

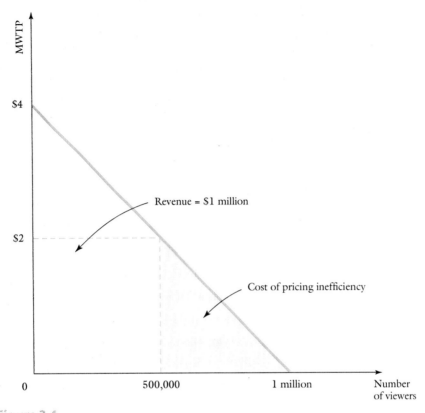

Figure 3.4
The Inefficiency of Charging a Single Price for a Public Good
The cost of a pay-per-view program is the same regardless of the number of viewers. Viewers are ranked according to their MWTP to see the program and, together, they would be willing to pay $2 million to watch the program. If the cost of the program is less than this, the program should be produced and no consumers excluded. However, private firms charge $2 to view the program, excluding 500,000 viewers whose MWTPs are less than $2. These extra viewers would not increase cost, so excluding them causes an inefficiency cost. It is equal to $500,000, which is the area of the shaded triangle.

unlikely in practice. With public goods, unlike private goods, no automatic mechanism is present that leads consumers to reveal their MWTPs so that the efficient quantity can be produced.

Congestible Public Goods

A **congestible public good** is a good that is nonrival when there are not too many users, but the marginal cost of an extra consumer rises when the number of consumers becomes too large. That is, when too many people consume a congestible public good at one time, they impose a cost on the other users because of crowding. We call this a *congestion* cost.

A bridge is a good example of a congestible public good. When it is not busy, it is nonrival because an extra car crossing the bridge does not reduce the availability of the bridge to others. However, when the bridge is clogged with cars, it is almost a rival good. If a bridge is crowded enough, one car crossing the bridge precludes another from crossing at the same time. Drivers must wait and take their turn, so each driver imposes a waiting-time cost on the others. Even if an extra car will fit onto the bridge without displacing another, it can slow the speed of the traffic and again impose a waiting-time cost on the other drivers.

The bridge may also be a mixed public good in another sense. A bridge may be excludable, meaning that it is feasible to charge tolls and prevent drivers who do not pay from crossing the bridge. Of course, charging tolls is costly, because toll collectors must be hired and a means of stopping drivers who refuse to pay is needed. A bridge is an example of a good that is excludable, but the cost of excluding drivers may be high.

If prices can be charged for a congestible public good, economic efficiency requires that a price be charged and that the price depend on the number of users at the time. When the bridge is not crowded, the marginal cost of a user is zero, so rationing the bridge with a toll is inefficient. In addition to incurring the costs of collecting the toll, we lose the benefits to the drivers whose MWTP is low and who consequently do not pay the toll to cross the bridge. When the bridge is crowded, efficiency requires that access to it be rationed by charging a toll. The toll or price should be equal to the marginal congestion cost of an extra user. It is efficient to charge a toll because the toll encourages efficient decisions by the drivers. If MWTP to cross the bridge is not as high as the toll, a driver won't cross the bridge. The reduced usage by drivers with low MWTPs reduces the congestion costs on others. Later in this chapter, we will examine how to set prices for congestible public goods like roadways.

Congestible public goods that become congested when there are relatively small numbers of users and for which consumers can be excluded are sometimes called **club goods.** Club goods, such as golf courses and marinas, are often provided by private firms. Typically, consumers must pay a fixed annual fee to become a member, which makes them eligible to pay to use the club facilities. In addition, user fees are charged when a member uses the facilities. The membership fee is levied to cover the fixed or capital cost of the facilities. The user fees are set to ration the availability of the facilities during periods of peak demand when congestion costs are high. During off-peak times, user fees for club members may be quite low. Other examples of club goods include tennis facilities and swimming pools. Because they are a form of mixed public good, club goods are often provided by local governments as well as privately—for instance, public tennis courts and swimming pools.

Local Public Goods

A nonrival good that allows every person in the country to consume it without incurring extra cost, such as national defense, is called a *national* public good. In fact, in some cases the benefits may spill over to people in other countries, in which case the good is a transnational (or international) public good. However, many public goods are available only to consumers who live within (or visit) a limited geographic area. Public goods with this property are called **local public goods.**

A broadcast TV signal is a local public good because consumers must live within a certain distance of the transmitting station to receive the signal. In some cases, the locality of a public good can be quite small. For example, a park providing a green space in a particular part of a city is a neighborhood public good, perhaps benefiting only families living within a few blocks. There is a limit to the property of being local: A good that benefits only one person or family becomes a private good.

As we might expect, some public goods have mixed properties, being both national and local at the same time. The section of the Interstate Highway 80 passing through Des Moines, Iowa, is largely a local public good, because it benefits mainly the people living in the vicinity of Des Moines who use it for commuting. It is also a national public good that benefits travelers from outside Des Moines who need to drive from, say, New York City to San Francisco. It also benefits people living anywhere in the country who consume goods shipped by trucks that use the highway.

In this way, public goods may have a geographic dimension. Local public goods are usually provided by local governments, since the benefits do not extend to other people in the country. Sometimes the domain of a public good does not correspond to the jurisdiction of the local government. In this case, the benefits of a local public good may spill over to people living outside the political boundaries (and the taxing authority) of the government providing it. For example, a larger police force to reduce crime in the city may benefit people living in the suburbs. Such effects are called **jurisdictional spillovers.**

Typically, local governments cannot charge (that is, levy taxes on) people living outside their jurisdiction for the spillover benefits of a public good. As a result, a local government providing a local public good with jurisdictional spillovers is somewhat like a person who provides a public good that benefits others. Local governments have incentives to free ride in providing public goods that have jurisdictional spillovers. To prevent this, higher levels of government or cooperative agreements among local governments are needed. The special problems associated with providing local public goods are discussed further in Chapter 18.

APPLICATIONS OF PUBLIC GOODS THEORY

In this section, we consider three national public goods: national defense, the national highway system, and knowledge capital. Our purpose is to draw insights from the theory of public goods that help us better understand government policy with respect to these three goods.

Defense Spending in the United States

National defense is one of the most important public goods provided by any national government. Indeed, it is often a primary function of a national government. The need to "provide for the common defense" is listed prominently in the preamble to the Constitution of the United States.

As you can see from Figure 3.5, the percentage of the gross domestic product (GDP) spent on national defense by the United States has varied widely over the

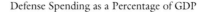

Defense Spending as a Percentage of GDP

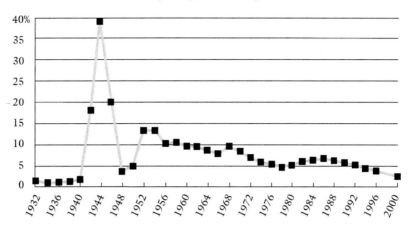

Figure 3.5

Defense Spending as a Percentage of GDP
As a percentage of GDP, spending on national defense has mostly declined since the early 1950s, except for a small peak during the Vietnam War and a rise during the 1980s.
Source: Economic Report of the President, various years

past six decades. Most of this variation is explained by international events. During the Great Depression of the 1930s, defense spending was only about 1% of GDP. With the outbreak of World War II, spending jumped dramatically, reaching nearly 40% of GDP at the height of the war. After the war, the percentage fell sharply when the country demobilized its military forces. It rose again with the onset of the Cold War and the Korean War in the early 1950s. In the 45 years following the Korean War, defense spending as a percentage of GDP has steadily declined, except for a small increase during the Vietnam War and a still smaller peak during the 1980s. The latter represents the defense buildup during the Reagan administration. With the collapse of the Soviet Union and the Warsaw Pact (the military alliance between the Soviet Union and the countries under its influence) in 1992, the fraction of GDP devoted to national defense has resumed its downward trend. In 1999, the federal government spent $275 billion on national defense, which is about 3% of the GDP. This is the lowest percentage since World War II.

DOES THE UNITED STATES SPEND "TOO MUCH" ON NATIONAL DEFENSE?
Although current defense spending as a percentage of GDP is low in terms of the postwar history of the United States, it still could be "too much." For one thing, it is three times greater as a percentage than it was in the 1930s, the last era of peace in which the United States did not face a world adversary. In addition, real GDP is much larger now. Measured in dollars of constant purchasing power, the level of defense spending in 1999 was 18 times greater than it was in 1938.

But if we use the 1930s as a benchmark, how do we know that "too little" wasn't being spent back then, rather than too much now? Some historians believe the lack of national preparedness by the United States and other countries was partially to blame for World War II, an event that caused the death of 292,000 Americans and claimed the lives of 50 million worldwide. Perhaps with the benefit of hindsight, we want to spend more on defense now to forestall a similar or worse catastrophe. Also, modern defense is more technologically advanced and hence more costly than it was in the 1930s.

Another approach is to look at what industrial countries like the United States spend on defense. Estimates of defense spending as a percentage of GDP for several countries in 1997 are listed in Table 3.4. As this table shows, the fraction of GDP devoted to defense spending in the United States is higher than that in most other industrial countries. The United Kingdom and France are second and third, with 3.4% and 3%, respectively. Some industrial countries spent much less, such as Germany and Japan, with only 1.6% and 1%, respectively. Furthermore, because these other countries have lower GDPs than the United States, the dollar amounts they spent on defense are much lower. France, the second-largest defense spender in this group, spent only one-sixth as much as the United States.

Again, we could ask whether other countries spend too little, rather than the United States too much. Defense spending by allied countries is a form of transnational public good. That is, defense spending by the United States benefits its allies and their defense spending benefits us by deterring common threats to world peace.[8] As always in the case of a public good, providers may get a "free ride" on the defense spending of others. Countries like Germany and Japan may well free ride on the defense provided by the United States, which would explain why they spend so little.[9] Perhaps the United States spends more because it has less incentive to free ride than other countries, since it has a leading role in world affairs.

If nothing else, the question of how much should be spent on national defense reveals the limitations of the theory of public goods in answering this type of question. The theory provides the following correct, but not very informative, answer: *The United States should provide defense at a level such that the sum of the MWTPs for*

Table 3.4 Defense Spending in Selected Countries

Country	1998 Defense Spending billions $ (1995) US	1997 % GDP
Canada	7	1.3%
France	46	3
Germany	38.9	1.6
Italy	22.8	2
Japan	51.3	1
United Kingdom	39.7	3.4
United States	251.8	3.4

Source: The SIPRI Military Expenditure Database, http//www.sipri.se:8020/IRSIS/owa/.

---

[8]Perhaps this is less true today, with the demise of the Soviet Union and the end of the threat it represented.

[9]Japan has a constitutional limit on its military spending.

defense by everyone in the country is just equal to the marginal cost of defense. How do we determine at which level this happens? Perhaps it is possible to determine the marginal cost of defense by asking how much we save by building one less submarine or by closing a military base, but how can we determine the sum of the MWTPs for defense by the population? Not only does the preference revelation problem mean that people have no incentive to reveal their true MWTPs for defense; the highly technical nature of modern national defense also makes it doubtful that even a truthful citizen could answer the question correctly. Knowing the value of national defense requires technical knowledge about weapons systems, foreign threats, military strategies, and so on, that the average citizen lacks. We must rely on specialists to make these assessments, and unfortunately these specialists may also try to influence the decision in a particular way. For example, the Joint Chiefs of Staff have expert knowledge on the subject of defense but may also be inclined to favor more rather than less spending on defense. So might legislators from districts that depend on military bases or defense industries as an economic base.

In the final analysis, the only way citizens can express their views about the values they place on defense spending is at the ballot box. As we will see in Chapter 5, voting is not likely to lead to an efficient quantity of a public good either, even if people are well informed and can vote directly on the issue of defense spending (which they cannot).

Roads and Highways

The role of government in providing for "internal improvements" (or "infrastructure," in modern jargon) has long been debated in the United States. The use of federal tax revenues to finance such projects was championed by the first secretary of the Treasury, Alexander Hamilton. Also, there have been some who question the desirability of this type of federal involvement. In 1830, President Andrew Jackson vetoed the Maysville Road Bill, which would have provided federal underwriting for a road that lay entirely within a single state.

The mass production of the automobile in the twentieth century created a public demand for hard-surfaced roads. In turn, the availability of more and better roads increased the demand for automobiles, leading to a powerful lobby—car manufacturers—that has long promoted government investment in roads. The federal government's involvement in highways increased significantly with the passage of the *Federal Road Aid Act* in 1916. This act provided for 50% federal financing for some rural roads, even roads lying entirely within a state. During the Great Depression, federal financing of highways increased further as part of the National Recovery Act, and during World War II the federal government financed highways for defense purposes, like the Alaskan Highway.

The national system of controlled-access highways, popularly known as "the interstate," is the largest government construction project in American history. When the interstate highway system was first proposed in the early 1950s, critics questioned the large federal involvement because it was uncertain whether the highways were a national public good. One deciding factor was national defense. Indeed, the official name of the interstate highway system is the National System

3.1   Defense Spending by Countries in an Alliance

Part of defense spending by allied countries is a multinational public good because it contributes to a common defense. That is, spending by one country to deter aggression and preserve world peace benefits the other countries as well. In addition, countries may contribute to multinational defense with foreign assistance, cost sharing, and/or providing military assets for world peace-keeping operations. However, as we saw in the section on the private provision of public goods, countries have an incentive to "free ride." If countries determine defense spending unilaterally, their combined spending is less than the efficient amount. To mitigate this problem, countries belong to cooperative organizations such as NATO and the Gulf Cooperation Council.

We can apply the theory of the private provision of public goods outlined earlier to defense spending by countries in an alliance. Suppose a country's MWTP for multinational defense is given by the equation $P^i = a \cdot (Y^i + q^0) - b \cdot q$, where P^i is the MWTP of country i, $\%$ is the fraction of additional national income spent on multinational defense, Y^i is an index of the country's income, q^0 is multinational defense spending by other countries, q is the combined alliance level of defense spending, and b is the absolute slope of the MWTP curve. For simplicity, assume two countries with identical demand curves. If countries act individually, the total spending on multinational defense is equal to $q^A = \dfrac{a \cdot Y - 2}{2b - a}$

where Y is an index of the combined income of the alliance. Thus, if Y is 100, a equals .06, and b equals .53, the noncooperative alliance would spend 4 units (or 4% of its income) on multinational defense.

However, the efficient level of multinational defense is given by the equation $q^* = \dfrac{a \cdot Y - 2}{2b - a}$

At the given parameter values, the efficient defense spending is 5 units (or 5% of allied income). To achieve a more efficient (and higher) level of multinational defense, countries act cooperatively through treaties and other arrangements. These arrangements require members to devote a larger percentage of their national incomes to defense and/or share the costs of some operations carried out by other members. To prevent free riding, defense spending and other contributions by members are monitored, and countries that fail to bear their responsibility could be expelled from the alliance. For example, the Secretary of Defense periodically issues a *Report to Congress on Allied Contributions to Common Defense.* The last report on March 1997 can be obtained at http://defenselink.mil/pubs/allied_contrib97/index.html.

Critically analyze the following:

- If the allied countries have the same income, and are similar in other respects, they will typically spend the same percentage of their income on the common defense in the non-cooperative case (4% in the example). However, if a country has more income than another, it will spend a higher percentage while the other country spends a smaller percentage. Explain why.

- In the *Report to Congress,* the United States determines whether allies are sharing the common defense burden by comparing the percentage of national income spent by each country on four categories—defense spending, military assets used for world peace-keeping, cost sharing, and foreign assistance—to its own spending. Given the preeminent position of the United States in the world, is this a good way to assess free riding?

- Some countries, such as Canada and Japan, spend a much smaller fraction of their incomes on defense than the United States, but contribute disproportionately for world peace-keeping forces and foreign assistance. Should such activities compensate for lower defense spending?

of Interstate and Defense Highways. Few motorists commuting to work today know that one justification for building the road they are driving on was the need to rapidly evacuate cities in the event of a nuclear attack.

Two features of the interstate system were controversial from the beginning. One was the decision to route the highways through densely populated urban areas rather than around them.[10] This decision increased the cost of the system because of the high cost of urban land for right-of-way. It also involved the federal government in financing urban roads, which were traditionally considered *local* public goods. About a quarter of the mileage in the present national highway system (which includes the interstate system and other federal highways) is located in urban areas. On a typical urban stretch of interstate highway, most of the traffic is local. Even in rural sections, nearly half of the traffic is short-haul local.

The second controversial issue was the decision not to charge tolls. The entire interstate highway system is toll-free, except for some stretches in a few states, mostly in the Northeast. If a state charges tolls on its portion of the interstate highways, the federal government reduces its share of the cost. Is the absence of tolls an efficient policy? To answer this question, it must be recognized that a highway is not a completely nonrival good but a mixed public good. The marginal cost of a highway user is not zero, because of pavement wear and traffic congestion. When the marginal cost of a user is positive, it may be efficient to charge tolls for the use of the highway.

Pavement wear caused by a user depends on vehicle weight per axle, not total vehicle weight. A significant fact is that pavement wear rises exponentially with axle load. Thus a loaded truck that is (say) 10 times heavier than a passenger car can cause 1000 times as much wear per axle, depending on the number of axles. Traffic engineers use a standardized measure of the damaging power of a vehicle called an *equivalent standard axle load* (ESAL). One estimate of the marginal cost of a user due to wear and tear on rural interstates is 1.5 cents per ESAL-mile.[11] Thus a truck weighing in at 2 ESALs that travels 1000 miles on a rural stretch of interstate causes pavement wear costing about $30. The equivalent cost of a passenger car is less than $1.

The congestion cost of a highway user does not depend on the weight of the vehicle, although it may depend on the vehicle's size. More important, it depends on the number of other vehicles on the highway, as well as other traffic conditions. On a sparsely used stretch of rural interstate, the congestion cost is practically zero. On a heavily used urban stretch during a rush hour, it is quite high. Each extra car on a crowded highway can slow down hundreds, perhaps thousands, of other vehicles. In 1996, the average congestion cost on roads and highways due to delay and extra fuel was about $630 per driver. In congested areas, it was over $1000 per driver.[12]

---

[10]Supposedly President Eisenhower, who signed the Federal Highway Act of 1956, authorizing the interstate system, thought that it would bypass the densely populated urban areas. He was surprised and distressed to discover otherwise when he noticed construction under way in Washington, D.C.

[11]See Kenneth A. Small et al., *Road Work: A New Highway Pricing and Investment Policy*, 1989.

[12]U.S. Bureau of the Census, *Statistical Abstract of the United States 1999*, Table 1040.

The theory of public goods concludes that it is efficient to base the toll to a highway user on the marginal cost of pavement wear plus the marginal cost of congestion. Therefore, the efficient toll depends on the axle load of the vehicle, and on the volume of traffic at the time it uses the highway. Charging such a toll is efficient because it ensures that the user incorporates the economic cost of using the highway into the decision to use it.

Of course, a toll is efficient only if it can be collected at low cost. This includes the financial cost of collecting the toll as well as the cost imposed on highway users who are delayed by paying it. The traditional method of collecting tolls is toll booths. While the cost of collecting tolls this way is relatively low on rural sections of the highway, because the access and egress points are widely spaced, it is costly or impractical to have toll booths within urban areas. Because of the high costs of collecting tolls, the interstate highway is a nonexcludable good within urban areas. At the same time, it is likely to be crowded in urban areas, and therefore rival. To summarize, the interstate highway system is likely to be a nonrival good on uncongested rural sections where toll collection is feasible and a nonexcludable good in urban areas where toll collection is costly.

EFFICIENT ROAD PRICES WITH ELECTRONIC TOLL COLLECTION (ETC).   ETC is a new technology that makes it possible to charge for using an expressway without the need for toll-collection gates and the delays they cause. ETC systems are already in use in Singapore, Hong Kong, and some European cities. With ETC, the motorist carries an electronic transponder that identifies the user and informs a roadside computer that the motorist is using the road. The time of day, miles traveled, the volume of traffic on the road, and the average speed of traffic flow is recorded for each use, and a toll is charged accordingly. In this section, we examine how the electronic toll should be determined so that the road, a congestible public good, is used efficiently.

We will ignore the costs of roadway wear and concentrate on congestion cost. To determine the toll, we first need to know the relationship between the speed of the traffic flow and the volume of traffic. As the volume of traffic increases, the average speed decreases. To make things concrete, let N denote the number of cars (in hundreds) on a road of fixed length. If N is less than 5 (hundred), we assume that the road is not congested and traffic flows at the maximum speed possible (60 miles an hour). As N increases above 5, the road is increasingly congested and we assume the traffic speed (S) is determined by the speed curve $S = \dfrac{300}{N}$. Thus if there are 1000 cars on the road (N equals 10), the speed of the traffic flow is 30 miles an hour.

The time (in fractions of an hour) it takes a motorist to travel one mile on the road when it is congested is $\dfrac{1}{S} = \dfrac{300}{N}$, or simply $\dfrac{1}{60}$ when the road is not congested.

The time cost of traveling one mile on the road for the average motorist (AC) is equal to the value of an hour of the motorist's time (W) times the time spent on the road, or $AC = \dfrac{W \cdot N}{300}$. In Figure 3.6, we plot the average time cost of a motor-

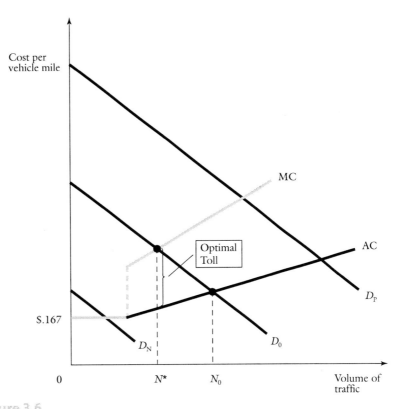

Figure 3.6

The Optimal Congestion Toll on a Roadway

The optimal congestion toll is equal to the difference between the time cost of an extra vehicle on the road to all users (MC) and the time cost to the individual user (AC).

ist of traveling one mile at different volumes of traffic assuming that W is $10 an hour. For N less than or equal to 5, traffic flows at a constant 60 mph and average time cost of traveling a mile is equal to $.167. For traffic volumes greater than 5 (hundred), the average time cost of the motorist increases at $3\frac{1}{3}$ cents for every extra hundred cars on the road.

Although AC is the time cost perceived by the motorist, it is not the marginal cost of a motorist using the road. To determine the marginal cost, We first find the total cost (TC) of the N motorists using the road at the time by multiplying AC per motorist times N to get $TC = \dfrac{WN^2}{300}$. We can now find the marginal cost (MC) of an extra motorist using the road when it is congested

$$\frac{\Delta TC}{\Delta N}\left(\text{for small changes in } N\right) = \frac{2WN}{300}, \quad \text{or } MC = 2 \cdot AC. \quad \text{. The marginal time}$$

cost is higher than the average time cost because the extra motorist slows all traffic, increasing the time cost of other motorists. The difference between MC and AC is the marginal congestion cost. When N is less than 5, the marginal congestion cost is zero, so MC = AC.

In Figure 3.6, we plot the AC and MC of traveling one mile at different values of N. We also plot the marginal willingness to pay to travel a mile by motorists at a particular time of day as a demand curve.[13] Some motorists have a higher MWTP than others (for example, motorists who are commuting to work versus those who are out for a pleasure drive). If we rank all motorists from those with the highest MWTP to those with the lowest, we obtain the downward-sloping schedule labeled D_0. Motorists will not use the road unless their MWTP is greater than or equal to their time cost, AC. Without tolls, the volume of traffic on the road is N_0 where MWTP is equal to AC. In Figure 3.6, we can see that the volume of traffic on the road is greater than the efficient volume. The reason is that motorists ignore the congestion cost they impose on other motorists. The efficient volume of traffic on the road is N^* where MWTP is equal to MC. In order to price this congestible public good efficiently, a toll is needed. In particular, the toll should be set equal to marginal congestion cost at the efficient volume of traffic. The marginal congestion cost is MC minus AC, which, in this example, is AC when N is greater than 5. Note that the optimal toll depends on the demand for the roadway. In the middle of the night, the demand is very low, as shown by the schedule D_N, and the road is not congested so the optimal toll is zero. At peak commuting times, the demand for the road is high (say as shown by the demand curve labeled D_P) and the toll is higher.

Technology Policy: Patents Versus Government R&D Spending

Recently, economists and lawyers have become more interested in government policies that protect intellectual property rights, mainly the granting of patents and copyrights. These policies attempt to assign property rights to knowledge capital, which is a nonrival good. If a farmer invents a process that increases the crop yield of his or her land, that knowledge can be used by other farmers to increase the yields of their land as well at no further cost to society. However, sharing such knowledge is not in the interest of the first farmer, who would lose the competitive advantage of the invention. If all farmers can increase their crop yields, crop prices are driven down, and the benefit of the invention is enjoyed by consumers rather than the inventor. In this case, the individual farmer has little incentive to incur the high costs of invention. In other words, there is a free-rider problem in the creation of knowledge capital that leads to too little of it being created.

In fact, the farmer who invents a way to increase crop yields has an incentive to prevent other farmers from using the knowledge. Likewise, commercial firms use secrecy to safeguard the benefits of their research and development (R&D) activities. Although inventors may view disseminating the knowledge they create as disadvantageous to themselves, dissemination is actually a benefit to the economy because knowledge is a nonrival good. These twin problems—inadequate incentives for producing inventions that become public knowledge, and the incentive to

---

[13] The MWTP is measured net of other variable costs of driving, such as gasoline expenses.

3.2   ETC on a California Highway

Electronic Toll Collection (ETC) has been used in Singapore and Hong Kong for several years now, but ETC has only recently been introduced into the United States. State Route 91 near Yorba Linda, California, now has four express toll lanes (two in each direction) in a heavily traveled ten-mile stretch. The toll lanes have flexible barriers separating them from parallel public lanes. To use the toll lanes, a driver must possess an electronic transponder that he or she receives when they open a prepaid account with the California Private Transportation Company (CPTC), which owns and manages the toll lanes. The transponder emits a radio signal that opens the gates to let the vehicle enter the lanes and records the time of day and traffic flow. The motorist pays a toll to use the ten-mile stretch of road that depends on the time of day and traffic volume, varying from $.25 at night to $2.50 at peak traffic hours for a one-way trip. The company sets the toll so that no traffic delays will be encountered. Indeed, the company offers a money-back guarantee of a delay-free trip.

The tolls are set according to the profit motives of the CPTC. The company is authorized to collect tolls for 35 years, but its annual profit cannot exceed 17% of the amount it has invested in the road (currently $126 million). Private toll roads must be next to freeways so that they do not constitute a monopoly. Indeed, motorists in the SR-91 toll lanes zip right by the slow-moving traffic in the congested freeway lanes.

Critically analyze the following issues:

- Given that motorists in the freeway lanes could obtain a transponder and use the toll lanes, what is their maximum marginal willingness to pay to avoid delays?

- The tolls are set presumably to maximize the profit of the company. Are these tolls efficient during peak traffic times? To answer this, assume that lower tolls would attract motorists currently using the congested freeway lanes but would slow traffic in the toll lanes.

- Suppose that, in the middle of the night, neither the freeway lanes nor the toll lanes are congested. Is the $.25 nighttime toll efficient?

prevent the dissemination of knowledge through secrecy—are the reasons for government policies regarding intellectual property rights. The market failure arises because of the public-good nature of knowledge.

The traditional way that the government tries to encourage R&D is by protecting the inventors of new products and processes with patents. Patents provide a 17-year period during which other firms cannot use an invention unless they pay royalties to the inventing firm. This allows the inventing firm to appropriate the benefits of the invention. Unfortunately, it also grants the inventor a monopoly, causing another form of market failure. The main advantage to society of issuing a patent is that it provides commercial incentives for invention and reduces the incentive to keep knowledge secret. In order to receive a patent, the inventing firm must make public the knowledge of its invention. Although other firms cannot use the invention without paying royalties, they can build on the knowledge so that technical progress can proceed.

In addition to patent policy, the government produces public-good knowledge capital with R&D activities financed at the taxpayers' expense in government laboratories. It also subsidizes the costs of R&D in private and university laboratories. This method is useful for "basic" research, where the benefits are indirect and cannot be appropriated with a patent. In 1995, nondefense R&D spending by the federal government amounted to over $30 billion. In addition, the government subsidizes private R&D spending with a tax credit that lowers the taxes paid by firms based on increases in their R&D spending.

One problem with government financing of knowledge capital is knowing how much to spend (the same problem we encountered in national defense) and deciding what types of knowledge to finance. Former senator William Proxmire of Wisconsin was famous for handing out his "golden fleece" awards to highlight cases where the government had spent money on research that he thought was worthless, or at least lacking any compelling public interest. On the other hand, when R&D has an immediate and tangible commercial benefit, it does not need government financing, providing it can be protected with patents, because there are adequate private rewards for such investment. Basic, rather than applied, research is more likely to yield benefits that cannot be appropriated by the firm, so the case for government intervention is the strongest for basic research. Unfortunately, it is also difficult to determine the social benefit of much basic research, and that makes it a candidate for the golden fleece award.

CONCLUSION AND SUMMARY

This chapter has argued that the existence of public goods provides a rationale for government allocative policies. Although private production of nonrival goods is not likely to be efficient, this need not imply that it is always a good idea for the government to produce them. For instance, we saw that inefficiency is created when fees are charged to view television programs, but this doesn't mean that the government should take over the broadcasting industry. (It does form the basis for government funding for public television, however.) Market failure is a matter of degree. In some cases, like national defense, market failure is so serious that the economy would be extremely inefficient (and vulnerable) without government production. In other cases, such as TV programs, public goods may best be produced by private firms. Although the market outcome is not likely to be fully efficient, the degree of inefficiency may not warrant government production. The best outcome might be for the government to subsidize private production to increase the quantity of the public good, or perhaps not intervene at all.

- While public goods are often provided by government, some are provided by private firms. Public goods and services possess the properties of nonrivalry and nonexcludability. Nonrivalry means that all consumers can enjoy the good without adding to its cost. Nonexcludability means that it is impractical to exclude consumers who do not pay.

- The properties of public goods typically lead to market failure. Nonexcludability means that private firms cannot appropriate the benefits from producing the good, so they have little or no commercial incentive to provide it. Nonrivalry means that it is inefficient to exclude consumers who do not pay from enjoying the benefits, because they do not add to the cost of producing the good.

- At the efficient quantity of a public good, the sum of the MWTPs of all consumers in the economy is equal to the marginal cost of producing the good. All consumers enjoy the total quantity of the public good, so differences in their tastes show up as differences in their MWTPs, rather than as differences in the quantities consumed.

▪ To provide a public good at the efficient quantity, the government must solve two problems. First, it must learn the community's MWTP for the public good; second, it must decide how to share the burden of the cost among the members of the community.

▪ Congestible public goods are subject to crowding (congestion costs) when the number of consumers is large. Local public goods are available only to consumers within a limited geographic domain.

▪ National defense is an important national public good provided by the federal government. Defense spending in the United States is currently less than 4% of gross domestic product. Although this is low by its own postwar standards, the United States spends more on national defense than any other country in the world.

▪ The interstate highway system is the largest domestic construction project in American history. Controlled-access highways are neither completely nonrival nor nonexcludable, so tolls could be charged. However, most of the interstate highway system is toll-free.

▪ The main objective of government policies toward intellectual property rights is to encourage private firms to create knowledge capital, by allowing them to commercially exploit their inventions, without discouraging the dissemination of knowledge. For this reason, firms must reveal the details of their invention to receive a 17-year patent monopoly.

QUESTIONS FOR DISCUSSION AND REVIEW

1. Identify whether the following goods are nonrival, nonexcludable, or both.

   a. Movie shown in an uncrowded theater.

   b. Viewing the Statue of Liberty from New York Harbor.

   c. Space in the overhead bins on an airplane.

2. Natural resource economists often speak of an "existence value," which is a value that people place on a natural asset not because they use it but merely because it exists. For instance, a person who never visits the Florida Everglades, nor plans to, may nonetheless place a value on preserving it. Is existence a rival or nonrival good?

3. Suppose a new submarine for the Navy cost $10 billion. Half the population (130 million people) are willing to pay $100 each to have it, and the other half are willing to pay $30 each *not* to have it. Should it be built?

4. Identify whether each of the following provides a national, transnational, or local public good or service.

   a. Hubble space telescope.

   b. Earthquake preparedness center in California.

   c. National Weather Service.

5. Everyone hates finding a table in the cafeteria where the previous user has left a mess of dirty dishes. And after cleaning up someone else's mess, it is tempting to leave yours for the next person too. We'd all be better off, and do no more work, if individuals bused their own tables, yet this rarely happens. Explain this phenomenon, using the prisoner's dilemma.

6. Some national parks do not charge entrance fees during the winter, except on weekends. Is this an efficient pricing policy?

7. Internet Exercise and Class Experiment. Free riding and the private provision of public goods have been studied by experimental economists. A good example of a classroom experiment is found at http://mcnet.marietta.edu/~delemeeg/games/games101-113.htm#g109 (experiment #109). With your instructor's permission, here is a version you can try. Ask your instructor to assign some bonus points for doing the experiment. Each student in the class is given four playing cards, two red and two black. Each student can "spend" two of these playing cards. A red card (a private good) earns the individual student one bonus point. A black card (a public good) earns $2/N$ bonus points for every student in the class, where N is the number of students in the class. (Thus, if there are 20 students in the class, each black card earns one-tenth of a point for everyone in the class.) The number of bonus points earned by student i is equal

to $R_i + \frac{2}{N} \cdot B$ where R_i is the number of

red cards spent by student i and B is the number of black cards spent by all students in the class. Thus if *all* students spend two red cards they will get two bonus points each whereas if *all* students spend two black cards they will receive four bonus points each. Although a red card has a higher private rate of return, the black card has a higher public rate of return. How much free riding occurred in your class? Did your instructor let the class consult prior to spending their cards? Would it have made a difference? Do you think it would have made a difference if the instructor had announced each student's decision to the class?

8. Internet Exercise. Many of the public-good issues discussed in this chapter apply to the Internet. One example is the software that chooses the best route for the traffic on the network. The backbone of routing software is GateDaemon (known as GateD), developed at Cornell University using public funds from the National Science Foundation. An excellent discussion of the public-good properties of GateD is found in "A Model for Efficient Aggregation of Resources for Economic Public Goods on the Internet" by Martyne Hallgren and Alan McAdams. This easy-to-read paper is available at http://www.press.umich.edu/jcp/works/HallgModel.html. Read the first half of this paper and answer the following questions. Why is GateD a public good? Is it an excludable public good? Does Cornell practice price exclusion? How does Cornell finance the costs of enhancing GateD? Is there a free-rider problem? How does Cornell try to mitigate the free-rider problem?

SELECTED REFERENCES

A classic book on free riding and public goods is Mancur Olson, *The Logic of Collective Action,* 1965. More up-to-date, and more technical, is Richard Cornes and Todd Sandler, *The Theory of Externalities, Public Goods, and Club Goods,* 2nd ed., 1996.

The cost of "winning the Cold War" is documented in Stephen I. Schwartz ed. *Atomic Audit: The Costs and Consequences of U.S. Nuclear Weapons Since 1940,* Brookings Press, 1998.

The entire subject of the economics of national defense is surveyed in Todd Sandler and Keith Hartley, *The Economics of Defense,* 1995.

The history of the interstate highway system is described in David J. St. Clair, *The Motorization of American Cities,* 1986.

USEFUL INTERNET SITES

The Center for Defense Information has data and policy papers on defense spending by the United States and other countries at http://www.cdi.org/issues/usmi/. See also the Defense Budget Studies section of the Center for Strategic and Budgetary Assessments site at http://www.csbaonline.org/. The Federal Highway Administrations Office of Transportation Studies at http://www.fhwa.dot.gov/policy/hptshmpg.htm has a lot of information on the economics of highways including its Highway Cost Allocation Study that provides detailed information on the social user cost of highways. The State of Minnesota DOT's Value Pricing and Congestion Pricing Homepage at http://www.hhh.umn.edu/centers/slp/conpric/conpric.htm has some very interesting material on new methods of highway pricing to reduce congestion. ETTM is a site dedicated to electronic road pricing at http://www.ettm.com/.

A P P E N D I X   T O   C H A P T E R   3

Efficiency Conditions in a Production Economy with a Public Good

Chapter 3 explained the efficiency conditions for a public good in terms of summing vertically the individual MWTP schedules for the good. The efficient quantity is found by equating the summed MWTP to the marginal cost of production. This Appendix analyzes the same problem in terms of consumers' preferences (indifference curves) and the economy's production possibilities curve.

In Figure A.3.1, an economy can produce a private good (food) and a public good (defense) according to the production possibilities curve PP. The slope of the production possibilities curve at each point is the marginal cost (MC) of defense measured in units of food (the numeraire good). To determine the efficient quantity of defense, we must consider the preferences of the consumers, represented by indifference curve maps. We assume two consumers (or two classes of consumers), George and Martha. Figure A.3.1(a) shows one of George's indifference curves U^G. The slope of this indifference curve (ignoring the minus sign) is George's MWTP for defense.

An efficient quantity of defense is Pareto optimal, so to find it we must exploit all opportunities to make Martha better off (give her higher utility) while holding George on his indifference curve. To do this, we determine the quantity of food available to Martha at each quantity of defense. For instance, if D units of defense are produced, a maximum of F units of food can be produced, according to the PP curve. To keep George on this prescribed indifference curve, he must consume F^G units of food, leaving F minus F^G units of food for Martha. Of course, both George and Martha consume the D units of defense because it is a nonrival good.

Figure A.3.1(b) plots the amount of food available to Martha for each quantity of defense. For example, as we saw, when D units of defense are produced, Martha consumes F minus F^G units of food. This quantity is the vertical distance between the production possibilities curve and George's indifference curve at quantity D.

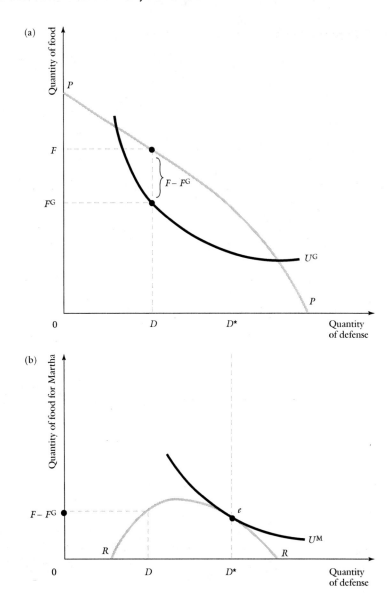

Figure A.3.1

Finding the Efficient Quantity of National Defense for Two Consumers

Given the production possibilities curve *PP* for defense and food in (a), we can fix George's utility and subtract the height of U^G from *PP* to find the amount of food left over for Martha at each level of defense. This is shown in (b) by the height of *RR*, which has a slope equal to the MC of defense minus George's MWTP for defense. Martha's utility is maximized at point *e*, where D^* units of defense are produced. At D^* units, the slope of Martha's indifference curve ($MWTP^M$) is equal to the slope of *RR* ($MC - MWTP^G$) and the equality can be rearranged as the Samuelson condition.

Subtracting the height of George's indifference curve from the height of the production possibilities curve at each quantity of defense and plotting it, we find the food available to Martha. Of course, the food available to Martha is positive only when George's indifference curve lies below the *PP* curve.

In Figure A.3.1(b) the curve showing the quantity of food available to Martha at each quantity of defense is *RR*. Since *RR* is constructed by subtracting the height of George's indifference curve from the height of the *PP* curve, the slope of *RR* is equal to the slope *PP* (the marginal cost of defense, MC) minus the (absolute) slope of George's indifference curve (George's marginal willingness to pay for defense, $MWTP^G$).

As mentioned, to find the efficient quantity of defense we want to exploit all possibilities of making Martha better off. This means we want to find the maximum utility (highest indifference curve) for Martha along *RR*. The maximum utility that Martha can have is found at the quantity of defense $D^{\star}$, where *RR* is tangent to Martha's highest possible indifference curve (at point e on *RR*).

At point e the *RR* curve is tangent to Martha's indifference curve, so the slopes of the two curves must be the same. As we saw, the slope of *RR* is equal to MC − $MWTP^G$. The slope of Martha's indifference curve is her marginal willingness to pay for defense, $MWTP^M$. Rearranging the equation MC − $MWTP^G$ = $MWTP^M$, we find

$$MWTP^G + MWTP^M = MC.$$

This is the condition defining the efficient quantity of defense. Economists refer to this equation as the **Samuelson condition,** in honor of the Nobel laureate Paul Samuelson, who worked out the condition in the 1950s, and who devised the diagrammatic derivation outlined above.

Finally, we should not think that the efficient quantity of defense is unique. We found the quantity $D^{\star}$ by starting with a given level of utility for George. Generally, if we start with a different level of utility for George, we obtain a different efficient quantity of defense because George, and Martha's preferences for the public good may differ. For instance, if George is a hawk and Martha is a dove on defense, the efficient quantity of defense will be smaller if George is held to a lower indifference curve. In other words, as for private goods, the efficient quantities of public goods depend on the distribution of utilities in the economy.

Reference

Paul A. Samuelson, "A Diagrammatic Exposition of a Theory of Public Expenditure," 1955.

4 Externalities and Public Policy

When the European settlers arrived on the Atlantic coast of North America, they found one of the richest cod fisheries in the world on the Grand Banks and Georges Bank off Newfoundland and New England. This fishery proved to be a rich economic resource, and it played no small role in the early economic development of North America as a source of exports. By 1992, the government of Canada had to close the Grand Banks fishery because of plummeting fish harvests; in New England, the Georges Bank fishery was closed two years later. What went wrong here? Why didn't the invisible hand of market forces lead those who were dependent on the fishery for their livelihood to husband this valuable resource to prevent its depletion?

A fishery is a good example of an industry plagued by an externality. An **externality** is present when an action by an individual producer or consumer affects other parties, without payment or compensation for the cost or benefit affecting them. An externality exists in the fishery because one person's fishing activity decreases the stock of fish, making it necessary for others to fish longer in order to catch a given quantity of fish. The individual fisher ignores this external cost on others when deciding how much to fish. Many economic activities, as well as fishing, have external costs. These costs may result from the excessive depletion of resources, hazards to the public's safety, the pollution of air and water, and other things. The presence of externalities is a form of market failure, meaning that the market allocation of resources is not efficient. The inefficiency caused by externalities means that the government can improve efficiency and potentially make everyone in the economy better off. The government does this with policies controlling the activities that have externalities. For example, a large body of government regulation is directed at controlling activities that pollute the environment.

TYPES OF EXTERNALITIES

The concept of an externality is quite general, and economists have identified and classified many different types of externalities. In this section, we identify and describe externalities according to the most common classifications.

Cost and Benefit Externalities

Perhaps the most important defining characteristic of externalities is whether they are cost or benefit externalities. An activity with a *cost externality* imposes net costs on other people without their being compensated. The fishing industry has a cost externality, and so does producing or consuming goods that cause pollution, such as gasoline. An activity with a *benefit externality* confers a benefit on other people without their having to pay for it. Immunization against a communicable disease confers a benefit externality. For example, when a child is immunized against polio, other children benefit because the immunized child cannot contract polio and infect them. Since the children who benefit indirectly do not have to pay the child who is immunized, the benefit is uncompensated and therefore an externality.

Sometimes benefit and cost externalities are described as positive and negative externalities respectively. We should not think, however, that a benefit externality is a positive thing for the economy. As we see below, benefit externalities create inefficiencies just as cost externalities do. Benefit and cost externalities are also called external economies and external diseconomies.

Consumption and Production Externalities

Another classification is based on whether an externality is caused by consuming or producing a good. In some cases, externalities are caused by both processes. For example, gasoline consumption imposes a cost externality because motorists pollute the air when they drive, and gasoline production imposes a cost externality because air quality is reduced around the oil refineries. On the other hand, paper consumption does not cause significant externalities (except, perhaps, litter), while paper production causes air pollution and puts hazardous wastes, such as dioxin, into rivers and lakes. Hence we can classify the paper industry as subject to a production externality.[1] The distinction between consumption and production externalities may be important for the design of the government policies that control the problem.

Production externalities can be further classified as *output* externalities and *input* externalities. The distinction concerns whether the external benefit or cost is directly related to the output of the firm or to the firm's use of particular factors of production (inputs). For example, the production of electricity often causes a cost externality by polluting the air, but this externality depends on the quantities of inputs used—for instance, the amount and type of fuel used by the generating plant (say, high- or low-sulfur coal)—and not on the output of electricity per se. The quantity of electricity produced by hydroelectric plants causes little or no air pollution. In contrast, the externality in the fishing industry is an output externality because the external cost depends on the quantity of fish caught rather than the means used to catch them.

[1]For example, imported paper does not cause an external cost in the country where it is consumed—only in the country where it is produced.

Network Externalities

An interesting type of externality is called a **network externality,** because there is an external benefit (or cost) associated with being part of a "network." With this type of externality, the benefit or cost of a good or service to one user depends on the number of people using the good, rather than on the amount consumed or produced. A good example is a person's decision to get a telephone or to subscribe to an e-mail service. When individuals get a telephone, not only can they call others, but others can call them.[2] A telephone would be of no use if no one else had one. The consumer's benefit from a telephone depends on the number of users on the telephone network.

Recently, economists have focused their attention on network externalities because of the importance of technology adoption and communication in modern economies. Network externalities introduce the phenomenon of the *industry standard,* which develops when a product or a technology is adopted by a new user simply because "everyone else uses it." Even if a cheaper and better substitute is available, consumers will choose a good or process that is established as the industry standard because it is more costly for individuals to "go it alone." That is, a network externality may create an inefficiency when an inferior good is established as the industry standard. Examples of an industry standard include the VHS videotape format (which eclipsed the earlier beta format by the late 1980s), PC computer technology (which accounts for about 85 percent of personal computers sold), and the "QWERTY" keyboard on the computer, which is a holdover from typewriter technology.

EXTERNALITIES AND THE EFFICIENCY OF MARKETS

Externalities are a major reason that an economy might not rely solely on an unfettered market system to allocate resources (hence the interest by public finance economists in them). Specifically, the market quantity of a good is greater than the efficient quantity when an external cost is present, whereas the market quantity of a good is less than the efficient quantity when an external benefit is present. That is, too much of the economy's resources is devoted to producing goods with cost externalities, and too little is devoted to producing goods with benefit externalities.

Inefficiency caused by a cost externality is shown in Figure 4.1, which gives supply and demand for a good with an external cost: the car burglar alarm. This is a good with an external consumption cost because it disturbs the neighbors when it goes off accidentally in the middle of the night. The height of the demand curve indicates the marginal willingness to pay (MWTP) by the buyer of the car alarm, and the height of the supply curve indicates the marginal cost of producing the alarms. The market equilibrium quantity of alarms, found by the intersection of the supply and demand curves, is Q_e. The prevailing market price of alarms is P_e, which is equal to the MWTP of the buyer and the marginal cost of production.

---

[2]Of course, that external benefit may be a cost to person getting the telephone, as those annoying telemarketing calls at dinner time illustrate.

[3]This assumes that the costs of waking up the neighbors are not directed back to the alarm owner—say, in the form of nasty phone calls.

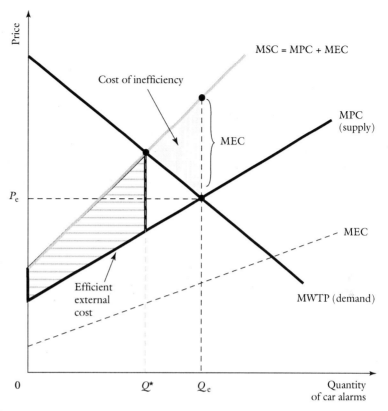

Figure 4.1

A Good with a Cost Externality

The marginal social cost (MSC) of car alarms exceeds the marginal private cost (MPC) because of the marginal external cost (MEC) caused by annoyance to third parties. The market equilibrium quantity Q_e is greater than the efficient quantity Q^* because market participants buy alarms as long as their MWTP exceeds the MPC of the alarm. The cost of inefficiency (or deadweight loss) is equal to the area of the shaded triangle. At the efficient quantity Q^*, the external cost of alarms is not zero. However, the MWTP of a buyer of an alarm is equal to the MSC of the alarm.

The marginal external cost (MEC) of a car alarm, caused by disturbing the neighbors, is not included in the market price and is disregarded by the consumer when choosing to buy an alarm.[3] If we add MEC to the supply price (the marginal private cost, MPC), we get the *marginal social cost* (MSC) of a car alarm. In Figure 4.1, the vertical distance between the MSC curve and the supply curve is MEC per alarm.

The efficient quantity Q^* of car alarms is the one at which the buyer's MWTP is equal to MSC. The efficient quantity is found by the intersection of the demand curve and the MSC curve. As we see, Q^* is smaller than the market equilibrium quantity because of the external cost. The reason the market quantity is greater than the efficient quantity is that the buyer does not take into account the marginal external cost of the alarm, only its market price. Car alarms appear cheaper to the buyers than they really are to the economy as a whole. The disturbance cost borne by the neighbors is part of the cost of a car alarm to the economy, but it is external to the buyers and they disregard it.

The cost of the inefficiency caused by the externality is measured by the area of the shaded triangle in Figure 4.1. This area is the excess of the MSC of the alarm over the MWTP of the buyers for the excess quantity of car alarms purchased (Q_c minus Q^*). The area of this triangle is equal to half the excess quantity of car alarms times the marginal external cost at the market output. In other words, we can measure the cost of the inefficiency created by a cost externality as

$$\frac{1}{2} \cdot \text{MEC} \cdot (Q_c - Q^*).$$

Note that the cost of inefficiency caused by the externality is not the same as the total cost imposed on the neighbors. At the efficient quantity Q^* there is no cost from inefficiency, but the neighbors still suffer the nuisance of car alarms going off in the night, albeit fewer of them. In other words, the existence of an external cost does not mean we should ban car alarms in order to eliminate the external cost altogether. Nor does efficiency require that the neighbors be compensated for being disturbed. While compensating disturbed neighbors seems like a fair thing to do, it is not necessary for efficiency, because equity and efficiency are different things. The inefficiency caused by the cost externality simply means that too many car alarms are purchased as a result of market forces. Efficiency requires that the quantity of car alarms be that at which the total cost of the alarm, including the external cost, is equal to the buyer's willingness to pay for it.

Figure 4.2 illustrates the case of a good with a benefit externality: smoke alarms in apartments. This is a good example of a private good with a benefit externality. When individuals buy smoke alarms for their apartments, they confer a benefit on their neighbors. The early detection of a fire in the purchaser's apartment reduces the danger and loss of property for the neighbors, even if they have their own alarms. Therefore everyone in an apartment building, not just the person purchasing the alarm, derives benefits from the purchase.[4]

In Figure 4.2 we see the demand and supply curves for smoke alarms by people in the apartment building. The height of the demand curve equals the purchaser's marginal *private* willingness to pay (MPWTP) for a smoke alarm, and the height of the supply curve is the marginal private cost (MPC) of producing smoke alarms as given by the market price of smoke alarms. The market equilibrium quantity of smoke alarms Q_c is found by the intersection of the supply and demand curves, and the equilibrium market price is P_c. At this price, everyone with an MWTP for a smoke alarm at least as high as the market price will purchase one.

The marginal *social* willingness to pay (MSWTP) for a smoke alarm is greater than the purchasers' MWTP because of the marginal external benefit (MEB). The marginal external benefit is the marginal willingness of everyone living in the building to pay for a smoke alarm in the purchaser's apartment. This marginal external benefit is ignored by the purchaser of the alarm, who cannot charge the other apartment dwellers for the benefit he or she confers on them by purchasing an alarm.

---

[4]The smoke alarm is not a public good in the sense that one smoke alarm is enough to benefit everyone. Each apartment dweller has his or her own smoke alarm, but an alarm in another apartment provides some benefits as well.

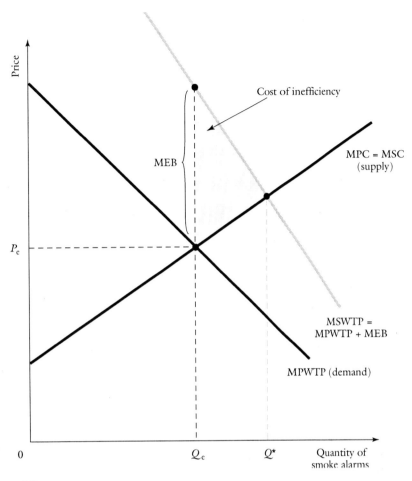

Figure 4.2

A Good with a Benefit Externality

The marginal social willingness to pay (MSWTP) for smoke alarms is greater than the marginal private will-ingness to pay (MPWTP) by the buyers because of the marginal external benefit (MEB) conferred on neigh-bors. The market equilibrium quantity Q_e is less than the efficient quantity Q^* because market participants buy alarms only if their MWTP is equal to the MPC of the alarm. They ignore the external benefit for the neighbors. The cost of inefficiency (or deadweight loss) is equal to the area of the shaded triangle.

Adding the marginal external benefit to the purchaser's MWTP gives the MSWTP. The vertical distance between the MPWTP (demand) curve and the MSWTP curve is the MEB. The efficient quantity of smoke alarms Q^* is found where the MSWTP curve intersects the supply curve.

In Figure 4.2, we see that a benefit externality causes a cost from inefficiency, just as a cost externality does. In this case, market forces bring forth a quantity of smoke alarms that is less than the efficient quantity, causing an inefficiency cost. It is equal to the area of the shaded triangle in Figure 4.2, which is the amount by which the market quantity falls short of the efficient quantity (Q^* minus Q_e units) multiplied by one-half the excess of the MSWTP over the marginal cost at the market equilibrium quantity.

Relevant and Irrelevant Externalities

An old adage says that "when you have a hammer in your hand, everything looks like a nail." This is true for externalities. Because of the importance of externalities to policy, once the concept is understood there is a tendency to find them everywhere. This is not hard to do because the modern economy is very interdependent—"everything depends on everything." However, we must be careful because many of the "externalities" are not a cause of market failure after all. For this reason, economists often identify externalities as *relevant* and *irrelevant* to the question of economic efficiency.

An example of an irrelevant externality is a good that has an inframarginal externality. An **inframarginal externality** occurs when the size of the external benefit or cost imposed on others does not depend on small changes in the quantity of the good around the market equilibrium quantity. With an inframarginal externality, changes in the market quantity do not affect efficiency. To give a unimportant example, when people walk by a newspaper box they often read the headlines. This is an external benefit from selling newspapers, but it does not depend on the quantity of newspapers sold (assuming the same number of boxes). Whether 1 paper or 20 papers are sold does not affect the benefits to the passersby.

No inefficiency is caused by inframarginal externalities. We see this result in Figure 4.3. Instead of newspapers, we consider a more important case: education. It is sometimes argued that education is a positive externality activity because educating people benefits others as well as the people educated. This observation is no doubt true, but it may not mean that people choose too little education.[5] For example, one external benefit from education comes from literacy. When an individual is made literate, this benefits others in the economy because they can communicate in writing with him or her. Imagine, for example, how inconvenient it would be not to write letters (or e-mail) to friends because they are illiterate.

If the external benefit from literacy is realized after fewer years of education than people would acquire for themselves, literacy is an inframarginal benefit. For instance, suppose people are fully literate after 10 years in school, but everyone goes to school for at least 12 years. Increasing education will increase private benefits but not the external benefit from literacy. In Figure 4.3, the private MWTP for education is shown by the downward-sloping curve, and the marginal cost of education is assumed to be constant. We assume that an inframarginal benefit externality is generated by the first 10 years of education. Adding the external benefit to the private MWTP, we obtain the curve labeled MSWTP, which is equal to the marginal social willingness to pay for a year of education less than 10 years. No marginal external benefit is present in education beyond 10 years. As shown, the individual has an incentive to acquire more than 10 years of education, so the full external benefit has

---

[5]The following example is meant to suggest, not that education does not have a marginal external benefit, but that some of the external benefits of education do not necessarily lead to inefficient private decisions.

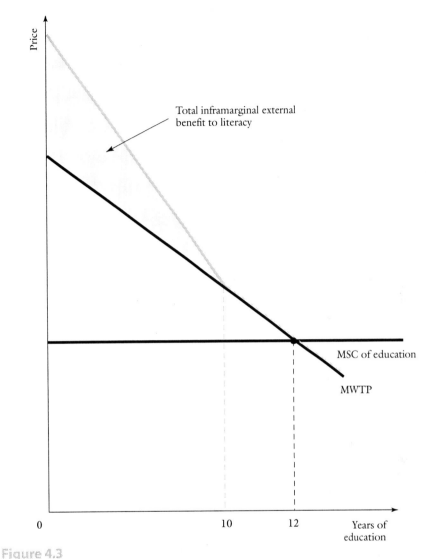

Price

Total inframarginal external
benefit to literacy

MSC of education

MWTP

0   10   12   Years of
education

Figure 4.3

An Inframarginal Externality

The market equilibrium is efficient if an external benefit or cost is *inframarginal*. In this example a marginal external benefit (perhaps from increased literacy) is present for the first 10 years of an individual's education, but not for more. The MSWTP is equal to the MPWTP beyond 10 years of education. Since the MSWTP for education is equal to the MC of education at 12 years, the quantity of education chosen by the individual is efficient.

been realized, and the government need not provide incentives to increase educational attainment.

Another example of an irrelevant externality is a pecuniary externality. A **pecuniary externality** occurs because an individual's decision affects others through a change in market prices. Suppose a consumer who wants a brighter smile decides to buy more toothpaste. The position of the market demand curve, which includes the purchase decisions of all consumers of toothpaste, determines the market price. The change in the consumer's demand shifts the market demand curve slightly to the right, which increases the price of toothpaste if the supply curve is upward-sloping. Of course, the effect on price is very small, perhaps a fraction of a cent, so the individual ignores it when deciding to buy more toothpaste. That sounds like an externality. Millions of other toothpaste consumers pay a slightly higher price because this consumer decided to buy more toothpaste. How is this different from the case of the individual fishing boat that catches more fish and creates external costs for other fishing boats?

The difference is that an *offsetting* externality is present in this case. Although an individual's increase in consumption raises the price slightly, this does not cause a net loss to the economy. Consumers pay more, but toothpaste producers receive a higher price and earn a higher profit (that is, higher producer's surplus). In other words, the decision to consume more toothpaste just transfers consumer's surplus into producer's surplus.[6] This affects the distribution of income in the economy but does not make it more or less efficient.

EXTERNALITIES AND PROPERTY RIGHTS

Sometimes an institution is so ingrained and so natural that we don't notice it until it is missing. Such is the case with the institution of property rights. A *property right* is a legal rule of entitlement that grants the owner of a property the right to enjoy the benefits it provides, to command payment (emolument) if the property is used for the benefit of others, to prevent trespass, and to sue for compensation (damages) in the event that he or she loses the benefits from the property because of actions by others. Although the fundamental theorem of welfare economics described in Chapter 2 does not mention property rights, the existence of property rights is presumed for a well-functioning market system. For market forces to direct an economic resource into its highest-valued use, a complete and unambiguous system of property rights to the resource is needed. Property rights allow the owner to appropriate the benefits of finding the more highly valued use. When property rights are missing or ambiguous, the market is not likely to perform this function. The main point of the subsequent discussion is that the absence of property rights is one reason externalities exist.

The Tragedy of the Commons

In the medieval English village there was a pasture, or commons, where all villagers were free to graze their cattle. Villagers were allowed to graze as many cattle as they liked on the commons, and the result was severe overgrazing. In comparison with the commons, privately owned pastures were rich with grass. Despite an overgrazed commons that supported few cattle, no villager had an incentive to restrain his or

---

[6]Consumer's surplus was explained in Chapter 2. Producer's surplus is the area above the supply curve below the price received by the sellers. It is equal to the economic profit of the producers.

her own grazing and let the grass grow. Any benefits from an act of conservation would mostly benefit the other villagers, while the cattle of the person who showed restraint would get less food.

In 1968, the ecologist Professor Garrett Hardin of the University of California at Santa Barbara described seemingly irrational outcomes like that of the overgrazed commons as the "tragedy of the commons." In fact, the tragedy of the commons is just the prisoner's dilemma problem explained in Chapter 3. When a pasture is owned in common, the individual villagers make a rational decision to let their own cattle graze as much as possible, even if that outcome is inefficient and makes everyone in the village worse off. More than a decade before Hardin, the tragedy of the commons in the unregulated fishery was described by Professor H. Scott Gordon of Indiana University. Gordon showed that free access to a common fishing ground will lead to overfishing, even to the point of depleting the stock of fish. It is ironic that in light of this knowledge, and despite government regulation, we should see the tragedy of the commons at the Grand Banks and Georges Banks fishery 40 years later.

Gordon was the first to point out that a stock of fish swimming in the water of a fishery to which everyone has free access is a **common property** resource. A common property resource is rival and nonexcludable: When more is used by one person, less is available for others; and because a common property resource is owned by everyone, no one can be excluded. In this case, no one has an incentive to conserve the resource because he or she cannot reap the benefit of conservation. Gordon pointed out that the problem in the fishery is that no property right is assigned to a fish until it is caught. Just as medieval villagers could claim rights to the pasture only by letting their cattle graze on the commons, so fishers can claim rights to the fish only by catching them. The result is competitive overfishing of the commons and drastic reductions in the stocks of fish, to the detriment of all.

How does the fact that fish in the sea are common property show up as a cost externality? The cost of catching a fish is determined largely by how long it takes the fisher to catch it. When the stock of fish is small, it is necessary to fish longer in order to catch a fish. If the fishing ground is severely depleted, it may be difficult or impossible to land a catch of a given size. In other words, when one fisher takes a fish from the sea, he or she imposes a cost on the others in the fishery. However, individual fishers do not bear the costs they impose on the others, unlike the "private" costs they must pay (such as the costs of the boat, fuel, gear, and labor). Since individual fishers do not bear this "external" cost, they ignore it and catch more fish than they would if they had to pay it. In other words, we have a cost externality in fishing, so the amount of fishing activity is too high for efficiency.

In this section we have seen that the externality in the fishing industry is a symptom of a deeper problem—the absence of property rights to a rival resource. If the fishery were privately owned, no externality would be present. For example, if fish are raised in a privately owned lake rather than roaming free in the sea, the owner has no incentive to overfish. In fact, the private ownership of fisheries has become common in the form of aquaculture, or "fish farming." The owner of a fish farm lets fish reproduce and grow, and then catches them at the best possible time. Owners do not overfish, because the cost of depleting the stock is borne wholly by themselves. Even if an owner lets many other people fish in the lake, no externality occurs: The price charged to each customer includes the cost an additional fisher imposes on others, so all costs of catching a fish are private costs.

The Reciprocal Nature of Externalities

It is perhaps human nature to perceive social problems in terms of victim and perpetrator, or right and wrong. This is no less true for externalities. When smokers light up in a public place, they impose an external cost on nonsmokers, who prefer smoke-free air. It is natural to view the smoker as the perpetrator of a wrong, and the nonsmoker as a victim who should be compensated. The same is true when a factory chimney spews noxious pollutants into the air.

However, as we have seen, the concept of economic efficiency is silent about the desirability of different distributions of utilities. As a result, we can understand the inefficiency of externalities without considering the philosophical issue of who should pay. Instead, we can explain externalities as simply an inefficient resolution to a conflict about how a resource is used. On this view, rather than being perpetrator and victim, the smoker and nonsmoker are simply people with conflicting desires over how the air in the room is to be used. The nonsmoker wants to keep the air smoke-free. The smoker gets enjoyment by smoking, which requires (among other things) exhaling used smoke into the air in the room.

An important insight following from this view is that all externalities are reciprocal in their impact, rather than having a one-way impact from perpetrator to victim. It is true that when smokers exhale smoke, they impose a cost on the nonsmoker, but it is also true that the nonsmokers' desire for a smoke-free room imposes a cost on the smoker. The smoker cannot enjoy smoking. We do not need to make a moral judgment about smoking in order to analyze the externality. If smokers have the right to light up in public places, they will consider only their own enjoyment and ignore the external cost they impose on the nonsmokers around them. The externality may lead to too much smoking (that is, inefficiently high levels of smoking) in public places. On the other hand, if nonsmokers have the right to demand that smokers do not smoke in public areas, they too consider only their own benefits and ignore the external cost they impose on the smokers. As an economic problem, externalities are a two-way street.

As economists, the question we want to answer is: What is the efficient amount of smoking, and how can it be brought about? To answer this, we'll consider a simplified case. Suppose two people—one smoker and one nonsmoker—occupy a room. The smoker wants to smoke and has a willingness to pay of $5 to light up. The nonsmoker wants the room smoke-free and has a willingness to pay of $10 to keep it that way. We assume that both people are fully informed about the dangers of tobacco smoke to their health and take these costs into account in their willingness to pay. No one else is in the room.

Is it efficient for the scarce resource—the air in the room—to be used for smoking or kept smoke-free? The answer, given the specified willingness to pay, is that it should be kept smoke-free because the nonsmoker's willingness to pay for clean air is more than the smoker's willingness to pay to light up. Keeping the air smoke-free is the highest-valued use for the air; therefore, not allowing the smoker to smoke is the efficient outcome. Will this outcome be realized? It seems that it will be realized only by making the room nonsmoking. If smoking is allowed, the smoker will light up and enjoy the $5 benefit while ignoring the $10 external cost on the nonsmoker. However, if the smoker has a willingness to pay of $10 and the nonsmoker has a willingness to pay of only $5, making the room nonsmoking is inefficient. If nonsmokers have the right to clean air in this case, it seems that the outcome is inefficient. Apparently we have to know the efficient outcome before we assign property rights. Or do we?

Bargaining and the Coase Theorem

Professor Ronald Coase of the University of Chicago, who won the Nobel Prize in economics in 1991, recognized that if people act rationally, and if bargaining (or transactions) costs are sufficiently low, the assignment of transferable property rights to a resource will lead to an efficient outcome regardless of who is given the property rights. A *transferable* property right is one that the owner has the right to sell.[7] In other words, whether the property rights to the air in the room are given to the smoker or the nonsmoker, the air in the room will be put to its highest-valued use.

The main idea is illustrated as follows. Suppose again that the smoker's willingness to pay to light up is $5 and the nonsmoker's willingness to pay for clean air is $10. Obviously, if the nonsmoker is given the rights, the room will be nonsmoking, and that is the efficient outcome. But what if the smoker is given the rights? Coase argued that if bargaining costs are low and the property rights are transferable, the room will still remain nonsmoking. The reason is that the nonsmoker is willing to pay up to $10 to keep it that way and thus can bribe the smoker not to smoke. For instance, if the nonsmoker offers the smoker $6 not to smoke, the smoker will accept (that is, sell his or her right to smoke). Refusing a $6 bribe to refrain from smoking is equivalent to paying $6 to smoke, which is more than the smoker's willingness to pay.

Why don't we ever see this happening—in a restaurant, say? If the smokers in a no-smoking restaurant have a higher willingness to pay to smoke than the nonsmokers have for clean air, why don't they offer a payment? Several reasons come to mind. First, to the extent that a no-smoking policy gives rights to the nonsmokers, these are not likely to be transferable rights. In other words, nonsmokers cannot sell their right to a smoke-free environment. Second, tradition and custom constrain the things people do and do not bargain for. Just as it is customary to haggle over the price in a store selling Persian rugs but not over the price of a garment in a clothing store, it is not customary to bargain over the right to smoke. Third, and most important, bargaining and transactions costs are present, and the total amount to be gained by the people in the restaurant is not likely to be great. If there are many people in the restaurant, the bargaining costs are likely to be very high. How do the smokers decide what payment to make and how to divide the payment among themselves? At the same time, even if the smokers can organize and collectively agree to make the payment, one of the nonsmokers may threaten to veto the

---

[7]Not all property rights are transferable. For instance, we each have the property rights on our labor, but we cannot sell ourselves into slavery.

agreement unless he or she gets a bigger share of the payment. In other words, when many nonsmokers are in a room, a smoke-free environment is a public good, with all the difficulties of private provision that we discussed in Chapter 3.

The difficulties of applying the Coase theorem in everyday life are illustrated well in A Case in Point 4.1.

ENVIRONMENTAL POLLUTION AS A COST EXTERNALITY

Perhaps the most important cost externality in the United States economy is pollution. Many economic activities cause the quality of the environment to be

A CASE IN POINT

4.1   Coase Goes to Hollywood

A news item on how filmmakers on location pay residents thousands of dollars to keep quiet while they are shooting a scene illustrates the Coase theorem in action, and its shortcomings.

> In his seven years as a location manager in the film industry, Patrick McIntire has rented noisy chain saws just so he could turn them off and paid lawn crews to stop clacking their shears and revving their leaf-blowers. Loud radios, barking dogs and immovable people have cost him a bundle.
>
> Mr. McIntire is not alone. In Los Angeles and other California areas popular for filming, residents are sometimes making thousands of dollars from movie crews by promising to vacate outdoor sets, tone down noise or otherwise stop harassing them. The problem has become so acute that the state legislature has stepped in, drafting laws to make harassing film crews for profit a criminal offense.
>
> "It's gotten to the point where at almost every shoot, somebody has their hand out," said State Senator Herschel Rosenthal, Democrat of Van Nuys, the sponsor of one such bill. "People blow horns, walk through shots, make their dogs bark or crank their stereos. And they all demand money to stop." (*New York Times*, July 27, 1995.)

The noise and disturbance of activities by residents are a cost to filmmakers on location, but keeping quiet is a cost to the residents. (Note the reciprocal nature of the externality.) The residents effectively have the property rights and can make whatever noise they want within the law. Filmmakers adopt the Coasian solution of paying them to keep quiet near the set. If the value of quiet to filmmakers is more than the cost to the residents, an efficient outcome is reached. But filmmakers claim that people are manipulating the system by creating noise or causing disturbance on purpose, simply to elicit a payment from the filmmakers. Such "attracting the nuisance" is a form of bargaining cost.

Critically analyze the following:

- If passed, how would Senator Rosenthal's bill alter the distribution of property rights? Do you think the amount of on-location filming would be affected by the change in property rights?

- If Rosenthal's bill passed, is it likely that residents would bribe filmmakers not to shoot in their neighborhoods? Why or why not?

- Suppose that, before shooting, filmmakers must report to a third party (such as the local government) how much it is worth to them to shoot, and that residents must report how much it is worth to them to avoid the disruption. The assignment of property rights will be determined afterwards by the flip of a coin. As a result, none of the parties knows, at the time they report their valuations, whether they will receive payment or be required to pay. Would this lead to a more efficient outcome? Why or why not?

degraded. Exhaust from automobiles and fumes from fireplaces create smog, along with pollutants from industry chimney stacks. Sulfur dioxide from coal-fired electricity-generating plants creates acid rain that destroys fish, trees, and marble buildings. Phosphorus and nitrogen from detergents in wastewater nourish plants that remove oxygen from lakes, making the lakes anaerobic and foul-smelling. Pesticide runoff from irrigated fields and toxic wastes dumped from industrial plants pose significant health-related hazards.

Many environmentalists view pollution as something that is simply wrong, perhaps immoral. While many economists share the environmentalists' concerns about pollution, they view the problem differently. In the economist's view, the problem is that the level of pollution is too high (that is, it is inefficiently high) because the costs of pollution are mainly external to the polluter. Since a firm that causes pollution does not have to pay the costs of increased air or water pollution, it has no profit incentive to reduce them. If the firm considers these costs at all, it is because of a desire to be a "good citizen." Such a sentiment may not be strong enough to warrant spending millions of dollars on equipment to abate pollution, especially if the firm's competitors don't—the expenses would then place the firm at a competitive disadvantage in the marketplace.

The argument that an individual polluter ignores the costs of pollution remains valid even when the polluter, such as a commuter in a smoggy city, suffers along with everyone else. The individual commuter driving to work contributes a very small amount to the total pollution in the air, but the cost of even this small increase affects everyone in the city. If an individual's decision to drive to work increases the cost of air pollution to everyone by only one-hundredth of a cent, the external cost of the decision is $100 in a city of 1 million. If the commuter were charged $100 to drive to work, he or she probably wouldn't do it.

Commuters drive to work because the private cost of polluting (that is, the cost to themselves) does not outweigh the benefits they get from driving. They ignore the external cost of their decision on everyone else. Like the medieval villagers who found it rational to graze their cattle and not to worry about overgrazing the commons, modern commuters find it rational to drive to work and not to worry about the brown haze hanging in the air.

Is it possible to have too little pollution? The idea that pollution is a problem of economic efficiency rather than morality leads naturally to the concept of an "efficient" level of pollution. Many people may think that the best level of pollution is none at all, but this is not the case. Some amount of pollution is one of the costs we must pay to enjoy a given material standard of living. Just as we need to get up at 7:00 A.M. each weekday to feed, clothe, and shelter ourselves, so we need to suffer some level of environmental pollution as part of the economic cost of enjoying goods and services. The problem is to make sure that this pollution is not excessive in the sense that the cost outweighs the benefits from having more consumer goods.

As always, consumers prefer more of everything, but the reality of life dictates that this is not possible. To have a cleaner environment, the economy must produce less output or use some of its economic resources to produce pollution-abatement equipment rather than consumer goods. For example, cleaner air requires that we drive less or have costly emissions control equipment installed in our cars.

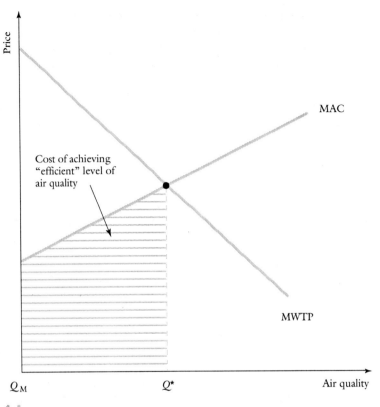

Figure 4.4

The Efficient Level of Air Quality

Although the market equilibrium air quality Q_M is less than the efficient level, the efficient outcome is not to have no air pollution at all. Air quality is a good for which people have an MWTP, but abating pollution has a cost. At the efficient level Q^*, the MWTP for air quality by citizens is equal to the marginal abatement cost (MAC). A higher level of air quality would be inefficient because the MAC is greater than the MWTP.

The concept of an efficient level of air quality is illustrated in Figure 4.4. We measure the level of air quality (visibility, absence of pollutants, etc.) on the horizontal axis. The level of air quality at the origin is assumed to be the level corresponding to the unregulated market level Q_M. At Q_M, air quality is low because most of the cost of pollution is external and people and firms have no incentive to reduce activities that cause pollution. The marginal cost of achieving better air quality is given by the height of the curve labeled **marginal abatement cost (MAC)**. The marginal cost of air quality is the marginal cost of abating pollution either by reducing production of consumer goods or by installing abatement equipment. As more abatement is done (giving higher air quality), the marginal abatement cost rises because firms exhaust "cheap fixes" and must resort to more costly alternatives. The community's marginal willingness to pay for air quality is shown by the downward-sloping demand curve labeled MWTP. The MWTP slopes downward because as air quality gets high, people are willing to pay less to make it a little bit higher.

The efficient level of air quality is not pristine air. Instead, we want to increase air quality up to the point where the MWTP for air quality is equal to the marginal abatement cost, MAC. The efficient level of air quality is denoted Q^* in Figure 4.4, and the pollution remaining in the air at this point is the efficient level of pollution. The area under the MAC curve is the cost of abating pollution to its efficient level.

Even without making the air pristine, the cost of abatement is large. One estimate of total cost in 1997 incurred by firms to comply with environmental regulations, including those that require firms to purchase and install pollution-abatement equipment—such as precipitators, filters, and scrubbers in factory chimney stacks—is $210 billion, or 2.6 percent of GDP.[8]

GOVERNMENT POLICIES FOR CONTROLLING EXTERNALITIES

Given that externalities cause economic inefficiency and impose costs on the community, we are not surprised to find that societies have devised various means of controlling them. Sometimes the means is a social convention, like etiquette. In the United States and other countries, children are taught from a young age to "give a hoot—don't pollute." In old Hawaii, society was governed by a rigid convention called *kapu*, administered by a priestlike *kahuna*. Many of the strictures concerned fishing. It is likely that these rules were used to control the problem of externality in the Hawaiian fishery, especially given that it was the mainstay of the Hawaiian economy.[9] Another way of controlling externalities is the law. Activities with external costs can be outlawed, while those with external benefits can be made compulsory. In industrial countries, child labor is illegal and basic schooling is compulsory. While this is done mainly to protect children, adult society benefits because children who are denied education can impose a large cost on everyone else.

Government in the United States has a long history of controlling externalities through regulation. The federal government's involvement in controlling water pollution dates back to the *Refuse Act* of 1899; its involvement in controlling air pollution began in 1955 with the *Air Pollution Control Act*, the predecessor of the Clean Air Act. Regulations controlling air pollution by local governments began as early as the 1880s. The federal government has regulated and managed the offshore fisheries since the *Magnuson Fishery Conservation and Management Act* of 1976. A large amount of regulation also protects people from hazards at home, in public, and in the workplace. For brevity, however, we restrict our discussion of government policies to those dealing with pollution and the management of fisheries.

Policies to control externalities can be grouped into two types: correction or internalization. A policy of **correction** adjusts activities with externalities by creating a corrective penalty or reward. A policy of **internalization** adjusts activities with externalities by changing the institutional arrangements that led to the externalities in the first place.

With a cost externality, firms do too much of the activity, so a corrective policy might subject them to a penalty unless they reduce it. The penalty could be a fine

---

[8]United States Environmental Protection Agency, "Environmental Protection: Is It Bad for the Economy?" July 1999.

[9]Of course, the rules also served to reserve the lion's share of the fish for the priestly class.

or punishment for exceeding specified limits, or a tax on the activity. Alternatively, the industry could be rewarded for reducing the activity. A corrective policy for activities that have a benefit externality is to reward the firm for increasing the activity, as by a subsidy. Alternatively, the firm could be penalized for reducing the activity below prescribed levels.

In contrast, a policy of internalization changes institutional arrangements so that the external cost or benefit becomes internal to the firm doing the activity. Suppose several firms operate in an industry and some activities by individual firms cause benefits or costs to all firms in the industry. For instance, when a firm provides training for its employees, the other firms in the industry may benefit because the employee may work for them in the future. Since the individual firm takes into account only its own benefit and not the benefit to the other firms, it "free rides" and provides too little training. However, if the firms are merged into one, the external costs and benefits become internal costs and benefits to the merged firm. For instance, if many firms are merged into one multiplant firm, so that employees have no place to work other than at one of its plants, the managers of the merged firm no longer have an incentive to free ride on training. All of the benefits will accrue to the merged firm no matter where the employees work.

Of course, the firms should not need any help from the government to plan an efficiency-improving merger. The presence of externalities makes it profitable for the firms to merge of their own accord. The internalization policy of the government might be to remove any artificial barriers that prevent the firms from merging. Another form of internalization policy is where the government creates property rights for common property resources or creates markets for permits that allow firms to engage in externality-generating activities. A good example of the latter is a recent policy that allows firms to trade permits for emitting sulfur dioxide. We discuss this type of policy below.

Command and Control Policies

In the United States, most government policies toward externalities are **command and control** policies, consisting of regulations that command polluters to do certain things, such as purchase pollution-control equipment, and to control their polluting activities. For instance, the amounts and types of waste products (effluents) that a firm can discharge into the environment are controlled and must be less than specified limits. Some substances, such as hazardous wastes, cannot be dumped at all.

A typical command and control policy specifies *quantity standards* that set limits on the externality-generating activities of firms and individuals. Technology standards specify the equipment and processes that firms and individuals must use. For example, two types of quantity standards limit the levels of air pollutants the firms can emit under the Clean Air Act. First, the ambient quality standards set the acceptable levels of pollutants in the environment in total. For clean air regulation, the National Ambient Air Quality Standards (NAAQS) specify upper limits on the amounts of particulate matter, sulfur dioxide, ozone, and other pollutants that can be present in the air on average over a period of time. Second, emissions standards specify the maximum level of pollutants that can be discharged by individuals or firms over a period of time. The emissions standards are set so as to attain the ambient standards. If the ambient standards are not attained, the emissions standards are tightened. An example of a technology standard is rules that require firms to use the best available control technology (BACT) for controlling emissions.

Setting standards is one thing; enforcing them is another. In the case of air pollution, enforcement requires monitoring both the ambient levels of pollution (*ambient monitoring*) and the level of compliance by individual emitters (*compliance monitoring*). It also must provide for punishment of polluters who violate the standards. Ambient monitoring is done mainly to gauge the overall success of compliance monitoring (if the air is bad, perhaps a lot of violators are not being caught) as well as to judge the overall achievements of the policy.

Variable and Tradable Permits

With a command and control policy, ambient quality standards are attained by setting fixed quantitative limits (emissions standards) on the amount of pollutants that can be discharged by a stationary source, such as an industrial plant. The limit is fixed regardless of the cost the firm must incur to comply with the standard. Such a policy almost certainly makes the cost of pollution abatement higher than it needs to be.

The reason for the excessive cost is shown in Figure 4.5. Suppose that there are two plants in a region, and that in order to attain the ambient standard, a certain reduction in the total emissions of the two plants is needed. The total pollution abatement that must be done by the two plants combined is measured by the horizontal distance 0^A0^B. For instance, this distance could represent the combined reduction in sulfur dioxide emissions needed to attain the NAAQS for this pollutant set by the EPA. The amount of abatement by plant A is measured to the right of the origin 0^A, and the amount by plant B is measured to the left of the origin 0^B. Thus any point on the line divides up the total abatement into the amounts done by each plant.

The marginal abatement cost (MAC), which is the cost to the plant of reducing emissions by 1 unit, for plant A is shown by the curve MAC^A. The curve is upward-sloping because as plant A's abatement increases (moving to the right along the horizontal axis from 0^A), it gets more costly per unit. The marginal abatement cost of plant B is shown by curve MAC^B. The marginal abatement cost curve of B is also upward-sloping as B's abatement increases (moving to the left of 0^B).

Although the MAC schedules of the two plants have the same general properties, they may be different. As shown, MAC^B is higher and rises more rapidly than MAC^A, perhaps because of B's location. Typically, regulators will set emissions standards for the individual plants that require them to abate equal amounts of pollution.[10] Point M denotes the midpoint of the axis 0^A0^B, so at this point the plants abate equal amounts.

The total cost of abatement to a plant is equal to the area under its MAC curve at each level of abatement. The height of MAC is the cost of the next unit of abatement, so the area under the curve sums the costs over all units. The lightly shaded area in

[10]Alternatively, the required amounts of abatement may be proportional to the size of the plant.

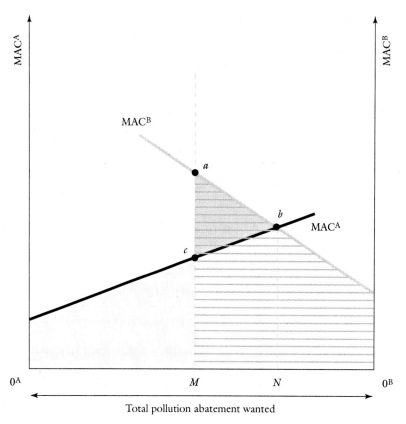

Figure 4.5

Minimizing the Cost of Pollution Abatement

To minimize the cost of reducing pollution, abatement should be allocated to the firms with the lowest marginal abatement cost (MAC). When firms A and B do the same amount of abatement, firm A has a lower MAC than firm B. The cost of this inefficient allocation of abatement is equal to the area of the shaded triangle *abc*. The efficient allocation of abatement is for firm A to do 0^A *N* units of abatement and firm B to do 0^B *N* units. At this allocation, the MACs of the two firms are the same.

Figure 4.5 is the total abatement cost of plant A, and the horizontally shaded area is the total abatement cost of plant B. When the two plants do equal amounts of abatement, the combined total abatement cost is the sum of the two shaded areas. We can easily see that the combined abatement cost (the sum of the areas under the two MAC curves) is smaller if plant A does one unit more of abatement and plant B does one unit less. B's abatement cost falls by MAC^B while A's rises by the smaller amount MAC^A. In fact, the total abatement cost is minimized by letting B reduce its abatement to $0^B N$ and letting A increase its abatement to $0^A N$. At this point, the marginal abatement costs of the two plants are equal and no further cost saving is possible by reallocating abatement. The total saving in abatement cost by using this minimum abatement cost allocation is equal to the area of the triangle *abc*.

The Clean Air Act of 1990 introduced what is now called *emissions trading* into the realm of environmental regulation in the United States. The amendments to the Clean Air Act allowed the creation of a market in **transferable discharge permits** for sulfur dioxide. Economists have promoted the concept of transferable discharge permits for the last 25 years. The main idea is that rather than setting emissions standards for individual firms and plants, the government issues transferable discharge permits equal to the total level of emissions that it wishes to allow and then lets firms buy the permits they need in order to emit. The firms with the highest cost of abating pollution will bid the most for the permits, whereas the firms with lower abatement costs will choose to sell their permits and reduce their emissions instead. This ensures that a given total abatement is achieved at least cost, as described in Figure 4.5. If one plant has a higher abatement cost than another, the first will purchase more permits while the second does more abatement. In the market-clearing equilibrium, the distribution of permits will be allocated to the highest bidders, and the combined abatement cost of all emitters is minimized.

A highly debated question about transferable discharge permits is how to determine the initial allocation of permits. The Coase theorem implies that the initial allocation of permits is not important for the purpose of achieving economic efficiency. The final distribution of permits will bring about the least costly allocation of abatement and the initial allocation simply determines who bears the cost of abatement.

One distribution of permits, called the **polluter-pays policy,** leaves the entire initial allocation of permits with the government and requires the polluters to purchase permits for all emissions they make. A second distribution is called the **government-pays policy,** though it would more properly be called a "taxpayer-pays" policy. This second approach allocates permits to polluters in sufficient quantities for them to continue at the unregulated emissions levels. The government must buy permits back from the polluters to reduce the total emissions to the desired level. A third alternative, called the **Pareto improving policy,** grants polluters sufficient transferable permits to emit at the emissions standards that exist under regulation. Plants that want to emit above the emission standard must purchase permits from other plants. This is a Pareto improvement because no plant is worse off than emitting at the existing standards (since any plant can retain its permits), and the plants that trade in permits must be better off doing so. Therefore the policy is viewed favorably by all plants, making it easier to enact. Probably for this reason, the Clean Air Act amendments of 1990 adopted the Pareto improving policy by allocating most of the tradable sulfur dioxide permits to existing electricity utilities.

Why do we need to issue tradable permits to reduce the cost of abatement to a minimum? Wouldn't it be easier for the government to simply maintain the regulation policy but lower the emissions standards for plants with high abatement costs and raise them for the plants with low costs? The problem is that the government cannot readily ascertain which are the high- and low-costs plants. The advantage of tradable permits is that it doesn't have to determine this. The plant owners, who know their costs of abatement, will determine how the permits are ultimately allocated.

Another advantage of transferable permits is that this policy rewards plants who invest in abatement equipment or find other ways of reducing their emissions below the existing standard. With command and control regulation, a polluter that reduces emissions below the existing standard gets no reward. A polluter that emits more than the standard, and is caught, is punished, so there is an incentive to reduce emissions to the standard. But if a plant's emissions are at or below the standard, no action is taken by the regulators. Since abatement is costly, and no rewards are given for further reductions, plants will emit at levels equal to the standard—no higher or lower. Tradable permits do provide incentives for plants to find ways to reduce emissions further. Suppose a plant uses its permits to emit at 100 percent of the standard. If the firm finds a way to reduce emissions further, it can sell some of its permits in the market for cash. Thus it reaps a reward for reducing its emissions.

Effluent Charges and Corrective Taxes

A policy similar to transferable permits is one that imposes on polluters an **effluent charge or fee,** a dollar price charged to plants per unit of effluent (smoke or dirty water) they discharge into the air or watershed. (The basic idea should be familiar to people who have a wastewater charge added to their utility bills each month.) An effluent charge has been used in Germany since 1976.

The effect of an effluent charge on a plant's decision to dump is shown in Figure 4.6, where the quantity of effluent dumped is measured on the horizontal axis. The downward-sloping curve MWTP indicates the plant's marginal willingness to pay to dump effluent. This MWTP is determined by the marginal abatement cost of the plant, since abatement is the alternative to dumping. A smaller quantity dumped means more abatement, and the marginal abatement cost increases with the amount of abatement. For this reason, the MWTP to dump curve is downward-sloping. The upward-sloping curve MEC is the marginal external cost, or marginal damages, caused by dumping. If no effluent charge or standard is set, the plant would dump Q_M units of effluent into the environment. Because the firm ignores the marginal external cost of dumping, the amount it dumps is greater than the efficient quantity of dumping Q^*. If the government can monitor the quantity of dumping and charge the plant accordingly, it can set an effluent charge (price) per unit of effluent dumped—say, P dollars. Facing this price, the plant dumps only if the effluent charge is less than its MWTP to dump. If the effluent charge is P dollars, the plant dumps Q' units, and abates Q_M minus Q' units. The firm pays P dollars times Q' for dumping.

By setting the effluent charge, the government can achieve whatever quantity of dumping it wants. For instance, it could stop dumping altogether by setting a very high charge. A better policy is to set the effluent charge at the estimated marginal external cost of dumping, measured at the efficient quantity of dumping Q^*. The efficient effluent charge is shown as MEC* in Figure 4.6. Facing this effluent fee, the firm dumps Q^* units of effluent, which is the efficient quantity to dump.

Since an effluent charge generates revenue for the government, it is a *polluter-pays* policy. Oddly, some people concerned about the environment condemn effluent charges (and transferable discharge permits) because they allow plants to "pollute for a price." However, the existing system of standards allows plants to pollute up to the standard without paying a price. Since the same amount of pollution can be achieved with an effluent charge, and the government gets a source of revenue as well, effluent charges are viewed positively by economists.

4.2   Polluting for a Price: How Well Does It Work?

Tradable pollution permits have advanced from academic idea to real-world fact. Several pollution permit markets now exist, the most visible being the Regional Clean Air Incentives Market (RECLAIM) in southern California and the EPA's Acid Rain Program. Title IV of the 1990 Clean Air Act Amendments created a national market in tradable sulfur dioxide (SO_2) allowances for electricity-generating plants. (Tradable allowance programs also exist for other pollutants such as Nitrogen Oxide [NO_2].) Each SO_2 allowance permits the owner to emit one ton of SO_2. These allowances are traded privately, purchased through brokers, or bought through an EPA auction administered by the Chicago Board of Trade.

Phase I of the program, which began in 1995, placed caps on the SO_2 emissions of the nation's largest and most polluting coal-fired electric power plants. In exchange, the plants received annual allocations of tradable SO_2 allowances based on their fossil-fuel consumption between 1985 and 1987. The allowances can be used by the plant, transferred to another plant within the company, sold to another party, or banked for future use. The emissions of the plants are continuously monitored, and each plant must hold allowances of no less than its emissions during the year. Excess emissions are subject to a penalty of $2000 per ton. In Phase II, which began January 2000, the caps are tightened, and the program is extended to all fossil-fuel plants larger than 25 megawatts. This brings many smaller, cleaner plants into the program.

Economists are now assessing the success of the program. Overall, the program is a major success. SO_2 emissions have been reduced nearly 50% at less than 50% of the estimated cost under command and control regulation.[1] The General Accounting Office has confirmed these benefits and projects that allowance trading will yield cost savings as much as $3 billion per year over the command and control approach. Nonetheless, some results have puzzled analysts. The volume of transactions has been less than anticipated and the price of the allowances is less than the marginal abatement cost (MAC) of most plants.

Further information on the program including prices and transactions is available on the EPA's Acid Rain Program site at http://www.epa.gov/docs/acidrain/overview.html.

Critically analyze the following questions:

■ SO_2 allowances traded at about $150 each as of December 1999. This is much less than the estimated marginal abatement cost of the plants in the program, which is around $300 per ton of SO_2.[2] Many theories have been proposed to explain this divergence. One theory stresses that most of the electric utilities are subject to rate-of-return regulation, which limits the profit the company can make. Why would this depress the price of allowances? (Hint: Under rate-of-return regulation, who would be the beneficiaries of abatement cost savings?) Would the allowance price have been higher if the government had adopted a polluter-pays policy of allowance allocation?

■ As the Phase II plants join the program in 2000, how do you expect this will affect the allowance price? Remember that they will receive allowances as well as will need them. (Hint: Do you think the marginal abatement cost of newcomers will be higher or lower than that of the Phase I plants?)

■ Individuals and groups may purchase allowances to reduce the level of SO_2 and NO_x emissions. For example, the Clean Air Conservancy (CaC) will purchase an allowance on your behalf and issue you a "Clean Air Certificate" at their homepage http://www.cleanairconservancy.org/. Suppose that a group of citizens has a combined marginal willingness to pay for a one-ton reduction in SO_2 that exceeds the market price of an allowance. Will they necessarily buy an allowance? Why or why not?

[1] Dallas Burtraw, "Trading Emission to the Clean the Air; Exchanges Few but Savings Many," *Resources for the Future*, Winter 1996, p. 1 (available at http://www.rff.org/resources_articles/files/trade_emit.htm).
[2] Carlson, Curtis, et al. "Sulfur Dioxide Control by Electric Utilities: What Are the Gains from Trade?" Discussion paper 98-44, *Resources for the Future*, July 1998.

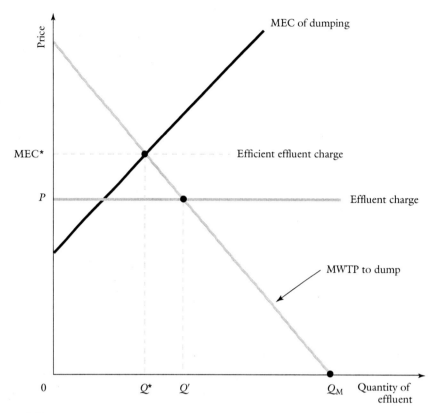

Figure 4.6

The Effect of an Effluent Fee

At the efficient quantity of effluent, the marginal external cost (MEC) of dumping on citizens is equal to the MWTP to dump by the firms. Without a policy, firms dump Q_M units of effluent because they ignore the MEC. If faced with an effluent fee of P, firms would dump Q' units where their MWTP is equal to the fee. An efficient policy charges the firms a fee equal to MEC*, the MEC at the efficient quantity of effluent Q^*. Facing this fee, firms dump the efficient quantity of pollution.

Closely related to effluent charges are corrective taxes and subsidies.[11] A **corrective tax** is imposed on a good or service subject to a production or consumption cost externality, and a **corrective subsidy** is imposed on a good subject to a production or consumption benefit externality. An example of a good with a cost externality is gasoline, which causes air pollution when used in automobiles. We saw earlier, in Figure 4.1, that the equilibrium quantity is too high for economic efficiency in a market with a cost externality. In Figure 4.7, the equilibrium quantity of gasoline Q_e is greater than the efficient quantity Q^*. The equilibrium quantity is found by the intersection of the demand and supply curves; the efficient quantity is found by the intersection of the demand curve and the marginal

---

[11]Corrective taxes and subsidies are also called Pigouvian taxes and subsidies, after the great welfare economist A. C. Pigou, who first suggested them in his book *The Economics of Welfare*, 1918.

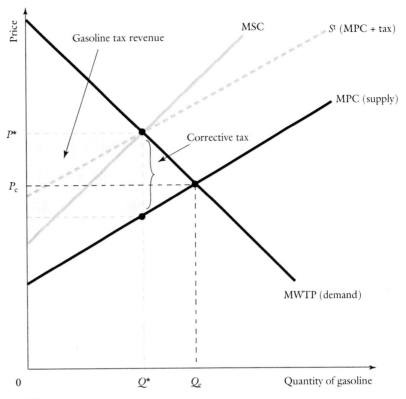

A Corrective Excise Tax on Gasoline

The equilibrium quantity Q_e of gasoline determined by supply and demand is greater than the efficient quantity because the MSC of gasoline exceeds the MPC. The MEC of gasoline consumption is ignored by market participants. A corrective excise tax set equal to the MEC at the efficient quantity shifts the supply curve up so that the market equilibrium quantity is reduced to the efficient quantity Q^*. In the process the government collects tax revenue, which can be used to reduce other taxes for a "double dividend."

social cost curve MSC. The MSC curve is found by adding the marginal external cost of gasoline consumption (from the increase in air pollution caused by consuming a gallon of gasoline) to marginal private cost (MPC) given by the supply curve.

There are several ways that the government can improve efficiency by reducing air pollution caused by consuming gasoline. The federal government has adopted a policy of commanding automobile manufacturers to install pollution-control equipment in new cars so that these cars emit less pollution per gallon of gasoline. Firms are also required to build cars that get better gas mileage, so less gasoline is used per mile. (Regulations also require gasoline manufacturers to change the formulation of gasoline in urban areas during winter months.) These technology standards for cars have significantly reduced the amount of pollution per mile driven. For instance, a 1994 automobile emits just 2 percent of the volatile organic compounds (a major cause of smog) per mile emitted by a pre-1970 automobile. However, these policies have not reduced the number of miles people drive; in fact, they have increased the number of miles driven by lowering the cost per mile. The cost of the new abatement equipment is built into the price of the car as a fixed cost, and it does not increase the variable cost of driving. However, the higher fixed cost has caused people to delay buying new, less polluting cars. The increase in the number of miles driven has offset much of the gain in air quality obtained through reduced emissions per mile.

Many economists believe that the best way to reduce air pollution is to reduce the number of miles people drive by significantly increasing the price of gasoline. Although gasoline is already taxed, the revenue from this tax goes into the highway trust fund and is spent on road improvements and maintenance. Thus, the existing tax is more a user fee than a tax. A still higher tax on gasoline is needed to reduce gasoline consumption toward the efficient level.

The impact of a corrective tax on gasoline is shown in Figure 4.7. The supply curve facing gasoline consumers, including the corrective tax, is labeled S^t. If the gasoline tax rate is chosen properly, the supply price of gasoline including the tax is high enough so that S^t intersects the demand curve at Q^*. That is, with the appropriate corrective tax, the market equilibrium quantity of gasoline will be equal to the efficient quantity.

With this policy, the cost of the inefficiently high levels of gasoline consumption is avoided, although the policy does not eliminate the automobile as a source of air pollution. The objective of a gasoline tax is more modest. It ensures that the level of air pollution created is efficient given the current technology. Also, more expensive gasoline provides a profit incentive for firms to develop cars that emit less pollution, and for consumers to embrace them when they arrive.

Policies like effluent fees and corrective taxes are said to yield a "double dividend." Unlike command and control policies, they encourage polluters to abate pollution in the least costly way. (For example, the least costly way of reducing vehicular air pollution for many people is to drive less, but current policies have not encouraged this.) Second, the revenue collected by effluent fees and corrective taxes is a source of revenue to the government and can be used to reduce other taxes, like the income tax. As we discuss later, in Chapter 12, most taxes have an "excess burden" because they distort economic decisions. For instance, high income tax rates discourage work and production in general. Proponents of environment taxes argue that it is better to discourage activities with cost externalities and improve efficiency than to discourage work and reduce efficiency.

Assigning Property Rights

We'll end this chapter where it began, at the fishery. Even before H. Scott Gordon's classic article on the externality in the fishery, governments recognized the dangers of overfishing and subjected the industry to regulation. These regulations provide for quotas that limit the total harvest of fish in a season. By limiting the annual harvest to a sustainable yield, the regulators hope to prevent overfishing. A *sustainable yield* is one that maintains the stock of fish so that a constant harvest is possible from year to year.

Because fisheries span international waters and because regulators are under constant pressure from the fishing industry to increase quotas, or to maintain quotas in the face of declining stocks, overfishing has remained a problem. One reason is the way individual rights to fish are acquired under existing regulation. In most fisheries, an overall quota on the size of the harvest is imposed and individual fishing boats can land fish until the overall quota is reached. Once the quota is reached, the fishery is closed for the season. This is called the "derby system" because it allots individual rights to the fish to the first boats that catch them, creating a race (or derby) to catch the fish.

The derby system causes an inefficient race among fishing boats to catch the fish. As soon as the fishing season opens, the boats try to land as many fish as possible as soon as possible. This floods the markets with fresh fish, driving down prices. As soon as the overall quota is reached, the supply of fresh fish stops, and consumers can buy only frozen fish. This causes at least two large inefficiencies. First, the timing of the supply of fish to the market is inefficient. Instead of getting a steady supply of fresh fish throughout the fishing season, the consumers get a flood of fresh fish at the beginning and must consume inferior frozen fish after that. Second, the derby system encourages firms to invest large sums in bigger and faster fishing boats. With the allowable seasonal harvest disappearing fast, no fishing boat wants to leave the fishing grounds to land its catch, so a large boat capacity is desired. And the bigger the boat motor, the faster the boat can go to and return from the fishing grounds. All this has added to the cost of fishing.

The derby system has also exacerbated the natural conflict between the fishing industry and the regulators. Fishers with large amounts of capital invested in their boats cannot afford to have the overall catch reduced. It is understandable that they will pressure regulators to maintain or even increase the fishing quotas, despite evidence of declining stocks.

The shortcomings of the derby system make clear the advantages of an alternative policy, sometimes called "privatizing the fishery."[12] This is done by assigning individual transferable quotas to fishing firms. An **individual transferable quota (ITQ)** is the right to catch a given fraction of the total fish catch each year. Only fishing boats with ITQs can enter the fishery, and they can catch only the quantity of fish allowed by their quotas. A one-time allocation of ITQs is assigned or sold to the individual fishing firms. Since the rights to the fish are preassigned, there is no early-season rush to catch fish (as there is under the derby system), nor do the firms have an incentive to invest in expensive large, fast boats. In fact, the firms that have the lowest cost of catching fish can land more fish by purchasing the ITQs from other, higher-cost fishers. The ITQs in fishing are analogous to individual transferable permits for discharging pollutants. They ensure that a given harvest is caught when it is most appropriate according to market conditions, and in the least costly manner. This system has been adopted in the Pacific halibut and sablefish fisheries with good results.

A fishery is privatized because ITQs give a right to catch a given *percentage* of the annual harvest in the future as well as in the current year. In effect, each fishing firm owns a fraction of the stock of fish in the fishery, just as a condominium owner owns a fraction of the building. As co-owners, the fishing firms find it in their own interest

---

[12]See "One Answer to Overfishing: Privatize the Fisheries" by Peter Passell, *New York Times*, May 11, 1995.

to conserve the stock in order to achieve a sustainable yield. The common property externality is eliminated because property rights to the fish stock are assigned.

A divisive practical problem that remains is the method of initially assigning the ITQs. Should they be sold to the highest bidders, or given to the fishing firms already in the industry? And if they are given to firms already in the industry, how should they be allocated? Although the Coase theorem predicts that the initial assignment does not matter for achieving economic efficiency, it is of intense interest to those in the industry. Recently the Magnuson Act, the main federal legislation controlling American fisheries, was amended to prevent further ITQ policies from being considered until October 2, 2000. This amendment was instigated by Senator Ted Stevens of Alaska primarily because the Alaskan fishing industry believes that it loses out on the assignment of ITQs.

CONCLUSION AND SUMMARY

In Chapter 3 we saw that certain goods, described as public goods, are likely to lead to market failure. In the present chapter, we have seen that external costs and benefits lead to market failure. The discussion of environmental pollution suggests that these two concepts, although distinct, overlap. On the one hand, pollution is an economic problem because the costs of pollution are external costs and are disregarded by individuals in deciding on private actions. On the other hand, the quality of the environment is a good example of a public good because it is both nonrival and nonexcludable.

What exactly is the difference between externalities and public goods? For one thing, the concept of externality is somewhat broader than the concept of a public good. Although public goods can cause externalities, other things—such as an absence of property rights—cause them as well. A more important difference is the matter of emphasis. The analysis of public goods and services concentrates on the *properties of the goods and services* to explain market failure. The analysis of externalities concentrates on the properties of *markets and institutions*. For instance, it is the absence of property rights that causes the tragedy of the commons, but it is the nonrival and nonexcludable property of national defense that explains why governments provide it and finance it with taxes.

The distinction between externalities and public goods has implications for government policies. The implication of public goods is that market forces will produce little or none of them, so the government can improve efficiency by providing them and financing them by taxes. The implications of externalities are somewhat broader. In addition to government production and tax finance, the policies that can be used to correct for externalities include institutional changes such as the creation of property rights.

■ An externality is present when an activity causes an uncompensated cost or confers an unpriced benefit on persons and firms that are not parties to a market transaction. Because consumers and producers ignore the external costs and benefits, the market equilibrium quantities of the goods may be, respectively, too high or too low for efficiency.

- Externalities can be classified in several ways, including whether they are consumption or production externalities. If the total benefit or cost to others is fixed, an externality is called inframarginal, meaning that the external cost or benefit is not affected by changes in market quantity. Inframarginal externalities do not cause market failure.

- An important cause of externalities is poorly defined property rights. A rival resource to which everyone has free access is called a common-property resource. Typically, externalities reflect conflicting desires over how a common-property resource is to be used. As such, externalities are reciprocal in nature.

- The Coase theorem states that if property rights to a resource are clearly defined and bargaining costs are low, the resource will be used efficiently regardless of who gets the property rights.

- One reason pollution is considered a social problem is that pollution is an external cost in many production processes. As a result, the level of pollution in a market economy is inefficiently high. At the efficient level of pollution, the marginal willingness to pay (MWTP) for environmental quality is equal to the marginal cost (MC) of reducing pollution.

- Most policies directed at externalities are command and control policies that regulate the activities of persons and firms. Alternatively, the government can control externalities with market incentive policies that charge firms for the external costs they cause and reward them for external benefits they confer.

- An unregulated fishery is a common-property resource, so overfishing results. Overfishing can be eliminated by assigning property rights to the fish in the sea, a policy called individual transferable quotas (ITQs).

QUESTIONS FOR DISCUSSION AND REVIEW

1. Identify the type of externality associated with each of the following activities: (a) using a leaf blower to clear your driveway; (b) shoveling the snow off the sidewalk in front of your house; (c) learning to play bridge.

2. Citing the health hazards from smoking, the Clinton administration recently expressed interest in tightening the regulation of the tobacco industry. To what extent is such regulation of tobacco justified by the theory of externalities?

3. Some people object strenuously to government policies that promote "safe sex," beyond an informational role, on the grounds that sex is a personal matter and the government should stay out of it. Use the theory of externality to identify the public interest in this matter. What sorts of corrective policies does the theory suggest?

4. Farmers in the dry Western states irrigate their crops by drilling wells into the Ogallala aquifer, a huge underground reservoir left after the last Ice Age. As farmers pump more and more water from the aquifer, all must drill deeper to reach water; and the deeper the well, the more costly it is to pump the water. Identify the missing property rights in this instance. Is there an economic argument for limiting the amount of water farmers can pump from their wells? What kind of policy do you suggest?

5. In Japan, the government-owned mass transit system employs people to push the crowds of commuters into the departing trains. Does this make sense? Doesn't each person have ample incentive to get into the train quickly before it leaves?

6. To combat unsightly graffiti, some cities have adopted a policy of fining property owners unless they promptly remove graffiti on their property. Indignant property owners have complained that they are being victimized twice—once by the vandals and then by the city. Use the Coase theorem to discuss this policy as a response to an externality.

7. To comply with the Clean Air Act, a region must abate (reduce) pollution emissions by 300 units. Before regulation, two firms emit 600 units of pollutants. The marginal abatement cost (MAC) of firm A is given by the schedule

$$MAC^A = \frac{1}{2} Q^A$$

where Q^A is the quantity of pollution abated by the firm. The MAC for firm B is $MAC^B = Q^B$.

   a. Suppose the EPA requires each firm to abate by 150 units. What is the MAC for each firm under this command and control regulation? Is it the least-cost allocation of abatement?

   b. What is the least cost (efficient) allocation of abatement for the two firms? What is the reduction in the abatement cost made possible?

   c. Suppose the EPA auctions off 300 pollution permits at a competitive auction. Each permit allows a firm to pollute by one unit. What is the market price of these permits?

8. A pulp mill has the right to discharge waste into a river. The waste reduces the number of fish, causing damage for recreational fishing. Let Q denote the quantity of waste dumped. The marginal damage (the value of lost fish for an extra unit of waste), denoted MD is given by the equation

$$MD = 2 + 5Q.$$

The marginal benefit (MB) of dumping waste (the cost of shipping an extra unit of waste to another dump site) is given by the equation

$$MB = 30 - 2Q.$$

   a. Draw a diagram showing the efficient quantity of waste that can be dumped in the river, and the quantity dumped by a firm that ignores the damage it causes for fishing.

   b. Calculate the efficient quantity of waste. What is the effluent fee in dollars per unit of waste that would cause the firm to dump only an efficient quantity of waste?

8. Internet Exercise. Table 405 of the *Statistical Abstract of the United States, 1999* (http://www.census.gov/prod/www/statistical-abstract-us.html) lists levels of National Air Pollutant Emissions from 1970 to 1997. Which of the major emissions fell the most between 1970 and 1997? Nitrogen oxide emissions from automobiles have remained relatively constant. How does this compare with the rise in vehicle miles traveled in Table 1047? Are these data sufficient for you to conclude that environmental policy in the United States has been very successful? What other data would you need to draw a conclusion?

9. Internet Exercise. Read about the history of the U.S. lobstering industry at http://www.gma.org/lobsters/allaboutlobsters/lobsterhistory.html. In Colonial times, lobsters were so plentiful that they were considered "poverty food." Immigrant indentured servants, who were required to work for seven years in exchange for

their passage, wrote into their contracts that they not be required to eat lobster more than three times a week. With the depletion of the natural stocks of lobsters, lobster is now an expensive delicacy. How do the Maine "lobster gangs" limit the harvest of lobsters? How can this be considered a response to an externality? The lobster gangs of Monhegan Island limit their fishing to the winter months—the worst time of year to be in a lobster boat. Why might this be more efficient?

SELECTED REFERENCES

A classic early treatment of externalities and policies regarding them is A. C. Pigou, *The Economics of Welfare*, 1918. The fishery as a common property resource is described clearly in H. Scott Gordon, "The Economic Theory of a Common Property Resource: The Fishery," 1954.

The Coase theorem is enunciated in Ronald H. Coase, "The Problem of Social Cost," 1960. Practical problems with the Coase theorem are discussed in Joseph Farrell, "Information and the Coase Theorem," 1987.

A good discussion of recent issues about externalities is found in "Symposium on Network Externalities," 1994.

Chapter 7, "Making Markets Work for the Environment," *Economic Report of the President, 2000* (http://w3.access.gpo.gov/eop/index.html) is a good discussion of market incentive–based environmental policy.

USEFUL INTERNET SITES

Sites specializing in environmental economics include EPA's Economics and Environment at http://www.epa.gov/economics/, World Bank Group's Environmental Economics and Indicators at http://www-esd.worldbank.org/eei/ and Resources for the Future at http://www.rff.org/.

As anyone living near an airport or freeway knows, noise is another externality. Everything you want to know about noise pollution is available from the Noise Pollution Clearing House at http://www.nonoise.org/.

Professor Stan Liebowitz at the University of Texas at Dallas has much information on network externalities at http://wwwpub.utdallas.edu/~liebowit/ netpage.html.

PART THREE

Government

Decision

Making

Unlike private decisions that are made by people or organizations with a relatively narrow set of interests, government decisions are collective decisions that affect everyone in the community. For example, a government decision to require automobiles to use unleaded gasoline affects everyone. Individuals are not free to make separate decisions as to whether or not to use unleaded gas. In Part III we consider two different aspects of how government makes such policy decisions. In Chapter 5 we examine the political demands for government programs as expressed through voting. Voters presumably vote for certain programs, or for legislators who favor those programs, based on the benefits they expect to receive and the taxes they expect to pay. We also examine how the politicians and the government bureaucracy respond to these political demands. Presumably, politicians propose or make legislative decisions that maximize their chances of getting or staying elected. Managers of government departments are motivated to please the legislators who control their departmental budgets, unlike the managers of private firms who are motivated to earn profits for shareholders.

In Chapter 5 we learn that, like market decisions, government decisions may fail to allocate resources efficiently. In Chapter 6 we learn a set of techniques, called benefit-cost analysis, that enables government to determine whether a particular policy or program decision is efficient in terms of its benefits and costs to the members of the community. Because the need for government programs is often the result of market failure, benefit-cost analysis must measure the benefits and costs of intangible, nonmarket goods and services like saving lives or providing national parks. Also, many government programs are forms of investment requiring society to incur current costs in order to enjoy future benefits. In Chapter 6 we learn the criteria that are used by government to determine whether a public investment is worthwhile.

5 Voting and Public Choice

Making public choices is a decidedly messy business. Unlike private decisions made by households and firms, government decisions often require protracted negotiations in committees and legislative bodies. "Experts" testify before congressional committees, and representatives of the affected groups lobby politicians to pay attention to their concerns. The lobbyists use money as well as rhetoric to influence the politicians. Many voters view the political process as partisan bickering and fear that the politicians are beholden to those who make large campaign contributions. Every year, opinion polls report that voters lack confidence in the political process, and in some states voters increasingly make public choices directly through ballot initiatives rather than through political representatives. For their part, politicians wonder, "What do the voters want?" In some opinion polls, voters say that they want the government to reduce spending and taxes, and in others they say that they want the government to enact new programs or enhance existing ones.

Welcome to the world of **public choice,** the theory of how government makes decisions. In previous chapters, we discussed how the government can improve economic efficiency by, say, choosing the efficient quantity of a public good. In this chapter, we focus on the outcomes that government will choose, given the incentives facing the policy decision makers. Whatever improvements in economic efficiency are possible because of market failure, such gains provide little justification for government intervention unless the right decisions can be made through the process of public choice.

The reason public choice is not as tidy as private choice is that governments must compromise between many conflicting interests. For instance, in Chapter 3 we saw that everyone consumes the same amount of a public good like defense, so deciding how much to produce might involve the interests of millions of households. In contrast, each household decides for itself how much to consume of a private good like carrots, and no one cares about the outcome except the household consuming the good.

Because of the large number of conflicting interests, it is difficult to model the process of public choice as maximizing a single objective as we do for households and firms. Perhaps this explains why so many public finance economists prefer to concentrate on how the government *should* make decisions—for example, to achieve greater efficiency or equity—rather than how it *does* make decisions. Unfortunately, this normative approach tends to focus on market failure and ignores the possibility of government failure. **Government failure** describes the fact that government may make decisions that reduce economic efficiency or fail to correct for inefficiencies caused by market failures.

This chapter can be described as the *positive* theory of government decision making, as compared with Chapter 6, on benefit-cost analysis, which focuses on the *normative* theory of government decision making. Our primary purpose in this chapter is to understand how public decisions are made and develop a theory that predicts how governments respond to the demands placed on them by voters. We also discuss the causes of government failure and the implications for the role of government in the economy.

HOW VOTERS DECIDE

The study of how collective decisions are made and outcomes are realized through the democratic political process is called *public choice;* it is also known as *political economy.* The main players in the process are voters, political action committees (PACs), politicians, and bureaucrats. The politicians are the decision makers, and they are influenced by the interests of various groups in the population as expressed through voting and lobbying. The bureaucrats are the administrators and managers who implement the decisions made by politicians.

Because the democratic political process is complicated, public choice theorists try to simplify it as much as possible. One way to simplify it is to assume direct voting. **Direct voting** (as the term implies) describes a process whereby people vote on government decisions and outcomes directly rather than voting for decision-making representatives. Representative voting is more common, and all national decisions are made by representatives. However, ballot initiatives and plebiscites are examples of direct voting and are familiar to voters in state and local elections. Public choice theorists believe (or at least hope) that theories of direct voting cast some light on the public choice process. Accordingly, we begin by assuming that people vote directly on government decisions, such as how much to spend on a certain public good, and we postpone until later the complications of representatives and bureaucrats.

The main advantage of direct voting theory is that we can focus on one group—the voters—and ignore the politicians and the bureaucrats. In particular, we examine how the voters' behavior, along with a voting rule, determines the government outcomes. The **voting rule** is the criterion, agreed on in advance, that determines the winner in an election. A common voting rule is that a simple majority of the votes determines the winner. In this case, an alternative approved by more than half the voters is the winner. Before we examine the outcome of majority-rule voting, we must analyze the behavior of the individual voter.

Voting One's Pocketbook

As in the theory of consumer choice, we assume that voters are motivated by self-interest and vote according to their "pocketbooks." Voting is a civic activity, and most people do not equate the polling place with the marketplace. Nonetheless, economists believe that the motives that lead a person to vote a certain way on a given issue—say, whether to increase spending on local schools—are like the motives that determine whether he or she buys more or fewer groceries. We describe such behavior as "voting one's pocketbook." People who vote their pocketbooks on school spending weigh the benefit they expect to receive against the cost they expect to pay, just as when they make a purchase at the market. In this example—school spending—the cost to the voters is the increase in their tax bill when school spending is increased. If the benefit to voters from increased school spending exceeds the increase in taxes, they vote for the increase.

Time and again, we see people voting their pocketbooks. People with school-age children in public schools are more likely to vote for higher school spending than retired people without school-age children. Similarly, lawyers vote against tort reform and no-fault automobile insurance, university professors vote for more spending on higher education, and union members vote for legislators who pass laws favoring collective bargaining. No doubt, all can justify their vote as a civic virtue, but it is hard to deny that self-interest plays a role.

Figure 5.1(a) illustrates voting one's pocketbook on the subject of public school spending. On the horizontal axis we measure the number of teachers in a school district. The downward-sloping schedule $MWTP^v$ represents the marginal willingness-to-pay schedule (or demand schedule) for teachers by voter v. The more teachers are hired, the lower the voter's MWTP for another teacher. In other words, the MWTP for teachers decreases like the MWTP of other goods. To vote one's pocketbook, the voter compares his or her MWTP for a teacher against the tax price. The **tax price** is the voter's share of the increase in taxes needed to pay for a teacher, or the teacher's salary multiplied times the voter's share of an increase in community taxes. For example, if a teacher can be hired for $40,000 per year and the voter's tax share is 1 percent (the voter's tax bill increases by $1 when the community's taxes are increased by $100), the tax price of the teacher to the voter is $400 per year.

Suppose the tax price of a teacher to voter v is T^v in Figure 5.1. For simplicity, we assume that the tax price of a teacher is the same whatever the number of teachers hired. Suppose currently there are Q_0 teachers in the district and the individual votes on the question of whether to hire one more. Clearly, the pocketbook voter votes for this proposal because his or her MWTP for a teacher is greater than the tax price. The net benefit to the voter of an extra teacher is shown by the shaded area in Figure 5.1(a). On the other hand, if there are Q_1 teachers in the school, the individual votes against hiring an extra teacher because the MWTP for a teacher is less than the tax price. Indeed, the voter would approve a proposal to reduce the number of teachers.

The voter's most preferred outcome is Q^v teachers. With this number of teachers, the voter opposes a proposal to increase or decrease the number of teachers. The most preferred outcome of the voter is the outcome at which his or her total

Figure 5.1

Pocketbook Voter with Single-Peaked Preferences

(a) MWTP schedule for public school teachers and tax price T^v of voter v. The voter's most preferred quantity is Q^v where MWTP is equal to T^v. (b) For Q^v the voter's total net benefit (TNB) from schoolteachers is maximized. At $Q < Q^v$ the voter votes to increase the quantity of schoolteachers; at $Q > Q^v$ the voter votes to decrease the quantity of schoolteachers.

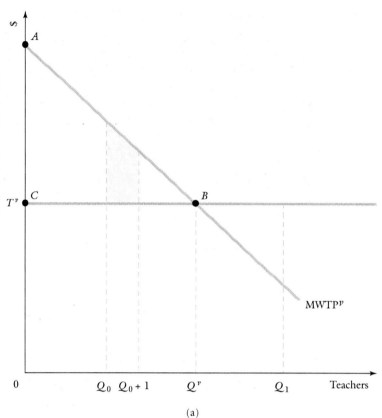

(a)

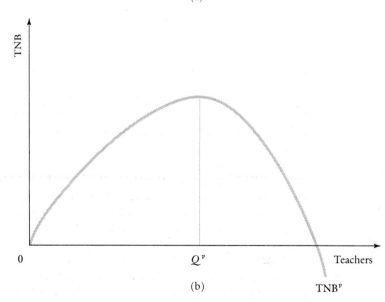

(b)

net benefit (TNB) is a maximum. The voter's total net benefit from Q teachers is total willingness to pay (TWTP) for Q teachers minus total tax cost. The voter's TWTP for Q teachers is the area under the MWTP schedule up to Q teachers, and the cost is the area under the tax price line up to Q teachers. At the preferred outcome Q^v, the voter enjoys a TNB equal to the consumer's surplus measured by the area of triangle ABC. In Figure 5.1(b) we plot the TNB to the voter for each quantity of teachers on the vertical axis. The level of the TNB for different numbers of teachers is shown by the curve labeled TNB^v. It is a maximum at Q^v teachers and declines steadily as the number of teachers increases or decreases. This voter is described as having unimodal or **single-peaked preferences** about the number of teachers to hire.

Multiple-Peaked Preferences

Many people think that if a voter is rational, the TNB curve must be single-peaked. After all, a voter who likes 30 teachers best is apt to like 20 better than 10 and 10 better than none. On closer examination, however, we find that this is not always the case. The TNB curve can have more than one peak, even when the voter is rational. This fact is important because, as we see later, single-peakedness plays an important role in determining whether the outcome of the voting process is stable and consistent.

To see why the TNB curve can have more than one peak, suppose that besides voting on the number of teachers, the voters make a private decision whether to send their children to a public or private school. The main reason they would send a child to a private school is that they think the public school is of poor quality. This is likely if it has too few teachers. Thus we'll assume when the number of teachers in the public school is low, a voter sends his or her child to private school. In this case that voter's MWTP for a public school teacher is zero, assuming the voter is self-interested and does not care about the benefits to others. Of course, this voter still must pay school taxes. Thus, voters' tax price for a public school teacher is the same whether or not their children attend public school.

This situation can result in more than one peak for the voter's TNB curve, as shown in Figure 5.2. Assume that if the number of teachers is fewer than Q', the voter sends the child to a private school. The voter's MWTP schedule has the shape shown in Figure 5.2(a). When there are fewer teachers than Q', the voter's MWTP is zero because he or she derives no benefit. When the number of teachers is Q' or more, MWTP is positive because the child goes to public school. The voter's TNB schedule for public school teachers is shown in (b).

Remember that the TNB is equal to the area under the MWTP schedule minus the area under the tax price line. As the number of public school teachers increases from zero to some low but positive level, the voters' TNB falls because they pay taxes for more schoolteachers but do not use them. When the number of teachers reaches Q', they send their children to public school, so if the number of teachers is increased above Q' the voters' MWTP is greater than their tax price. Above Q' the voters' TNB schedule increases as the number of teachers increases until the most preferred quantity Q^v is reached. At this point, the TNB schedule has another

Figure 5.2

Pocketbook Voter with Multiple-Peaked Preferences

When the quantity of public school teachers is less than Q', the voter sends his or her child to private school because the quality of public schools is too low. Increases in public school teachers from 0 to Q' lower the TNB to the voter. If there are more than Q' public school teachers, the TNB of the voter increases with the number of teachers up to Q^v. This voter is rational but has a preference profile with two peaks, the first at zero teachers and the second at Q^v teachers. The least preferred quantity is Q' teachers.

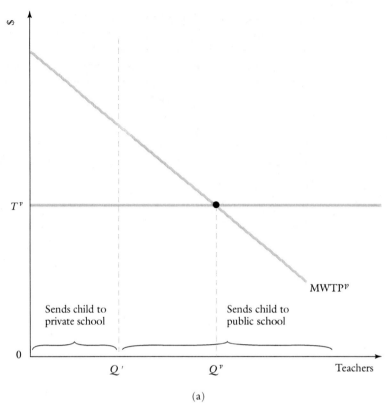

(a)

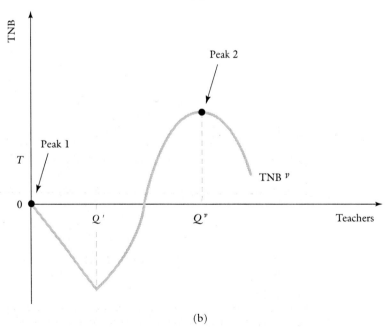

(b)

peak. Note that the TNB curve has two peaks: one at zero teachers and another at Q^v teachers. As drawn, the peak at Q^v teachers is higher, but this need not be the case, nor does it matter. The important point is that the TNB has multiple peaks for voters with rational and consistent preferences.[1] Later in this chapter, we will see that the existence of multiple-peaked preferences has important implications for the outcome of majority rule voting.

Are Voters Apathetic or Rational?

Now that we know what outcomes pocketbook voters prefer, we should ask whether they will vote on election day. In almost every election year, newspaper editorials complain about "voter apathy." In years when the turnout is good, about 60 percent of eligible voters participate in presidential elections. Usually, the turnout is far less than this. In local elections, voter turnout is abysmal: usually between 20 percent and 30 percent, even for important issues like school funding. In addition, polls show that many voters know little about the candidates or the issues on which they vote.

Many people are surprised and disappointed that voters are apathetic and ignorant about public issues. Why aren't voters more concerned about government programs that cost them millions of dollars a year? In most instances, voters put less effort into learning whether to support or oppose a new tax and spending program than into buying a new pair of shoes. Voters form their opinions about the issues from "sound bites" on television and, if sufficiently motivated, they may go to the polls on election day—provided it doesn't rain.

Surprisingly, however, public choice theorists are puzzled about why voters are not even *more* apathetic toward and ignorant of the issues. It is not really hard to see why many voters are apathetic. Few, if any, can think back to past elections and conclude that the outcome would have been different had they not bothered to vote. The fact is that one vote is not likely to influence the outcome of an election unless the number of voters is very small or the election is very close. Public choice theorists calculate that the probability that one vote will change the outcome in the average election is about comparable to the chance of winning a state lottery.

On the other hand, voters must incur costs to learn how an issue affects them. Given the tiny chance of affecting the election, a voter who remains uninformed is **rationally ignorant.** The benefit of being informed is too low relative to the costs. Similarly, given the cost—in time and inconvenience—of going to the polling place, a voter's decision to stay home on election day is **rational voter apathy.**

The existence of rational voter apathy is a problem for the theory of the pocketbook voter. The pocketbook theory assumes people vote out of self-interest, yet a truly self-interested person would not bother to go to the polls. Of course, many people vote out of civic duty. However, it seems contradictory to assume that people vote out of civic duty but that how they vote depends on self-interest. This issue

---

[1]In this example, the multiple peaks occur because decisions are made on at least two dimensions—how many public school teachers to hire and whether to send one's child to public or private school. Multiple peaks can also occur when a decision is made on only one dimension.

remains unresolved, but public choice theorists use the pocketbook voter theory anyway. People vote despite the overwhelming odds against affecting the outcome, just as they buy lottery tickets despite the overwhelming odds against winning. In addition, observed voting patterns are consistent with pocketbook motives for many groups of voters. Perhaps the simplest explanation for the discrepancy is that people get utility (satisfaction) from the act of voting.

THE OUTCOME OF DIRECT MAJORITY VOTING

Suppose a public decision, such as what quantity of a public good to produce, is submitted directly to a population of pocketbook voters. A voting rule is needed to decide the outcome, and as mentioned, the majority voting rule is the most common.[2] Later we will explore why this voting rule is so common and discuss the merits of alternative voting rules. For now, we'll simply assume that the outcome is determined by majority vote.

We can ask several questions about the outcome of majority voting on the quantity of a public good by pocketbook voters. Is the outcome *determinate* in that a proposal to produce a particular quantity of the good can defeat all others in head-to-head contests? If not, how does a majority vote determine the quantity of the public good? Does the outcome reflect the preferences for the public good by all voters? If majority voting determines a particular quantity of the public good, is the quantity the efficient quantity? If not, how does it compare?

The Voting Paradox

If consumers were to make inconsistent choices over different market goods, preferring one good to another in one instance and the opposite in another, we might describe them as "fickle." Inconsistency in political choices is often blamed on "fickle voters" who do not know what they want. In this chapter we see that majority voting can lead to inconsistent outcomes even if all voters are relentlessly consistent. The inconsistency may lie not in the voters but in the voting process.

The inconsistency of voting outcomes, known as the **voting paradox,** was first pointed out by the Marquis de Condorcet in 1785. For this reason, it is also called Condorcet's paradox. It is ironic that Condorcet, an aristocrat by birth and a democrat by conviction, discovered a basic flaw in the democratic process.[3] To make things simple, suppose there are three alternatives A, B, and C, and three voters: Tom, Dick, and Harriet. The alternatives could be different quantities of a government good—say, low (L), medium (M), and high (H) numbers of public school teachers. The total net benefit curves of the three voters for the alternatives are labeled TNB^T, TNB^D, and TNB^H in Figure 5.3. In each case, a voter's total net benefit is high for

---

[2]Actually, the *plurality* voting rule is the most common way of voting for representatives in the United States. The candidate who gets the most votes—not necessarily a majority—wins the election. Of course, if there are only two candidates, the plurality and majority rules amount to the same thing.

[3]Condorcet, the only *philosophe* to participate in the French Revolution, died in prison during the Reign of Terror, possibly by his own hand. A good work to read about this remarkable man and his ideas is *The Noble Philosopher* by Edward Goodall, 1994.

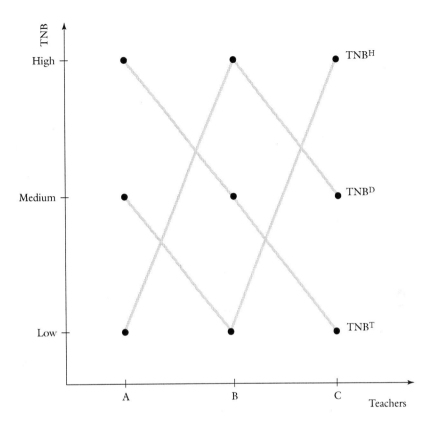

Preference Profiles of Three Voters
Three voters have different preferences over three alternative quantities of teachers: A, B, and C. All voters
have rational and consistent preferences, but Harriet has multiple-peaked preferences. She prefers alternative C (most teachers) best, alternative A (no teachers) second-best, and alternative B (average number
of teachers) least.

one alternative, medium for another, and low for the third. All voters have different
preferences, but each has consistent preferences. That is, if a voter prefers C to A and
A to B, he or she must prefer C to B.

Suppose voters choose between alternatives A and C in an election. A majority, consisting of Dick and Harriet, prefers C to A, so C wins the first-round election. Now suppose the voters choose between C and the remaining alternative B in
a second-round election. In this case a majority, consisting of Dick and Tom,
chooses B over C. So far, we find that a majority of voters prefers C to A and B to
C. It seems entirely reasonable, therefore, that a majority should prefer B to A, satisfying a principle of rationality called **transitivity.** However, when alternative A and
the second-round winner B are put to a head-to-head contest, a majority, consisting of Harriet and Tom, chooses A over B.

This example shows that although individual voters have consistent preferences,
the majority voting process can display inconsistency. As a result, **cyclical majorities**

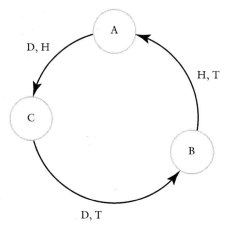

Figure 5.4

Cyclical Majorities

Although individual voters have consistent preferences, majority voting can lead to cycles. A majority
(Harriet and Tom) prefers A to B; a majority (Dick and
Harriet) prefers C to A; but a majority (Dick and Tom)
prefers B to C.

can occur in which a majority votes for C in preference to A and for B in preference
to C, yet a majority votes for A in preference to B. The cyclical majority for this example is shown in Figure 5.4. The arrows point to the alternative that wins a majority
vote in a head-to-head contest between adjacent pairs of alternatives. The initials of
the voters making up the majority are shown in each case.

Normally we'd expect that voting stops once one alternative has beaten all others. However, if a cyclical majority is present, no alternative can beat all others. How
is voting stopped and the outcome determined? One possibility is that voting stops
after three elections in which all possible pairs of alternatives have been voted on.
With this stopping rule, and the order of voting in the above example, alternative A
is the ultimate outcome because it is the winner in the third round of voting.

IMPLICATIONS OF THE VOTING PARADOX.   The voting paradox has several
implications for public decision making. Perhaps the most important is that
considerations unrelated to the preferences of the voters can determine the
outcome. For example, a factor unrelated to preferences, such as the order in which
the alternatives are presented to the voters, may determine which alternative wins.
In Figure 5.4, suppose the voters choose first between alternatives A and C, then
between C (the first-round winner) and B, and finally between B (the second-round
winner) and A. With this order of voting, A is the final winner. Suppose instead that
the voters first choose between alternatives C and B (B wins), then between A and
B (A wins), and finally between A and C (C wins). A different order of voting yields
a different outcome.

This is very strange. For instance, alternative A might be a decision to spend
nothing on public school teachers and alternative C a decision to spend a lot on
them. Hence, whether the community decides to do one thing or its opposite
depends on the order of the vote. The outcome has nothing to do with voters' preferences because the preferences are the same whatever the order in which the alternatives are presented.

The fact that the order of voting matters makes possible **agenda manipulation,**
which is the ability to control the outcome of an election by controlling the agenda.

It is well known that agenda control is a powerful tool because the person who controls the agenda can determine whether an issue comes to a vote. But even if all issues are voted on, the presence of voting cycles provides another reason that agenda control is important. If the person who controls the agenda knows the preferences of the other voters, he or she can determine the outcome by choosing the voting order. For example, if Harriet controls the agenda, she can arrange for an election between B and C in the first round, then B and A, and finally A and C. With this order, her most preferred outcome, C, is the ultimate winner.

Another way the agenda can be controlled is with strategic voting. **Strategic voting** describes a situation where people vote contrary to their true preferences in early rounds of voting so as to achieve a more preferred outcome in the later rounds. To see how this might happen, assume that voting stops when one alternative beats all others, or after all possible pairs of alternatives have been put to the vote, whichever comes first. Consider the case in which alternatives A and C are voted in the first round and the winner (C) faces alternative B in the second. If C beats B in the second round, voting stops; otherwise, B faces off against A. Dick knows that if he votes his true preferences in the second round of voting (he really prefers B to C), in the third round A will win. Dick prefers A least of all, so he'd prefer C to this outcome. If "tricky" Dick votes for C rather than B in the second round, C beats both alternatives and the voting stops, with C as the winner.

REASONS FOR THE VOTING PARADOX.   Many people find it surprising that the voting process can have inconsistent outcomes, so we should understand why it happens. Two factors are responsible. The first is that the "majority" is not the same group of people in each election. In our example, the majority consists of Dick and Harriet in the contest between A and C, Dick and Tom in the contest between B and C, and Tom and Harriet in the final contest. Once we recognize that the majority consists of different people in different election rounds, the inconsistency is not so surprising.

The second factor explaining the inconsistency of majority voting is that some of the voters do not have single-peaked preferences. In this example, Harriet has multiple-peaked preferences, with a peak for alternative C and a lesser peak for alternative A. The necessity of multiple-peaked preferences for the voter's paradox is seen if we assume that all voters have single-peaked preferences. Suppose Harriet likes alternative C best, B second-best, and A least in our example. Now cyclical majorities do not occur, because B beats both A and C in head-to-head contests. No matter in what order the alternatives are presented to voters, B is the winner. In the public choice literature, an alternative that can beat all others in head-to-head contests is called a **Condorcet winner.** If voters have single-peaked preferences over a single-dimensional issue, such as the quantity of a public good, majority voting always has a Condorcet winner.

The Median Voter Theory

When the voting paradox is ruled out, an interesting candidate for the majority voting equilibrium emerges. The most preferred outcome of the median voter is a Condorcet winner and the equilibrium of majority voting.

5.1 Cyclical Majorities and Coalition Busting

While the voting paradox can occur in popular voting, it is more common in legislative and committee voting, where it gives rise to a phenomenon known as the "coalition-busting" amendment. Suppose Tom, Dick, and Harriet are the only members of a school board, and currently the district has a low number of teachers (A). Harriet might make a motion C to hire a lot more teachers, which would pass if it came to a vote because both Dick and Harriet would approve. (See Figure 5.4.) Tom recognizes the coalition of Dick and Harriet, so he quickly proposes amendment B to hire a few more teachers. If this coalition-busting amendment came to a vote, Tom and Dick would approve it. Harriet likes this outcome the least so she proposes to table the motion (stay with the status quo). The motion to table would be approved by Harriet and Tom, and no action would be taken.

Professors Kenneth A. Shepsle and Mark S. Bonchek argue that the first U.S. income tax levied in 1861 to finance the Union's prosecution of the Civil War came about from coalition busting. Here is their story.

"The interesting thing about the income tax is that it resulted from a preference cycle (and was not even part of the original suggestion for raising revenue). There was a motion in the House of Representatives to raise federal revenue by taxing wealth. To this motion was offered an amendment to raise revenue instead by taxing land. And, of course, if neither the original motion nor

the amended version passed, the status quo of no taxes would prevail. Different majorities preferred the land tax to the wealth tax, the wealth tax to no tax, and no tax to the land tax. There was much confusion and to-and-fro during the debate as this majority preference cycle wreaked havoc. Finally, someone introduced the idea of taxing income. This swept to victory primarily because, unlike each of the other taxes (in which politicians knew exactly whose ox would be gored), there was much uncertainty about how an income tax would impact various constituencies. Politicians preferred the 'lottery' of an income tax to no tax at all or a tax on either land or wealth."[1]

Critically analyze the following:

- Would Tom's coalition busting amendment work if Harriet had single-peaked preferences (say she preferred B to A and C to B)?

- Sometimes, to prevent cyclical majorities, the right to make amendments to congressional bills is restricted. In this case, however, agenda control becomes more important. Why?

- Draw a diagram, similar to Figure 5.4, showing how the land tax, wealth tax, and no tax alternatives were ranked by the majority in the House of Representatives in 1861.

[1]Kenneth A. Shepsle and Mark S. Bonchek, *Analyzing Politics: Rationality, Behavior, and Institutions,* Norton Webbook at http://www.wwnorton.com/college/polisci/analyzing/webbook/cases-1.html.

THE CONCEPT OF THE "MEDIAN VOTER." The **median voter** is a person whose most preferred outcome in an election on a single issue occupies the midpoint of voters' opinions. Suppose voters have single-peaked preferences over the quantity of a public good and Q^m is the quantity most preferred by the median voter. Half the remaining voters prefer a quantity equal to or greater than Q^m and the other half prefer a quantity equal to or less than Q^m. Because Q^m occupies the midpoint, it is the only quantity that can command majority approval over the other alternatives.

Consider a voting process where sequential votes are taken to incrementally increase or decrease the quantity of a public good. If an incremental change is supported by a majority of votes, it is approved. When the existing quantity is less than

Q^m, more than half the voters, including the median voter, will approve a proposal to increase it. Similarly, if the existing quantity is greater than Q^m, a majority of voters will approve a proposal to decrease it. The ultimate outcome of this sequential voting is Q^m, the quantity preferred by the median voter. If a community has Q^m units of the public good, proposals to increase or decrease the quantity are defeated, so the preferred outcome of the median voter is the equilibrium.

Note that Q^m is not necessarily the quantity preferred by the most voters. In fact, apart from the median voter, most voters prefer a different quantity altogether. The quantity Q^m is selected by voters not because it is the outcome preferred by most of them, but because it is the *only* quantity that can win a majority of votes in contests against all others. This distinction is important because it explains an apparent paradox. Many, if not most, voters may be dissatisfied with the outcome of the election because they do not get their most preferred quantity. Nonetheless, Q^m is the only quantity that wins a majority of the votes.

Figure 5.5 illustrates the median voter theorem for three voters, each of whom bears a per capita share of the marginal cost of the public good. If the marginal cost is $1, the tax price to each voter is one third of a dollar. The MWTP schedules for the public good by Dick, Harriet, and Tom are labeled $MWTP^D$, $MWTP^H$, and $MWTP^T$, respectively. At each quantity of the public good, Tim has the lowest MWTP, Harriet the highest, and Dick is in between. This could reflect the fact that they have different incomes or different tastes. The most preferred outcomes of the voters are Q^T, Q^H, and Q^D, respectively.

In this example, Dick is the median voter. Below quantity Q^T, the voters unanimously vote to increase the quantity of the public good. Between quantities Q^T and Q^D, a majority of the voters, Harriet and Dick, will vote to increase the quantity further. Between Q^H and Q^D, a majority of the voters, Tom and Harriet, will vote to decrease it. Above Q^H the voters vote unanimously to decrease the quantity. Thus Dick's most preferred quantity is the equilibrium outcome of direct voting. Still, a majority of the voters, consisting of Harriet and Tom, is not totally happy with the outcome. Tom complains that the quantity is too high, and Harriet complains that it is too low.

What sorts of things affect the voting equilibrium quantity, according to the median voter theorem? First, an increase in Dick's income increases the equilibrium quantity if the public good is normal. (We must assume that Dick remains the median voter after the change in his income because "median voter" is not a person, but a position occupied by a voter.) Second, an increase in Dick's tax price decreases the equilibrium quantity of the public good. Dick's tax price could increase because the marginal cost of the good increases, or because Dick's tax share increases. Note that changes in other voters' incomes and tax prices do not affect the outcome, unless they change Dick's status as the median voter. If Tom's MWTP schedule shifts, changing his most preferred quantity, the equilibrium quantity is not affected. Tom could rightfully complain that the voting process is not responsive to his preferences.

THE MEDIAN VOTER THEOREM AND ECONOMIC EFFICIENCY.   How does the equilibrium quantity of a public good compare with the efficient quantity, as described in Chapter 3? The fact that the equilibrium quantity does not depend on

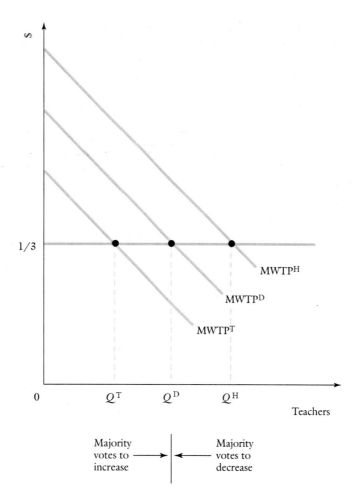

Figure 5.5

Median Voter Theorem

All the voters have the same tax price but different MWTP schedules for teachers. Their most preferred numbers of teachers are Q^T, Q^D, and Q^H. Dick is the median voter because his most preferred alternative occupies the midpoint of voters' preferences. If the number of teachers is less than Q^D, a majority consisting of Harriet and Dick will vote to increase the number of teachers. If the number is greater than Q^D, a majority consisting of Dick and Tom will vote to decrease the number. Only Dick's most-preferred alternative can command a majority against all challengers.

changes in demands by anyone except the median voter provides a clue. From the Samuelson condition, which defines the efficient quantity, we know that an increase in the demand for the public good by anyone in the community increases the efficient quantity. However, the quantity determined by vote depends only on the MWTP of the median voter. Therefore, only by accident would the efficient quantity and the median voter's quantity be the same.

In our example, the Samuelson condition requires that the efficient quantity of a public good satisfy the condition $MWTP^D + MWTP^H + MWTP^T = 1$ where we assume that the marginal cost of the public good is 1. Dividing both sides by 3 (the number of voters), we can rewrite the Samuelson condition as $\overline{MWTP} = ⅓$ where $\overline{MWTP}$ is the mean (average) value of the MWTP across the voters. In other words, at the efficient quantity, the average MWTP of the population for a public good is equal to a per capita share of marginal cost. By comparison, at the voting equilibrium quantity, the MWTP of the median voter is equal to his or her tax price. The equilibrium and efficient quantities are the same if the MWTP of the median voter is equal to the average MWTP and the median voter's tax price is equal to a per capita share of the marginal cost.

Is this likely? To simplify, assume that voters have the same tastes and the MWTPs for the public good differ only because voters have different incomes. Further, assume that voters' MWTP for the public good is proportional to their income. Under these assumptions, the distribution of MWTPs across the voters has the same shape as the distribution of incomes across voters. The distribution of incomes in the United States is skewed to the right, as shown in Figure 5.6, so the distribution of MWTPs is skewed the same way. This means that the median MWTP of the voters (the MWTP for which half the voters have higher and half have lower MWTPs) is less than the average $\overline{MWTP}$. If the median voter has the

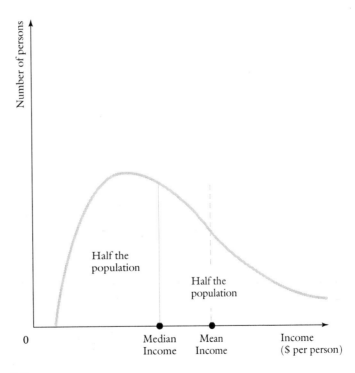

Figure 5.6

Median and Mean Incomes

Because the distribution of income is skewed to the right as shown, the mean income (total income divided by the population) is greater than the median income (the income for which half the population has more and half has less). If the median voter has median income, he or she has less than the mean income.

median MWTP and his or her tax price is equal to a per capita share of the marginal cost, Q^m is less than the efficient quantity, so majority voting approves a quantity of public good that is "too small."

Offsetting this bias is the fact that the tax price of the median voter is likely to be less than a per capita share of the marginal cost of the public good. In the United States, as in many other countries, people with lower incomes have small tax shares because the tax system is progressive (see Chapter 11). Because the income distribution is skewed, the median income is less than the mean, so the tax price of the median voter is likely to be less than a per capita share of the marginal cost.[4] This means that, other things being equal, the median voter prefers a quantity of a public good greater than the efficient quantity because he or she views the good as cheaper than the average person does. Combining the effects of skewed incomes and a lower tax share, we find that the median voter's most preferred quantity of a public good can be either greater or less than the efficient quantity.

OTHER VOTING RULES

Majority voting is one of many voting rules. Instead of requiring 50 percent of the voters plus one to win an election, a voting rule could require 60 percent. When more than 50 percent of the voters plus one are needed to approve an initiative, the voting rule is called a **supermajority voting rule.** This type of voting rule is required in some states on proposals to raise local taxes.

The *unanimity voting rule* sets an even stiffer requirement. It requires every voter to agree in order for a proposal to be approved. In practice, the unanimity voting rule is used only for special decisions. For example, the unanimous consent of the states is needed to amend the equal representation of the states in the Senate under the Constitution.[5] The unanimity voting rule is of interest because of its relationship to economic efficiency. Recall that a change in the allocation of resources that makes everyone in the community better off is called a Pareto improvement. In principle, an increase in economic efficiency allows the government to make a Pareto improvement, so efficient policies should command unanimous approval.

Does this mean that the unanimity voting rule can be used to determine the efficient quantity of a public good? Although a proposed Pareto improvement would be approved unanimously if everyone voted truthfully, unanimity invites strategic voting. Recall that people vote strategically if they oppose a proposal that benefits them in the hope of doing better on subsequent rounds of voting. Voters are not usually faced with a single ballot alternative offering a Pareto improvement. Instead, voters realize that many Pareto-improving alternatives are possible, even if they are not on the current ballot, and some of these may offer higher benefits to the individual voter than the alternative under consideration. With unanimity voting, each voter can veto an alternative. Voters may veto a proposal that offers a Pareto improvement because they think that they can get an even greater benefit from another alternative that will

---

[4]We assume that the median voter has the median income.

[5]For all practical purposes, unanimity is required. Conceivably, a state can be deprived of its equal representation if it agreed to that, even if some other states were opposed.

be placed on the ballot if the current one fails. Under a unanimous voting rule, endless rounds of voting might take place as voters jockey for advantage. This raises the cost of voting, perhaps making it impossible to agree on a Pareto improvement.

CHOOSING A VOTING RULE

We have seen that different voting rules have different disadvantages. Majority voting is insensitive to many voters' preferences at best, and inconsistent at worst because of the voting paradox. The unanimity voting rule invites strategic voting. How do we decide which voting rule to use? Is the majority voting rule the best we can do, or can we do better?

ARROW'S POSSIBILITIES THEOREM.   A voting rule can be thought of as a way of aggregating (summing) individual preferences for outcomes that must be enjoyed collectively. The resulting aggregation of preferences could be considered the preference function for society. It seems reasonable that a good voting rule should provide a preference function for society that is rational and consistent. The following properties seem desirable for this purpose.

- *Society's preference function should be complete* in that it can compare all pairs of alternatives and decide which is preferred or whether they are equivalent (the case of indifference).

- *Society's preferences between any two alternatives should be independent of irrelevant alternatives.* For instance, suppose a group of diners must decide whether dinner (served to all) is steak or fish. Why should the group's preference between steak and fish depend on their preferences between steak and chicken or fish and pork? According to the irrelevant alternatives requirement, it should not. The same should be true for society's preference function.

- *The preference function should be transitive.* That is, if society prefers A to B, and B to C, then society should prefer A to C. In other words, no voting paradox should occur.

- *Society should prefer a Pareto improvement.* If everyone prefers a particular alternative to another, it should be also preferred in the society's preferences.

- *There should be no dictator of society's preferences.* That is, no one individual's preferences should always take precedence over the preferences of others.

- *The voting rule should not be restricted* to specific forms of individual preferences. For instance, we cannot insist that all individuals have single-peaked preferences as required for the median voter theorem.

If we study this "wish list" for the process of choosing society's preference function, all the properties seem desirable and reasonable. Together they guarantee that collective decisions can be made rationally and consistently. Some people might even believe that these properties are the *least* we should settle for. Unfortunately, they are mutually inconsistent, which means that not all the properties can exist simultaneously. This was first proved by the Nobel laureate Kenneth Arrow several decades ago. The implication of Arrow's result is that when choosing a voting rule among all possible voting rules, we must accept the fact that the rule we choose will be unsatisfactory in some way or other. At least one of the properties listed above cannot be present. The result is sometimes called **Arrow's possibilities theorem** because it limits the set of feasible voting rules from which society can choose.[6]

IS THE MAJORITY VOTING RULE A HAPPY "MEDIAN"?   The most important implication of Arrow's theorem is that any practical voting rule is less than ideal. In view of this, perhaps the majority voting rule is not so bad after all. The majority vote is the most common voting rule we encounter, if we include two-way races under a plurality voting rule. (With a plurality voting rule, the alternative with the most votes wins, even if it gets less than half of the votes.) Majority voting is found not only in government elections but also in corporate and committee elections. Perhaps there are good reasons that it is so prevalent.

Several theories purport to explain why majority voting is the rule, not the exception. To understand these arguments, let's suppose that a society wants to decide in advance what percentage of the votes should be needed to win future elections. With the simple majority voting rule, the criterion is 50 percent plus one vote. With a supermajority voting rule, substantially more than 50 percent of the voters must agree. With the unanimity voting rule, 100 percent of the voters must agree, so each voter has veto power. Why is the majority voting rule better than these other rules?

According to one influential theory, proposed by the Nobel laureate James M. Buchanan and Gordon Tullock, formerly of the University of Virginia, majority voting is prevalent because it is the lowest-cost voting rule. Buchanan and Tullock argue that two important costs are associated with any voting rule. The first is the *decision-making cost,* which is the time and effort needed to reach an agreement with voting. As the fraction of voters needed to win an election increases toward unanimity, the decision-making cost increases because it is easier for a small number of voters to block an outcome favorable to everyone else and necessitate further rounds of voting. The second cost is the *frustration cost,* which is the cost to voters of getting an outcome that makes them worse off. The frustration cost decreases as the fraction of voters needed to approve an action increases toward unanimity. If a voting rule requires only a small percentage of voters to approve, a special interest group can approve outcomes that make themselves better off but are very inefficient, so the frustration cost to other voters is high. On the other hand, with unanimity voting only Pareto improvements (which benefit everyone) are approved, so the frustration cost is very low. However the decision-making cost with unanimity voting is very high because of strategic voting.

The voting rule that makes the sum of the decision-making and frustration costs as low as possible is called the least-cost voting rule. Because the frustration cost is high when the fraction of voters needed to win is low while the decision-making cost is high when the fraction of voters needed to win is high, the least-cost voting rule is one where the fraction needed to win is neither too low nor too high. Of

---

[6]Arrow's theorem actually applies to *collective choice rules,* which are more general than voting rules. This technical detail is not important for our purposes. Also, the result is sometimes called Arrow's *impossibilities* theorem.

course, the majority voting rule is right in the middle, so it may represent the "happy median" that trades off the decision-making cost of the voting rule against its frustration cost.

The Lindahl Equilibrium

We have stressed that a major problem in public choice is the existence of divergent interests. Some people might like a public good a lot and others only a little, but they all must consume the same quantity. How do we get them to vote for the efficient quantity of the public good? A Swedish economist, Erik Lindahl, thought of a way, and we call the outcome of his scheme a **Lindahl equilibrium** in his honor. In a Lindahl equilibrium, people vote unanimously for the efficient quantity of the public good.

The Lindahl equilibrium for three voters is shown in Figure 5.7. We assume that the marginal cost of the public good is equal to $1 and that it is financed with a per capita levy so each voter faces a tax price equal to ⅓ of a dollar. The equilibrium outcome of majority voting on the quantity of a public good is Q^D, which is the quantity at which median voter's—Dick's—MWTP for the public good is equal to ⅓.

The efficient quantity of the public good is $Q^\star$ (which we assume is smaller than Q^D) where the average of the three MWTP schedules, shown as the $\overline{\text{MWTP}}$ schedule, is equal to ⅓. If the average of the MWTPs is equal to one-third, the sum of the MWTPs is equal to the marginal cost of the public good, so it is provided at the efficient quantity. If the government knows the MWTP schedules of the voters, it can get them to unanimously agree to $Q^\star$ by charging them the right tax prices. Dick and Harriet both want a quantity greater than $Q^\star$ so the government reduces their demands by raising their tax prices. Tom wants a quantity less than $Q^\star$, so the government increases his demand by lowering his tax price. As shown in Figure 5.7, when tax prices are set at T^T, T^D, and T^H for Tom, Dick, and Harriet, respectively, they unanimously vote for $Q^\star$. The efficient quantity is the most preferred outcome for every voter, so it is the Lindahl equilibrium quantity. The tax prices that must be set for the voters are called the **Lindahl tax prices.**

The Lindahl equilibrium seems too good to be true. Simply by setting the right tax prices, the government gets voters to agree unanimously on the efficient quantity of a public good! If that were the case, politics would be less interesting and certainly less divisive. The difficulty with the Lindahl equilibrium is the problem of setting the tax prices in the first place. For one thing, the government must discover the MWTP schedules of the voters. Lindahl described an iterative process for discovering the tax prices: If unanimous agreement on the quantity of the public good is not reached on a given round of voting, the tax prices are adjusted, and so on. However, as a practical matter, the tax prices to the voters are a public choice decision and subject to all of the problems we discussed earlier.

Lindahl ignored the question of how tax prices are set by the political process. The fact is that voters will not unanimously approve the Lindahl prices. Each voter would like a lower tax price for himself or herself and higher tax prices for everyone else. If the voting process sets tax prices for voters as well as the quantity of the public good, people have an incentive to vote strategically in order to get a lower

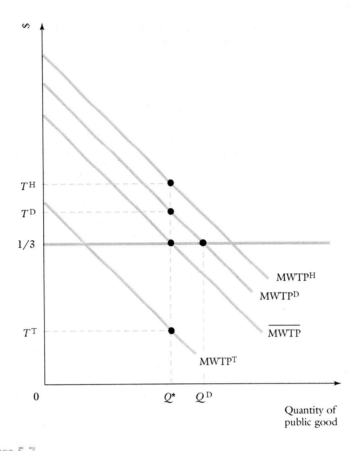

Figure 5.7

Lindahl Equilibrium for a Public Good

The efficient quantity of a public good is found where the mean MWTP for it by the population is equal to the per capita marginal cost ($^1/_3$ in the example). As drawn, the efficient quantity Q^* is less than the median voter outcome Q^D when the tax price for all voters is the per capita share. If the government sets personalized tax prices T^D, T^H, and T^T equal to the MWTPs of the respective voters at Q^*, they will vote unanimously for the efficient quantity. This is called the Lindahl equilibrium.

tax price. In other words, the free-rider problem arises again. We now discuss a method of getting people to truthfully reveal their preferences for a public good.

A Method for Learning Voters' Preferences

Consumers derive no advantage by concealing their MWTP for goods purchased in a competitive market, because they must buy a good in order to enjoy it. However, this "take it or leave it" approach to learning a consumer's MWTP does not work for public goods, because price exclusion cannot be practiced. Economists have devised a complicated way of asking voters for their MWTPs for a public good so that they get true answers. The procedure is called a **preference revelation mechanism.** Although the mechanism is hypothetical at present, because no practical means of implementing it has been devised, it is interesting enough to describe briefly.

The key feature of a preference revelation mechanism is the way in which a voter's tax price is determined. With this method, unlike the median voter model or the Lindahl model, the voters do not face a fixed tax price. Instead, they are told that the tax price they must pay per unit depends on reports by the other voters of their MWTP schedules. Specifically, the tax price for a unit of public good is equal to the marginal cost of the public good minus the sum of the reported MWTPs of all other voters for that unit.

The voters are also informed that once they have all reported their MWTP schedules, the government will add the MWTPs at each quantity of the public good (it will vertically sum the MWTP schedules as in Chapter 3) and produce a quantity at which the sum of the reported MWTPs equals the marginal cost. In other words, the voters are told that the Samuelson condition is used to determine the quantity of the public good according to their revealed preferences. It turns out that, facing these conditions, individual voters can do no better than truthfully report their MWTP schedules.

A preference revelation mechanism is illustrated in Figure 5.8 for three voters. The quantity of the public good is measured on the horizontal axis, and the upward-sloping line shows Harriet's tax price for the public good. The height of this line is equal to the marginal cost of the public good minus the sum of the reported MWTPs by Dick and Tom. Since their MWTPs decrease as the quantity increases, the curve is positively sloped. The quantity Q_0 is the amount of the public good that is produced if Harriet does not report her schedule. At Q_0 the sum of the MWTPs of the other two voters is equal to the marginal cost of the public good.

Also shown is Harriet's true MWTP schedule for the public good. If Harriet reports this schedule, Q^* of the public good is produced. By reporting her true schedule, Harriet enjoys a net benefit equal to the area of the shaded triangle. The net benefit to Harriet is equal to the excess of her MWTP over the tax price she pays for the difference in the quantity of the public good produced because of her report (Q^* minus Q_0). If Harriet reports a false schedule, say MWTP′, a different quantity Q' is produced and she gets a smaller net benefit. Dick and Tom are asked to reveal their MWTP schedules under the same terms, so they too report their true schedules.

Despite this impressive result, the preference revelation mechanism has not been employed by any government. The difficulty with using the mechanism is practicality. Rather than simply voting yes or no, voters must report their MWTP schedules. This imposes significant information costs on voters and on the government to collect and compile the information. Understanding the procedure requires patience, as the reader can confirm, so rational voter ignorance and apathy would lead many voters to abstain. The net benefit to be gained by voters who report their schedules is not likely to compensate them for the costs of participating in such a complicated process.

Registering the Dimensions of Voters' Preferences

An important shortcoming of the majority (or plurality) voting rule is that it incorporates little information about a voter's preferences. Individual voters express their preference for one of the alternatives on the ballot, and the alternative that receives the most votes wins. This type of voting ignores information in two ways. First, *it*

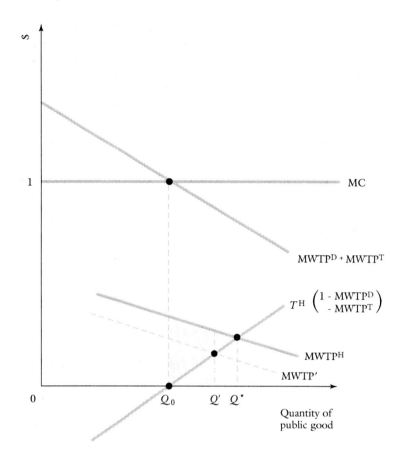

Figure 5.8

Preference-Revelation Method

Each voter is faced with a tax price schedule that is determined by subtracting the sum of the reported MWTP schedules by all other voters from the marginal cost of the public good. T^H shows the tax schedule facing Harriet on the assumption that Dick and Tom report their true MWTP schedules, as they will under this mechanism. The government produces the quantity of public good where the reported MWTP schedule of the voter intersects the tax price schedule for the voter. This condition satisfies the Samuelson condition (see Chapter 3) for an efficient output if all voters report their true schedules. As seen in the figure, Harriet can do no better than report her true schedule, since it maximizes her total net benefit.

does not register the intensity of preferences. If a voter strongly favors a certain outcome and another voter is mildly opposed, their votes nonetheless cancel in the final count. Second, if more than two choices appear on the ballot, the voters' *secondary preferences are not counted.* This can lead to some odd electoral outcomes.

Suppose 30 percent of the voters want 100 public school teachers (alternative A), 30 percent want 90 (alternative B), and 40 percent want no teachers at all (alternative C). Suppose the first group prefers alternative B if it can't have A and the second group prefers alternative A if it can't have B. If the three alternatives are on a single ballot and voters vote for their most preferred alternative, C wins a plurality vote (gets the most votes) even though 60 percent of the voters want many more teachers. The voters who want more teachers don't win, because they "split their votes" between A and B. The voting outcome does not take into account the secondary preferences of the voters who want more teachers.

As a result of these oddities, alternatives to the majority and plurality voting rules have been studied. One type of voting rule attempts to make the voting process more sensitive to the intensity of voters' preferences, and another attempts to make it sensitive to their secondary as well as their primary preferences. We'll consider each in turn.

The intensity of voters' preferences can be expressed within the majority voting rule if voters are allowed to trade votes. One form of vote trading is known as **logrolling.** Logrolling occurs when one voter agrees to vote for an alternative he or she mildly opposes if another voter, who strongly wants this alternative, will vote for an alternative strongly desired by the first voter. In other words, logrolling is "You scratch my back and I'll scratch yours" at the ballot box.

Vote trading can lead to a more efficient voting outcome in some cases. Suppose three voters—Dick, Harriet, and Tom—can vote yes or no on two initiatives, A and B. Each initiative is a public project that costs $3000. To be specific, suppose A is a sidewalk and B is a park in a public place. Each voter must pay a per capita share of the cost of the projects, so each initiative will cost a voter $1000 if passed. The MWTPs for the projects by the voters are shown in Table 5.1. We assume the voters' MWTPs for project A do not depend on whether B is done, and vice versa.

Note that it is efficient to do both projects because the sum of the MWTPs of the three voters is $3200 for each project and each costs only $3000. Nevertheless, given the equal per capita tax prices, majority voting defeats both projects. The votes of Dick and Tom defeat project A, and the votes of Harriet and Tom defeat project B.

Now suppose that Dick and Harriet engage in vote trading. Harriet agrees to vote for project B if Dick agrees to vote for A. In this case both projects are approved. The net benefit to Dick (his MWTP for A plus his MWTP for B minus his $2000 increase in taxes) is positive ($500), and the same is true for Harriet. Both are happy with the vote trade. Granted, Tom is unhappy, but in principle Dick and Harriet could each give him a little over $300 so that a Pareto improvement occurs. Of course, the transfer is not necessary to win a majority vote with vote trading.

Vote trading could just as easily lead to an inefficient outcome. Suppose Tom's MWTP for both projects is $0 rather than $700. Neither project is efficient because the sum of voters' MWTPs is less than the cost. If Dick and Harriet engage in vote

Table 5.1   Voters' MWTP for Two Projects

Voter	MWTP for Project A	MWTP for Project B
Dick	$500	$2,000
Harriet	2,000	500
Tom	700	700

trading, the two projects nonetheless receive majority approval. Dick and Harriet are better off by $500 each, but they cannot transfer enough to Tom to compensate him for his loss. If they each were to give him $500 (the maximum they would pay to have the two projects), Tom would still be worse off by $1000 because he is forced to pay $2000 more in taxes for projects that do not benefit him.

Vote trading requires a small number of voters and an open (nonsecret) voting system, because it is costly to find opportunities for trading votes and necessary to ensure that agreements are carried out. For this reason, the phenomenon is found mainly in legislative bodies. However, a voting rule that directly allows many voters to express the intensity of their preferences is **point voting.** Rather than a single vote, voters are given an allotment of point votes that they can allocate across different alternatives. For example, each voter might be given 10 point votes, which can be cast for a single strongly preferred alternative or spread over several less intensely desired alternatives. The total of the point votes cast on all alternatives must add up to 10, like a budget constraint. Negative preference can be registered with negative votes, which cancel out positive votes by other voters. Negative point votes are subtracted from the voter's allotment, just like positive point votes. Voters who strongly dislike an alternative can cast their entire point allotment against it.

Another type of point voting, used by the Associated Press football poll to rank teams, is designed to consider the voters' secondary preferences. Suppose voters are asked to rank the alternatives on a ballot and points are assigned to the alternatives according to the ranking given. For instance, if N alternatives are on the ballot, an alternative receives N points for each first-place ranking it receives from a voter, $N - 1$ for each second-place ranking it receives, etc. The alternative that receives the greatest number of points wins. This is called the **Borda voting rule** after Jean-Charles de Borda, another French voting theorist, who first proposed it in 1770.

Other voting rules allow transferable votes. An informal example is the *runoff* election used in some state elections. If several alternatives are on the ballot and only one can win, another election is scheduled when no alternative receives a majority of the votes. The two alternatives receiving the most votes in the first election face off in the runoff election. Those who chose an alternative receiving too few votes in the first election can transfer their votes to their preferred alternative in the runoff election.

A formalized type of transferable voting known as "Cincinnati rules" has been used to elect officials in that city, and variations are used in some European and Australian elections. As with the Borda rule, the voters rank the candidates, but points are not assigned on the basis of the rankings. Rather, an alternative wins if it receives a majority of first-place votes. If no alternative has a majority, the alternative with the fewest first-place votes is eliminated and the alternatives ranked second by these voters are promoted to first-place votes. This process continues until some alternative receives a majority of first-place votes.

VOTING FOR REPRESENTATIVES

So far we have looked at systems where the public votes directly on government decisions. More realistically, voters elect representatives (politicians) who vote on these decisions in legislative bodies. Public decision making requires gathering and assessing information, which is costly. It also may require considerable vote trading. For these reasons, direct voting is too costly and cumbersome for making many public decisions. Also, the rational ignorance of voters would mean that direct voting on public decisions would not be very informed.

In the United States, people vote nationwide for an executive—the president—and by state and district, respectively, for legislative representatives in the Senate and House. The governments of the states are determined in a similar way. With representative government, decision-making costs are reduced because a much smaller group of people propose and vote on the alternatives. We describe the decision-making parts of government as the administrative-legislative branch.

The politicians or representatives are only part of the political scene we observe. The administrative branch of government is organized into departments, or bureaus, staffed with people who implement the programs and policies decided on by the politicians. Sometimes this is done by separate government agencies. Most of these government employees are nonpolitical or "civil service," though a department is usually administered by a political appointee, such as a cabinet member. We describe the part of government that implements government decisions as the **bureaucracy.** The judicial branch is another part of government that interprets and enforces the laws, although we will not be concerned with it here. In addition to these parts of government, the politicians are organized into private political parties. Also, private households and firms with intense interests organize into **political action committees (PACs)** that raise money and lobby the politicians to achieve their objectives.

Politicians as Vote-Seekers

Politicians are the main decision makers in the political process, analogous to entrepreneurs in the theory of the firm. Unlike entrepreneurs, however, they are not motivated by personal monetary profit except in corrupt regimes. What objectives do they seek? A realistic assumption is that their primary motive is to maximize their chance of being elected or reelected to political office. This does not mean that politicians always put their desire to be elected before a higher "public interest," but cases where politicians put principles before election are rare enough to be considered newsworthy.

The theory that politicians maximize their chances of being elected leads naturally to the **vote competition hypothesis,** which postulates that politicians compete for votes by promising to work in the legislative body for programs that please a majority of the voters in their districts. This is not simply a matter of trying to maximize the number of votes they receive. Rather, it is a matter of attracting enough votes to be elected. It is the nature of politics that some voters are made unhappy by policies that please others. A politician who tries to please everyone may end up pleasing no one. Also, the marginal benefit to politicians of attracting more votes declines as the number of votes they already have increases. Once they have enough votes to win an election, the benefit of attracting more votes is low. Furthermore, politicians risk alienating their existing supporters by announcing policies to attract new voters. If they have enough votes to win, why try?

What type of political behavior do we expect on the basis of the vote competition hypothesis? According to a theory first proposed by Harold Hotelling in 1929 and developed further by Anthony Downs in 1957, politicians propose policies that lie at the center of public opinion. This is the median voter theorem as it applies to representative government.

In general, politicians make decisions on many programs during their term in office, so voters must assess the candidates on a package of programs—a "platform"—not on a single issue. For simplicity, let's assume that on the basis of their platforms, politicians can be ranked in terms of a single dimensional measure: say, how liberal or conservative they are.[7] In Figure 5.9, the numbers of voters who prefer politicians at different points on this political spectrum are measured on the vertical axis. For simplicity, we assume that this distribution is unimodal or single-peaked. The point on the political spectrum labeled M (for median) is one

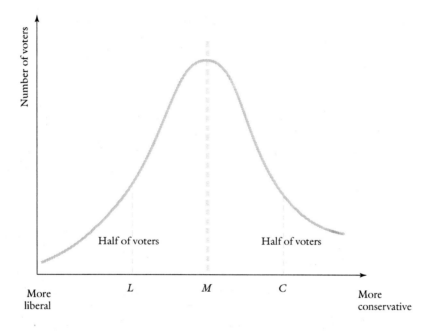

Figure 5.9

Middle-of-the-Road Politics

Suppose that voters are arrayed from more liberal to more conservative. The median voter has political persuasion M. Vote-seeking politicians do best by pitching their platform at the median voter. For example, a liberal espousing platform L will appeal to voters at L or to the left but alienate the more numerous voters to the right of L—and conversely for a conservative politician espousing platform C.

---

[7]Such a measure is the politician's approval rating by the Americans for Democratic Action (a high number indicating liberal) or the League of Conservative Voters (a high number indicating conservative).

at which half the voters hold a view that is more liberal than *M* and half hold a view that is more conservative.[8]

Suppose two politicians compete for votes from this distribution of voters' preferences, and one stakes out a conservative position at *C* and the other a liberal position at *L*. More than half the voters think the politician located at *C* is too conservative, so he or she cannot win a majority. To get elected, this politician must move toward *M* to attract more voters. The same thing happens for the liberal politician, who is considered too "left-wing" by a majority of voters. The equilibrium platform is the median *M,* which could also stand for "me too" because there both politicians espouse the same centrist views.

Of course, when both politicians espouse platform *M* neither has an advantage, so they may not fully converge on the same platform. The candidates want to distinguish themselves in a way that appeals to the voters without abandoning the middle ground. One way is to "go negative" and label the opponent "too liberal" or "too conservative," depending on which voters the politician is trying to attract. Each candidate stakes out the middle ground and represents the opponent as "too extreme." For example, a "conservative" candidate may argue that the opponent is a "left-wing extremist," or vice versa, even though both candidates support the same popular programs, such as Social Security. This explains why politics contains so much "sound and fury" yet few things change when one politician replaces another in office.

Another fact about politicians is that they belong to political parties. With the rare exception of an independent, the congressional representatives belong to one of two rival political parties. The political party functions somewhat like the firm in the theory of production. It is an organization within which the politicians work to achieve their objectives. It also plays an informational role. The party affiliation of a candidate is like a brand name on a consumer product—it informs the voter that the candidate holds a certain political philosophy and will vote accordingly on legislative issues. Also, as we saw earlier, voters are likely to remain rationally ignorant and not expend much effort or resources on becoming informed. Through advertising and in other ways, political parties put the issues (but perhaps not *just* the issues) before the voters in order to attract them to the party's candidates.

A distinguishing feature of politics in the United States is the remarkable stability of the two-party system. Third parties are short-lived and usually unsuccessful. According to the Hotelling-Downs theory, the plurality voting rule is responsible for this. With a unimodal distribution of voters' preferences like that in Figure 5.9, and with two established parties occupying the middle ground, a third party can attract voters only from the tails of the distribution. Under the plurality voting rule, people who vote for the smaller third party because they like its message waste their votes and do not get their views represented in the legislative body.

---

[8]Position *M* itself may be described as liberal or conservative according to the temper of the times. At the present time, a majority of U.S. voters describe themselves as "conservative," so *M* would be described as conservative. Whether *M* is or is not conservative is not important; it is the relative position of the candidates on the spectrum that matters.

In contrast, under the proportional voting systems favored in some European countries, smaller parties survive and often hold the balance of power.[9]

Political Action Committees

As mentioned, demands for political action may be expressed through means other than voting. Individuals give money to their preferred candidates or perform volunteer labor, such as stuffing envelopes. People with a common interest band together to form lobbies and political action committees (PACs). In 1998, there were nearly 4600 PACs ranging from the Association of Trial Lawyers of America to the National Rifle Association Political Victory Fund. Together they spent over $470 million on their activities, including $220 million in campaign contributions to their preferred candidates for federal government offices.

Ever since James Madison's *Federalist* papers, political theorists have complained about the role of factions and "special interests" in the American political process. Many people believe that such groups exert too much influence. One reason for the formation of such factions is the rational voter ignorance and apathy mentioned earlier. Since one vote doesn't matter much, people with strong political demands must find other ways of influencing the outcome of the political process. By organizing and contributing money they can inform and encourage others to support the actions they desire. As representatives of blocs of voters, PACs can exert greater influence over politicians than individual voters can.

Despite their seeming ubiquity, PACs must overcome a serious obstacle to their formation. Promoting a political action is costly in terms of both organization and resources. Moreover, the people who stand to gain from the actions of the PAC have an incentive to freeride. For example, older citizens may gain politically from the efforts of American Association of Retired Persons (AARP), but they can freeride by not joining AARP and avoid paying the annual dues. So why are there so many PACs?

One reason is that the PACs are sometimes a side product of groups organized to serve other purposes. For example, AARP provides a package of benefits to its members, including discounts at commercial establishments. Similarly, labor unions are organized to serve the interests of employees in contract negotiations with employers, and the National Rifle Association is organized to provide information and facilities for hunters and gun enthusiasts. Once formed, these groups may also find it useful to pursue their objectives through political actions.

Another reason for the formation of PACs is that some government policies may concentrate visible benefits on small groups of people and have costs that are spread over the population at large. In addition, the costs may be indirect and less visible. Suppose a subsidy to firms in an industry costs each of the 120 million taxpayers $1 a year. The taxpayers have little incentive to organize to oppose the subsidy because it is not worth their time and effort. Also, rational voter ignorance

---

[9]Proportional representation means that the distribution of political views of the representatives reflects the distribution of political views of the voters. Thus if *X* percent of the voters subscribe to certain political views—say, a religious political party line—then *X* percent of the representatives in the legislative body hold those views.

5.2   The Art of Buying Votes: Pork Barrel Politics

Slot machines were the subject of a recent ballot initiative in Washington state. In particular, casinos run by Native Americans in the state wanted them, and the voters were asked to approve. Backers offered all voters a share of the profits, regardless of how they voted, if the initiative was approved. It wasn't, but the opponents charged the backers with buying votes—an illegal act.

The fact is that votes are bought all the time, albeit indirectly. This is called pork barrel politics. Members of Congress who are successful at bringing federal projects into their districts are well liked by pocketbook voters living in the district. The projects typically benefit the people in the district, but the taxes needed to pay for them are spread over the population of the whole country, so the tax price to the constituents is negligible. Of course, when every politician in the country does this, everybody pays for everyone else's pork as well.

Economists have long sought evidence of the electoral benefits of pork to the politicians who deliver it. A clear positive relationship between the amount of federal pork brought home and the success of members of Congress seeking reelection is muddled by another political fact. Politicians who are only weakly supported by voters in the polls or who face strong challengers are likely to try that much harder to get federal money for their constituents. Recently, two economists thought of a way to get around this omitted variable—political desperation—by looking at the success of politicians in districts adjoining those that got the pork. These econo-

mists reasoned that the benefits of pork are likely to spill over to adjoining districts, and the local members of Congress are likely to claim the credit. By including the pork spillover from adjoining districts as a variable determining reelection, Steven Levitt of Harvard and James Snyder Jr. of MIT estimated that an extra $100 of pork per voter yields an incumbent politician 2% more votes.

Critically analyze the following:

- It is often claimed that "one person's pork is another person's beef." No one can agree on an exact definition of "pork barrel spending," but most people reserve the term for national spending that serves a narrow, local interest. How does pork barrel spending relate to national versus local public goods described in Chapter 3?

- It is easy enough to see why a politician from a district that receives pork barrel benefits would vote for the project, but why would politicians from districts that don't benefit and have to pay extra taxes vote in favor? (Hint: Might vote trading, considered in this chapter, be a factor?)

- Many people equate pork barrel spending with government waste. Is it necessarily the case that pork barrel spending is more wasteful that non–pork barrel spending?

Steven D. Levitt and James M. Snyder Jr., "The Impact of Federal Spending on House Election Outcomes," *Journal of Political Economy*, Feb. 1997, pp 30–53.

means that the individual taxpayer may be unaware of the extra tax. However, the smaller number (perhaps 10,000) of employees and shareholders of the firms that receive the subsidy may gain hundreds or even thousands of dollars each. This benefit makes it well worth while to organize a PAC to lobby for the subsidy, especially if freeriding can be controlled in the smaller group.

The concentration of benefits and the dilution of costs mean that some public decisions may be motivated by rent-seeking behavior rather than social welfare maximization. **Rent-seeking** describes support for policies that redistribute income from taxpayers to special interest groups, rather than creating wealth. Rent-seeking policies may be fiercely supported by PACs even though they are inefficient and reduce social welfare overall.

BUREAUCRACY AND THE SUPPLY SIDE OF GOVERNMENT

So far we have concentrated on the demand for government actions by voters and political action committees and how politicians win and keep office by responding to these demands. As in the theory of markets, we must also consider the supply side. Let's start by asking why politicians are so anxious to seek office.

Unless politicians are altruists who care only about serving the public, there must be more for them in their jobs than simply pleasing the voters. Politicians are paid, of course, but many earn lower salaries in government than they could earn in the private sector. Obviously, political office does confer benefits in the form of power and prestige; and some political offices, such as being the chair of a congressional committee, offer more power and prestige than others. Also, politicians in important positions can control the public agenda to some degree, and as we saw earlier, control of the agenda is often tantamount to control of the outcome. Although politicians are held in check by the demands of the voters, they have a long leash, so to speak. Within the constraints imposed by their need to get elected, politicians can pursue their own objectives, and the government policies they choose reflect those preferences.

Another group of people in government whose preferences matter are the bureaucrats who implement the policies chosen by the politicians. Although the bureaucrats are not concerned about getting elected, they must please the politicians by implementing their programs. But implementing a political program is not like executing a computer program. The bureaucracy is not simply a machine that blindly follows orders. As with the other actors in our drama, we need to look at the objectives and behavior of government bureaucrats.

Together, decisions made by the politicians and bureaucrats are described as the "supply side" of government. Although the supply side of government concerns the production or provision of government goods and services, several things distinguish "government work" from similar activities occurring in private firms.

First, compared with those of private firms, the outputs of the government are often hard to measure, and sometimes even hard to define. The programs that the bureaucrats must implement may have multiple, perhaps conflicting, objectives. For example, education is one of the more easily defined government outputs, but the managers of public schools are required to attain both quality and equality objectives. Furthermore, they are not told what weight to give each objective, so they have some discretion. The output of national defense, unlike the output of automobiles, is almost impossible to measure. As a result, we measure it using the quantity of inputs, such as the number of military personnel on active duty or the number of bombers ready to fly. Second, bureau managers—unlike private managers—do not worry about competition, because the government is often a monopolist provider of its outputs. For example, access to the unique natural areas of the country is available only from the National Park Service, and only the postal service can deliver first-class mail. Third, and perhaps most important, profit is not the objective of government. This means that a bureaucrat monopolist acts quite differently from a private monopolist who would use this power to earn monopoly profit. For one thing, bureaucracies are under far less pressure to minimize their costs, because they do not seek profit and are not concerned about bankruptcy.

Bureaucrats as Budget Maximizers

If bureaucrats do not maximize profit, what do they maximize? Perhaps nothing in particular, or perhaps the "public interest." However, economists find it useful to assume that human beings act with a purpose or objective, and that a tangible self-interest often takes precedence over an abstract public interest. The study of bureaucratic behavior is no exception. Bureaucrats, like almost everyone else, try to achieve personal success and satisfaction in their jobs. What kind of behavior do we expect from this?

An influential theory, proposed by William A. Niskanen, who was a member of the Council of Economic Advisors during the Reagan administration, is that the bureaucrats try to maximize the size and budgets of their departments. Niskanen defines a **bureau** as any nonprofit organization financed by an appropriation or grant, rather than revenue from sales. Because the people controlling a bureau cannot earn a profit, the personal goals of the managers and employees are their main concern. These goals include higher salaries for employees, perquisites and amenities, prestige, power, and the potential for advancement and promotion. Niskanen argues that such things are all associated with larger departments and larger budgets. Thus the bureau manager associates personal and professional success with success in obtaining the largest possible appropriation or grant for his or her department.

The theory of budget-maximizing behavior is illustrated in Figure 5.10. The bureau produces a government good or service whose output is measured on the horizontal axis. The demand for this good, expressed through voting and lobbying by the population, is shown by the downward-sloping curve labeled MWTP. The marginal cost to the bureau of producing the output is labeled MC, which we assume is constant. The output of the public good preferred by the voters is Q^* where their marginal willingness to pay is equal to the marginal cost. This quantity maximizes the total net benefit (or consumers' surplus) measured by the area of the triangle ACE. We'll call this the *potential* total net benefit because, according to Niskanen, it will not be realized.

If the bureau were a profit-maximizing monopolist,[10] it would generate monopoly profit by producing a quantity that is less than the efficient Q^*. However, the manager of a government agency cannot benefit by earning a profit, because the funds simply go into the general revenue of the government. Instead, the manager's interests lie in making the agency's budget as large as possible by supplying a larger quantity than Q^*. This is done by producing the largest output possible given the demand curve. This quantity is Q_B. The agency cannot produce

---

[10]The profit-maximizing output of a monopolist is found at the intersection of the marginal revenue curve derived from the demand curve (not shown) and the marginal cost curve.

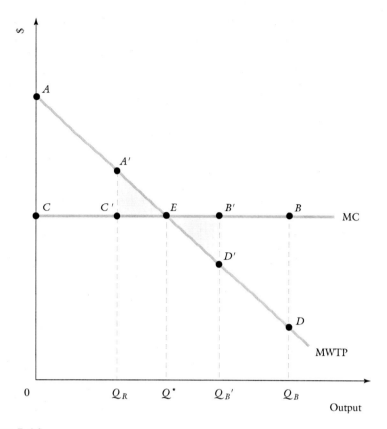

Figure 5.10

Equilibrium Output of a Bureaucracy

If the voters (or politicians) reject the bureau manager's proposed budget, a "reversion" budget is adopted that allows an output other than Q^*, which is the output preferred by the voters. If the reversion output is zero, the maximum output that can be proposed by the bureau manager is Q_B where the area of triangle BED is just equal to the area of triangle ACE. If the reversion output is Q_R, the maximum output that can be proposed is $Q_{B'}$ where the area of $B'D'E$ is equal to the area of $A'C'E$. A larger budget would not be approved, because the voters prefer the reversion output Q_R.

more than Q_B, because the voters are worse off with more than Q_B than with no output (and no bureau) at all, so the vote-seeking politicians will not approve the budget. The excess cost over the marginal willingness to pay for the excess output must be paid in taxes. At Q_B this excess cost, measured by the area of triangle BDE, exactly offsets the potential consumers' surplus.

The outcome preferred by a budget-maximizing bureaucrat can be expressed in another way. At output Q_B the total benefit to the consumers (equal to the area $A0Q_BD$) is equal to total cost of producing it (the area $C0Q_BB$). That is, the total net benefit to the consumers is zero. By comparison, at Q^* the consumers' total net benefit is maximized. To maximize the net benefit, the bureau would have to produce where the marginal benefit (marginal willingness to pay) is equal to marginal cost, not where the total benefit is equal to total cost.

At this point, we should ask: How do the bureaucrats get away with this? Why don't the politicians, as representatives of the voters, instruct the managers to produce Q^* and no more? One answer is that the output of a government department is hard to measure. The managers have better information about the operation of their departments and their cost structures than the politicians do. The politicians are to some extent at the bureaucrats' mercy. For example, politicians rely on the bureaucrats to appear before review committees to inform them what is going on in their departments. For this reason, a bureaucrat has leeway to exercise budget-maximizing behavior.

The bureaucrat's leeway may not be as great as that described above. He or she may not be able to expand output enough to wipe out the entire potential consumers' surplus ACE. A bureaucrat with less leeway is also shown in Figure 5.10.[11] Suppose that when the bureaucrat makes an appropriation request to the politicians, a smaller "default budget" is adopted if the bureaucrat's budget request is refused. For example, the default budget might be the level of funding provided in an earlier year. We assume that this default budget is too small to produce Q^*, so output Q_R is produced when the bureaucrat's request is refused. Quantity Q_R is called the *reversion* output.

According to this argument, bureaucrats have reasons to make reversion outputs painfully small, if they can. The National Park Service once limited public access to popular sights like the Statue of Liberty because of "inadequate funding." If the reversion output is produced, consumers of the government output lose consumers' surplus equal to the area of the shaded triangle $A'C'E$ (compared with their most preferred quantity Q^*). Therefore, given the reversion output, the bureaucrat can request a budget sufficient to produce Q_B' and expect to get it approved. At output Q_B', the excess cost of the bureaucrat's oversupply (equal to the area of the shaded triangle $ED'B'$) is just equal to the loss in consumers' surplus if the budget is refused. Any larger appropriation requested by the bureaucrat is refused.

An implication of this theory is that a bureau manager has greater power to expand the size of a department if the reversion output is low relative to the voters' preferred quantity (Q^*) and the loss of benefits to the voters at the reversion output is high. For instance, if the demand curve for the output is steep to the left of Q^*, the loss of consumers' surplus is large when the reversion quantity is produced. This is the reason essential departments, like the Department of Defense, have more power to get their budget requests accepted and can expand in size relative to other departments.

The Inefficiency of the Government Bureaucracy

A bureaucracy's tendency to overexpand is not the only concern. As a supplier, the government is viewed as inefficient and rigid. Stories about government waste, or inaction due to ridiculous rules and regulations, are reported regularly in the news. Indeed, the very word "bureaucratic," which once implied "well organized," is now

---

[11]This generalization of Niskanen's argument was proposed by Thomas Romer and Howard Rosenthal (1979).

a pejorative term synonymous with the rulebound, impersonal, and unresponsive operation of many government departments and agencies. People have complained about the government bureaucracy for decades, and for just as long reformers have promised to "reinvent" government. Is government as inefficient as people think? If so, why? And what can be done about it?

We are concerned here with the cost inefficiency of bureaucracies, rather than the allocative inefficiency associated with producing too much of a public good. That is, do bureaucracies produce their outputs using excessive amounts of inputs and incur higher costs than they need to? Three factors can cause cost inefficiency in government supply.

First, because government does not maximize profit, bureau managers do not have an incentive to reduce the costs of production and operation. If bureau managers can provide the same level of output with fewer employees, they are not likely to do it. They cannot keep the money saved by being cost-efficient, and they end up with a smaller department and a smaller budget. In fact, under prevailing budget rules, departments lose budget money allotted to them if they do not spend it by the end of the fiscal period. For this reason, bureaucrats are encouraged to spend money left in their budgets, whether the expenditures are needed or not. A second reason for cost inefficiency is that the government is usually a monopoly producer of its outputs. As monopolists, bureaucrats do not have to worry about losing their "customers" (the people they serve) to other suppliers because their costs are too high. The customers have no other place to go. Third, because many government outputs are difficult to measure, bureau managers' performance is assessed on whether they have followed all the rules and correct procedures, not on whether they have delivered good value to the taxpayers.

Another fact about bureaucracies is that government employees often have "tenure" and cannot be removed from their jobs without cause. In this environment, bureaucrats are more likely to worry about errors of commission than omission. That is, they worry about being blamed for decisions that lead to bad outcomes, not for failing to make decisions that would have led to good outcomes. For this reason, bureau managers are willing to incur higher costs and impose rigid rules to ensure that nothing can go wrong, at least nothing that can be blamed on them. This is why bureaucracies have so much "red tape."

The rigid rules and red tape are not the fault of the bureaucrats alone. Some of the rules are imposed by the politicians to limit the bureaucrats' ability to exercise discretion in their decisions. Recall that bureaucrats can be considered the agents of politicians who, as principals, have given the bureaucrats a job to do for them. Because of imperfect information, the bureaucrats may make decisions that further their own interests rather than those of the politicians. To keep control, politicians install an elaborate system of accountability, which typically makes the bureaucracy very slow to respond to new circumstances.

If the bureaucracy is inefficient, what can be done about it? Some people believe that government is inefficient by nature, so the best thing is to limit its role in the economy as much as possible. Government should perform only those functions that cannot be carried out by private firms. The government might see to it that a certain good or service is provided—say, garbage collection—but should leave the actual production of the output to private firms.

Other people believe that government can be "reinvented" in an entrepreneurial mode that would make it more efficient. Suggested reforms include the following: (1) Force government agencies to compete with private firms to supply government outputs wherever possible. For instance, make city sanitation departments compete with private firms for city contracts to collect garbage. (2) Establish a clear purpose or mission for government departments and agencies and base their budgets on whether they achieve the desired results. (3) Allow government agencies to "earn a profit" by cutting their costs. This profit cannot be used to enrich the bureaucrats but can be saved and applied toward improving the department's service in the future. While many anecdotes describe remarkable improvements when these reforms have been tried, no systematic and comprehensive study of the effects of such reforms has yet been done.

CONCLUSION AND SUMMARY

Given the prevalent cynicism about government in the United States today, we hope that this chapter is not misinterpreted. We do not mean that government will always do things wrong. Rather, our purpose is to identify the incentives facing government decision makers and analyze how they behave under given institutional rules. In this regard, it should be remembered that people in government are likely to have the same self-interest as people in the private sector. To paraphrase Madison, a nation of angels does not need government and a government run by angels does not need rules and restrictions, but a nation and government made up of people do. It is not enough that government *may* improve economic efficiency when there is market failure. It is necessary that government decision makers have the information and the incentives to make the right decisions. A method for improving the government decision-making process is described in Chapter 6.

- The theory of public choice seeks to explain how public decisions about the allocation of resources are made through the political process. The main actors in the political process are voters, political action groups, politicians, and bureaucrats.

- Direct voting theories simplify the analysis by assuming that the public votes directly on government decisions rather than for representatives. Pocketbook voters vote according to the benefits they receive from a public expenditure relative to the tax price they face.

- The outcome of direct majority voting may be inconsistent, a result called the voting paradox. The voting paradox does not occur if voters have single-peaked preferences; in this case the equilibrium outcome of majority voting is the outcome preferred by the median voter. The median voter occupies the midpoint of voters' opinions, but the outcome may or may not be efficient.

- Majority voting is just one of many voting rules. Although majority voting is a low-cost voting rule, other voting rules may have the advantage of registering the intensity of voters' preferences or the voters' secondary preferences. Arrow's possibilities theorem shows that no voting rule can satisfy all desirable conditions.

"We can't come to an agreement about how to fix your car, Mr. Simons. Sometimes that's the way things happen in a democracy."

- ▓ With a unanimity voting rule, only Pareto improvements can be approved, because each voter has a veto. An efficient quantity of a public good would be approved by all voters if the government sets Lindahl prices equal to each voter's marginal willingness to pay for the good.

- ▓ To produce the efficient quantity of public goods, the government must know the voters' preferences. Under most voting rules, voters may conceal or lie about their preferences. Economists have devised preference revelation mechanisms that elicit truthful responses.

- ▓ Because of the costs of popular voting and because voters remain rationally ignorant, most government decisions are made by politicians who act as the voters' representatives. Politicians are assumed to maximize their chances of being elected to political office by competing for the votes of their constituents. One theory states that politicians maximize their chances for election by advocating centrist platforms.

- ▓ Groups of households and firms try to influence politicians through political action committees. This is especially true when the benefits of a program are focused on a narrow group and the costs are diffused over the whole population. Rent-seeking is behavior by a group that attempts to derive benefits at the expense of the taxpayers through political action.

- ▓ Bureaucrats further their self-interest by maximizing the size and budgets of their departments. Bureaucracies are likely to be cost-inefficient because they do not maximize profit and are sheltered from competition.

QUESTIONS FOR DISCUSSION AND REVIEW

1. What is the likely effect of each of the following on the number of acres of parks favored by a pocketbook voter?

   a. The voter enjoys picnics outdoors with his or her family.

   b. The voter thinks that, as a matter of principle, parks are good for a community.

   c. The parks are financed with a flat-rate tax on the value of homes, and the voter has an expensive home.

   d. Cheap land is readily available for purchase in the community.

2. Marilyn Vos Savant writes a column inviting readers to stump her by asking difficult questions. She was recently asked the following question. In the 1992 election, suppose a majority of the voters preferred Clinton to Bush, and a majority preferred Bush to Perot. Does this mean that a majority of voters prefered Clinton to Perot? Savant, who was not stumped, said it does not and gave an example. Can you do the same?

3. Suppose voters cast their votes for the presidential candidates in question 2 strictly on the basis of how liberal or conservative they were. All voters agreed that Clinton was the most liberal, Bush was the most conservative, and Perot was in the middle. Can the case described by Savant occur if all voters have single-peaked preferences over political philosophies?

4. The media and politicians are often criticized for using "sound bites" when presenting political opinions. Explain why "sound bites" are so common, using the concept of rational voter ignorance.

5. Recently Congress passed and the president signed a bill that gives the president a type of "line-item veto" over the budget. A line-item veto allows the president to approve the budget as a whole, while vetoing specific line items. Without the line-item veto, the president must accept or veto the whole budget. How will giving the president such power probably affect the ability to logroll on budget issues in Congress?

6. Sometimes opinion polls find that a number of government programs are opposed by a clear majority of the voters. Is this evidence of "government failure"? Why or why not?

7. Quotas on imports raise the price of sugar in the United States to nearly twice the world price. This increases the earnings of domestic sugar producers but also the cost of living of the consumers. Consumers outnumber sugar producers by more than 10,000 to 1. Why does this legislation get passed in a democratic political system?

8. Suppose a means of producing the same level of output using fewer employees is discovered by the United States Post Office (for first-class letters) and United Parcel Service (for parcels). Which enterprise is more likely to implement the discovery? Explain why.

9. Canada has two transcontinental railways. One is privately owned and the other government-owned, but the government-owned railway self-finances its operating costs. The two railways appear equally costefficient since both operate at about the same cost per ton-mile of freight. Is the fact that both have the same operating cost evidence that government firms are no less efficient than private firms are, generally?

Would you expect the government railway to operate as efficiently if it were the only transcontinental railway in the country?

10. *Internet Exercise.* Acquire data on voter turnout from Section 8 of the *Statistical Abstract of the United States, 1999*, which is found at http://www.census.gov/prod/www/statistical-abstract-us.html. From Figure 8.1, what percentage of eligible voters participated in elections for president and representatives in 1996? Does voter turnout for electing representatives depend on whether or not it is a presidential election year? Explain this pattern in terms of the benefits and costs of voting.

11. *Internet Exercise.* We learned in this chapter that the free-rider problem limits the incentive to form PACs, so many PACs represent groups that are organized for other (nonpolitical) purposes. Information on the number and types of PACs and how much they spend is available from the Federal Elections Commission at http://www.fec.gov/. Find the table that lists PACs grouped by total spent. From this table, what percentage of all PACs are either Corporate, Labor, or Trade/Member/Health? Is the free-rider problem as important for these PACs? Although there are 4599 PACs in 1997–1998, what fraction of these PACs accounted for about 85 percent of PAC spending?

SELECTED REFERENCES

A technical but comprehensive text book on public choice and voting is Dennis C. Mueller, *Public Choice II,* 1989. A nontechnical discussion of different voting rules is found in Jonathan Levin et al., "Symposium: The Economics of Voting," 1995. The idea that the majority voting rule minimizes the cost of voting is found in J. M. Buchanan and G. Tullock, *The Calculus of Consent,* 1962.

The general principle of the median voter equilibrium in voting is found in H. Hotelling,

"Stability in Competition," 1929, and A. Downs, *An Economic Theory of Democracy,* 1957. The theory of bureaucracy was introduced by William A. Niskanen, Jr., *Bureaucracy and Public Economics,* 1971.

A plan for improving incentives in government is presented in David Osborne and Ted Gaebler, *Reinventing Government,* 1993.

USEFUL INTERNET SITES

Professor George Hwang at George Mason University maintains a website called the Internet Center for study of Public Choice at http://www.iso.gmu.edu/~ghwang/pcnofram.htm#organizations. This site has links to journals and people interested in public choice and political economy. Also see

The Center for Voting and Democracy at http://www.fairvote.org/ for information on voting systems. In an interview, Nobel laureate James Buchanan traces the development of public choice theory at http://woodrow.mpls.trb.fed.us/pubs/region/int959.html.

6 Evaluating Programs Using Benefit-Cost Analysis

In many opinion polls, people express concern about how well the government functions, and more than a few express the belief that much of government spending is wasted. In Chapter 5 we considered theories that explain why government might make inefficient decisions. In this chapter we consider a methodology designed to help the government function more efficiently. To function efficiently, households and firms try to achieve their objectives at least cost and undertake ventures only when the benefits they receive are greater than the costs they pay. To do the same, the government must determine whether the costs of a government pro gram are as low as possible and whether the benefits are greater than the cost. However, the government has a much bigger job than an individual. Individuals need consider only the benefits and costs to themselves or their families, but the government must consider costs and benefits for everyone in the economy.

While the theory of market failure, covered in Chapter 2, implies that government can implement programs that increase economic efficiency, it says nothing about how big a program should be or how strict a regulation should be. Although the economy may be inefficient without intervention, the government can make things worse. At most, market failures provide *opportunities* for government to carry out programs that improve economic efficiency; to achieve economic efficiency, the government must make good policy decisions. To help the government make good policy decisions, various methods of evaluating government programs have been developed over the years.

In this chapter we study one of the most important and useful of these methods—benefit-cost analysis. **Benefit-cost analysis** is a systematic methodology for measuring the benefits and costs of government programs to the population as a whole. An important feature of benefit-cost analysis is the inclusion and valuation of nonmonetary benefits and costs that should be considered in government decisions even if they would be ignored in commercial decisions. Benefit-cost analysis is now used widely by national and subnational governments, as well as international agencies like the World Bank.[1]

---

[1]In March 1978, President Carter's Executive Order 12044 introduced an informal type of benefit-cost analysis for evaluating regulations. This was strengthened in February 1981 when President Reagan issued Executive Order 12291, making all new regulatory rules subject to a "regulatory impact analysis" that, among other things, requires the regulatory agencies to make "a determination of the potential net benefits of the rule, including an evaluation of benefits that cannot be quantified in monetary terms." Executive Order 12291 was superceded by Executive Order 12866 issued by President Clinton in 1993.

Although there are earlier precedents, benefit-cost analysis was first used in the decision-making process of the United States government in the 1930s. Large public works projects to develop the nation's water and land resources were proposed under President Roosevelt's "New Deal" program, and because these projects were very costly it was important to determine whether the benefits were large enough to justify the costs. Benefit-cost analysis was part of a collection of techniques used to evaluate government projects. In the 1950s, the federal government standardized its techniques for program evaluation in a document known as the "Green Book." The Green Book recommended that the benefits and costs of government programs be measured according to their impact on gross national product (GNP).

Subsequently, benefit-cost analysis was modified to include some nonmonetary benefits and costs that would not be measured in national product accounting. In the late 1950s and the 1960s, economists further developed and rationalized the method, leaving it roughly in the form it takes today. These refinements completed the earlier trend that shifted the emphasis of benefit-cost analysis away from measuring a program's impact on GNP and toward measuring its impact on social welfare. Social welfare is a more general measure of economic well-being than GNP, so modern benefit-cost analysis is best described as applied welfare economics.

SIX STEPS IN BENEFIT-COST ANALYSIS

The basic outline of benefit-cost analysis is relatively easy to describe in terms of six steps. In this overview we try to see the forest, not the trees. The terms introduced and the procedures described are explained in greater depth in the rest of the chapter.

Identify Objectives and Alternatives

The first step is to identify the objectives to be achieved by a program and the different ways in which the objectives could be achieved. Suppose a city wants to make it easier to commute between the central business district and the suburbs. The main objective is to reduce commuting time, although there may be other objectives, such as reducing air pollution and traffic congestion on city streets. There are several ways of achieving these objectives, including building a commuter rail system, expanding the bus system, and creating high-occupancy-vehicle (HOV, or car-pool) lanes on the expressway. Even if the benefit of a new commuter rail system is greater than its cost, it is not a good use of economic resources if an alternative (say, an expanded fleet of buses) can achieve the same objectives at less cost. In other words, a well-designed benefit-cost analysis should determine that the objectives are achieved at *least* cost, as well as whether they are worth achieving at all.

Identify Inputs and Outputs

Typically, a government program requires the economy to give up things of value, which we call program *inputs,* in order to make available other things of value, which we call program *outputs.* The inputs determine the program's cost, and the outputs determine its benefits. In benefit-cost analysis, we begin by measuring the program inputs and outputs in physical units, rather than monetary values. We will call the inputs and outputs in physical units the program *quantities.*

The advantage of starting with program quantities is that we are less likely to overlook outputs and inputs that give rise to nonmonetary benefits and costs. Also, "double counting" of benefits or costs is less likely, as are other errors. Double counting means measuring the same benefit or cost, in different guises, more than once. For example, suppose an irrigation project raises the crop yields on farms in a region, generating greater farm revenue. This would also increase the value of the farmland. An analyst who starts with monetary benefits might be tempted to count both the increased farm revenue and the increased value of the farmland. This is double counting because the project increases the value of farmland only because the land is capable of producing higher revenues from crops. By starting with the physical outputs of the project, the analyst identifies the increased crop yield as the cause of both monetary gains and counts the output only once.

Value the Inputs and Outputs at Their "Shadow Prices"

Of course, you cannot compare the benefits and costs of a program using physical quantities, because you cannot "add apples and oranges." It is necessary to convert the program quantities into units of common value. In benefit-cost analysis this is done by multiplying each physical quantity by its shadow price. The **shadow price** of an output or input is its value to the economy as a whole. The shadow price of a unit of output is consumers' marginal willingness to pay (MWTP) for it, and the shadow price of a unit of input is its marginal opportunity cost (MOC). The MOC is the input's value in its best alternative use outside of the government program.

Because of the effects of market externalities, shadow prices are not always equal to market prices, even when the goods and services to be valued are exchanged in markets. We can find the shadow prices of market outputs and inputs by adjusting their market prices for the value of the external benefits and costs. Nonmarket outputs and inputs are not exchanged in any market, so they do not have market prices at all. We must infer the shadow prices of nonmarket goods and services by other means.

Discount Benefits and Costs Occurring in the Future

Usually, the benefits and costs of a program occur over several years. In fact, sometimes the consequences of a program may last decades, or even centuries. Adding up benefits and costs occurring in different years is another case of "adding apples and oranges." A million-dollar benefit in the future is worth less than a million-dollar benefit occurring in the present.

To compare current benefits and costs with benefits and costs occurring in future years, we must discount them by multiplying their value in the year they occur by a discount factor. A **discount factor** is a number less than 1 and smaller the further in the future the benefit or cost occurs. The product of a future value and its discount factor is its **present value.** Once expressed in units of present value, the benefits and costs in different years can be added and subtracted.

Calculate Net Present Value

The purpose of benefit-cost analysis is to ensure that the government allocates resources wisely in the public sector. The critical step is to recommend to the policy decision makers whether a program should be accepted or rejected. A recommendation to implement is made if the sum of the discounted benefits, or present value of benefits, is larger than the sum of the discounted costs, or present value of costs. The present value of benefits minus the present value of costs is called the **net present value** (**NPV**) of the program. A program with a negative NPV should be rejected. A program with a positive NPV should be implemented, unless an alternative program is available that has a higher NPV. Ultimately, the resources of the economy are used best if the government chooses programs that maximize NPV.

Deal with Limited Information

Finally, benefit-cost analysis is typically conducted under conditions of informational uncertainty. We use **sensitivity analysis** to determine the effects of such uncertainty on the recommendation about whether to implement a program. This is done by calculating the NPV of the program under alternative assumptions about values of the uncertain variables.

MEASURING ECONOMIC BENEFITS AND COSTS

As we have just seen, the economic benefits and costs of a government program are determined by their physical quantities multiplied by their shadow prices. These must be measured for the whole economic jurisdiction, which depends on the level of government undertaking the program. For the federal government the economic jurisdiction is the whole nation, so benefits and costs to everyone in the country must be considered. Typically, a state or local government is interested only in the benefits and costs accruing to its own residents.

We now discuss four important issues that arise in measuring program benefits and costs for an economy: (1) treatment of transfers; (2) willingness to pay for program outputs; (3) the opportunity cost of program inputs; and (4) distribution of benefits and costs among the members of the community.

Treatment of Transfers

Transactions that simply transfer purchasing power among the members of the economy are not economic benefits and costs, because they do not augment or reduce the amount of goods and services available in the economy as a whole. Usually we ignore transfers altogether in benefit-cost analysis, although they may be considered separately if the distributional impact of the program is important (we discuss this later).

A good example is the treatment of taxes in benefit-cost analysis. Suppose a program increases the amount of revenue the government collects from an existing tax. Is this increase counted as a benefit of the program? For example, suppose a program that increases commercial logging in the national forests increases the fees paid by the logging companies to the government. Is this a benefit of permitting more logging activity?

Taxes and fees paid to the government are not economic benefits to the economy because they are transfers of purchasing power between the private sector and the government. While the government gains tax revenue, taxpayers have less to spend. In dollar terms, the two effects cancel out. The benefit of expanded logging is properly measured as the economic value of the increased timber harvest, and the impact on government revenue is ignored.

Measuring Economic Benefits Using Willingness to Pay

The economic benefit of a program is equal to program outputs valued at their shadow prices. The shadow price of an output is the marginal willingness to pay (MWTP) for it by the people who enjoy it. The MWTP is the amount of income (i.e., the value of other goods) the consumer is willing to give up in order to consume one extra unit of the program output.

To measure consumers' MWTP, two problems must be solved. The first is to find a way in which the MWTP is revealed by the consumers. This problem is discussed later. The second problem is to determine the value of a benefit when the consumers' MWTP varies with the amount consumed. To solve this problem, consumers' surplus is used. **Consumers' surplus** is the excess of the consumers' total willingness to pay for a given quantity of output over the amount that they actually do pay.

The first known use of consumers' surplus for measuring the benefits of public works was in 1844, by the French engineer Jules Dupuit, who explained how to find the "utility" (the benefits) of a bridge that is crossed without tolls. He did this by determining the number of trips over the bridge people make and summing the amounts that the individual users are willing to pay for a trip.

This is shown by the downward-sloping MWTP schedule (or demand schedule) in Figure 6.1. If no toll is charged, people cross the bridge whenever their MWTP is positive, so they make Q_0 trips. Consumers' surplus is equal to the area $0CQ_0$ under the MWTP curve, where $0C$ is the most anyone will pay to cross the bridge and Q_0 is the number of crossings when the toll is zero. This is the economic benefit of the bridge per interval of time, even if no toll revenue is collected. If a toll is charged, the benefit of the bridge is the toll revenue plus the consumers' surplus. For example, if a toll T is charged for each crossing, the number of crossings is Q_1. The benefit of the bridge when a toll is charged is equal to the toll revenue T times Q_1 plus the consumers' surplus, which is equal to the triangular area under the MWTP curve above T.

Consumers' surplus is also used to measure the economic cost or benefit when a government program increases or decreases the price of a good to the consumers. For instance, to improve air quality, the federal Clean Air Act required that reformulated gasoline be sold in certain parts of the country after December 1994. Reformulated gasoline costs about 5 cents more per gallon than ordinary gasoline. The economic cost of this regulation on the consumers of gasoline is measured by the loss in consumers' surplus, shown in Figure 6.2. The price of ordinary gasoline

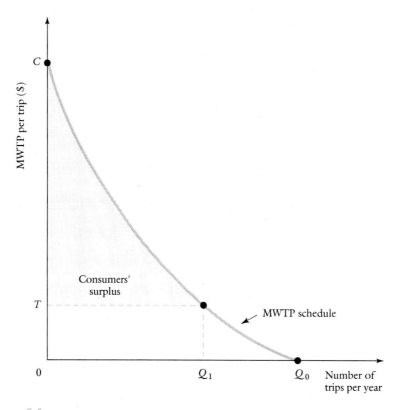

Figure 6.1

Figure 6.1

Consumers' Surplus from Crossing a Bridge

The MWTP schedule for consumers crossing the bridge determines the annual benefit of the bridge. The height of the schedule determines the value of a crossing at each number of crossings. If no toll is charged, consumers make Q_0 trips each year and the annual benefit of the bridge is the area under the schedule. If toll T is charged, consumers make Q_1 trips each year and the benefit of the bridge is the area under the MWTP schedule above T plus the toll revenue T times Q_1.

is P_0, and Q_0 gallons are consumed. Reformulating raises the price to P_1, and consumption drops to Q_1 gallons. The lost consumers' surplus is equal to the area of the trapezoid P_1BAP_0.

Measuring Economic Cost Using Marginal Opportunity Cost

The shadow prices of program inputs are determined by their marginal opportunity costs. An input's opportunity cost is its value in uses outside the government program. For example, the opportunity cost of workers hired to build a bridge is the amount they would have earned (and produced) working elsewhere had the bridge not been built. Perhaps the workers are paid more than this on the govern-

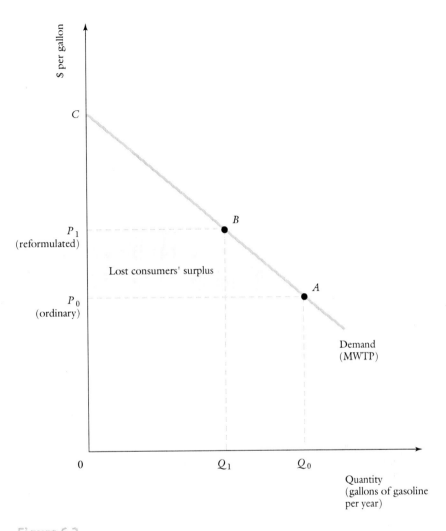

Figure 6.2

Economic Cost of Reformulated Gasoline

The cost of a regulation requiring reformulated gasoline is the loss in consumers' surplus from the higher price of gasoline. Reformulating raises the price of gasoline from P_0 to P_1. The lost consumers' surplus is equal to the shaded quadrilateral P_1BAP_0.

ment project, but the lower amount is their opportunity cost nonetheless. The excess payment is a transfer from the taxpayers to the workers.[2]

In Chapter 2, we saw that the marginal opportunity cost of a good produced by private firms is the supply price of the firms (the height of the supply curve). Typically, the supply curve of a good—say, cement—slopes upward. As more cement

---

[2]The Davis-Bacon Act requires that workers on federally funded construction projects earn the local union wage. However, the opportunity cost of these workers may be much less than this.

is used in a government project (say, building a dam), the price of cement rises and so does its MOC.

In Figure 6.3, the upward-sloping supply curve of cement is labeled MOC. To simplify, assume that no cement would be produced without the dam, and that the construction of the dam requires Q_0 units of cement over the construction period. The monetary cost of the cement to the government is P_0 times Q_0, which is the area of the rectangle $0P_0BQ_0$ in Figure 6.3. However, the economic cost of the cement is less than the monetary cost. The economic cost is the area under the MOC curve, or $0ABQ_0$. The area AP_0B, though it is part of the monetary cost to the government, is not part of the economic cost but increased producers' surplus. **Producers' surplus** is the economic (supernormal) profit received by the producers. The monetary cost is equal to the economic cost if the MOC schedule is horizontal.

Weighing Benefits and Costs to Different People

We have stressed that in benefit-cost analysis, it is necessary to consider benefits and costs accruing to everyone in the economy. The government cannot consider just the effect of the program on its own revenue and outlays but must measure the impact of the program on all persons in the economy. This raises another "apples and oranges" question—How do we add up benefits and costs accruing to different people?

There are two alternative approaches. The first is to "treat a dollar as a dollar" and add up benefits and costs regardless of who receives or incurs them. The justification of this practice lies in the **compensation principle** enunciated by the British economists John Hicks and Nicholas Kaldor. An alternative—less common in practice—is to weight the benefits and costs accruing to different people using a system of **distributional weights.** We will compare the two methods.

THE COMPENSATION PRINCIPLE: A DOLLAR IS A DOLLAR. Suppose a government program benefits person A by $100 but costs person B $50. Using the compensation principle, we subtract the cost from the benefit to get a net benefit of $50, even though different people are affected. With the program, it is argued, A can make a side payment of $50 to B that covers B's loss and leaves a net gain to A of $50, which is an increase in economic efficiency.

There are some problems with the compensation principle. For one, what if the side payment isn't made? Some economists argue that this does not matter for efficiency—only the potential for compensation matters, and whether compensation is made is a separate distributional question. In other words, benefit-cost analysis is used to determine whether the "cake" is bigger, not how it should be shared. Others argue that such a separation of efficiency and equity is not legitimate. If compensation does not occur and someone is made worse off by a government program, we have no basis for deciding whether a program is desirable by summing benefits and costs to different people.

A second problem is that compensation, if it does occur, may be costly to implement. Redistribution of the type needed by the compensation principle is done through government tax and transfer policy. In a second-best economy, tax-transfer policies are like carrying water in a leaky bucket. Something is lost in the process

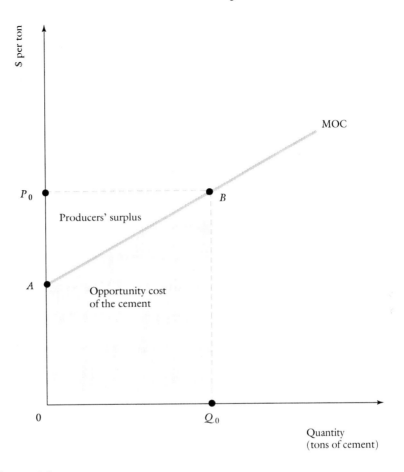

Figure 6.3
Cost of a Program Input
If a project uses Q_0 units of a good as an input, the economic cost is the area under the MOC curve. Although the government pays P_0 times Q_0 for the input purchased, the area of the triangle P_0BA is an increase in producers' surplus, or economic profit, and not a cost to the economy.

because such policies are costly to administer and create disincentives to work. Therefore it is necessary to tax the gainers more than \$1 to compensate the losers by \$1. We cannot conclude that the gainers can compensate the losers by subtracting the loss to one person from the gain to another because the costs of implementing the compensation scheme must be counted as well. For a program to be efficient, the benefits must be large enough to outweigh the economic costs plus the implementation costs of compensating the losers.

THE USE OF DISTRIBUTIONAL WEIGHTS.   The *distributional weights* approach treats the distribution of gains and losses resulting from the program as given and ignores the possibility of compensation. The value of the economic benefits and costs is measured as a *weighted* sum of the benefits and costs to different people.

6.1   The Benefits to the Urban Water Supply from the Central Arizona Project

The Central Arizona Project (CAP) is a huge aqueduct and dam authorized by Congress in 1968. One of the project "outputs" is water supplied to residents of rapidly growing cities, like Tucson, which are dependent on groundwater. By the year 2010 and for 100 years thereafter, CAP will supply over 100,000 acre feet of water per year to Tucson.

Professor R. Bruce Billings of the University of Arizona, Tucson measures the benefit of CAP water using an estimated household water demand function as the MWTP schedule. The impact on the water consumption of a representative Tucson household in the year 2010 is shown in the accompanying figure. Without CAP, water is scarce, and a typical household consumes 3.9 ccf of water per month (1 ccf = 100 cubic feet). Its MWTP for an

extra ccf is $16.87. With CAP, water is plentiful and the household consumes 12.9 ccf per month, with an MWTP of $2.06 for 1 extra ccf.

What is the benefit of the extra 9 ccf of water per month consumed by this Tucson household? Valuing it at $2.06 (to get $18.54 per month, the area of rectangle *AEFG*) will understate the benefit of the water. On the other hand, valuing it at $16.87 per ccf would greatly overstate the benefit. The correct reasoning is as follows. The drop in the price of water resulting from CAP increases the household's consumer surplus by the area *ABCD*. The rectangle *BCDE* is just a transfer from the water utility to the consumer. The net increase in consumers' surplus to the household is the area of the curvy "triangle" *BAE*, which is approximately

Value of CAP Water to a Typical Tucson Household

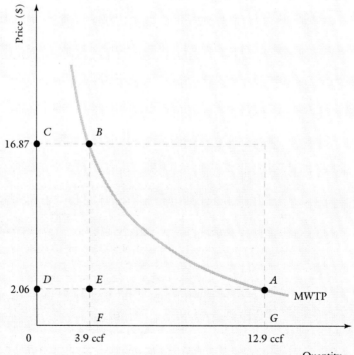

(continued)

A Case in Point (continued)

$33 per month. This, plus the $18.54 the household spends on the water, gives the total monthly benefit of $51.54. Summing over households and months yields the annual benefit occurring in the year 2010.

Critically analyze the following:

- The value of the extra water depends on the shape of the demand curve. In this example, Billings assumed the demand curve for water is of a constant elasticity form. Alternatively, we could assume that the demand curve is linear and has a constant slope. Would this increase or decrease the estimated value of the extra water?

- Environmentalists point out that water conservation can be considered an extra supply of water. Suppose the cost of conserving water (water-saving toilets and showers, etc.) is reduced. How would this affect the demand curve for CAP water? How would this change the estimated value of CAP water?

- Water is a normal good, so presumably people will demand more water if their incomes rise. How would a rise in household income affect the estimated value of CAP water?

R. Bruce Billings, "Demand-Based Benefit-Cost Model of Participation in a Water Project," 1990.

These distributional weights take into account the economic circumstances of the people affected. Benefits and costs affecting poor people typically receive a weight greater than 1 and those affecting well-off people receive a weight smaller than 1. This reflects the idea that a dollar of income to a poor person is more socially valuable than a dollar of income to a rich person.

To the extent that distributional weights are used in benefit-cost analysis, they are usually applied at an additional, separate stage of the analysis. Benefits and costs are first summed without weights to find the *economic value* of the program. Then the benefits and costs to different people are weighted by their distributional weights and summed to find the *social value* of the program. The social value of the program includes its impact on the distribution of economic well-being.

The use of distributional weights is somewhat controversial. Some economists believe they introduce inconsistency into benefit-cost analysis and create a potential for misuse because there are no agreed-upon weights. Another criticism is that the use of distributional weights would lead to inefficient, wasteful public works programs implemented for distributional reasons that can be achieved at lower cost with tax and transfer policies. For instance, it seems silly to build a large hydroelectric dam simply because it might benefit low-wage workers. It is more efficient to help the workers with government transfers.

DETERMINING THE SHADOW PRICES USED IN BENEFIT-COST ANALYSIS

Determining shadow prices is perhaps the most important part of benefit-cost analysis, and a variety of methods are used, depending on the type of good or service that must be valued. For goods exchanged in markets, market prices are used with adjustments for market distortions like externalities and taxes. Many government programs involve **nonmarket goods and services** (also called *intangibles*) that are not exchanged in markets. Special methods must be used to find their shadow prices.

Shadow Prices of Goods and Services Exchanged in Markets

We begin with an economy where all goods and services are traded in *well-functioning* markets. The first theorem of welfare economics (see Chapter 2) implies that the shadow price of a good is equal to the market price in a well-functioning market because the market price is equal to both the MWTP of the consumers and the MOC of the producers. Since there are no externalities, the private benefits and costs to the consumers and firms are equal to the benefits and costs for the whole economy. Furthermore, if markets are functioning well, there are no missing markets, so there are no nonmarket goods.

The equality between shadow prices and market prices in well-functioning markets can help us better understand the role of benefit-cost analysis in government decision making. In market decisions, private benefit-cost analysis is carried out by the individual or firm, which pursues its own self-interest. In a well-functioning market, this private benefit-cost analysis is equivalent to a benefit-cost analysis for the whole economy because there are no externalities. That is why an efficient allocation of resources is achieved without centralized decision making. But with market failure, the market prices of goods and services are not equal to their respective shadow prices, so the private benefit-cost analysis leads to an efficient allocation of resources. Market failures cause inefficiency and provide a potential for government programs to benefit the economy. Governmental benefit-cost analysis, using shadow prices rather than market prices, determines whether a program increases economic efficiency and should be implemented.

Since there is no need for governmental benefit-cost analysis if all markets are well-functioning, the need to find shadow prices when markets are distorted or missing is central to such analysis.

ADJUSTING FOR MARKET DISTORTIONS.   When markets are distorted or imperfect, finding a shadow price involves more than checking market prices. For example, what is the shadow price of gasoline if the refineries that produce it create pollution? What is the shadow price of unionized labor or labor that would have been unemployed had it not been employed in the program?

Where there is an external cost to producing a good, as in the case of gasoline, it should be added to the firm's marginal cost to obtain the shadow price. The firm's marginal cost plus the external cost per unit is the total MOC of the good to the economy.[3] Similarly, external benefits in consumption are added to market price in order to get its shadow price. A good's market price reflects only the MWTP of the person consuming it, and if the consumption of the good benefits others in the economy, their MWTP must be considered as well. In the case of a nonrival good, the MWTP of all consumers must be summed to find the good's shadow price.

Adjustments are made for noncompetitive behavior of private firms as well. If the market price of a good (say, a supercomputer) purchased by the government

---

[3]If a corrective tax policy is pursued by the government, the tax-inclusive price of the good in the market can be used as the shadow price. Ideally, with such a policy the tax is set equal to the external cost per unit, so the tax-inclusive price measures the MOC of the good to the economy.

includes a monopoly markup, the markup should be estimated and subtracted from the market price to find the shadow price. Alternatively, the firm's marginal cost of the good can be estimated directly. The monopoly markup is not part of the MOC of the good, because it is a transfer from the government to the owners of the firm. Although the monopoly markup is part of the monetary cost to the government, it is not part of the shadow price of the good.

THE SHADOW WAGE.   The wage paid by a profit-maximizing firm is equal to the value of the goods produced by a unit of labor. Of course, labor is not homogeneous, so the wage depends on the level of skills required for the job. In a well-functioning labor market, the wage is also the value of the worker's time in alternative uses, including leisure. If a government program draws labor from a well-functioning labor market, the shadow wage is the market wage. Adjustments must be made for distortions in labor markets, such as income taxes, but these adjustments are similar to those made for taxes in other markets.

A special problem in finding the shadow wage is the existence of unemployed labor. A certain level of unemployment is considered normal in a labor market, because of labor turnover and other "friction." Although the exact rate is uncertain, the "natural" unemployment rate lies between 4 and 6%. At some times, and in some places, the level of unemployment is so high that the labor market must be considered to be in disequilibrium, because not everyone who wants to work at the market wage can do so. These workers are involuntarily unemployed.

The shadow wage for labor drawn from a labor market with widespread involuntary unemployment may be quite low compared with wage rates paid to employed workers. The most the economy gives up by employing unemployed workers in a government program is the value of their leisure time. This is less than the market wage—that is why they are involuntarily unemployed.

Sometimes a shadow wage equal to zero is used for labor by previously unemployed workers. This is probably too low, because even unemployed workers value their leisure time in various uses. For example, unemployed workers may look after their children or maintain their homes. An even more serious error than using a shadow wage of zero is to count wages paid to previously unemployed workers as a program benefit, rather than a cost. Labor used in the government program is displaced from alternative uses, so it is a cost and not a benefit even if the alternative use is unwanted leisure. Although the individual workers may be happy to get work because they are involuntarily unemployed, providing jobs is *not* a benefit for the economy. To treat it as such is equivalent to assuming that people will pay to work. Since politicians routinely get elected by promising "jobs, jobs, jobs," it is easy to see how this error is made.

Shadow Prices of Intangibles

The biggest challenge in benefit-cost analysis is to determine the shadow prices of nonmarket goods (sometimes called intangibles), such as changes in environmental quality, the recreational use of natural areas, and improvements in public safety. There are three common methods—the hedonic method, the travel-cost method, and the contingent valuation method.

THE HEDONIC METHOD.   The **hedonic method** looks for indirect ways that people might reveal their MWTP for a nonmarket good. For a market good, people reveal their MWTP by their decision to buy it at the market price. How do people reveal their MWTP for a nonmarket good? One way occurs when a nonmarket good is consumed in conjunction with a market good for which a price can be observed.

A good example is the **property-value method** for obtaining the shadow price of environmental quality in a residential area. The hedonic method assumes that the price of a market good is the value placed on the "bundle" of desirable characteristics provided by a unit of the good. For example, the value of a house is determined by its structural characteristics, such as living area, lot size, number of rooms; its accessibility characteristics, such as the distance to downtown and the proximity of commuting facilities; and its neighborhood characteristics, such as the crime rate and the quality of local schools.

Important neighborhood characteristics include local air quality and the absence of noise from planes and automobile traffic. Even within a city, air quality can vary dramatically from neighborhood to neighborhood. And, as everyone knows, neighborhoods near airports and expressways are much noisier. The property-value method isolates the impact of environmental-quality variables by comparing property values in different neighborhoods and controlling for the effect of all other characteristics on price. In doing so, it attributes differences in the willingnesses to pay for properties in different neighborhoods to differences in environmental quality.

To find the impact of a local environmental variable on the price of a house, we must control for the other characteristics that affect its value. Typically, this is done by econometric methods. A house price equation is estimated using multivariate regression techniques on observations of the variables expected to determine property value. The dependent variable is property value. The estimated coefficient for the environmental variable in the regression equation is the MWTP for environmental quality.

THE TRAVEL-COST METHOD.   The **travel-cost method** is a technique for estimating the value of intangible recreational benefits. It was first suggested by the famous economist Harold Hotelling in a letter to the National Park Service in 1947. The main idea is that the "price" paid to use a natural area, such as a state or national park, has an explicit component equal to the park fee (if any), and an implicit component equal to the travel cost incurred by the visitor getting to and from the park. Hotelling recognized that the travel-cost component varies from user to user because people come to the park from different geographic locations. Assuming that people respond to differences in the travel cost the same way they respond to changes in the park fee, it is possible to construct a marginal willingness-to-pay schedule for the recreational services provided by the park and estimate the consumers' surplus resulting from the recreational use of the park.

To illustrate, suppose that people visit a park from two cities N and F, each with a population of 1 million. City N is nearby, and the travel cost is $10 per visit; F is farther away, and the travel cost is $20. Travel cost includes the cost of the visitor's time in getting to and from the park, as well as out-of-pocket expenses such as fares or gasoline. To simplify, suppose that the park does not charge an entrance fee.

Suppose a survey reveals that 80,000 visits to the park are made by people from city N (8% of its population) and 40,000 visits are made by people from city F (4%

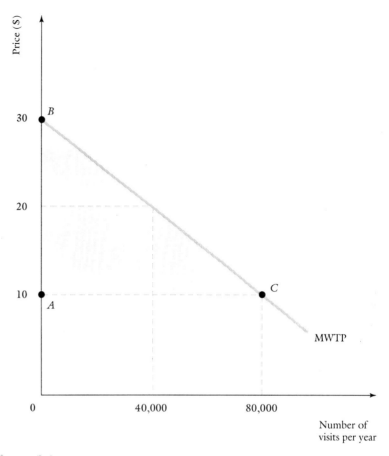

Figure 6.4

Using the Travel-Cost Method to Value a Recreation Area

People from nearby region N pay a travel cost of $10 per visit to use a recreational area and make 80,000 visits. People from farther-away region F, with a travel cost of $20, make half as many visits as a fraction of population. Controlling for other factors, we conclude that only 40,000 visits would be made by people from the first region if a $10 entry fee were charged, making the total price $20. From information about travel cost, we can construct the entire MWTP curve for region N and find the benefit of the recreation area to region N as the shaded area under the constructed curve.

of its population), for a total of 120,000 visits per year. If we control statistically for differences in family income and other economic variables that might influence a person's decision to visit the park, we can attribute the difference in the rates to the different travel costs faced by visitors from the two cities.

We construct the MWTP schedule for visitors from city N (shown in Figure 6.4) in the following way. At a travel cost of $10 there are 80,000 visits from city N. How many visits would there have been if the park had set a fee of $10? If we assume that people living in N respond to a hypothetical extra $10 fee in the same way that the people living in F respond to the actual extra $10 in travel cost, we conclude that only 40,000 visits (4% of the population) are made from N when the park fee is $10. Continuing in this way, we can construct the MWTP schedule for residents of city N. The consumers' surplus they get from visiting the park is the area of the triangle *ABC*, which is $800,000 per year. Similarly, we can estimate the consumers' surplus of visitors from city F as $400,000 per year, giving a total recreational value of the park of $1.2 million per year.

THE CONTINGENT VALUATION METHOD.   In 1947, the same year that Hotelling wrote his letter to the National Park Service, an economist named S. V. Ciriacy-Wantrup suggested a new method for measuring the benefits of preventing soil erosion. This method, now called the **contingent valuation method (CVM)**, determines the population's willingness to pay for a nonmarket good by asking people for their valuation in a highly structured survey. The survey must give the respondents a clear picture of the good in question and then ask, in various ways, how much each respondent is *willing to pay* (WTP) to receive, or is *willing to accept* (WTA) to give up, a unit of the nonmarket good. The exact circumstances under which the good is to be consumed are carefully specified—hence the term *contingent* valuation.

The CVM is considered controversial by economists for at least two reasons. First, many economists are dubious about survey methods, arguing that "hypothetical questions receive hypothetical answers." Second, even if people make an honest attempt to determine and express their values, many subtle and some not-so-subtle biases affect their answers and make those answers unreliable.

One source of bias in a survey, known as *sampling bias*, is a result of the way the respondents are sampled. Actually, concern about sampling bias is not great, because it can be virtually eliminated by choosing a large enough random sample. More worrisome is *response bias*, where a sample fails to be random because only certain people choose to respond to the survey. For example, people who are very concerned about the environment may be more likely than others to respond to a survey that tries to measure the value of environmental variables.

Also worrisome is *strategic bias*, which occurs when survey respondents believe that they can affect a decision with their answer. If respondents believe that they can affect the decision in a way that favors them, such as how much they have to pay or how much they receive in compensation, the value they report is not reliable. They may deliberately understate or overstate the value in order to influence the expected payment. There are many other potential sources of response bias in the CVM.

Economists who use the CVM are aware of these biases and attempt to minimize them. The question is whether they have been successful. One reason for doubt is the fact that reported WTPs for a good are typically much less than reported WTAs. For example, Richard Bishop and Thomas Heberlein of the University of Wisconsin asked a sample of hunters how much they would pay for a hunting permit they didn't have (their WTP), and how much they would need to be paid to give up a permit they did have (their WTA). The mean WTA for a permit was nearly $1200, whereas the mean WTP was less than $50. People's expressed valuations seem to depend on the prior distribution of property rights.

A second reason for doubt is known as the "embedding effect." This term describes the possibility that people "embed" a larger and more general question in the specific question that is asked by the survey. Evidence of embedding includes the fact that people often express almost the same WTP to clean and improve the quality of many rivers as they do to clean and improve a single river. This seems implausible. It suggests that once one river is cleaned up, their WTP to clean up another is zero. The interpretation of this phenomenon is that people, when asked for their WTP for cleaning up a single river, embed in that question the larger question of how they value clean rivers in general.

One of the more controversial uses of the CVM is to elicit a special value for a resource, known as its **existence value.** The existence value of a resource is the value of its mere existence and does not depend on whether the respondent uses the resource. The CVM makes it possible to ask people how much they value something they have never used and perhaps never will use. In contrast, the travel-cost method measures the value of a park to people who visit and use it for recreation, and the property-value method measures the value of environmental quality to people who want to occupy the property.

For example, in surveys people often express high values for environmental quality in places that few will ever visit, such as remote parts of Alaska or Antarctica. Furthermore, because the existence of something is a nonrival good (see Chapter 3), the MWTP for its existence by the whole population can be very large. Economists who are skeptical about the CVM believe that the values expressed are unreasonably high and demonstrate the unreliability of the method. Economists who use the method believe that, in many cases, the CVM is the only way of valuing nonmarket goods and that, with care, its faults can be eliminated or minimized.

An Application of Valuing Nonmarket Goods: The Value of a Life

In 1987, 18-month-old "baby Jessica" McLure fell into an abandoned water well in Midland, Texas. For days, hundreds of men and women, and lots of heavy equipment, labored to rescue her while millions anxiously watched their progress on TV. No one thought to ask about the cost of rescuing baby Jessica, nor should anyone have asked. When the life of a baby trapped 22 feet underground is at stake, price is no object.

The attitude that life is priceless, while admirable when saving the life of a particular person, is a luxury we cannot afford in the broader realm of public policy. One estimate places the cost of "saving a life" by removing asbestos from the innards of public buildings at $100 million. But each year, more than 40,000 lives are lost on the nation's highways and roads. If we really valued every life at $100 million, we would spend over half our gross domestic product making our roads and cars safer.

Since human lives saved (and lost) are an important part of many government programs, it is often necessary to place a value on human life in benefit-cost analysis. But what is the shadow price of human life? Most of us would spend anything to save our own lives. Is there any meaningful answer to this question?

Fortunately, in benefit-cost analysis we never need to value the certain loss of a particular life. However, we often must place a value on risk to life. In constructing a dam, some workers may die in accidents. Although we may know that one worker in a thousand will die, no individual faces certain death. Similarly, government regulation of hazardous materials, foods and drugs, and the safety of the workplace changes the risk of dying and does not cause or prevent the certain death of a particular person.

Two methods are commonly used to place a value on a life. The first method, used in wrongful-death lawsuits, values a life as the value of the lost earnings of the deceased. According to this method, the value of an old teacher's life would be far less than the value of a young plastic surgeon's life because the latter would have earned much more over his or her remaining life. The second method, preferred by benefit-cost analysts, uses the value that people place on a reduction in their risk of dying. Arguably, this is a better measure of the value of a life than the amount an employer is willing to pay people for their services.

The second method places a value on a unit known as a **statistical life**. A statistical life is not the life of an identifiable person but an anonymous life saved or lost among a population. For example, suppose 100 thousand drivers face an annual mortality risk of .02% on a dangerous stretch of road. This means that we can expect 20 of them to die (the loss of 20 statistical lives) in traffic accidents over the year. If a government road-safety project (say, installing traffic dividers) reduces the mortality risk to .015%, 5 statistical lives are saved as a result. If we know the value of a statistical life (VSL), we can place a value on the benefit of lives saved by the project.

We can use either the hedonic or contingent valuation method to find the VSL. The hedonic method uses the values people reveal in their everyday activities such as buying safer automobiles or choosing between more risky and less risky occupations. Cars with more safety equipment cost more than cars with less, and riskier occupations pay more than safe ones. We can use the differences in the amount people are willing to pay to reduce mortality risk to calculate the VSL.

Most hedonic estimates of the VSL are based on observed wage differentials among occupations that have different mortality risks. To illustrate, suppose we observe the wages of 10,000 firefighters and 10,000 bus drivers. After adjusting for differences in wages that reflect the skills needed for the job, suppose firefighters earn $31,000 and bus drivers earn $30,000 a year. The annual wage cost is $310 million for the firefighters and $300 million for the bus drivers. If we assume the $10 million differential reflects compensation for the higher mortality risk faced by firefighters, we can calculate the VSL using the mortality rates for the occupations. Suppose four of the 10,000 firefighters die each year doing their jobs as compared with only two bus drivers. This means there are two more statistical lives lost in the firefighter occupation. Since this requires an extra $10 million in wage compensation for the same size group, we can determine the VSL at $5 million.

We face several difficulties in calculating the VSL this way. For one, we must try to control for all factors that determine employee compensation (skills, experience, etc.) other than mortality risk. Also, we must assume that people in different occupations have the same attitude toward risk. If the risky occupation attracts people who are thrill-seekers, the differential we observe will not be an accurate measure of the VSL for the population as a whole. For example, as a group, test pilots are likely to be less risk averse than are university professors. Therefore, the difference in their wages, even after adjusting for skill, is not likely to measure accurately the compensation the average person needs to assume the higher mortality risk of flying experimental aircraft.

The alternative contingent valuation method (CVM) avoids these problems by directly asking a random sample of people for the annual payment they would be willing to pay (WTP) or willing to accept (WTA) for a specified decrease or increase, respectively, in their mortality risk. The general problems associated with the CVM were discussed earlier. In its application to the VSL, the CVM has an additional problem in that respondents may have difficulty understanding the question asked. People may have difficulty interpreting and answering questions about changes in mortality risk, particularly if such changes are conditional or occur at some time in the future. Numerous studies have attempted to calculate the VSL using both hedonic and contingent valuation methods. These studies show a wide range of estimates from 750,000 to 13 million 1998 dollars, although the value does not seem to depend on whether the hedonic method or CVM is used. The Environmental Protection Agency (EPA) compared studies, 5 of which use the CVM and the rest the hedonic wage method, and found that the mean VSL in the studies was $6 million (1998). While a precise value is elusive, such an average is useful for many benefit-cost purposes (see A Case in Point, 6.2).

DECISION CRITERIA USED IN BENEFIT-COST ANALYSIS

The ultimate purpose of benefit-cost analysis is to recommend a decision to government policy makers. This requires a criterion or standard to determine whether a program should be implemented. The general principle, as the term *benefit-cost analysis* suggests, is that a program is desirable if its economy-wide benefits outweigh its economy-wide costs, and it should be implemented if no alternative programs have greater benefits relative to costs.

Many programs have costs and benefits that occur in different years. Public works projects, for example, are public investments that usually require large outlays in the present with the benefits spread out over the life of the project. The project's life may extend decades into the future. To evaluate whether benefits are greater or less than costs over the life of a program, benefit-cost analysts use net present value (NPV) as a criterion. To understand this criterion and its alternatives, we must understand the process of discounting and the meaning of present value.

Discounting and Present Value

Suppose someone offers you a choice between $1000 now or $1100 (with certainty) next year. If the sums were the same, the choice would be easy, but is it worth waiting a year for a larger amount? A good way to decide is to use the concept of present value. The present value of a future sum is a present sum that is equivalent to the future sum.

Assume that you have money in the bank, or can easily borrow, and the interest rate in either case is 5%.[4] How much money can you take from your account

---

[4]Of course, the interest rate at which you can borrow is greater than the rate the bank pays on your savings account, but let's ignore this complication.

6.2   Benefits and Costs of Testing Donated Blood for HIV

In the mid-1980s, when the dimensions of the AIDS epidemic were first recognized, a national debate ensued about the merits of testing the nation's donated blood supply for HIV, the virus that causes AIDS. Some people argued that the costs of testing the blood supply were too high to justify the program.

By analyzing data drawn from Red Cross samples, Professor Gregory Gelles of the University of Missouri estimated the cost of saving a statistical life by testing the nation's donated blood supply for HIV. In the data, two types of tests were used. First, the enzyme-linked immunoassay (EIA) test was applied. About one-third of 1 percent of donated blood tested positive (was potentially infected). Further EIA tests and a Western blot (WB) test were applied to these reactive samples to determine, with high sensitivity and specificity, the fraction of donated blood infected with HIV. Gelles estimated that testing the entire blood supply in this way detects about 1375 units of infected blood, and each unit could infect 1.54 patients. Given that some of the infected blood would not be used for transfusions (it was donated for testing only), that not all patients receiving an infected transfusion would develop the virus, and that some patients would die before developing it, Gelles estimated that testing the nation's blood supply prevents as many as 1500 HIV infections per year from transfusions of infected blood. This translates into about 600 AIDS cases per year.

On the other hand, testing is not cheap. The biggest cost is the primary EIA test that must be applied to more than 12 million units of blood per year. The cost of this test varies, but at most it is about $13 per unit of blood. All told, testing the nation's blood supply has an annual economic cost no higher than $158 million per year. This equals about $322,000 per prevented case of AIDS. Assuming that everyone who contracts AIDS dies prematurely, this is well below most estimates of the value of a statistical life, suggesting that the benefits of testing blood for HIV outweigh the costs.

Critically analyze the following:

- Since HIV is infectious, the 1500 people who could be infected each year through an untested blood supply could infect others. How would this fact alter the estimated benefit of testing the nation's blood supply?

- Thanks to AIDS awareness programs, the percentage of people infected with HIV has been dropping in recent years. How does this affect the estimated benefit of testing the nation's blood supply?

- Suppose a contingent valuation survey asked a random sample of the nation's 120 million families how much they are willing to pay a year to avoid the risk of a family member being infected by HIV through the blood supply. What is the reported average WTP per family that is needed to conclude that the benefits of testing the nation's blood supply outweigh the costs? Would you be willing to pay this amount to protect you and your family members from HIV-contaminated blood?

Gregory M. Gelles, "Costs and Benefits of HIV-1 Antibody Testing of Donated Blood," 1993.

now (or borrow) and repay the principal plus interest with the $1100 you will receive next year? The answer is $1100 divided by 1.05, or $1047.62, which is the present value of $1100 coming one year hence.[5] This exceeds the $1000 received today, so in the choice between $1000 today and $1100 next year it is best to receive $1100 next year.

The procedure just described is called **discounting.** To discount a future sum, we multiply it by a discount factor, which converts it into a present value that can be compared with sums received or paid in the present. The discount factor for money received in one year is 1 divided by 1 plus the discount rate. The discount rate is the monetary rate of interest (5% or 0.05 in this example). The discount factor, $(1.05)^{-1} = 0.952$, is the price of $1 next year in terms of money this year when the market interest rate is 5%. If the interest rate is higher, the price (present value) of future money is lower because more interest is forgone by waiting a year to receive the money.

What if someone offers you $1000 now or $1100 in two years? The discount factor for money received in two years must take into account the longer waiting period and the fact that interest gets compounded. Assuming that interest is compounded annually and is 5% in both years, the two-year discount factor is

$\left(\dfrac{1}{1.05}\right)^2 = 0.907.$ The present value of $1100 received in two years is 0.907

times$1100 or $997.73. Since this is less than $1000, you are marginally better off choosing the $1000 now.

More generally, the present value of $1 received in t years when the discount

rate is i is given by the formula $\left(\dfrac{1}{1+i}\right)^t$.   Using this formula it is possible to

find the present value of complicated combinations of receipts and outlays, because the discounted values are all in present values and are comparable to one another. That is, they can be added and subtracted.

Social Discount Rate

Benefit-cost analysis discounts the future benefits of a government program and adds them together in order to find the present value of the benefits (PVB) over the life of the program. Similarly, the present value of program costs (PVC) is found. The discount rate used to do this is called the **social discount rate.** What rate should be used as the social discount rate in benefit-cost analysis? There is no agreement on the answer to this big question, so let's divide it into several smaller questions to see where the agreements and disagreements lie.

Should a real or nominal discount rate be used in benefit-cost analysis? A nominal interest rate is the interest rate on money, such as that prevailing in the bond market or quoted by your bank. However, the purchasing power of money (its command over goods and services) is not constant over time, because of inflation. If prices rise by 3% over the year, the purchasing power of money is that much less after one year. A real interest rate takes into account the change in the purchasing power of money by subtracting the rate of inflation from the nominal interest rate.

---

[5]$1047.62 plus 5% interest is equal to $1100.

The real interest rate is used to discount sums that are expressed in units of constant purchasing power (for example, constant dollars). Thus, if the nominal interest rate is 7% and the inflation rate is 3% the real interest rate is 4%. Typically, in benefit-cost analysis the economic benefits and costs occurring in different years are expressed as dollars of constant purchasing power. Therefore we discount these "real" benefits and costs using a "real" discount rate.

Should the social discount rate be high or low? There is a long standing controversy about the level of the discount rate to be used in government benefit-cost analysis. Over time the discount rate recommended for government programs has risen steadily. In the 1950s, the Army Corps of Engineers used a discount rate of 2½%. In 1972, the Office of Management and Budget (OMB) directed federal agencies to use a discount rate of 10%, although it has been lowered to 8% since then.

Usually, the cost of a government program is concentrated in the first few years of the program, whereas the benefits are spread into the future. This means that the level of the discount rate makes a very big difference to whether the PVB is greater or less than the PVC. The higher the discount rate, the smaller the PVB relative to the PVC. This was expressed in a little verse by the economist Kenneth Boulding, testifying to the Congressional Subcommittee on Irrigation and Reclamation in 1965:

> *The long-term interest rate*
> *Determines any project's fate:*
> *At 2 percent the case is clear,*
> *At 3 percent some sneaking doubts appear,*
> *At 4 percent it draws its final breath,*
> *While 5 percent is certain death.*

Boulding probably exaggerated, but it is certain that many of the projects found acceptable by the Corps of Engineers at 2.5% would not pass muster at the OMB's rate of 8%. For example, suppose a project costs $10 million in the current year and provides a benefit of $14 million in five years. Discounting at 2.5%, the $14 million benefit in five years has a present value of about $12.4 million, so the present value of benefits exceeds the present value of cost by $1.6 million. Discounting at 8%, the $14 million benefit in five years has a present value of $9.5 million, so the present value of costs exceeds the present value of benefits by $500,000.

How does the theory of benefit-cost analysis help us decide how high the social discount rate should be? Perhaps the most important insight is that *the social discount rate used in benefit-cost analysis is a shadow price,* and therefore it is not necessarily equal to the market rate of interest at which the government borrows. If financial markets were well-functioning, we could use the market interest rate as a shadow price, but financial markets may not function well enough for this approach.

One distortion in financial markets is the presence of income taxes that drive a wedge between the **investment rate of interest** and the **consumption rate of interest.** The consumption rate of interest is the rate that is received by private savers after all taxes have been subtracted. Although it varies over time, it averages around 3%. The investment rate of interest is the rate of return on private investments before taxes are taken out. It can easily be twice as large as the consumption rate of interest, or even higher.[6] Traditionally, those advocating a high discount rate for benefit-cost analysis have favored the high investment rate of interest.

We can think of the government as entering the capital market to borrow the resources to be "invested" in a government program. It competes with private firms for the supply of investible funds made available from the savings of the population, so the amount borrowed by the government must come from more saving (less consumption) or from less borrowing for private investment.[7] The latter is sometimes called **crowding out.**

If the amount borrowed by the government comes from increased saving, the lower consumption rate of interest is the appropriate discount rate for the benefit-cost analysis because this measures the cost to the savers of delaying their consumption by one year. On the other hand, if government borrowing comes from crowded-out private investment, the social discount rate is the investment rate of interest. This is the rate lost on private investment because resources are diverted into the government program. Unfortunately, little is known about the ultimate source of money borrowed by the government, so the debate about the level of the discount rate to be used in benefit-cost analysis continues.

Some benefit-cost analysts believe that even the consumption rate of interest is too high for discounting the benefits and costs of government projects, particularly if the benefits and costs extend far into the future. They think that the consumption rate of interest observed in financial markets is too high for government benefit-cost analysis because people are mortal. Consumers discount future values because they may die before they receive the benefit or incur the cost. However, future generations will enjoy the benefits or bear the costs of government programs, even if they occur in the distant future when generations currently alive will be gone. The government should not discount these benefits and costs the way private households do. For example, radioactive plutonium from nuclear reactors lasts thousands of years and presents a potential cost to generations in the distant future. Discounting costs occurring in the far distant future at the consumption rate of interest would make them insignificant in present value terms, but they will not be insignificant to generations alive then. For this reason, some benefit-cost economists propose that the government choose a **social rate of time preference** to discount future values in benefit-cost analysis. This social rate of time preference is typically very low, even zero, so that future benefits and costs are worth almost as much as current benefits and costs.

Net Present Value Criterion

To determine whether the benefits of a program outweigh its costs, we calculate the net present value (NPV) of the program. Let r be the real social discount rate

---

[6]These real interest rates are for safe investments and do not include a **risk premium.** This is appropriate because risk and uncertainty are best treated separately in benefit-cost analysis (as discussed later in this chapter).

[7]For simplicity, we ignore the possibility that the amount borrowed by the government is obtained from foreign savers by international borrowing.

for discounting future benefits and costs. If we discount the benefits occurring in each year of a program and sum their present values, we find the present value of benefits (PVB) of the program. Discounting and summing the costs occurring over the life of the program gives the present value of costs (PVC). The *net present value* (NPV) of a program is PVB minus PVC. In other words, it is the surplus of the benefits over the costs.

A program is desirable if its NPV is positive and should be implemented if there are no alternative programs that have a higher NPV. The NPV is a good criterion for deciding whether to implement or reject a program because it measures the net increment to the "economy's wealth" created by the program. The efficiency objective of the government is to make the country's economic wealth as high as possible.

A numerical example of calculating the NPV is shown in Table 6.1 for a government project that lasts four years beginning in year 0, the present year. The first row shows the discount factors applied to benefits and costs in their respective years, assuming a 5% social discount rate (that is, the discount factor in year t is equal to $\left(\dfrac{1}{1.05}\right)^t$). We assume benefits of $350 start in the second year and continue to the end of the project, while a cost of $1000 occurs only in the current year. As we can see, although the sum of the dollar benefits exceeds the cost, the sum of the discounted benefits (PVB) is less than the PVC, and hence the NPV (PVB minus PVC) is negative. Consequently, the government should not implement the project.

The formulas expressing PVB and PVC are complicated in the general case, so let's simplify by considering a simpler *perpetuity* program. A perpetuity program is one where the costs of the program, C dollars, occur only in the present year and are zero thereafter. The yearly benefits, B dollars, begin after one year and continue for every year forever. For a perpetuity program, it can be shown that $\mathrm{PVB} = \dfrac{B}{r}$. That is, the present value of benefits is equal to the annual benefit divided by the shadow discount rate. Therefore, $\mathrm{NPV} = \dfrac{B}{r} - C$. For example,

Table 6.1   Illustraton of the NPV Calculation

	Year 0	Year 1	Year 2	Year 3	Sum
Discount factor for year t (at 5%)	1	.952	.907	.864	
Benefit in year t ($)	0	350	350	350	1050
Benefit in year t times the discount factor (PV$)	0	333.33	317.46	302.34	935.14 (PVB)
Cost in year t ($)	1000	0	0	0	1000
Cost in year t times the discount factor (PV$)	1000	0	0	0	1000 (PVC)
NPV (PV$)					−46.86

if the social discount rate is 5% a perfectly durable road built in the current year at a cost $1 million that provides benefits of $75,000 every year thereafter has NPV equal to $\dfrac{\$75,000}{0.05} - \$1,000,000$, or $500,000.

With a perpetuity program, it is also possible to **annualize** the first-year costs so that they can be compared with the annual benefits, rather than discounting. This is done in some studies—for example, the Tellico dam study we discuss toward the end of this chapter. The annualized cost is equal to r times C. In the example of the road, the annualized cost is $50,000 a year, which is less than the $75,000 annual benefit. If the road depreciates and has to be maintained, the annualized cost is equal to $(r + d)$ times C, where d is the annual depreciation expressed as a fraction of the cost. For example, if d is 0.1 (a depreciation rate of 10%) the annualized cost of the road is $150,000.

The NPV is positive if the annual benefits of a program exceed its annualized cost, and vice versa, so the two methods are equivalent. By either method, the program should be implemented, provided there is no alternative program that has higher benefits relative to its costs.

Other Benefit-Cost Criteria

In modern benefit-cost analysis, the NPV is the most widely used decision criterion. In older benefit-cost studies, we sometimes encounter other criteria such as the benefit-cost ratio or the internal rate of return. These criteria are no better than the NPV, and in some cases they are inferior, so most benefit-cost analysts prefer to use the NPV. We discuss the alternatives briefly.

BENEFIT-COST RATIO. Fifty years ago, the **benefit-cost ratio** (**BCR**) was the main criterion used in benefit-cost analysis. The BCR is simply the ratio of program benefits to program costs. For example, $\text{BCR} = \dfrac{\text{PVB}}{\text{PVC}}$. In the perpetuity case, where the costs can be annualized, we can also express the BCR as the ratio of benefits per year to the annualized cost. According to the BCR criterion, a program is desirable if the BCR is greater than 1. Obviously this is closely related to the NPV criterion. In fact, the BCR is greater than 1 whenever the NPV is positive, and less than 1 whenever the NPV is negative.

INTERNAL RATE OF RETURN. Another decision criterion that is sometimes used is the **internal rate of return** (**IRR**). The IRR is the implicit interest rate "paid" by the program on the value of the resources invested in it. It is found by solving the expression for the NPV of the program for a hypothetical discount rate for which the NPV is zero (that is, PVB is equal to PVC). In contrast to calculating the NPV, where the social discount rate is given, the IRR is found by letting the value of the discount rate be an "unknown variable" to be found. The discount rate that solves this problem is the program's IRR. The program is desirable if the IRR is greater than a benchmark interest rate, such as the social discount rate.

The relationship between the IRR and the other criteria can be easily seen for the case of a perpetuity program. The IRR (denoted ρ) for a perpetuity program is found by solving $0 = \dfrac{B}{\rho} - C$. This can be rearranged as $\dfrac{\rho}{r} = \dfrac{B/r}{C}$, where r is the social discount rate. In other words, the ratio of the IRR to the social discount rate is equal to the BCR. From this expression, we see that the IRR is greater than r when the BCR is greater than 1. Since the BCR is greater than 1 when the NPV is positive, all three criteria are equivalent for determining whether benefits exceed costs. For projects that are not perpetuities, calculating the IRR is more complicated, and in some cases the IRR for a program can take many values.

In Table 6.2 we show the NPV, BCR, and IRR for two perpetuity projects. Project A costs $1000 in the first year and earns a benefit of $100 every year in perpetuity beginning in year 2. Project B costs $500 and earns a benefit of $60 every year in perpetuity beginning in year 2. We assume that the appropriate discount rate is 5%

Choosing Among Alternative Projects

If the government can do both projects listed in Table 6.1 all three criteria indicate that they should be done. But rather than analyzing individual projects and deciding whether they should be done, a benefit-cost analyst must also analyze the choice among alternative projects. For example, an analyst might be asked to determine whether project A *or* B (but not both) in Table 6.2 should be done. In this case, the benefit-cost criteria give different answers. Project B has a higher BCR and IRR than project A, but A should still be done in preference to B because A has a higher NPV. That is, project A creates more wealth for the economy.

Projects can be alternatives for several reasons. First, projects may be mutually exclusive—that is, doing one precludes another. For instance, the government can tear down the dam that floods the Hetch Hetchy valley in Yosemite National Park so as to restore the natural wonders of the valley, or it can use the dam to generate electricity. It can't do both. Second, projects may be alternatives because they are substitutes: for example, whether to build a bridge or a car ferry to enable traffic to cross a river. If a bridge is built, it is not desirable to have the ferry, and vice versa. Third, the total amount of money the government can spend on a group of projects may be limited, so policy makers have to pick and choose among projects within a budget constraint.

Table 6.2   **The NPV, BCR, and IRR of Two Hypothetical Projects**

Project	First-Year Cost	Perpetuity Benefit	NPV	BCR	IRR
A	$1000	$100	$1000	2	10%
B	$100	$20	$300	4	20%

When the government must choose among alternatives, a project must satisfy two criteria to be worth implementing. First, as before, the NPV of the project must be positive. However, in the presence of alternatives, a positive NPV is only a necessary condition. In addition, doing the project must maximize the NPV over all projects. For instance, suppose that building a bridge has an NPV of $1 million, whereas building a car ferry has an NPV of $2 million. Notwithstanding the fact that the bridge has a positive NPV, it should not be built, because an alternative project—the car ferry—has a higher NPV. If we build the bridge, we give up the opportunity to create $2 million in wealth for the economy by building a car ferry (since we do not want to do both). Together, the condition that the NPV is positive and that it is the highest over all alternatives is called the **generalized net present value criterion.**

In government programs and projects, there are nearly always alternatives. Suppose the government has a blueprint to build a dam on a particular river site to provide irrigation for agriculture, and we have determined that the blueprint dam has a positive NPV. What are the alternatives? It might be possible to tap sufficient groundwater with a system of wells, of course, but even if the dam is the only possibility, there are still alternatives to be considered.

First, the government can build the dam at different heights, providing more or less irrigation. Building a dam at one height precludes building it at another, so dams of different heights are alternatives. In other words, the choice of *scale* is a choice among alternatives. Second, the dam can be built of concrete with a long life, or of earth with a shorter life. Again, one type of dam precludes the other, so the choice of *durability* is a choice among alternatives. Third, and less obvious, the dam can be postponed and built in the future when the surplus of benefits over costs may be even greater. Building the dam in the present precludes building it in the future, so the choice of *starting time* is a choice among alternatives.

In other words, even if a dam should be built, we must consider "alternative dams" to ensure that society is to get the largest possible increase in wealth. The generalized net present value criterion is used to choose among these alternative scales, durabilities, and starting times so as to get the greatest excess of benefits over costs. Using the BCR or IRR to choose among these many alternative projects can lead to erroneous decisions.

Uncertainty and Limited Information

Usually, the benefits and costs of a project are uncertain because the analyst has limited information about the project. For example, future benefits and costs may depend on unpredictable events. The cost of constructing the Eurotunnel between England and France was several times higher than originally estimated when the project started. Benefits and costs occurring in the far future are especially uncertain because so many unpredictable events can occur in the meantime.

Uncertainty introduces two important considerations into benefit-cost analysis. The first is how to decide whether to implement a project when it is evaluated with uncertainty and limited information. The second is how to measure the cost of risk in evaluating a project.

LIMITS ON INFORMATION.   Typically, a benefit-cost analyst has limited information and must make "educated guesses" about the values of some variables. This uncertainty is sometimes made explicit by performing a sensitivity analysis. A sensitivity analysis calculates how sensitive the NPV of a project is to the values of the uncertain variables.

For example, estimates of the future benefits of a road may depend on assumptions about regional population growth rates, future gasoline prices, etc. Furthermore, the present value of these benefits depends on the social discount rate used. Since the analysts may not know the values exactly, they may try a range of values. Typically, "conservative" and "optimistic" estimates of benefits and costs are made. In the case of the road, a conservative estimate of the benefits would use a low estimate of population growth rate, a high estimate of gasoline prices, and a high discount rate.

Sensitivity analysis makes the uncertainty of a project's NPV explicit. A decision is then made by informally weighing the possibilities, or by formally incorporating the cost of risk.

THE COST OF RISK.   Every day, people incorporate the cost of risk into the decisions they make. They keep money in a low-interest, insured bank account rather than holding more risky equity shares; or they take the bus on an icy morning rather than risk fender bender. This aversion to risk should also be reflected in benefit-cost analysis, as a cost if the project increases the risk facing the population, or as a benefit if the project reduces the risk the population faces.

Suppose a government wants to improve weather forecasting by launching a new weather satellite into orbit. The benefits of this project are risky—they depend on whether the satellite is successfully launched or blows up on the launch pad. How should this risk be measured and valued?

Generally, the risk of a government project is determined by how much it contributes to the unpredictable variability in a household's consumption. Households dislike unpredictable variability in their consumption and are said to be **risk averse.** The contribution of a government project to variability in household consumption depends on several things. First, it depends on the variability of the benefits and costs of the project itself, as in the case of the weather satellite. Second, the variability of the government project may offset or reinforce the variability of the other components of the household's income or consumption, depending on whether the variability of the project values are positively or negatively correlated with other consumption.

In the case of the satellite, the variability of the project benefits and costs is not likely to be correlated to the variability of other consumption, so the satellite risk is said to be independent. On the other hand, consider a government project that retrains unemployed workers. The cost of the program is certain, but the benefit is risky because the effectiveness of the retraining may be high (H) or low (L). In addition, the private consumption of the workers may be uncertain because they may find themselves employed (E) or unemployed (U). If H is more likely when U happens (negative correlation), the variability in the government project offsets the variability in private consumption and reduces variability. On the other hand, if L is more likely when U happens (positive correlation), the variability of the government project reinforces the variability in private consumption.

Professors Kenneth Arrow and Robert C. Lind of Stanford University argued that if the benefits and costs of government projects are independent of the economy, the government should ignore the cost of risk in benefit-cost analysis. In this case, the government can diversify and spread the variability of project benefits and costs over the population so that each household incurs a very small fraction of the variability. The effective risk of the project is zero. In other cases, however, the variability of project benefits and costs is positively correlated to the rest of the economy and cannot be diversified and spread away. For example, the benefits of a new road may be high when income is high (because people drive more) and low when income is low. In this case, the risk of the government project is not zero and the cost of the risk should be evaluated.

When the cost of risk must be evaluated, it is usually measured as the difference between the expected value of a benefit or cost and its **certainty equivalent** value. The expected value of a variable is its actuarial value. For instance, the expected value of a benefit that has a 75% chance of being $100 and a 25% chance of being zero is $75. The certainty equivalent value of a benefit is equal to the certain amount of money that a household would treat as equivalent to the uncertain benefit. If the household were indifferent between $60 for certain and the above benefit offering a 75% chance of $100, the cost of the risk would be $15. This is the amount the household is willing to pay to avoid the unpredictable variability of the benefit.

PUTTING IT TOGETHER: THE TELLICO DAM PROJECT

In this section we put together some of the pieces of benefit-cost analysis by examining the evaluation of a famous Tennessee Valley Authority (TVA) hydroelectric project—the Tellico dam on the Little Tennessee River.[8] Although it was funded by Congress in 1966, and the land to be flooded was purchased shortly thereafter, the building of the dam itself was delayed into the late 1970s. The benefits and costs of the dam were reevaluated after this lengthy delay.[9]

The main outputs of the Tellico dam are electric power and flood control. Also, the long reservoir created by the dam provides a navigable waterway for barge traffic, as well as an area for boating and recreational use. The reservoir supplies irrigation water to the bordering agricultural land. The main cost incurred is the building of the dam and the value of the flooded land. Also, the Little Tennessee was one of the few remaining "wild" rivers in the region and was heavily used for sport fishing. This was lost by building the dam.

In its analysis in 1968, the TVA estimated that the annual benefits of the project would exceed costs by about $11.5 million (here measured in 1978 purchasing

---

[8]The dam is famous because it was challenged in 1976 under the then-new Endangered Species Act of 1973 in order to protect a tiny fish known as a "snail darter."

[9]The story of the evaluation of this project, and role that politics played, is interesting and instructive. However, space limits me to a brief outline of how the economic benefits and costs of the dam were determined.

Table 6.3   **Benefits and Costs of the Tellico Dam ($1978)**

	TVA 1968	ESC 1978
B1 Power	$0.9 million	$2.7 million
B2 Navigation	0.9 million	0.1 million
B3 Flood control	1.1 million	1.0 million
B4 Recreation (travel-cost method)	3.7 million	2.5 million
B5 Agriculture and water supply	0.2 million	0.15 million
B6 Employment	8.1 million	0
B7 Enhanced value of surrounding land	1.6 million	0
C1 Dam cost (annualized)	5.0 million	3.2 million
C2 Opportunity cost of flooded land	0	4.0 million
Benefits minus costs	11.5 million	(0.75 million)

power). An enumeration of these benefits and costs is given in Table 6.3.[10] The annualized cost of the dam was estimated using a *nominal* interest rate of 10%. The cost of the land flooded was excluded from the TVA's estimates on the ground that it was already purchased and was therefore a "sunk" cost.

There are several errors in the analysis done by the TVA. Fortunately for us, they are the type of errors from which we can learn. There are two offsetting errors on the cost side. A nominal, rather than a real, interest rate was used to annualize costs. Annualizing investment cost is the reverse of discounting annual benefits, and since all values are measured in real terms (i.e., dollars of constant purchasing power) a real discount rate should be used. Although real discount rates as high as 10% have been used by the OMB, such rates are at the upper end of the scale. So for this reason, the annualized cost of the dam is probably overstated by the TVA.

An offsetting error on the cost side was the exclusion of the opportunity cost of the land to be flooded. Although the land had already been purchased, it was available for alternative uses until flooded by the dam.[11] Therefore the opportunity cost of the land should be counted as a cost of building the dam, notwithstanding the fact that the government already owned it. This opportunity cost is estimated at about $4 million per year.

There are also errors on the benefits side. The biggest error was counting the $8 million of employment as a benefit. This is a holdover from the Green Book methodology of the 1950s, mentioned at the beginning of this chapter: estimating benefit as the change in gross national product. Whatever the merits of counting employment as a benefit during the Depression era, it is not valid to count it as a benefit in the high-employment economy of the 1970s. Most persons employed on the project would have been employed elsewhere had the dam not been built.

The inclusion of enhanced land values as a benefit was a classic case of double counting. The land values are enhanced only because of the recreational and irrigation benefits of the reservoir created by the dam, but these benefits are already

---

[10]These figures and the subsequent discussion are based on material in Edward Gramlich, *A Guide to Benefit-Cost Analysis,* 2nd ed., chap. 8.

[11]In fact, even after the dam was built, the land was available until the floodgates were closed.

counted once and should not be counted again. In fact, the recreational benefits of the reservoir were overestimated by the TVA because many similar recreation sites are available at other TVA dam sites in Tennessee. Many of the people using the new site would have used another reservoir for recreation had the Tellico dam not been built. In addition, the lost recreation benefits of the river in its wild state, mainly for trout fishing, were not subtracted from the recreation benefits of the reservoir.

The TVA also underestimated the power benefit, because it did not foresee the rise in energy prices; and it overestimated the navigation benefit because it did not foresee the decline in barge traffic. A sensitivity analysis could have been used to determine how sensitive the value of the project was to these unknown variables. A later evaluation of the Tellico dam by the Endangered Species Committee (ESC) found that the costs exceeded the benefits by about $750,000 a year. The ESC estimates are given in the right-hand column of Table 6.3. According to the ESC study, the Tellico dam should not have been built.

CONCLUSION AND SUMMARY

We began this chapter by asking how we can ensure good value for our tax dollars. Benefit-cost analysis, which we have described in some detail, is designed to help policy makers achieve that. However, it is not a panacea. Because of imprecision and unverified assumptions, estimates of benefits and costs are prone to margins of error. Nonetheless, in the opinion of many economists, benefit-cost analysis is the best tool available for the purpose. The methods have been improved and refined over the past 50 years, though there is still work to do. In an economy where the demands on government are great and the resistance to taxes is high, benefit-cost analysis is well suited to improving government decision making.

- Benefit-cost analysis is a method of evaluating government programs in terms of their economic benefits and costs. The economic benefit is the value of the program's outputs (things acquired), and the economic cost is the value of the program's inputs (things given up).

- Benefits and costs to everyone in the economy should be counted, whether or not they have pecuniary value. Transactions that merely reflect transfers of purchasing power between members of the economy are excluded.

- The compensation principle is used to justify "treating a dollar as a dollar" and to sum benefits and costs to different people as if they were one person. An alternative approach is to use distributional weights to reflect the value of benefits and costs to people whose circumstances differ.

- In benefit-cost analysis, goods and services are valued at their shadow prices, which are equal to marginal willingnesses to pay for outputs and to marginal opportunity costs of inputs.

- In well-functioning markets, shadow prices are equal to market prices. When markets are distorted, market prices must be adjusted to find shadow prices. Two broad methodologies are used for finding shadow prices of nonmarket goods: revealed-preference techniques, such as the property-value and travel-cost methods; and survey techniques, such as the contingent valuation method.

■ In order to compare economic benefits and costs occurring in different years, they must be converted into their present values by discounting at the shadow discount rate. The net present value of a program is equal to the present value of benefits minus the present value of costs.

■ If the net present value of a program is negative, it should not be implemented. Among alternative programs with positive net present values, those with the highest net present values should be implemented.

QUESTIONS FOR DISCUSSION AND REVIEW

1. Suppose 80% of the $8 billion construction cost of the new urban transit system in Los Angeles is paid by the federal government. From the perspective of the state of California, what is the economic cost of construction? What is this cost from the perspective of the federal government?

2. Before 1996, the federal government stored over 32 billion cubic feet of helium in an underground mine near Amarillo, Texas. Some people argue that this Federal Helium Reserve (FHR) was a perfect example of government waste. Others claim it was not because it makes money for the government. Revenue of $28 million a year was received from selling helium to government agencies, like NASA, at $55 per thousand cubic feet. The market price of helium was $46 per thousand cubic feet. Critics say the profit is spurious because it was a transfer from one pocket of the government to another. Moreover, the government lent the FHR the money to buy the helium in the first place, and the uncounted interest cost was over $100 million a year. How can benefit-cost analysis help us understand who is right in this debate?

3. Suppose the city you live in adopts a newspaper recycling program. This program is presented to the public as having two benefits. First, the newspapers collected are sold, generating revenue for the city; second, the cost of disposal (landfill, etc.) is saved. However, the program turns out to be too successful because the large amount of newspaper made available drastically reduces the price at which it can be sold to recyclers. Suppose the price of newspaper drops from $10 a ton to almost nothing because of the program. Is the saved disposal cost the only benefit of the program? Explain.

4. The National Park Service is considering removing two dams in Olympic National Park. These dams provide nearly 40% of electricity used by the Daishowa pulp and paper mill in Port Angeles, Washington; the mill gets the rest of its power from the Bonneville Power Administration (BPA). If the dams are torn down, all of the mill's electricity will have to be purchased from the BPA. To evaluate the economic cost of the power lost if these dams are torn down, is the commercial rate for electricity charged by the BPA a good measure of shadow price of electricity? Why or why not?

5. Suppose a city is considering building a public swimming pool in a section of town

where the average income of a family is very low. The pool will cost $150,000, which will be raised by increasing taxes on property owned by wealthy residents. A study finds that total willingness to pay for the swimming pool by the poor residents is only $50,000, although they will be able to use the pool without charge. Should this pool be built, according to the compensation principle approach? Should it be built according to the distributional weights approach?

6. There is pressure on the United States and other countries to reduce emissions of greenhouse gases like carbon dioxide in order to forestall global warming. Suppose that at current rates of emission,

average global temperature will rise, causing large economic costs, such as lost agricultural production, in about 40 years. The cost of reducing emissions is also high, and it begins right away if the emissions are reduced. How does the shadow discount rate affect whether it is a good idea to reduce emissions? Is it likely to be a good idea to reduce emissions if the shadow discount rate is high or low?

7. Suppose an eccentric rich aunt offers you a choice between two certain investments, one paying 20% interest per year and the other paying 100% interest per year. Which would you choose? (Before you answer, remember to ask her how much you can invest in each alternative.)

SELECTED REFERENCES

The roots of benefit-cost analysis are found in the pioneering work of Jules Dupuit, "De la Mesure de l'Utilitie des Travaux Publics," 1844. Important contributions are found in John Krutilla and Otto Eckstein, *Multiple Purpose River Development*, 1958.

The compensation principle was proposed by Nicholas Kaldor, "Welfare Propositions in Economics and Interpersonal Comparisons of Utility," 1939; and John Hicks, "The Valuation of Social Income," 1940. The use of distributive weights in benefit-cost analysis is explained in Lyn Squire and Herman G. van der Tak, *Economic Analysis of Projects*, 1975.

Residential property values are used to estimate the benefits of improved air quality by

Ronald Ridker, *Economic Costs of Air Pollution: Studies in Measurement*, 1967. The travel-cost method suggested by Harold Hotelling was further developed in Marion Clawson, *Methods of Measuring the Demand for and Value of Outdoor Recreation*, 1959.

On the difference between WTP and WTA, see Richard C. Bishop and Thomas A. Heberlein, "Measuring Values of Extra Market Goods: Are Indirect methods Biased?" 1979.

A textbook on benefit-cost analysis with many applications is Anthony Boardman et al., *Cost-Benefit Analysis: Concepts and Practice*, Prentice-Hall, 1996.

USEFUL INTERNET SITES

The EPA's Economy and Environment site at http://www.epa.gov/economics/ has numerous benefit-cost studies of environmental issues.

See also U.S. Department of Agriculture's Risk Assessment and Cost Benefit Analysis page at http://www.usda.gov/agency/oce/oracba/.

PART FOUR

Government

Transfer

Programs

The largest spending programs of government are not on public goods and services, but for the purpose of redistributing income from one group of people to another. Such transfer programs do not reallocate spending in the economy between private and public uses. Rather, they change the distribution of private spending (or the ability to spend) among households. In Chapter 7, we learn the facts about the distribution of income across households in the economy, and the theory of how it is determined. We then consider the arguments for government programs that redistribute income. The three main arguments for government redistribution are (i) government redistribution is a public good, (ii) government redistribution is needed to ensure equity or fairness, and (iii) government redistribution provides a "safety net" or social insurance.

In addition to being unequal, the market distribution of income leaves many families in poverty. In Chapter 8, we learn how the federal government officially defines and measures poverty, and the ways in which poverty measurement could be improved. We then study the government transfer programs directed at alleviating poverty. Such transfers are means-tested, meaning they give benefits only to families who have limited incomes. The antipoverty programs, commonly termed "welfare," provide cash, vouchers such as food stamps, and direct goods and services such as medical care to families who are classified as poor. Antipoverty programs are controversial because many people believe they remove private incentives to avoid poverty. The chapter describes recent welfare reforms that were designed to make poor people more self-reliant.

Unlike the antipoverty programs, Social Security and Medicare provide benefits for retired persons regardless of their income. In Chapter 9, we examine the economic reasons for these social insurance programs, as well as the effects they have on household behavior, particularly saving.

7 Government and the Distribution of Income

Inequality is a pervasive fact of life. Perhaps this is best illustrated by the so-called 20/80 rule popular in business and engineering. Examples of the 20/80 rule abound. About 20% of real estate agents account for 80% of all real estate sales, and about 20% of books published each year account for 80% of all sales. The 20/80 rule is sometimes called Pareto's rule after Vilfredo Pareto, the great nineteenth-century economist and sociologist whose contribution to the concept of economic efficiency we discussed in Chapter 2. Pareto observed that the distribution of wealth in most societies is unequally distributed, with about 20% of the population controlling 80% of the wealth. He went on to formulate a more general principle stating that "a small fraction in terms of number of the elements almost always accounts for a large fraction in terms of effect."

While inequality of effects may be a fact of life, the inequality of incomes that emerges is a major government policy issue. Much of the analysis and commentary that surrounds existing and contemplated government spending and tax policies focuses on the effect of the policies on the distribution of incomes and on the question of whether the policies are fair or equitable on those terms. In fact, many of the largest government spending programs are transfer programs whose main purpose is to redistribute income from one group of people to another, like Social Security and Temporary Assistance to Needy Families (welfare). In this chapter, we study the existing inequality of the distribution of income and examine the economic reasons that the government undertakes programs to change the distribution of incomes. In the two chapters that follow, we consider the two major categories of government programs that redistribute incomes—the means-tested programs that redistribute income to the poor (Chapter 8) and the social insurance programs that redistribute income to the elderly (Chapter 9).

THE FACTS OF THE DISTRIBUTION OF INCOME

Everyone knows that income and wealth are not distributed equally across people or families in the United States. How do we measure inequality? How much do people move up and down the income "ladder"? Has inequality increased, as many people think, and why? How does income inequality in the United States compare with that in other countries? The answers to these questions help us better understand the extent to which inequality is a social problem that calls for government redistribution.

Measuring Inequality in the Size Distribution of Income

Information on the distribution of income is available from several sources, but the most important is data on the incomes of households and families in the U.S. Census. According to the Census, a household is a person, family, or group of unrelated persons residing under one roof. A family is two or more related persons residing together. Both households and families come in different sizes.

Table 7.1 shows the **size distribution** of income across families for selected years as reported in Census data. To obtain the size distribution, families are ranked according to their annual cash income and then divided into groups, called quintiles, each containing a fifth of the total population of families. Since there were 71.6 million families in the United States in 1998, each quintile contains about 14.3 million families. The first quintile contains the 14.3 million families with the lowest cash incomes, which are those with income less than $21,600 in 1998. The second quintile contains the 14.3 million families with the next lowest incomes, and so on up to the fifth quintile, which contains the 14.3 million families with the highest incomes—those with more than $83,694 in 1998.

Table 7.1 reports the share of total family income received by the families in each quintile, called **quintile shares.** Income is measured as cash income, which includes cash transfers from the government like Social Security and welfare checks, but excludes noncash forms of income such as fringe benefits from employers and government transfers in kind, like Medicare or Medicaid benefits. This measure of income also excludes capital gains and is measured before taxes are taken out. The table shows that the share of the families in the lowest quintile was 4.2% in 1998, whereas the share of the fifth, or highest, quintile was 47.3%. If we think of the total income of all families as a pie of a given size, the table shows that the first quintile gets a slice equal to under 5% of the pie, the second quintile receives a slice equal to nearly 10% of the pie, and so on. Each quintile contains the same number of families; therefore, the different sizes of the slices of the pie indicate the inequality in the distribution of income. Since quintiles are rather large groups of families, the table also shows the share of the top 5%, which contains the 3.6 million families with the highest incomes—above $145,200 in 1998. As shown in the table, this top 5% of families received over 20% of all cash income in 1998.

Table 7.1   Quintile Shares of Family Cash Income for Selected Years

	Quintile					
Year	1	2	3	4	5	Top 5%
1998	4.2%	9.9%	15.7%	23.0%	47.3%	20.7%
1990	4.6	10.8	16.6	23.8	44.3	17.4
1980	5.3	11.6	17.6	24.4	41.1	14.6
1970	5.4	12.2	17.6	23.8	40.9	15.6

Source: U.S. Census Bureau, *Statistical Abstract of the United States,* various years.

THE LORENZ CURVE.   They say a picture is worth a thousand words, so it is useful to have a graphical representation of the size distribution of income. This is provided by the **Lorenz curve** in Figure 7.1. Along the vertical axis we measure the cumulative percentage of income received by the families, and along the horizontal axis we measure the cumulative percentage of the number of households ranked according to income. The diagonal is the **equality line,** which represents the hypothetical case where each quintile of families would receive 20% of all income. Because income is not equally distributed, the Lorenz curve lies below the equality line. The greater the inequality, the further the Lorenz curve lies below the equality line.

The Lorenz curve in Figure 7.1 is constructed as follows. The first point, labeled *a*, shows the lowest quintile families received 4.2% of income, point *b* shows that the lowest two quintiles received 14.1%, point *c* shows that the lowest three

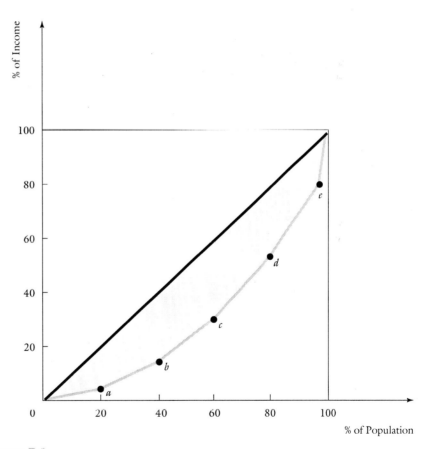

Figure 7.1

Lorenz Curve for 1998

With families ranked according to their incomes, the Lorenz curve plots the percentage of total income received by the percentage of families with the lowest incomes. For instance, point *c* indicates that the 60% of families with the lowest incomes received about 30% of total income. The further the Lorenz curve lies from the diagonal, called the *equality line*, the more unequal the distribution of income.

quintiles combined received 29.8%, and point *d* shows that the lowest four quintiles combined received 52.7%.

THE GINI RATIO.   Sometimes it is useful to collapse the information on the size distribution into a single number. The most popular way to do this is to calculate the **Gini ratio,** also known as the **coefficient of income concentration.** The Gini ratio would equal zero if income were equally distributed across families, and one if it were concentrated in the hands of a single family. In 1998, the Gini ratio was .43. Changes in the size distribution over time and differences across countries can be measured using the Gini ratio.

The exact formula for calculating the Gini ratio is too complicated to give here, but it can be explained and calculated using the Lorenz curve. The Gini ratio is equal to the ratio of the shaded lens-shaped area between the Lorenz curve and the equality line in Figure 7.1 to the area below the equality line. Using elementary geometry, we can approximate the Gini ratio using the quintile shares. In particular,

$$G = 0.8 - \frac{(1.6s_1 + 1.2s_2 + 0.8s_3 + 0.4s_4)}{100}$$

where G is the approximate Gini ratio and s_1, s_2 ... are the percentage income shares for the respective quintiles from the size distribution in Table 7.1. This approximate Gini ratio is an underestimate of the true Gini ratio since it is calculated from a limited number of points and the Lorenz curve is concave up.

Is Income Inequality Increasing in the United States?

The average person senses that income inequality is greater in the United States than it used to be. Is this perception correct, and, if so, what are the reasons for the increased inequality? The fact is that measured income inequality has increased significantly since 1970. This development is of great interest to economists, because prior to 1970 the distribution of income was remarkably stable. One economist described following the data back then as like "watching the grass grow." The changes in the distribution of income since 1970 have been anything but slow.

Perhaps the most dramatic change has been the increase in the share of income received by families in the highest quintile. In 1970 these families received 40.9% of all income, but by 1998 they received 47.3%, an increase in their share of 15.6%. Over the same period, the share of the top 5% of families increased from 15.6% to 20.7%, an increase of 32.7%. This means, of course, that the share of income going to families in the other four quintiles must have fallen by an equal amount (although the numbers listed here may not add up due to rounding). In fact, the share of income going to families in the lowest quintile fell from 5.4% to 4.2%, a decline of 22%. One also hears about the "shrinking middle class." Although there is no official definition of the middle class, many economists use the combined second, third, and fourth quintiles as the middle class. Since 1970 the combined share of these three quintiles has dropped from 53.6% to 48.6%, a decline of 9.3%.

We mentioned earlier that the Gini ratio is a popular summary measure of the amount of inequality in the size distribution, with higher values of the Gini ratio meaning greater inequality of incomes. Figure 7.2 shows the values of the Gini ratio between 1970 and 1998. As we can see, the Gini ratio rose slowly during the 1970s from a value of .353 in 1970, accelerated in the 1980s and again in the 1990s, but has leveled off since 1993 and stands at .43 in 1998. Overall, the Gini ratio rose nearly 22% between 1970 and 1998. This figure dramatically illustrates how the income distribution, as conventionally measured, has become more unequal over the past three decades.

What is the cause of this increase in income inequality? Some people think it is the result of changes in government policies that redistribute income, such as a reduction in welfare payments or the lowering of income tax rates for high-income taxpayers. However, economists who have studied the phenomenon believe the main reason for the increase in income inequality is an increase in wage and earnings disparities. Between 1970 and the mid-1990s, wage and earnings dispersion has increased dramatically within all demographic and skill groups. Although the wage differential between men and women and between whites and nonwhites has actually narrowed, the wage and earnings differences within each group have increased. The earnings differential between skilled, educated workers and unskilled, less-educated workers has widened most of all. Economists attribute these changes

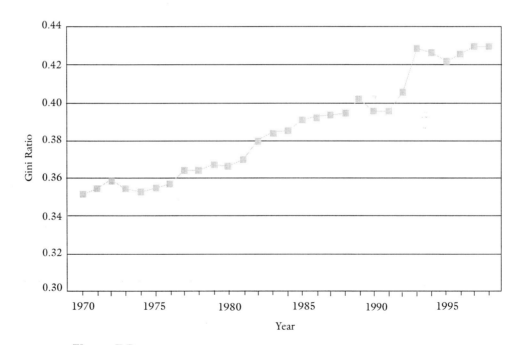

Figure 7.2

Gini Ratio of U.S. Family Income Concentration: 1970–1998

The Gini ratio is a summary measure of income concentration. Since 1970, the Gini ratio has increased 22%. *Source:* U.S. Bureau of the Census, *Historical Income Tables*, Table H.4, at http://www.census.gov/hhes/income/listing/ho4.html.

to a variety of factors including technological change and deindustrialization, globalization of markets, and changes in business organization. All of these have put a premium on the skills, education, and experience of workers.

Interpreting the U.S. Distributional Facts

The picture of the U.S. income distribution described above is one of considerable inequality coupled with the disturbing fact that inequality has been rising over the past three decades. How concerned should we be about this inequality? The answer depends on how we interpret this picture as well as our judgments about equity. The size distribution of income in any given year is a snapshot and does not capture the dynamic element that people can and do move from one place in the income distribution to another. A popular American myth is the so-called Horatio Alger story of an individual moving from poverty to riches through equal opportunity and superior effort.

The economic historian Joseph Schumpeter used a different metaphor. He compared the income distribution to a hotel with many rooms of differing qualities. Although every room in the hotel is occupied, people can move between rooms. Our concern about the income distribution depends on the different qualities of the rooms and also on the amount of movement between rooms. If everyone moves from room to room, sometimes occupying a room of high quality and sometimes occupying a room of low quality, our concern is different (perhaps less) than if everyone remains in the same room for life. Schumpeter's analogy suggests that to interpret the facts about the income distribution, we should focus on two things. The first is the degree of mobility between the rooms (income quintiles). The second is the quality of the rooms (how we measure income).

UNEQUAL INCOMES AND UNEQUAL OPPORTUNITIES. It is important to recognize that income inequality would exist even if everyone had the same ability and opportunity to earn income. One reason is age. Earnings follow a common pattern over a person's life. When people are young and starting out, their earnings are usually low, whereas in middle age most people reach the peak of their experience and their earning power. When people become old and retire, their income falls again. For instance, in 1998 the mean income of a male worker between the ages 25 and 34 was $33,334. The mean income when the worker is between 45 and 54 and at the peak of his earning ability was $49,910, while for men over age 65 it was $27,997. A similar pattern is found for women. This suggests that people move from one place in the income distribution to another over time as their earnings change.

Incomes also change over time according to how much people work and how much they saved and invested in the past. People who sacrifice leisure in order to work longer hours earn more. Similarly, people who saved a large fraction of their past earnings to acquire income earning assets have more interest and dividend income, and people who forgo current income to acquire education or skills will have higher incomes in the future. Because of differences in age, work effort, saving, and education decisions, people who have the same lifetime opportunity to earn income may have different amounts of income in any given year.

To assess how much income inequality depends on unequal opportunities, economists study the degree of economic mobility. In particular, they try to determine how likely it is that a household or family that occupies a particular place in the income distribution in any given year will occupy the same place in other years. A study by the U.S. Treasury identified and followed the same taxpayers as they moved within the income distribution between 1979 and 1988. It found that a third or fewer of the taxpayers that were in the lowest income quintile in 1979 were also in the lowest income quintile in 1988. In fact, a larger fraction of the taxpayers moved from the lowest quintile in 1979 to the highest quintile in 1988 than remained in the lowest quintile.[1]

A limitation of the Treasury study is that it includes only taxpayers and therefore excludes some of the poorest people in the country, who do not pay income taxes. However, similar although less dramatic mobility is found in studies that follow a more representative group of households. Isabel V. Sawhill and Mark Condon of the Urban Institute used the Panel Study of Income Dynamics (PSID), which includes both taxpayers and nontaxpayers, to examine economic mobility of individuals over a decade beginning in 1967 and 1977. They found that in both decades, substantial mobility occurred and that the amount of mobility was roughly the same in both decades. Sawhill and Condon found that over 60% of individuals occupied a different family income quintile at the end of a decade from the one they occupied at the beginning of the decade.[2] Other researchers have found similar rates of long-term mobility and substantial short term mobility as well. One study found that over 27% of individuals occupy a different income quintile after one year and about 45% occupy a different quintile after five years.[3] Another finding of these studies is that people with at least a college education are more likely to be upwardly mobile in the income distribution than people without. Moreover, the upward mobility of college-educated people has increased over time.

The Census Bureau uses a different method of measuring economic mobility. It calculates the year to year change in people's **Income-to-Poverty Ratio (IPR)**. The IPR divides a family's income by the **Official Poverty Threshold (OPT)** for a family with the same characteristics. We will examine how the OPT is determined in the next chapter. For now we will simply state that it is equal to the minimum amount of income needed by a family of given size to afford a basic standard of living. In 1994, the average IPR for people in the lowest income quintile was .92 while for people in the highest quintile it was 4.67. That is, people in the lowest quintile had, on average, income equal to 92% of the OPT, whereas people in the highest quintile had income equal to nearly 5 times the OPT. The Census Bureau finds that, between 1994 and 1995, the IPR changed by less than 5% for 22.7% of persons, declined by more than 5% for 36.8% of persons, and increased by more than 5% for 40.5%. These changes vary little by the race or gender of the person. Thus, as was

[1]Reported in the *Economic Report of the President,* February 1992, pp. 124–5.
[2]Sawhill and Condon, "Is U.S. Income Inequality Really Growing?" 1992.
[3]Burkhauser et al., "Labor Earnings Mobility in the United States and Germany" 1996. A comparison of various studies of income mobility is found in Sawhill and McMurrer, "How Much Do Americans Move Up and Down the Economic Ladder?" December 1996. This article and its companion piece can be viewed or downloaded on the Urban Institute's web site at www.urban.org.

found for economic mobility between quintiles, the Census finds that people's economic circumstances vary considerably over time.

Because people's incomes change over time, the measured inequality of the size distribution of income is less when income is measured over a longer interval of time than one year. For instance, when income is measured over a seven-year interval rather than one year, the Gini ratio is nearly 8% less than the Gini ratio of annual income.[4] This means that part of the inequality we observe in annual incomes is temporary and reflects differences in family incomes over time rather than differences between families.

ALTERNATIVE MEASURES OF INEQUALITY.   As stated earlier, interpreting the distribution of income requires us to consider the quality of the hotel rooms as well as mobility among them (to continue Schumpeter's analogy). We can measure the quality of the rooms (the actual status of people in a given quintile) using different measures of income. The official measure used by the Census Bureau is cash income before taxes, including cash transfers received from the government like Social Security and welfare checks. The Census definition of income is narrow in the sense that it excludes many receipts that are equivalent to cash income. Excluded components of income include capital gains, employer-paid fringe benefits, and noncash government transfers like Medicare and Medicaid health benefits. In addition, the Census measures income before taxes, so the amount reported does not actually equal what households have to spend. Table 7.2 shows the size distribution of household (information on families is not available) *comprehensive* after-tax income. The comprehensive measure used by the Census (second row) adds capital gains income, the value of noncash government transfers like Medicare and Medicaid, and also the imputed return on homeowner's equity. The latter is the implicit income homeowners receive from living in their own home rather than

Table 7.2   Inequality: Alternative Income Measures

Income Measure	Quintiles					Top 1%	Gini Ratio
	1	2	3	4	5		
Cash income, before taxes	3.6	9.2	14.9	23.3	49.0	n.a.	.446
Census comprehensive after taxes (1998)*	4.9	10.7	16.0	23.0	45.4	n.a.	.399
CBO (projected 1999) after federal taxes⁺	4.2	9.7	14.7	21.3	50.4	12.9	.41**
CBO (1977) after federal taxes⁺	5.7	11.5	16.4	22.8	44.2	7.3	.35**

Sources: *Census Bureau, *Money Income in the United States—1998,* September 1999, p. xix.
*Calculated by the Center on Budget and Policy Priorities, "The Widening Income Gulf," figure 2, September 1999 (www.dopp.org/9-4-99 taxrep.htm), using CBO daa available on the CBO web site.
**Approximate Gini ratio calculated by author using the formula in the text.

---

[4] *Economic Report of the President,* February 1992, p. 125.

paying rent to a landlord. Federal and state personal income and payroll taxes are subtracted. As we can see from the table, the size distribution of after-tax comprehensive income is more equal than the distribution of before-tax cash income. The lowest and highest quintiles of households receive 4.9% and 45.4% of comprehensive income respectively, compared with 3.6% and 49% of cash income before taxes. Similarly, the Gini ratio is .399 for household comprehensive income as compared with .45 for cash income.

A significant shortcoming of the Census data is that it fails to adjust for household or family size. A household with six persons has a different level of need than a single person, and an income of (say) $25,000 would impose greater hardship on the bigger household. The Census data puts both households in the same quintile. Economists attempt to adjust for a family's need using an **equivalence scale.** The Congressional Budget Office (CBO) measures a family's comprehensive income and divides it by the Official Poverty Threshold income for a family of the same characteristics for this purpose. The resulting index, called Adjusted Family Income (AFI) by the CBO, is just the Income-to-Poverty Ratio mentioned earlier. The CBO uses the AFI to rank families and classify them into the appropriate income quintile (as compared with the Census, where the families are ranked on their cash income). This way, a family of six with $25,000 income would be classified in the lowest income quintile rather than the second quintile, and a single person with this income would be classified into a higher quintile. The CBO uses a comprehensive measure of family income that includes capital gains but not the value of in-kind transfers. All federal income, payroll, and excise taxes are subtracted.[5] Fortunately, the CBO provides historical data that can be compared with current data so that we can examine changes in the income distribution over time.

Whereas the Census data for households indicate that after-tax comprehensive income is more equally distributed than before-tax cash income, the CBO data reveal that, after applying an equivalence scale, after-tax comprehensive income is as unequally distributed across families as Census cash income (third row). In fact, the CBO data show that inequality of after-tax comprehensive income has increased over the past two decades at about the same rate as the inequality of before-tax cash income.

So far we have measured the quality of the "rooms" only in terms of income, which is the most usual. We can also measure inequality in terms of consumption and wealth. Some economists argue that consumption is a better measure of a household's economic status because it is most directly related to its standard of living. Households in lower income quintiles typically spend more on consumption than their incomes. How is this possible? One possibility is that income is underreported or does not include all the receipts of the household, such as gifts from family members. It also reflects the fact that households can consume more than they earn by running down their savings. Similarly, households in higher

---

[5]The incidence of taxes is analyzed in Chapter 11. The CBO assumes personal income and payroll taxes are borne by the families that pay them, corporate income taxes are borne in proportion to a family's income from capital (dividends and capital gains), and excise taxes are borne in proportion to a family's consumption of the taxed goods.

income quintiles spend less than they earn, typically because they save the remainder, thereby increasing their net worth. For this reason, some economists view wealth or net worth as a better measure of the household's economic status. Net worth is equal to the value of the household's assets (bank accounts, stock portfolio, home, etc.) less its liabilities (debts, mortgage, etc.) and is a measure of the household's *capacity* to consume. Wealth also provides advantages in terms of liquidity, which allows a household to maintain consumption levels when its income fluctuates, and financial independence.

Table 7.3 reports the size distribution of expenditure as reported in the *Consumer Expenditure Survey* published by the Bureau of Labor Statistics and the size distribution of net worth as calculated by Professor Edward N. Wolff of New York University. The first two rows show the share of total consumption spending by each quintile, where each quintile represents 20% of the "consuming units" (roughly equivalent to households) in the survey. In these rows, the quintiles are determined by income, so quintile 5 (Q5) represents the 20% of consuming units with the highest reported incomes. The last two rows show the share of total net worth by each quintile, where each quintile represents 20% of households ranked according to their net worth. In this case, Q5 represents the 20% of households with the highest net worth.

The first thing we learn from Table 7.3 is that Pareto's 20/80 rule applies well to the distribution of wealth in the United States. Second, by comparing Table 7.3 with Table 7.1 or Table 7.2, we see that the size distribution of consumption expenditure is more equal than income, whereas the size distribution of net worth is more unequal. Thus actual consumption is more equal across households than income, but the capacity to consume, as measured by net worth, is less equal. Finally, as in the case of income, inequality of consumption and wealth has increased over time. From 1984 to 1998, consumption by the highest-income quintile increased from a share of 37.2% of total spending to 42.8%, while from 1983 to 1995, the net worth share of the highest-net-worth quintile increased from 81.3% of total net worth to 83.9%. The increase in inequality in consumption and wealth is relatively less than that of income, however. Between 1984 and 1998, the Gini ratio of consumption increased by 7.7%, whereas the Gini ratio for household income inequal-

Table 7.3   Inequality in Consumption and Wealth

	Quintiles					Gini Ratio**
	1	2	3	4	5	
Share of consumption (1998)*	8.9%	12.7%	16.9%	23.5%	42.8%	.28
Share of consumption (1984)*	9.6	13.1	17.3	23.2	37.2	.26
Share of net worth (1995)+	.2		4.5	11.4	83.9	.72
Share of net worth (1983)+	.9		5.2	12.6	81.3	.70

Sources: *Calculated by author from *Consumer Expenditure Survey*, 1998 and 1984.
+Edward N. Wolff, "Recent Trends in the Size Distribution of Household Wealth," 1998, p. 136.
**Approximate Gini ratio calculated by the author.

ity increased 8.9%. Between 1983 and 1995, the Gini ratio for net worth increased 2.9% as compared with a 9.9% rise in the Gini ratio for income.

Comparisons of Income Inequality Across Countries

How does the distribution of income in the United States compare with that of other countries, and have other countries experienced the same increase in inequality we see in the United States? In the past, such questions were difficult to answer because comparisons of income distributions in different countries were beset with numerous problems, including the way income is defined and differences in family size and composition. In the past few years, however, comparative data have become available through the Luxembourg Income Study (LIS), and several studies comparing the income distributions in different countries are now available. Figure 7.3 shows the Gini ratios for disposable personal income in six industrialized countries.[6] The equivalence scale chosen by LIS is to divide family income by the square root of the number of family members. For all countries, income is defined as cash income, including cash transfers, minus direct taxes (personal income and payroll taxes). Figure 7.3 shows that income inequality in the United States is somewhat higher than in other countries, although roughly comparable with that in the United Kingdom. Russia, not shown in the figure, has considerably more income inequality than the United States or other countries, with a Gini ratio of .47 in 1995.

Figure 7.3 also shows that the United States is not the only country that has experienced an increase in income inequality. From 1979 to the mid-1990s, Sweden

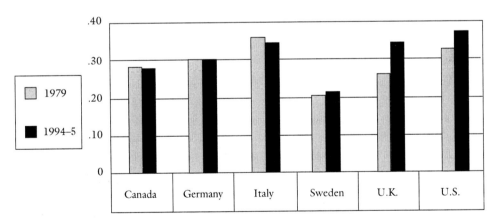

Figure 7.3

Gini Ratios by Country: 1979 and 1994–5

Income concentration, as measured by the Gini ratio, varies across countries and time.
Source: 1994–5 information from LIS Inequality Indices, Luxembourg Income Study, LIS Information Server at http://lissy.ceps.lu/ineq.htm. 1979 information is author's calculations based on Peter Gottschalk and Timothy M. Smeeding, "Empirical Evidence on Income Inequality in Industrialized Countries," Luxembourg Income Study Working Paper No. 154, Rev. February 1999, Table A-2.

[6]Because the LIS income data is disposable (after tax) and adjusted for family size, the Gini ratio reported for the United States in Figure 7.3 differs from that reported in Figure 7.2.

7.1   Do Census Data Exaggerate Inequality?

Robert Rector and Rea Hederman of the Heritage Foundation contend that even the Census's comprehensive measure of income exaggerates income inequality in the United States. The study is available at www.heritage.org/library/cda/cda99-07.html. The authors observe that the households in different quintiles differ in size and hours worked. For instance, although the bottom and top quintiles both contain 20% of all households, the quintiles contain different percentages of the population because household size varies across the quintiles. The bottom quintile contains only 14.7% of persons, while the top quintile contains 24.3% of persons. They also find that the average hours worked by working-age adults is only 14.4 hours per week in the bottom quintile as compared with 34.6 hours per week in the top. Rector and Hederman rank households by their incomes but adjust the Census data so that quintiles contain the same number of persons rather than households. For example, they raise the upper income limit on the lowest quintile to $23,124 household income from $18,195 so that it contains enough households to account for 20% of persons. Similarly, they raise the lower income limit for the top quintile to $66,501 from

$60,603. They also standardize for work effort by calculating the hypothetical income each quintile would receive if its working-age adults worked the average hours per week of all working-age adults. The standardized quintile shares for quintiles 1 to 5 are 12%, 15%, 17%, 20%, and 37%.

Critically analyze this issue by answering the following questions:

- The Gini ratio for the corresponding Census data is .40. How much less unequal is the distribution of income according to the Rector and Hederman study? (Use the formula for the approximate Gini ratio given in the text.)

- Rector and Hederman adjust for different numbers of persons in households by changing the income limits on the quintiles. The CBO adjusts by dividing each family's income by the Official Poverty Threshold for a family of the same size and then ranks families by Adjusted Family Income. Which method do you prefer and why?

- For the purpose of measuring inequality, do you agree or disagree that incomes should be adjusted to reflect different hours worked by working-age adults in each quintile? Why?

and the United Kingdom also experienced increased inequality; the increase was especially marked in the United Kingdom, where the Gini ratio increased by 33% as compared with 15% in the United States. Income inequality remained relatively constant over the same period in both Canada and Germany and declined in Italy.

REASONS FOR GOVERNMENT REDISTRIBUTION

Whatever the facts about income inequality, what can and should the government do about it? Some people argue the government should do nothing about it—the role of government is to establish rights and provide the judicial institutions needed for society to function or, at most, provide public goods and correct market failures. Nonetheless, in the United States, as in nearly all industrialized countries, the government does carry out significant redistribution policies including Social Security, welfare and other forms of public assistance for the poor, and Medicare and Medicaid. Distribution considerations influence public education policies and the structure of the tax system. Moreover, government spending on programs such as national defense alters the income distribution even if the effect is unintended.

Given that government does redistribute income, what principles can explain this role and help us evaluate whether the amount and type of redistribution achieved is desirable? The normative reasons for government redistribution can be grouped into two broad classes: redistribution that improves economic efficiency, and redistribution that improves distributional equity. Of course, in addition, the government may redistribute income for political reasons, such as when politically powerful groups convince legislators to pass programs that benefit them.

Efficiency-Improving Redistribution

Two arguments contend that at least some amount of redistribution would improve economic efficiency. The first argument hinges on the idea that charity is a type of public good discussed in Chapter 3. The second argument is based on market failure in private insurance markets. We consider each in turn.

THE PUBLIC GOOD ARGUMENT.   Although economists often assume that people are motivated by self-interest, we know that a desire to help others is not uncommon. Individuals, corporations, and institutions made philanthropic gifts of nearly $175 billion in 1998.[7] And we often witness outpourings of gifts in money and goods in response to national and international tragedies. It seems that people care about the utilities of others as well as themselves.

Economists analyze this type of behavior by assuming that people have altruistic preferences—that is, they derive utility from giving charity to others as well as from spending on their own consumption. Consequently, people have a marginal willingness to pay (MWTP) for charitable gifts for the less fortunate. As in the case of any other form of spending, it is reasonable to assume that the MWTP for charity is lower the greater the level of charity. However, the level of charity depends not only on a person's own charitable gifts but on the gifts as others as well. In other words, charity is a nonrival good and one person's gift to the less fortunate benefits all others who care about the less fortunate.

Suppose, for example, Florence N. sees homeless families on the street and is moved to help them by giving them money. Although she may do this to increase her own utility (because she is altruistic), she also benefits her altruistic neighbor M. Teresa. However, in addition to being a nonrival good, charity is also a nonexcludable good. That is, Florence is not able to charge Teresa for the benefit she enjoyed from Florence's gift. Moreover, Florence's gift may reduce Teresa's incentive to make her own gift to the poor, because her MWTP for charity declines as the total amount of charity increases. Despite their altruism for the poor, Florence and Teresa are inclined to "free ride" and each gives less to charity in the hope that the other will give more. As a result, the total level of charity will be less than either person actually desires.

To see this more clearly, let's apply the analysis of the private provision of public goods described in Chapter 3. Assume both Florence and Teresa have the same

---

[7]American Association of Fund-Raising Counsel, *Giving USA*. See chart at www.aafrc.org.

Figure 7.4

The Private and Efficient Levels of Charity

Although the efficient level of charity for Florence and Teresa is $60, free riding leads to a lower level of charity ($10) provided voluntarily by the participants.

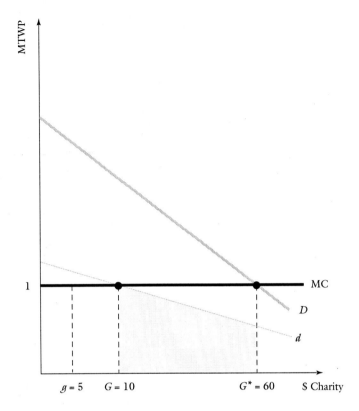

marginal willingness to pay schedule for charity, labeled d in Figure 7.4, where (say) each person's $MWTP = 1.1 - \dfrac{G}{100}$ and G is the total level of charity (gifts) for the poor. Because Florence and Teresa have identical schedules, $G = 2g$ where g is the amount of the gift made by each person. The marginal cost of making a one-dollar gift to the poor is $1, so the two donors are in equilibrium when $1.1 - \dfrac{2g}{100} = 1$, which can be solved for $g = \$5$. Thus, total charity provided privately by Florence and Teresa combined is $10, which is shown where schedule d intersects the horizontal line with height equal to 1 (the marginal cost of charity) in Figure 7.4. It is easy to see that this level of charity is inefficient. When total charity is $10, Florence and Teresa each have a MWTP of $1, so their combined MWTP for an increase in charity is $2. This is greater than the marginal cost of charity ($1).

To be efficient, the level of charity should be such that the *sum* of the marginal willingness to pay for charity by Florence and Teresa is equal to the marginal cost of charity. This is the "Samuelson" rule for the efficient amount of a public good described in Chapter 3. By vertically summing the individual MWTP schedules, we obtain the schedule labeled D in Figure 7.4, and the efficient level of charity is found where D intersects the marginal cost of charity line. Because Florence and Teresa have identical schedules, the intersection occurs where $2\left(1.1 - \dfrac{G}{100}\right) = 1$, which can be solved for an efficient level of charity G^* equal to $60. Thus, in this case of two persons, total private charity is equal to one-sixth the efficient level of charity.

The level of private charity is even more inadequate if more people are involved. If N people have the MWTP schedule specified above, private motives would lead to an outcome where $1.1 - \dfrac{N \cdot g}{100} = 1$. In this case, g equals $\dfrac{10}{N}$.

Note as N becomes large, the individual's gift g becomes small, although total private charity remains $10 because there are more people who give. The efficient level of charity satisfies $N\left(1.1 - \dfrac{G}{100}\right) = 1$ or $G^* = 110 - \dfrac{100}{N}$. Thus, in this example, when the number of people is sufficiently large the efficient level of charity is approximately $110, whereas the amount of private charity is just $10.

The government can increase efficiency by taxing the population to provide more charity (transfers to the poor). For example, if the government taxes Florence and Teresa $30 each and gives the $60 to the poor, both of them are made better off. When charity is socialized in this way, neither Florence nor Teresa will make private gifts because at $60 their MWTP is just $.50, which is less than what it costs them to give a dollar to the poor. Since they no longer contribute $5 to charity voluntarily, the net cost of the government program to each is $25. However, the increase in charity from $10 to $60 benefits each of them by an amount equal to the shaded area under their MWTP schedule shown in Figure 7.4. Using geometric reasoning, we can calculate this area as $37.50. Thus Florence and Teresa are each made better off by the government redistribution program by $12.50.

THE SOCIAL INSURANCE ARGUMENT.   Many government programs that redistribute income are structured somewhat like insurance contracts. Indeed, sometimes the government programs that provide income support are described as a "social safety net" or social insurance. The fact that people benefit from and demand a social safety net is easy enough to understand. Everyone faces various risks and uncertainties in life and fears the consequences of misfortune, whether it is one's house burning down or a primary family earner becoming disabled and unable to earn a living. In many cases people protect themselves from such risks by purchasing insurance from private companies. Most people have life insurance to protect their families against loss of income in the event of the death of a primary earner, automobile insurance to insure against a loss from a traffic accident, homeowner's insurance to protect against the loss of one's residence, and many other forms of insurance. Private specialty insurance companies have insured everything from Tina Turner's legs to being abducted by aliens.

Given the prevalence and variety of private insurance contracts, why is there a need for social or government insurance? To understand this, we need to briefly consider how the insurance industry operates. Private firms can offer insurance against large losses because many of the risks that people face are independent. For example, the chance that one person's house will burn down does not depend on the chance that someone else's house will burn down (assuming they are not neighbors). Private insurers can pool the risk of house fires and other independent risks by selling insurance to a large number of households, called the risk pool. The premiums from these insurance policies are placed in a fund, and the few unlucky households whose homes burn down receive a payment from the fund to offset their loss. Because the risks are independent, the amount that has to be paid out to the unlucky households is highly predictable, providing the risk pool is large. In this case, insurance companies can charge an insurance premium determined by the fraction of policy holders whose homes will burn down times the amount the company has to pay out in that event (plus a profit for the company). Note that these private insurance arrangements can be viewed as a type of redistribution. Households whose homes don't burn down pay premiums but never receive a payment, whereas households whose homes burn down receive payments much larger than the premiums paid.

To provide insurance on reasonable terms, the risk pool should include as many households with independent risks as possible. For example, if the risk pool included only those households who have a high probability of suffering a loss, insurance would be unavailable or prohibitively expensive. Insurance market failure can occur if the risk pool becomes concentrated with households who pose higher than average risks. In this case, the private insurance market would yield an inefficient outcome, and government or social insurance arrangements could increase economic efficiency to the benefit of society. Two phenomena can account for insurance market failure: adverse selection and moral hazard. Both of these phenomena can arise when the insurance sellers have incomplete information about their customers.

Adverse Selection.   Insurance is more attractive to people who are likely to need it. The probability that a household will experience a loss or harmful event often depends on certain characteristics possessed by the household. For instance, the chance of a person dying within a given year depends on the person's age, sex, state of health, whether he or she smokes, genetic factors, and other things. Obviously, a person who has a high chance of dying is likely find life insurance more attractive than someone who has a low chance of dying. If life insurance were sold to everyone for the same price, people who are more likely to die would buy more life insurance and people who have a low chance of dying would buy less or none. Consequently, the fraction of high-risk persons in the risk pool would increase, and the price of life insurance would have to rise. As the price of life insurance rises, low-risk people would find life insurance even less attractive, and drop out of the risk pool. This process, called **adverse selection,** would ultimately lead to a shrinking risk pool that contains only high-risk people, and insurance companies could offer insurance only at exorbitant prices. In an extreme case, private companies would stop offering insurance altogether.

We do not see this happening in the life insurance industry, because firms can and do distinguish high- and low-risk people and can charge different premiums for life insurance accordingly. Younger people, women, people who have no history of serious illness, nonsmokers, and people whose parents live to a ripe old age are offered life insurance at lower rates than older people, men, people with serious illnesses, smokers, and people whose parents died young. In some insurance markets, such as automobile insurance, firms assess a person's risk from his or her past history and charge premiums accordingly. This is called **experience rating.**

When private insurance firms can accurately observe the risk level of a household, insurance is usually readily available, although it may be expensive for those in high-risk groups. In other words, for adverse selection to cause insurance market failure, private insurers must be incapable of observing a household's risk, or at least incapable of charging different insurance premiums based on such observations. For certain types of risk, adverse selection is a serious problem and insurance would be unavailable unless provided by the government.

Moral Hazard.   **Moral hazard** is the name given to the simple fact that people tend to act differently when they are insured against a loss. In particular, they are less likely to be careful or take preventive actions to avoid the loss for which they are insured. For instance, drivers may be less careful to avoid an accident when they have collision insurance and homeowners may be less careful to lock their doors when they have burglary insurance. Another type of moral hazard also is present when people have medical insurance. People are more likely to visit the doctor or demand expensive treatments when the insurance company pays the cost rather than the patients themselves. Although this may be good in some cases, such when the person has an illness that requires early diagnosis, in other cases it results in unnecessary medical costs.

If insurers cannot observe whether insured households take preventive actions, their costs are higher and insurance is more expensive. Insurers may require the households to pay part of the loss out of their own pockets in the form of co-payments, so insurance coverage is partial rather than full. In some cases, moral hazard may be so extreme that insurance is unavailable. If insurers can observe preventive actions and set insurance premiums accordingly, no moral hazard is present. For example, many insurers offer lower rates to homeowners who have burglar and smoke alarms installed. In this case, the insured household has no less incentive to be careful.

Moral hazard can be viewed as a type of externality (see Chapter 4). When an insured person takes care to prevent a loss, he or she incurs a private cost and lowers the cost of insurance. However, people who take care do not reap the full benefit of their actions, because insurance premiums do not depend on their actions. Instead, the lower cost of insurance benefits everybody in the risk pool whether they take care or not. As a result, insured households have little incentive to undertake preventive actions.

What Can the Government Do?   Insurance market failure due to adverse selection and moral hazard means that insurance is more costly than necessary, coverage is incomplete, and many people may be uninsured even though they would choose to be insured if insurance was less costly. The government can increase economic efficiency by supplying more insurance and increasing the number of people who are covered. When the government provides social insurance, it may take the form of a tax and transfer redistribution program. For example, Social Security, Medicare, and unemployment insurance are all government transfer programs funded by levying payroll taxes on employers and employees. These programs pay a benefit to an individual when a certain event occurs such as retirement, illness, or job loss. Typically, too, government insurance programs are compulsory and cover nearly everybody. This prevents the risk pool from shrinking through adverse selection. The government can also undertake policies to mitigate moral hazard. Penalties are imposed for early retirement under Social Security and co-payments are required for hospital stays under Medicare. Unemployment insurance programs in some states are experienced rated, so employers who lay off more workers pay a higher unemployment payroll tax.

Equity-Improving Redistribution

The public good and social insurance arguments both justify government redistribution as a means of improving economic efficiency. Another concern underlying government redistribution is fairness or equity. Whenever tax reform, health care, welfare, or practically any government economic policy is debated, someone is bound to ask, "Is it fair?" Because equity is such a subjective concept, some economists hesitate to enter the debate and prefer to concentrate on positive economics or economic efficiency. Increasingly, however, economists incorporate equity into their policy evaluations. To do this, they have identified several principles of equity that they believe are acceptable to most people, and have formalized some these principles in the economic models they use to evaluate policy.

PRINCIPLES OF EQUITY.   Four main principles underlie most discussions about equity. We call them the process principle, the benefit principle, the horizontal equity principle, and the vertical equity principle. As we will see, these principles are sometimes in conflict, which is why there is so much disagreement about what is fair and equitable.

The Process Principle.   Even as children, we learn early that fairness requires that we "play by the rules." And changing the rules in the middle of a game is certainly unfair. This principle extends to matters of state. The "rule of law," for example, demands that the laws apply equally to everyone in the land regardless of their status or position of power. The **process principle** defines fairness or equity in terms of the process by which an outcome is determined, rather than by the outcomes that result. Thus, by this principle the distribution of income is fair if people earned their incomes "fair and square" and did not violate the rules or laws in the process of acquiring them. Another example of the process principle is the perceived unfairness of *ex post facto* or retroactive taxes, where the government taxes you on the basis of actions you took in the past. Such taxes are considered unfair (and, indeed, are unconstitutional) because they would change the rules after the fact.

The Benefit Principle.   The **benefit principle** of equity requires that consequences depend on actions. For example, many people believe that a person who works hard deserves to be rich whereas a person who is lazy deserves to be poor. Thus if a person believes that differences in incomes among families reflect differences in how hard family members work, he or she might judge the income distribution as equitable according to the benefit principle. In taxation, the benefit principle requires that those who benefit the most from a government program should pay the largest share of the taxes needed to finance it. Thus, for example, a tax on gasoline may be considered fair if the revenue from the tax is used to improve roads. People who drive the most and benefit from the improved roads also bear the bulk of the tax.

The Horizontal Equity Principle.   The principle of **horizontal equity** is often expressed as "equals should be treated equally." In other words, a policy is unfair if it has different impacts on people in similar economic circumstances. For example, a tax policy that required two families with the same income to pay considerably different amounts of tax violates the principle of horizontal equity. A weaker form of horizontal equity states that household characteristics other than income or ability to pay (such as family name, sex, ethnicity, or national origin) should not be used as a basis for differential treatment under a government policy.

The Vertical Equity Principle.   The principle of **vertical equity** states that an increase in the economic well-being of people who have more income should count less than an increase in the economic well-being of those who have less income. Thus a policy that increases the income of the needy is more equitable than a policy that increases the income of the rich. In taxation, the principle of vertical equity requires that the taxes levied on a household be in accordance with its ability to pay. Thus, for example, a per capita tax that required every household to pay the same amount of tax would be considered inequitable under the vertical equity principle.

The principle of vertical equity has a long history in economics. Nearly **200** years ago, the dominant philosophy of welfare economics was **utilitarianism.** Utilitarians, such as the British philosopher Jeremy Bentham, believed that an ideal society would maximize the sum of the utilities of the population. Furthermore, they believed in the "law of diminishing marginal utility of money," which holds that an extra dollar of income increases the utility of a poor person more than an extra dollar of income increases the utility of a rich person. Thus a policy that takes a dollar from a rich person and gives it to a poor person would increase the sum of utilities and society would be happier. As reasonable as the assumption of diminishing marginal utility of money sounds, economists now know that it cannot be verified by any observation of human behavior. Nonetheless, the idea that redistributing income from the rich to the poor increases the welfare of a society survives in the form of a social welfare function.

EQUITY AND THE SOCIAL WELFARE FUNCTION.   The challenge facing economists is to formalize the different concepts of equity in a consistent way. Because the principles may conflict with each other, this proves to be an impossible task. For example, according to the benefit principle, two households who have the same income should pay different amounts of tax if they receive different benefits from the government, but horizontal equity requires that they pay the same amount of tax. Similarly, the process principle states that income disparities are equitable if all households play by the rules, but the vertical equity principle requires redistribution from the rich to the poor. Because of these conflicts, most economists focus on equity as determined by outcomes rather than by process, and on the horizontal and vertical equity principles rather than the benefit principle.

The horizontal and vertical equity principles can be expressed in the form of a **social welfare function (SWF)**. An SWF is simply a way of expressing the level of social welfare in the society as a function of (i.e., depending on) the levels of utilities of the people in the society. In a two-person society consisting of George and Martha, the SWF can be written

$$W = F\left(U^{\,G}, U^{\,M}\right)$$

where W is the level of social welfare, U^G is the level of utility enjoyed by George, and U^M is the level of utility enjoyed by Martha. The utility of any individual can be scaled so that it is equal to the real consumption of the individual.[8] Thus, $U^G = I^G$ and $U^M = I^M$, where I^G and I^M are indexes of the real income levels of George and Martha respectively.

Figure 7.5 illustrates the SWF using social welfare indifference curves. Along a social indifference curve, the level of social welfare is a constant, so every distribution of I^G and I^M along the curve is equally good in terms of social welfare. Social indifference curves lying farther from the origin represent higher levels of social welfare and are therefore more desirable. The 45-degree line is the equality line, because at every point on this line George and Martha have the same level of real income.

The slope of a social welfare indifference curve at any point is equal to the decrease in the real income by Martha needed to offset a small increase in the real income of George while holding social welfare constant. An increase in the real income of George without a change in Martha's income would be an improvement in social welfare according to Pareto's criterion (see Chapter 2), so social welfare must be higher for all distributions in the northeast quadrant to a point on an indifference curve. Therefore, the social welfare indifference curves must be negatively sloped in order to be consistent with Pareto's criterion.

The principles of horizontal and vertical equity are reflected in the shape of the social welfare indifference curves. Typically, these indifference curves are symmetric around the equality line.[9] This means that if we swap George and Martha's income levels (giving George what Martha had and vice versa), the level of social welfare would not change. This is consistent with one interpretation we gave to horizontal equity earlier—that people's incomes, not their identities or personal characteristics, should determine their equitable treatment.[10]

The principle of vertical equity is reflected in the curvature of the social welfare indifference curves. The social welfare indifference curve has an absolute slope of 1 where it intersects the equality line. This indicates that a unit increase in George's

---

[8]We can scale utility this way because utility numbers can be assigned to indifference curves in any way we like as long as the curves farther from the origin have higher numbers.

[9]Symmetry means that a mirror placed along the equality line would reflect the upper half of the indifference curve so that it exactly overlies the lower half.

[10]Martin Feldstein, "On the Theory of Tax Reform," 1976, argues that the stronger definition of horizontal equity (equals must be treated equally) can conflict with vertical equity.

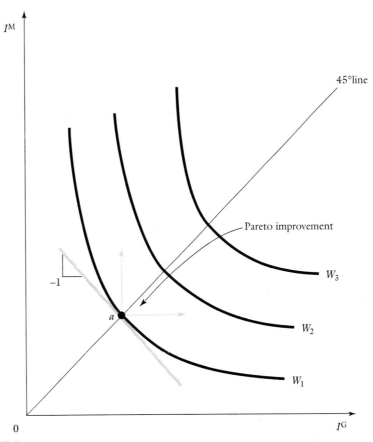

Figure 7.5

The Social Welfare Function and the Distribution of Income
If we identify the consumers' utilities with their income levels respectively, the level of social welfare in an economy depends on the distribution of income. The social welfare function can be illustrated by social welfare indifference curves that show distributions yielding the same level of social welfare. At point a, both George and Martha get equal amounts of income and social welfare is equal to W_1. An increase in income by either person, ceteris paribus, or by both yields a Pareto improvement. More generally, a distribution of income above W_1 gives an increase in social welfare.

income is worth the same as a unit decrease in Martha's income when they have equal incomes. Above the equality line, Martha has more income than George and the indifference curve has an absolute slope greater than 1. This indicates that a unit decrease in Martha's income requires less than a unit increase in George's income to hold social welfare constant. In other words, a greater weight is placed on the change in George's income than Martha's when Martha is relatively better off. The reverse is true below the equality line.

The amount of curvature in the social welfare indifference curves measures the degree of **inequality aversion** in the SWF. If the indifference curves are quite flat, the demand for vertical equity is weak and disparity in the distribution of incomes does not matter much. In the extreme case, the indifference curves are right angles and the degree of inequality aversion is infinite. Such an SWF puts a positive weight only on the income of the poorest person in the economy.

THE DISTRIBUTIONAL WEIGHTS APPROACH. The social welfare function is a rather abstract idea. The most practical application of the SWF is the use of **distributional weights** to evaluate small changes in the distribution of income.

The distributional weight for person H, denoted ω^H, is the increase in social welfare that occurs if H's income is increased by one unit. The weight ω^H is a positive number that is larger when person H is poor relative to others in the society. Using the distributional weights approach, the change in the social welfare in the two-person economy is

$$\Delta W = \omega^G \cdot \Delta I^G + \omega^M \cdot \Delta I^M.$$

The distributional weights approach provides a linear approximation to the change in social welfare obtained by changing the income distribution. In fact, the ratio ω^M / ω^G is equal to the slope of a social welfare indifference curve in Figure 7.5. The curvature of the indifference curve means that the weights are not constant but depend on the existing distribution of income.

Let's work through a simple example to see how the change in social welfare is found using the distributional weights approach. First, we need the distributional weights. One simple (but arbitrary) way of choosing distributional weights is to set the distributional weight for a family equal to the median family income in the economy ($56,061 in 1998 for a family of four) divided by the family's own income. By this method, a family receiving the median family income gets a distributional weight equal to 1, while families whose incomes are greater than (less than) the median get distributional weights that are less than (greater than) 1.

In 1998 the Official Poverty Threshold income (the level of income below which families are considered to be in poverty) was $16,530 for a family of four. Using our method of distributional weights, a family on the poverty threshold gets a weight of $56,061 divided by $16,530, or about 3.4. This means we are willing to give up $3.40 of income to a family with median income to increase consumption of a family at the poverty threshold by $1. On the other hand, the family income for affluent families who are in the top 5% of the income distribution is at least $145,200. The distributional weight of a family with this income is about .39 ($56,061 divided by $145,200). This indicates that we are willing to give up only 39 cents of the income of a median income family to increase the income of an affluent family by $1.

To make things interesting, assume that the poverty threshold family receives an extra $100 but the affluent family must pay $400. This seems like a poor bargain, yet it can increase social welfare when we take distributional weights into account. Using the weights calculated above, the increase in income of $100 to the poverty-line family increases social welfare by $340 (3.4 times $100). The $400 loss to the affluent family decreases social welfare by $156 (.39 times $400). The net change in social welfare is $340 minus $156, or $184. The gain is attributable to the fact that the smaller income gain of the poor family is weighted far more heavily than the income loss to the affluent family.

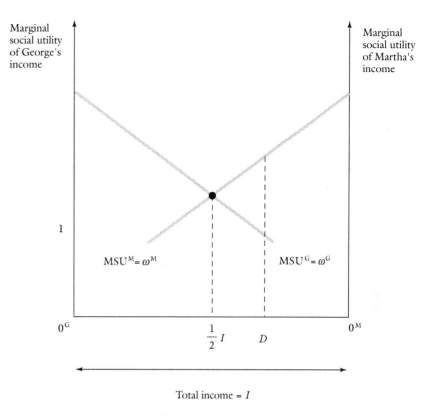

Figure 7.6

"Optimal" Redistribution

If the total income in the economy is fixed and George and Martha have the same marginal social utility (MSU) schedules, the optimal distribution of income is one of complete equality.

EDGEWORTH'S "OPTIMAL" DISTRIBUTION OF INCOME.   If the distributional weight of a family with lower income is greater than one with higher income, should the government redistribute income until their incomes are equalized? Seventy-five years ago, F. Y. Edgeworth showed that, under certain assumptions, equality is indeed the "optimal" distribution of income. Edgeworth's analysis is illustrated for a two-person economy in Figure 7.6. The total amount of income in the economy, assumed to be a constant, is equal to distance $0^G 0^M$; the amount of income received by George is measured to the right of 0^G, while the amount of income received by Martha is measured to the left of 0^M. The increase in social welfare from an extra dollar of income to George, called the marginal social utility (denoted MSU^G) of George's income, is measured on the left-hand vertical axis and that of Martha (MSU^M) on the right-hand vertical axis. The MSUs are just the distributional weights discussed above. The downward-sloping curve labeled MSU^G shows that the marginal social utility of income to George declines as his income increases because the social welfare indifference curves exhibit inequality aversion (vertical equity). The curve labeled MSU^M shows the same thing for Martha.

7.2   The Marginal Cost of Redistributing Income

Professors Edgar K. Browning and William R. Johnson, then at the University of Virginia, calculated the cost of redistributing income from upper-income households to lower-income households using the tax system. In particular, they assumed revenue is collected using a flat rate tax on income (that is, all income is taxed at one rate, say 20%), which can be used to finance a universal transfer payment. The universal transfer payment, sometimes called a **demogrant,** is a lump-sum payment that is received by every household, rich or poor. Since lower-income households pay less income tax than higher-income households, this effectively redistributes income to them.[1] Browning and Johnson consider the effect of an increase of one percentage point in the income tax rate with the revenue used to increase the demogrant. Taking into account the effects of the tax and the demogrant on the incentive to work, they estimated the effect on a household's utility measured as an equivalent change in its income. The changes in income based on 1976 data for households in each quintile from this experiment are shown below.[2]

Critically analyze the following questions:

- Suppose the distributional weight on upper-income households is .5 and the distributional weight on lower-income households is 2. Would it be desirable to increase the tax rate by one percentage point and use the revenue to increase the demogrant? What if the distributional weight on lower-income households is 1.5?

- In a later study, Professor Charles Ballard of Michigan State University calculated that it would cost upper-income households between $1.50 and $2.30 to increase the income of lower-income households by $1 using the tax-demogrant scheme.[3] Thus, between 33% and 57% of income is lost. Ballard assumed that the household's labor supply is less sensitive to its after-tax wage rate than did Browning and Johnson. Why is the cost of redistribution less when it is assumed that the labor supply is less sensitive to the wage rate?

- Would you support raising the income tax rate to redistribute income if Ballard's estimate is correct? Would you be more or less likely to support the idea if Browning and Johnson's estimate is correct? Explain.

	Quintile 1	Quintile 2	Quintile 3	Quintile 4	Quintile 5
Change in equivalent income	$47.30	$32.60	−$11.49	−$71.59	−$196.21

The ratio of the total loss to the upper three quintiles to the total gain for the lower two quintiles is 3.5. Consequently, they concluded that it costs upper-income households $3.50 to redistribute $1 to lower income households. Put differently, Browning and Johnson conclude that the "holes" in the redistribution bucket are quite large—about 71% of income is lost in redistributing it.

[1]Public finance economists call this tax-demogrant system a Negative Income Tax system, or NIT. The NIT is explained further in Chapter 12.
[2]Browning and Johnson, "The Trade-off Between Equality and Efficiency" 1984, Table 8, p. 200.
[3]Charles Ballard, "The Marginal Efficiency Cost of Redistribution," 1988, p. 1019.

(Remember that Martha's income is measured to the left from 0^M.) The MSU curve of Martha is a mirror image of George's because the social welfare indifference curves are symmetric about the equality line (horizontal equity). The combined area under the two MSU curves is equal to the level of social welfare.

Suppose the existing distribution of income is at D, where George gets income $0^G D$ and Martha gets a smaller income $0^M D$. At this distribution, the MSU of income to George is less than that of Martha because George has more income. The level of social welfare (the area under the combined curves) is increased if income is taxed away from George and the revenue given to Martha as a transfer. Social welfare is maximized where the two curves intersect, which under Edgeworth's assumptions occurs when the total income in the economy is split evenly between the two people. When George and Martha receive the same income, their MSUs are the same. Apparently, vertical equity requires that the government carry out an extreme tax and transfer policy that equalizes incomes across families.

THE EQUITY-EFFICIENCY TRADE-OFF.   Edgeworth was troubled by this answer, because it does not seem like a practical or desirable policy. The problem lies in his assumptions, particularly that the total income in the economy remains the same when the government tries to redistribute it. The total income in the economy depends on how much people work, and if everyone received the same income (after taxes and transfers) regardless of whether or how hard they work, no one would have much incentive to work.

The fact that redistribution reduces the incentive to work means that the economy faces an equity-efficiency trade-off. Authur Okun, the late economist, called it the "big trade-off." He pointed out that as the government redistributes income to achieve greater equity, work incentives are impaired, which reduces economic efficiency and creates a deadweight loss (or efficiency cost). In addition, redistribution programs have administration costs that absorb some of the taxes levied to finance redistribution. For example, the administration cost of a typical welfare program in the United States is about 16 cents per dollar of benefits distributed. Because of these costs, Okun compared redistributing income to carrying water in a leaky bucket. When we carry water from one place to another, some of it is lost through the holes in the bucket. Similarly, when the government redistributes income from one family to another, income is lost due to the deadweight loss from reduced work incentives and the administrative costs of the programs.

Just as more water is lost the farther we carry the bucket, the amount of income lost is greater the more redistribution the government undertakes. Because of the holes in the redistribution bucket, it is never optimal for the government to redistribute income to the point where everyone gets the same income, as in Edgeworth's analysis. According to the leaky bucket model, income should not be redistributed if the costs of redistribution outweigh the gains of increased vertical equity. For example, if the government must reduce a rich family's income by $10 so that it can increase a poor family's income by $1, it should not do so unless the distributional weight of the poor family is at least ten times that of the rich family.

Economists have attempted to estimate the size of the hole in the redistribution bucket. One estimate indicates that the hole is quite large, and 71% of income is lost in redistributing it. Another study found a smaller hole—about 33% to 57% is lost (see A Case in Point 7.2).

CONCLUSION AND SUMMARY

In this chapter we have presented methods of measuring inequality in the distribution of income and a consistent method of analyzing the role of government in redistributing income. Government redistribution policies remain problematic and controversial nonetheless. Partly this is because the government does not seem to follow consistent policies. While many programs, like welfare, redistribute from higher-income families to low, some programs do the opposite. For example, many provisions in the income tax system called tax expenditures subsidize higher-income families much more than lower-income families. (We will study tax expenditures at some length in Chapter 14.) Even where government is consistent in its pursuit of equity, it faces the difficulty of reconciling different notions of equity. Moreover, there is no set of distributional weights that is widely agreed on so that the government can rationalize its policies. Although most people might agree on the abstract idea of vertical equity, agreement breaks down when it comes down to a specific issue like the values of the distributional weights.

In the next two chapters we examine the two main directions of redistribution policy that do show some consistency. The first are the antipoverty programs that redistribute income in cash or benefits in kind, like food and health care, to people who meet certain standards of need. The second are the social insurance programs that redistribute income to the elderly in the form of Social Security checks and Medicare benefits.

- Income inequality is summarized by the size distribution, which reports the income shares of given percentages (such as quintiles) of families ranked by income. In 1998, families in the bottom quintile (the 20% of families with the lowest incomes) received just over 4% of all cash income, whereas the families in the top quintile received over 47% of cash income.

- The Lorenz curve is a graphical representation of the size distribution, and the Gini ratio is a numerical measure of overall income inequality. The Gini ratio is convenient for making inequality comparisons over time and across countries.

- Income inequality has risen over the past 30 years in the United States and in some other countries. In the United States, the income share of the highest quintile has increased nearly 16% between 1970 and 1998, while the Gini ratio increased 22% over the same period.

- When considering the social implications of income inequality, it should be remembered that the size distribution is a snapshot of the income distribution at a point in time. Families can and do move up and down the income ladder. In fact, most studies show significant mobility over a decade.

- Broader measures of income show a similar pattern of inequality. Consumption is more equally distributed than income, but wealth is more unequally distributed. Inequality has increased over the past 30 years by all measures.

- Income in the United States is somewhat more unequally distributed than in most other industrialized countries. Changes in inequality over time vary across countries. In the United Kingdom, the level of inequality grew faster than in the United States, whereas in Canada and Germany the level of inequality remained constant.

- The main arguments for government redistribution are to improve economic efficiency and increase equity. Government redistribution can increase efficiency because charity is at least partly a public good and because insurance market failure provides a need for social insurance (or a social safety net).

- There are several principles of equity (or fairness), and sometimes these principles conflict with each other. Economists concentrate on horizontal equity (the equal treatment of equals) and vertical equity (giving greater weight to the needs of the poor over the needs of the rich).

- Horizontal and vertical equity can be expressed in a social welfare function that provides distributional weights for changes in the incomes of families, with lower-income families receiving higher weights.

- Although vertical equity requires the government to redistribute income from higher-income families to lower-income families, redistribution is limited by its cost. Estimates of the costs of redistributing a dollar of income to families in the lowest quintile range from $1.50 on high-income families to nearly $3.50.

QUESTIONS FOR DISCUSSION AND REVIEW

1. According to Table 7.1, the share of income received by families in the top quintile has increased since 1970. The table shows that the top 5% did even better. What happened to the share of the other 15% of families in the highest quintile between 1970 and 1998?

2. How would you expect each of the following events to affect the position of the Lorenz curve in Figure 7.1 and why?

   a. The fraction of students dropping out of high school and the fraction of high school graduates going on to college both increase.

   b. The government takes 1% of every family's cash income and gives it to other countries as foreign aid.

   c. The government takes 1% of every family's income and gives every family a check for $400.

3. Suppose the Lorenz curves for two countries are different, but the Gini ratios for the two countries are the same. What can we say about the Lorenz curves (e.g., does one lie wholly above or below the other)?

4. The formula for the approximate Gini ratio given in the text using quintile shares underestimates the true Gini ratio. Why? Hint: Draw the smooth Lorenz curve that would be obtained with complete family data through the quintile points.

5. Assume you can choose to live in either of two different countries, both of which have the same average per capita income. The income distribution is more unequal in country A than in country B, but mobility between income classes is high in A and low in B. Not knowing which income class you will occupy after you move there, which country would you prefer to live in and why?

6. In 1979, the United States, Canada, and Germany had roughly the same levels of after-tax income inequality (see Figure 7.3), but now the United States has greater inequality than Canada and Germany. Two possible hypotheses are the decline in the relative strength of labor unions in the United States (they remained stronger in Canada and Germany) and more government redistribution in Canada and Ger-

many. What data would you collect to decide between these hypotheses?

7. "There is no virtue in compulsory government charity. And no virtue in advocating it. A politician who commends himself as 'caring' and 'sensitive' because he wants to expand government's charitable programs is merely saying that he's willing to do good with other people's money. Who isn't? A voter who takes pride in supporting such programs is telling us that he'll do good with his own money—if a gun is held to his head." (P. J. O'Rourke, *Rolling Stone Magazine*, July 12, 1995). Use the public good theory of charity to explain why a voter may support compulsory rather than voluntary charity.

8. Affirmative action programs, which give preferences to people according to their race or gender, are the subjects of intense debate. Some people think such programs fair because they help disadvantaged groups. Others think them unfair because someone might receive preference over an equally qualified and disadvantaged white male. Explain this controversy in terms of differing opinions on the importance of vertical and horizontal equity.

9. Suppose the social welfare function for a society is $W = \log I^G + \log I^M$ and George has twice as much income as Martha ($I^G = 2 \cdot I^M$). What is the maximum income loss that George can suffer to increase Martha's income by $1 without lowering social welfare? (Hint: For small changes, $\Delta \log I = \frac{\Delta I}{I}$)

10. Internet Exercise. Most people know that the average income of African-American families is less than that of white families. In 1998, the mean income of an African-American family was $38,563 while the mean income of a white family was $62,384. Do you think income inequality is greater or less among African-American families than among white families? Gini ratios for families of different ethnicity are found on the U.S. Census web site at www.census.gov/. Click the "Income" link under "People" and look up table f04.txt in the "Detailed Historical Tables" from the Current Population Survey. Draw a graph of showing the Gini ratios for selected years for "white" and "black" families from information in this table. What do you conclude about income inequality among African-American and white families?

11. Internet Exercise. The World Bank inequality page at www.worldbank.org/poverty/inequal/index.htm has a wealth of information on inequality measurement as well as data from around the world. The Deininger-Squire data set provides quintile shares and Gini ratios for many countries and different years in spreadsheet form. Download the spreadsheet at www.worldbank.org/poverty/inequal/index.htm and choose two different countries you find of interest. Use the data in the table to chart the Lorenz curves for these two countries, and report the difference in income inequality. Choose a country that has Gini ratio data for several years and create a chart showing the change in its Gini ratio over time. Compare this country's experience with that of the United States.

SELECTED REFERENCES

A classic reference on the theory and measurement of income inequality is A. B. Atkinson, *The Economics of Inequality,* 2nd ed. 1983. Income and earnings inequality has been the subject of much discussion. See the symposium on wage inequality in *The Journal of Economic Perspectives,* Spring 1997; also see *Income Inequality: Issues and Policy Options,* a symposium sponsored by the Federal Reserve Bank of Kansas City 1998. It is available on its web site at www.kc.frb.org. Peter Gottschalk and Timothy M. Smeeding provide a survey of inequality studies in different countries in "Cross-National Comparisons of Earnings and Income Inequality," 1997.

The public good theory of charity is explained in Richard J. Zeckhauser, "Optimal Mechanisms for Income Transfers," 1971. The concept of the social welfare function was introduced by A. Bergson, "A Reformulation of Certain Aspects of Welfare Economics," 1938. M. Rothschild and J. E. Stiglitz worked out the theory of insurance market failure due to moral hazard and adverse selection in "Equilibrium in Competitive Insurance Markets: An Essay in the Economics of Incomplete Information," 1976.

The trade-off between equity and efficiency was examined by Authur Okun in *Equality and Efficiency: The Big Trade-off,* 1975. Edgar K. Browning and William R. Johnson estimate the marginal cost of redistribution in "The Trade-off Between Equality and Efficiency," 1984.

USEFUL INTERNET SITES

Numerous web sites are devoted to income inequality. The World Bank's is one of the best, at www.worldbank.org/poverty/inequal/index.htm; another site, www.inequality.org/ has numerous links. Information for the United States is found on the Census Bureau site at www.census.gov/hhes/income/. Also, see www.inequality.org for a more lively (and political) site devoted to issues of income inequality in the United States.

8 Spending on Programs to Alleviate Poverty

Sometimes a few simple statistics tell a big story. In 1998, despite an extended economic boom, over 34 million people, or 12.7%, of the U.S. population lived in poverty as officially defined by the federal government. Nearly 13 million of these, or 38.5% of the total poor, were children (under 18 years old). Shockingly, 4 out of every 10 African-American children under 6 years old and 7 out of every 20 Hispanic children under 6 years old lived in poverty. All levels of government provide public assistance ("welfare") to alleviate the distress caused by poverty. Combined, governments spent $368 billion on means-tested programs to assist the poor in 1996, or just over 15% of all government spending. These programs provided benefits to poor families both above and below the poverty line in the form of cash, medical care, food, housing, education, and job training.

Deprivation amid plenty has always raised conflicting opinions among people. Most Americans find abject poverty, homeless families, and hungry children unfitting in a country as rich as the United States. In 1964 President Lyndon Johnson declared an "unconditional war on poverty," vowing to eradicate it within a generation. Johnson's war on poverty vastly expanded the network of programs designed to help the poor. These programs seem essential to prevent genuine misery for a significant fraction of the population, yet many people are concerned that they are abused by some people, or that they institutionalize poverty and dull people's efforts to improve their own well-being. In 1992, popular resentment against welfare programs led then presidential candidate Clinton to promise to "end welfare as we know it." In 1996, he made good on this promise and signed the *Personal Responsibility and Work Opportunity Reconciliation Act* (PRWORA), which ended the federal program that was the mainspring of national assistance to the poor for more than 60 years. This program was replaced with federal support for welfare programs administered by the individual states.

In this chapter, we describe how poverty is measured in the United States and consider several of the large federal and state programs that assist the poor with cash and benefits in kind. We examine how these programs affect the behavior of the recipients, look at the problems with the welfare system that led to the 1996 reforms, and assess how the newly structured state welfare programs are progressing.

MEASURING POVERTY

What does it mean to be poor? John Nash, the 1994 co-winner of the Nobel Prize in economics for his work on game theory, had a personal observation. Nash was struck with paranoid schizophrenia when he was 30 years old, and spent much of his adult life in grinding poverty. After winning about $200,000 after taxes, he observed that "[now] I feel like I can go into a coffee place and spend a few dollars. If I was really poor, I couldn't do that. Previously, I was like that."[1] Poverty, of course, is more than doing without "frills," like espresso, movies, and vacations, or amenities like VCRs and dishwashers. It can mean living in crowded, substandard housing in neighborhoods with low-quality schools and a high incidence of crime. For the very poor, it means living on the street or spending the nights in a public shelter. It can also mean an inadequate diet, limited or no access to health care, and the inability to afford child care or job training so a parent can work.

Poverty can be measured both relatively and absolutely. Measured relatively, people are poor if they are at the bottom of the income "ladder" we studied in Chapter 7. For example, we might define a family having income in the first (lowest) quintile of the size distribution of income as poor. By this criterion, a family with income less than $21,600 in 1998 was poor. Measuring poverty this way has its problems, however. For one thing, it does not take into account family size or special need. Also, if poverty is defined relatively, it can never be reduced or eradicated. No matter how rich Americans may become, there will always be a lowest quintile. Families currently in the lowest quintile in the United States would not be considered poor in most developing countries or, for that matter, a few generations ago in this country.

Perhaps for these reasons, the federal government uses an absolute measure of poverty. Put simply, an absolute measure of poverty is the inability to afford what most people would consider a minimally adequate standard of living.

The Official Poverty Threshold

Mr. Micawber, in Charles Dickens's *David Copperfield,* had what perhaps is the simplest definition of poverty. He said, "Annual income twenty pounds, annual expenditure nineteen nineteen six, result happiness. Annual income twenty pounds, annual expenditure twenty pounds ought and six, result misery." Poverty, it seems, is having less income than you spend. The federal government goes about things somewhat differently. It estimates the minimum amount a family *needs* to spend and compares this with what the family has available to spend. As in Micawber's definition, however, a family that has a dime less than it needs to spend is poor and a family with a dime more is not.

Using a method introduced by Mollie Orshansky of the Social Security Administration in 1963, the official poverty threshold is determined by the share of income spent on food by an average family with a given number of family members. Orshansky reasoned that an absolute definition of poverty is a family's inability to afford basic nutrition. Using data from the Department of Agriculture, we can calculate

---

[1] *New York Times,* December 5 1999, p. B17.

the cost to a family of given size of a no-frills adequate diet called the "economy food plan." Surveys done in 1955 found that a typical family spent one-third of its income on food (the share is much smaller today), so multiplying the cost of the economy food plan by 3 gives the Official Poverty Threshold (OPT) or **poverty line.** Changes in the OPT from year to year are calculated from changes in the cost of living. In 1998 the OPT for a family of four persons was $16,530.

The **poverty rate** is the percentage of people or families with money income (before taxes and plus cash transfers from the government) below the OPT. In 1998, 34.4 million persons (7.2 million families), or 12.7% of the population (10.0% of families), were officially poor. However, a simple body count of the number of persons with income below the Official Poverty Threshold can be misleading. For example, is it worse to have two people with incomes $2000 below the threshold or one person with $5000 less? To handle this problem, the government measures the poverty gap. The **poverty gap,** also known as the **income deficit,** is the hypothetical amount of income needed to bring everyone below the Official Poverty Threshold up to it. Thus, if there are two persons with incomes $2000 below the threshold, the poverty gap is $4000. One person with income $5000 less than the threshold would mean that the poverty gap is $5000.

To measure the poverty gap, the government measures family income before means-tested government transfers. The difference between this before-tax, before-transfer income and the Official Poverty Threshold is the poverty gap (in dollars) for the individual family. The poverty gap for all families below the Official Poverty Threshold in 1998 was $47.6 billion. The average income deficit for families below the OPT was $6,620 per family.

Figure 8.1 shows how the official poverty rate of families has changed over time. The poverty rate fell steadily from a high of 18.1% in 1960 to a low of 8.8% in the mid-1970s. The poverty rate climbed again in the 1980s and has since fluctuated in a band between 10% and 12%.

The Incidence of Poverty

Who are the poor? Although 12.7% of persons and 10% of families are poor according to the official definition, poverty rates are much higher for certain demographic groups.[2] The poverty rate (persons) was 26.1% for African Americans and 25.6% for people of Hispanic origin as compared with 10.5% for whites in 1998. The poverty rate was 18.9% for persons under age 18 and 10.5% for persons over age 65 as compared with 6.9% for people aged 45 to 54. Over 20% of children under age 6 live in poor families. Poverty is also concentrated among immigrants. Twenty-two percent of noncitizens were poor in 1998 as compared with 12.1% of native-born Americans. Poverty is highest in the West and South, where the 1998 rates were 14% and 13.7% respectively, and lowest in the Midwest, where the poverty rate was 10.3%. It is also more concentrated in the cities. The poverty rate inside central cities was 18.5%, compared with 8.7% outside of the central cities. Not surprisingly,

---

[2]The following statistics are from *Poverty in the United States, 1998,* U.S. Census Bureau, September 1999.

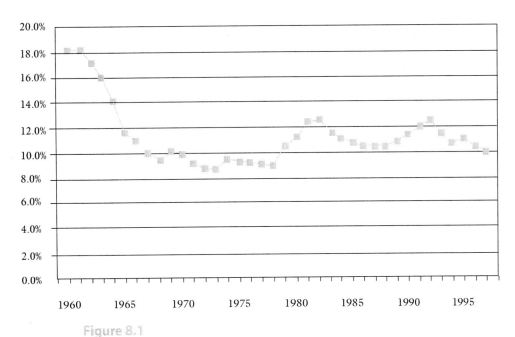

Figure 8.1

Poverty Rate of Families, 1960–98
Source: Historical Poverty Tables   Families, U.S. Census Bureau, Table 13, www.census.gov/hhes/poverty/histpov/ hstpov13.html.

poverty rates are higher for single-parent families. For single-mother families the poverty rate was 29.9% in 1998, compared with 10% for all families. Poverty rates also vary according to work experience and education. In 1998, 21.1% of people who had not worked during the year were poor as compared with 6.3% of people who had worked sometime during the year. In 1994, 23.9% of people age 18 and over who had less than four years of high school were poor, compared with only 6.3% of people who had one or more years of college.

Alternative Definitions of Poverty

Poverty depends on how we measure it. Debate has long raged about whether the official measure of poverty accurately detects who is poor and who is not. Many people believe that the official measure underestimates the extent of poverty in the United States, while probably an equal number believe that it overstates the extent of poverty. In the early 1990s, the Joint Economic Committee of Congress began a review of the official poverty measure, and in 1995 a panel of academic experts from the National Academy of Sciences (NAS) issued a report identifying the main problems with the official measure.

The main criticisms of the official measure focus on the way the OPT is determined and on how family resources are measured. Recall that in the 1960s the OPT was set equal to three times the cost of a minimally nutritious diet for a family of given size and adjusted for general inflation since then. Family income is measured by cash income, including cash transfers from the government but before taxes. The main criticisms of the OPT are as follows:

■ It ignores changing patterns of consumer spending. Although the average family spent a third of its income on food in the 1950s, the average family spent about 12% of its before-tax income on food in 1998.

■ The cost of other necessities such as housing, health care, and clothing are ignored. As a result, the OPT disregards regional variation in the cost of living because housing costs differ greatly according to the city in which the poor live in, or whether they live in rural areas where the cost of housing is lower.

■ It ignores the cost the poor incur in earning income, such as child-care costs.

The main criticisms of the measurement of family income are the following:

■ It excludes in-kind benefits such as food stamps, Medicaid, and housing assistance received by the poor. It also excludes capital gains, although presumably the poor have little of those.

■ It ignores income and payroll taxes paid by the poor.

■ It ignores assets that the poor may own, including homes, cars, and bank accounts.

Some of these identified problems, such as the failure to consider the cost of non-food necessities, child-care expenses, and taxes, would lead to an underestimate of poverty; others, such as failure to exclude in-kind transfers, would lead to an over-estimate. The NAS panel made various recommendations to improve the method of detecting poverty, including changing how the OPT adjusts for family size and the survey methodology used to canvas the poor.

The U.S. Census Bureau has recently reported six new "experimental" measures of poverty based on the panel's recommendations.[3] All of these experimental methods show higher poverty rates than the official rate (12.7%), ranging from 14.6% to 15.7% of the population. However, comparing the official and experimental rates is like comparing apples and oranges. More important is what these experimental rates reveal about how poverty changes over time. To learn more about this, the Census Bureau adjusted the experimental poverty rates so that they report the same level of poverty as the official measure (13.7%) in 1997. The adjusted experimental rates from 1990 to 1998 indicate that poverty declined more during the 1990s than shown by the official rate. The official poverty rate declined from a decade high of 15.1% in 1993 to a decade low of 12.7% in 1998. According to the standardized experimental rates, poverty declined from a decade high of 15.5 to 15.7% in 1993 to a decade low of 12.5 to 12.7% in 1998.

Other researchers, using different methods, claim that the official measure of poverty vastly overstates the hardship suffered by poor families and fails to consider genuine improvements in their standard of living over time. Robert Rector of the

---

[3]Kathleen Short, John Iceland, and Thesia Garner, "Experimental Poverty Measures: 1998," September 1999.

Table 8.1   Percentages of Households Having Various Goods

Type of Good or Asset	Percent of All Households	Percent of Poor Households
Own home	65.0%	41.0%
Car or truck	90.2	69.7
Refrigerator	99.7	99.3
Telephone	93.7	86.8
Microwave oven	83.0	63.7
Dishwasher	53.7	28.1
Air conditioner	75.4	66.3
Color television	98.7	97.3
VCR	87.6	73.8

Source: "The Myth of Widespread American Poverty," Table 1, p. 5.

Heritage Foundation analyzes the conditions of the poor in terms of their spending and ownership of assets and amenities.[4] His data are difficult to compare directly with those of the Census Bureau because they are drawn from different sources and for different years. Table 8.1 indicates patterns of ownership of homes, cars, and amenity-providing appliances for poor households and households in general. Although the table shows, as expected, that poor families have less of most goods, it also indicates that some of the amenities we associate with middle-income households are enjoyed by the poor as well. The Rector study also shows that 84.1% of poor households report having enough to eat, compared with 96.1% of all households.

MEANS-TESTED GOVERNMENT TRANSFER PROGRAMS

In the United States in 1996, all levels of government combined spent about $368 billion on **means-tested transfer programs.** These programs gave benefits in cash and in kind to persons and families with limited incomes. The major assistance programs and the amounts spent (measured in constant 1996 dollars) for fiscal years 1978 and 1996 are shown in Table 8.2. The percent of total spending on each program that was financed by the federal government in 1996 and the growth rate in real spending from 1978 to 1996 are shown in the last two columns.

Table 8.2 reveals that most government spending on the poor is in the form of **transfers in kind.** Three-quarters of government spending on means-tested programs is of this type. In fact, the largest single form of assistance to the poor is the Medicaid program, which provides assistance in the form of health care. Also, we see that transfers in kind have been the most rapidly growing type of means-tested transfers. Real spending on means-tested transfers in kind rose 120% over the 18-year period, as compared with only 54% for cash transfers. Over this period, real GDP rose about 55%, so both types of spending grew as fast or faster than the economy.

---

[4]Robert Rector, "The Myth of Widespread American Poverty," September 18, 1998.

Table 8.2   Cash and Non-cash Benefits to Persons with Limited Income (in 1996 dollars)

Program	Spending FY 1978 ($1996 billions)	Spending FY 1996 ($, billions)	Percent Federally Financed FY 1996	Percent Growth, 1978–96
Transfers in cash				
Aid to Families with Dependent Children (AFDC)	28.5	23.7	53.6%	(16.8)%
Supplemental Security Income (SSI)	17.2	30.4	85.5	76.7
Earned income tax credit (refundable portion)	2.4	21.6	100	800
Other *	11.3	16.0	52.5	41.6
Total in cash	59.5	91.7	75.9	54.1
Transfers in kind				
Medicaid and other medical care	57.1	177.6	58.3	211
Food stamps and other nutrition	22.4	39.0	95.1	74.1
Housing	16.7	27.2	92.2	62.9
Education	10.1	16.3	93.8	61.4
JOBS and other job training	9.6	4.6	87.0	(52.1)
Other **	9.5	11.3	58.4	18.9
Total in kind	125.6	276.0	69.5	119.7
Total	184.6	367.7	71.1	99.2

* Includes foster care, pensions for needy veterans, and general assistance.
** Includes general and energy assistance.
Source: Author's calculations based on U.S. Bureau of the Census, *Statistical Abstract of the United States, 1998* (Table 605) and *1982–1983* (Table 517). Spending in 1978 was converted into 1996 dollars using the CPI-U series.

Means-Tested Cash Transfers

Although it was not the largest cash transfer program, the program most people meant when they talked about "welfare" was Aid to Families with Dependent Children (AFDC), a federal welfare program begun in 1935. As of July 1997, AFDC was replaced by **Temporary Assistance for Needy Families (TANF),** which turns the implementation of welfare programs over to the state governments and provides a federal **block grant** (see Chapter 18) to help with the financing. Because most states have inherited welfare programs based on AFDC, it is useful to describe how AFDC was constructed.

The AFDC program was enacted under the Social Security Act of 1935 as a cash grant program for needy children without fathers. As part of the "war on poverty," it became a shared federal and state entitlement providing monthly cash payments to families with dependent children. The federal government provided each state with a matching grant (see Chapter 18) to finance its AFDC spending. The federal share averaged 55%, although it was as high as 78% in the poorer states. In its last full year, 1996, AFDC paid a benefit averaging $374 per family per month to about 4.6 million families.

Under AFDC, the federal government set the general eligibility rules, although states could set the numerical limits or receive waivers from some requirements. To receive AFDC benefits, a family had to pass two means tests and satisfy several eligibility rules. First, its gross monthly income had to be less than 185% of the **need standard** set by the state, which was based on the state's definition of the cost of meeting basic living needs. Not all families that met the need standard received AFDC benefits. In addition, the family's **countable income** had to be less than the state's **payment standard.** Countable income equals the family's gross income, including child support payments, minus "disregarded" income such as $120 work expenses, $100 child-care expenses, and a third of earned income during the first four months the family receives benefits. The payment standard is the maximum benefit the family can receive (if the family has zero countable income), which ranged from $120 a month in Mississippi to $923 in Alaska. In addition, to receive benefits under AFDC, families must have limited assets. In particular, a family could not receive AFDC benefits if it owned cash assets exceeding $1000 in value or a vehicle worth more than $1500. Finally, to receive benefits a family had to have an absent, unemployed, or incapacitated parent. In most cases, the recipient family was a single mother with children.

In most states, the AFDC benefit was equal to the payment standard minus countable income. This meant that, for all intents and purposes, a family receiving benefits would lose $1 for every extra dollar it earned.[5] For instance, in a state with a payment standard of $400 a month, a family with $200 countable income would receive a benefit of $200. If the parent worked more so countable income rose to $300, the family would receive a benefit of only $100. In either case, the family has $400 a month to spend.

TEMPORARY ASSISTANCE FOR NEEDY FAMILIES (TANF). The *Personal Responsibility and Work Opportunity Reconciliation Act* (PRWORA) of 1996 ended the 60-year-old federal entitlement to assistance under AFDC and created the Temporary Assistance for Needy Families (TANF) block grant to finance cash assistance programs administered by the states. A block grant is a fixed sum of money given to the state for a prescribed purpose, in this case public assistance. The total federal TANF block grant is $16.8 billion per year for the years 1998 to 2002, which the states can use in any way "reasonably calculated to accomplish the purposes of TANF." Under TANF, the states are given wide latitude to design their own programs and the federal government cannot regulate the conduct of the states except as expressly provided under the statute.

The stated purposes of TANF are to provide assistance to needy families so that children can be cared for in their own homes; to reduce dependency on welfare by promoting job preparation, work, and marriage; to prevent out-of-wedlock pregnancies; and to encourage the formation and maintenance of two-parent families. To achieve these purposes, the state programs funded by TANF are subject to some general restrictions. In particular:

- The state programs must impose work requirements on the recipients. With the exception of single parents with young children, recipients must work

---

[5]Ten states used a "fill the gap" method that allowed the recipient to keep at least part of any extra earnings.

after two years on assistance. Twenty-five percent of all recipient families in a state must be engaged in work activities or off the welfare rolls by July 1, 1997, rising to 50% by 2002. Work activities can include on-the-job training, work experience, community service or providing child care to individuals participating in community service, and 12 months of vocational training.

- The state programs must place limits on how long recipients can receive cash assistance. Families who have received assistance for five cumulative years (or less, if the state chooses) will be ineligible for cash aid. The states can exempt up to 20% of their caseload from this time limit or provide noncash assistance and vouchers to avoid undue hardship.

- The states must maintain spending on welfare from their own funds at 80% or more of 1994 levels.

- States are penalized for failing to meet the above requirements and receive performance bonuses for moving welfare recipients into jobs and reducing out-of-wedlock births.

- Contingency funds and supplementary grants are available for states experiencing economic downturns.

By the end of 1997, all states had enacted TANF programs. Although these programs bear some resemblance to the AFDC program that preceded them, many states have used their new leeway to introduce several innovations in their assistance programs. Some of the most important are as follows:

- Most states have maintained the maximum monthly benefit levels set under AFDC, but have increased income eligibility limits (the maximum earnings level for which families can receive benefits). States have done this in different ways, but the most significant change is that more than 30 states now disregard part of earnings in determining countable income for an indefinite period. Some states also disregard part of child support payments. This means that rather than losing a dollar of benefits for every dollar of extra earnings, a recipient can keep up to 50 cents in some states.

- Thirty-nine states have increased the asset limits for recipients and introduced restricted savings accounts. Eleven states and the District of Columbia have maintained the $1000 limit, but the rest have increased the limit, as high as $10,000 in Oregon. Forty-eight states increased the vehicle exemption, with a majority allowing one vehicle of any value. Fifteen states have introduced individual development accounts that allow recipients to accumulate savings for post-secondary education, home ownership, and business formation.

- Most states have eliminated the single-parent requirement, with 35 states now applying the same eligibility rules to two-parent families as used for one-parent families.

- To comply with the TANF regulations, all states have imposed time limits on cash assistance. Most states have a 60-month (five-year) lifetime limit, although some are more restrictive. In some states, eligibility terminates after the time limit (the most common), whereas in others benefits are reduced. All states have exemptions to their limits, but some states are more generous than others. Exemptions may be given for age, disability, caring for a young child or disabled person, job unavailability, and victims of domestic violence.

- Again to comply with TANF regulations, all states have imposed work requirements. PRWORA requires all adult recipients to participate in work activities (as defined by the state) within two years, except for single parents caring for a young child. The states vary in their definitions of "work activities" and in the age of the child that exempts the parent from work. Most states exempt a parent with a child under one year old, although 14 states set the exemption age younger and 5 states provide no exemption.

The most significant impacts of the new welfare rules have been a sharp decline in the number of recipients and a significant increase in employment of current recipients. The number of recipients fell 40% from 12.2 million before PRWORA to 7.3 million by March 1999. In 1998, 23% of recipients were employed as compared with 7% in 1992. Partly this is due to the booming economy, but most experts also credit the new welfare rules. The poverty rate fell only 10% between 1996 and 1998.

SUPPLEMENTAL SECURITY INCOME.   Supplemental Security Income (SSI) is the largest means-tested cash benefit program. SSI is a federal program that was created in 1974 to combine a number of smaller federal and state programs paying cash benefits to the disabled. States can supplement the SSI payment out of their own funds. In 1998, the federal SSI payment standard was $494 per month for individuals and $726 for couples. Recipients include eligible individuals and couples over age 65, blind or disabled persons of any age, and the parents of children who are blind or physically or mentally disabled. Of the 6.1 million recipients in 1998, over 82% were eligible because they were blind or disabled and 18% were eligible because of their age. About 18% of the disabled recipients were children.

As with all means-tested transfers, to receive SSI a recipient must have limited income and assets. The SSI benefits are reduced by the amount of other income. Recipients of SSI can also receive Social Security benefits. In fact, SSI recipients are required to apply for any benefits for which they are eligible under other programs, since SSI is supposed to be a "program of last resort." Recipients may also receive in-kind benefits, like food stamps and Medicaid.

EARNED INCOME TAX CREDIT.   The third important means-tested cash transfer program is the earned income tax credit (EITC). Unlike TANF and SSI, the EITC is administered through the income tax system and is an example of what economists call a tax expenditure, or spending through the tax system. The EITC is a refundable tax credit. A tax credit is an amount that is subtracted from the amount of income taxes that a family must pay. A refundable tax credit refunds the excess of the tax credit over and above the taxes owed by the taxpayer. For instance, a taxpayer with an EITC of $500 who owes only $300 in taxes receives a cash payment from the government of $200.

In 1998, a family with two children and an annual earned income (wages and salaries) of $9390 received an EITC of $3756 per year. The tax credit rate for this family is 40% on earned income up to a maximum of $9390. The EITC was reduced for families with incomes greater than $12,255. In this way, the payment is means-tested. However, unlike TANF and SSI, which reduce the benefit by $1 for every $1 of excess income, the EITC is reduced by about 21 cents for each extra dollar. Hence two-child families with incomes up to $30,095 received some EITC in 1998.

The EITC was introduced in 1975 to offset the increasing burden of higher payroll (FICA) taxes on low-income working families. Since then, it has expanded to provide actual assistance, not just a tax offset, to needy families and individuals. The growth of this program was particularly fast in the 1990s. In 1990, 12.6 million families received an average annual EITC benefit of $549, for a total cost of $6.9 billion. By 1998, 18.8 million families received an average annual EITC benefit of $1473 each, for a total cost of $27.7 billion (all amounts are in current dollars). This represents a growth of 300% over the period.[6]

Means-Tested In-Kind Transfers

We saw in Table 8.2 that 75% of government spending on the poor provides in-kind benefits to the poor in the form of medical care, food stamps, housing, education, and job training. We briefly describe the major programs.

MEDICAID.   Established in 1965, Medicaid is the largest single spending program assisting the poor and nearly poor. In 1998, the federal and state governments spent $184.7 billion on Medicaid, which provided health and long-term care to nearly 41 million recipients, 21 million of them children. Federal assistance is provided to states through a matching grant based on the state's per capita income. The federal share averaged 57% in 1998, ranging from 50% for 12 states to 77.2% for the state of Mississippi. Services mandated by the federal government include inpatient and outpatient hospital care, physician's services, laboratory tests and X-rays, and nursing home care. States can opt to cover additional services like prescription drugs and dental care and receive a federal matching grant to help them finance the cost.

Eligibility to receive Medicaid is determined by the states, but the federal government requires that certain "categorically needy" people be covered. These include SSI recipients, pregnant women and infants in families with income less than 133% of the OPT, and all children under 18 living in families with income equal to or less than the OPT. Beginning in 1999, a new supplementary federal-state program, called the Children's Health Insurance Program (CHIP), extends medical coverage to all children living in families with income less than 200% of the OPT who are not covered under Medicaid.

Medicaid is not automatic for families who receive TANF cash assistance as it was under the old AFDC program, although TANF recipients are eligible in most states. Most Medicaid recipients must have income and assets below specified

---

[6]These figures are taken from *Overview of Entitlement Programs, 1998 Green Book,* Table 13-14.

amounts. These amounts vary from state to state but are determined within federal guidelines. Forty states provide Medicaid to groups whose incomes are too high to be categorically needy, but are deemed "medically needy" because of high hospital or nursing home care expenses. Table 8.3 shows the percentage of families covered under Medicaid according to family income. The table indicates that most Medicaid recipients are poor or nearly poor, but some are well above the official poverty threshold.

Despite Medicaid, a significant fraction of poor people does not have health insurance. In 1998, 32.3% of poor people were without health insurance, and nearly 50% of those between the ages of 25 and 34 were uninsured. Sadly, 25% of poor children did not have health insurance even though they are eligible for Medicaid.

Spending on Medicaid grew rapidly during the 1990s, although the rate of growth slowed toward the end of the decade. Between 1990 and 1998, Medicaid spending grew 155%, or about 11% per year. This rapid growth in Medicaid spending prompted policy makers to seek ways to control costs. One solution was to rely on managed care to deliver Medicaid services. Under a managed care system, a health provider like a **Health Maintenance Organization (HMO)** is paid a fixed monthly fee to provide comprehensive services to the Medicaid patient, rather than being paid a fee for service. An alternative is a **Primary Care Case Management (PCCM)** plan in which a provider, usually the primary care physician, acts as a gatekeeper to approve and monitor services to the patient. Both methods attempt to control costs by eliminating inappropriate or unnecessary services. In 1991, only 9.5% of Medicaid beneficiaries were enrolled in managed care plans, whereas 53.6% were enrolled in these plans in 1998.

THE FOOD STAMP PROGRAM.   After Medicaid, the largest category of in-kind transfer programs is those providing food and nutrition to needy families. Included are the Food Stamp Program, established in 1964 (the largest single program in this category), the National School Lunch and Breakfast Programs, and the Special Supplemental Food Program for Women, Infants, and Children (WIC). The Food Stamp Program gives coupons exchangeable for food to individuals and families with low income and assets. In 1996, $27.3 billion was spent on the Food Stamp Program including administration costs and 25.5 million persons, or 8.6% of the population, received benefits in some amount. The average monthly benefit was $71 per person; the maximum monthly allotment for a four-person household was $408 in the 48 adjoining states and the District of Columbia.

Table 8.3   **Medicaid Coverage by Family Income**

	Family Income			
	100% OPT or Less	100–133% of OPT	133–185% of OPT	Greater than 185% of OPT
Percent of families covered	44.6%	24.2%	14.4%	3.8%

Source: Overview of Entitlement Programs, 1998 Green Book, Table 15-12, p. 957.

8.1   How Much Will It Cost to Insure the Poor?

Although Americans devote a larger share of national income to health care than any other country, the government does not provide universal health insurance coverage, unlike governments in the other wealthy industrialized countries. As a result, a significant fraction—16.3% in 1998—of the population is without health insurance. An even larger fraction of the poor is uninsured—32.2% in 1998. Some Americans, presumably the young and healthy, may remain uninsured by choice. Others are uninsured because they cannot afford it or because they have existing health conditions that make them uninsurable. Others, mainly children in poor families, are eligible for coverage under Medicaid but are not enrolled, for whatever reason. Many of these uninsured poor must rely on charity health care in the event of illness or injury.

Universal health care has been proposed for the United State several times in the past, the most recent being President Clinton's failed 1993 proposal. A major objection to insuring the uninsured is the cost. The table at right shows the numbers of poor children, elderly, and other (nonaged adults) in the United States and the percentage of each uninsured in 1998. Also shown is the per person cost of providing Medicaid to those children, elderly, and others who were enrolled in Medicaid in 1997. As you can see, it costs nearly nine times as much to provide Medicaid to an elderly person as to a child.

	Number of Poor (1998) (thousands)*	Percent Uninsured (1998)*	Per Person Medicaid Cost per Year (1997)+
Children	13,467	25.2%	$1,047
Elderly	3,386	3.2	8868
Other (Nonaged Adults)	17,623	43.4	2285

Source: *Health Insurance Coverage: 1998, U.S. Census, at www.census.gov/hhes/hlthins/hlthin98/hi98t2.html.
+1998 Green Book, Committee on Ways and Means, Table 15-18, p. 978.

Assuming it will cost the same to provide Medicaid to the uninsured as it does to those already enrolled, critically analyze the following:

■ Poor children are already eligible for Medicaid, and advocates argue that an outreach program is needed to enroll those children remaining uninsured. If such an outreach program is successful, how much will it cost the government in increased Medicaid spending per year?

■ How much would it cost the government to cover all of the uninsured poor under Medicaid?

■ Would the cost to the economy as a whole of extending coverage to the uninsured poor be greater or less than the cost to the government? Why?

To receive food stamps, a household must have income low enough to qualify. First, its gross income must be less than 130% of the OPT. For the Food Stamp Program, gross income includes earned income such as wages and cash transfers such as TANF and Social Security benefits. Hence cash benefits reduce food stamp benefits—but not vice versa, because countable income for TANF benefits does not include in-kind tranfers. Next, the household's countable income must be less than the OPT. Countable income is gross income less certain deductions, including a standard deduction (which is $134 per month regardless of household size), shelter expenses, deductions for employment-related child-care expenses, and 20% of earned income.

The recipient household is expected to contribute 30% of its own cash income to the purchase of food. The difference between this amount and the expenditure needed for a low-cost but adequate diet, known as the "thrifty food plan," is the household's food stamp benefit. Because the household is expected to contribute 30% of its own resources to food purchases, each extra $1 of counted income of the household reduces its food stamp benefit by 30 cents.

The PRWORA of 1996 placed new limits on food stamp eligibility. Able-bodied adults with no children can now get stamps only for three months every three years if they do not work. The act also restricted the eligibility of noncitizens.

HOUSING AND OTHER IN-KIND BENEFITS.   Several programs provide housing assistance to very-low-income renters and homeowners. These programs include the construction and rehabilitation of low-cost housing units (public housing) and the so-called "Section 8" rental assistance. The latter provides subsidies to low-income families seeking housing in the private sector. The rent paid must be within certain guidelines called fair market rents (FMRs). Assistance to low-income homeowners takes the form of low-interest mortgages.

There are also programs that give aid to needy families in the form of education. These include the Head Start program, which provides pre-schooling to children of needy families; and the Pell Grant and Stafford Loan programs, which provide tuition assistance for undergraduate higher education. Other in-kind programs provide job training for disadvantaged adults and young people, as well as adults in families receiving TANF.

THE IMPACT OF MEANS-TESTED TRANSFERS ON RECIPIENTS

How do the programs that assist the poor change their behavior? Does welfare reduce the incentive of the poor to work? Do the poor become dependent on welfare? Do food stamps increase the nutrition of the poor more than would a cash transfer? In this section, we analyze and attempt to answer these questions using economic theory.

The Impact on Work

Many people believe means-tested programs like TANF, food stamps, and Medicaid reduce work participation by the poor. It was for this reason that the welfare reforms of 1996 stressed welfare-to-work measures. We analyze the impact of means-tested transfers on the incentive to work using the theory of the labor-leisure choice. Suppose a household gets utility from leisure as well as from consuming goods. Leisure includes productive activities, such as providing parental care, as well as recreational activities. The quantity of leisure consumed is measured as the number of hours spent not working for monetary compensation.

In Figure 8.2, we consider a household that can choose the number of hours it works, and hence the number of hours of leisure it enjoys, over the course of a week. The total hours available for work and leisure are measured on the horizontal axis. There are 168 hours in a week, which is shown as the household's endowment of

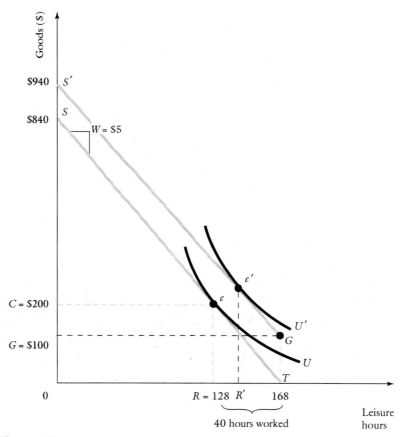

Figure 8.2
Utility-Maximizing Labor Supply
A worker can take a maximum of 168 hours of leisure a week, or consume goods equal in value to the
wage rate ($5) times hours worked. The budget line *ST* between goods and leisure is determined by
the wage rate. A worker maximizes utility at point *e*, which is tangent to the highest indifference curve along
ST. The worker maximizes utility by supplying 40 hours of labor, which allows $200 in consumption and 128
hours of leisure. A lump-sum transfer at $100 shifts the budget line to *GS'*. The worker maximizes utility at
point *e'* by working fewer (168–*R'*) hours.

time *T*. If the household does not work at all, it enjoys all 168 hours as leisure. Consumption of market goods is measured on the vertical axis. At point *T* the household does not work and has no income, so its leisure is probably not that enjoyable.
By working, the household earns the money needed to buy goods. This is shown by
the budget line *ST*. The (absolute) slope of *ST* is equal to the real wage *W* (money
wage divided by the cost of living) earned by working for 1 hour. For simplicity we
assume that the wage is the same regardless of the number of hours worked. Also,
we assume that the cost of living is equal to 1, so the money wage and the real wage
are the same. If the household earns $5 an hour, point *S* ($840 per week) is the maximum income it can earn. Of course, no household works this many hours, nor
would it want to. At point *S* it can buy the most market goods but has no time to

consume them, let alone sleep. The household's preferences between goods and leisure are shown by an indifference curve map. The slope of an indifference curve at each point is the household's marginal willingness to pay for leisure.

The household maximizes utility at point e on its budget line, where it gets R hours of leisure and works T minus R hours to earn W times $(T - R)$ dollars. If R is 128 hours, the household works 40 hours a week at $5 an hour and earns $200. Left of e on the budget line, the household's MWTP for 1 hour of leisure is greater than the wage, so the household would increase utility by working less and consuming more hours of leisure. The opposite is true to the right of point e. Consider the effect of a lump-sum transfer of G (say $100 per week). The household's budget line between market goods and leisure is the line labeled $S'GT$ when it receives a lump-sum transfer. Typically, the household works fewer hours when it receives such a transfer. The utility-maximizing point on the budget line $S'GT$ is point e'. Assuming that leisure is a normal good (a good consumed in greater amounts as income rises), the transfer causes the household to increase its leisure hours, which it does by working fewer hours.

THE IMPACT OF TANF. The lump-sum transfer in Figure 8.2 is not means-tested—the family receives it regardless of how much it works and earns. Nonetheless, the family works fewer hours per week (in theory) because it feels richer and can afford more leisure. A means-tested transfer, like TANF, has an even greater impact on hours worked because extra earnings reduce the size of the benefit received by the family.

Figure 8.3 illustrates the impact of the TANF program on a hypothetical family of three persons in Pennsylvania. The income eligibility limit, called the **breakeven income,** in Pennsylvania is $800 a month or $200 a week (1997). A family earning $200 a week would receive no TANF benefit. Pennsylvania has an earnings disregard of 50%, so a family with less than $200 a week receives $.50 in benefits for every dollar less than $200 it earns, assuming it satisfies the other eligibility criteria. Put differently, the **benefit reduction rate** for Pennsylvania TANF is 50% because each dollar of earnings reduces the benefit by $.50. For instance, a family with no earnings receives a benefit of $100 a week, and a family with $100 earnings receives a benefit of $50 a week for a total cash income of $150.

The budget line between goods and leisure for this family is the segmented line labeled $SBGT$. The slope of the line labeled $S'G$ is $2.50, which is the family's wage rate times the 50% benefit reduction rate. At point B (for breakeven) where line $S'G$ intersects the budget line TS, the family loses welfare eligibility, so the dashed segment $S'B$ is irrelevant. (In this particular example, point B happens to coincide with the initial equilibrium point e.) Facing this budget line, the family maximizes utility by choosing hours of work somewhere along the segment BG. In the figure, we show the case where the family chooses not to work at all.[7] The family does this even though it would have had more to spend if it worked 40 hours a week. Although the family has only $100 per week to spend from its TANF benefit, it has more time to spend for leisure and looking after children.

---

[7]We are ignoring the work requirement features of TANF in this example.

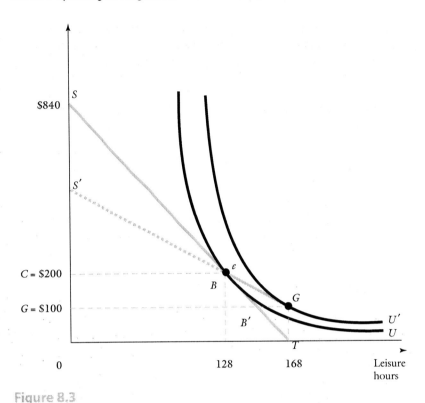

Figure 8.3

The Impact of TANF on Labor Hours

A welfare program with a 100% benefit reduction rate, like the old AFDC program, faces the recipient with the budget line *SB'GT*. The recipient maximizes utility at point G by not working. With a 50% benefit reduction rate, the recipient faces budget line *SBGT* and maximizes utility by choosing some point between *B* and *G*.

Thus a means-tested program is likely to discourage work more than does a lump-sum transfer. In fact, under the old AFDC program, work discouragement was even more extreme. Under AFDC, the benefit reduction rate was 100% (after four months of benefits) so the welfare family's budget line would be *SB'GT*. Facing this budget line, the family would have been almost certain not to work. In fact, in 1994 only 8.9% of adults receiving AFDC had earnings. Under TANF, 20.6% of adults had earnings in fiscal year 1998. This may be due in part to the lowered benefit reduction rate in most states, but also to the work requirements of TANF.

The decline in hours worked by welfare recipients creates an efficiency cost or deadweight loss on the economy. Efficiency requires that a person's marginal willingness to pay (MWTP) for an hour of leisure (the slope of the indifference curve) be equal to his or her gross wage rate. As can be seen in Figure 8.3, the MWTP for leisure by a welfare recipient is equal to or less than the gross wage rate multiplied by the benefit reduction rate. As a result, welfare recipients are inclined to consume an inefficiently large number of leisure hours. Welfare recipients would be better off, and the economy more efficient, if the transfer were a lump sum (not means-tested). In this case, however, the transfer would be available to everybody and the government would have to levy high income tax rates to fund the program. As we will see in Chapter 12, high tax rates also create a deadweight loss.

Most econometric studies support the hypothesis that means-tested transfers discourage work effort by recipients. However, different studies find different magnitudes for the impact, ranging from slight to significant.[8]

THE IMPACT OF THE EITC.   The Earned Income Tax Credit enjoys broad support, even by people who disparage welfare, because it "rewards working families." How does the EITC affect work effort? We will consider the effect of the EITC on a hypothetical family of three that earns $5 an hour and has no other income. In 1997, a family of three received a 34% EITC rate on $125 per week (based on $6500 earnings per year), giving it a maximum credit of $42.50 per week. If the family earned more than $230 per week (based on $11,930 per year), the EITC was reduced about 16 cents for each extra dollar of earnings. The breakeven income under the EITC for this family is $495 per week ($25,750 per year). Income and payroll taxes are ignored.

With the EITC, the budget line between goods and leisure for this family is the segmented line $SBG'GT$ in Figure 8.4 (without the EITC, the budget line is ST). In the segment GT, the family takes home $6.70 for each extra hour of work ($5 wage plus the 34% EITC). At point G, the family works 25 hours a week and receives the maximum EITC; each extra hour of work earns the family $5. At point G', the family works 46 hours a week and reaches the point where its EITC is phased out as earnings rise. In the segment BG', the family takes home $4.20 for each extra hour of work ($5 wage less the 16% phaseout). Point B is the breakeven point at which the family no longer receives the EITC.

The impact of the EITC depends on how many hours the family would work in its absence. For example, if leisure is a normal good (the family wants more when its income rises) and the family works at least 25 hours a week without the EITC, the EITC causes the family to work fewer hours. In this case, shown in the figure, the take-home wage of the family is unchanged or reduced by the EITC (segment $G'G$ or BG'). The EITC increases family income but not the take-home wage rate for an extra hour of work. In the figure, the family maximizes utility at point e' and the EITC acts like a lump-sum transfer that reduces hours worked. If the family worked more hours so it was in the segment BG', work effort would be discouraged further by the 16% benefit reduction rate. Theoretically, the EITC could only increase hours worked (and even this is uncertain) if the family worked less than 25 hours a week. In this case EITC increases the take-home wage to $6.70 an hour, raising the price of leisure to the family. This discussion compares the impact of the EITC with no assistance at all. The EITC is less likely to discourage working than would conventional welfare (like TANF) with a high benefit reduction rate applying to the first dollar of earned income.

---

[8]Two surveys of empirical work on the work disincentives of welfare are available. See Moffitt, 1992, and Danziger et al., 1981.

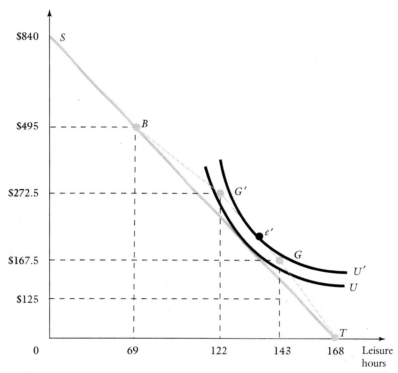

Figure 8.4

The Effect of the EITC on Labor Hours
At low incomes (few hours worked) the EITC increases the take-home wage and the recipient faces a steeper budget line, segment *TG*. At a higher level of income, the EITC is phased out. The phaseout is like a tax on income and lowers the take-home wage. The phaseout region is segment *BG'* of the budget line.

The Effects of Welfare on Family Structure

Although the effect of welfare on work effort is the most thoroughly studied, other impacts must be considered. One of the most important is the possibility that welfare encourages family dissolution. Under AFDC before 1990, benefits were available only to single-parent families. After 1990, benefits were extended to two-parent families if one of the parents was disabled or unemployed. Many people believe that the ineligibility of (or restrictions on) two-parent families encourages single-parent families. To receive welfare, the parents might postpone or avoid marriage, or married parents might separate. In fact, single females headed 89% of families who received AFDC in 1995.

Some people also believe welfare encourages recipient families to have more children. For both TANF and food stamps, the monthly benefit is higher the more children in the recipient family. In July 1997, the maximum monthly TANF benefit for a family with three persons was $379. Another child would increase the benefit by $84 a month to $463. The maximum food stamp benefit would increase by $90 a month.

Several econometric studies support the hypothesis that AFDC causes family dissolution. Such studies examine the relationship between the likelihood that a single female is the head of a recipient family, or that a divorce has occurred, and the maximum level of the AFDC benefit. The studies find a significant positive relationship. The evidence that welfare encourages recipients to have more children is less convincing. Economists expect that the increased benefit from one more child is not likely to encourage births solely for the purpose of getting the higher benefit. Rather, they hypothesize that the higher benefit may reduce, albeit slightly, any qualms a poor mother may have about having another child, or influence her decision not to have an abortion. Econometric studies have found a positive relationship between the likelihood of out-of-wedlock births and the maximum benefit level under AFDC. It is not clear, however, whether this reflects a higher level of births or a higher probability that they occur out of wedlock because AFDC was not available to two-parent families. Most economists think the latter is more probable.

Another major concern is that means-tested programs encourage a culture of **welfare dependency.** Welfare dependency describes a recipient's long-run attachment to welfare benefits as the family's primary means of support. Several things can lead to welfare dependency. First, recipients of welfare may simply "get used to it." Any perceived stigma or embarrassment about receiving welfare declines once a person has received it for a while. Second, in using the welfare programs, recipients learn how the system works and learn to take better advantage of it. Third, and perhaps most important, welfare recipients lose their attachment to the labor force and their human capital. Continuous employment is an important source of acquiring and maintaining human capital, like the working skills that make people employable. The longer people remain out of the labor force, the harder it is for them to reenter, and the more dependent they become on welfare.

Facts about the length of time a typical recipient spends on welfare provide disturbing evidence about the reality of welfare dependence. A period of time spent on welfare is referred to as a welfare "spell." Surveys of persons receiving welfare have found that a large fraction of them were in the midst of a long period of welfare assistance. In fact, 50% of recipients enrolled at any point in time were in the midst of a spell lasting eight years or longer. It can be argued that such lengths of time do not reflect temporary assistance to recipients, but a way of life.

An observation at a given point in time shows a biased picture of the duration for a typical welfare recipient because it is not a random sample of recipients—long-term recipients are overrepresented and short-term recipients are underrepresented. If we choose a sample from people who were *ever* on welfare (including those not on it at the time of sampling), we find that half left the welfare system within a year. Using data that follow the recipients over a longer period (such data is called "longitudinal"), we find that 48% of recipients entering welfare remained on it for less than two years. This suggests there have been two types of welfare recipients: the more numerous short-term recipients who entered welfare for temporary assistance, and the long-term recipients who could be described as welfare-dependent. Although less numerous, the long-term recipients have accounted for the greater share of welfare costs.

Many of the provisions in the PRWORA that reformed welfare in 1996 are directed at the sorts of problems discussed above. Under TANF, many states have abolished the 100% benefit reduction rate that applied under AFDC so that recipient families will have more incentive to earn. To help keep families intact, most state TANF programs now apply the same eligibility criteria to two-parent families as they do to single-parent families. Also, as part of the TANF program, Congress offers a bonus as high as $25 million to states that reduce the ratio of out-of-wedlock births to total births measured over two-year intervals. Perhaps, the most important change is the emphasis on the "T" in TANF, for temporary. Under the new welfare rules, families face a time limit on the cumulative number of months they can receive benefits and, while receiving benefits, must engage in work participation unless exempted. These measures are directed at the problem of welfare dependency and loss of labor force attachment.

The Impact of In Kind Versus Cash Transfers

We saw in Table 8.2 that three-quarters of the dollar value of benefits for the poor take the form of in-kind transfers, mainly $276 billion in health care, food, housing, and other goods and services. Would it make a difference if the government used this $276 billion to give more cash benefits, rather than Medicaid and food stamps? In both cases the cost would be the same, and the recipients should be no worse off since they could use the cash to purchase health insurance or food if they desired. In this section we examine the difference between cash and in-kind benefits and discuss some of the reasons that in-kind benefits are so prevalent.

WHEN IS A TRANSFER IN-KIND EQUIVALENT TO CASH?   The difference between receiving cash and receiving an equal dollar value of food stamps is shown in Figure 8.5. The amount spent on food is measured on the horizontal axis and the amount spent on other goods on the vertical axis. The household's budget line when it receives no transfer is labeled MM. The household's preferences between spending on food and spending on other things are shown in the form of an indifference curve map. The household maximizes utility at e, where it spends $F on food and $C on other goods. The level of household utility is given by the indifference curve labeled U.

Suppose the household receives a cash transfer from the government of $G. The budget line is shifted to $M'M'$ and the household maximizes utility at point e', where it spends F' on food and C' on other things. Household utility rises to U'. What if the household is given $G in food stamps rather than in cash? If the amount it spends on food with a cash transfer (F') is greater than $G, this would make no difference to the household. With $G in food stamps, the recipient's budget line is the kinked budget line MNM'. Along MNM', utility is again maximized at point e' and F' is spent on food and C' on other goods, just as with the cash transfer. The household simply uses the food stamps in place of the money it spends on food. The food stamps reduce the amount of money the household spends on food by $G, making that amount available to buy other goods. In other words, food stamps are as good as cash, and the amounts spent on food and other goods are the same with both cash and in-kind transfers.

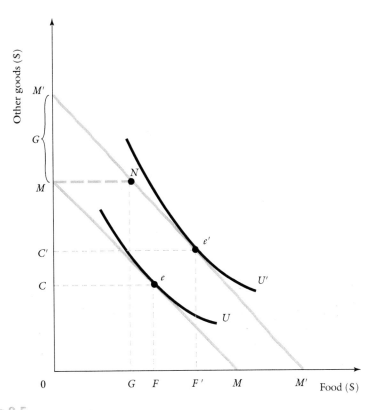

Figure 8.5

Equivalence of Transfers in Cash and Food Stamps

A cash transfer shifts the recipient's budget line between food and other goods from *MM* to *M'M'*, and the recipient spends *F'* on food. A transfer in food stamps of the same amount shifts the budget line to *MNM'*, where bundles between *M'* and *N* to the northwest of *N* are not available. Since the recipient wants to spend more on food than the allotment of food stamps, the food stamps are as good as cash, and the recipient buys the same amount of food.

On the other hand, if a household receives a food stamp benefit that is greater than the amount it would spend on food with an equal amount of cash, it purchases more food with food stamps than with cash. This is shown in Figure 8.6, where the food stamp benefit is larger than the desired food expenditure. With a cash transfer of $\$G$, the household would maximize utility at point e' by spending $\$F'$ on food. With food stamps worth $\$G$ (more than $\$F'$), the household consumes more food than it would if given the cash, because the food stamps cannot be used for other goods. The recipient maximizes utility at point N, where it gets a lower utility level U''.

When the household consumes more food with stamps than with cash, the value of the food stamps to the recipient is less than their face value. The value of the food stamp allotment to the recipient is equal to a cash transfer that gives an equal increase in utility. In Figure 8.6, we see that a cash transfer of $\$E$ (less than $\$G$) gives the recipient the same level of utility as the $\$G$ food stamp allotment. With a cash transfer of $\$E$, the household's budget line is $M''M''$, and the

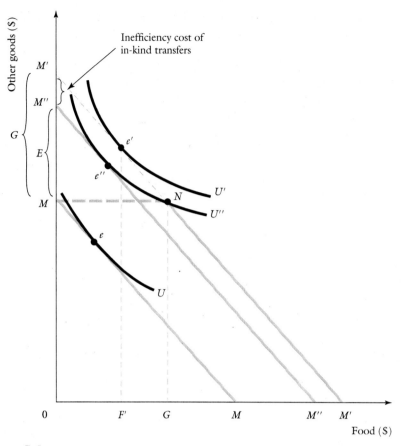

Figure 8.6

Nonequivalence of Transfers in Cash and Food Stamps

Given a cash transfer of G that shifts the budget line to M'M', the recipient spends only F' on food, which is less than the transfer. Given a food stamp allotment of G, the individual would spend more on food because the dashed segment NM' of the budget line is not available. The recipient gets less utility with food stamps, causing an inefficiency cost equal to the loss in income of M'M'' measured on the vertical axis. That is, the recipient gets the same utility from the smaller cash transfer E as from a food stamp transfer of G.

utility-maximizing household just reaches the indifference curve U'' (the level of utility it gets with $\$G$ in food stamps).

What is the evidence on the equivalence or nonequivalence of food stamps and cash? Consumer theory proposes that food stamps will increase food consumption relative to cash if the two types of transfers are not equivalent but will make no difference if they are equivalent. Empirical studies of actual behavior yield mixed results. Most of the evidence comes from states where food stamps have been "cashed out"—that is, replaced with an equal amount of cash.

One study of a food stamp cash-out program in the state of Washington, where some households were given cash while others received food stamps, found that the average budget share spent on home food expenditures was 30.3% for households receiving food stamps, but only 27% for those receiving cash.[9] This difference is statistically significant. However, studies of cash-out experiments in other states have found that the differences in the budget shares spent on food before and after food stamps were cashed out were not statistically significant. If the study in Washington state is accurate, food stamps do increase food consumption more than an equal cash transfer. However, it also implies a deadweight loss of the kind shown in Figure 8.6. It means that people use food stamps to consume food that they value at less than its cash price.

WHY IN-KIND TRANSFERS?   If a transfer in kind is never preferable to cash for the recipient, why does the government assist the poor with so many in-kind benefits? Several explanations have been suggested.

- *Parentalism.* Parentalism (also called paternalism) means that the government, or the taxpayers that pay for the poverty programs, know better than poor families themselves how they should spend their resources. Many people fear that if the poor are given cash rather than goods and services, they will spend it on frills like cable TV or "sins" like alcohol or drugs. A parentalist believes we should help the poor by ensuring they have better health, nutrition, and a roof over their heads.

- *Merit Goods.* Nobel Laureate James Tobin pointed out that people's desire for equality is greater for some goods than for others. For example, many people believe that the poor should have equal access to health care and food, but not to expensive watches, designer clothes, and luxury cars. Tobin called this sentiment **specific egalitarianism.** The goods and services we believe should be more equally available are called **merit goods.** The in-kind transfer programs assist the poor by giving them these merit goods.

- *Targeting.* Most of us are concerned that the benefits of poverty programs actually go to the poor rather than to those who are not poor. A problem with any program that offers assistance to needy families is that those who are not needy may misrepresent themselves (welfare fraud), or impoverish themselves, so that they can receive benefits. The ability to police this sort of behavior is limited, so it is an advantage for the government to offer benefits that are more attractive to the truly needy than to the nonneedy. For instance, the nonneedy may be willing to stand in line to get a $20 bill, but not to get a bag of canned food costing $20. If the government offers canned food rather than cash, only the needy would apply. This idea is commonly called the **target efficiency** of in-kind transfers.

  In-kind transfers can be used to target benefits within families as well as among families. For instance, one argument for providing school meals to poor children rather than giving cash to their parents (so their children can buy meals) is that the school meals are more likely to reach their targeted recipients—the children.

---

[9]Barbara Cohen and Nathan Young, *Evaluation of the Washington State Food Stamp Cashout Program*, 1992.

8.2   Welfare Reform: Has It Helped or Hurt?

Proponents of the 1996 welfare reform extol its successes. Caseloads dropped dramatically; between August 1996 and March 1999, the number recipients receiving AFDC/TANF assistance dropped 44%, from 4.8% of the population to 2.7%. Work participation by recipients has increased fourfold since 1992, and the earnings of those on the welfare increased 11% between 1997 and 1998. Between 1996 and 1998, employment of former welfare recipients has increased 34%. Through all of this, the poverty rate has dropped 15% since 1993.

Welfare advocates express grave concerns about the reforms. They argue that much of the improvement is attributable to the good state of the economy and plentiful jobs. They warn that an economic downturn could bring about real hardship. They also point out that falling enrollments in cash assistance programs have reduced access to programs that provide benefits in kind. Between May 1996 and May 1999, people receiving food stamps fell 32% from 26.5 million to 18 million recipients. And after years of rapid growth, the number of Medicaid recipients fell 13% for adults and 11% for children in 1997. Welfare advocates attribute these declines to increased restrictions in the programs (for exam-

ple, many resident aliens are no longer eligible for food stamps and able-bodied adults have short time limits) and the de-linking of eligibility for Medicaid from that for cash assistance. They also point out that low-income working adults are much less likely to have health coverage than their unemployed counterparts. Thus, the success of welfare reform in moving people from welfare to work is likely to increase the percentage of poor families without health insurance.

Critically analyze the following questions:

- Suppose the economy enters a recession. What do you expect will happen to welfare caseloads under TANF and the number of people enrolled in the Food Stamp Program and Medicaid? Would the length of the recession affect whether real hardship results?

- Both welfare reform proponents and opponents stress changes in caseloads as criteria for judging success or failure. What criteria would you use to determine whether the effects of welfare reform are favorable or not?

- How would your view of the fall in Medicaid enrollees depend on whether former welfare recipients are covered under employer-paid health care plans?

In order for targeting to work, in-kind transfers cannot be equivalent to cash for all recipients. Ideally, an in-kind transfer should be inferior to nonneedy families but as good as cash to needy families. Public housing is a case where this might be true. A nonneedy family is unlikely to find public housing attractive and, therefore, would not misrepresent or impoverish itself to obtain it. However, homeless families might treat public housing as equivalent to cash.

- *Moral Hazard.* People can invest in human capital (better health, education, and skills), which increases their potential future earnings. Such investments have a cost, so poor people who receive and expect to continue to receive cash transfers have an incentive to invest too little of their resources in human capital. The reward on human capital to a welfare recipient is reduced by the fact that the higher future earnings would be offset by the loss of welfare benefits (therefore benefiting the taxpayer rather than the investor). For this reason, the government may find it efficient to give poor people benefits in the form of health care, education, and job training.

▓ *Interests of Producers.* In-kind programs may indirectly benefit the producers of the goods and services as well as the poor. The Department of Agriculture administers the Food Stamp Program, and the domestic food industry as well as farmers lobby hard to keep and enhance the program. It is probably significant that food stamps cannot be used for imported food items. This suggests that the nutrition of the poor is not the only motivation of the program.

CONCLUSION AND SUMMARY

Absolute measures define poverty by comparing a family's resources with the cost of socially defined "needs.' But economists argue that the distinction between "needs" and "wants" is subjective—needs are simply intense wants. Moreover, needs depend on individual perceptions. For example, a drug addict "needs" heroin and kids "need" Pokemon cards. Socially defined needs, like food, clothing, decent shelter, and health care, are simply wants that a majority of the population is willing to define as needs. In this sense, they are as much merit goods as needs. As an economy grows richer, what were once merely wants (more living space, car, television, telephone, etc.) become socially defined needs. In this sense all measures of poverty are relative measures, so poverty, as we define it, will not soon vanish.

Perhaps no better example is retirement. Before the twentieth century, retirement was rare. People worked until they were too old and frail to carry on, and retirement, as such, was short and brutish. Today, people live longer and expect to retire with more than a decade of healthy life ahead of them. Two of the largest federal spending programs—Social Security and Medicare—provides benefits to retirees. We consider these programs in the next chapter.

▓ In 1998, 34.5 million people, or 12.7% of the population, were living "in poverty." Poverty rates vary according to age, ethnicity, and geographic location, with poverty rates as high as 26% for some groups.

▓ The federal government defines poverty by comparing a family's cash income with the Official Poverty Threshold (OPT). In the 1960s, the OPT was set at three times the cost of a minimally nutritious diet for the family and has been adjusted for inflation since that time. The OPT depends on family size; in 1998, the OPT for a family of four was equal to $16,530.

▓ The current measure of poverty is criticized for many reasons, including: (i) it ignores the costs of necessities other than food, such as clothing and housing; (ii) it does not take into account geographic differences in housing costs; (iii) measured family income does not include earnings and transfers in kind, such as food, health, and housing benefits; and (iv) mandatory family outlays, such as taxes, work expenses, child-care costs, and out-of-pocket medical expenses, are ignored.

▓ In fiscal year 1996, the federal and state governments combined spent nearly $370 billion on programs that assist the poor with means-tested transfers. Three-quarters of the dollar value of these transfers are in kind, mainly food, health care, and housing.

▓ The main sources of cash assistance to the poor are the state-administered Temporary Assistance for Needy Families programs, which are partly financed by a $17 billion block grant from the federal government; the federally funded Supplemental Security Income program, which provides means-tested cash benefits to the blind, disabled, and aged; and the Earned Income Tax Credit, which provides a refundable tax credit to working families based on their earned income.

▓ The main sources of in-kind assistance are Medicaid, which provides health insurance for the poor, the Food Stamp Program, and several programs that provide housing, education, and job training assistance.

▓ Means-tested transfers are likely to reduce the incentive to work, because benefits are reduced as earnings increase. Both TANF and the Food Stamp Program require able-bodied persons without small children to engage in some form of work participation. The Earned Income Tax Credit may increase or decrease work effort.

▓ Means-tested transfers may have contributed to family dissolution, illegitimate births, and welfare dependency. Many of the welfare reforms of 1996 are directed at these concerns.

▓ In theory, in-kind transfers are no better than, and perhaps inferior to, cash transfers to the recipient. However, in-kind transfers may be preferred by the government because of parentalism, specific egalitarianism, targeting, moral hazard, and producer interests.

QUESTIONS FOR DISCUSSION AND REVIEW

1. According to the Bible (John *xii. 8.*), "The poor always ye have with you." Evaluate this hypothesis assuming poverty is measured relatively. What if it is measured absolutely?

2. To determine the poverty rate, the government counts a family as poor if its income before taxes including cash transfers from the government is less than the OPT. Do you think that in-kind transfers from the government such as food stamps and Medicaid benefits should also be counted? Why or why not?

3. In 1996, the government reported that 7.7 million families lived below the Official Poverty Threshold. In the same year, all governments combined spent $367 billion on means-tested transfers, which

amounts to $47,662 per family in poverty! How is it that we still have poor families in the United States?

4. Under TANF, many states have dropped the requirement that two-parent families are ineligible for cash welfare benefits (which prevailed under the old AFDC program). Under TANF, the percentage welfare recipient families that are two-parent families rose from under 10% to 16%. Is this evidence that the old AFDC program encouraged family dissolution?

5. In the accompanying figure, the demand for food by a food stamp recipient is shown as an MWTP schedule. The quantity of food (in baskets) is measured on the horizontal axis, and the price of a basket of food is measured on the vertical

axis. A basket of food costs $10 at the supermarket. Suppose the recipient is given an allotment of food stamps sufficient to buy 10 baskets. Consuming these, he or she would be willing to pay $4 at most for another basket. Given cash instead of food stamps, this individual would buy five baskets at the going price. What is the cost of the food stamp allotment to the government (not counting administrative costs)? What value does the recipient place on the food stamps relative to an equal dollar amount of cash? What is the deadweight loss associated with food stamps?

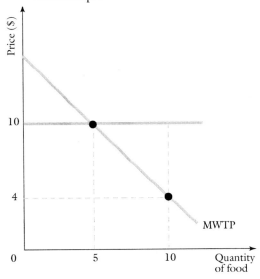

6. In 1999, the federal government became alarmed about the sharp drop in food stamp recipients from 28 million four years earlier to less than 19 million people. At the same time, the federal government boasted about the fall in cash welfare caseloads after welfare reform. Shirley R. Watkins, undersecretary of agriculture, put it this way: "The goal was to get people off welfare programs, but people may have failed to understand that the food stamp program is not a welfare program. It's nutritional assistance" (The

Times Herald Record, Middletown, NY, February 25, 1999). Given that people must prove financial need to get food stamps, is Ms. Watkins' assessment accurate? Why might the federal government be concerned about the drop in food stamp caseloads but not the drop in TANF caseloads?

7. Beginning in 2000, paper food stamps are being replaced with a type of debit card, embossed with the recipient's identity. Given that there is an extensive black market in paper food stamps where recipients can sell stamps to others, how will this affect the equivalence or nonequivalence between food stamp transfers and cash transfers? How will this affect the ability of food stamps to target benefits to the poor? How do you think it will affect the level of food consumption by the poor?

8. Despite an expansion in eligibility, the number of children enrolled in states' Medicaid programs declined about 1.5% from 1995 to 1998. Propose some possible reasons for this.

9. Internet Exercise. At 12.7%, the poverty rate for persons in 1998 is slightly lower than it was in 1989 (13.1%). However, the aggregate figure does not reveal larger changes in the poverty rates of the different groups who make up the poor. Use U.S. Census Bureau data at http://blue.census.gov/hhes/poverty/poverty98/pv98est1.html to answer the following questions:

   a. How did poverty among African-Americans change from 1989 to 1998 as compared with whites?

   b. In what regions of the country did poverty decline? Did poverty increase in any region?

   c. In which age groups did poverty decline? In which age groups did it increase?

10. Internet Exercise. The author Scott Fitz-
gerald once told Ernest Hemingway "The
rich are not like us," and he replied "Yes,
they have more money." Many nonpoor
Americans believe the poor are unlike
themselves in more ways than a simple
lack of money. Many studies compare
families who are poor with those who are
nonpoor. The Urban Institute's National
Survey of American Families at http://
newfederalism.urban.org/nsaf/cpuf/

index.htm provides a public use data set
that allows the user to compare characteristics of children in poor and nonpoor
families. Access the site and download the
easy-to-use NASFTabulator. Use it to
compare the percentage of children in
families above and below the poverty line
"who always do their homework" or
"have feelings of inferiority." Do you
think the results reflect the fact that the
poor are different, or simply lack money?

SELECTED REFERENCES

The effects of cashing out food stamps on food
consumption are studied in Barbara Cohen and
Nathan Young, *Evaluation of the Washington
State Food Stamp Cashout Demonstration*, 1992.

A summary of research on the effects of
welfare on behavior is found in Robert Mof-

fitt, "The Incentive Effects of the U.S. Welfare System: A Review," 1992. An excellent
discussion of different aspects of welfare
reform is found in Sheldon H. Danziger et
al., *Confronting Poverty: Prescriptions for
Change*, 1994.

USEFUL INTERNET SITES

The Institute for Research on Poverty at the
University of Wisconsin, Madison, maintains a
site with excellent information on the measurement of poverty at http://www.ssc.wisc.
edu/irp/.

The latest information on the impact of
the 1996 welfare reforms and how the states
are modifying their programs can be found

at the Urban Institute's Assessing the New
Federalism site. The address is http://
newfederalism.urban.org/

Data and information on welfare reform
can also be found on the Department of
Health and Human Services site at http://
www.acf.dhhs.gov/news/welfare/

9 Social Security and Medicare

On January 31, 1940, Ida May Fuller, a legal secretary from Ludlow, Vermont, entered the history books when she received the first Social Security check ever issued—for $22.54. Fuller had worked for three years under the new Social Security system introduced just three years earlier. She and her employer had paid a grand total of $45.50 in Social Security payroll taxes. Before she died at age 100 in 1975, she collected nearly $23,000 in benefits. No doubt, Ida Fuller thought she got her money's worth from Social Security and she was not alone in thinking this. Most people retiring before 1990 received benefits of greater value than the payroll taxes they paid. For this reason, Social Security is a popular program with older Americans. In fact, many politicians consider it the "third rail" of American politics: touch it and they die. Medicare, which provides medical insurance for retirees, is equally popular. But many young Americans today fear that they will benefit little from these programs when they reach old age. Political discussions about Social Security and Medicare focus on the need to reform or even "save" these programs.

Social Security and Medicare are the largest social insurance programs in the United States. Unlike transfer programs that provide assistance to the poor, these **social insurance** transfer programs are not *means-tested*. Retired people who have contributed to Social Security and Medicare receive benefits no matter how wealthy they are. Another social insurance program is unemployment compensation. To receive unemployment compensation, workers do not have to be poor; they just need to lose their jobs.

WHY SOCIAL INSURANCE?

Social insurance programs differ from means-tested programs in several ways. First, the benefits usually depend on the past earnings or contributions by the beneficiaries or their employers. For example, workers with higher past incomes, called **insured earnings,** receive higher Social Security benefits. Second, social insurance programs are funded with special taxes levied on earnings and payrolls (sometimes called "contributions"), not from general revenue. Also, the revenue from these taxes is "earmarked" and is not supposed to fund government spending other than the program for which the taxes are intended.

In other words, social insurance programs function somewhat like private insurance policies. Contributions are made to a trust, or reserve fund, and when events occur in the lives of contributors—such as retirement, unemployment, or illness—benefits are paid to the contributors. However, unlike private insurance, social insurance is compulsory: workers cannot opt out of the Social Security program.[1]

Because these programs are so large, they always figure prominently in the budget debate. Many people—including the members of the Bipartisan Commission on Entitlement and Tax Reform, a congressional commission that recently examined the long-term solvency of the social insurance programs—believe the programs cannot continue unchanged. Eventually, they say, the benefits will outstrip available funds and the programs will become insolvent. What can be done to forestall such a fate? The answers depend on how serious the observer thinks the problems are. Suggested reforms for the Social Security program range from investing some of the trust fund's $800 billion surplus in the stock market to privatizing the program—which effectively means abolishing it and replacing it with a program of compulsory saving.

Why does government provide social insurance programs? Are the programs simply to insure people against particular risks, or are there other objectives? Do the programs benefit some people more than others? To answer these types of questions, we first review reasons for government insurance. We then study the structure of the Social Security and Medicare programs in this context. We also examine the economic effects of the programs and evaluate the need to reform them, especially Social Security.

As we learned in Chapter 7, the economic reason that government provides social insurance is insurance market failure. Insurance market failure occurs when moral hazard (the fact that insured people are less likely to avoid losses) and adverse selection (the fact that people who are more likely to make a claim are more likely to buy insurance) are present. Because of moral hazard and adverse selection, private insurance against some types of risk are prohibitively expensive or even unattainable. If the government did not provide the insurance, most people would be uninsured.

Medical insurance is a good illustration. Medical insurance is likely to be purchased by people who, perhaps because of poor health, are in need of it, rather than people in good health (adverse selection). Moreover, people who have insurance are more likely to demand medical services than are those who have to pay for the services out of their own pocket—a form of moral hazard. Of course, the need for medical services increases as people age. In fact, end-of-life health care for people who die during the year (less than 1% of the population) accounts for more than 7% of annual national health care expenditures. Private insurers are reluctant to sell medical insurance to the elderly and to people with existing health conditions, or do so only at very high premium rates.

Clearly, Medicare is a type of health insurance, but how is Social Security insurance? Social Security can be considered insurance against the risk of outliving one's retirement savings. A woman (man) retiring at age 65 in the year 2000 can look

---

[1]Some forms of private insurance are compulsory as well. Certain professions cannot be practiced without malpractice insurance, and automobile insurance is required in some states.

forward to living about 19.3 (15.7) more years on average. However, the number of years an individual will actually live is very uncertain. He or she might die a year later at age 66, or live to 106. Although it is prudent for people to retire with sufficient savings to cover their expenses over the period of their life expectancy, what if they live much longer than average? They could exhaust their savings and spend their last years in poverty.

Private insurers sell insurance against this type of risk in the form of life annuity contracts. A life annuity contract guarantees the buyer a specified periodic payment (monthly or annual) for the rest of his or her life. Adverse selection raises the cost of annuity contracts to people of average life expectancy. People who have longevity and good health are more likely to buy life annuities than people with health conditions and family histories of dying young, so the price charged for a life annuity by an insurer must be high enough to cover the costs of these longer-than-average-life buyers. According to one estimate, the price of life annuities is increased 10% by adverse selection.[2] Another 10% is absorbed in administration fees. Social Security is a type of life annuity because its pays benefits for the life of the beneficiary and his or her spouse. Workers "purchase" this annuity by paying payroll taxes during their working years. Some people argue that Social Security is a more cost-effective way of providing such an annuity. The Social Security Administration reports that the annual administrative cost of the program was less than 1% of contributions (Social Security taxes) in 1998.[3]

SOCIAL SECURITY: THE NATION'S BIGGEST GOVERNMENT PROGRAM

The main social insurance programs that benefit the elderly are grouped together under the title OASDHI, which stands for Old Age, Survivors, Disability, and Health Insurance. The OASI part, commonly called Social Security, pays lifetime cash benefits to retirees over the age of 62 or to the survivors of deceased retirees. The DI part extends the benefits to people under 62 if they are unable to work because of a disability. The HI part, commonly called Medicare, which provides hospital insurance for people over age 65, is discussed later in this chapter.

Total government spending on Social Security, all of it by the federal government, was $390 billion in 1999. This was 23% of all federal spending, making Social Security the largest single spending program of the federal government; indeed it is the largest government spending program in the nation. In 1998, 44.5 million people received Social Security benefits. Of these beneficiaries, 70% were retired workers and their dependents, who received an average benefit of $780 a month.

A Brief History of Social Security in the United States

The nation's largest spending program was created by the Social Security Act of 1935. Although Social Security was enacted mainly to alleviate the high rate

---

[2]Olivia Mitchell et al. "New Evidence on the Money's Worth of Individual Annuities," 1999.
[3]Social Security Administration, *Fast Facts and Figures About Social Security, 1999,* October 1999, p. 2.

of poverty among the elderly who outlive their resources, it was not structured as a means-tested program. The most important element was a contributory plan that entitled contributors to benefits regardless of their incomes. The Social Security Act proposed a lifetime monthly pension benefit for retired workers who made contributions for at least five years. The "contributions" were a 2% tax, split equally between the employer and the employee, on the first $3000 of earnings per year. Membership was compulsory for most people, and initially about half the workforce was required to contribute. The benefits, scheduled to begin in 1942, depended on the contributors' accumulated wage earnings after 1936. As it was designed in 1935, Social Security was a "funded" program, with the contributions saved in an "old-age reserve account" to pay future benefits.

Before the scheduled benefits were paid, the Social Security Act was amended in 1939 in significant ways. Most importantly, the government began paying benefits immediately, so that workers retiring in 1940 received benefits even though they had not paid five years of contributions. This amendment turned the Social Security program into a **pay-as-you-go** system, which is a system in which the contributions collected by the government in a year are used to pay benefits in that year, rather than accumulated for future benefits. A second amendment further broke the link between contributions and benefits by granting a benefit to a spouse of a covered worker even if the spouse made no contributions.

A third amendment created the **Social Security Trust Fund,** a separate government account to receive contributions and pay out benefits. Despite the name, the trust fund was not like a savings account in which contributions were saved for future benefits. Instead, it was like a checking account in which contributions were received each month and the same amount was paid out as benefits. The fund served to separate the revenues and outlays of the Social Security program from the general accounts of the government.

In redesigning the Social Security program, the government sought to achieve two conflicting goals. The first goal was *individual equity,* which means that a contributor has an earned right to receive benefits in accordance with his or her contributions. To achieve this, the benefit was based on past covered earnings and therefore on past contributions. This decision had political as well as economic motives. In a much-quoted passage, President Roosevelt said that the link between contributions and benefits was

> ... politics all the way through. We put those payroll contributions there so as to give the contributors a legal, moral, and political right to collect their pensions ... [so] no damn politician can ever scrap my Social Security program.

The second objective, *social adequacy,* required that contributors receive an adequate pension benefit even if they had low earnings in the past. The objective of social adequacy meant that the Social Security program would function as a redistributional program as well as a social insurance program. To achieve social adequacy, the benefit increased with the average monthly wage (AMW) of the contributor at a decreasing rate. The first $50 of the AMW increased benefits at 40 cents per dollar, whereas the next $150 of AMW increased benefits at only 10 cents per dollar. The change in the benefit rate at $50 is called a *bend point.*

Converting Social Security into a pay-as-you-go system was necessary to achieve these two conflicting objectives. When the Social Security program was young, the number of beneficiaries was small relative to the number of covered workers (6 per 100 covered workers in 1950 as compared with 27 per 100 in 1999), so the annual contributions were more than enough to pay every retiree a benefit sufficient for individual equity and leave enough for social adequacy by paying higher benefit rates to retirees with low AMWs.

Although the Social Security program was small in 1940, its main features have remained largely unchanged to the present day:

- The program is compulsory, and eligibility to receive benefits is not means-tested.
- The program pays out a cash benefit based on an accumulated measure of the contributor's past earnings, and a benefit is available to a noncontributing spouse.
- The rate at which the benefit increases with past earnings is less as accumulated past earnings increase because of bend points in the formula for calculating benefits.
- The program is financed by a flat percentage rate tax on the worker's earnings up to an earnings limit. The tax is split equally between the employee and the employer.
- The tax revenue collected is used to pay out current benefits; that is, the system is a pay-as-you-go system. The taxes and outlays are separated from other government accounts by means of the trust fund.

Since 1940, the Social Security Act has been amended many times in order to broaden the coverage, change the eligibility requirements, alter the benefits (usually increasing them), and change the formula by which benefits are calculated. The amendments have also changed the Social Security tax rates and the amounts of earnings subject to tax. The most important amendments were those in 1954, which extended benefits to disabled covered workers; those in 1972, which indexed benefits to the cost of living; those in 1977, which introduced the current formula for calculating benefits; and those in 1983, which changed the age of eligibility in the future and introduced partial funding for the program.

Since the program started, spending on Social Security has increased vastly. As a percentage of GDP, it has increased from less than 0.3% in 1950 to 4.5% in 1998. Projected Social Security benefits in the year 2030 amount to about 8% of projected GDP.

The Social Security Benefits Structure

Workers with 40 quarters (10 years) of coverage are eligible to receive Social Security benefits when they reach age 62. In 1999, a quarter of coverage was credited if a worker had at least $740 dollars of covered earnings (on which Social Security taxes were paid) during the quarter. To receive a full Social Security benefit, a worker must retire after the normal retirement age (65 in 1999). If an eligible worker retires before the normal retirement age, the benefit is reduced for each month before age 65. A worker retiring at 62 receives a benefit that is only 80% of the full benefit. Workers who delay retirement beyond the normal retirement age receive a **delayed retirement credit.** For someone turning 62 in 1999, the delayed retirement credit increased the Social Security benefit by 5½% per year of delay past age 65, until age 70.

CALCULATING THE BENEFIT FOR A RETIRED WORKER.   The full benefit for a single retired worker is the **primary insurance amount (PIA),** which is based on the worker's **average indexed monthly earnings (AIME).** The AIME is a measure of the retiree's average earnings, in dollars of constant purchasing power, over his or her working life. The covered earnings in each of the best 35 years of the working life are multiplied by an indexing factor to convert them into dollars of constant purchasing power as of the year the worker turns 62, and then summed. The summed indexed earnings are then divided by 420 (the number of months in 35 years) to get the worker's AIME.

An increase in the worker's AIME increases PIA at a decreasing rate because of two bend points. Figure 9.1 shows the schedule relating PIA to AIME for someone retiring at age 65 in 2002. The PIA is determined in the year the worker turns 62 (1999 in this example). If the worker's AIME is $3265, PIA is calculated by taking **90%** of the first $505 of AIME plus 32% of the next $2538 plus 15% of the remaining $222, for a PIA of $1300 as of 1999. The PIA for subsequent years is indexed to the cost of living. For instance, if the worker retires at age 65 in 2002 and the cost of living rose 10% between 1999 to 2002, the benefit in the first year of retirement is $1430 ($1300 times 110%).

As is apparent in Figure 9.1, the schedule for calculating the PIA from the AIME has three brackets. In the first bracket, the PIA increases at 90% of AIME, so a worker with a low AIME (under $505) gets a benefit equal to 90% of AIME. Workers with higher AIMEs get higher benefits, but less than 90%. For instance, the worker with an AIME of $3265 receives a Social Security benefit that is about 40% of AIME. In the third bracket, the PIA increases at only 15 cents per dollar of AIME. Since workers pay the same Social Security tax on covered earnings, the benefits schedule means that the *net* Social Security benefit (benefits minus contributions) is higher for low earners than for high earners. This is the income redistribution element of the Social Security program.

The PIA is the Social Security benefit for a single worker retiring at age 65. A married worker's spouse also receives a benefit (upon reaching 65) equal to 50% of the covered worker's PIA. This benefit is paid even if the spouse has made no contributions. A divorced spouse who was married to a covered worker for at least 10 years also receives the spousal benefit providing he or she has not remarried while the covered worker is alive. If both spouses contributed to Social Security, they are *dually entitled*. A dually entitled contributor can choose a benefit equal to 100% of his or her own PIA or 50% of the spouse's, whichever is greater. If a covered worker dies, the surviving spouse can receive 100% of the worker's benefit upon reaching 65, or his or her own benefit, whichever is greater.

The Distributional Impact of Social Security

Social Security is not just a social insurance program; it is also a vast redistribution program. Although everyone pays the same Social Security tax rate, the benefits depend on past earnings, year of retirement, number of years lived after retirement, whether the contributor has a spouse, and whether the spouse is dually entitled. In this section, we will study who benefits most and least from Social Security.

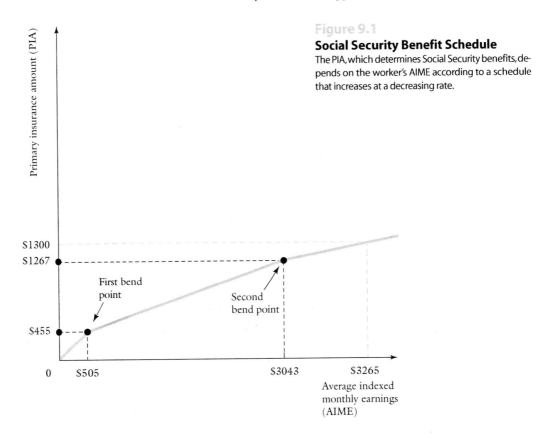

Figure 9.1

Social Security Benefit Schedule

The PIA, which determines Social Security benefits, depends on the worker's AIME according to a schedule that increases at a decreasing rate.

To examine the distributional impact of the Social Security program, we need to measure each person's level of benefits. This can be done in several ways. Because the program is supposed to "insure" against the loss of earnings upon retirement, a natural measure is called the replacement rate. The gross **replacement rate** is the fraction of a retiree's before-tax earnings that is "replaced" by pretax Social Security benefits. Most commonly, the replacement rate is based on the retiree's earnings in the year immediately preceding retirement, adjusted for changes in the cost of living. For example, if a worker's earnings were $30,000 a year before retirement (adjusted for inflation) and his or her annual Social Security benefit is $10,000, the gross replacement rate is 33⅓%. In 1995, a worker with average earnings retiring at age 65 received a gross replacement rate of 41%.

Less readily obtained, but of greater interest, is the *net* replacement rate provided by the program, which is the fraction of the retiree's *after-tax* earnings that is replaced with after-tax benefits. Typically, the net replacement rate is higher than the gross because people receive lower income in retirement and the income tax system is progressive.

The distributional impact of Social Security among workers with different earnings is seen from the gross replacement rates. Single male workers with average earnings received a gross replacement rate of 41%, those with earnings 45% of the average received a gross replacement rate of 55%, and those with the maximum earnings covered by the program have a gross replacement rate of only 24%.

Although the replacement rate is a useful number, it is not always the most useful for measuring differences in benefits received. Economists prefer the **benefit-to-tax ratio.** The benefit-to-tax ratio is the *actuarial* value of benefits received divided by the value of Social Security taxes paid over one's lifetime. Actuarial values are based on the probability that a person will die at each age. Also, because we are summing benefits and taxes in different years, we must convert them into units of present value. This conversion takes into account that receipts or payments occurring earlier in life have greater value because of the possibility of earning interest on them. The details of present-value calculations are discussed in Chapter 6. A benefit-to-tax ratio of 100% means that the present value of a recipient's expected benefits in retirement is equal to the present value of contributions made while working.

The main distributional features of the Social Security program are summarized in Figure 9.2, which shows the lifetime benefit as a percentage of lifetime contributions for low-earnings workers (45% of median covered earnings), average-

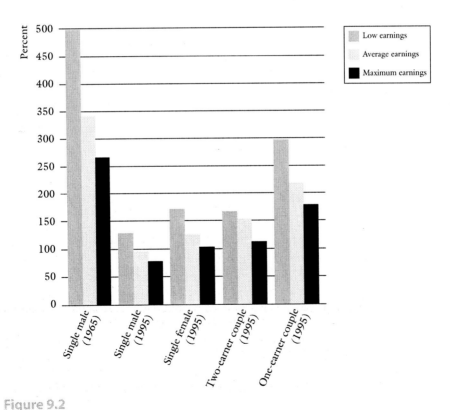

Figure 9.2

Benefit-to-Tax Ratio (BTR) for People Retiring at Age 65
The BTR is higher for persons retiring earlier rather than later, for persons earning less rather than more, for females rather than males, and for one-earner couples rather than singles or two-earner couples.

earnings workers (median covered earnings), and high-earnings workers (maximum covered earnings). Differences in the benefit-to-tax ratio are shown according to the worker's sex, normal retirement date, and marital status. Present values are calculated discounting at 2% per year.

A male worker with average earnings retiring at age 65 in 1995 received a benefit-to-tax ratio of 95%, indicating that the present value of his Social Security benefits is just 95% of the present value of his past contributions. A male with earnings 45% of average received a benefit-to-tax ratio of 128%. A male with the maximum covered earnings received only 78%. We see from these figures that, relative to contributions, Social Security is a much better "investment" for workers with low earnings than for workers with high earnings.[4]

The redistribution of income from high- to low-income groups is a design feature of the Social Security program, but its other distributional impacts are no less important for having been unintended (if they were unintended). In particular, the program redistributes income from people who remain single to those who marry, from two-earner couples to one-earner couples, from men to women, and from those who are born later to those who are born earlier.

Income is redistributed from single people to married people because a benefit is paid to a retiree's noncontributing spouse. Single and married workers make contributions at the same rate, yet the married worker with a noncontributing spouse gets an extra benefit. Two-earner married couples can also benefit from this feature because a low-earner worker may receive a higher benefit as the spouse of a high-earner worker. The lifetime benefit per beneficiary in a two-earner couple with average earnings retiring in 1995 at age 65 is 153% of lifetime contributions, as compared with 127% for a single female and 95% for a single male. A one-earner couple does best of all, with a lifetime benefit equal to 221% of contributions.

Redistribution from men to women occurs because women of age 65 will live four years longer than men on average. In 1990, the average woman reaching age 65 would live 19 more years, whereas the average man would live 15 more years. Unlike private insurance policies, Social Security ignores actuarial differences in the life spans of men and women. Men and women pay the same contribution rate, and their benefits are calculated by the same formula. As a result, the benefit-to-tax ratio for a single woman with average earnings retiring at age 65 in 1995 is 127% whereas a man with comparable earnings gets just 95%.

One of the most widely discussed features of Social Security is the difference in benefit-to-tax ratios across generations. The benefit-to-tax ratio is higher the sooner a person reaches normal retirement age. A single man with average earnings who retired at 65 in 1950 had a benefit-to-tax ratio equal to 966% compared with a single man who retired at 65 in 1995, who had 95%. A single man who turns 65 in 2025 will have a benefit-to-tax ratio of only 71%. This same pattern across generations is found for men and women, whether married or single, with high or low earnings. The generational impact partially reflects the way in which

---

[4]Figures on the distributional effects of Social Security were taken from C. Eugene Steurle and Jon M. Bakija, *Retooling Social Security,* appendix.

the program is funded, which allowed it to pay benefits in excess of contributions in its early years. It also reflects the large numbers of retirees expected in the future. Since the number of beneficiaries will grow rapidly after the year 2010, future retirees will be less fortunate than past or present retirees.

Financing Social Security

Unlike most federal spending programs, OASDI (and part of Medicare as well, as discussed later) is financed with an **earmarked tax** on payrolls known as the Federal Insurance Contributions Act (FICA) tax. An earmarked tax is one for which the revenue collected is dedicated for a specific program, in this case Social Security. OASDI is financed with a 12.4% tax on earnings (up to $72,600 in 1999) split equally between the employee and his or her employer. That is, the employee pays 6.2% on salary and wages received and the employer pays 6.2% on salaries and wages paid. An additional 2.9% tax, split equally between employees and their employers, is levied to finance Medicare. There is no upper limit for the Medicare part of the payroll tax. Self-employed people pay the entire 15.3% FICA tax on their self-employment earnings. The revenue from the FICA tax flows into the Social Security and Medicare Health Insurance (HI) trust funds, which are separate from the general revenues of the federal government. Social insurance benefits and administrative costs are paid out of these trust funds.

The FICA tax is now the second-largest source of revenue for the federal government. In 1999, the FICA tax collected $612 billion, or 33.5% of all federal receipts. Since the FICA tax has no deductions or exemptions, unlike the personal income tax, it is the largest tax paid for most low- and low-middle income families. Moreover, between 1955 and 1995, it was also the most rapidly growing major tax. In 1955, the FICA tax rate was only 3% (combined employee and employer), and a maximum of $3000 earnings was taxed. In the same year, the FICA tax accounted for only about 12% of federal revenue. Between 1955 and 1995, FICA tax revenues grew an average of 7% a year.

The rapid growth in the FICA tax reflects the rapid growth in spending on the social insurance programs that it finances. Part of the growth is attributable to the introduction of new programs such as Medicare, which was introduced in 1965. Part of the growth is attributable to the increase in the number of people eligible to receive benefits and to increases in size of the real benefit (measured in dollars of constant purchasing power) paid. Finally, part of the growth in the FICA tax is attributable to a policy decision in 1983 to accumulate a surplus in the Social Security trust fund in order to maintain the solvency of the Social Security program. That is, the FICA tax now collects more revenue than is needed to finance the social insurance programs. The annual surplus, which was over $100 billion in 1999, is accumulated in the trust fund, which had a closing balance of nearly $800 billion at the end of 1999.

FUNDED VERSUS PAY-AS-YOU-GO PROGRAMS. Pay-as-you-go is an important feature of the Social Security program. As a result of demographic developments, this feature will place financial strain on the program several decades from now. For this reason, many people believe that Social Security is in danger of "going broke" in the future. To understand this concern, we need to understand the difference between a pay-as-you-go and a funded Social Security program.

To explain, we use a simple **overlapping generations model,** in which people are born in every time period, live for two periods, and then die. In the first period of life people are young and work; in the second period they are old and retired. As time passes, old generations are replaced with young ones, who in turn grow old and are replaced by young generations. In each period, two generations overlap, so younger working people coexist with older retired people. Although real-world demographics are more complicated, this model captures the basic demographic facts needed to understand the difference between the two types of programs.

The overlapping-generations model is illustrated in Figures 9.3 and 9.4. The columns represent successive periods moving to the right, and rows represent successive generations moving down. A generation is labeled by the period of its birth; thus a generation born in period 1 is called generation 1. Period 1 represents where

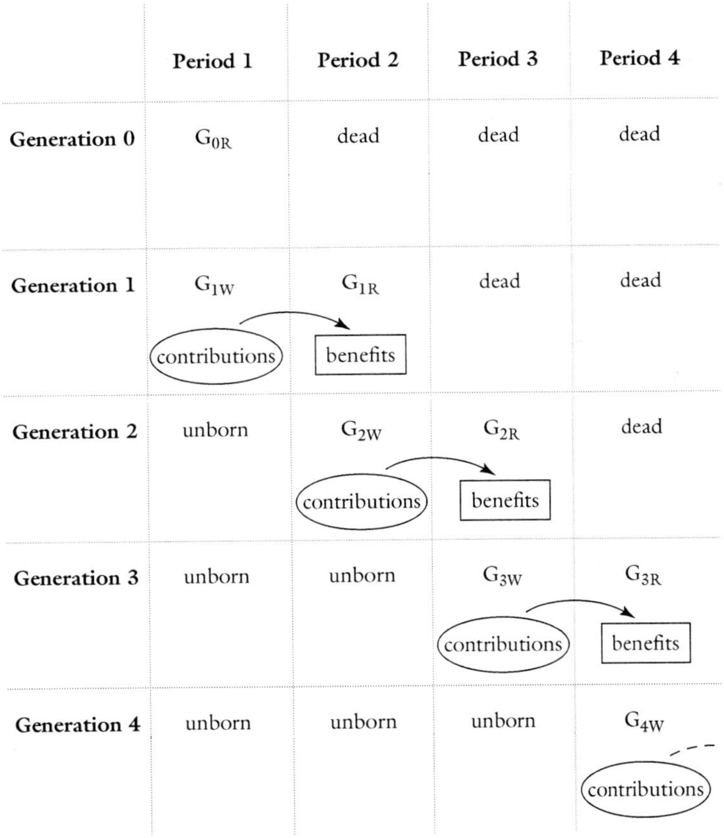

	Period 1	Period 2	Period 3	Period 4
Generation 0	G_{0R}	dead	dead	dead
Generation 1	G_{1W}	G_{1R}	dead	dead
	contributions → benefits			
Generation 2	unborn	G_{2W}	G_{2R}	dead
		contributions → benefits		
Generation 3	unborn	unborn	G_{3W}	G_{3R}
			contributions → benefits	
Generation 4	unborn	unborn	unborn	G_{4W}
				contributions

Figure 9.3

Funded Social Security Program

Under a funded program, contributions made during a generation's working years are saved in a trust fund and used to pay benefits to the members of the same generation when they retire.

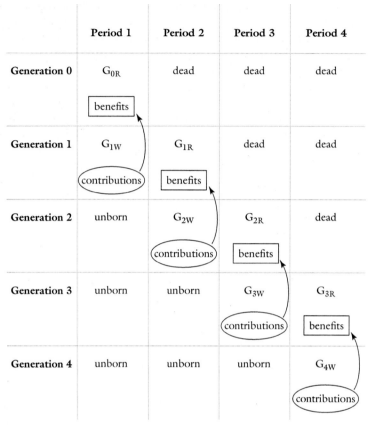

	Period 1	Period 2	Period 3	Period 4
Generation 0	G_{0R}	dead	dead	dead
	benefits			
Generation 1	G_{1W}	G_{1R}	dead	dead
	contributions	benefits		
Generation 2	unborn	G_{2W}	G_{2R}	dead
		contributions	benefits	
Generation 3	unborn	unborn	G_{3W}	G_{3R}
			contributions	benefits
Generation 4	unborn	unborn	unborn	G_{4W}
				contributions

Figure 9.4

Unfunded or Pay-As-You-Go Social Security Program

Under a pay-as-you-go program, the contributions of the working generation are used to finance benefits to the retirees of the older generation in the same period. The trust fund has no appreciable balance, so each generation must rely on the contributions of future generations to finance its benefits.

the diagram starts, not where the generations start. In period 1 we find two generations overlapping, the generation born a period earlier and now retired, represented by G_{0R}; and the generation born in period 1 and presently working, represented by G_{1W}. Earlier generations are dead, and later generations are yet to be born. Similarly, the column labeled period 2 shows the generation 1 retired and generation 2 working.

A **funded** Social Security program beginning in period 1 is shown in Figure 9.3. Generation 1 (G_{1W}) works and makes contributions, but no benefits are paid out. The contributions accumulate in a trust fund that is invested in the capital market. The proceeds, including the interest earned on the balance, are used to pay benefits to generation 1 when it retires in period 2 (G_{1R}). The generation that is already retired in period 1 (G_{0R}) when the program begins receives nothing and must rely on its own savings or private pensions.

A pay-as-you-go Social Security program beginning in period 1 is illustrated in Figure 9.4. With this program, the contributions made by generation 1 (G_{1W}) are used to pay out benefits to those already retired (G_{0R}). This is the **start-up bonus** of pay-as-you-go Social Security. Because contributions are used to pay the start-up bonus, they do not accumulate in a fund, so the pay-as-you-go program is **unfunded.** A trust fund may exist in name, but it is simply a temporary repository for contributions until the benefits are paid out in the same period. With a pay-as-you-go program, the benefits paid to generation 1 when it retires in period 2 are financed by contributions of generation 2, which is young and working in period 2. This process continues indefinitely with contributions of the working generation paid as benefits to the retired generation each period. With a pay-as-you-go program, it is pointless for current workers to worry about whether the money in the fund will "run out" before they retire. There is no money to run out! The current working generation relies on future workers to finance its retirement benefits.

Can a pay-as-you-go program pay interest on contributions? Not if the population or its earnings do not grow over time, because interest would require ever-higher contribution rates by future generations. However, if the total earnings grow over time, because of a larger workforce or higher earnings, a pay-as-you-go program can pay interest even if the contribution rate remains the same. The "interest" rate is the rate of growth in the total earnings of the workforce, so it is sometimes called the "biological" interest rate.

For example, suppose the population of each generation is 10% bigger than the generation before it. The G_{2W} population in Figure 9.4 is 10% larger than generation G_{1R}, so the revenue from the contributions of G_{2W} are 10% greater than the contributions of G_{1R}. Thus if all of the contributions in period 2 are paid out as benefits, generation G_{1R} receives a biological interest rate of 10% on its contributions. As long as growth continues, each generation receives interest on its contributions at the growth rate.

Note that a mature pay-as-you-go program doesn't appear much different from a mature funded program. In period 2, generation G_{2W} pays contributions and generation G_{1R} receives benefits in both programs. With growth, both programs pay interest; and if the growth rate is equal to the interest rate on investment, the benefits are the same under both programs. The differences are that the funded program has an accumulated fund and the pay-as-you-go does not, and the pay-as-you-go program has a start-up bonus and the funded program does not. It was the temptation of the start-up bonus that led to the 1939 amendments creating the pay-as-you-go system we have today. The price of the start-up bonus is the absence of a trust fund balance to invest in the capital market.

Economic Effects of Social Security

Social Security is a big program, and we expect that it has a significant impact on the economy. Economists have studied the impact of Social Security on household decisions, including its effects on decisions about retirement, which affect the labor supply of older workers, and decisions to save.

EFFECTS ON RETIREMENT AND LABOR SUPPLY.   In 1950 the average worker retired at age 68; by 1995 the average worker retired before age 64. This earlier retirement age has significantly reduced working by older people. For example, in 1950, 46% of men over age 65 were in the labor force, whereas this figure had fallen to 17% by 1995.

What determines when a worker decides to retire? And how does Social Security affect this decision? The decision to retire can be considered, for the most part, a decision to consume more leisure, so the impact of Social Security on retirement is analyzed using the labor-leisure model. As we saw in Chapter 8, this model implies that government programs can affect the choice between labor and leisure by altering incomes and the cost of leisure.

The income effect occurs because Social Security increases the retirement income of a potential retiree. Because leisure is a normal good (consumption rises with income), the demand for leisure increases if people are made better off by the program. This increases their desire to retire. For workers approaching retirement age, the income effect of Social Security on the retirement decision depends on the benefits they expect from Social Security over the remainder of their lifetime.

The Social Security program also changes the cost of retirement leisure to the worker. The cost of retiring a year earlier is the earnings lost. For instance, if the replacement rate is 100%, the price of leisure is zero because no income is lost by retiring. With no Social Security benefits at all, the cost of a year of retirement is equal to the worker's after-tax earnings. Since replacement rates are less than 100%, there is a price to be paid by retiring, equal to some fraction of the worker's annual earnings.

Empirical work examined retirement rates by age. First, the number of workers of a given age retiring in a year is expressed as a percentage of the number of workers of the same age who *could have retired* that year. The latter is measured as the number of workers aged one year younger working one year earlier. This percentage, known as the **retirement hazard rate,** measures the probability that a worker of given characteristics will retire in a given year. The retirement hazard rate is observed to rise for people in their late fifties and jumps sharply at age 62, the year they become eligible for Social Security benefits. It then declines until age 65, the age for full Social Security benefits, when it jumps even more dramatically. This pattern seems to suggest that the availability of Social Security benefits increases the probability that an eligible worker will retire.

Several considerations make it difficult to conclude firmly, from age profiles of retirement hazard rates, that Social Security increases the probability of retirement. For one thing, many private companies also have mandatory retirement at age 65, and private pension plans also begin paying benefits at that age. Other empirical studies attempt to quantify the effect of Social Security on retirement using a variable called **Social Security wealth.** Social Security wealth is the present value of benefits to which a worker is entitled once eligible for retirement. Studies find that workers at age 62 with greater Social Security wealth have higher retirement hazard rates than those with less. For instance, 62-year-old men with Social Security wealth between $20,000 and $25,000 had retirement hazard rates of 0.21 (meaning that about two workers retire for every 10 in a 1971 sample that could retire), which was twice as high as the retirement hazard rate for similar men with Social Security wealth between $15,000 and $20,000.[5] Most economists cite these results

---

[5]See Michael Hurd, "Research on the Elderly: Economic Status, Retirement, and Consumption and Saving," 1990, p. 598.

as evidence that the presence of Social Security benefits increases the probability that a worker of a given age will retire.

EFFECTS ON NATIONAL SAVING.   The impact of Social Security on household saving decisions and the implications for national saving have been widely studied and debated. Household saving rates are lower in the United States than in many other countries, and many economists believe that government policies—Social Security among them—may be partly to blame. For instance, one influential study in 1974 found that Social Security reduced personal saving by as much as 50%, although later studies found an error in the calculations that reduced the estimated impact. If the studies finding that Social Security significantly decreases saving are correct, the nation's private capital stock is much smaller than it would have been without the program. Economists and others believe that a capital shortage of this magnitude could cause low growth rates and lagging labor productivity.

The Theory of Social Security and Saving.   The impact of Social Security on saving is analyzed using the **life-cycle theory** of consumption. The central idea in the life-cycle theory is that people save in order to smooth consumption over their lifetimes. People receive income unevenly over their lives, earning a low income when starting out, a higher income during middle age, and a low income again in retirement. People desire a more even consumption level from year to year, so they save or dis-save (run down their savings) to achieve this.

Figure 9.5 illustrates the life-cycle theory for a person who lives two periods, working in the first and retired in the second. Income and consumption in the first period are measured on the horizontal axis, and consumption in the second (retirement) period is measured on the vertical axis. Assume that the person has E earnings in the first period and no earnings in the second. If the worker saves none of the first-period earnings, he or she would have no retirement consumption without Social Security. A worker who saves consumes less in the first period and consumes the savings plus interest in retirement. The **intertemporal budget line,** EE', indicates the amount of retirement consumption the worker can enjoy for each level of first-period consumption. The absolute slope of this line is 1 plus the interest rate i. For simplicity, we assume no income taxes or inflation.

To determine how much income is saved in the first period, we need to know the person's preferences. People get utility over a lifetime by consuming in each year **Lifetime utility** is a measure of a worker's satisfaction over a lifetime and depends on the levels of consumption in every year. Combinations of working-period consumption and retirement consumption that give the same level of lifetime utility are shown as lifetime indifference curves. These indifference curves have the same properties as ordinary indifference curves.

The life-cycle theory assumes that a person chooses how much to save during the working period so as to maximize lifetime utility. Thus the person chooses point e on the budget line, consumes C during the working period, and saves the rest. Saving, denoted S, is equal to E minus C, and retirement consumption RC is equal to saved wealth $S(1 + i)$ upon retirement. At point e the intertemporal budget line is tangent to the highest attainable lifetime indifference curve.

Suppose the government introduces a Social Security program with contributions T in the first period and giving benefits of A (for annuity) in the second. Then

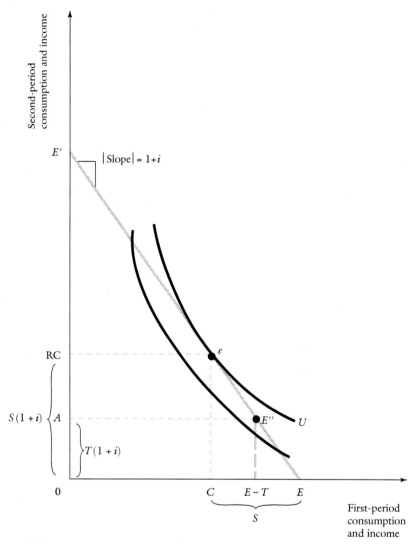

Figure 9.5

Effect of Social Security on Personal Saving
A person earns E dollars in the first period and nothing in the second period, when retired. Without Social Security, the person maximizes lifetime utility by saving S dollars to finance retirement consumption. A Social Security program that levies taxes of T in the working period and provides an actuarially fair annuity A in retirement simply shifts the endowment point from E to E'' and does not change the budget line EE'. The person reduces personal saving by the amount of the Social Security tax and consumes the same over time.

A represents the worker's Social Security wealth. For simplicity, we'll assume that the Social Security program pays the same rate of interest earned in financial markets, so $A = T(1 + i)$. The effect of the program is to change the intertemporal budget line[6]

---

[6]If the worker is unable to borrow against Social Security wealth, consumption points to the right of E'' are not available.

facing the individual to $(E - T)E''E'$. Although after-tax earnings fall to E minus T in the first period (which shifts the budget line to the left), the worker receives the annuity A in the second period (which shifts the budget line vertically). In Figure 9.5, we assume that the Social Security contribution T is less than the amount that would be saved without Social Security. Because Social Security pays the same interest rate as that earned on saving, Social Security wealth is actuarially fair and a perfect substitute for private wealth. This means that the worker's intertemporal budget line is not changed, and the current and retirement consumption levels that maximize lifetime utility are the same with and without Social Security.

Although the worker's first-period consumption is not changed, saving is affected because the Social Security program changes the timing of receipts. To consume the same amount in the first period, the worker must reduce saving by the amount of Social Security contributions. As a result, the worker has less private wealth in the second period, but this is made up by Social Security wealth. This is called the **wealth substitution effect.** This effect reflects the fact that workers treat Social Security wealth as a substitute for private wealth as a source of finance for retirement consumption.

According to the wealth substitution effect, personal saving falls by the amount of Social Security contributions. The model can be generalized to allow for Social Security wealth that is *not* a perfect substitute for private wealth because it is less liquid or pays a different interest rate. Even if Social Security wealth is not a perfect substitute for private wealth, we expect the wealth substitution effect to occur to some degree.

Although the wealth substitution effect predicts that Social Security decreases personal saving, the program can affect saving in other ways as well. We have already seen that Social Security may encourage people to retire earlier. If people who retire earlier want to spend more than their Social Security benefits (as most do), they must save. This is called the **retirement effect** of Social Security on saving, which increases personal saving. We also saw that Social Security redistributes income from younger to older people. Of course, the older generations are the parents and grandparents of the younger generations, and parents usually care about their children. If parents and grandparents perceive that the Social Security program has made them better off at the expense of their children or grandchildren, they may leave larger bequests to their heirs when they die. In order to leave a larger bequest, the parents must save more over their lifetime. Therefore, Social Security may increase personal saving because of the **bequest effect.**

Empirical Studies of Social Security and Saving.   Given that, in theory, Social Security has offsetting effects on personal saving, empirical studies are needed to answer the question of whether saving has been reduced by Social Security. An influential study by Professor Feldstein of Harvard University found that household saving was significantly depressed by Social Security "wealth," perhaps by as much as 50%. Using annual time series data, Feldstein used econometric methods to estimate the impact of Social Security wealth on consumption. (Once the effect on consumption has been found, the effect on saving is easily calculated because saving is equal to income less consumption and taxes.) He constructed a variable to measure the total Social Security wealth of households in each year and estimated the impact of this variable—along with other variables, such as income—on aggregate household consumption. He found that Social Security wealth increased consumption, ceteris paribus, and therefore reduced saving.

Feldstein's work stimulated much research on the effect of Social Security wealth on personal saving. Some of this work has cast doubt on his original results. It seems that the observed effect of Social Security wealth on saving depends on the years of data used, the way the Social Security wealth variable is constructed, and the other variables that are included as determinants of consumption. Also, Feldstein made a mistake in calculating the value of the Social Security wealth variable. After correcting for this error, Professors Leimer and Lesnoy found that Social Security wealth has a much smaller effect on saving. As a result, no firm conclusion can be drawn from empirical studies using time series data as to whether Social Security significantly reduces household saving.

Other evidence comes from cross-sectional data on the consumption behavior of a sample of households and longitudinal data on the behavior of a sample of households over consecutive years. Using these data, economists have estimated the impact of Social Security wealth on the level of private wealth held by a household. One study, using cross-sectional data, also done by Feldstein, found that each $1 of Social Security wealth reduces private asset holdings by $1. This result implies that the wealth substitution effect is complete. Another study, by Professor Laurence Kotlikoff of Boston University, using longitudinal data, found a smaller effect. This study divided Social Security wealth into components. Each dollar of the "actuarially fair" component of Social Security wealth (the component equal to the lifetime value of Social Security contributions) reduced private asset holdings by about 67 cents.

Evaluating Social Security

Over the past 50 years, Social Security has grown from a tiny program in the federal budget to the largest single government spending program in the nation. The economic status of the elderly has also changed remarkably. Since 1950, the percentage of people over age 65 receiving Social Security benefits has risen from 22.5% to 90% in 1999. In 1998, Social Security benefits accounted for 38% of the income received by the average retiree, and 66% of the income received by the elderly poor. Forty-eight percent of Social Security beneficiaries would have income below the poverty threshold in the absence of their benefits. Since 1959, the poverty rate for persons 65 or older has dropped from over 35% to under 10.5% in 1998. The poverty rate for the population as a whole fell from 22% to 12.7% over the same period. Thus, rather than being at greater risk of poverty, as a group the elderly are now at less risk of poverty.

Although other factors no doubt contributed to reducing poverty among the elderly, it is almost certain that the increased benefits and coverage of Social Security have been important factors. Some people argue that if the primary purpose of the program was to reduce poverty among the elderly, it should be pronounced a success. Yet many economists and others have serious concerns about the program and argue that it must be reformed. In fact, a recent study concluded that reform is "inevitable." Why should Social Security be reformed, and what sorts of changes are needed?

DEMOGRAPHIC EVENTS AND PAY-AS-YOU-GO SOCIAL SECURITY.   Perhaps the main reason analysts believe there is a pressing need for Social Security reform is the impending retirement of the "baby-boom" generation. What happens to the contributions and benefits of a pay-as-you-go Social Security program if a generation that is abnormally large is followed by a generation that is much smaller? This demographic event happened in the United States when the baby-boom generation born between 1945 and 1960 was followed by the "baby-bust" generation born between 1960 and 1975. In 1940, the total fertility rate began rising, reaching over 3 by 1945.[7] It remained over 3 until the early 1960s, when it declined sharply, falling below 2 by 1975.

During the years in which the baby-boom generation is in the workforce, the pay-as-you-go program receives a large inflow of contributions. However, when the abnormally large baby-boom generation ages, the fraction of older persons of retirement age will begin to grow quickly. In 1999, 12.7% of the population was age 65 or older. By 2020, 16.4% of the population will be over 65, and the proportion of people over 65 will continue to grow until 2030. Since the large generation is followed by a smaller one, the ratio of beneficiaries per worker will grow quickly once the baby-boomers begin retiring. In 1999, there were 27 Social Security beneficiaries per 100 covered workers paying contributions. By 2030 this will rise to 43 per 100 workers.

Clearly, when a smaller generation follows a larger one, a pay-as-you-go program will encounter difficulties because the contributions of the smaller generation finance benefits to the larger one, a reversal of the growing population example we considered earlier. In this case, it may not be possible to pay benefits equal to the contributions made by the larger generation. One estimate of the contribution rate on future workers needed to finance the benefits to retiring baby boomers is 25%, double the current rate. This is what people mean by the long-run "insolvency" facing Social Security. The baby-boom problem is aggravated by the fact that people are now retired for a longer time because they retire earlier and live longer.

In 1983, the Social Security program was amended to address this looming problem. These amendments increase the normal retirement age from 65 to 67 beginning in the twenty-first century. For workers turning 62 after the year 1999, the normal retirement age will increase by 2 months per year, continuing until 2022 when the retirement age for a worker to receive a full benefit reaches 67. The 1983 amendments also increase the penalty for early retirement and the reward for delaying retirement. The delayed retirement credit increases by half a percentage point a year until 2005, when it will be 8% on an annual basis.

The most important amendment in 1983 was the decision to partially fund the program. Since 1984, Social Security taxes have collected more than enough revenue to pay benefits each year. The surplus contributions will continue until the year 2020, when the bulk of the baby-boom generation begins to retire. The annual surplus on the Social Security trust fund, consisting of the excess contributions and

---

[7]The total fertility rate in a year is the average number of children that a woman would have over her lifetime if she bore children at the birthrate prevailing in that year. Barring immigration, a constant population requires a total fertility rate slightly greater than 2.

interest on the fund balance, was $117 billion in 1999. These surpluses are accumulated in the fund and invested in government bonds. Since 1984, accumulated surplus on the trust fund has risen, from $25 billion to $800 billion by the end of 1999.

Figure 9.6 shows the balance in the trust fund, including projections by the Social Security trustees, up to the year 2030. As we see, the trust fund balance will steadily increase until 2018, when it will reach a maximum of $2900 billion. In dollars of 1996 purchasing power, the assets of the fund will top out in 2015 at $1315 billion (1996 dollars). After 2020, the benefits paid out to the retired baby boomers will outstrip the contributions, and the fund balance will drop precipitously, reaching zero by the year 2030.

The partial funding of Social Security implemented in the reforms of 1983 is intended to make the baby-boom generation partially pay in advance its own Social

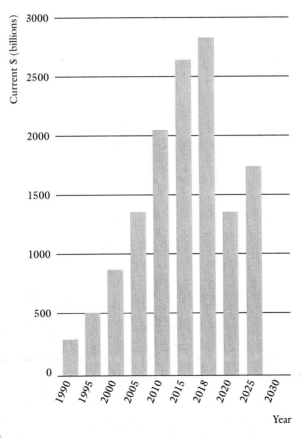

Figure 9.6

Projected OASDI Trust Fund Reserves, 1990–2030

Because of reforms put in place in 1983, contributions to Social Security exceed benefits paid with the surplus accumulated in the trust fund. The fund will top out at $2900 billion in 2018 and then drop sharply, reaching zero in 2030.

Source: Committee of Ways and Means, U.S. House of Representatives, *1996 Green Book,* 1996, p. 62.

Security benefits. As mentioned earlier, continuing Social Security on a pay-as-you-go basis would require higher contribution rates by future workers to provide benefits to baby boomers at current levels. This would place a large burden on future workers and threaten the continuation of the program.

SHOULD SOCIAL SECURITY BE REFORMED?   Several concerns motivate those who believe that Social Security should be reformed. The first is concern about the national saving rate. As we learned earlier, many economists believe that Social Security has reduced saving because households find the need to save for retirement less pressing. To a certain extent, concern about Social Security and saving reflects a changed view about the needs of the economy. In the 1930s, when the Social Security program was designed, inadequate spending was thought to be the major economic problem facing the nation. Reduced saving and increased spending were a benefit, not a problem. In the last quarter of the twentieth century, the main concerns have been slower growth and stagnant wages due to static labor productivity. One possible cause is an inadequate level of business investment, perhaps because of a smaller supply of domestic investible funds from household saving.[8] In this economic climate, the possibility that Social Security has reduced household saving is a problem.

Another concern is that Social Security benefits are more generous than the program can support over the long run. The real level of benefits provided by the Social Security program has increased greatly since the program began. The plentiful supply of contributions when the program was immature and had few beneficiaries per contributor made it easy to increase benefits in response to political demands. Also, when benefits were indexed to the cost of living in 1972, a flawed method was used that allowed benefits to rise faster than the cost of living. Although this was corrected in 1978, other factors have also increased benefits. Perhaps most important are earlier retirement and longer life expectancy among older people. In 1940 the average male worker retired at 69 and had a remaining life expectancy of 9 years. In 1999, he retired at under age 64 with a remaining life expectancy of nearly 16 years. The average female worker retired at about the same age in 1999, but had a remaining life expectancy of 20 years.

As mentioned, the main concern about Social Security is the threat to its long-run financial solvency posed by demographic events that will affect the program over the next quarter-century. As we have learned, the viability of a pay-as-you-go Social Security program depends on the size of the population of contributing workers relative to the number of retirees drawing benefits. At present, people retiring were born in the 1930s, a decade with a low birthrate. However, this situation will change dramatically by 2010, when the first members of the postwar baby-boom generation begin to retire. As the number of beneficiaries per covered worker rises sharply, the pay-as-you-go Social Security program will face increasing financial strain.

The Social Security reforms of 1983 addressed the long-run demographic problem by partially funding the system. Social Security now runs a healthy surplus, and

---

[8]Of course, investment in the United States could be financed with the savings of foreigners, but a reliance on foreign saving is considered by many to be undesirable.

the trust fund balance is expected to rise to nearly $3000 billion by 2020 and remain positive until at least 2030. Social Security seems solvent for the next three decades, so what is the problem? One problem is that, according to projections, the trust fund will be exhausted by 2030, but enormous outlays will continue for decades after. The second problem is that the trust fund is invested in government bonds, which means that it holds "IOUs" from another branch of the government (the Treasury). This casts doubt on whether the fund is really solvent. Some argue that the trust fund is merely hiding government debt.

WHAT ARE THE OPTIONS?   Several reforms have been proposed for Social Security. We will briefly describe and assess some of them.

Reduce Benefits, or Subject Them to a Means Test.   Some people favor reducing benefits as a means of restoring long-run solvency to the program, because they believe that current benefits are more generous than intended or needed. There are several ways of reducing benefits: increase the age of eligibility; subject benefits to a means test, as is done for welfare; change the cost-of-living index used to increase dollar benefits each year; and increase the portion of benefits subject to income tax. Some of these suggestions would be difficult to implement, for political reasons.

Any attempt to reduce benefits will be unpopular with retirees and those nearing retirement. Opposition to reduction of benefits is politically effective because the structure of Social Security encourages the view that benefits are simply a return of the retiree's earlier contributions. In addition, changes in the benefit schedule

*"By the way, Sam, as someday you'll be paying for my
entitlements, I'd like to thank you in advance."*

create horizontal inequities among those retiring near the time of the change. For instance, when the government corrected for the overindexing of benefits in 1977, people reaching age 62 between 1979 and 1983 (known as the "notch" generation) believed that they were badly treated relative to people who turned 62 shortly earlier. A person who turned 62 in January 1979 received a smaller benefit than a person with the same earnings who turned 62 in December 1978.

For these reasons, a reduction in benefits, if it occurs, is likely to take the form of a change in the index used to adjust benefits to changes in the cost of living, or an increase in the fraction of benefits subject to income tax. Both methods are indirect ways of reducing benefits and may be politically possible. In 1996, an advisory council chaired by Professor Michael Boskin, the former chairman of the Council of Economic Advisors, concluded that the current method of measuring changes in the cost of living overstates the change by a percentage point or more. A reduction in the cost-of-living adjustment to Social Security benefits to reflect this overstatement would reduce dollar benefits to retirees by tens of billions of dollars over the next decade, increasing the long-run solvency of the program. In 1993, the portion of benefits subject to income taxes was increased to 85% for some beneficiaries, with surprisingly little opposition. Some people advocate making Social Security benefits fully taxable.

Raise Social Security Taxes.   If benefits are not reduced, solvency of the Social Security program can be maintained by raising the OASDI payroll tax rate. The big question is: How much would the rate have to increase in order to pay benefits when the baby boomers retire? Under the "high-cost" projection—increased life expectancy and slow wage growth—the rate would need to be increased by 50% immediately and permanently from 12.4% to 18.4% to raise sufficient revenue to pay future benefits. An even larger increase would be needed, as much as 100%, if tax rates are not increased until 2020. Furthermore, as we will see in the next section, a similar problem looms for the Medicare program. Many people argue that the combined increase in Social Security and Medicare taxes would overwhelm future working generations and would not be politically viable.

Under a more optimistic scenario, known as the "low-cost" projection, tax rate increases are more manageable. The low-cost projection assumes faster wage growth and a smaller increase in life expectancy. This projection, combined with some cuts in benefits, implies that relatively modest increases in the OASDI tax rate are sufficient to maintain solvency. Another way of augmenting revenue without increasing the tax rate is to eliminate the cap on earnings subject to the tax ($72,600 in 1999). However, since earnings above the cap do not contribute to increased Social Security benefits, such a change would further weaken the link between contributions and benefits.

Tax rate increases do not come without an economic cost. In addition to the burden on workers, tax rate increases cause an excess burden that rises with the square of the tax rate (see Chapter 12). This excess burden reflects the fact that taxes on wages discourage the labor supply. The extent to which the OASDI tax creates such an excess burden depends on whether workers perceive a Social Security benefit equal to the increased taxes they pay. Since it is necessary to raise tax rates while holding benefits constant to make Social Security solvent, workers are not likely to perceive a compensating rise in benefits.

Privatize Social Security.   The most radical plan to reform Social Security proposes to "privatize" it. What does "privatizing" Social Security mean, and how would privatizing the program solve its long-run problems?

A fully privatized Social Security program, such that implemented in Chile (see A Case in Point 9.1), requires that workers save money in an employer-provided or personal pension plan rather than pay Social Security taxes. One such plan has been advanced by Professors Laurence Kotlikoff and Jeffrey Sachs of Boston University and Harvard University respectively.[9] Under the Kotlikoff-Sachs plan, the OAI part of the payroll tax is eliminated and workers would deposit an amount equal to the employee's share of the tax in a Personal Security System (PSS) account. The government would match a worker's PSS contributions in a progressive manner (i.e., a higher match rate for low-income workers). The PSS accounts would be regulated, supervised, and invested in inflation-indexed government and high-grade corporate bonds. Workers would not be able to withdraw funds before age 65. Upon turning 65, the balance in the worker's PSS account is pooled with that of other workers of the same age and converted into a life annuity.

Proponents of privatization argue that such a system would benefit society by increasing saving, encouraging individual responsibility, and permitting people with different attitudes toward risk to invest in different portfolios. As we learned earlier, a pay-as-you-go Social Security substitutes the promise of future tax-financed benefits for retirement saving. The lost saving could have been invested at a higher rate of return than the government pays in benefits, so the pay-as-you-go system imposes a deadweight loss on the economy. In addition, the payroll taxes needed to finance a pay-as-you-go system cause an excess burden by discouraging the labor supply. According to Professor Feldstein of Harvard University, the present value of these economic costs is equal to $10 trillion dollars.[10] By privatizing Social Security, society stands to gain this through greater efficiency.

Opponents of privatization believe that the benefits of privatization are illusory and that the existing system can be preserved with some modest reforms. They argue that the administrative costs of individual accounts like the PSS accounts are much higher than the administrative costs of the Social Security system. These higher administrative costs would absorb much of the alleged benefits of privatization. They also fear that privatized Social Security would expose workers to market risks. Current Social Security is a defined benefit plan, which means that when they retire, individuals can expect to receive a benefit calculated by a known formula. Privatized Social Security is a defined contribution plan, and the benefit an individual can expect depends on how well the money is invested and the performance of the investments. Opponents of privatization argue that the current Social Security system is less risky because the government can manage and pool risk through the tax-transfer system better than individuals can through portfolio diversification.

---

[9]Laurence J. Kotlikoff and Jeffrey Sachs, "It Is High Time to Privatize Social Security," 1997.
[10]Martin Feldstein, "Richard T. Ely Lecture," *American Economic Review,* May 1996.

The strongest argument against privatizing Social Security is known as the "transition problem." While privatization may be an option for countries starting new Social Security systems, a country that already has a mature pay-as-you-go system faces the problem of how to finance the benefits that have been promised to retired individuals and those nearing retirement. If young workers stop paying OAS taxes and put their money into PSS accounts, who pays for the benefits to existing beneficiaries? Under the Kotlikoff-Sachs plan, the transition would be financed with a national sales tax. They calculate that, initially, the sales tax rate would have to be around 10% but would decline to about 2% within 40 years. Opponents argue that such a sales tax would be as onerous as increasing payroll taxes to preserve the existing system.

Invest the Trust Fund in the Stock Market.   In 1997, a federal advisory panel stated that part of the growing surplus in the Social Security trust fund should be invested in stocks rather than solely in government securities as is presently done. The managers of the trust fund would choose a portfolio of stocks that mirrors the performance of the overall stock market. How does investing trust funds in stocks address the long-run problems of Social Security?

The advisory panel noted, as have others before them, that stocks have outperformed government bonds historically. In fact, the real (inflation-adjusted) rate of return on stocks has averaged 6.3% over the postwar period, as compared with 2.3% for government bonds. If this continues in the future, the higher reward on the trust funds invested in stocks would increase the balance in fund and allow it to remain solvent longer.

The plan to invest the trust fund in stocks raises several questions and concerns. First, although it is true that stocks earned a higher rate of return than bonds in the past, will this remain true in the future? The "bull" market in stocks has had its longest run in history, and many analysts think that most stocks are currently overvalued. If the stock market were to level off or decline, the future rate of return on stocks would be lower than that on bonds. Second, stocks are considered riskier than bonds. In fact, that is why they pay a higher rate of return. The risks of stocks in the trust fund would imply risks in a worker's Social Security benefits and/or taxes. If the stock market were to crash, the balance in the trust fund would be reduced, and lower benefits or higher taxes would be necessary. A third concern is that ownership of stocks in the trust fund would invite "social investing" and government meddling in corporate governance. The trust fund would become one of the largest shareholders in U.S. corporations, and politicians may use that power to pressure corporations into conducting their affairs for political rather than economic ends. The advisory panel believes that this problem could be minimized by creating a quasiprivate institution, like the existing Thrift Savings Plan for the pension funds of government employees, to avoid political interference.

From an economic point of view, one could also ask whether it would really make a difference if the trust fund were invested in stocks. To invest in stocks, the trust fund would need to sell bonds and buy stocks. Since all transactions have two sides, this means that individuals would buy bonds and sell stocks. Individuals would own fewer stocks in their own portfolios, but they would own more stocks in "their" trust fund. If individuals treat the trust fund as simply an indirect part of their own portfolios, nothing would be changed. This is an example of what economists call the Modigliani and Miller theorem. However, individuals are not likely to treat stocks in the trust fund as equivalent to stocks in their own portfolios, because their Social Security benefits are determined by the benefit formula, not by the performance of the stock market.

A CASE IN POINT

9.1   Privatizing Social Security in Chile

In 1981, Chile privatized its state-run pay-as-you-go social security system, the oldest in the hemisphere. Other countries have watched the Chilean experiment, and some—mostly other Latin American countries—have privatized their own programs. Advocates of privatizing the U.S. system also cite the apparent success of the Chilean system as "proof" that privatization works.

Before 1981, Chile had a patchwork of separate state-run pension programs for workers in different occupations. The benefits received bore little relationship to taxes paid, and eligibility requirements were different for different workers. In 1981, Chile replaced this public system with a private system in which workers make contributions to individual accounts similar to 401(k) plans in the United States. Workers are required to contribute 13% of their earnings tax-free (10% for pensions and 3% for disability) and have the option of contributing another 10%. The individual accounts are managed by about a dozen mutual funds known as Pension Fund Administrators (AFPs is the Spanish acronym), which compete for the workers' accounts. Upon retirement, workers can use the money in the account to purchase life annuities from private life insurance companies or make programmed withdrawals based on their life expectancy. Workers with insufficient funds for retirement receive a minimum pension guarantee if they have contributed for at least 20 years.

When the plan was introduced, all new workers entering the labor force were enrolled in the privatized system. Workers already in the workforce could elect to remain in the state-run system or switch to the new system. Workers who switched were issued nontransferable "recognition bonds" for credits earned under the old system. Upon retiring, workers can redeem these bonds, which pay a real (inflation-adjusted) interest rate

of 4%, and deposit the balance in their retirement accounts. General tax revenue, the budget surplus, and proceeds from the sale of the assets of state-owned enterprises are used to finance the recognition bonds, pensions to individuals who were already retired, and pensions for workers who chose to stay under the old system.

Advocates of privatization tout the successes of the Chilean experiment. The real rate of return on money invested in the individual accounts has averaged 12%, and the Chilean savings rate jumped from 10% in 1986 to nearly 29% in 1996. Also, it is argued, the elimination of the payroll tax that financed the old state-run system has encouraged the labor supply.[1]

Critically analyze the following:

- How did Chile manage its transition problem? Are the same options available in the United States?

- Chile has a younger and faster growing population than does the United States. Also, in 1981 Chile was governed by the Pinochet dictatorship. Would these factors make it easier for Chile to adopt a privatized system?

- The unfunded liability of the U.S. Social Security system (the value of future benefits the government owes individuals covered by Social Security) is estimated at $8 trillion. Suppose the U.S. privatized Social Security in the same way that Chile did. If everyone in the United States opted out of the existing system in exchange for recognition bonds, how much would the national debt increase?

---

[1]Much of the information in the case is drawn from Peter Passell, "How Chile Farms Out Nest Eggs," *New York Times*, March 21, 1997, and National Center for Policy Analysis, "Privatizing Social Security in Latin America," *Policy Report No. 221*, January 1999.

Use Fiscal Policy to "Save" Social Security.   Although it is not a plan to reform Social Security, many people—including all of the candidates in the recent presidential primaries—believe that the government should reserve most or all of the budget surplus to "save" Social Security. The budget surplus, discussed in Chapter 16 is the excess of federal tax revenue over outlays (spending). As mentioned earlier, all of this surplus reflects the excess of Social Security taxes over Social Security spending generated as part of the 1983 reforms to "advance fund" the baby boomers' benefits. Some analysts believe that the government should take advance funding a step further and create an even bigger surplus by cutting spending programs other than Social Security. How do greater surpluses "save" Social Security?

Surpluses help save Social Security by reducing the government debt. At the end of 1999, the federal government debt held outside the Social Security trust fund was $3633 billion, and the interest payments necessary to service this debt were $265 billion for the year. If the government were to balance its non–Social Security budget over the next ten years, the Social Security surpluses could pay down a large part of this debt before the baby boomers retire. If a surplus on the non–Social Security budget were added, the entire national debt could be paid off, freeing up the $265 billion currently spent on interest payments for paying Social Security benefits. However, a means is needed to direct these savings to the Social Security program instead of being used for other spending or tax cuts. In his budget for the 2000 fiscal year, President Clinton proposed such a means—transfers of special U.S. Treasury obligations to the Social Security and Medicare HI trust funds. Each year the Treasury would issue about $100 billion of special securities and give them to the trust funds. However, as several analysts have noted, such a transfer is little more than a bookkeeping trick unless the government runs a non–Social Security surplus of a comparable amount. This issue is discussed at greater length in Chapter 16.

MEDICARE FOR THE AGED

The United States spends more on health care than any other country. In 1998, health care spending in the United States amounted to $1228 billion ($4300 per capita), or nearly 14% of GDP. In most other countries, spending on health care is less than 10% of GDP, except Germany and Switzerland, where health spending is 10.7% and 10% of GDP, respectively. In the United States and most other countries, health care spending has risen more rapidly than GDP over the past three decades. In 1965, health care spending was less than 6% of GDP in the United States. Current projections indicate that health care spending will continue to grow faster than GDP, reaching over 16% of GDP by the year 2008.

While the United States spends more on health care than other countries, government spending on health care accounts for a smaller fraction than in other countries. In 1996, government health care spending accounted for just over 46% of national health care spending, as compared with 70% or more in most other countries. In Germany and Switzerland, government health care spending accounts for 77.1% and 69.9%, respectively, of national health care spending. The reason is that, unlike other countries, the United States does not have universal government-provided medical insurance. The government provides medical insurance in the United States only for the aged under the Medicare program and the poor under the Medicaid program. Everyone else, except for about 15% of the population that is uninsured, is insured privately, usually through his or her employer.[11] The Medicaid program, which is means-tested, was discussed in Chapter 8. Medicare, which is not means-tested and is available for nearly all people over age 65, is a social insurance program. People earn the right to receive Medicare by paying a payroll tax during their working years.

The Role of Government in Health Care

What explains the large government involvement in the health care and medical insurance industry? Two explanations are usually cited. First, many people argue that health care has features that make it different from ordinary market goods. Second, market failure in the medical insurance market provides a social insurance argument for government involvement.

How is health care different from other goods? Some argue that health care is different because people need it rather than want it, and might die if they do not have access to it. For this reason, it is argued, health care should not be left to market forces. However, people also need food and shelter and could die without them, but government involvement in these industries is much less. Others argue that health care is a special good because the seller (doctors and other health care providers) have better information about the product being sold than the buyer (the patient). But this is true for many other market goods as well.

One feature that could justify government involvement would be that health care is a public (i.e., nonrival and nonexcludable) good. Unfortunately, this is true only for certain types of health care expenditures, like medical research. Finding a cure for cancer is a nonrival good because it would benefit everyone afflicted with cancer. However, most types of health care services are rival rather than nonrival. The time a doctor spends with one patient cannot be spent with another, and a hospital bed cannot be occupied by more than one person. Moreover, health care is excludable—that is, service can be denied unless the patient pays. For these reasons, health care is more like a private good than a public good.

A better argument for government involvement is that health care is a good that provides positive externalities. In Chapter 4 we learned that the government can increase economic efficiency by providing or subsidizing goods that have benefit externalities. Some types of health expenditures, such as flu shots, do provide benefit externalities. If a person with an infectious disease is immunized or treated, he or she will not infect others. Again, however, most types of health care services do not have this feature.

Both the public good and externalities arguments justify government involvement in health care to improve efficiency. Equally important, and perhaps more compelling, is the argument that government involvement is justified to improve equity. In other words, many people believe that health care is a **merit good** that

---

[11]However, the government "subsidizes" private insurance through the tax system, as we will see in Chapter 12. This tax subsidy is equivalent to the government spending an additional $70 billion on medical insurance.

should be consumed more equally by all. This could reflect a preference for **specific egalitarianism,** which is the opinion that people should be able to consume some goods and services, like health care, regardless of their ability to pay for them. These egalitarian sentiments are likely to be particularly strong when it comes to health care for the poor and the elderly, hence the Medicaid and Medicare programs. Considerations of vertical equity may also be important. Vertical equity requires putting a greater weight on the consumption of the needy, and a person might be considered needy because he or she has big medical expenses.

Although these special features of health care as a good provide some role for government in the health care industry, they do not seem to explain the massive involvement we observe. Probably the main reason for government involvement in the health care industry is insurance market failure. Illness and its accompanying expense is one of life's biggest uncertainties, and most people want insurance against the risk of large expenses should they find themselves in need of medical treatments. Although many people buy medical insurance from private companies, the medical insurance industry will provide inefficiently low levels of coverage because of adverse selection.

As we learned in Chapter 7, adverse selection occurs when sellers of insurance cannot distinguish good health risks from bad among those buying insurance. Families with bad health or with existing medical conditions are more likely to buy insurance than those who are in excellent health. As people with good health drop out of the risk pool, medical insurance becomes increasingly expensive because the only people buying it are likely to incur medical expenses. To prevent adverse selection from driving out all of the good risks, insurance companies may exclude certain demographic groups from medical insurance coverage. Older people are likely to be in the excluded group because they are more likely to become ill and incur medical expenses. Government can limit adverse selection by forcing people to purchase insurance, such as with payroll taxes.

Moral hazard can take three forms in the medical insurance industry. First, people who have medical insurance may take less care in maintaining their health. Second, people may not buy medical insurance because they expect to receive uncompensated care if they are injured or become sick. If someone shows up at a hospital emergency room with a heart attack, it is difficult to deny admission simply because he or she does not have insurance. Third, people who have medical insurance are more likely to overconsume health care services because they do not have to pay the cost themselves. Since the insurance company pays the cost, the patient perceives health care as a free good.

Although moral hazard is an insurance market failure that raises the cost of medical insurance to consumers, it is not clear how government can improve on the situation. Unlike adverse selection, which the government can control by making medical insurance compulsory, moral hazard is likely to afflict social insurance programs as well as private. Like private insurance companies, the government can control the overconsumption of health care services through cost-sharing arrangements. Cost sharing could require three types of payments by the patient in addition to any insurance premiums. A **deductible** is a fixed amount per year that the patient pays before the insurer pays anything—for example, the first $100 of medical expenses each year. A **co-payment** is a fixed dollar amount the patient must pay per unit of health care provided—for example, $10 for each visit to the doctor's office. **Co-insurance** is like a copayment but is a fixed percentage of the service fees charged—for example, 10% of the doctor's bill. Co-payments and co-insurance give the patient an incentive to economize on the use of health care services. The Medicare program has all three of these cost-sharing payments.

The Structure of the Medicare Program

Medicare is a federal program that pays for hospital, physician services, and other medical services for people over age 65, people with disabilities, and people with severe kidney disease. Medicare is not a comprehensive insurance program because it has cost sharing and limits on coverage. For example, hospital coverage is limited to 90 days per benefit period, which begins when the patient enters the hospital and ends when he or she has not received benefits for 60 days. The patient pays a deductible of $776 (in 2000) per admission and a copayment of $194 per day after 60 days. The patient also has a 60-day lifetime reserve, which have a copayment of $388 a day. Patients can also receive care from a skilled nursing facility for up to 100 days, with a copayment of $97 a day after 20 days. Patients with terminal disease also receive hospice care. However, long-term care in a nursing home is not covered, nor are outpatient prescription drugs. Medicare beneficiaries can purchase supplementary medical insurance from private companies, called *Medigap* insurance, to cover some of these out-of-pocket costs.

"TRADITIONAL" MEDICARE.   Traditional Medicare, which was the only form of Medicare available before 1997, consists of two parts. **Part A Medicare** covers the cost of health care facilities including hospitals, skilled nursing facilities, home health care, and hospice care for the terminally ill. **Part B Medicare,** also known as Supplementary Medical Insurance (SMI), covers the cost of physician's services, outpatient services, laboratory tests, and ambulance transportation. Part A Medicare is automatic for recipients of Social Security and their spouses who are over 65 years old or have received disability benefits for at least two years. In 1999, over 39 million people were enrolled in Part A Medicare. Of these, 34 million were over age 65, or 98% of the population over age 65. People who are over age 65 but not eligible for Medicare (because they were not in covered employment) can receive Part A Medicare by paying a monthly premium ($301 in 2000). Part A Medicare is financed with a payroll tax of 2.9% split evenly between the employee and his or her employer. The revenue from the payroll tax is received in the Medicare HI trust fund and all benefits of Part A Medicare are paid from the trust fund, as well as the administrative costs of the program. Expenditures on Part A Medicare were $131 billion in 1998.

All people enrolled in Part A Medicare and all persons over age 65 can enroll in Part B Medicare by paying a monthly premium ($45.50 in 2000), which is deducted from the Social Security benefit checks of most enrollees. These premiums cover about 25% of the cost of Part B Medicare. The rest is financed out of the general revenue of the federal government, which amounted to $85 billion in 1998.

Since Part B Medicare is heavily subsidized, just about everyone enrolled in Part A is also enrolled in Part B. Like Part A, Part B has cost sharing arrangements. In 2000, the annual deductible was $100 and patients are required to make a co-insurance payment equal to 20% of the physician's bill.

MEDICARE + CHOICE PLANS.   The Balanced Budget Act of 1997 introduced some new options for Medicare called Medicare + Choice (M+C). M+C allows beneficiaries to choose a managed care plan rather than traditional Medicare.[12] For a managed care plan, the government pays a capitation fee per enrollee to a health care provider, unlike traditional Medicare that pays the provider for the services rendered to the patient ("fee-for-service"). A capitation fee is a fixed amount of money per period of time (say, a month or year) paid to a health care organization for providing health care services of the enrollee, which must include all of the services provided under traditional Medicare. The fee is the same regardless of the amount of services actually provided to the enrollee. The health care provider, usually a Health Maintenance Organization (HMO) or a Preferred Provider Organization (PPO), makes a profit if the enrollee requires little care but assumes the extra cost if the enrollee requires a lot of care. Hence, the cost risk is transferred from the government to the health care provider. The supposed advantage of the capitation fee compensation scheme is that the health care provider has incentives not to provide unnecessary services, unlike the fee-for-service compensation scheme.

If a Medicare enrollee chooses an M+C plan, he or she surrenders the right to receive the fee-for-services benefits under the traditional Medicare program. He or she must obtain health care services from the chosen HMO or PPO and must pay for services rendered by any other provider. At the end of 1999, about 17% of Medicare beneficiaries were enrolled in M+C plans. This percentage is expected to increase to over 30% by 2008. The attraction of M+C to the enrollee is that many plans offer benefits not offered by traditional Medicare, including discounts on prescription drugs, routine physical examinations, and hearing aids and eyeglasses. The provider can charge co-payments and additional premiums, although these are low, at least as of 1999. The downside is that the HMO or PPO can withdraw from M+C and drop the enrollee if it chooses. In this case, the enrollee must find another M+C provider or switch back to traditional Medicare.

Economic Issues

One of the main economic issues concerning Medicare is the projected growth in spending. In 1998, the federal government spent an amount equal to 2.7% of GDP on Medicare for 38.8 million beneficiaries (13.8% of the population). As the pop-

---

[12]M+C also includes a Medical Savings Account (MSA) plan in which beneficiaries buy a high-deductible medical insurance policy from a private company, presumably at low cost. They can deposit the difference between the Medicare benefit the government would have paid and the cost of the plan in an MSA and use the money to pay out-of-pocket costs. This is a type of "voucher" system.

ulation ages, this is expected to rise to 5.3% of GDP for 69.3 million beneficiaries (20.6% of the population) by 2025.[13] Medicare is funded in the same way as Social Security—it is a tax-financed pay-as-you-go system. Therefore it poses the same long-run solvency problems. Future generations of workers will be required to pay higher taxes in order to finance the Medicare benefits of the disproportionately large baby-boom generation. Unlike the Social Security trust fund, the Medicare HI trust fund does not have a growing surplus to help finance future expenses.

GOVERNMENT COST-CUTTING POLICIES.   In view of the rapidly rising Medicare expenses in the past and those projected for the future, the government has taken several steps to reduce program costs. In 1983, the hospital reimbursement system was changed from a cost-plus recovery system to the **Prospective Payment System (PPS)**. The PPS pays hospitals a fixed amount based on the diagnosed illness of the patient, not the actual cost incurred by the hospital. Under PPS, a hospital's patients are grouped into diagnostic-related groups (DRGs) according to their illness. Different DRGs are given different weights relative to some standardized case on which the hospital fee is set. For instance, a simple appendectomy has a weight of .78 whereas a heart transplant has a weight of 13.5 times the standardized case fee. The purpose of the PPS is to make hospitals more cost-conscious in treating Medicare patients whose bills are paid by the government. Since the PPS went into effect in 1983, the average hospital stay by Medicare patients declined over 36%, from 10.1 days in 1982 to 6.4 days in 1997.

The Balanced Budget Act of 1997 took further steps to trim the growth in Medicare spending. In addition to introducing the Medicare + Choice plans, the Balanced Budget Act froze the fees paid to hospitals under the PPS system and other Medicare compensation rates. In addition, the Balanced Budget Act increases the premium for Part B Medicare gradually between 1998 and 2007. These changes will slow the annual per capita growth in Medicare spending from a projected 6.9% per year over the ten-year period to 5.5% per year. This amounts to a $200 billion reduction in Medicare spending over a ten-year period.[14] As a result of these changes, and because of the strong economy, the Board of Trustees of the Medicare HI trust fund estimates that fund receipts will exceed outlays until 2010, rather than 2003 as projected earlier.

The efforts to reduce Medicare spending are controversial. Hospitals complain that the PPS system does not compensate them adequately for the costs of caring for Medicare patients, and some private insurance companies that once welcomed Medicare patients no longer do so because they believe the compensation is too low. Out-of-pocket costs to beneficiaries are increasing, and many beneficiaries may be forced to choose managed care plans to reduce these costs. Beneficiaries in managed care plans complain that the providers ration medical services.

---

[13]Marilyn Moon, "Growth in Medicare Spending: What Will Beneficiaries Pay?" The Urban Institute, May 1999

[14]Moon et al. "An Examination of Key Medicare Provisions in the Balanced Budget Act of 1997," Urban Institute, September 1997.

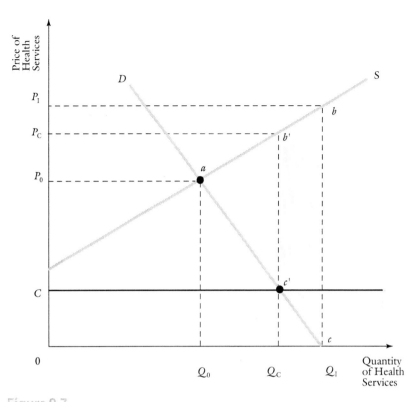

Figure 9.7
Effect of Insurance on the Price and Quantity of Health Care Services
Without insurance, the market for health services is in equilibrium price P_0 and quantity Q_0. If fully insured, patients would demand Q_I services and the per unit cost of health services would rise to P_I. A copayment C reduces the quantity demanded and the cost of health care services.

ARE COST-CUTTING POLICIES JUSTIFIED?   What are the causes of rising Medicare costs, and do they justify the cost-reducing measures adopted by the government? Some economists think that Medicare itself is partly to blame for the rising cost of medical services. Although the prices of services in general rose faster than the overall price level, the price of medical services rose particularly fast. One possible reason is that Medicare, and other government health insurance programs like Medicaid, have increased the demand for medical services and contributed to overutilization.

The argument is illustrated in Figure 9.7, which shows the supply and demand curves for medical services. If individuals are not insured and have to pay for all services out of their own pockets, the equilibrium price and quantity of medical services are P_0 and Q_0. If individuals are fully insured and do not pay any part of the cost of medical services, they would increase consumption to Q_I units and the equilibrium price charged by suppliers to the insurance companies is P_I. Overutilization of medical services not only raises the price, it also creates a deadweight loss (inefficiency cost) because the extra medical services consumed cost more than the individuals are willing to pay for the services. The deadweight loss, equal to the area of the triangle *abc,* represents the excess of the cost of the extra services (the height of the supply curve) over the marginal willingness to pay for the extra services (the height of the demand curve).

In the presence of such moral hazard, the insurer can reduce costs and increase efficiency with cost-sharing arrangements. The case of a co-payment of C dollars per unit of medical services is shown in Figure 9.7. With an out-of-pocket expense equal to the co-payment for each extra unit of service, the insured individual reduces consumption of services to Q_C. This reduces the price charged by the suppliers to P_C and reduces the deadweight loss from overutilization to the area of the triangle $ab'c'$. The shaded area in Figure 9.7 is equal to the reduction in the deadweight loss of overutilization. However, since cost sharing reduces the effective insurance to the individual, the copayment must be less than P_0; otherwise, the individual is not insured. For this reason, insurance like Medicare does raise the price of medical services and imposes a deadweight loss from overutilization.

The amount of overutilization of medical services and the amount by which the co-payment reduces the price of medical services depend on the slope of the demand curve. It also depends on whether the individual purchases supplementary insurance, like Medigap insurance. In an experimental study by the RAND Corporation, 5809 individuals were randomly assigned to insurance programs with different cost-sharing arrangements. The study found that higher co-insurance rates decreased utilization. The price elasticity of the demand for medical services was around .22 in the range of moderate co-insurance rates. If this elasticity value were constant over the whole demand curve, it would imply that a fully insured individual consumes about 22% more services than an uninsured individual.[15] Other types of health services, such as dental care, are more sensitive to price, with an elasticity of .4

For individuals with Medigap insurance, the insurance company pays the co-payment or co-insurance. Such individuals are fully insured and therefore have no incentive to economize on their demand for medical services. Medigap insurance imposes a type of externality that raises the cost of Medicare to the government. For example, because Medigap pays the 20% co-insurance payment under Part B Medicare, beneficiaries demand more services than if they had to pay the co-insurance themselves. But 80% of the cost of the services is borne by the government. The Congressional Budget Office estimates that Medigap coverage increases the use of services by close to 24%.[16] The increase in the cost of Medicare to the government is approximately equal to the shaded area in Figure 9.7 and is mostly deadweight loss. Since these extra

---

[15]The magnitude of the elasticity is actually like to rise as the co-insurance rate rises; therefore, insurance is likely to increase use of medical services by more than 22%.

[16]Congressional Budget Office, "Long-Term Budgetary Pressures and Policy Options," May 1998.

services would not have been demanded if the beneficiary had to pay the 20% co-insurance payment out of his or her own pocket, the marginal willingness to pay for the extra services is at most 20% of the costs charged by the health care provider.

Medicare Reform.

Although Social Security reform gets more attention, many people believe that the need to reform Medicare is just as great, and perhaps more urgent. Those who argue for Medicare reform can be classified into two groups: (1) people who want to radically restructure Medicare to contain costs and make the program less bureaucratic, and (2) people who want to expand benefits and access. The first group is motivated by the fact that Medicare spending is projected to rise dramatically when the baby boomers retire, and the outlays for the program will exceed the revenues collected by the Medicare part of the FICA tax. The second group is motivated by the hardship many elderly beneficiaries face in affording the out-of-pocket costs of Medicare, such as prescription drugs, and the fact that many older people who have lost their jobs or retired before age 65 have difficulty buying medical insurance.

The proposal of the National Bipartisan Commission on the Future on Medicare, issued in March 1999, is a good example of the reforms favored by the first group. The Commission, in a divided vote, proposed several controversial changes, including increasing the age at which an individual is eligible for Medicare to conform with the eligibility age for Social Security (which increases by 2 months per year to age 67 by 2022). The most controversial change is to change Medicare into a premium support system. In effect, this would eliminate traditional Medicare and expand Medicare + Choice. Private insurers, HMOs, and other managed care organizations would compete on equal terms to provide the same services as the government's fee-for-service program. Medicare beneficiaries can "shop" for the plan they prefer as they can do now under M+C. In economic terms, this turns Medicare into a type of "voucher" program. In a voucher program, like food stamps, the government provides the beneficiary with a claim for a fixed amount of goods and services, in this case health care, that he or she can present to a private firm.

The Bipartisan Commission did not reach a bipartisan conclusion and had insufficient votes to issue a final report. President Clinton has made proposals to reform Medicare, along with other parts of the government health care system. His proposals are a good example of the reforms favored by the second group. One proposal is to allow a Medicare "buy-in" option for individuals between 55 and 65 years of age. Everyone over age 62 and displaced workers over age 55 could receive Medicare benefits by paying an annual premium. To increase affordability, individuals would receive a tax credit equal to 25% of the premium, meaning that the government pays a quarter of the cost. In addition, Clinton proposes adding a Part D Medicare that provides a prescription drug benefit of $1000 a year, rising to $2500 by 2008. As mentioned earlier, outpatient prescription drugs are not currently covered by Medicare. Under the proposal, Medicare beneficiaries could choose to enroll in Part D Medicare by paying an annual premium. Half of the

A CASE IN POINT

9.2   Canada's Single-Payer National Health Care System

Pressures for reform in U.S. government health policy go beyond Medicare. The United States is the only major industrial country without a universal medical insurance system that covers all of the population. About 15% of the population is uninsured, including many children, and people who receive medical insurance through their employers risk losing their coverage if they change employers or lose their jobs. Many people have pointed to Canada's universal national health care system as a model for reform. All Canadians are entitled to medical insurance provided by the government with no out-of-pocket deductibles, co-payments, or co-insurance payments. Indeed, such cost-sharing arrangements are explicitly precluded. The coverage is portable, so Canadians are insured no matter where they work or live in the country. Moreover, Canadians spend less on health care than Americans do— 9.3% of GDP in Canada as compared with 14% in the United States.

Proponents of a Canadian-style system argue that it can provide medical coverage to all citizens at less cost for two reasons. First, the net cost of administering the Canadian program is much lower at .9% of benefits than the cost of administering private health insurance in the United States, where it is 7.6% of benefits. Second, since the government is the largest purchaser of health services, the **single-payer system** holds down prices charged by health care providers. Economists call this monopsony power. In Canada, the provincial governments control the growth of health care expenditures by dictating hospital, operating budgets and negotiating physicians fees with provincial medical associations.

Opponents of a Canadian-style system argue that many of the costs of the system are hidden. For one thing, Canadians often have to wait to receive health care services. Patients can-

not receive specialist services directly, but must obtain referral from a general practitioner who acts as a gatekeeper. The Fraser Institute of Vancouver, British Columbia, conducts an annual survey of how long people have to wait for different types of services in the different provinces. In 1998, patients had to wait more than three months on average between the referral and the time the services were received. The waiting time was much longer in some provinces—for example, over five months in Saskatchewan.[1] Some Canadians have died waiting for treatment, and others have sought treatment in the United States at their own expense. In addition to waiting times, the provincial governments restrict access to technology outside hospitals. On a per capita basis, the United States has eleven times as many cardiac catheterization units (for treating heart disease) as Canada, ten times as many magnetic resonance imaging (MRI) machines, and three times as many CAT scanners and open-heart surgery units.[2]

Critically analyze the following:

- How is overutilization of health care services controlled under the Canadian system?

- Do you think nonprice rationing is likely to be more or less efficient than cost sharing? More or less fair?

- The provincial governments put caps on the fees doctors can charge for office visits. Since the introduction of universal health insurance, the time of the average office visit has declined 16%, while the number of office visits has increased 32%. Explain why.

[1]Fraser Institute, *Waiting Your Turn: Hospital Waiting Lists in Canada* (9th edition), September 1999.
[2]Patricia M. Danzon, "Hidden Overhead Costs: Is Canada's System Really Less Expensive?" *Health Affairs*, Spring 1992.

cost of the program would be financed by revenue from the premiums, and half by general tax revenues. The Congressional Budget Office estimates that the program would increase Medicare spending by $136 billion through 2009. When the baby boomers retire, the cost would increase significantly. As we can see, the reform proposals that enhance benefits are seriously at odds with the reforms that attempt to contain cost.

CONCLUSION AND SUMMARY

Social Security and Medicare are among the largest spending programs of the federal government, with over 15 cents of every dollar earned by workers going to pay cash and health care benefits to the elderly. As entitlements, these programs also pose the greatest challenge for present and future policy makers. Since both are mainly pay-as-you-go programs, the impending retirement of the baby-boom generation beginning in 2015 will significantly increase the cost of the programs. According to the high-cost (pessimistic) projections of the trust fund trustees, by the year 2045 over 30 cents of each dollar earned by workers will be needed to support the programs. However, these problems are far off in an uncertain future. At present, more than enough revenue is collected to finance the benefits of these highly popular programs. Unless the political will to address these problems is found, we cannot know how the future crisis in entitlement spending will be resolved and who will pay.

- Social Security and Medicare are social insurance programs because eligibility and benefit levels depend on retirement and past contributions, not need.

- One reason for social insurance is insurance market failure due to adverse selection and, possibly, moral hazard. Adverse selection in annuities markets and medical insurance markets means that government Social Security and Medicare programs can improve economic efficiency.

- Social Security (OASDI) pays cash benefits to retirees, their dependents, and disabled workers. Medicare (HI) provides hospital benefits for retirees, and Medicare (SMI) pays for the costs of physician services.

- Social Security and Medicare are mostly pay-as-you go programs, which means that payroll taxes on current workers are used to pay benefits to current retirees. The future benefits for current workers will be paid by payroll taxes on future workers.

- Social Security is partially funded in advance because current payroll taxes collect about $100 billion per year more than is needed to pay current benefits. The surplus is accumulated in the Social Security trust fund, which had a balance of $800 billion at the end of 1999, all of which was invested in U.S. Treasury securities.

- Social Security redistributes income among different groups. Women and married couples receive higher benefits per dollar of contribution than men and single people, respectively. People who entered the system earlier also received higher benefits than people who entered the system later.

■ Individuals are likely to substitute future Social Security benefits for retirement saving; hence Social Security discourages personal saving and decreases national saving. Social Security may also induce earlier retirement and reduce the labor supply of older workers.

■ Demographic facts have raised concern about the long-run solvency of Social Security, prompting calls for reforms. Suggested reforms include reduction of benefits, higher payroll taxes, privatization, diversification of the trust fund balance into stocks, and budget surpluses to save Social Security.

■ Medicare expenditures have risen rapidly in the past due to the rising cost of health care. In response, the Balanced Budget Act of 1997 cut the growth in Medicare spending by freezing Medicare compensation rates to hospitals and private plans. It also introduced Medicare + Choice to encourage beneficiaries to enroll in managed care plans.

QUESTIONS FOR DISCUSSION AND REVIEW

1. In France, one can buy real estate "en viager," which allows sellers to live in their homes rent-free and receive a monthly payment for as long as they live. In exchange, the buyer takes possession of the property when the seller dies. In 1965, 47-year-old Andre-Francois Raffray bought the apartment of 90-year-old Jeanne Calment en viager by agreeing to pay her 2500 francs (about $500 a month) for the rest of her life. In 1995, M. Raffray died at age 77 after paying $184,000 to Mme Calment over 30 years. Mme Calment, then 120 years old, was still alive and living in the apartment. How would buying property en viager invite adverse selection? Use this example to explain.

2. Which of the following are examples of adverse selection, and which are examples of moral hazard?

   a. Someone whose parents lived to 100 is anxious to buy a life annuity.

   b. People in hurricane-prone areas are more likely to build homes on the seashore because hurricane damage is insured through the Federal Emergency Management Agency (FEMA).

   c. A person with disability insurance is less likely to be careful lifting heavy objects at work.

   d. People with existing health conditions are more anxious to buy medical insurance.

3. Can individual equity and social adequacy be combined in a fully privatized Social Security program? Why or why not?

4. One recent study by the Social Security Administration claimed that Social Security is a good deal, even for younger male workers. It calculated lifetime benefits from Social Security as a percentage of lifetime contributions by the employee alone and showed that everyone gets back more than his or her own contributions. Evaluate this argument.

5. How does immigration policy affect the viability of a pay-as-you-go Social Security system? If you were to adopt an immigration

policy for the purpose of maintaining the long-run solvency of Social Security, what types of immigrants would you prefer?

6. Suppose that in every year real earnings (in dollars of constant purchasing power) grow faster than the real rate of interest (the nominal rate less the rate of increase in the cost of living) on investment. Which do you think is better and why: a pay-as-you-go Social Security program or a privatized Social Security program?

7. A recent cartoon showed a person opening a locked safe labeled "Social Security trust fund" to find an IOU signed by Congress. Explain what this cartoon means.

8. In estimating the cost of allowing a Medicare "buy-in" option for people between age 55 and 65, the government assumes that the per capita cost of the potential beneficiaries is the same as the average cost of people already in the program. Is this likely to be accurate? Why or why not?

9. The government often complains that the Medicare program "subsidizes" private sellers of Medigap insurance. Explain why.

10. Suppose that the quantity demanded of visits to a doctor per year is given by $Q = 12 - 0.05P$ where Q is the number of visits and P is the price the patient pays for a visit. How many visits would a patient make if he or she had to pay the full price of a visit, $100? How many visits would a patient make if he or she was insured and had to pay only a 20% co-insurance payment per visit?

11. Retirees can obtain supplemental private insurance to cover Medicare co-payments more easily than private insurance for long-term care. Explain how moral hazard may explain this fact.

12. Internet Exercise. The 1999 Report of the Trustees of the Social Security trust fund is available at http://www.ssa.gov/OACT/TR/TR99/triiib.html. Using Table III.B2, in what year does the outgo of the fund exceed the income according to the intermediate projection? How does this compare with the low-cost and high-cost projections? What is the maximum value for the assets (in 1996 dollars) of the trust fund and in what year is it reached under the intermediate projection? What percentage of this value is outgo for that year? What is the level of projected outgo in the year the fund is exhausted?

13. Internet Exercise. The *1998 Data Compendium* on the Health Care Financing Administration Internet site at http://www.hcfa.gov/stats/ is a good source of information on government health care policy. On page 6, the growth in total Medicare benefit payments, enrollees, and benefits per enrollee from 1980 to 1999 are listed. What percentage of the growth in total payments is the result of the increase in the number of enrollees? What percentage is the result of increased spending per enrollee? What implications do these trends have for the need to control health care spending before the baby boomers retire?

14. Internet Exercise. Projections of future health care spending are available at http://www.hcfa.gov/stats/NHE-Proj/proj1998/tables/. Table 1 shows projected health care spending to the year 2008, and Table 3b shows the projected composition. Using these data, how much is national health care spending expected to rise between 1999 and 2008? How much is Medicare spending expected to rise? What about out-of-pocket spending on health care?

SELECTED REFERENCES

A good description of the Social Security program, and its history, is found in C. Eugene Steurle and Jon M. Bakija, *Retooling Social Security for the Twenty-First Century*, 1994. The problems faced by Social Security are discussed in Eric Kingston and James Schulz (eds.), *Social Security in the Twenty-First Century*, 1997.

The economic effects of Social Security are summarized in Michael D. Hurd, "Research on the Elderly: Economic Status, Retirement, Consumption and Saving," 1990; and Henry J. Aaron, *The Economic Effects of Social Security*, 1982.

The effect of Social Security on retirement savings was estimated by Martin Feldstein, "Social Security, Induced Retirement, and Aggregate Capital Accumulation," 1974. Also see Dean R. Leimer and Selig D. Lesnoy, "Social Security and Private Saving: New Time Series Evidence," 1982; and Laurence J. Kotlikoff, "Testing the Theory of Social Security and Life Cycle Accumulation," 1979.

A textbook on health economics is Charles E. Phelps, *Health Economics*, 1992. A book that covers all aspects of Medicare is Marilyn Moon, *Medicare Now and in the Future*, 2nd ed., 1996.

Different points of view by economists on health care reform are found in "Health Care Reform Symposia," 1994; and Charles T. Carlstrom, "The Economics of Health Care Reform," 1994.

USEFUL INTERNET SITES

Data on the Social Security program are available on the Social Security Administration's web site at http://www.ssa.gov/.

For health care data, see HCFA's web site at http://www.hcfa.gov/. More health care statistics and information are available at the University of Michigan's Public Health Statistics site. See http://www.lib.umich.edu/hw/public.health/health.stats.html.

Information on all entitlement programs can be found in the *1998 Green Book* at http://www.access.gpo.gov/congress/wm001.htm/.

A good site for economic studies of social insurance programs is the National Academy of Social Insurance at http://www.nasi.org/.

PART FIVE

The Basic

Theory

of Taxation

Chapters 10, 11, and 12 provide a framework for understanding the main economic issues surrounding the government revenue system. Avoiding the details and complications of the existing revenue system, these chapters develop the main ideas in terms of simple taxes like excise taxes.

In Chapter 10, we discuss and classify the different taxes that could be levied in a market economy. We consider the effects of an excise tax on the economic decisions of households and firms, and the ultimate impact on market prices and quantities. We also discuss the relationship between tax rates and tax revenues.

In Chapter 11, we analyze one of the most important aspects of a tax—how the burden is distributed across people in the economy. The "incidence" of a tax, as it is called, may vary according to where taxpayers live, how much income they have, and when they were born. The most important idea is that the person who bears the tax burden is not necessarily the person who pays the tax, because tax burdens can be shifted.

Chapter 12 outlines how we can evaluate tax policy using three criteria: economic efficiency, distributional equity, and administrative cost. First, we investigate how to measure the excess burden of a tax that causes economic inefficiency. The excess burden is used to develop the idea of an optimal tax system that minimizes the burden of collecting a given amount of revenue. Second, we define principles of tax equity and examine how equity is achieved in the tax system. Finally, we discuss the administration and compliance costs of different tax systems.

10 Taxation and the Allocation of Resources

"Taxes are what we pay for civilized society." These words by Supreme Court Justice Oliver Wendell Holmes Jr. in 1927 sum up what many people believe about taxes. Although no one likes to pay them, taxes are a necessary evil. In a market economy the government does not own the means of production and must obtain the resources it needs by exacting payments from private individuals and firms. In earlier societies, the authorities simply seized what they needed or wanted, but in modern society the government obtains the resources it needs by legislating taxes.

The power to tax is perhaps the most obvious display of the government's coercive power. Private contracts require consent and voluntary exchange among the parties involved, but the government can force us to do things, such as pay taxes. Taxes do require consent by the voters through their elected representatives but are involuntary from the standpoint of the individual. For the remainder of this textbook, we study the impact on the economy of the government's need to raise revenue through tax policy. The taxes the government levies have as important an impact on the economy as the programs they finance. We begin by explaining the basic theory of taxation and leave to later chapters the details about the existing tax system in the United States.

WHAT IS A TAX?

Sometimes a simple question is hard to answer. Such a question is "What is a tax?" Unlike private businesses, which obtain revenue by selling products to willing buyers, governments rely on taxes for most of their revenue. We all recognize that the income tax deducted from our paychecks is a tax, but what about the tuition that students pay at state universities or the price of a state lottery ticket? Is every payment to the government a tax? If not, what makes a tax different from other payments to the government?

Economists define a **tax** as an involuntary payment to the government by an individual or firm that does not entitle the payer to a *quid pro quo* benefit or to an equivalent value of goods and services in exchange. Tuition is not a tax, because it is paid only by people who attend the state university in exchange for the services they receive. Tuition is a **user fee** and is no different from the prices charged by private firms for goods and services. Although the government receives some revenue from user fees, it gets most of its revenue from taxes. Taxes are needed because user fees cannot be charged for most government goods and services.

If taxes are involuntary, what about lottery tickets? Isn't the price of a lottery ticket just a user fee because it is voluntary and the buyers get a chance to win a prize in exchange? For that matter, aren't all taxes voluntary? People pay cigarette taxes only if they choose to smoke and income taxes only if they choose to work. These arguments carry the meaning of *voluntary* payments too far. Although the amount we pay in taxes may depend on our actions, taxes are involuntary. We may benefit generally from the goods and services the government provides, but the benefits we, as individuals, receive from the government are independent of the taxes we pay. There is no *quid pro quo*.

Taxes and user fees are polar cases; some payments to the government are a mixture of both tax and user fee. A lottery ticket is a good example. Although part of the lottery ticket price is a user fee in exchange for a chance to win a prize, most of it is tax because the government sets the price far above the expected value of the prize.[1] The state can charge a higher price because the state makes it illegal for private companies to sell lottery tickets. In contrast to lottery tickets, tuition at state universities is well below the value of the services provided to the students, so all of it is a user fee.

Closely related to user fees are benefit taxes. A **benefit tax** is an involuntary payment to the government that entitles the taxpayer to a benefit. The social security tax is a benefit tax because the taxpayers are eligible to receive Social Security benefits when they retire, and the size of the benefit depends on the amount of social security taxes paid. People would be willing to pay part (but probably not all) of their Social Security tax in exchange for the increased benefits.

CLASSIFYING TAXES

Governments in the United States levy many different types of taxes. As individuals, we pay taxes on the income we earn from working and on income from savings and investments. We pay taxes when we sell assets that have increased in value, and when we die and leave an inheritance to our heirs. We also pay taxes when we purchase many goods and services. Businesses pay taxes on the wages they pay workers and on the revenue they receive from customers.[2] In other countries, businesses pay taxes on the value they add to the goods and services they produce.

Generally, when scientists encounter a bewildering variety of phenomena they try to classify them. For instance, zoologists classify fauna and physicists classify particles. Public finance economists do the same thing with taxes.

---

[1] The expected value of the prize is the prize multiplied by the probability of winning it.
[2] Taxes are also levied on the import of goods from foreign countries. Although such duties raised over $10 billion for the federal government in 1998, they are usually ignored in public finance because their primary purpose is assumed to be commercial policy, not raising revenue.

Taxes Classified According to Who Pays Them

One of the oldest ways of classifying taxes is to group them according to who pays them. In the United States, taxes are typically divided into those paid by persons and those paid by businesses. In fact, when taxes are raised or lowered, political arguments rage about whether it should be taxes on persons or taxes on businesses that are changed. A related classification is between direct taxes and indirect taxes. **Direct taxes,** such as income taxes, are levied on persons (or artificial persons like corporations); **indirect taxes,** such as sales taxes, are levied on goods and services.

Ultimately, it is people who pay the taxes, whether they are direct or indirect or levied on persons or businesses, so these classifications seem contrived. In fact, most public finance economists think classifying taxes according to who sends the payment to the tax collector is not particularly meaningful, and prefer to classify taxes according to the economic activity on which the tax is levied.

The main difference between direct and indirect taxes is that indirect tax rates, by their nature, are anonymous, so all taxpayers pay the same rate of tax. In contrast, the personal income tax rate depends on the taxpayer's total income and on the taxpayer's personal characteristics, such as marital status.[3] Another difference is that the tax base (the amount subject to tax) of a direct tax usually includes the amount of the tax (a **tax-inclusive** base), whereas the tax base of an indirect tax usually excludes the amount of tax (a **tax-exclusive** base).[4] A third difference is visibility. People usually know how much they pay in direct taxes, but indirect taxes are sometimes "hidden" because they are included in the prices of the goods, so the taxpayers may be unaware of the amount of tax they are paying.

Taxes Classified According to Economic Activity

Occasionally, journalists write humorous articles listing taxes the government *should* collect, like taxes on people who talk too much or tell bad jokes. If governments could generate sufficient revenue from these taxes, the subject of taxation would have little to do with economics. The fact is that, with few exceptions, all taxes are levied on market activities like incomes and sales. It is for this reason that taxation is studied so extensively by economists.

To understand the impact of taxes on economic activities, economists compare them to a tax that is not levied on an economic activity—the lump-sum tax, also known as a poll or head tax.[5] A **lump-sum tax** is a fixed amount of money (a lump sum) that

---

[3]In fact, the income tax of 1894 was a flat rate tax (that is, not graduated with different tax brackets) in order to forestall a constitutional challenge on the grounds that it was a direct tax with a need for apportionment.

[4]For instance, a person who earns $10 and pays a 20% income tax pays $2 tax and is left with $8 to spend. A person who spends $8 and pays a 20% sales tax pays $1.60 tax and makes a total outlay of $9.60. The taxpayer has $8 in goods, and tax rates are 20% in both cases, but the income tax base is tax-inclusive and the sales tax base is tax-exclusive.

[5]*Poll* is an old English word for head. The poll tax we are describing here should not be confused with the infamous poll tax that was levied in some states prior to the Twenty-fourth Amendment to the Constitution. This poll tax was levied when a person showed up at the polls to vote, and its purpose was to deprive poor citizens, usually African Americans, of their right to vote.

the taxpayer must pay to the government regardless of circumstances. With a lump-sum tax, taxpayers can do nothing to change the amount of tax they must pay, so they have no incentives to change their economic behavior in order to reduce the amount of tax paid. A poll or head tax, which is a fixed tax per person, is an example of a lump-sum tax. Poll taxes have been levied at different times in various countries throughout history and have sometimes been followed by civil unrest or even rebellion. During the 1980s, Prime Minister Margaret Thatcher tried to levy a poll tax in England, which eventually led to riots in the streets of London and Thatcher's resignation as Conservative Party leader. Oddly enough, economists view the lump-sum tax as an ideal tax in some ways because it does not affect people's economic behavior.

In any case, lump-sum taxes do not exist in the United States at present, so they are purely hypothetical. Had the combined governments in the nation raised their revenue with lump-sum taxes in 1999, the tax would have been $10,250 per person or $41,000 for a family of four. This is probably the main reason lump-sum taxes are not levied in any significant amounts by any country. To rely on them would be impractical and grossly unfair. How would a family with income less than $41,000 pay such a tax? Still, the lump-sum tax serves as a useful benchmark for analyzing real-world taxes levied on economic activities.

Nearly all taxes levied in the United States, whether direct or indirect or levied on households or businesses, are levied when the taxpayer engages in an economic activity. Income and payroll taxes account for over 90% of federal government revenue and 45% of the tax revenue collected by the states, so they are by far the most important. Taxes on incomes are also called **factor taxes** by economists, because the taxes are levied on the incomes earned by the factors of production in the economy (labor, capital, and land).

Taxes on goods and services may take the form of general sales taxes, such as the familiar retail sales tax levied in many states, or excise taxes. An excise tax is a sales tax that is levied on a particular good or group of goods, such as gasoline, tobacco products, and telephone calls. Taxes on goods and services amount to only about 5% of federal revenue, all from excise taxes, but collect nearly half of the revenue collected by state governments. In many countries, governments levy a type of general sales tax called a **value-added tax** (**VAT**). Unlike a retail sales tax, which is levied on goods sold at the retail stage, the VAT is levied on the increase in the value of goods and services as they pass from firm to firm on their way to the final consumer.

In the United States, taxes on wealth and property are levied primarily on real estate (land and buildings), although in some states the property tax includes personal property like cars and boats. Such taxes account for most of the revenue collected by cities and school districts. Federal and state taxes on transfers of wealth are levied on large gifts, estates, and inheritances. In some other countries, a tax on the taxpayer's net worth (assets minus liabilities), called a personal wealth tax, is levied.

Taxes on economic activities can be general or selective. A **selective tax** is levied on a narrow range of economic activities, such as an excise tax levied on a single good. The retail sales tax levied by most states is a **general tax** because it includes most goods and services purchased by consumers. Income taxes vary in their degree of selectivity. The personal income tax is the most general because it covers most forms of income, including earnings (wages and salaries), royalties, interest, dividends, and capital gains. In contrast, a payroll tax is more selective because it is levied on labor's earnings only. A very selective form of income tax, called a **partial factor tax,** is levied on the income of a particular factor employed in a particular use. Economists analyze the corporation income tax as a partial factor tax, because the tax applies only to the earnings of shareholder capital (a particular factor) employed by incorporated firms (a particular use).

In Table 10.1, we classify taxes according to whether they are general or selective. Within each category, we further classify according to the economic activity that is taxed and whether the tax is direct or indirect. Examples of taxes in each classification are shown.

Excise Taxes Levied by the U.s. Government

Although excise taxes are not a large source of revenue for governments in the United States , we concentrate on them in this section. An excise tax is a good model for understanding the more important, and more complicated, taxes such as the personal income tax. An excise tax is selective because it applies to a particular good (service) or group of goods, but not to others. That is, we can easily identify taxed and untaxed goods. As we will see in later chapters, most or all taxes are selective in one way or another. For example, some types of income are taxed and others are not taxed under the personal income tax system, and the sales of some goods are taxed under a general sales tax and others are not.

In 1999, the federal government collected $68.1 billion in excise tax revenue and another $18.3 billion in customs duties on imported goods and services. Together, these taxes account for less than 5% of all federal revenue. The importance of federal excise taxes as a source of revenue has declined over time. For example, in 1960 the federal government collected over 14% of its revenue from excise taxes.

The excise taxes levied by the federal government can be classified into four main categories. The first category is the so-called "sin taxes" on alcohol, tobacco, and

Table 10.1   Classification of Taxes with Examples

General Taxes	Selective Taxes
Direct factor taxes	*Indirect factor taxes*
federal and state personal income tax	employer payroll tax
Indirect goods and service taxes	*Direct factor taxes*
state retail sales tax	employee wage tax
value-added tax	
Direct wealth taxes	*Partial factor taxes*
federal estate tax	corporation income tax
personal wealth tax	
	Indirect sales taxes
	federal and state excise tax
	Direct wealth taxes
	local real estate property tax

Table 10.2   Some Goods and Services Subject to Federal Excise Taxation (1999)

"Sin" taxes

Distilled spirits	$13.50 per proof gallon
Beer	$18 per 31-gallon barrel
Cigarettes (2000)	$17 per thousand
Wagers except parimutuel	25% of amount wagered

Transportation and communication

Gasoline	18.3 cents per gallon
Trucks	12% of manufacturer's sale price
Transportation of persons by air	8% of ticket price
International departures	$12.20 per departure
General and toll telephone service	3% of amount paid

Environmental and resources

Fishing equipment and firearms	10% of manufacturers sale price
Coal (underground)	$1.10 a ton
Coal (surface)	$.55 a ton
Ozone-depleting chemicals	$7.15 per pound

Luxury

Jewelry	10% of retail price
Furs	10% of retail price

Source: U.S. Congress, Joint Committee on taxation, Schedule of Present Federal Excise Taxes, 1999, available as JCS-2-99 at www.access.gpo.gov/congress/joint/hjoint01cp106.html.

wagering. These taxes are levied partly to discourage those activities, a well as to force the consumers who buy such goods to pay for the privilege. The second category is taxes on transportation and communication facilities, which include taxes on gasoline, other motor fuels, tires and trucks, air transportation, air freight and aviation, and fuel used on inland waterways, as well as taxes on telephone service and long-distance calls. The transportation and communication taxes can be viewed as user fees that finance federal government support for highways, air transportation, and communication facilities. A third category includes environmental and resource taxes on hunting and fishing equipment, "black lung disease" taxes on coal production, taxes on ozone-depleting chemicals, and "Superfund" taxes on crude oil and chemicals.[6] These corrective taxes are levied as a policy for market failures, as we discussed in Chapter 4. The fourth category is taxes on luxury goods. This category, sometimes called *sumptuary taxes,* is rather small and includes only jewelry, furs, and expensive automobiles.

Some of the more important federal excise taxes and their rates are shown in Table 10.2. In this table, note that the tax rate for some excise taxes (such as those on tobacco and gasoline) is fixed in dollars per unit of the good, whereas the tax rate for others (such as jewelry) is a fixed as a percentage of value (*ad valorem*). Generally, it does not make a difference at a point in time whether an excise tax rate is levied

---

[6]The "Superfund" was created under the Comprehensive Environmental Response, Compensation, and Liability Act of 1980 to clean up toxic waste sites in the aftermath of the catastrophe at Love Canal, New York, in 1978.

per unit or on percent of value. It does make a difference over time, however, if inflation is present. For instance, to keep the federal excise tax rate per gallon of gasoline constant in terms of dollars of purchasing power, Congress must increase it, whereas a percentage excise tax automatically keeps pace with inflation.

Because of erosion by inflation, the real excise tax rate has decreased on some goods taxed per unit. For instance, the excise tax rate on cigarettes was $4 per 1000 cigarettes in 1954. If the same tax rate in dollars of constant purchasing power were levied on cigarettes in 2000, the tax rate would have to be nearly $25 per 1000 cigarettes, rather than $17 per 1000. Inflation has eroded the federal excise tax on cigarettes as a percentage of value.

Excise taxes are more important as a source of revenue for state governments. In 1998, state governments collected $71 billion in revenue from selective excise taxes, which is about 11% of general revenue derived from state sources (i.e., excluding intergovernmental transfers). Many of the same goods subject to federal excise taxes are subject to state (and sometimes local) excise taxes, including alcoholic beverages, tobacco, motor fuels, and telephone service. In addition, many state governments levy excise taxes on admissions to amusement parks, parimutuel wagering, insurance premiums, hotel accommodations, and car rentals.

THE IMPACT OF TAXES ON INDIVIDUALS' DECISIONS

A major task of a public finance economist is to discover how a tax affects the allocation of the economy's resources among competing uses. In a market economy, the allocation of resources is determined mainly by decisions of households and firms. These decisions are reflected in market prices and quantities. As a result of a tax, the economy produces less of some goods and services and more of others. Our goal in this chapter is to understand the effect on resource allocation and its implications. To do this, we examine first how a tax affects the decisions made by consumers and firms.

Impact of Taxes on Consumers' Decisions

Suppose a consumer has a fixed amount of money M each month to spend on two goods—apples and bagels. The market prices of the goods are fixed, and the quantities consumed per month are denoted A and B. In Figure 10.1, the quantity of bagels is measured on the horizontal axis and the quantity of apples on the vertical axis. We choose apples as our numeraire good, or unit of account, and fix the money price of an apple at $1.[7] Assume that the price charged for a bagel by producers is $\bar{P}$ dollars, which is fixed. Without taxes, the consumer's budget line is the one labeled MM'. Since we've normalized the price of apples at $1, the vertical intercept of the budget line is the consumer's income M and the horizontal intercept is $M/\bar{P}$. The slope of the budget line (ignoring the minus sign) is $\bar{P}$, the money price of bagels.

According to the theory of consumer choice, the consumer chooses among the bundles of goods available on the budget line to maximize utility. The consumer's

---

[7]We do this by our choice of the unit for apples. For example, if an apple costs 50 cents, our apple unit consists of two apples.

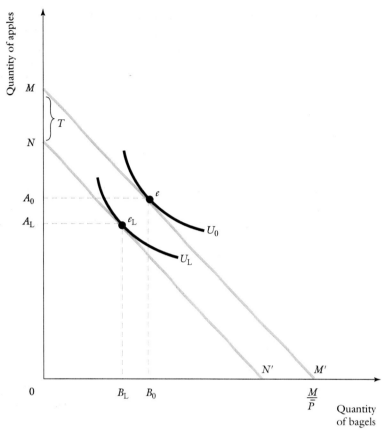

Figure 10.1
Effect of a Lump-Sum Tax on Consumers' Choices
A lump-sum tax shifts the budget line facing the consumer to the left from *MM'* to *NN'* without changing its slope (the relative prices of the goods). The consumer responds to the tax in the same way as a reduction in income, and he or she reduces consumption of both goods if they are normal goods.

utility, or preferences, can be represented by the indifference curves shown in Figure 10.1.[8] The consumer maximizes utility by purchasing the bundle where the budget line is tangent to the highest possible indifference curve. This utility-maximizing bundle, labeled e, consists of A_0 apples and B_0 bagels. At e, the consumer's marginal willingness to pay (MWTP) for a bagel is equal to the price of a bagel,[9] and maximum utility is U_0.

IMPACT OF A LUMP-SUM TAX.   In Figure 10.1 we analyze the impact of a lump-sum tax of T dollars on the consumer's choice of apples and bagels. Recall that a lump-sum tax is a fixed amount that consumers must pay regardless of how they

---

[8]The properties of indifference curves are reviewed in the main Appendix.
[9]The slope of the indifference curve is also called the marginal rate of substitution.

choose to spend their income. The lump-sum tax shifts the consumer's budget line down by the amount T and leaves the relative prices of apples and bagels unchanged (a parallel shift in the budget line). After the tax is imposed, the consumer has disposable income of $M - T$ to spend each month and can choose any point on the budget line NN'. The consumer now chooses the bundle labeled e_L and gets a maximum utility U_L. In response to the decreases in disposable income caused by the lump-sum tax, the consumer reduces the consumption of apples and bagels to A_L and B_L, respectively.

The impact of a lump-sum tax on consumption is determined solely by the income effect on the quantities of goods demanded. The **income effect** of a tax on a good is measured by the good's income elasticity, which is equal to the percentage change in the quantity demanded divided by the percentage change in disposable income. For example, if a lump-sum tax reduces disposable income by 10% and the income elasticity of bagels is 1, the consumer purchases 10% fewer bagels. *Normal* goods have positive income elasticities, so lump-sum taxes decrease consumption of normal goods. A *luxury* good has an income elasticity greater than 1, so the consumption of a luxury good falls by more than 10% when disposable income is decreased by 10%. A *necessity* good has an income elasticity less than 1, so the consumption of a necessity good falls by less than 10%. Some necessities, called *inferior* goods, have negative income elasticities.[10] A lump-sum tax causes the consumption of inferior goods to rise.

IMPACT OF AN EXCISE TAX.   Unlike a lump-sum tax, for which the amount of tax is fixed, the amount of excise tax depends on the quantity the consumer purchases of the taxed good. For instance, no tax at all is paid if the consumer does not buy the taxed good. An excise tax rate may be set in dollars (or cents) per unit of the good or in dollars per unit of value.[11] For example, the federal excise tax on gasoline is 18.3 cents per gallon (a per unit excise tax) and the federal excise tax on pistols and revolvers is fixed at 10% of the manufacturer's price (a percentage excise tax).[12] Generally, the economic impact of an excise tax is the same whether it is levied at a per unit or percentage rate (another form of tax equivalence), although the taxes will have different impacts if prices change over time.

Suppose that the government decides to levy a per unit excise tax of t on bagels. If the price charged for bagels by the firms is not affected by the tax, the consumer now must pay $\bar{P} + t$ for each bagel. Since the consumer has M dollars to spend, he or she can now buy at most $\dfrac{M}{\bar{P} + t}$ bagels, so the new budget line is the one labeled

---

[10]The term *inferior* does not refer to the quality of the good; it is an economic term that describes the response of the good to a change in income. For example, consumption of margarine tends to drop as incomes rise because consumers prefer butter and exercise that preference when they can afford it.

[11]When the excise tax is fixed per unit of good, it is sometimes called a *specific* excise tax, whereas if the excise tax rate is fixed per unit of value, the tax is called an *ad valorem* excise tax.

[12]The reason the excise tax on firearms is per unit of value is that one pistol (unlike a gallon of gasoline) is not the same as another. All general sales tax rates are set per unit of value, because there is no way to set the same tax rate in per unit terms when a tax is imposed on many different goods.

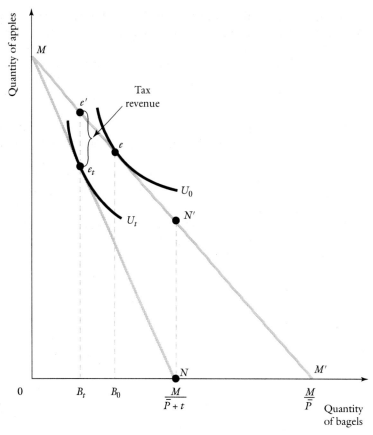

Figure 10.2

Effect of an Excise Tax on Consumer's Choices

Given the seller's price, an excise tax on bagels raises the price of bagels and changes the budget line facing the consumer from MM' to MN, making it steeper as well as shifting it to the left. The amount of tax paid,
measured as the vertical distance between MM' and MN, depends on the quantity of bagels consumed. The
quantity of bagels consumed falls more than it would with a lump-sum tax because the excise tax raises
the price of bagels, causing a substitution effect.

MN in Figure 10.2. The consumer can still consume M apples because apples are
not taxed. With the bagel excise tax, the amount of tax the consumer pays depends
on the quantity of bagels consumed. At point M on the budget line, the amount of
excise tax paid is zero, and at point N it is the vertical distance NN'. In general, the
amount of tax *measured in apples* is the vertical distance between the MM' and MN
budget lines at each quantity of bagels.

The effect of an excise tax on the consumer's budget line is more complicated
than that of a lump-sum tax. As noted above, not only is the budget line shifted, it
is made steeper. The absolute slope of budget line MN is equal to $\bar{P} + t$, which is
the price of a bagel plus the excise tax. The consumer maximizes utility by choosing the bundle e_t on MN, where B_t bagels are consumed. The total amount of excise

tax paid is equal to the quantity B_t times the per unit bagel tax rate t, which is equal to the vertical distance between MM' and MN at quantity B_t, or $e_t e'$.

As compared with a lump-sum tax that collects the same amount of tax from the consumer, the taxpayer consumes fewer bagels under the excise tax. The reason is that the excise tax has two effects on the consumer's choice. The consumer can afford fewer bagels (the income effect of the tax); also, the consumer substitutes consumption away from bagels toward apples because apples are untaxed (the sub-stitution effect of the tax). The substitution effect is caused by the rise in the price of bagels *relative* to apples, which prompts the consumer to choose more of the cheaper, untaxed good.

The effect of an excise tax on the quantity of a taxed good is measured by **price elasticity** of the good. The price elasticity is equal to the negative of the percentage change in the quantity consumed of a good divided by the percent-age change in the consumer's price.[13] For example, if the excise tax raises the con-sumer's price of bagels by 10% and the quantity of bagels consumed falls by 10%, the price elasticity is 1. Since the quantity falls in the same proportion that the consumer's price rises, total spending on the good, including the tax, remains constant. If the price elasticity is less than 1, the good is *price inelastic* and the quantity demanded falls by less than 10% in response to a 10% increase in its price. In this case, total spending on the good rises in response to the tax. If the price elasticity is greater than 1, the good is *price elastic* and the quantity demanded falls by more than 10% in response to a 10% increase in its price. With an elastic demand, the amount spent on the taxed good falls even though the consumer's price rises.

We now examine the effect of a tax on the market demand curve for bagels. The market demand curve for bagels, labeled D in Figure 10.3, plots the quantity of bagels on the horizontal axis against the consumer's price of bagels on the ver-tical axis. The quantity demanded is found by summing the quantities demanded by all consumers, but for simplicity we consider the demand curve of the single con-sumer we analyzed above.

When the market price is $\bar{P}$, the consumer demands B_0 bagels. The imposi-tion of a lump-sum tax shifts the market demand curve for bagels to the left; at each price, the consumer demands fewer bagels because of the income effect of the tax. The quantity of bagels demanded by the consumer decreases to B_L because the lump-sum tax reduces the consumer's income. In contrast, when an excise tax is levied on bagels, the consumer's price rises to $\bar{P} + t$ and the quantity demand falls to B_t. The total amount of excise tax paid by the consumer is equal to the area of the shaded rectangle, which is the per unit tax t on bagels times the quantity of B_t bagels demanded. If the total tax paid by the consumer is the same as the lump-sum tax, the consumer demands fewer bagels with an excise tax than with a lump-sum tax, as shown in the figure. The larger decrease in the demand for bagels when an excise tax is imposed (from B_L to B_t) is the substitution effect of the excise tax.

---

[13]Multiplying by -1 simply expresses the elasticity as a positive rather than negative number.

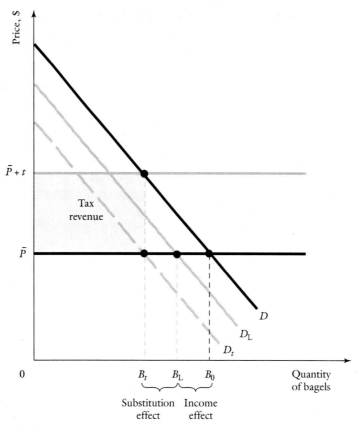

Figure 10.3

Effect of a Lump-Sum Tax and an Excise Tax on Demand

The effects of a lump-sum and an excise tax that collect the same revenue are shown in terms of demand curves. Without taxes, the demand curve is labeled D and B_0 bagels are consumed. A lump-sum tax shifts the demand curve to D_L and consumption of bagels falls to B_L. The excise tax raises the price of bagels, and consumption falls to B_t. Subtracting the excise tax rate from the demand curve gives the after-tax demand curve D_t facing sellers. The income effect of the excise tax is the fall in consumption from B_0 to B_L and the substitution effect is the fall from B_L to B_t. The tax revenue collected by the excise tax is shown by the shaded rectangle.

In a later section of this chapter we examine the impact of an excise tax on the equilibrium price and quantity in a market. To do this, we make use of the dashed curve labeled D_t in Figure 10.3. This dashed line is the "after-tax" demand curve facing bagel producers after the excise tax is paid by the consumers. Curve D_t is obtained by subtracting the excise tax per bagel from the height of the market demand curve. The height of the bagel demand curve is the maximum price consumers will pay per bagel to consume a given quantity, so the height of D_t is the net price received by the bagel producers. For instance, at quantity B_t the consumers are willing to pay a maximum of $\bar{P} + t$ per bagel, so the producers receive $\bar{P}$ after the excise tax is paid. The D_t demand curve is drawn parallel to the market demand curve on the assumption that the excise tax is a per unit tax. If the excise tax is a percentage tax, the after-tax demand curve is flatter than the market demand curve.

Impact of a Tax on Firms' Decisions

To examine the effect of an excise tax on consumers, we assumed that the tax is paid by the consumers; that is, producers received the same net price regardless of the tax. To determine how an excise tax affects production decisions, we assume now that the excise tax is levied on the producers and the price they receive for the good is fixed. Firms are competitive and can sell as many or as few bagels as they like at the prevailing market price $\bar{P}$. Since the price is fixed, the price of a bagel is also the firm's marginal revenue. **Marginal revenue** is the addition to the firm's total receipts from selling an extra unit of output.

In Figure 10.4, the curve labeled MC is the marginal cost of bagels to the firm. The **marginal cost** is the increase in the firm's total cost when it increases output by one unit. For most goods, the marginal cost curve slopes upward, so the marginal cost is higher the greater the firm's output.[14] A firm maximizes profit at the output where marginal cost is equal to marginal revenue (MR). When the market price is $\bar{P}$, the firm maximizes profit by producing B_0 bagels. A change in the market price causes the firm to move along its marginal cost curve, so the MC curve is the firm's supply curve.

Suppose the government levies an excise tax at rate t on every bagel produced by the firm. The firm treats this tax as just another variable cost, so its marginal cost rises by the tax per bagel. The tax-inclusive marginal cost curve is labeled MC + t in Figure 10.4. To maximize profit, the firm produces B_t bagels where the tax-inclusive marginal cost is equal to marginal revenue. The increase in marginal cost due to the tax causes the firm to produce less of the taxed good.

THE EFFECT OF AN EXCISE TAX ON MARKET OUTCOMES

Having examined the impact of an excise tax on the individual decisions made by consumers and firms, we now examine the impact of an excise tax on the market where the consumers and firms come together. This is the most important part of the analysis, because economists are most likely to observe market outcomes. If market participants act competitively, we can study the market using the familiar supply and demand analysis. Without taxes, the market demand and supply curves for bagels are shown as D and S in Figure 10.5. To simplify, we assume that the market demand and supply curves are linear. The market equilibrium is found where the curves intersect at point e, and the price of bagels P_0 clears the market at the quantity B_0 bagels.

Now suppose the government levies a per unit excise tax on bagels of t per bagel. Assume that the tax is levied on the consumers, so whenever they purchase a bagel a tax is rung up on the cash register along with the seller's price. Since the height of the market demand is the gross price that consumers are willing to pay per unit at each

[14]At a low level of outputs, it is possible that the marginal cost falls as quantity rises because of "economies of scale." We ignore that possibility in this discussion.

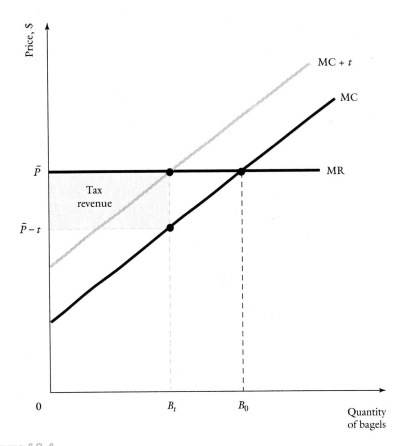

Figure 10.4

Effect of an Excise Tax on Supply
An excise tax on production of bagels is equivalent to an increase in marginal cost (MC), shifting the marginal cost curve up by the tax per unit of output from MC to MC + t. If the seller's market price is fixed, the price $\bar{P}$ also the marginal revenue (MR) curve. Since the firm maximizes profit where marginal revenue equals marginal cost, the output of bagels falls from B_0 to B_t.

quantity, we can subtract the excise tax from this price to find the after-tax demand curve D_t that the bagel producer receives. With the excise tax, the market equilibrium is found at e_t, where the after-tax demand curve intersects the supply curve. After the excise tax is levied, the equilibrium quantity of bagels is B_t and the equilibrium price charged by the producers is P_t. The gross price of a bagel to the consumers is $P_t + t$.

Using Figure 10.5, we can summarize the impact of the excise tax on the market prices and quantity. These results are described for the general case where the demand curve is downward-sloping and the supply curve is upward-sloping.

■ The equilibrium price received by the producers is reduced by the excise tax. If producers were to receive the same price as before the tax was imposed, consumers would have to pay a gross price that is higher by the full amount

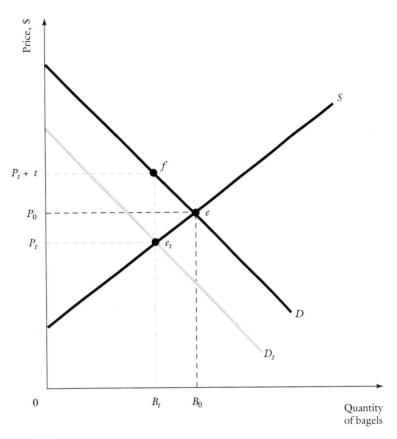

Figure 10.5
Effect of an Excise Tax on the Market
Without taxes, the market equilibrium is at point e, where the demand curve D intersects the supply curve S. With an excise tax, the market equilibrium is at point e_t, where the after-tax demand curve D_t intersects the supply curve. The tax reduces the equilibrium quantity from B_0 to B_t, lowers the seller's price from P_0 to P_t, and increases the consumer's price from P_0 to $P_t + t$.

of the tax. But at a higher price, consumers demand a lower quantity, so the price charged by the firms must decline.

- The excise tax increases the gross price paid by consumers (including the excise tax), but not by the full amount of the tax. If the price to the consumers were to stay the same, the producers would receive a net price that is reduced by the full amount of the tax. At a lower price, firms are not willing to produce as many bagels, so the gross price to the consumers must rise. The gross price charged to consumers does not rise by the full amount of the tax because the price charged by the producers is lower.

- The equilibrium quantity must decline as a result of the excise tax. If the net price of the producer is lower and the gross price to the consumer is higher, the quantity produced and consumed must be smaller in order to be consistent with the joint desires of the market participants.

Tax Equivalence

In the above example, we levied the excise tax on the consumers of bagels. Would it make a difference if we had levied the tax on the producers instead? In other words, rather than assuming that the excise tax is rung up at the cash register when a consumer buys a bagel, suppose that the government levies the tax of t dollars on the firm whenever it sells a bagel. We shall see that the effect on the market equilibrium is exactly the same in either case—an example of **tax equivalence.**

If two taxes have the same effects on the quantities of goods and services bought and sold, market prices, and the distribution of the tax burden across households, they are said to be equivalent, notwithstanding any other differences between them. For example, a percentage excise tax levied at (say) 10% on a good that has a price of $2 is equivalent to a per unit excise tax levied at 20 cents per unit on the same good. Less obviously, a tax on revenue received by sellers is equivalent to a tax at the same rate on spending by buyers. In either case, the government is taxing the transaction and all transactions have two sides, so the money received by sellers is the same money spent by buyers. The point in the transaction at which the government decides to levy the tax does not alter the economic effects of the tax.

The equivalence between taxing consumers and taxing producers is illustrated in Figure 10.6. Suppose that initially the excise tax is levied on the consumers so the market equilibrium is determined by the intersection of the after-tax demand curve D_t and the supply curve S at point e. The seller receives price P_t per bagel and the consumer pays $P_t + t$ once the tax is rung up. Now suppose the tax on the consumers is removed and a tax is levied at the same rate on the sellers every time they produce and sell a bagel. When the tax on consumers is removed, the sellers face the demand curve D, but now they must pay tax of t per bagel, which adds to their marginal cost. The excise tax on the sale of bagels vertically shifts the producers' supply curve to S_t. The vertical distance between curves S_t and S is equal to the tax per bagel.

When the excise tax is removed from the buyers and levied on the sellers, the market equilibrium is found at point f, where demand curve D intersects the tax-inclusive supply curve S_t. Since S_t lies the same distance above S as D lies above D_t (in both cases the distance is t), f lies vertically above point e. Therefore, exactly the same quantity of bagels is bought and sold when the sellers pay the tax as when the consumers pay the tax. The bagel sellers now charge a higher price P_t^C to the consumers, which includes the excise tax per bagel. The consumer pays the same gross price as before; the only difference is that the tax is not rung up separately on the register but is included in the price of the bagel. After paying the excise tax to the government, the sellers receive the same net price per bagel as well.

A good example where tax equivalence is important is the payroll tax that finances Social Security and Medicare. Half of the tax (7.65%) is levied on the money paid by employers, and half is levied on the money received by the employ-

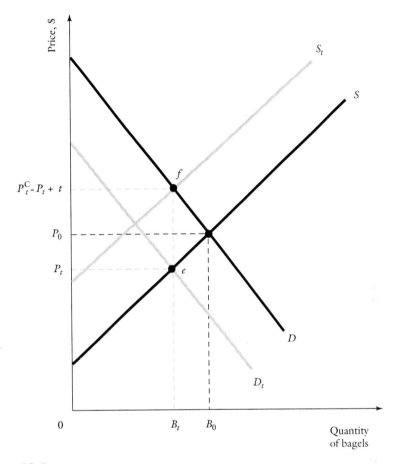

Figure 10.6

Equivalence of Taxing Buyers and Sellers

When an excise tax is levied on buyers, the market equilibrium is at point e where the after-tax demand curve D_t intersects the supply curve S. If the tax on buyers is replaced with a tax on sellers, the equilibrium is at point f where the demand curve D intersects the after-tax supply curve S_t. The vertical distance between D and D_t is equal to that between S and S_t, so point f lies directly above point e, and the impact on quantities and prices is the same. However, when the tax is levied on the sellers, an "all in" price is charged that includes the tax passed on to the buyers.

ees. According to tax equivalence, how the payroll tax is split between the employers and employees is irrelevant. The tax would have the same effects on labor costs to employers, take-home wages to employees, and the level of employment if it were levied entirely on the employers or entirely on the employees, rather than being split between them. For instance, if the employers' half of the tax were removed and levied on the employees, firms would be willing to pay that much more to their employees (since they do not care whom they are paying). After paying the full tax, employees would take home the same amount.

10.1   The Supreme Court and Tax Equivalence

In a recent ruling by the United States Supreme Court, the issue of whether one tax is equivalent to another played a pivotal role in both the majority and the dissenting opinions. In *Oklahoma Tax Commission v. Jefferson Lines Inc.* (Case No. 93-1677), the Supreme Court ruled that an Oklahoma sales tax on the full value of tickets for interstate bus travel does not violate a constitutional ban on taxes detrimental to interstate commerce (Article 1, Section 10). In an earlier case in New York, *Central Greyhound Lines* v. *Mealey* (1948), the Supreme Court had ruled that a tax on interstate bus companies' receipts was unconstitutional by the interstate commerce clause.

In a dissenting opinion to the recent case, Justices Stephen Breyer and Sandra Day O'Connor argued that the tax on bus tickets and the tax on bus company receipts are "for all relevant purposes, identical"; therefore, if one is unconstitu-

tional so is the other. Writing for the majority, Justice Souter argued that the two taxes are not equivalent. According to Justice Souter, the New York tax was a form of income tax whereas the Oklahoma ticket tax was a "garden variety" sales tax. He argued that the New York tax was unconstitutional because many states could tax the same bus company receipts, causing multiple taxation, to the detriment of interstate commerce.

Critically analyze the following:

■ If the Jefferson Lines bus company received its revenue only from selling tickets in Oklahoma, would a tax on tickets be equivalent to a tax on bus company receipts?

■ How does the possibility that the bus company receives revenue from selling tickets in other states affect the equivalency of these taxes?

■ Was Justice Souter correct in calling a tax on bus company receipts an income tax?

Who "Pays" the Tax—The Buyer or the Seller?

In late 1996, Congress reinstated a 10% federal excise tax on airline tickets that it had let expire earlier. In the travel sections of newspapers, puzzled journalists reported that the price of airline tickets rose only about 4% after the tax was levied. Why didn't the increase in airline ticket prices fully reflect the tax? The answer is, as we have already seen, that an excise tax puts downward pressure on the prices received by the producers as well as increasing the price to consumers. In other words, the producers typically have to absorb part of a tax levied on their goods. In this case, the net fare received by airline companies fell by 6% as a result of the airline excise tax.

What determines how an excise tax is divided between a higher gross price to consumers and a lower net price to producers? In other words, who really "pays" the excise tax? Although this question is the main subject of Chapter 11, we will trespass on it briefly here. We have already seen that the effect of a tax on market prices and quantities does not depend on whether the tax is levied on the buyers or the sellers, so what does it depend on? Economists argue that it is the conditions in the market that determine how an excise tax is divided between higher gross prices to consumers and lower net prices to producers. For some goods, market conditions are such that all or most of an excise tax shows up as a higher consumer price; for other goods, some of an excise tax is absorbed by the producers, and consumers see a smaller increase in price.

In the competitive world of supply and demand, the market conditions that determine the effect on prices are summarized in terms of the relative slopes (or elasticities) of the supply and demand curves. Generally, the steeper the demand curve, the greater is the rise in the gross price to the consumer as a result of the tax. Alternatively, the steeper the supply curve, the greater is the fall in the net price that is received by producers.

Two special cases of the bagel market help us understand this result more clearly. In the first case, shown in Figure 10.7a, market conditions are such that the supply curve is horizontal (has a slope of zero). This would be the case if bagels are produced at a constant marginal cost. When the supply curve is horizontal, an excise tax on bagels causes the gross price to consumers to rise by the full amount of the tax. The reason is that a horizontal supply curve means producers are unwilling to produce bagels below their constant marginal cost $\bar{P}$. The constant marginal cost fixes the net price that producers must receive, so all of an excise tax must be passed

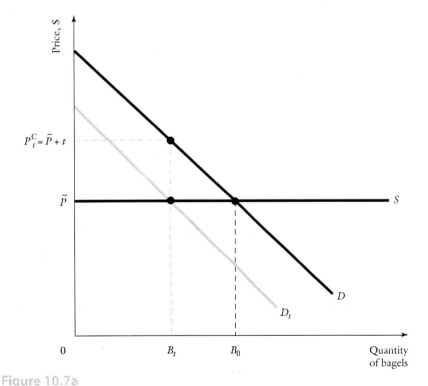

Figure 10.7a

Effect of an Excise Tax on Consumer and Producer Prices Under Alternative Supply Conditions

The impact of an excise tax on consumer and producer prices depends on the relative slopes of supply and demand. (a) When the supply curve is horizontal, all of the tax is reflected in a higher price to consumers.

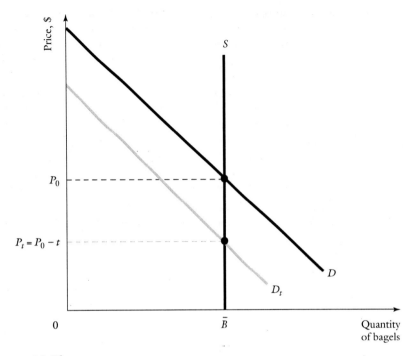

Figure 10.7b

(b) When the supply curve is vertical, all of the tax is reflected in a lower price to the producers.

on to consumers as a higher price. The equilibrium quantity of bagels sold decreases

until consumers are willing to pay the gross price of $P_t^C = \overline{P} + t$.

In the second case, shown in Figure 10.7b, the supply curve of bagels is vertical (it has an infinite slope) at quantity $\overline{B}$. This would be the case if producers have
a given quantity of bagels that they must sell regardless of price. Under these conditions, an excise tax on bagels causes the price to producers to fall by the full amount
of the tax, so the consumers' price is unchanged. At a given quantity, the gross price
consumers are willing to pay per bagel is fixed by the height of the demand curve,
so to sell $\overline{B}$ bagels the producers must absorb the whole tax. The consumer price
remains P_0 and the producers' price falls to $P_0 - t$.

Although we do not show it, the same analysis can be used to demonstrate that
the consumers' gross price rises by the full amount of the excise tax when the
demand curve is vertical. On the other hand, when the demand curve is horizontal the producers' net price falls by the full amount of the tax.[15]

---

[15]This is most easily shown by assuming that the tax is levied on the producers (and shifts the supply
curve) rather than being levied on the consumers. Because of tax equivalence, it does not matter whether
the tax is levied on the consumers or the producers. We are free to assume whatever is easiest for the
purpose of economic analysis.

For a general result, let d denote the absolute slope of the demand curve and s denote the slope of the supply curve. If the government levies an excise tax of t dollars per unit, the gross price to consumers rises by $\dfrac{d}{d+s}$ times t while the net price to producers falls by $\dfrac{s}{d+s}$ times t. Alternatively, let η denote the price elasticity of demand and ε the price elasticity of supply. The increase in the gross price to consumers is $\dfrac{\varepsilon}{\eta+\varepsilon}$ times the tax rate, and the decrease in the net price to producers is $\dfrac{\eta}{\eta+\varepsilon}$ times the tax rate.[16] For example, if the quantities demanded and supplied are equally sensitive to price, an excise tax would be divided evenly between an increase in the consumers' price and a decrease in the producers' price. If the quantity demanded is more (less) sensitive to price than the quantity supplied, the fall in the net producers' price absorbs a larger (smaller) fraction of tax.

Price-Setting Behavior and the Impact of a Tax

So far, market conditions have depended only on the slopes (or elasticities) of the supply and demand curves. Another market condition of interest is the power of the sellers to set prices, or noncompetitive behavior. In a competitive market, the sellers have no power to set the prices of their goods and prices are determined by the forces of supply and demand. How does an excise tax affect the market equilibrium when the sellers have price-setting power?

It is tempting to conclude that when sellers have price-setting power, they will pass on to the consumer a larger fraction, perhaps all, of the excise tax. After all, if sellers have the power to set the price, won't they pass the entire tax on to their customers? Surprisingly, the answer is "not necessarily." In fact, in some cases price-setting power leads to smaller increases in the consumers' price than would have occurred in a competitive market! This paradoxical conclusion is helpful in understanding the effects of taxes on markets, so we will discuss it at more length.

An extreme case of price-setting power is a market dominated by an unregulated, profit-maximizing monopolist. This is a market where a good or service with no close substitutes is sold by a single firm with no existing or potential competitors. Nor does the firm worry about government regulators' controlling its prices, as in the case of public utilities. Although rare, this type of market captures the

---

[16]The demand and supply curves can be expressed $P^C = a - d \cdot Q$ and $P = b + s \cdot Q$, respectively, where $P^C = P + t$. These can be solved for $P^C = a - d \cdot Q_0 + \dfrac{d}{d+s} \cdot t$, so $\dfrac{\Delta P^C}{\Delta t} = \dfrac{d}{d+s}$. The expression in terms of elasticities is derived using $\eta = -\dfrac{1}{d} \cdot \dfrac{P^C}{Q}$ and $\varepsilon = \dfrac{1}{s} \cdot \dfrac{P}{Q}$ at the point where $t = 0$.

extreme of price-setting power, so we can use it to study the implications of price-setting power on the effects of a tax. Since it does not matter whether the tax is levied on the producer or consumer, we assume that the tax is levied on the output of the monopolist.

Suppose a monopolist produces a good or service—say, telephone service—at constant marginal cost. In Figure 10.8, the quantity of telephone service (in minutes per month) is measured on the horizontal axis, the marginal cost curve is labeled MC, and the downward-sloping demand curve for the service by consumers is labeled *D*. For simplicity, we assume that the demand curve is linear and the marginal cost curve is horizontal. Because the monopolist has the entire market, it takes into account the fact that the demand curve slopes down and recognizes that the

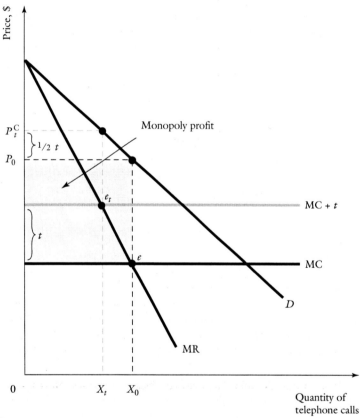

Figure 10.8

Effect of an Excise Tax on a Monopoly Market
Without taxes, a monopolist maximizes profit at output X_0, where marginal revenue (MR) equals marginal cost (MC). An excise tax raises the marginal cost to MC + *t*, and the monopolist moves along its marginal revenue curve to point e_t. Because the marginal revenue curve is twice as steep as the demand curve, the price charged by the monopolist increases by exactly half of the tax rate. As we saw in Figure 10.7a, the consumers' price rises by the full amount of the tax in a competitive industry with a horizontal supply curve.

more it sells, the lower the price it receives. To determine what quantity to sell, and what price to set, the monopolist considers the marginal revenue of output. The firm's marginal revenue is the increase in its total receipts (price times quantity) when it sells an extra unit of output. Because the firm can sell an extra unit of output only by lowering its price on all units sold, the marginal revenue is less than price. The marginal revenue curve is labeled MR in Figure 10.8. When the demand curve is linear, the marginal revenue curve is also linear and downward-sloping. Furthermore, it is exactly twice as steep as the demand curve.[17]

The monopolist maximizes profit by producing where the marginal revenue curve intersects the marginal cost curve at point e in Figure 10.8. At this point, the monopolist produces X_0 units and sets the consumers' price at P_0 per unit. This allows the firm to earn a maximum profit equal to P_0 minus MC times output X_0, which is equal to the area of the shaded rectangle in Figure 10.8.

When the government levies an excise tax on the monopolist of t cents per minute on every telephone call, the firm treats the tax as a rise in its marginal cost. The marginal cost plus the tax is shown in Figure 10.8 by the horizontal line labeled MC + t. After the tax is imposed, the producer maximizes profit by producing where MC + t is equal to marginal revenue at point e_t. Thus it produces output X_t and sets the price to consumers at P_t^C.

From Figure 10.8 we see that a producer with price-setting power reduces output when an excise tax is levied, just as a competitive producer does. The monopolist reduces output until marginal revenue rises by the tax per unit t. Since the marginal revenue curve is twice as steep as the demand curve, and marginal cost is constant, the price to the consumer rises by exactly half the tax rate. In other words, despite its price-setting power, the monopolist does not pass on all of the tax to the consumers. Even stranger, the monopolist increases the consumers' price by less than a competitive industry would have increased price. Since marginal cost is constant, the supply curve of a competitive industry (created, say, if a multiplant monopolist is broken up into separate firms by a successful antitrust suit) is horizontal. We saw earlier that when the supply curve is horizontal, the consumers' price increases by the full amount of the tax.[18]

The reason this result is paradoxical is that the monopolist could increase the consumers' price by the full tax if it wanted to, but it chooses not to do so. We should remember that the objective of the monopolist is *not* to pass on the tax; it is to maximize profit. The firm will pass on a tax only if doing so maximizes profit. However, the monopolist knows that when it raises the consumers' price, it sells less output. Because the firm receives a monopoly markup on each unit it sells, it does not want output to fall too much. Competitive producers receive no monopoly markup, so they do not have such a concern.

---

[17]An exact derivation of this result can be found in most microeconomics textbooks. For example, see Jeffery M. Perloff, *Microeconomics*, 2nd ed., 2001, pp. 345–7.

[18]The result that a monopolist raises the price by less than a competitive industry would raise it is not general. If the demand curve is nonlinear, we can find some forms where the monopolist raises its price by more than a competitive industry would.

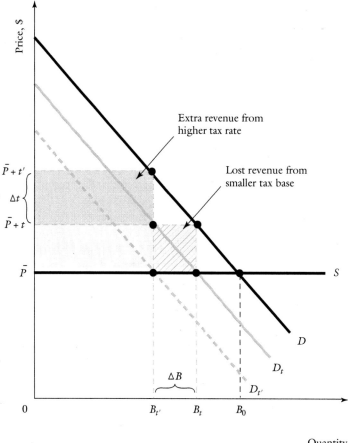

Figure 10.9

Effect of an Increase in Excise Tax Rate on Amount of Revenue Collected

An existing excise tax on bagels is increased from rate t to t'. The increase causes the quantity of bagels consumed to fall from B_t to $B_{t'}$, losing revenue equal to the crosshatched area. On the other hand, the government taxes the remaining $B_{t'}$ bagels at a higher rate, gaining revenue equal to the dark-shaded rectangle. At high tax rates, the crosshatched area is greater than the area of the dark rectangle, so an increase in an already high tax rate causes revenue to fall.

The Relationship Between Tax Rates and Tax Revenues

In Figure 10.9, the tax revenue collected by the excise tax of t per bagel is equal to the area of the lightly shaded rectangle. The height of this rectangle is the tax rate in dollars per bagel, and the width is the equilibrium quantity of bagels B_t. Since the area of a rectangle is equal to its height times its width, this area is equal to the tax revenue collected.

Governments are particularly interested in the amount of revenue that they receive from levying a tax. When they need more revenue, they typically increase

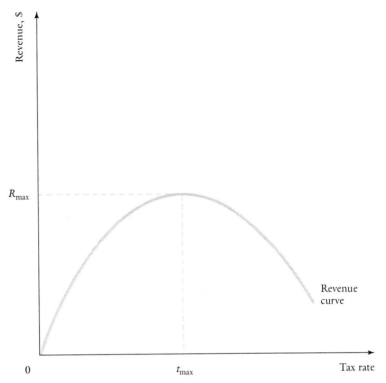

Figure 10.10

Revenue Curve

Given the argument in Figure 10.9, the relationship between the excise tax rate and the amount of revenue collected is given by the revenue curve plotting the tax rate on the horizontal axis against tax revenue on the vertical axis. This curve increases at low tax rates but decreases at tax rates above the revenue-maximizing tax rate t_{max}.

the tax rate. What happens to the amount of tax revenue collected when the government increases the tax rate on bagels to t'? Normally we expect tax revenue to increase, and if the tax rate is low enough to begin with, this will be the case. However, as the tax rate on bagels is successively raised, a form of diminishing returns sets in. The increase in revenue from subsequent increases in the tax rate become smaller and smaller, and eventually a tax rate is reached at which further increases in the tax rate actually reduce the tax revenue collected.

The relationship between the excise tax rate levied on bagels and the revenue collected by the tax is shown by the **revenue curve** in Figure 10.10. The tax rate in dollars per bagel is measured on the horizontal axis and the tax revenue in dollars is measured on the vertical axis. When the tax rate is zero, an increase in the tax rate increases tax revenue, so the revenue curve is positively sloped at the origin. However, as the tax rate is raised further, revenue increases at a decreasing rate (the revenue curve flattens out). At some critical tax rate t_{max}, the tax revenue

10.2   The Economics of Taxing Tobacco[1]

In January 2000, the wholesale price of cigarettes was $2.35 per pack (standard premium brand), up 60% from mid-1998. The sharp rise in wholesale cigarette prices is due mainly to increases in the federal tobacco excise tax and settlement charges from the agreement between the tobacco companies and the states. The federal excise tax rose 42%, from $.24 to $.34 per pack, in 2000 and is scheduled to rise to $.39 in 2002. In addition, cigarette manufacturers must pay about $10 billion a year (about $.44 per pack at 1999 consumption rates) in settlement charges. States are increasing their excise taxes as well, with some states taxing cigarettes over $1 per pack. As of January 2000, the median state levied an excise tax of $.34 per pack. However, most of the larger states have high excise tax rates so the average is closer to $.40 a pack, up about 33% from $.30 in 1998. In fiscal year 1997–1998, all governments combined collected about $12 billion from excise taxes on cigarettes. This does not count state receipts from the settlement charges.

In 1998, annual cigarette consumption in the United States was about 23 billion packs (115 packs per resident over age 19), down 8% from 1991. No doubt, the decline in cigarette consumption is caused by several things besides the rise in the price of cigarettes, including an increased perception of health risk and restrictions on advertising and smoking in public places. What will be the impact of the sharp rise in the price of cigarettes starting in 1998? Economists have estimated that the demand for cigarettes is quite price inelastic—around .4 in the short run.[2] This is expected, given the addictive properties of nicotine. It implies that cigarette

consumption would fall about 4% for every 10% rise in price. The price elasticity is higher for some groups of people (for example, teenagers are more sensitive to price) and in the long run. The long-run price elasticity, estimated at around .8, takes into account that price affects whether people start smoking. The fact that cigarette consumption falls as price increases implies that tax revenue will not increase as much as the increase in excise tax rates.

Critically analyze the following:

- Assuming a price elasticity of .4, how much will cigarette consumption decline if the recent tax hikes and settlement charges raised the average price of cigarettes 50% from 1998 to 2000? What is the predicted level of consumption in 2000?

- What is the predicted impact on combined government excise tax revenue (not counting receipts from settlement charges), given the combined federal and average excise tax rate rose from $.53 in 1998 to nearly $.75 per pack in 2000?

- Ignoring growth in population, what is the predicted long-run impact on excise tax revenue if the price elasticity is .8? Does this mean that the government has raised cigarette excise tax rates to more than the revenue-maximizing rate?

1The information in this case is based on data drawn mainly from the Department of Agriculture http://www.econ.ag.gov/Briefing/tobacco/. State excise tax rates are found on the Federation of Tax Administrators site at http://www.taxadmin.org/fta/rate/ cigarett.html. 2These estimates are drawn from Becker et al., American Economic Review, 1994.

is the greatest amount possible, R_{max}. Any further increase in the tax rate causes the amount of revenue to fall. This is shown by the negatively sloped segment of the revenue curve.

Why do increases in the tax rate eventually cause decreases in the tax revenue collected? To answer this, return to Figure 10.9, in which an excise tax on bagels initially at rate t is increased to a higher rate t'. To simplify the analysis, we assume that the supply curve of bagels is horizontal at $\bar{P}$, and the demand curve for bagels is linear. The demand curve facing the firms after the tax rate is increased is labeled $D_{t'}$ and the equilibrium quantity of bagels falls from B_t to $B_{t'}$ as a result of the increase.

The change in tax revenue from an increase in the tax rate can be divided into two components. First, the increase in the tax rate causes the equilibrium quantity of bagels to fall from B_t to $B_{t'}$. Since bagels were already taxed, the government loses the tax on the bagels no longer purchased because of the higher tax rate. For each bagel not purchased the government loses t dollars of revenue, so the higher the tax rate to begin with, the greater the loss in revenue from this component. The revenue loss component is shown by the crosshatched area of the initial tax revenue rectangle in Figure 10.9. The area is equal to the initial tax rate t times the decrease in bagel consumption (B_t minus $B_{t'}$) resulting from the tax increase.

The second component is a revenue gain. The government receives a higher tax rate t' on the bagels that are still consumed after the tax rate is increased. This revenue gain component is equal to the area of the darkshaded rectangle in Figure 10.9, or the increase in the tax rate (t' minus t) times the new equilibrium quantity of bagels $B_{t'}$. When the tax rate is high to begin with, $B_{t'}$ is smaller, so the gain in tax revenue from this component is smaller at higher tax rates.

Whether the revenue of the government increases or decreases as a result of an increase in the tax rate depends on whether the revenue gain component is larger or smaller in magnitude than the revenue loss component. When the base tax rate (the tax rate before the increase) is low, the revenue gain component is larger and the revenue loss component is smaller, so the revenue curve is positively sloped. As the base tax rate increases, the revenue gain component grows smaller and the revenue loss component grows larger, so the revenue curve becomes flatter. At $t_{\max}$ in Figure 10.10, the revenue gain and loss components are equal in magnitude, so the revenue curve is flat and the government collects the maximum possible revenue. If the tax rate is increased further, revenue will decline.[19]

CONCLUSION AND SUMMARY

Governments collect tax revenue by levying taxes on economic activities, especially activities taking place in markets. In this chapter we have examined how taxes affect the allocation of resources as determined by market forces. In Chapter 11, we apply the principles learned in the present chapter to the question of tax incidence, or the question of who bears the tax burden. In Chapter 12, we use the principles to develop a normative theory for evaluating tax policy.

■ A lump-sum tax is a tax of a fixed amount levied on persons regardless of their income or spending. Such a tax is hypothetical, since most taxes are imposed on market activities.

---

[19]The revenue gain component (dark-shaded rectangle in Figure 10.9) is equal to $B_t \cdot \Delta t$ and the revenue loss component (crosshatched rectangle) is equal to $-t \cdot \Delta B$. At $t_{\max}$, the two components are equal, and we can solve the resulting equation for $\dfrac{t_{\max}}{P_t} = \dfrac{1}{\eta}$ where η is the price elasticity of bagel demand.

- Taxes can be classified according to whether they are levied on households or businesses, or according to the economic activities that are taxed. Economists believe that the second classification is more useful.

- An excise tax raises the price of the taxed good to consumers, causing them to decrease their consumption. The decrease in consumption of the taxed good results from the fact that the consumer cannot afford to consume as much (the income effect), and from substitution of untaxed goods owing to the change in relative prices (the substitution effect).

- An excise tax decreases the equilibrium quantity bought and sold in the market. The gross price to consumers increases by some fraction of the tax, and the net price received by producers falls by the remaining fraction.

- The apportionment of the tax between price changes to consumers and producers depends on the relative slopes or elasticities of the market supply and demand curves, not on whether the tax is legally imposed on the buyers or the sellers. A tax imposed on the buyer is, in fact, equivalent to a tax imposed on the seller.

- As a tax rate increases, the tax revenue collected increases at a decreasing rate. Above a critical tax rate, the revenue falls for further increases in the tax rate. The relationship between the tax rate and the revenue collected is called the revenue curve.

QUESTIONS FOR DISCUSSION AND REVIEW

1. Which of the following is a lump-sum tax?
   a. Tax on your weight
   b. Tax on your age

2. Which of the following fees charged by the government is best described as a "tax"?
   a. Parking meter fee
   b. Entrance fee at a national park
   c. Driver's license fee

3. Gifts and inheritances from parents to their children are subject to a federal tax. Both are taxed at the same rate, which, for simplicity, we assume is 50%. Suppose the parents have $1.5 million to give. If the parents give their children $1 million while they are alive (a gift), they pay tax of $500,000. If, instead, they leave the

$1.5 million as a bequest to their children, they pay $750,000 tax and the children receive $750,000. The tax rate is 50% in both cases, but the children receive more if the parents make a gift rather than a bequest. Why? (Hint: What is the difference between a tax-exclusive and tax-inclusive tax base?)

4. Suppose a consumer buys only bread and butter and buys one pound of butter with every loaf of bread, no more or less (his or her indifference curves are right angles). Show that an excise tax on bread and a lump-sum tax that collects the same revenue are equivalent taxes for this consumer.

5. A consumer with $2000 monthly income buys 200 gallons of gasoline each month

at $2 a gallon. The price of gasoline includes an excise tax of $.50 per gallon. The price elasticity of gasoline for this consumer is −.4 and the income elasticity is 1. How much gasoline tax does this consumer pay each month? Suppose the government abolished the excise tax and levied a lump-sum tax on the consumer to collect the same revenue. How many gallons of gasoline would he or she consume? (Assume the supply curve of gasoline is horizontal in this question.)

6. Explain the difference between the income effect and the substitution effect of an excise tax on recordings on compact discs. Which effect depends on the availability of the same recordings on untaxed tape cassettes? Which effect depends on whether compact discs are a necessity or a luxury for consumers?

7. A federal excise tax known as the "gas guzzler tax" is levied on the manufacturers (and importers) of cars with low fuel economy. The tax is $1000 on cars that get between 21.5 and 22.5 miles per gallon, $1300 on cars that get between 20.5 and 21.5 mpg, etc., all the way up to $7700 on cars getting less than 12.5 mpg.

   a. Would it make a difference if the tax were levied on the buyers of gas-guzzling cars rather than the manufacturers? Why or why not?

   b. Suppose that fuel consumption is directly proportional to the size of a car. How would this tax affect the prices and average sizes of cars sold in America?

8. We mentioned that airline fares increased about 4% when Congress reimposed the 10% federal excise tax on airfares. Assuming that the airline industry is competitive, what does this imply about the slope of the demand curve for airline tickets relative to the slope of the supply curve?

9. Suppose that in question 8, the airline companies were to collude and set airfares as a monopoly. Would you expect a larger fraction of the 10% federal excise tax to be reflected in higher ticket prices? Why or why not?

10. The algebraic expression for a linear demand curve is $P^C = a - d \cdot Q$ where P^C is the price to the consumer and d is the slope of the demand curve. The expression for the supply curve is $P^F = b + s \cdot Q$ where P^F is the price to the firm and s is the slope of the supply curve. Q is the market quantity. In equilibrium, $P^C = P^F + t$. Suppose a is 6, d is 0.1, b is 0, and s is 0.05. Determine the impact of an excise tax of $1.50 per unit on the equilibrium quantity and prices paid by consumers and received by the firms.

11. Suppose the government is considering taxing video rentals. Video rentals are currently untaxed, and consumers rent 10 billion videos a year. They would reduce the quantity of rentals by 1 billion for each dollar of excise tax that the government levies per video rental. Construct a table showing the quantity of video rentals and the amount of tax revenue the government collects at each of the following tax rates per video: $1, $2, $3, $4, $5, and $6. At which of these tax rates does the government maximize its revenue from the tax?

12. Internet Exercise. Many consumers are bewildered by the many taxes and charges they see on their phone bills, including the Universal Service Charge (USC) on long-distance services. Long-distance companies impose the USC, sometimes dubbed the "Gore tax," to pass on charges levied on them to subsidize Internet connections for schools under a program called e-rate. Many people claim the USC is unconstitutional because it is a tax and was never

authorized by Congress (see, for example, the National Taxpayers Union Gore Tax site http://www.goretax.com/news/admin.html). Others claim the USC is a charge and not a tax (see, for example, the National PTA site http://www.pta.org/programs/0717action.htm). Research this topic on the Internet and use the concepts in this chapter to decide whether or not the USC is a tax.

SELECTED REFERENCES

The idea that an excise tax is reflected in consumers' or producers' prices depending on the relative slopes of supply and demand dates back to Fleeming Jenkin, 1887.

Gary Becker, Michael Grossman, and Kevin Murphy examine the effect of price on smoking in their paper "An Empirical Analysis of Cigarette Addiction," 1994.

USEFUL INTERNET SITES

Two sites with numerous links to useful tax information on the Internet are the homepage of teh National Tax Association at http://www.ntanet.org/ and the Tax and accounting Sites Directory at http://www.taxsites.com/.

For a Lighter touch, visit Dr. Quiggly's Museum of Tax Oddities at http://www.progress.org/banneker/museum.html or Tax analysts' Tax History Museum at http://www.ax.org/museum/default.htm.

11

Tax Incidence: Who Bears the Tax Burden?

Hotel and real estate billionaire Leona Helmsley, who was sent to prison in 1993 for evading taxes, allegedly claimed that "only the little people pay taxes." Helmsley was making a statement about tax incidence, although she was wrong, as we will see. Tax incidence describes who pays, or more correctly who bears the burden of, the taxes levied by the government. People are intensely interested in how tax burdens vary for different families and how the distribution of the tax burden is affected by changes in the tax system. As the presidential candidates campaigned in early 2000, they all seemed to have a plan to cut taxes. In debating the different proposals, one question seemed to dominate all others in deciding which is best—Who gets the biggest tax cuts? Most importantly, how are low-income families affected relative to high-income families? Economists are interested in other questions about tax incidence, too. For instance, how is the tax burden distributed across families living in different parts of the country? How do tax burdens on younger generations (or generations yet to be born) compare with those on older generations?

Questions such as these concern what economists call the incidence of a tax. **Tax incidence** describes how the burden of a tax is distributed across the population. In addition to being important, questions about tax incidence are among the most difficult to answer. One reason is the fact that the individual or firm who *pays* the tax to the government does not necessarily *bear the burden* of the tax. To use a trivial example, the chief financial officer of a corporation may sign the check to the IRS for corporation income taxes, but he or she does not bear the burden of the tax. Likewise, the property tax on an apartment building may be borne, in the form of higher rents, by the people renting the apartment rather than by the owner who pays the tax to the city.

This chapter uses economic analysis to determine who bears the burden of a tax. We concentrate here on general principles of tax incidence and illustrate them with a few examples. The incidence of particular taxes is discussed in later chapters.

DIFFERENT MEASURES OF TAX INCIDENCE

Analyzing the incidence of a tax is like peeling an onion: it has many layers and causes lots of tears. The complexity of the problem, along with the political importance of the findings, means that there is lots of room for disagreement. In part, the disagreement about tax incidence reflects the different ways in which tax incidence can be measured. We begin there.

Analysis of Statutory Versus Economic Incidence

The **statutory incidence** of a tax describes its incidence solely in terms of the taxes actually paid by different groups. If no taxes are paid, no tax burden is incurred. Economists are primarily interested in the economic incidence of a tax. **Economic incidence** takes into account not only the taxes paid by different groups in the economy, but also the effect on real incomes caused by changes in wages and prices when the tax is levied. A group's real income is its money income adjusted for changes in the cost of living.

Economic incidence differs from statutory incidence because of tax shifting. **Tax shifting** describes changes in rewards and prices that reduce the burden of the people paying the tax and increase the burden on others. For instance, if apartment rents increase when property taxes are increased for apartment owners, we would say that the property tax burden has been shifted (at least partly) from the owners to the tenants.

Economic incidence is more difficult to analyze than statutory incidence because in order to determine whether a tax is shifted we need an economic theory of how prices and rewards are affected by the tax. The analysis may also require assumptions about unknown parameters, such as the exact price elasticity of the demand for apartment rentals. Whether an economist does a statutory or an economic incidence study of a tax depends on the resources available and the extent to which tax shifting is anticipated.

In many studies, arbitrary assumptions are made about tax shifting. For instance, one study of the incidence of the property tax simply assumed that half of the tax is borne by the property owners and half is borne by the tenants. Most studies assume that the burden of the personal income tax is not shifted, although in principle nothing prevents this tax from being shifted. On the other hand, the corporation income tax burden is certainly shifted, since corporate financial officers do not bear the burden of the corporate tax.[1] Economic models are used to determine how much of the corporate tax burden is shifted to the firms' shareholders, consumers, or employees. It is also possible that the burden is shifted to people not directly associated with the corporation.

Analysis of Absolute and Differential Incidence

To identify the distribution of a tax burden, we need to specify an alternative to the tax. To conclude, for example, that the owners of capital bear the burden of the corporate income tax begs the question "Compared with what?": compared with no tax at all, or compared with some other tax? **Absolute tax incidence** determines the incidence of a tax assuming that no other tax would be levied in its absence.

---

[1] Unless their wages are reduced by it.

The assumption is that without the tax the government collects less revenue, so various groups in the economy bear smaller tax burdens. **Differential tax incidence** determines the incidence of a tax on the assumption that a benchmark alternative tax is levied in its place. The alternative tax may be hypothetical, such as a lump-sum tax, or an increase in an existing tax. Differential tax incidence is the difference between the absolute incidence of a tax and the absolute incidence of the benchmark tax.

Economists prefer differential to absolute incidence because this approach allows us to analyze the burden of a tax separately from how the revenue is spent. What does it mean to say that the absolute incidence of (say) the corporate income tax is on capital owners? If the government does not levy another tax to replace the corporate tax, it has less revenue to spend. To determine the absolute incidence on different groups, we would also have to consider how each group is affected by the reduced government spending. Most tax revenue goes into a general fund, so it is not usually possible to determine what programs would be cut if the government had less revenue. Without such information, the change in the burden on different groups cannot be established. With differential incidence we do not have this problem, because the same amount of revenue is collected by the benchmark tax.

Tax incidence is measured in other ways as well. Later in this chapter, we discuss the difference between annual incidence and lifetime incidence, partial and general equilibrium incidence, and other ways of measuring tax incidence. Keep in mind that no method is superior in all respects to others. Some methods measure incidence more accurately in principle, but they are more difficult to perform or subject to greater uncertainty. Knowing the best way to measure tax incidence in any given situation requires experience and judgment.

THE PEOPLE WHO BEAR THE TAX BURDEN

Here is a truism that is useful to remember when addressing any question of tax incidence: *Only people—not goods or organizations—can bear the burden of a tax.* Sometimes you hear talk about a "need for business to pay its fair share of taxes." While businesses can certainly pay taxes, they do not bear the burden of the taxes they pay. A business is merely an organization. Ultimately it is people—perhaps the owners of the businesses, the customers, or the employees—who bear the burden of taxes, whether those taxes are paid by people or businesses. A good tax incidence study should start by looking at tax burdens on people.

Policy officials and economists are not interested in the incidence of a tax on a particular person; rather, they examine tax burdens on identifiable groups of people. People are grouped according to some relevant characteristic such as their income, where they live, or how old they are. For example, reductions in capital gains tax rates have been criticized as shifting the tax burden from richer to middle-income taxpayers. Similarly, in 1993 when President Clinton proposed an increase in the gasoline tax, some economists claimed it would put a heavier burden on people who live in certain parts of the country. Debate continues about whether increases in Social Security taxes have put a heavier burden on younger workers.

Tax Incidence by Income Group

Many people believe that as a matter of equity, people should bear taxes in accordance with their ability to pay the taxes. The ability to pay is commonly measured by income, so most incidence analysis focuses on incidence by income group. The distribution of a tax burden across people grouped according to their incomes is called the **income incidence** of the tax. To study income incidence, people are ranked by their income, and the resulting distribution is known as the size distribution of income. The main question we usually ask about the income incidence of a tax is whether it is progressive or regressive. The statutory incidence of a tax is described as **progressive** if the tax paid rises *relative to income* as income rises; the incidence is described as **regressive** if the tax paid falls relative to income as income rises. If the tax burden remains constant relative to income as income changes, the tax has **proportional** incidence.

Note that progressivity means more than simply, "People with more income pay more taxes." It means that people with more income pay *a higher percentage of their income in taxes*. If one taxpayer has twice the income of another, a tax is progressive only if the first pays more than twice as much tax as the second. If the first taxpayer pays less than twice as much in tax, the tax is regressive even if he or she pays more dollars of tax.

The income incidence of taxation can be expressed in two ways. The first, shown in Table 11.1, calculates the average tax rate (ATR) for different income groups. The second, shown in Table 11.2, compares the share of total tax payments paid (or borne) by different income groups with their respective shares of total income.

Table 11.1 reports the federal average tax rates for 1999 by income quintile as estimated by the Congressional Budget Office (CBO). To construct this table, the CBO first ranks all families according to their Adjusted Family Income (AFI). As explained in Chapter 7, a family's AFI is equal to its income divided by the Official Poverty Threshold (OPT) for a family of the same size. Dividing by the OPT standardizes family income according to family size. After ranking families from those with the lowest AFI to those with the highest, the families are divided into equal size groups. In Tables 11.1 and 11.2, each group contains 20% of the families and is called a **quintile.** The first (or lowest) quintile contains the 20% of families hav-

Table 11.1 **Average Federal Tax Rate (Tax as a Percent of Income) by Adjusted Family Income Quintile (1999)**

Federal Tax	Bottom 20%	Second 20%	Middle 20%	Fourth 20%	Top 20%	Top 5%	Top 1%	All
Individual income tax	−6.8%	.9%	5.4%	8.4%	16.1%	19.6%	22.2%	11.1%
Social insurance (FICA) tax	7.9	10	10.8	11.4	7.7	5	2.7	9.2
Corporate income tax	.5	1	1.3	1.3	4.6	6.8	9.2	3
Excise taxes	2.9	1.8	1.3	1.1	.6	.4	.3	1
All federal taxes	4.6	13.7	18.9	22.2	29.1	31.8	34.4	24.2

Source: Congressional Budget Office Memorandum, *Estimates of Federal Tax Liabilities for Individuals and Families by Income Category and Family Type for 1995 and 1999*, May 1998, Table A.3, p. 40. The entire document can be downloaded from the CBO web site at http://www.cbo.gov.

Table 11.2   Percent of Federal Taxes Borne by Adjusted Family Income Quintile (1999)

Federal Tax	Bottom 20%	Second 20%	Middle 20%	Fourth 20%	Top 20%	Top 5%	Top 1%	All*
Individual income tax	−2%	1%	7%	16%	79%	50%	29%	100%
Social insurance (FICA) tax	3	9	16	26	46	15	4	100
Corporate income tax	1	3	6	9	81	64	44	100
Excise taxes	10	15	18	22	33	11	5	100
All federal taxes	1	5	11	19	65	37	21	100
Pre-tax income	3	9	14	21	54	28	15	100

*Figures may not sum to 100% due to rounding.
Source: Congressional Budget Office Memorandum, *Estimates of Federal Tax Liabilities for Individuals and Families by Income Category and Family Type for 1995 and 1999*, May 1998, Table A.3, p. 41. The entire document can be downloaded from the CBO web site at http://www.cbo.gov.

ing the lowest AFI. A family of four persons was in the lowest quintile in 1999 if its pre-tax income was less than $22,900. The fifth (or highest) quintile contains the 20% having the highest AFI. A family of four persons was in the fifth quintile if its pre-tax income was greater than $101,200. Also shown are the ATRs for the top 5% (income greater than $190,700 for a family of four) and the top 1% (income greater than $450,800 for a family of four) of families.

The CBO calculates the ATR for each quintile by dividing taxes paid by families in the quintile by the total pre-tax income they receive. Table 11.1 shows the ATRs for the federal individual income tax, social insurance (FICA) tax, corporate income tax, excise taxes, and for all federal taxes combined. The CBO makes several assumptions in determining the income incidence of the different taxes. It assumes (1) individual income taxes are borne by the taxpayer, (2) both the employer and employee shares of social insurance taxes are borne by the employee, (3) the corporate income tax is borne by the shareholders of the corporation, and (4) excise taxes are borne by the consumers of the taxed goods.

We can analyze the income incidence of the different federal taxes by comparing the ATRs for the different income quintiles. For example, we see that the individual income tax has a progressive incidence because the ATR is higher for higher-income quintiles. In 1999, the lowest quintile had an ATR of −6.8% for the individual income tax, whereas the highest quintile had an ATR of 16.1%. The ATR for all quintiles combined is 11.1%. The ATR is negative for the lowest quintile because of the refundable **Earned Income Tax Credit** (discussed in Chapter 13), which allows tax refunds to families with low earned incomes in excess of the taxes they owe. The corporation income tax is also progressive, with ATR in the highest quintile equal to 4.6% as compared with .5% for the lowest quintile. The social insurance tax is progressive over the lowest four quintiles, but the ATR drops sharply in the highest quintile. This is because the Social Security part of the tax is cut off above a certain earnings level.[2]

---

[2]Since the Social Security tax is a flat rate up to the earnings cutoff, you may wonder why the ATR rises over the first four quintiles. The reason is the Social Security tax is paid on earnings only. The lower quintiles get a significant fraction of their income from transfers not subject to the tax.

Of the four main federal taxes in Table 11.1, only the federal excise taxes are regressive. As we can see, the ATR falls as income rises, with the ATR equal to 2.9% in the lowest quintile and .6% in the highest. Excise taxes are regressive because the amount of tax paid (or borne) by a family depends on the amount it spends on the taxed goods. High-income families tend to spend a smaller fraction of their pre-tax income than low-income families overall, so the excise tax is regressive. This is explained further later in the chapter.

Although excise taxes are regressive, they are not a large component of federal revenue; thus the income incidence of all federal taxes combined is progressive, but not as progressive as the individual income tax or corporate income tax. For all federal taxes, the ATR is 4.6% for the lowest quintile rising to 29.1% for the highest. The ATR for all quintiles combined is 24.2% when all federal taxes are included.

The incidence of federal taxes is presented in a different way in Table 11.2. This table reports the fraction of the total revenue collected by each tax paid (or borne) by the families in each quintile. For example, in 1999 the federal government collected $1800 billion in tax revenue. Table 11.2 shows the families in the highest income quintile (20% of all families) paid 65% of the all federal taxes. In fact, a mere 5% of all families (those with the highest incomes) paid (or bore the burden of) 37% of all federal taxes.

Table 11.2 reveals some interesting information. First, note that the 20% of families with the highest incomes bore the largest share of each federal tax and the 20% of families with the lowest incomes bore the lowest share. Second, the highest quintile's share of the individual and corporate income taxes is about 80%, compared with a share of less than 1% for the lowest quintile. Third, the largest share of excise tax revenue is borne by the families in the highest quintile even though these taxes are regressive. This is because high-income families spend more on these goods even though it is a smaller fraction of their income.

Whether a tax is progressive or regressive can be determined in Table 11.2 by comparing the share of tax paid with the share of pre-tax income received by the families in each quintile. The last row of the table shows that the families in the bottom quintile received just 3% of all pre-tax income whereas the families in the top quintile received 54%. Under a proportional tax, the bottom quintile would bear 3% of the tax and the top would bear 54%. If a tax is progressive, the top quintile bears a larger fraction of the tax than the share of income it receives, and vice versa for the lower income quintiles.

Tax Incidence by Other Household Groupings

While the income incidence of taxation is by far the most important, we are also interested in how the tax burden is distributed across households grouped in other ways, such as geographic location and age.

REGIONAL INCIDENCE.   When households are grouped according to where they live, we describe the distribution of the tax burden as its **regional incidence.** The regional incidence of the income tax, for example, would find that families living in high-income states have higher ATRs than families living in low-income states because of the graduated income tax rate structure (see Chapter 13). Of particular concern to the founders of the Constitution was the regional incidence of excise taxes, which were a major source of government revenue at the time the Constitution was written. The Constitution requires that import duties and excise taxes levied by the federal government be uniform (that is, levied at the same rate) throughout the nation. Nonetheless, different excise taxes have varying regional incidence because of differences in spending on taxed goods from region to region.

For example, the regional incidence of excise taxes on fuel and energy is a concern whenever changes in these taxes are contemplated. People in the West and South bear a larger fraction of the gasoline excise tax because they drive more, and people living in the Northeast would bear a larger fraction of excise taxes on natural gas and fuel oil because their winters are colder. Similarly, people in the South bear more of an excise tax on electricity because they use more air conditioning.

GENERATIONAL INCIDENCE.   Taxes may impose different burdens on people of different ages even though the tax rate is the same for everyone. For example, a tax on interest and dividends places a larger burden on older, retired taxpayers than does a tax on earnings, because most of their earnings are low and many retirees live off of their investment income. Similarly, an excise tax on motor homes has an older incidence than, say, a tax on mountain bikes.

Although the burden of a tax may vary by age, a more relevant issue is the incidence of a tax across people of different generations—the **generational incidence** of the tax. A person's generation is defined by birth date. To determine the generational incidence of a tax, it is necessary to consider the taxes that must be paid over a person's lifetime. Even if a certain tax imposes a heavier burden on young people than old people in a particular year, it may treat all generations the same if the present old people paid higher taxes when they were young and the present young people will pay lower taxes when they are old. In other words, to understand generational incidence, we must first measure the effect of a tax over each generation's lifetime.

The **lifetime burden** of a tax on a person or group of people is equal to the present value of taxes paid over the lifetime, which is the sum of the discounted values of the future annual tax burdens.[3] Discounting is necessary because taxes paid later in a person's life cause a smaller burden per dollar than taxes paid earlier in life. The reason is that a taxpayer could have invested taxes paid earlier in life and earned interest on the balance.

Generational incidence measures the distribution of lifetime tax burdens across different generations. Again, these tax burdens are typically compared with the taxpayer's ability to pay the taxes. Just as we measure the lifetime burden of a tax, we also must measure a lifetime ability to pay the tax. One such measure is the taxpayer's lifetime income, which is the present value of income earned over a lifetime.

Because of the need to measure lifetime taxes and incomes, calculating the generational incidence of taxation is a difficult job. In the past 15 years or so, studying

---

[3]Discounting future values to find present values is discussed in Chapter 6 in the context of benefit-cost analysis. The procedure for discounting is the same in lifetime incidence, except that future values are discounted using market interest rates rather than a public sector discount rate.

generational incidence has become a major area of research for public finance economists. One reason for this interest is the emergence of large and persistent federal budget deficits, which many people believe shift the burden of taxes to future generations. The effect of deficits on generational incidence is considered in Chapter 16. Another federal program that has a large impact on the generational distribution of the tax burden is Social Security. The incidence of Social Security across generations was discussed in Chapter 9.

To measure generational incidence, a technique called generational accounting was developed by Alan Auerbach of the University of California, Berkeley, Jagadeesh Gokhale of the Federal Reserve Bank of Cleveland, and Laurence Kotlikoff of Boston University. **Generational accounting** calculates the expected net lifetime tax burden for the remainder of a taxpayer's life according to age and sex. The *net* burden is the present value of taxes *less transfers* received over the person's life. The future tax and transfers are based on projections of the population structure and government fiscal policies. These future payments and receipts are discounted using an appropriate interest rate.

Lifetime net tax rates for selected generations, calculated using generational accounting, are shown in Table 11.3. The second column reports the present value of lifetime gross tax payments as a percentage of lifetime income. The third column is lifetime transfers expressed as a percentage of lifetime income, and the fourth is the difference or net tax rate. The table shows that the lifetime net tax rate is higher for younger generations. This is not surprising, since government spending and taxes have risen over the course of this century and younger taxpayers have the bulk of their working (and taxpaying) years ahead of them.

One important conclusion from generational accounting is that "future generations" face very high net lifetime tax rates. Future generations include anyone born after 1995, the year for which the study was done. According to Table 11.3, the lifetime net tax rate on future generations is almost twice as high as that on current generations. This high number is based on the assumption that tax rates must rise or transfers must fall drastically in the future, because the current fiscal policy

Table 11.3   Lifetime Tax and Transfer Rates Based on Generational Accounting

Year of Birth	Percent of Lifetime Income		
	Gross Tax Rate	Transfer Rate	Net Tax Rate
1900	28.0%	4.0%	23.9%
1920	36.4	6.7	29.6
1940	40.3	7.8	32.5
1960	44.1	10.8	33.3
1980	43.0	12.2	30.8
1995	41.70	13.1	28.6
Future generations	n.a.	n.a.	49.2

Source: Jagadeesh Gokhale, Benjamin R. Page, and John R. Sturrock, "Generational Accounts for the United Staes: An Update," 1997, Table 3.

11.1   The Ethnic Incidence of Property Taxes

A study by Professor Andrew Beueridge of Queens College (City University of New York) caused a stir in 1994 when he reported that African Americans paid higher suburban property taxes than whites on homes of comparable market value. Since the property tax rate in a community is the same for everyone, how could this be the case? The main reason for Beueridge's finding is that many communities assess the value of homes at market value only when they are sold. People who have lived in their homes for many years usually have assessed values that are much lower than the market value. Many African Americans have only recently realized the dream of a home in the suburbs and are thus disproportionately represented in the group of new homeowners.

Beueridge surveyed 30 cities and 31 suburbs and found that African-American homeowners paid more taxes than whites with homes of comparable value in 58% of the suburbs. In the 30% of the cities, African Americans paid more. The disparities in average property tax rates ranged from 3% more in the Dallas-Fort Worth suburbs to 47% more in the Philadelphia suburbs.[1]

Critically analyze the following questions:

- Does the finding that the average property tax rate on homes of the same value is higher for African Americans imply that they pay a higher share of the property tax revenue than their share of income in the community? Why or why not?

- How would you reform the property tax so that African Americans do not pay higher property tax rates than others?

- What other types of taxes may be borne more heavily by minority groups than by whites?

---

[1]"Taxes Are Higher for Blacks, Analysis Shows," *New York Times,* August 17, 1994.

---

is "not sustainable." That is, present taxes are not high enough to fund government spending, interest payments on the debt, Social Security, and other transfer programs at current levels over the long run.

Generational accounting is not without its critics. Some economists believe that the numbers are unreliable because there are too many uncertainties with projecting tax and transfer policies into the distant future. Also, the present values calculated are sensitive to the interest rate chosen to discount future values. Generational incidence, like any tax incidence study, is based on certain economic assumptions, and all findings are subject to change as better information and data are obtained.

THE ECONOMIC INCIDENCE OF AN EXCISE TAX

Although it is a common practice to study the statutory incidence of taxes, we must consider the possibility of tax shifting and examine the economic incidence of the tax. The principles of economic incidence can be explained by analyzing the incidence of an excise tax. Recall that an excise tax is levied on a single good like cigarettes or on a narrow group of goods like tobacco products. In Chapter 10, we examined how an excise tax affects the gross price of the taxed good to consumers and the net price received by the producers. In the present chapter, we use that analysis to determine the economic incidence of the excise tax.

The first step is to determine whether the excise tax is shifted forward as a higher price to the consumers or backward as a lower price to the producers. Many noneconomists often assume that an excise tax is always shifted to the consumers. In Chapter 10 we learned that an excise tax on a good bought and sold in a competitive market may increase the price to the consumers, lower the price to producers, or most likely, produce some combination of both effects. Whether an excise tax is shifted forward or backward makes a big difference to its economic incidence.

What Determines Degree of Tax Shifting?

What determines whether a tax can be shifted and to whom? There is a general principle to keep in mind when answering this question: The burden of a tax is shifted away from persons or firms who can easily alter their economic behavior in response to the tax, and toward those who are least able to alter their plans. We will see several applications of this principle throughout this chapter.

A good illustration is shown in Figure 11.1. In this figure we assume that the demand curve for a certain good—say, insulin—is completely price inelastic (vertical).[4] A tax levied on such a good is shifted forward completely to the consumers. That is, the excise tax increases the gross consumer's price from P_0 to $P_0 + t$, where t is the excise tax rate. This result is easily interpreted in terms of the general principle of tax shifting. A consumer of insulin has few or no alternatives to insulin. In other words, consumers of insulin cannot avoid the tax by buying substitutes, because insulin has no good substitutes. Therefore, the consumers of insulin bear the whole burden of the tax.

In Figure 11.2, we show the opposite case, in which an excise tax is imposed on a good that has satisfactory substitutes for the consumers. The demand curve for this good—say, a particular brand of cola—is nearly completely elastic (horizontal). Any rise in the price of brand X cola causes the consumer to substitute other brands of cola. In this case, a tax on the good cannot affect the consumer's price, so the entire tax is shifted back to the producers of brand X cola in the form of a lower price for their product.

This result is easily understood in terms of the general principle of tax shifting. The consumers of brand X cola can easily alter their consumption and substitute other, untaxed brands of cola to avoid the tax. Producers of brand X cola cannot easily produce the other brands in response to the tax, so their price must fall by the full amount of the tax if they are to continue to sell their good.

In general, an excise tax is reflected partly as a higher price to the consumers and partly as a lower price to the producers. As we learned in Chapter 10, the actual degree of shifting depends on the relative magnitudes of the slopes of the supply and demand curves. A larger fraction of the tax is shifted to consumers if the demand curve is steeper than the supply curve (i.e., it has a bigger absolute slope), and vice versa. Again, this illustrates the general principle of tax shifting: When the demand curve is steeper than the supply curve, the consumers are less able to alter their plans than the producers, so they bear a disproportionately large share of the tax burden.

---

[4]Actually, even an essential good like insulin is unlikely to have a demand curve that is vertical. We are making this assumption for the purpose of illustration.

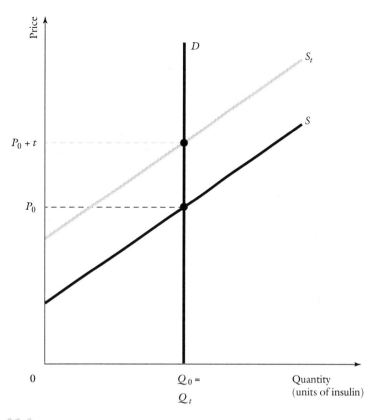

Figure 11.1

Effect of an Excise Tax on Consumer's Price Under Alternative Demand Conditions—Inelastic Demand

Without a tax, the consumer's price is determined by the intersection of the supply curve S and the vertical demand curve at P_0. When the good is taxed, the consumer's price rises by the full amount of the tax to $P_0 + t$ where the supply curve S_t intersects the demand curve.

INCOME INCIDENCE WHEN EXCISE TAXES ARE SHIFTED TO CONSUMERS. Determining whether an excise tax is shifted to consumers or producers is a useful first step, but does not tell us what we really want to know about the incidence of the tax: How is the burden distributed across people with different abilities to pay, or what is the income incidence of an excise tax? To answer this question, it is necessary to gather more information. If the excise tax is completely shifted to consumers in the form of a higher gross price, we need to know how consumption of the taxed good varies across different income groups.

To find the income incidence, we need to know the share of income spent on the taxed good by people with different incomes. We will define the budget share of a particular good as the fraction or percentage of total income (or total spending) spent on that good. For instance, if a person with monthly income of $100

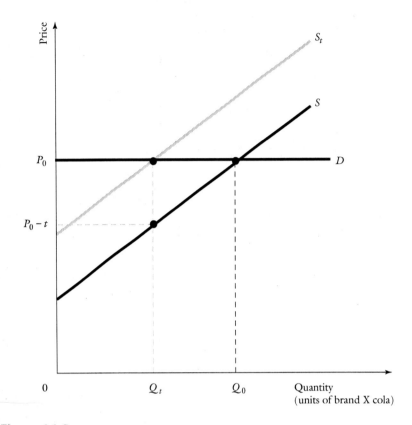

Figure 11.2

Effect of an Excise Tax on Consumer's Price Under Alternative Demand Conditions—Elastic Demand

Here the demand curve is horizontal. In this case, the consumer's price is not affected by the tax, and the producer's price falls by the full amount of the tax.

spends $20 a month on bagels, the bagel budget share is .20, or 20%. More

formally, let's denote the budget share of good X as s_X, where $s_X = \dfrac{P_X \cdot Q_X}{M}$ and

P_X is the price paid by the consumer, Q_X is the quantity consumed by the consumer, and M is the consumer's income. Typically, the budget share of a good varies with the amount of income the consumer has. If a good has an income elasticity greater than 1, the budget share increases with income, and we call the good a luxury.[5] If a good has an income elasticity less than 1, the budget share decreases with income and the good is called a necessity.

How does the incidence of an excise tax depend on the budget share of the taxed good? When analyzing the income incidence of a tax, we are interested in

[5]The budget share of good X is $\dfrac{P_X \cdot Q_X}{M}$. With P_X fixed, the budget share rises as M rises only if Q_X rises more than M. That is, the income elasticity is greater than 1.

whether the **average tax rate** (**ATR**) is higher or lower for consumers with higher incomes. The average tax rate is the tax paid by the consumer divided by income. If an excise tax is fully shifted to the consumers, the tax paid is equal to the tax rate per unit times the quantity consumed of the taxed good. That is, $T_X = t_X \cdot Q_X$, where T_X is the amount of the excise tax on good X paid by the consumer. The ATR$_X$ for a consumer is $\dfrac{T_X}{M}$. A little simple algebra shows that

$$\mathrm{ATR}_X = \frac{t_X \cdot Q_X}{M} = \frac{t_X \cdot P_X \cdot Q_X}{P_X \cdot M} = \frac{t_X}{P_X} \cdot s_X$$

In other words, the average tax rate paid by a consumer is equal to the excise tax rate (per unit of output) divided by the consumer's price, all times the budget share of the consumer for the taxed good. The excise tax rate divided by consumer price is just the excise tax expressed as a percentage of the price. An indirect tax like an excise tax is levied at the same rate for all consumers, so $\dfrac{t_X}{P_X}$ does not vary across consumers. The ATR is different for different consumers because their budget shares are different.

We can now understand the importance of the income elasticity of the taxed good to the question of its income incidence. If good X is a luxury, s_X is higher for consumers with higher incomes, so the ATR is higher for higher-income consumers and an excise tax on the good is progressive. If good X is a necessity, s_X is higher for consumers with lower incomes, so the ATR is higher for consumers with lower incomes. In this case, an excise tax on X is regressive. If s_X is the same across all income groups, the excise tax is proportional.

We should end this discussion with a qualification. The income elasticity of a taxed good determines the income incidence of an excise tax provided that the tax is fully shifted to the consumers. If the tax is shifted to the producers, the income elasticity of the good is irrelevant. For example, in 1991 Congress levied an excise tax on expensive pleasure boats. It was expected that this tax would be borne by the well-to-do buyers of such boats and would be progressive. Following the passage of the tax, sales of boats slumped sharply, and so did prices charged by boat sellers. This led some people to argue that the incidence of the "yacht tax" was on workers in the boat-building industry, rather than well-to-do boat buyers. Whether the slump in boat sales was due to the tax, or to the recession of 1991–1992, the event did focus attention on the possibility that excise taxes on luxuries can be shifted to producers and therefore are not necessarily progressive. Partly for this reason, Congress rescinded the "yacht tax" in 1994.

THE INCOME INCIDENCE OF TOBACCO TAXES. We will now learn how to create an incidence table like Tables 11.1 and 11.2 for an excise tax. Recently, people who are concerned about the health effects of smoking have advocated substantially raising the excise tax rate on tobacco products. In 2000, the federal government levied an excise tax of 34 cents on a package of cigarettes and the median state and county tax is about 40 cents a pack. President Clinton has proposed raising the federal tax to 55 cents per pack, and some states impose an excise tax as high as $1.00 a pack. In addition, the recent comprehensive agreement between the tobacco companies and the states imposes an indirect tax of about 40 cents on each pack of cigarettes. Not counting the tobacco settlement, excise taxes constitute 40% or more of the price a consumer pays for cigarettes. How is the burden of the cigarette excise tax distributed across households with different incomes?

To simplify, we assume that the tax is fully shifted to consumers. To determine how the burden is distributed across income groups, we compile data from the *Consumer Expenditure Survey* of 1998 in Table 11.4. This table shows income before taxes and spending on tobacco products for households classified into income quintiles. The third row shows the fraction of household income spent on tobacco products (s_X in the definition of the ATR) for each quintile. As we can see, the lowest income quintile spends a fraction equal to .03 (or 3%) of its pre-tax income on tobacco products, whereas the corresponding fraction for the top quintile is .003 (or .3%). The second to last row shows the ATR for the different quintiles (cigarette excise tax paid divided by income). It is obtained by multiplying the tobacco budget share of each quintile by 40%. The ATR declines as income rises, so the tobacco tax is regressive with an ATR of 1.2% for the bottom quintile falling to .12% for the top. Although the ATR is highest for the bottom quintile, these households do not pay the largest share of the cigarette tax. As shown in the last row, households in the fourth income quintile paid the largest share (23.7%) since they consume the largest share of cigarettes produced. Households in the bottom quintile paid 15.6% of the total cigarette tax burden.

ARE ALL EXCISE TAXES REGRESSIVE?   We found that the excise tax on tobacco products is regressive. Are there any excise taxes that are not? Assuming that an excise tax is shifted forward, and using the above methodology, we are likely to find that all excise taxes, and therefore all sales taxes, appear regressive. The reason is that for nearly all goods, the income budget share falls as we move up the income scale. This may exaggerate the regressivity of excise taxes..

Table 11.4   The Income Incidence of Tobacco Excise Taxes

| | Quintile | | | | | |
	1	2	3	4	5	All
Annual income	$7,170	$17,962	$30,981	$50,205	$101, 602	$42,622
Spending on tobacco	$217	$259	$307	$331	$282	$279
Tobacco budget share	.030	.014	.010	.007	.003	.007
ATR (%) (tobacco budget share times 40%)	1.2%	.56%	.4%	.28%	.12%	.28%
Percent of tobacco tax paid	15.6%	18.6%	22%	23.7%	20.2%	100%

Source: Calculations by author from Bureau of Labor Statistics, *Consumer Expenditure Survey, 1998,* available on the BLS web site at http://.stats.bls.gov/cxstnd.htm.

First, the share of income before taxes spent on goods is likely to fall because personal income and employment taxes take a larger fraction of income from these groups. According to Table 11.1, the lowest income quintile pays 1.1% of its income in income and payroll taxes, whereas the top quintile pays nearly 24%. Since higher income quintiles pay a larger fraction of their income as personal income taxes, a smaller fraction of pre-tax income is left to spend on goods. This is part of the reason budget share declines as income rises.

Second, higher-income people save a larger fraction of their income. Since a larger fraction of income is saved as income rises, it is likely that the budget shares of most goods fall as income rises. For this reason, some economists prefer to use budget shares calculated as a fraction of a consumer's spending rather than as a fraction of income. They argue that spending is a better measure than income of ability to pay taxes. Alternatively, economists can calculate the lifetime incidence of sales taxes, which is described in the next section.

Third, the calculations assume that the money income of the consumers is not affected by changes in the tax. But low-income consumers derive much of their purchasing power from government transfers, which are indexed to the cost of living. If excise taxes raise consumer prices, low-income consumers receive more dollars of transfers when the excise or sales taxes are increased. This automatically offsets a large part of the regressivity of the excise tax.[6] These considerations suggest that the standard method of determining the incidence of an excise tax is biased toward finding regressivity.

LIFETIME INCOME INCIDENCE OF EXCISE TAXES.   A difficulty with the methods we have described for determining the incidence of taxes on goods and services is the fact we consider *annual* taxes paid divided by *annual* income of the taxpayer. This raises two concerns. First, annual taxes paid may not be a good measure of the amount of excise taxes paid by a taxpayer. For example, we saw that budget shares spent on different goods decline with income because consumers with higher incomes save a larger fraction of their income. However, taxes on goods and services are not avoided by saving income; they are postponed. When consumers withdraw their savings and spend this money in the future, they pay taxes on the goods and services they consume then. Measuring taxes paid annually treats saving as if it were an untaxed good because it ignores taxes paid in future years when savings are spent.

Second, annual income may not be a good measure of a taxpayer's ability to pay. Measured income does not include all of a family's income. This is not just because of errors in reporting income, but also because the definition of income excludes some forms of income, such as transfers in kind from the government. Also, people can consume more than their income by spending down their savings. People are likely to do so if they believe their income in the year is temporarily low. Just as a person who is unemployed for a month and has no income does not stop consuming, people whose incomes are temporarily low during a given year maintain their consumption level by spending their savings. The permanent, or lifetime, incomes of these consumers is higher than their annual income.

---

[6]This point was made by Edgar Browning and William Johnson in *The Distribution of the Tax Burden*, 1979.

Because of these problems, economists have developed a methodology of measuring tax incidence on a lifetime basis. Lifetime tax incidence measures the total amount of tax that people pay over a lifetime and compares it with their lifetime income. The lifetime tax burden is equal to the *present value* of the annual tax burdens over the taxpayer's lifetime. Similarly, lifetime income is the present value of annual incomes received over the lifetime. Dividing the lifetime tax burden by the lifetime income gives the lifetime average tax rate of the taxpayer.

To study lifetime income incidence, we place people into income groups according to their lifetime incomes. An individual who is in a low annual income group in one year could be in a high lifetime income group, or vice versa. The distribution of the lifetime tax burden across lifetime income groups describes the lifetime income incidence of the tax. In some cases, the lifetime income incidence of a tax is quite different from its annual income incidence.

The difference between annual and lifetime incidence is especially important for sales taxes. The value-added tax (VAT) is a form of sales tax used in many countries, though not in the United States. The introduction of a VAT in the United States has been opposed largely because critics allege that it is regressive. In fact, using the annual incidence methodology, it seems very regressive. On the basis of annual incidence, a 5% VAT applying to all goods and services would mean a relative tax burden of 7.7% on the lowest income decile (a decile is 10% of the population), but only 2.75% on the highest income decile. However, using a lifetime incidence approach, the relative tax burden would be 3.9% on the lowest lifetime income decile of the population and 2.9% on the highest.[7] Although this is still regressive, it is much less regressive than the annual incidence calculations suggest.

Income Incidence when Excise Taxes Are Shifted to Producers

How do we determine the income incidence of an excise tax when it is passed back to the producers in the form of a lower net price? Remember that the producer is typically a firm, and we know that people—not firms—bear the burden of any tax. When the price received by sellers declines, their total receipts are reduced, so they can afford to pay out less to factor owners such as employees and shareholders. When all firms spend less on factors, the rewards to the factors (such as wages to employees and dividends to shareholders) decline in factor markets.

In other words, an excise tax that is shifted to the producers as a lower price for their products is eventually borne by people in the form of lower factor rewards. To determine the income incidence of taxes shifted to producers, we must know which factor rewards are reduced, by how much, and which households own the factors.

IMPACT ON FACTOR REWARDS. To discover which factor rewards are reduced, it is useful to apply the general principle of tax shifting. A reward to a factor will fall

---

[7]These numbers are taken from E. Casperson and G. Metcalf, "Is a Value-Added Tax Regressive?" 1994, Table 4.

10.2   Is the Gasoline Tax Regressive?

Many people argue that the federal excise tax on gasoline (just over 18 cents per gallon in year 2000) should be raised. In dollars of constant purchasing power, the excise tax rate is lower now that it was in past years, and it is much lower than the tax rate levied in most other countries. Economists argue that raising tax rates on gasoline is a good way for the government to improve economic efficiency while raising more revenue. Higher gasoline taxes would reduce the number of miles people drive each year, reducing both air pollution and traffic congestion. And the revenue raised could be used to reduce other distortionary taxes for a further improvement in economic efficiency. This is called the "double dividend" from taxing gasoline.

Despite these arguments, Congress seems loathe to raise the federal tax. Why is there so much resistance to higher gas taxes? Undoubtedly, resistance to higher gas prices is a major factor, but the argument that gasoline taxes are regressive adds weight to the opposition. Opponents of gas tax hikes argue that the gasoline tax is regressive and borne disproportionately by low-income families. Professor James Poterba of MIT has analyzed the regressivity of the gas tax and concludes that its incidence is closer to proportional than regressive.[1]

Poterba argues that the apparent regressivity of the gasoline tax arises because pre-tax income is used to measure ability to pay and transfer income is assumed not to change when gasoline prices rise. Although the income budget share of spending on gasoline falls from .11 (11%) for the first income decile (the 10% of families with the lowest incomes) to .024 for the highest decile, the pattern is different when annual expenditure is used as a measure of ability to pay. As a percentage of expenditure, spending on gasoline rises from about .04 (4%) for the lowest decile to nearly .07 for families in the middle deciles. The expenditure share then falls to .04 for families in the highest decile. This implies that the lowest and highest deciles pay the same amount of gasoline tax as a percentage of their annual expenditure, while middle-income families pay a higher rate. Poterba also calculates the fraction of income spent on gasoline under the assumption that government transfer income (welfare and Social Security) is fully indexed for changes in gas prices. In this case, he finds that the incidence of the gasoline tax is close to proportional.

Critically analyze the following questions:

- Do you think that expenditure or pre-tax income is a better measure of a family's ability to pay? Give reasons for your answer.

- Suppose the gasoline tax *is* regressive. Is this a good argument not to raise it, given the efficiency improvements that would result? Would your answer depend on whether the revenue raised by the tax is used to lower income taxes on low-income families?

- Federal gas taxes accrue to the Highway Trust Fund, not general revenue, and are used to finance highway improvements. Assuming people receive benefits from highways in proportion to how much they drive, would this alter the view that gasoline taxes are regressive?

---

[1] James M. Poterba, "Is the Gasoline Tax Regressive?" 1991.

more in response to a tax if the owners of the factor cannot easily employ their factors outside the industry where the tax is levied. Factor owners who can easily reemploy their factors in other industries will not bear much of the burden. We expect that the ability to employ a factor outside the industry of the taxed good depends on how important the industry is as a source of employment for the factor.

The importance of an industry to a factor depends on several things. One is whether the factor is **specific** to the industry. A factor is specific for producing a good if it cannot find employment producing other goods. For example, an architect is specific to the construction industry. Although architects could do other forms of work, they earn more working in their chosen field. If a tax were to depress the prices of buildings, it is likely that the wages of the architects who design the buildings would decline as well.

The effect of factor specificity in determining the tax incidence of an excise tax is shown in Figure 11.3. The supply and demand curves for a certain factor that is used in producing the taxed good are shown. The demand comes from firms producing the taxed good, and the supply from owners of the factor seeking to employ the factor in the taxed industry. Before the excise tax is imposed, the demand curve for the factor is that labeled D. If the factor is specific, the supply curve of the factor to the industry is steep (vertical in Figure 11.3), as shown by the curve labeled S^S. The supply curve is steep because the factor is not easily employed outside of the taxed industry. Before the excise tax is levied, the equilibrium reward to the factor is W_0 and the quantity of the factor used is Q_0. After the excise tax is imposed

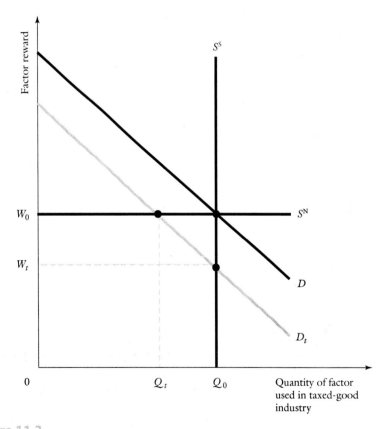

Figure 11.3

Incidence on Specific and Nonspecific Factors

If a factor is specific, the supply curve is vertical, such as S^S. Imposing the tax shifts the demand curve for the factor to D_t and the factor reward falls by the full amount of the tax, from W_0 to W_t. For a nonspecific factor, the supply curve is horizontal, such as S^N. In this case, the quantity of the factor falls to Q_t and the reward to the factor owner remains W_0

on output, firms demand less of the factor at every factor reward, so the demand curve for the factor shifts left to D_t. Because the factor is specific, its reward falls sharply to W_t and the quantity used of the factor is unchanged.

If the factor is completely nonspecific to the industry, the supply of the factor to the industry is very elastic, as shown by the flat factor supply curve S^N. Because the factor is nonspecific, it can be employed easily in other industries where it earns factor reward W_0, which also must be paid by firms in the taxed industry in order to attract the factor. When the excise tax is imposed on industry output, the firms demand less and the quantity of the factor used falls to Q_t. However, the reward to the factor remains unchanged at W_0 because the factor owners can easily employ the factor to produce other, nontaxed goods.

Another way a factor can be important in the taxed-good industry is when it accounts for a larger share of the cost of producing the good as compared with its cost share in other industries. In this case, the factor is said to be **intensive** in producing the taxed good. For example, land is intensive in producing agricultural products and labor is intensive in producing most services. The effect of factor intensity in determining tax incidence is shown in Figure 11.4. In this case we assume an upward-sloping supply curve of the factor to the industry, and the equilibrium factor reward and quantity of the factor used are respectively W_0 and Q_0 when the output is not taxed. When a tax is imposed on industry output, the demand curve for the factor again shifts to the left. If the factor is intensively used in producing the taxed good, the demand curve shifts by a large amount to D_t^I. As a result, the factor reward drops sharply to W_t^I. By comparison, if the factor is not used intensively in producing the taxed good, the demand curve for the factor shifts by less, say to D_t^N, and the factor reward declines by less, to W_t^N.

From Figures 11.3 and 11.4, we can conclude that when the burden of an excise tax is shifted back to producers, it will be borne most heavily by owners of factors that are specific to the taxed industry and/or used intensively in producing the taxed good. If a factor is specific to the taxed industry, its supply to the industry is inelastic and the factor reward falls by more as firms reduce their demand for the factor in response to the tax. If a factor is intensive in producing the taxed good, the demand for the factor will fall by more, again causing a larger decline in the reward to the factor.

INCOME INCIDENCE AND THE OWNERSHIP OF FACTORS.   So far, we have considered the impact of an excise tax on levels of factor rewards. The incidence of a tax according to factor rewards is known as its **functional incidence.** The functional incidence is the distribution of the tax burden on different factors—labor, land and capital, etc. Typically, we are interested in the income incidence rather than the functional incidence of a tax.

Once we know the functional incidence of a tax, we can determine the income incidence using information about factor ownership across income groups. Suppose, for example, that an excise tax on cigarettes is shifted to the cigarette companies as a lower net price for cigarettes, and this lowers the reward to owners of tobacco-growing land. If we have information about the ownership of tobacco-growing land (how much of it is owned by low-income households versus high-income households, etc.),

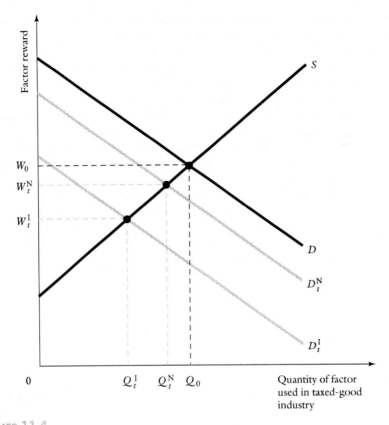

Figure 11.4

Incidence on Intensive and Nonintensive Factors
The demand curve for a factor shifts to the left due to the output effect. If the good is not intensive in the factor, the shift in the factor demand curve is small, such as to D_t^N, so the factor reward falls little. If the good is intensive in the factor, the shift in the demand curve is large, such as to D_t^I, and the factor reward falls a lot.

we can determine the income incidence of the cigarette tax. If tobacco-growing land is owned mostly by high-income people, we can conclude that the tax is progressive because it is reflected in lower rewards to rich landowners.

ADVANCED ISSUES IN ANALYSIS OF TAX INCIDENCE

The study of tax incidence has many layers, and the deeper we look into the question of tax incidence the more complicated things become. Although we cannot cover advanced issues in tax incidence in detail here, we can describe some general ideas that arise in advanced analyses.

Most of the tax incidence we discuss in this chapter is partial equilibrium analysis. **Partial equilibrium analysis** considers the effects of a tax in the market where it is levied and ignores the impacts on other markets. For instance, the partial equilibrium analysis of the gasoline tax assumes that only the price of gasoline is affected by the tax. The main reason we do partial equilibrium analysis is simplicity.

Although partial equilibrium analysis provides a good approximation for economic incidence in some cases, a tax that has wide-ranging impacts in the economy cannot be analyzed this way.

When many markets are affected by a tax, we must use general equilibrium analysis to find the economic incidence. **General equilibrium analysis** includes linkages between markets, so equilibrium (supply equals demand) in any one market depends on events in other markets. For example, a general equilibrium analysis of the gasoline tax would consider not only the effect on the consumers' price of gasoline, but also the impact of higher gas prices on the cost of transporting goods and the effects of the gasoline tax on prices of other goods as well.

The Incidence of the Corporation Income Tax

The incidence of the corporation income tax has long been a subject of debate. The Congressional Budget Office, in determining the incidence of federal taxes shown in Tables 11.1 and 11.2, assumed that the corporation income tax is borne by owners of corporate shares. As we saw in these tables, the corporation income tax is very progressive under the CBO's assumption. Managers of corporations make a different assumption about the incidence of the corporation income tax. They argue that their companies treat the tax as part of their cost of production, and as with other costs, it is reflected in the prices they charge for their goods. In other words, the corporation income tax is like an excise tax and is passed forward to consumers. Under this assumption, the corporation income tax would be regressive.

Arnold C. Harberger, now at the University of California, Los Angeles, applied general equilibrium analysis to the question of the incidence of the corporation income tax and found that this tax is borne primarily by owners of capital. Unlike the CBO's assumption, all capital owners, not just owners of corporate shares, bear the burden of the corporation income tax. Harberger divided the economy into two sectors, the corporate sector (C) and the noncorporate (NC), each producing different goods. He assumed two factors of production, labor (L) and capital (K); these are fixed in total supply to the economy but can easily be moved between the corporate and noncorporate sectors. (In words, Harberger assumed that factors are not specific.) As a result, the factor owners must receive the same reward for a factor whether it is employed in one sector or the other. In **Harberger's general equilibrium model,** the corporation income tax is treated as a tax on the reward to capital when it is employed in the corporate sector, but not when it is employed in the noncorporate sector. Such a tax is often called a **partial factor tax.**

Using general equilibrium analysis, Harberger showed that the corporation income tax has two effects on the after-tax reward to capital. The **factor substitution effect** arises because the corporation income tax increases the cost of capital to firms in the corporate sector, causing them to substitute labor for capital. The factor substitution effect can be understood from Figure 11.5. In this figure, the length of the horizontal axis is equal to the total capital stock available for use in the economy. The amount employed in the corporate sector is measured to the right of the origin 0^C, and the amount employed in the noncorporate sector is measured to the left of origin 0^{NC}. The reward to capital in the corporate and noncorporate sectors is measured on the vertical axes. The demand curves for capital by the corporate and noncorporate firms are labeled D^C and D^{NC} respectively. These demand curves are drawn oriented to their respective origins.

Without a corporation income tax, the reward to capital is R_0 in both sectors; the corporate sector employs $0^C K_0$ units of capital, and the noncorporate sector employs the rest ($0^{NC} K_0$ units). If we impose a tax on the reward to capital employed in the corporate sector, the height of the demand curve labeled D_t^C the maximum reward that corporations can pay capital owners after corporate taxes. The (vertical) distance between D^C and D_t^C is equal to the corporate tax on the income of a unit of capital. Since the after-tax reward must be the same in both sectors, the equilibrium is found where D_t^C intersects D^{NC}, and $0^C K_t$ units of capital are employed in the corporate sector. The after-tax reward to capital falls to R_t in *both* sectors, but the cost of capital gross of tax rises to $R_t + t$ in the corporate sector. Capital becomes more expensive to corporations, so they substitute labor for capital. Capital is less expensive to firms in

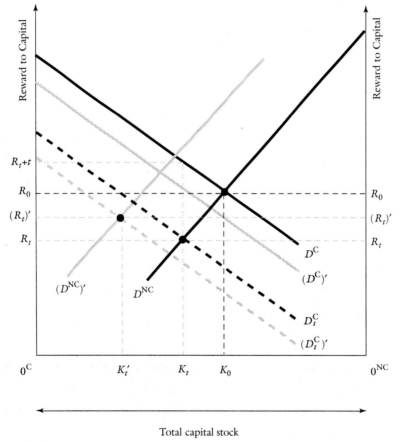

Figure 11.5

Harberger's General Equilibrium Model of Corporation Income Tax Incidence
The total capital stock is allocated between the corporate (C) and noncorporate (NC) sectors so that the after-tax reward is the same in both sectors. The effect of a tax on capital in the C sector depends on the slopes of the capital demand curves for each sector and the magnitude of the output effect, which shifts the capital demand curves.

the noncorporate sector, so they substitute capital for labor. The fall in the after-tax reward to capital depends on the strength of this factor substitution effect. The more substitutable labor is for capital in the corporate sector (the flatter the D^C curve) or the less substitutable labor is for capital in the noncorporate sector (the steeper the D^{NC} curve), the more the reward to capital falls as a result of the corporation income tax.

This is not the end of the story, however; Harberger pointed out that the increase in the cost of capital to corporate firms would mean that the price of corporate goods would rise relative to noncorporate goods. Consumers would thus want to consume less corporate goods and more noncorporate goods. As a result, output in the corporate sector would fall and output in the noncorporate sector would rise. Harberger called this the **output substitution effect.** As a result of the output substitution effect, the demand curve for corporate capital decreases to $(D^C)'$ and the demand curve for noncorporate capital increases to $(D^{NC})'$. The relative magnitude of the shifts in these curves depends on the capital intensity of the corporate and noncorporate sectors. If the corporate sector is less capital intensive than the noncorporate sector, the horizontal shift in D^C is less than that of D^{NC}, which is the case shown in the figure. Corporations can pay capital owners a maximum reward after corporation income taxes equal to the height of $(D_t^C)'$, so the equilibrium after-tax reward to capital is $(R_t)'$ in both sectors.

When the corporate sector is less capital intensive than the noncorporate sector, the after-tax reward to capital falls by less than it would as a result of the factor substitution effect alone. As the corporate sector contracts due to the output substitution effect, it releases less capital than is demanded by the expanding noncorporate sector. Thus the output substitution effect increases the demand for capital, raising its reward. In fact, the output substitution effect could be large enough to offset the factor substitution effect, in which case the after-tax reward to capital would not be changed by the corporation income tax. In this case, the corporation income tax is shifted to owners of labor or to consumers.

If the corporate sector is capital intensive, both the factor substitution and output substitution effects decrease the after-tax reward to capital. In this case, the shift in the corporate capital demand curve is greater than the shift in the noncorporate capital demand curve and the reward to capital is depressed more than caused by the factor substitution effect alone.

Harberger found that the corporate sector is less capital intensive than the noncorporate sector, so the factor and output substitution effects have opposite effects on the reward to capital. However, using estimates of the relative strengths of the factor and output substitution effects, he found that the after-tax reward to capital falls as a result of the corporation income tax. In fact, the fall in the total earnings of all capital earners is about equal to the amount of corporation income tax collected. Hence, Harberger concluded, the incidence of the corporation income tax is nearly all on capital owners.

Tax Capitalization

When a tax is imposed on the income of an asset, the incidence of the tax can depend on a phenomenon known as tax capitalization. **Tax capitalization** describes a situation in which the market price of the asset is reduced by the taxes that must be paid by the buyer in the future. If a tax is capitalized, its incidence depends on who owns the asset at the time the tax is imposed. If the taxed asset is subsequently sold, the buyer of the asset does not bear the burden of the tax on the income of the asset, because the purchase price is reduced by the tax rate.

To explain, we must use the concept of present value. Suppose an asset pays the bearer an untaxed return of $10 per year forever (a so-called perpetuity), and the market interest rate is 5%. The present value of $10 per year forever discounted at 5% is $10 divided by 0.05, or $200. Suppose Mr. Dow owns the asset and the government unexpectedly levies a tax of 20% on the income of Dow's asset and only his asset. Instead of receiving $10 a year, Dow now receives $8 after paying the $2 tax. Mr. Dow, perhaps angry about the tax, puts the asset up for sale. However, the most anyone will pay for the asset is now $160, which is the present value of $8 a year discounted at 5%.

If Ms. Jones buys the asset from Mr. Dow, she will pay $2 in taxes every year, but she does not bear the burden of this tax. She earns the same rate of return on the taxed asset, 5% or $8 divided by $160, that she could have earned from an untaxed asset. Mr. Dow bears the entire burden of all taxes, present and future, in the form of the capital loss he suffered at the time the tax was levied. The value of the asset fell by 20%, or $40, which is equal to the present value of $2 tax per year discounted at 5%.

Tax capitalization occurs when a particular asset or class of assets is singled out for tax. If a tax is imposed on all assets, capitalization does not occur. For instance, if a 20% tax is imposed on all other assets as well as the one Mr. Dow holds, the price of Dow's asset is not affected. Although the after-tax earnings on Dow's asset are only $8 per year after the tax, the tax also applies to bonds, which now pay an after-tax return of 4% (80% of 5%). Discounting the annual $8 using an after-tax market interest rate of 4% gives a present value for Dow's asset of $200 ($8 divided by .04), which was the price before the tax was imposed.

Tax Incidence in the Long Run

The economic incidence of a tax in the long run is sometimes different from that in the short run. In the short run, some economic quantities are fixed and cannot be changed, such as capital stock. This is not true in the long run. For instance, capital stock may rise or fall over time because of decisions regarding accumulation. The fact that the quantities of some variables are fixed in the short run but are variable in the long run has implications for tax incidence.

Suppose, for example, the government levies an excise tax on fuel oil for heating. In the short run, people with oil furnaces do not find it worthwhile to replace their serviceable oil furnace with a natural gas furnace. Their demand for fuel oil is reduced only to the extent that they turn down the heat, so the demand curve for fuel oil is relatively steep. In the long run, the oil-burning furnaces grow old and wear out, and many will be replaced with natural gas furnaces because of the higher price of fuel oil. This further reduces the demand for fuel oil, so the long-run demand curve is much flatter. As we learned earlier, the consumers' price of a good is more likely to rise in response to an excise tax when the demand curve is steep, while the producers' price is more likely to fall when the demand curve is flat. This suggests that in the short run, a tax on fuel oil is mostly borne by consumers, but in the long run, as oil furnaces wear out, it can be shifted to producers.

The difference between the short- and long-run incidence of a tax on the income from capital is of special interest. In the short run, a country's capital stock, which is the result of past decisions about savings and investment, is more or less fixed in quantity. As a result of this fixity, the short-run incidence of a tax on capital income is mainly on capital owners, who typically have higher incomes. In the long run, higher taxes on capital incomes reduce the incentives for owners to save and invest, and the capital stock grows at a lower rate, or even declines. Workers have less capital to work with in the long run, so their marginal productivity is reduced and employers are willing to hire them only at lower wage rates. In the long run, a tax on the capital income may be fully shifted to labor in the form of lower wages, and borne by wage earners rather than the capital owners.

This analysis is especially relevant to the incidence of the corporation income tax. Recall that Harberger's analysis found that the corporation income tax is borne by capital owners throughout the economy in the form of a lower after-tax return on their capital. However, Harberger assumed that the total capital stock in the economy was fixed, even though it could move freely between corporate and non-corporate firms. In the long run, a lower return on capital caused by the corporation income tax may discourage capital accumulation and reduce the economy's capital stock relative to what it would have been without the corporation income tax. As explained, this reduces wage rates in the economy, so the burden of the corporation income tax can be shifted to workers in the long run.

CONCLUSION AND SUMMARY

In this chapter, we learned the basic principles that determine how the burden of a tax is distributed across the population. Economic analysis is helpful, perhaps essential, to this task. The burden of a tax on a household is not just the amount of tax paid to the government, but the change in disposable real income caused by the tax. Real income is affected indirectly by changes in factor rewards and prices of goods and services, as well as directly by taxes.

Some empirical studies of tax incidence use the simplest type of incidence analysis, but more sophisticated ways of measuring incidence give a more complete picture. The simplest measures sometimes give misleading conclusions about tax incidence, although they have the advantage of being easy to do. Advanced analyses may be more exact in principle, but they are difficult to do and usually require many unverified assumptions. Although many theoretical uncertainties and practical problems permeate the study of tax incidence, keep in mind that tax incidence is an exercise in positive economics. With better and more careful empirical work, we can improve our knowledge and reduce the amount of disagreement. As the quantitative methods of modeling the economy improve, so too, it is hoped, will our knowledge of tax incidence.

- The distribution of the tax burden across different groups of people is called the incidence of a tax. Although people, and only people, bear tax burdens, the person who pays a tax need not bear the tax. A tax burden can be shifted by changes in equilibrium output prices and factor rewards caused by the imposition of the tax.

▨ Statutory incidence is the distribution of the tax burden according to who makes the tax payments to the government. Economic incidence is the distribution of a tax burden according to the changes in disposable real income caused by the tax. Absolute incidence is the incidence of a tax compared with no tax at all. Differential incidence is the incidence of one tax relative to the incidence of another.

▨ The most important question in tax incidence is how the tax burden is distributed across people with different incomes. There is also interest in the incidence of a tax on people in different regions and people in different generations. Generational accounting is a method of reporting the generational incidence of the tax and transfer system.

▨ A person's average tax rate is his or her tax burden divided by income. If the average tax rate rises as income rises, the incidence of the tax is progressive. If the average tax rate falls, it is regressive. The statutory incidence of the personal income tax is progressive.

▨ An excise tax on a particular good may be shifted as a higher price to consumers or as a lower price for producers. The division of an excise tax between consumers and producers depends on the relative slopes (or elasticities) of the supply and demand curves for the taxed good.

▨ The general principle of shifting a tax burden states that tax burdens are shifted to those with less flexibility in changing their economic behavior in response to the tax and away from those with greater flexibility.

▨ When an excise tax is shifted forward to consumers, its incidence depends on the fraction of income spent on the taxed good (budget share) by different households. If budget share falls (rises) with income, the incidence of the excise tax is regressive (progressive).

▨ When excise taxes reduce prices received by sellers, they are ultimately shifted to factor owners as lower factor rewards. A factor is more likely to bear the burden of an excise tax when it is specific to the taxed-good industry or when it is used intensively in that industry.

▨ General equilibrium analysis determines the economic incidence of a tax by determining the impact of the tax in all markets. General equilibrium analysis is needed when a tax, such as the corporation income tax, has wide-ranging effects in the economy.

QUESTIONS FOR DISCUSSION AND REVIEW

1. The Omnibus Budget Reconciliation Act of 1990 imposed a "luxury good" tax of 10% on certain goods purchased for non-business purposes. These goods included boats and yachts worth more than $100,000 as well as other goods, such as airplanes, expensive cars, and furs. The purpose was to obtain tax revenue from people who could well afford it. What crucial assumption about tax incidence is made here? The luxury tax on yachts and planes was repealed in 1994, partly because the yacht-building and airplane industries complained loudly. What does this suggest about supply conditions in these industries?

2. Which is more likely to be shifted forward completely to the consumer, an excise tax on gasoline imposed by the federal government or an excise tax on gasoline imposed by the government of a single state—say, Hawaii?

3. Suppose the market for long-distance telephone calls is competitive and the demand curve is twice as steep as the supply curve. How is the 10% federal excise tax divided between higher rates to consumer and lower rates for the carrier companies?

4. From an analytic perspective, a subsidy is nothing more than a negative excise tax that confers a benefit to certain groups rather than imposing a burden on them. For decades, the federal government has given fairly large subsidies to farmers for producing everything from grain to honey. Under what conditions of supply and demand do farmers enjoy all the benefit from these subsidies? Under what conditions do the farmers enjoy none of the benefit at all? Who does benefit from the subsidies in this case?

5. Interest on certain bonds issued by municipalities and hospitals is exempt from income tax. On average, these bonds earn an interest rate that is a couple of percentage points less than the interest rate on taxable-interest bonds. These bonds are held mostly by high-income taxpayers. Who is the ultimate beneficiary of this tax exemption?

6. What would be the generational incidence of the following policies?

   a. The government replaces the payroll tax on wages with a national sales tax.

   b. The government makes Social Security benefits fully taxable as income (at pre-

sent, part of Social Security benefits are exempt from tax) from now on, and uses the revenue to reduce the Social Security payroll tax.

7. In order to protect the ozone layer, the government puts a tax on coolants used in air conditioners. What is the likely regional incidence of this tax? In answering this question, what assumption did you make about forward and backward shifting?

8. Internet Exercise. Some people argue that the federal tax system has become less progressive over the past 20 years. They point to the reductions in personal income tax rates applying to high incomes during the Reagan administration and the growth in payroll taxes. Others dispute this and point to the fact that high-income families now pay a larger share of total federal taxes in 1999 than they did in 1977. Historical data on the incidence of federal taxes can be found in *Preliminary Estimates of Effective Tax Rates,* produced by the Congressional Budget Office. Access this document on the CBO web site (http://www.cbo.gov/showdoc.cfm?index=1545&from=4&sequence=0) and examine Tables 1 and 2. How did the federal ATR (Effective Total Tax Rate in the tables) change for the five quintiles between 1977 and 1999? What happened to the ATR for the 1% of families with the highest incomes? How did the share of total individual income taxes paid by high-income families change between 1977 and 1999? How do you reconcile the observed change in the share of taxes paid by high-income families with the observed change in their ATR?

9. Internet Exercise. To reduce the regressivity of the retail sales tax, many states exempt groceries from sales tax, or tax groceries at a lower rate. How regressive is a tax on groceries? To answer this question, access the 1998 *Consumer Expenditure Survey*

at the Bureau of Labor Statistics web site (http://stats.bls.gov/csxstnd.htm) and inspect the table that classifies households by income quintile. Use the data in this table on income before taxes and expenditures on "food at home" to determine the ATR for the different income quin-

tiles if groceries are taxed at 7%. Assume the tax on groceries is fully passed forward to consumers. Is taxing groceries significantly more regressive than taxing all expenditures? Is taxing "food away from home" more or less regressive than taxing "food at home"?

SELECTED REFERENCES

Information on tax incidence can be found in Joseph A. Pechman, *Who Paid the Taxes, 1966–85,* 1985; and Joel B. Slemrod, *Tax Progressivity and Income Inequality,* 1994.

Don Fullerton and Diane Lim Rogers study the lifetime incidence of different taxes in *Who Bears the Lifetime Tax Burden?* 1995.

The best place to learn about the structure of generational accounts is Laurence J. Kotlikoff, *Generational Accounting: Knowing Who Pays, and When, for What We Spend,* 1992. For differing views on the usefulness of generational accounts, see the symposium in *Journal of Economic Perspectives,* 1994.

A critical study of the incidence of the gasoline excise tax is James M. Poterba, "Is the Gasoline Tax Regressive?" 1991. A lifetime incidence analysis of VATs is found in Eric Casperson and Gilbert Metcalf, "Is a Value-Added Tax Regressive?" 1994.

The classic article on the general equilibrium incidence of the corporation income tax is A. C. Harberger, "The Incidence of the Corporation Income Tax", 1962. This famous article is also reprinted in various places.

USEFUL INTERNET SITES

The Economic and Social Research Council in the United Kingdom maintains a site that allows the user to perform interactive experiments to discover the generational incidence of different types of taxes. It can be accessed at http://www. generationalaccounting.com/DOCS/index.html.

12 Tax Policy Analysis

Most people worry about how much tax they pay. However, economists and other tax experts believe that the *way* in which the government collects taxes is as important as *how much* it collects, perhaps more so. Although the government can reduce the burden on taxpayers by reducing the amount of revenue it collects from them, the lost revenue means less government spending. What taxpayers gain in lower taxes, they lose in benefits from government programs. However, by aptly changing the way it collects the taxes, the government can reduce the tax burden and collect the same amount of revenue it needs.

How can different tax systems impose different burdens if they collect the same amount of revenue? If you ask different tax specialists this question, you are likely to get different answers, all of them correct. An economist would point out that different tax systems impose different burdens in terms of lost economic efficiency. An excess burden is caused when a tax system distorts private economic decisions adversely. A second expert—say, from *Citizens for Tax Justice,* an organization interested in the incidence of the tax system—might point out that different tax systems distribute the burden differently. Many people believe that a good tax system should place the tax burden on taxpayers who have the greatest ability to pay the tax, and a system that overly taxes the poor increases the overall burden of the tax system by taxing those least able to pay. A third expert, who favors a simpler tax system, emphasizes that different tax systems have different burdens of administration and compliance. With a complex tax system, the government incurs higher administrative and enforcement costs and the taxpayers bear a larger burden in complying with it.

Analysis of tax policy evaluates different tax systems in terms of three criteria: (1) economic efficiency, (2) distributional equity, and (3) costs of administration and compliance. In this chapter we explain how these criteria determine the overall burden of a tax system. We begin with the excess burden caused when a tax reduces economic efficiency and consider how the government can reduce this burden while collecting the needed revenue. We then address the problem of achieving equity in the tax system. Unfortunately, a more equitable tax system sometimes means a less efficient one and a higher excess burden. Finally, we discuss the administrative and compliance costs of a tax system, including the indirect costs caused by tax avoidance and evasion.

THE TAX BURDEN AND ECONOMIC EFFICIENCY

Although the revenue collected by a tax is its most obvious burden, taxes impose burdens above and beyond the money they take from taxpayers. These hidden burdens are worse than the obvious tax burden because they do not provide revenue for the government. To economists, the most important hidden burden is the excess burden caused when taxes distort market decisions in ways that cause less efficient allocations of economic resources.

The **excess burden** of a tax can be measured as the loss in the combined surpluses to consumers and producers minus the revenue collected by the government. The adjective *excess* indicates that the burden caused by lost efficiency is a burden above and beyond the revenue collected by the tax. The excess burden is caused by the fact that consumers and producers substitute untaxed goods for taxed goods in response to the tax. This is inefficient because the untaxed goods have a lower value to the economy as a whole than the taxed goods they replace.

The excess burden of an excise tax on bagels is shown in Figure 12.1. We assume that the market for bagels is well-functioning and that an efficient quantity B_0 is produced when the good is not taxed. At the pre-tax equilibrium, the consumers' price (MWTP for bagels) is equal to the producers' price (MC of bagels). When an excise tax is imposed on bagels, economic resources are driven out of bagel production and enter untaxed uses. Although these untaxed uses seem attractive to market participants, because they are untaxed, they have lower value for the economy as a whole. After the excise tax is levied, the equilibrium quantity of bagels is B_t. At this quantity, the consumers' MWTP for bagels is equal to the seller's price plus the tax $P_t + t$, which is greater than the MC of producing bagels. In a competitive market, the seller's price is equal to the marginal cost of producing the good. Because MWTP is greater than MC, the after-tax equilibrium is an inefficient allocation. The inefficiency is created because consumers perceive bagels as more costly than they are to the economy as a whole. The consumers must pay the tax, but the government receives revenue, which it can spend on public goods or use to make transfer payments that benefit the population. As individuals, consumers ignore these government benefits because from their viewpoint the benefits do not depend on the quantity of bagels they consume and the amount of bagel tax they pay.[1]

The Tax Burden as Lost Surplus

The excess burden of an excise tax can be explained using the concepts of consumers' and producers' surplus. **Consumers' surplus** is the excess of the consumers' total willingness to pay for a given quantity of bagels over what they actually do pay. For example, the total willingness to pay for B_0 bagels in Figure 12.1 is the area under the demand curve D. Since consumers pay only P_0 times B_0 to consume that

[1] If taxpayers perceived an extra dollar of government benefit from every extra dollar of tax they pay, they would have no incentive to avoid the tax. The fact that we, as taxpayers, think the benefits we get from government are independent of how much taxes we *individually* pay is crucial to this argument.

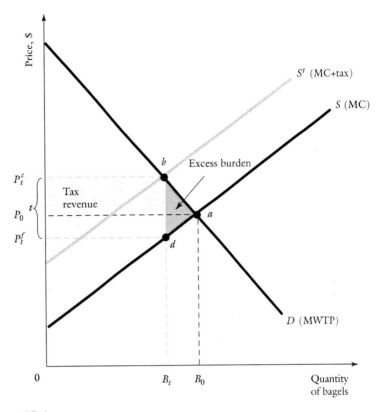

Figure 12.1

Excess Burden of an Excise Tax

An excise tax increases the consumer's price from P_0 to P_t^c and lowers the producer's price from P_0 to P_t^f, causing a combined loss in consumers' and producers' surpluses equal to the pencil-shaped area P_t^c bad P_t^f. Of this, the area of the shaded rectangle is transferred to the government as tax revenue. The remaining loss in surplus is the excess burden of the tax and is equal to the area of the triangle bad. The excess tax burden is attributable to the reduced economic efficiency caused by the excise tax.

many bagels, the consumers' surplus is equal to the area of the triangle formed by the demand curve above P_0.[2]

Producers' surplus, or economic profit, is the excess of the firms' receipts from selling a given output over the total costs of producing the output. The producers' receipts from selling B_0 bagels is P_0 times B_0, which is the area of a rectangle $0P_0aB_0$ in Figure 12.1. If we assume no fixed costs of production, the total cost of producing B_0 bagels is the area under the supply curve. This area is the total cost

---

[2]This statement is not strictly accurate in general, but it is a case where an ounce of inaccuracy saves a ton of explanation. Consumers' surplus is correctly measured using a "compensated" demand curve rather than the market demand curve. See the Appendix to this chapter for a discussion of the compensated demand curve. The analysis of consumers' surplus using the market demand for bagels is correct only if we assume that the income elasticity of bagels is zero.

because the height of the supply curve is the producers' marginal cost, so the area under the supply curve is the summed marginal costs of production. The area of the triangle above the market supply curve below P_0 is the total receipts of the firm minus total costs. When the market for bagels is untaxed, the sum of the consumers' and producers' surpluses is maximized at the market equilibrium.

When an excise tax at rate t is levied on bagels, the equilibrium quantity falls to B_t, the producers' net price falls to P_t^f and the consumers' gross price rises to P_t^c. The increase in the consumers' price reduces the consumers' surplus by the area of the trapezoid $P_0abP_t^c$. The fall in the producers' price causes producers' surplus to fall by the area of the trapezoid $P_0adP_t^f$. The combined loss to the market participants is the sum of the two trapezoids; however, part of this loss is recouped by the government as tax revenue. The tax revenue received by the government is t times B_t, or the area of the shaded rectangle $P_t^f dbP_t^c$. The excess burden of the excise tax on bagels is the sum of the areas of the two trapezoids minus the area of the tax revenue rectangle, or the area of the triangle *bad*.

Measuring the Excess Burden of an Excise Tax

The excess burden of a tax is of particular concern for policy because it is a loss to the consumers and producers but, unlike the revenue rectangle, does not provide the government with funds to spend. In fact, the excess burden does not benefit anyone in the economy—it is economic value flushed down the drain. Given the importance of the excess burden, we need to measure it.

From Figure 12.1, we see that the excess burden is equal to the area of a triangle. Although this is strictly true only if the demand and supply curves are linear, it provides a good approximation in most cases. The area of a triangle is equal to half its height times its base, so we can use this formula to obtain a quantitative expression for the excess burden. Imagine triangle *bad* in Figure 12.1 as lying on its side. The height of this reclining triangle is the distance $B_0 - B_t$, or the fall in the equilibrium quantity as a result of the tax (denoted $-\Delta Q$). The base of the triangle is the excise tax rate t. Using the formula for the area of a triangle, we obtain the expression for the excess burden (EB):

$$EB = -\frac{1}{2} \cdot t \cdot \Delta Q.$$

For example, if a tax of $2 per bagel causes the equilibrium quantity in the market to fall by 5 million bagels, the excess burden is $5 million.[3]

As we will see in Chapters 14 and 17, general income and sales taxes also cause excess burdens. Calculating the excess burden of these taxes is more complicated because the excess burdens must be calculated in many markets, and a tax in one market affects the excess burden in others as well. For this reason it is necessary to use general equilibrium analysis. A group of economists using an econometric model estimated that the excess burden of the whole United States tax system lies

---

[3]That is minus one half times $2 times minus 5 million units.

between 4% and 7% of GDP, or between 13% and 23% of the revenue collected by the tax system.[4]Using the lowest estimate, the excess burden of the tax system amounted to nearly $350 billion per year in 1999.

The Tax Rate and the Excess Burden

In Chapter 10 we saw that successive increases in the excise tax rate collect ever smaller increases in government revenue. (In fact, in theory, the revenue collected declines if the tax rate is increased above a critical level.) In contrast, successive increases in the excise tax rate cause the excess burden to increase at an *increasing* rate. When the supply and demand curves in the market are linear, the excess burden is proportional to the square of the tax rate, a relationship known as the **square rule.**

The square rule is illustrated by comparing the size of the excess burden triangles for tax rates t and t' in Figure 12.2. To simplify the diagram, we assume that the supply curve is horizontal, although this is not needed. Suppose tax rate t' is twice as large as t. Because the supply and demand curves are linear, the decline in the quantity from B_t to B_t' is equal to the decline from B_0 to B_t. A little geometric reasoning shows that the area of triangle $b'ad'$ is four times as great as the area of triangle bad. The area of $b'ad'$ exceeds the area of bad by the area of triangle $b'bc$, which is equal to the area of bad, and the area of rectangle $cbdd'$, which is twice the area of triangle bad.[5]

Combining what we have learned about the relationship between tax rate, revenue collected, and excess burden, we can draw a normative conclusion that is fundamental to the theory of tax policy: For the purpose of collecting revenue, high tax rates, particularly on a narrow category of goods, should be avoided. The higher the existing rate of tax, the less effective a further rate increase is for raising revenue and the more destructive it is to economic efficiency.

This discussion is summarized in Figure 12.3, where the revenue, excess burden, and total burden (the sum of the revenue and the excess burden) of an excise tax are plotted against the tax rate. These curves are plotted on the assumption that the demand and supply curves are linear. The revenue curve, showing the relationship between the tax rate and the revenue collected, increases as the tax rate increases but at a decreasing rate. Above a critical rate t_{max}, the revenue curve is negatively sloped. The excess burden increases with the tax rate at an increasing rate, reflecting the square rule, as shown by the curve labeled excess burden. The total burden curve is found by vertically summing the revenue and the excess burden curves.

The total burden of the tax increases steadily as the tax rate increases, but at higher tax rates more and more of the total burden is excess burden and less is revenue. Above the tax rate that maximizes tax revenue, the burden of the tax continues to rise as the tax rate rises because the increase in the excess burden outweighs the decline in the

[4]C. Ballard, J. Shoven, and J. Whalley, "The Total Welfare Cost of the United States Tax System: A General Equilibrium Approach," 1985.
[5]The result that the excess burden increases with the square of the tax rate depends on the assumption that the supply and demand curves are linear, but not on the assumption that the supply curve is horizontal. More generally, the percentage increase in the excess burden is more than the percentage increase in the tax rate.

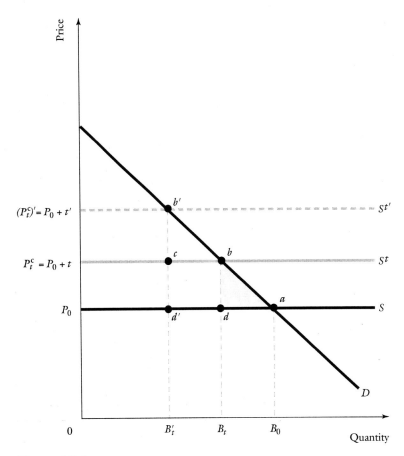

Figure 12.2

The Square Rule

When the tax rate is t, the excess burden is equal to the area of triangle *bad*. If the tax rate is increased to t', which is 2 times t, the excess burden is equal to the area of the larger triangle $b'ad'$. The larger triangle is 4 times the size of the smaller triangle. The area of the larger triangle includes that of the smaller triangle, plus the area of triangle $b'bc$, which has the same area, plus the area of rectangle $cbdd'$, which has twice the area of the smaller triangle.

revenue. At tax rate $\bar{t}$, the market equilibrium output is driven to zero (at least in the legal market—the good may be exchanged in an underground market) and no revenue is collected. The entire burden of the tax is excess burden. Such a tax rate is obviously a bad policy, unless the government wants to drive the good out of existence for another reason. For example, marijuana is taxed at high rates in some states for the purpose of making it prohibitively costly as well as illegal. Governments do not expect to raise revenue with this tax; they do it to suppress the use of marijuana.

Economic Efficiency and the Tax System

In practice, the government levies taxes on a broad range of goods and services. (From now on we understand the term *goods* to include both goods and services.)

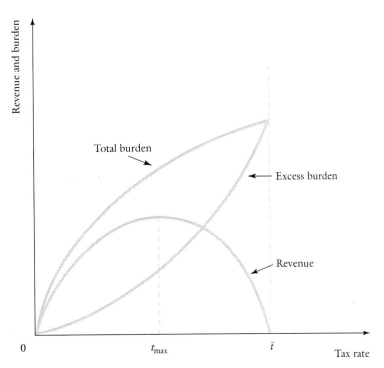

Figure 12.3

Burdens of an Excise Tax

As the tax rate increases, the total burden of the tax increases but its composition changes. The revenue component of the burden increases at a decreasing rate, and it decreases for rate increases above the critical rate t_{max}. The excess burden increases at an increasing rate, reflecting the square rule.

This is just as well, since we have seen that it is not a good policy to tax a single good or a narrow range of goods. We define a *tax system* as a set of taxes imposed on several goods. The government can get the same amount of revenue with different tax systems. For instance, under one tax system, good X might be taxed at a high rate and good Y at a low rate or not at all. Under another tax system, X is taxed at a low rate and Y is taxed at a high rate. Suppose both tax systems collect the same amount of revenue. What, if anything, is there to choose between them? Economic efficiency demands that we choose the tax system that imposes the smallest excess burden.

The excess burden of a tax system can be reduced in two ways. The first way is to exploit the square rule by broadening the tax base; the second way takes advantage of offsetting tax distortions.

REDUCING THE EXCESS BURDEN BY BROADENING THE TAX BASE. A straightforward advantage of taxing more than one good is that it allows the government to collect the same amount of revenue at lower tax rates. If two goods are independent, the excess burden of the tax system is the sum of the excess burdens created in each market. Goods are independent if the quantity demanded of each good depends on its own price only and not on the price of other goods. Although

A CASE IN POINT

12.1   The Excess Burden of Telecommunications Taxes

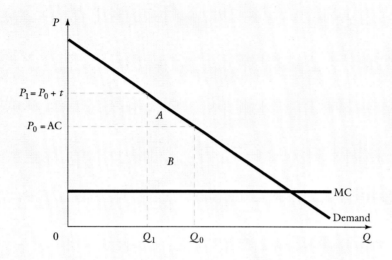

The federal government levies explicit and implicit taxes on telecommunications services. The explicit excise tax of 3% on the dollar amount of the taxpayer's phone bill dates back to 1898, when it was levied as a temporary tax to help finance the Spanish-American War. At that time, there was less than one telephone per 100 people and a telephone was considered an expensive luxury. An implicit (or hidden) tax levied by the Federal Communications Commission (FCC) requires telecom companies to contribute to the Universal Service Fund, which subsidizes the cost of providing phone service to rural and low-income customers as well as Internet connections for schools and other educational institutions. Most telecom companies pass on this cost to their customers as a Universal Service Charge (USC) of about 5% or 6% on their long-distance bill. The FCC also sets the subscriber line charge (SLC) that the companies charge customers. The SLC is a fixed monthly fee ($3.50 for residential customers) per phone line.

Professor Jerry Hausman of MIT estimates that the excess burden of USC is very high—

about $2.36 billion per year—which is more than $1.9 billion revenue collected. The reason for this high excess burden is shown in the figure. Telecom companies charge rates for long-distance service (P_0) that cover their average cost (AC) of long-distance service, rather than marginal cost (MC). Because of high fixed costs, MC is much less than AC (about one-quarter of AC, according to Hausman). Adding the USC (denoted t) to the long-distance rate raises the price to the consumer to P_1. The magnitude of the demand price elasticity for long-distance service is quite high— about .7—so the tax causes the quantity of long–distance calls to fall substantially, from Q_0 to Q_1. The excess burden is the sum of the areas A and B in the figure.

Critically analyze the following.

■ According to Hausman's estimates, the total burden of the $1.9 billion collected by the USC tax is $4.26 billion per year. Explain in words why the total burden of the tax can be so much more than the revenue collected.

■ Estimates of the price elasticity of phone service are very low, about .005, meaning that few

(continued)

A Case in Point (continued)

people would discontinue their phone line if the SLC were raised. Hausman argues that the total burden of financing the USF would have been much less had the FCC raised the SLC rather than the USC. Assuming that the price elasticity of phone service is approximately zero, what is the total burden of raising the SLC to collect $1.9 billion?

■ Given the large excess burden of the USC, it seems that customers would be better off if the USC were funded differently. Are there any reasons that such an inefficient tax is imposed? (Hint: The income elasticity of long-distance service is quite high (at least one), whereas the income elasticity of basic phone service is quite low (not much greater than zero).)

taxing two goods means that excess burdens are created in two markets rather than one, the government can collect the same revenue at lower tax rates. The sum of the areas of the two smaller excess burden triangles is smaller than the area of one large one, because of the square rule, so the overall burden is reduced. Taxing more goods in order to lower tax rates is called a **base-broadening** tax reform.

The advantage of base broadening is illustrated in Figure 12.4. In (a) and (b) we consider the markets for two goods X and Y, respectively. The quantity of each good is measured on the horizontal axis, and the demand curves are labeled D_X and D_Y, respectively. To simplify the diagram, we assume that the supply curves are perfectly elastic (horizontal) at the seller's price of $1. Suppose the government initially taxes good X at a high rate t_X', so the consumer pays $1 + t_X'$ for each unit of X. No tax is levied on good Y. The tax on X collects revenue equal to the area of rectangles A plus B, and the excess burden caused by the tax is the area of the triangle formed by the sum of the areas C, D, and E.

Suppose the tax rate on good X is reduced by a small amount to t_X and the lost revenue is made up by taxing good Y at t_Y. The revenue lost by reducing the tax rate on X is equal to the area of A minus the area of D. The tax rate on good Y must be set so the tax revenue collected by this tax (the area of F) is equal to the lost revenue from the reduced X tax. The advantage of changing the tax rates this way is the reduction in the excess burden. The excess burden in the X market falls by the sum of areas C and D. The excess burden created in the Y market is the area of triangle G. Because of the square rule, the area of G must be smaller than the area of C plus D when Y is initially untaxed. When both goods are taxed, the excess burden of the tax system is the sum of the areas of triangles E and G.

OFFSETTING TAX DISTORTIONS. When goods are not independent, the advantage of base broadening can still be exploited, although the excess burden of the tax system is not equal to the sum of the individual excess burdens. When the goods are not independent, increasing the tax on one good affects the quantity consumed of others. Suppose one good, video rentals, is already taxed. When we impose taxes on other goods, the excess burden caused by the tax on video rentals is affected even though the tax rate remains the same. Taxes on the other goods can either increase or decrease the quantity of video rentals, depending on whether the goods are substitutes or complements.

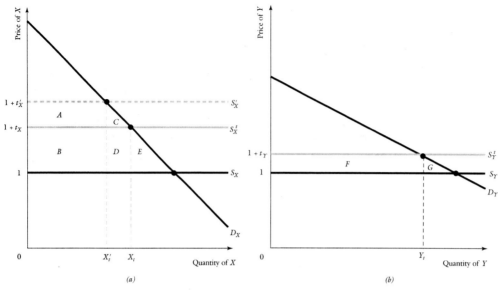

Figure 12.4

Efficiency Advantage of Base Broadening

Initially, the government gets all revenue by taxing only good X at a high rate t'_X. If the government decreases the tax on X to t_X and makes up the revenue by levying a tax on good Y, the excess burden in the X market is decreased by an amount equal to the sum of areas C and D. An excess burden created in the Y market is equal to the area labeled G, but it is smaller than the excess burden saved in the X market because of the square rule.

A tax on a substitute for video-taped movie rentals—say, pay-per-view (PPV) movies on cable TV—increases the quantity of video rentals and the revenue collected from taxing them. A tax on complements to video rentals—say, video recorders—decreases the quantity of video rentals and the revenue collected. When video recorders are taxed, fewer people buy recorders, so video rentals fall.

In Chapter 4 we saw that an excise tax can offset an existing market failure: for example, a cost externality associated with consuming gasoline. With a cost externality, the equilibrium quantity is greater than the efficient quantity, and a tax on gasoline can increase economic efficiency by reducing the quantity consumed. In the same way, a tax on one good can offset the inefficiency caused by a tax on another good.

Suppose an excise tax is imposed on red wine, which is bought and sold in a well-functioning market. The tax causes an excess burden because consumers substitute untaxed white wine for red wine. The substitution is made because the price of red wine is increased by the tax. However, since red wine is actually preferred, an excess burden is caused by the substitution. Too much white wine and too little red wine is consumed because of the tax. If the government also taxes white wine, it corrects (at least in part) for the distortion caused by the tax on red wine, because the tax raises the price of white wine and consumers have less incentive to substitute it for red wine. This reduces the inefficiency caused by taxing red wine alone. For this reason, the excess burden is always smaller when a given amount of revenue is collected by taxing two substitute goods rather than just one of them. By taxing both goods, the government gives consumers less opportunity to substitute untaxed goods for the taxed good. In addition, the government takes advantage of base broadening.

When the taxed goods are complements, taxing both goods reduces consumption of each good by more than by taxing that good alone. For instance, taxing both video rentals and video recorders causes consumption of both video rentals and recorders to fall more than taxing just one of the goods. The tax on video recorders reduces the demand for video rentals, and the tax on video rentals reduces the demand for recorders. Taxing complements together causes consumers to substitute untaxed goods for the complements, which *may* increase the excess burden. However, taxing both complement goods broadens the tax base, so it is possible, but not certain, that the excess burden can be reduced because taxing both goods permits lower tax rates.

Although a few goods may be complements in particular cases, generally goods are substitutes for each other. Although they may not perform the same functions, different goods are substitutes because they are alternative ways of providing utility to consumers. For example, wool and heating oil are substitutes because consumers can turn down the furnace and put on a sweater. For this reason, taxing more goods at lower rates rather than fewer goods at higher rates will generally reduce the excess burden of the tax system.

IS A UNIFORM TAX SYSTEM BEST?   The argument that it is better to tax more rather than fewer goods can be taken a step further. Suppose the government can tax *all* goods. The excess burden can be eliminated if it taxes all goods at the same percentage rate. When the government taxes all goods at the same rate, the tax system is called uniform. A **uniform tax system** is a **neutral tax system** because it does not alter relative prices and does not favor or hinder any particular good.

A uniform tax system on all goods can eliminate the excess burden, as shown in Figure 12.5. To simplify, we assume there are just two goods[6] in the economy, X and Y. A consumer with M dollars to spend faces prices P_X and P_Y on goods X and Y, respectively. When the goods are untaxed, the consumer's budget line BB intersects the horizontal and vertical axes at $\dfrac{M}{P_X}$ and $\dfrac{M}{P_Y}$. A tax on good X increases the price of X to the consumer, and the new budget line BB', intersects the horizontal axis at $\dfrac{M}{P_X + t'_X}$ where t'_X is the tax per unit of X. If good Y is not taxed, the budget line becomes steeper and the consumer chooses consumption bundle a. The amount of tax paid to the government (measured in units of good Y) is equal to the vertical distance ab between the two budget lines.

If the government taxes Y as well as X, the vertical intercept of the budget line shifts to $\dfrac{M}{P_Y + t_Y}$. When good Y is taxed in addition to X, the tax base is broader

---

[6]The argument extends to any number of goods and services.

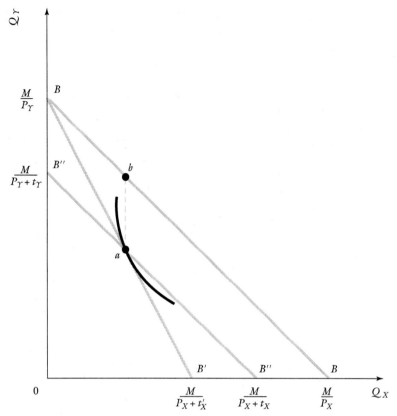

Figure 12.5

Neutrality of Uniform Taxes

When no taxes are levied, the budget line is *BB*. When only good *X* is taxed, its relative price is increased and the budget line is the steeper *BB'*, which provides an incentive to substitute good *Y* for good *X*. Taxing goods *X* and *Y* at the same percentage tax rate leaves the relative prices of the goods unchanged, and the budget line is *B"B"*. If goods *X* and *Y* are the only goods the consumer buys, the effect of uniform tax rates is equivalent to a lump-sum tax.

and so the government can reduce the tax rate on good X and collect the same amount of revenue. The new budget line $B''\ B''$ passes through point a, so the same amount of revenue is collected. When the tax rates on goods X and Y are uniform, the new budget line (with relative prices $\dfrac{P_X + t_X}{P_Y + t_Y}$) is parallel to the budget line where no goods are taxed (with relative prices $\dfrac{P_X}{P_Y}$). Algebraically, equating the relative prices requires that $\dfrac{t_X}{P_X + t_X} = \dfrac{t_Y}{P_Y + t_Y}$. That is, the tax per unit on each good represents the same fraction of the price paid by the consumer. For notational simplicity, we denote the per unit tax divided by the consumer's price (including the tax) by the Greek letter τ. That is, $\tau_X = \dfrac{t_X}{P_X + t_X}$ and $\tau_Y = \dfrac{t_Y}{P_Y + t_Y}$ A uniform tax system requires that $\tau_X = \tau_Y$.

In Figure 12.5, we see that taxing goods X and Y uniformly has the same effect on the budget line as imposing a lump-sum tax on the consumer. Recall that a lump-sum tax is a fixed amount consumers must pay no matter how they spend their income. No excess burden is caused by a lump-sum tax, because consumers cannot reduce the amount of tax by altering their consumption. Similarly, when consumers face uniform tax rates, they cannot change the amount of tax by substituting untaxed goods for taxed goods. By eliminating the excess burden, a uniform tax system allows the consumer to reach a higher indifference curve, as shown in the figure.

Proponents of broad-based tax systems, like the personal income tax, have long used this argument to support their case. A broad-based income tax is most efficient, they argue, because taxpayers pay the same amount of tax no matter how they spend their income. Does this mean that the personal income tax system has little or no excess burden? Unfortunately not. The problem is that even the broadest-based tax system cannot tax all the goods consumers enjoy. Leisure, for example, is a good because people enjoy it, but it is not a good that is bought and sold in commercial markets, so it is not easily taxed. Also, taxes on some goods are easily avoided or evaded. These include goods in the so-called *underground economy*, where cash transactions or barter are used to avoid the scrutiny of the tax collectors.

If for practical reasons some goods cannot be taxed, a truly uniform tax system is not feasible. Also, lump-sum taxes are viewed as arbitrary and unfair, so—as a matter of practicality—the government must choose among tax systems that are selective in one way or another. Except for corrective taxes, like a gasoline tax, real-world tax systems distort private decisions and reduce economic efficiency. Rather than eliminating the excess burden, the best the government can do is try to minimize it. This is an example of second-best economics, described in Chapter 2.

How can the government improve the tax system by avoiding unnecessarily large excess burdens? Should it uniformly tax those goods that it can tax? To answer these questions, we first develop the concept of the marginal burden of collecting tax revenue.

The Marginal Burden of Tax Revenue

The **marginal burden** of tax revenue is the increase in the burden on consumers and producers when the government collects $1 more of revenue by raising tax rates. The concept was developed by Professor Edgar Browning, now of Texas A&M, who called it the **marginal cost of public funds** because it represents the cost imposed on the private sector by an increase in the availability of funds for government programs. The marginal burden of tax revenue from raising the tax on good X is shown in Figure 12.6. The quantity of good X is measured on the horizontal axis, and the demand curve for X is labeled D_X. The price charged by the sellers for a unit of X by the firm is fixed at $1 by assumption, and the existing per unit tax on good X is

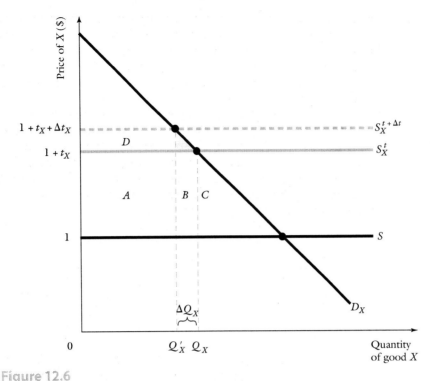

Figure 12.6

Calculating Marginal Burden per Dollar of Increased Revenue

An increase in the tax rate Δt_X causes the quantity of good X consumed to change by ΔQ_X. The increase in price reduces consumers' surplus by $Q'_X \cdot \Delta t_X$, which is the area of D (the small shaded triangle can be ignored for small tax changes), while tax revenue increases by $Q'_X \cdot \Delta t_X + t_X \cdot \Delta Q_X$, which is the area of D minus the area of B. Taking the ratio of the change in consumers' surplus to the change in tax revenue gives the expression for the marginal burden of tax revenue.

t_X. Because the supply curve is horizontal, the tax is fully passed on to the consumer, who faces a total price of $1 + t_X$ and consumes Q_X units. The revenue collected from the tax is equal to the area of the area of rectangle A plus the area of rectangle B. The excess burden caused by the tax is equal to the area of triangle C.

Suppose the government increases the tax by a small amount Δt_X so the new tax rate is $t_X + \Delta t_X$. The consumers' price rises by the increase in the tax, and the consumption of good X changes by ΔQ_X to Q'_X. The increased tax rate increases the burden on the consumer and the amount of revenue collected by the government. The burden on the consumer increases by the area of trapezoid D, which represents the reduction in consumers' surplus caused by the tax increase. For small changes in the tax rate, the increase in the burden is approximately equal to the area of the rectangle part of trapezoid D; that is, the small shaded triangle can be ignored for small changes in the tax rate, which we do throughout this discussion. The area of this rectangle is $Q'_X \cdot \Delta t_X$.

How much revenue does the government gain by increasing the tax on X? At the new tax rate, the revenue is $(t_X + \Delta t_X) \cdot Q'_X$ or the combined areas of rectangles A and D. The change in the tax revenue is equal to the area of rectangle D (the loss in consumers' surplus from the tax increase) minus the area of rectangle B. The government gains less revenue than the consumers lose in surplus because the area of rectangle B is lost when the tax rate is increased. The area of rectangle B (along with the ignored shaded triangle) becomes part of the larger excess burden, so it is lost to the economy as a whole.

The marginal burden of tax revenue is the loss in consumers' surplus divided by the increase in tax revenue. The loss in consumers' surplus is equal to the area of rectangle D or $Q'_X \cdot \Delta t_X$, and the increase in tax revenue is equal to the area of rectangle D minus the area of rectangle B. The area of rectangle B is equal to minus $t_X \cdot \Delta Q_X$, so the increase in tax revenue is $Q'_X \cdot \Delta t_X + t_X \cdot \Delta Q_X$. Dividing the loss in consumers' surplus by the gain in tax revenue gives the following expression[7] for the marginal burden (MB) of revenue from raising t_X:

$$MB_X = \frac{1}{1 + \dfrac{t_X}{Q'_X} \cdot \dfrac{\Delta Q_X}{\Delta t_X}} = \frac{1}{1 - \tau_X \cdot \eta_X}.$$

The right-hand expression for MB_X is fairly easy to interpret. The second term in the denominator is the price elasticity of demand for good X multiplied by the tax rate on good X expressed as a percentage of the tax-inclusive price paid by the consumer. Since price elasticity is positive, the denominator is less than 1 if the tax rate is positive. This means that the marginal burden of the tax on good X is greater than 1 except when the tax rate is zero, in which case it is equal to 1. Generally, an increase in the tax rate increases the burden on the economy more than it increases the government's tax revenue.

To illustrate the calculation of the marginal burden, we can use the middle expression. Suppose the tax on good X is initially \$1 and 100 units are consumed; when the tax rate is increased by 5 cents to \$1.05, consumption falls by 1 unit, to 99 units. In this case we can find the marginal burden of the tax as:[8]

$$MB_X = \frac{1}{1 + \dfrac{\$1}{99} \cdot \dfrac{-1}{\$0.05}} \approx 1.25.$$

That is, the loss in consumers' surplus from increasing the tax rate on good X to collect \$1 more of tax revenue is about \$1.25.

---

[7] The first equality is obtained using $MB_X = \dfrac{\text{area } D}{\text{area } D - \text{area } B} = \dfrac{Q'_X \cdot \Delta t_X}{Q'_X \cdot \Delta t_X + t_X \cdot \Delta Q_X}$.

Dividing the numerator and denominator of this expression by $Q'_X \cdot \Delta t_X$ gives the first equality in the text. The second equality is obtained by dividing the second term in the denominator of the preceding expression by $1 + t_X$. Also, since the supply curve is horizontal, $\dfrac{\Delta Q_X}{\Delta t_X} = \dfrac{\Delta Q_X}{\Delta P_X}$. Finally, the price elasticity of demand is defined by $\eta_X = -\dfrac{\Delta Q_X}{\Delta P_X} \cdot \dfrac{1 + t_X}{Q'_X}$.

[8] Alternatively, the price elasticity of demand is

$\eta_X = \dfrac{1}{0.05} \cdot \dfrac{2}{100} = 0.4$ and $\tau = 0.5$, so $MB_X = \dfrac{1}{1 - (0.5)(0.4)} = 1.25$.

The marginal burden of revenue depends on the existing level of the tax rate (and the amount of revenue collected). The more revenue we already collect from a tax, the higher the marginal burden of getting $1 more by raising the tax rate. This reflects the result, shown earlier, that the excess burden increases with the square of the tax rate. For example, suppose the tax on good X is initially $2 per unit, at which 80 units of X are consumed (assuming the demand curve is linear). If the tax rate is increased by 5 cents to $2.05, consumption falls by 1 unit, to 79. Evaluating the marginal burden using the above expression, we find $MB_X = 2.02$, which is larger than when the tax rate was $1.

The relationship between the marginal burden of revenue and the amount of revenue collected by the tax on X is shown by the curve labeled MB_X in Figure 12.7. The amount of revenue collected is measured on the horizontal axis, and the marginal burden is measured on the vertical axis. The marginal burden of the first $1 of revenue is $1, and MB_X increases steadily as the amount of revenue collected by the tax increases.

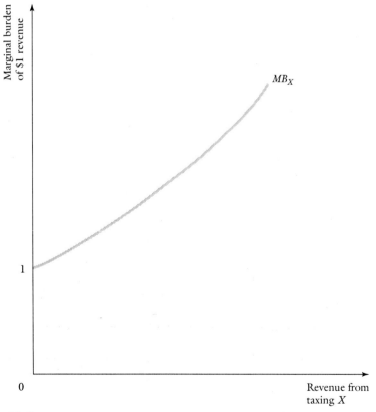

Figure 12.7

Marginal Burden of Revenue Schedule
The marginal burden of the first $1 of revenue from taxing good X is 1. As the amount of revenue collected from a tax on good X is increased, the marginal burden increases because the excess burden rises with the square of the tax rate.

Public finance economists use the concept of the marginal burden in many ways, from benefit-cost analysis to finding the cost of income redistribution through the tax system. In this chapter, we use it to find the tax system that minimizes the excess burden associated with collecting a given amount of tax revenue. One recent estimate of the marginal burden of the income tax—the most important source of tax revenue—suggests a marginal burden between 1.16 and 1.31, depending on assumptions about the elasticity of the labor supply and the supply of household savings.[9] This means that a government program that requires $1 million dollars of revenue from higher taxes does not cost $1 million dollars of lost private consumption—it costs between $1.16 million and $1.31 million. This includes the cost of greater economic inefficiency caused by the higher income tax rates. In order for the program to be worth doing, its benefits must exceed *this* amount, not the $1 million budgetary cost.

The Optimal Excise Tax System

The problem of finding a tax system that minimizes the burden of taxes on the economy can be analyzed in a simple economy with three goods and a single consumer. Goods X and Y are market goods that the government can easily tax, and a third good Z—say, leisure—cannot be taxed. The government taxes X and Y enough to raise a given amount of tax revenue R. The revenue is used to make lump-sum cash transfers to consumers or to provide them with a public good. Since the quantity of the public good is fixed, we can ignore it and concentrate on the three private goods X, Y, and Z.

In this framework, the government cannot avoid distorting private decisions with tax policy. Even if it taxes goods X and Y at the same percentage rate, so that their relative price is not changed, the tax system still alters the relative prices between the taxed goods and the untaxed good Z. As we will see, under these circumstances, taxing goods X and Y uniformly may not be the best tax system the government can choose.

The problem of finding the most efficient tax system is illustrated in Figure 12.8. Here the distance between 0_X and 0_Y is equal to R, the fixed amount of revenue the government must collect. The amount of revenue from taxing good X is measured to the right of 0_X, and the amount of revenue from taxing good Y is measured to the left of 0_Y. Together, the revenue from taxing the two goods adds up to R, and any point on the horizontal axis shows how much is collected by taxing each good. For instance, at 0_X all revenue is raised by taxing good Y, whereas at point m (equal to half of R), half the revenue comes from taxing good X and the other half from taxing good Y.

The marginal burden schedules are labeled MB_X and MB_Y, respectively. The marginal burden schedule for taxing good Y is drawn with respect to the origin 0_Y, so it is mirror-reversed. As derived above, the marginal burden of tax revenue from raising

the tax on good X is $MB_X = \dfrac{1}{1 - \tau_X \cdot \eta_X}$. Similarly, we can express the marginal

[9]C. Ballard, J. Shoven, and J. Whalley, "General Equilibrium Computations of the Marginal Welfare Costs of Taxes in the United States," 1985.

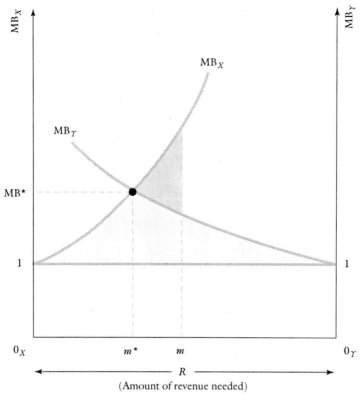

Figure 12.8

Optimal (Burden-Minimizing) Tax Structure

The base of the diagram is equal to R, the revenue the government must collect. The amount of revenue collected from taxing X (Y) is measured to the right of 0_X (left of 0_Y), and the associated marginal burden schedule MB_X (MB_Y) is also drawn. The burden of the tax structure is equal to the area under the marginal burden schedules. At point m the burden is not minimized, because MB_X is greater than MB_Y. By getting less revenue from taxing X and more from taxing Y at point m^*, the government minimizes the area under the marginal burden schedules.

burden of tax revenue from raising the tax on good Y as $MB_Y = \dfrac{1}{1 - \tau_Y \cdot \eta_Y}$. The burden of collecting R dollars in revenue is equal to the combined area under the two marginal burden curves, so in order to minimize the burden of collecting R dollars in revenue, the government chooses the tax structure that minimizes the combined area.[10] In Figure 12.8, we see that point m does *not* minimize the tax burden. At m, the marginal burden of taxing X is higher than the marginal burden of taxing Y, so by collecting less revenue from taxing X and more from taxing Y, the government reduces the burden of the tax by the difference between the mar-

---

[10]Since the marginal burden is the burden per dollar of revenue, we sum the areas under the curves to find the total burden.

ginal burdens. By choosing tax structure $m^\star$ rather than m, the government reduces the tax burden by the dark-shaded triangle.

At $m^\star$ the marginal burdens of each tax are equal to each other, so the tax burden cannot be reduced further unless the government reduces the amount of tax collected. At $m^\star$ the excess burden of the tax system is not zero, but it is as low as possible given that the government cannot tax all three goods and needs R dollars of revenue. The taxes on goods X and Y distort private economic decisions because the consumers substitute the untaxable good Z for the taxed goods, but the government cannot do any better. The minimized excess burden is shown in Figure 12.8 as the light shaded area. The rectangle below the excess burden is tax revenue R (since the height of the rectangle is 1 and the base is R).

THE INVERSE ELASTICITY RULE.   The tax rates on X and Y that minimize the excess burden in the problem above are the "optimal" tax rates. What can we say about these optimal rates? Are they equal to each other, or is one good taxed more than the other? If so, which good? These are the types of questions a policy maker must answer in designing an efficient tax system. The answer is found by substituting the expressions for the marginal burdens into the equality $\mathrm{MB}_X = \mathrm{MB}_Y$. Let $\mathrm{MB}^\star$ denote the equalized value of MB_X and MB_Y at $m^\star$ in Figure 12.8. Note that $\mathrm{MB}^\star$ is greater than 1. Substituting the expressions for the marginal burdens of each tax,[11] we find

that the optimal tax rate on good X must satisfy the equality $\tau_X^\star = \dfrac{\mathrm{MB}^\star - 1}{\mathrm{MB}^\star} \cdot \dfrac{1}{\eta_X}$ and

the optimal tax rate on good Y must satisfy the equality $\tau_Y^\star = \dfrac{\mathrm{MB}^\star - 1}{\mathrm{MB}^\star} \cdot \dfrac{1}{\eta_Y}$. The

asterisk on a variable indicates that it is set at its optimal level (that is, the level that minimizes excess burden). The expressions above describe the **inverse elasticity rule,** which states that the optimal tax rate on each good is proportional to the

inverse of its own price elasticity. The factor of proportionality, $\dfrac{\mathrm{MB}^\star - 1}{\mathrm{MB}^\star}$, is the

same for both goods.

When is it optimal to tax X and Y uniformly? The inverse elasticity rule provides the answer: it is optimal to tax X and Y uniformly when they have the same price elasticities of demand, or $\eta_X = \eta_Y$. The inverse elasticity rule also tells us that it is efficient to tax good X at a higher rate if $\eta_X < \eta_Y$ and vice versa. The optimal tax rate is higher for the good that has a lower price elasticity.

The logic of the inverse elasticity rule is rather obvious. Excess burdens are caused because in response to taxes, consumers reduce their consumption of taxed goods. If a good has an inelastic demand curve—say, because it has few good substitutes—consumption does not fall much when the good is taxed. Taxing a good with an inelastic demand curve causes a small excess burden, so it is best to tax it at a higher rate. On

---

[11]That is, we solve $\dfrac{1}{1 - \tau_i \cdot \eta_i} = \mathrm{MB}^\star$ to find $\tau_i{}^\star$, where $i = X, Y$.

the other hand, taxing a good with a high elasticity causes consumption to fall significantly, resulting in a large excess burden, so it is best to tax such a good lightly.

THE RAMSEY RULE AND TAX NEUTRALITY.

Although the inverse elasticity rule implies that, in general, tax rates may differ across taxed goods, the idea that the tax system should be neutral and not interfere with the consumers' choices among taxed goods is also compelling. Can the conflict between the inverse elasticity rule and the belief in tax neutrality be resolved? Frank Ramsey, the Cambridge economist who first analyzed this problem in 1927, provided an interpretation that reconciles the notion of different tax rates on goods with tax neutrality.

To understand Ramsey's interpretation, start by rewriting the inverse elasticity expression as $\eta_X \cdot \tau_X^* = \eta_Y \cdot \tau_Y^* = \frac{MB^* - 1}{MB^*}$. This expression states that the price elasticity of each good multiplied by its optimal tax rate is the same for both taxed goods. Given the definition of price elasticity, $\eta_X \cdot \tau_X^*$ is equal to the percentage fall in consumption of good X when it is taxed at the optimal rate, and $\eta_Y \cdot \tau_Y^*$ is the percentage fall in the consumption of good Y. In other words, when the goods are taxed optimally, consumers reduce their consumption of the taxed goods by an equal percentage. That is, $\frac{\Delta Q_X}{Q_X} = \frac{\Delta Q_Y}{Q_Y}$. This is known as **Ramsey's rule** for optimal taxation.

We can interpret Ramsey's rule as a desirable form of tax neutrality. Normally, we think of tax neutrality in terms of the tax system's not affecting relative prices. But economic efficiency does not concern relative prices; it concerns the use of economic resources. Ramsey's rule shows that the optimal excise tax system is neutral with respect to quantities. When goods X and Y are taxed optimally, consumers substitute away from them toward the untaxed good Z in equal proportions. The imposition of the tax system does not cause a bigger substitution of the untaxed good Z for X than Z for Y, or vice versa. Optimal tax rates have a uniform impact on the relative quantities of the taxed goods, though not necessarily on their prices.

EQUITY AND THE TAX SYSTEM

Although economists tend to focus on economic efficiency, many people are more concerned with the fairness of a tax system. Whatever improvements in economic efficiency a new tax system makes possible, if it is considered "unfair" by a large part of the population it has little chance of being enacted. For this reason alone, analysis of tax policy must consider the equity effects of different tax systems in addition to their effects on economic efficiency.

Principles of Tax Equity

In Chapter 7 we discussed several principles of equity or fairness that apply to the distribution of income. The same principles apply to the distribution of tax burdens. Historically, two notions of equity have dominated discussions of fairness in the tax system—the benefit and ability-to-pay principles. The **benefit principle of equity** is

A CASE IN POINT

12.2   The Double Dividend from the Green Tax Shift

The concept of the marginal burden helps us understand a major policy debate: do we get a "double dividend" with an environment-friendly tax structure? Many environmental groups (for example, see the Green Tax Shift Website at http://www.progress.org/banneker/shift.html) argue that a shift from the current reliance on income taxes to "green taxes" will yield two large benefits. The first comes from levying corrective (Pigouvian) taxes on goods with marginal external costs (MEC), as was explained in Chapter 4. The second comes from using the revenue from these taxes to reduce income tax rates. Income taxes cause an excess burden by reducing the taxpayer's incentive to work. (The effect of the income tax on the incentive to work is discussed in Chapter 14.) By reducing income taxes, the excess burden of the tax system is reduced, hence the double dividend.

Suppose, as in our discussion of the optimal tax system, that the economy has three goods—an "environmentally dirty" good Y with a marginal external cost (MEC), a "clean" good X, and an untaxable good Z (leisure). As we saw, the marginal burden of raising a dollar of revenue by raising the tax on X is the cost of the lost consumers' surplus divided by the change in revenue, which can be expressed

$$MB_X = \frac{1}{1 + t_X \cdot \frac{\Delta Q_X}{\Delta t_X} \cdot \frac{1}{Q_X}}$$

The marginal burden of raising a dollar of revenue by raising the tax on Y is

$$MB_Y = \frac{1 + MEC \cdot \frac{\Delta Q_Y}{\Delta t_Y} \cdot \frac{1}{Q_Y}}{1 + t_Y \cdot \frac{\Delta Q_Y}{\Delta t_Y} \cdot \frac{1}{Q_Y}}.$$

The second term in the numerator reflects the fact that the net cost of taxing this good is not the loss in consumers' surplus alone. It is the loss in consumers' surplus plus the gain from reducing the quantity of the dirty good, which is the marginal

external cost (MEC) times that change in the quantity of the dirty good. A small "green tax shift," which collects a dollar less by taxing X and a dollar more by taxing Y, provides a net benefit MB_X minus MB_Y. The economy saves the marginal burden from taxing X but pays the marginal burden from taxing Y.

Proponents of the green tax shift argue that current tax rates on dirty goods are zero, or very low.

If $t_Y = 0$, then $MB_Y = 1 + MEC \cdot \frac{\Delta Q_Y}{\Delta t_Y} \cdot \frac{1}{Q_Y}$, which

is less than one. The benefit from the shift

$(MB_X - MB_Y)$ is $(MB_X - 1) - MEC \cdot \frac{\Delta Q_Y}{\Delta t_Y} \cdot \frac{1}{Q_Y}.$

The second term is the benefit of reduced environmental costs. The first term is the difference between the marginal excess burden of taxing clean goods. As mentioned, economists estimate the marginal burden of income taxes to be around 1.3, so the double dividend from a green tax shift of $1 is 30 cents plus the environmental benefit.

Critically analyze the following:

- Green taxes proponents propose huge tax shifts—as much as a trillion dollars to goods that harm the environment. Would you expect a double dividend from such large shifts? (Hint: What happens to MB_Y as Y is taxed at higher and higher rates?)

- Critics of the double dividend hypothesis argue that a tax on income taxes both clean *and* dirty goods, so $t_Y = t_X$ rather than $t_Y = 0$. Show that there is still a double dividend from a small green tax shift if $t_Y < MEC$.

- Using a diagram like Figure 12.8, show the "optimal" green tax shift. If green taxes are initially zero, what is the maximum benefit according to the diagram? (Remember that when the tax on the dirty good is zero, the marginal burden is less than one.)

the belief that the burden on taxpayers should depend on the benefits they receive from government spending. Although this view is not as prevalent as it once was, in some cases people still perceive fairness in such terms. A good example is the federal excise tax on gasoline, which is used mainly to fund road construction and maintenance. In the minds of many people, the gasoline tax is fair because it is paid by the people who benefit from gasoline taxes—drivers. Note that the perception of fairness depends on the tax proceeds being spent on roads. As a source of general revenue, the gas tax is considered unfair because many people believe it is regressive.

In modern analysis of tax policy, the dominant principle of tax equity is the **ability-to-pay principle,** which requires that burdens on taxpayers be related to their ability to pay the tax. This principle of equity is based on two beliefs: First, the tax system should be impartial among taxpayers; second, the tax system should not overly burden taxpayers who have limited means.

Economists have formalized these beliefs in terms of two criteria. The first criterion, **horizontal equity,** requires that the tax system treat people equally if they have equal ability to pay. Hence, a tax system in which two taxpayers have the same ability to pay but pay different amounts of tax violates horizontal equity. The second criterion, **vertical equity,** requires that a tax system impose lighter burdens on people with less ability to pay and heavier burdens on those with more ability to pay. Vertical equity reflects the belief that a given dollar tax burden imposes a greater utility burden on people with less ability to pay than those with more ability to pay.

Achieving Equity in a Tax System

How does the government achieve equity as defined by these principles in the tax system? The problem is difficult because the equity principles may conflict with each other. For example, suppose people with low ability to pay receive greater benefits from a government program. The benefit principle requires that they pay more of the tax that finances the program than others do, but the ability-to-pay principle requires that they pay less. Another difficulty with the benefit principle is that it may be difficult or even impossible to determine how much different groups of people benefit from some government programs. For example, it would be very difficult to determine how much different groups of taxpayers benefit from national defense spending. Furthermore, most tax revenue goes into the government's general fund rather than being dedicated to a particular program.

Ability to pay is typically easier to measure than the benefits received from government spending, so this principle of equity is somewhat easier to apply. To make the tax system equitable in terms of ability to pay, the government must first decide how to measure ability to pay. Most commonly, the taxpayer's annual income is used to measure ability to pay, although some people argue that wealth is a better measure. Ideally, lifetime income is the best measure of ability to pay. Recall from Chapter 11 that lifetime income is a measure of a person's income over his or her lifetime rather than over a particular year. Lifetime income is better than annual income, because many people who have low income in a particular year might have higher incomes in other years, and vice versa. Such a person has higher ability to pay than someone whose income is low every year. For instance, a skilled professional who takes a "sabbatical" has a low income but a high ability to pay. Conversely, a construction worker may have high income in a particular year when he or she has lots of work and over-time pay, but lower income in other years. Since lifetime income is not easily measured, annual income is most commonly used to measure ability to pay.

ACHIEVING HORIZONTAL EQUITY.   Once some measure of ability to pay is adopted—say, income—horizontal equity requires that people with the same income pay the same amount of tax. To achieve this, people should pay the same amount of tax no matter the source of their income. For instance, if some sources of income are not taxed or are taxed more lightly than other sources, people with the same level of income from different sources would pay different amounts of tax. Suppose, for example, the income a taxpayer earns from a company in the United States is taxed, but not the income from a company in another country. Two taxpayers, one with income from the American company and another with income from the foreign company, would pay different amounts of tax even though they have the same income. For this reason, for an income tax to be horizontally equitable, taxable income should be defined as broadly as possible. That is, it should include income from all sources and tax it at the same rate. Lower tax rates on some types of income—say, capital gains—create horizontal inequity.

In addition, to achieve horizontal equity taxpayers with the same income should pay the same amount of tax, no matter how they spend it. If people pay less tax when they spend their incomes in certain ways, taxpayers with the same income would pay different amounts of tax. For example, in most states people pay sales tax when they spend their income. In most cases, these sales taxes apply to most goods but exempt many services. Two taxpayers with the same income, but one with a taste for goods and the other with a taste for services, would pay different amounts of tax. Therefore, to achieve horizontal equity, a sales tax should be as broad as possible and tax all goods and services.

Earlier we saw that taxing more goods and services at lower rates (base broadening) allows the government to collect the revenue it needs and imposes a lower excess burden. Now we also see that broad-based taxes achieve greater horizontal equity. For this reason, economists advocate uniform broad-based taxes and oppose provisions that give tax breaks to special industries, such as the one the U.S. Congress was considering in March 2000 to exempt Internet commerce from sales taxes. Economists argue that it is both fair and equitable to tax Internet commerce at the same rate as regular (brick-and-mortar) commerce.

ACHIEVING VERTICAL EQUITY.   At a minimum, vertical equity requires that people with more income pay more tax. However, most people believe that this is not enough. By this definition, a tax is vertically equitable if a person with $100,000 income pays $1 more in tax than does someone with $10,000 income. Most people would argue that a person with $100,000 tax should pay at least 10 times as much tax as does a person with $10,000 income. In other words, vertical equity requires that the tax system not be regressive (see Chapter 11). In fact, many people, though not all, believe that vertical equity requires the tax system to be progressive, so the person with $100,000 income pays *more* than 10 times as much tax as the person with

$10,000 income. In other words, the tax paid as a percentage of income should rise as income rises. Although the issue is debatable, let us accept the assumption that vertical equity requires the tax to be progressive. How is vertical equity achieved?

An income tax can be made progressive in three ways. One way is to exempt a given amount of income from taxation. An income tax that exempts a certain amount of income B and taxes all income above that level at a flat rate is shown as schedule T_E in Figure 12.9. In this figure, the income of the taxpayer is measured on the horizontal axis and the tax paid by the taxpayer on the vertical axis. The slope of a ray from the origin to the tax schedule measures the average tax rate (or the tax paid as a percentage of income) because it is equal to the rise (tax paid) over the run (income). For example, a taxpayer with income M_1 pays tax R_1 and has an average tax rate equal to R_1/M_1. Another taxpayer with a higher income I_2 pays tax R_2 and has a higher tax rate, as can be seen from the steeper slope of the ray. The higher a taxpayer's income, the steeper the slope of the ray, hence the higher the taxpayer's average tax rate. The taxpayer with less income pays a lower percentage of income in tax because the exempted income B is a larger percentage of his or her income.

The second way the government can make the income tax progressive is to make it a **negative income tax** or **NIT**. A NIT is illustrated in Figure 12.9 by extending the T_E schedule below the horizontal axis as shown by the dashed line.

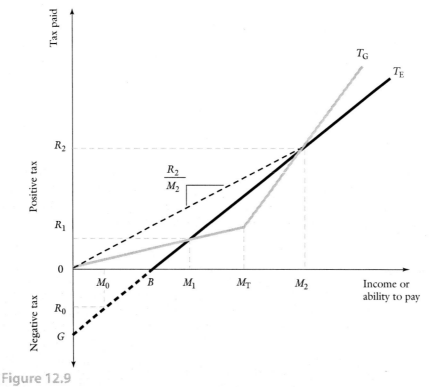

Figure 12.9

Progressive Taxes
An income tax system is progressive if it has a graduated rate structure (schedule T_G) or an exemption (schedule T_E). A negative income tax, illustrated by schedule T_E extended to G, is also progressive.

Rather than paying no tax, a person with income less than B pays a negative tax—that is, he or she receives a payment from the government. The payment is found by multiplying the tax rate by the difference between income B (called the break-even income) and the taxpayer's income. For example, a taxpayer with income M_0 would pay a negative tax (receive a payment from the government) equal to R_0. Again, as income rises, the slope of the ray becomes steeper, indicating that tax paid as a percentage of income rises with income.

The third way the government can make an income tax progressive is with a graduated tax rate structure. Such a tax is illustrated in Figure 12.9 by the schedule labeled T_G, which has two tax brackets. Income less than M_T, called the tax bracket threshold, is taxed at a low rate (say, 15%), whereas income above M_T is taxed at a higher rate (say, 28%). Again, the taxpayer with the higher income M_2 pays a higher percentage of his or her income in tax than does the taxpayer with income M_1.

In Chapter 13, we will see that the U.S. personal income tax is made progressive using all three methods. Taxpayers can deduct from their income a fixed amount called the standard deduction and additional personal exemptions for each family member. A family of four can earn over $16,000 before it pays any tax. In addition, taxpayers with limited incomes can receive the refundable Earned Income Tax Credit (EITC) discussed in Chapter 8. A tax credit is an amount the taxpayer can deduct from taxes owed. Because the EITC is refundable, a taxpayer receives it (in the form of a government payment) even if no tax is owed. This would be the case if the taxpayer's income is less than the sum of the standard deduction and the personal exemptions. The U.S. personal income tax rate structure is also graduated with five tax brackets ranging from 15% for taxpayers with low taxable income to 39.6% for taxpayers with the highest incomes. All of these features make the personal income tax very progressive, as we saw in Chapter 11.

Achieving vertical equity with a sales tax is more difficult because the tax is paid on transactions, and it is not possible to have exemptions and graduated rate structures. People do not reveal their ability to pay when making purchases at the store. In fact, most people consider the sales tax regressive because people with higher income tend to spend a smaller fraction of their income than do people with lower income. The regressivity of a sales tax can be mitigated by exempting those goods and services for which lower-income people spend a larger fraction of their income than do higher-income people. For this reason, many state sales taxes exempt groceries, rent, and in some cases, children's clothing.

CONFLICTS BETWEEN EFFICIENCY, HORIZONTAL EQUITY, AND VERTICAL EQUITY. While base broadening generally makes a tax more efficient and equitable, in many cases an attempt to make a tax more equitable will make it less efficient (and cause a larger excess burden). For example, greater vertical equity in an income tax can be achieved with a large exemption, but this makes the tax base less broad so a higher tax rate is needed to collect a given revenue. As we saw earlier, the excess burden of a tax rises with the square of the tax rate. Similarly, an attempt to make a sales tax less regressive by exempting groceries makes the tax bases less broad, so higher tax rates are needed on other goods to raise sufficient revenue.

In other cases, making a tax more vertically equitable can make it less horizontally equitable. If groceries are exempted from the sales tax in order to achieve greater vertical equity, people with the same incomes who spend different fractions of their income on groceries will pay different amounts of tax. This would be a violation of horizontal equity. As in most economic choices, trade-offs have to be made between these competing objectives.

THE BURDENS OF ADMINISTRATION AND COMPLIANCE

The third feature of a desirable tax system (along with efficiency and equity) is a low cost of administration and compliance. This includes the cost to the government of administering and enforcing the tax law, and the costs imposed on the taxpayers in obeying and complying with it. In addition, burdens are caused by the actions taxpayers take to minimize their tax payments through tax avoidance and tax evasion. These running costs depend mainly on the complexity of the tax system. If a tax system is efficient and equitable, but too complex for the government to administer and for the taxpayers to understand and comply with, it is not likely to be perceived as a good tax system. For this reason, a good tax system should be as simple and transparent as possible.

The burden of running a tax system consists of direct costs, which are costs of administration and enforcement incurred by the government agency that collects the taxes; and indirect costs imposed on the taxpayers and the economy. The costs of running a tax collection agency, such as the Internal Revenue Service (IRS), absorb a fraction of the revenue it collects. For example, the budget of the IRS was $7.6 billion in 1999, which is less than one-half of 1% the federal receipts it collects. However, these easily measured costs are just part of the costs of running the tax system. In addition, compliance costs are imposed on the taxpayers. The compliance cost is the value of the taxpayers' time and effort in keeping records, learning the tax laws and rules, and providing the necessary information to the tax collection agency.

The compliance costs of the income tax system are substantial, even for individuals. For instance, the IRS estimates that the average taxpayer filling out Form 1040—the main form for the personal income tax—spends about 11 hours and 38 minutes in keeping records, reading the instructions, and completing the return. With itemized deductions, the taxpayer also must fill out Schedule A, which takes another 4 hours and 35 minutes. Business income requires Schedule C, which takes another 10 hours and 16 minutes, according to the IRS estimates.[12] Using a conservative estimate of the taxpayers' time—say, $10 an hour—this part of the compliance cost amounts to nearly $14 billion, or nearly twice the IRS budget, for 125 million taxpayers.

The compliance cost imposed on business firms is even greater. A study by Arthur D. Little, Inc., commissioned by the IRS, found that the time taken by business taxpayers to comply with the federal income tax system is twice that of individuals, 3.6 billion hours versus 1.8 billion hours. Moreover, the taxation of business is more complicated than that of individuals, and it requires specialized knowledge, which is very costly. Recently, the total compliance burden of the federal income tax by individuals and firms was estimated at $200 billion by Arthur P. Hall, an economist at the Tax Foundation.[13] This figure is probably far too high. A more

---

[12]Internal Revenue Service, Form 1040 1995, p. 7.
[13] *Wall Street Journal*, July 12, 1995, p. 1.

recent study by Professor Joel Slemrod and Jon Bakija of the University of Michigan concludes that a "reasonable estimate" of the compliance cost of the federal income tax system is around $75 billion a year, which is still a sizable sum.[14]

The Burden of Tax Avoidance

Another burden is caused by tax avoidance. Tax avoidance means legal actions taken by taxpayers to reduce the amount of taxes they pay. Unlike tax evasion, tax avoidance is within the law, although some cases are murky and may be considered avoidance by the taxpayer and evasion by the government. The difference in opinion is usually settled in tax court.

One of the most common methods of income tax avoidance is *shifting* income. Taxes are reduced by shifting income to another person, usually a family member, who has a lower income tax rate. For instance, authors could arrange to have royalties from their books assigned to their children. Because children have little or no income, they have a lower tax rate than the parent under the graduated income tax system (the graduated income tax is described fully in Chapter 13). To be legally shifted, the full right to the income must actually be transferred to the child. Some form of trust must be used with this type of tax avoidance; otherwise, the "kiddie tax" applies. The kiddie tax provision of the Internal Revenue Code (IRC) requires that unearned income of children under age 14 be taxed at the marginal tax rate of the parent.

Deferring income is a common form of tax avoidance. In December, taxpayers can arrange to delay until January receiving income to which they are entitled. Since the income is taxed next year, taxpayers pay the tax later, perhaps at the end of next year, rather than sooner. Deferring tax payments is equivalent to paying less tax because taxpayers retain the use of the money longer. Moreover, if taxpayers have lower tax rates next year, perhaps because they have less income and are in a lower tax bracket, they pay less tax as well.

Another form of tax avoidance is to take advantage of different tax rates on income of different types. For instance, for many taxpayers capital gains income (income from appreciation in the value of sold property) is taxed at a lower rate than "ordinary" income like wage and salaries. Also, capital gains (unlike earnings) are not subject to payroll taxes. To taxpayers, $1 of income is the same regardless of the form in which they receive it, so if they can arrange to be paid in the form of capital gains rather than earnings, they will pay less tax.

Taxpayers take the most advantage of different tax rates by engaging in tax arbitrage. Arbitrage is making a profit by exploiting different prices for the same good, specifically by buying the good at the low price and simultaneously selling it at the high price. **Tax arbitrage** is reducing the amount of taxes paid by exploiting differences in tax rates applying to income and expenses. The income tax allows taxpayers to subtract expenses incurred to earn income. If taxpayers can arrange to receive income in a form that is taxed at a low rate and deduct expenses at a high rate, they can reduce their tax burden.

The more complicated forms of tax avoidance require specialized knowledge of the tax law, the way in which the tax authority interprets the tax law, and a vast body

[14]Joel Slemrod and Jon Bakija, *Taxing Ourselves,* 1996, p. 133.

of tax regulations. The taxpayer usually obtains this information by hiring the services of tax accountants and tax lawyers. Taxpayers can increase their net income if the tax saved by hiring professional help is greater than the cost. This is more likely the higher the taxpayer's marginal tax rate (the tax paid per $1 extra income). In Figure 12.10 we measure the amount of income the taxpayer shelters from tax on the horizontal axis. The schedule labeled MC plots the marginal cost of tax avoidance, which is the cost in accountants' and lawyers' fees of avoiding taxes on $1 of income.

It is reasonable that the marginal cost of tax avoidance is rising. To shelter more income, more sophisticated tax avoidance techniques must be used. If the taxpayer's marginal tax rate is t, the optimal level of tax avoidance is to shelter V dollars of taxable income where the marginal cost of tax avoidance is equal to the taxpayer's marginal tax rate. The marginal tax rate is the marginal benefit of sheltering $1 of income from taxation because t dollars of tax is saved per $1 of income sheltered.

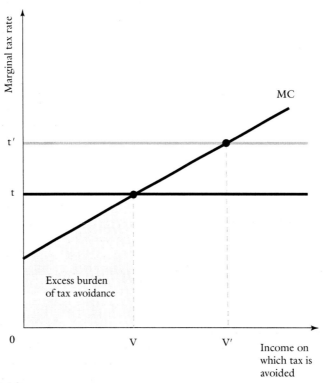

Figure 12.10

Excess Burden of Tax Avoidance
A taxpayer shelters V dollars of income from tax where the taxpayer's marginal tax rate t is equal to the marginal cost of tax avoidance (the cost of more services by tax accountants). At a higher tax rate t', the taxpayer shelters more income V'. Because avoided taxes represent a transfer, not an economic benefit to the economy, the resource cost of tax avoidance, shown by the shaded area under the MC curve, is an excess burden or deadweight loss.

At a higher tax rate, say t', the taxpayer engages in more tax avoidance, enough to shelter V' dollars of taxable income. From this we can draw a simple conclusion—higher marginal tax rates cause taxpayers to practice more tax avoidance.

Why should tax avoidance by the taxpayer be of concern in evaluating different tax systems? For one thing, a tax that is easily avoided is not likely to generate much revenue for the government. For another, the costs of tax avoidance are a deadweight loss to the economy, like the excess burden of an excise tax. When a taxpayer hires an accountant or lawyer to help with "tax planning" to reduce taxes owed, the cost of such professional help is a resource cost to the economy. The taxes saved by the taxpayer are simply a transfer from the government to the taxpayer. The amount the tax avoider saves is lost by the government and, therefore, by other taxpayers.

Accountants and lawyers may object, of course, to having their work described as a deadweight loss. Perhaps a more polite way to make the point is to recognize that trained people like tax professionals are a valuable resource to the economy. Accountants could use their time measuring a firm's profitability, allowing it to operate more efficiently, and lawyers could use their time arranging contracts that allow people to cooperate in commercial ventures with less conflict. If they are busy helping people avoid taxes, they are not available for these more socially useful activities.

The excess burden created when the taxpayer avoids taxes on V dollars of income is shown by the shaded area under the MC schedule in Figure 12.10. The excess burden is equal to the cost of resources used in tax avoidance. A good tax system minimizes the burden of tax avoidance as much as possible. As mentioned, tax avoidance is more likely to occur when tax rates are high and when more opportunities for tax avoidance are available. More opportunities for income tax avoidance are available when a tax system has multiple tax rates and taxes different types of income at different rates.

It is difficult to separate the cost of compliance from the cost of tax avoidance. Do taxpayers hire an accountant simply to calculate taxes owed, or to find ways of reducing the taxes they must pay? An estimate by Professor Joel Slemrod, an economist at the University of Michigan, of the combined compliance and avoidance burden of the federal and state income tax system found that it was between 5% and 7% of the revenue collected. If this fraction is applied to the $927 billion personal and corporation income taxes collected in 1994, the burden of avoidance and compliance that year amounted to between $46 billion and $65 billion.

The Burden of Tax Evasion

Will Rogers once remarked that the income tax made more people into liars than golf. In fact, it makes them into more than liars, because people who willfully do not pay their taxes are criminals. Nonetheless tax evasion, like smuggling, is a crime that many otherwise law-abiding people commit without remorse. Without effective enforcement of its tax laws, the government would collect far less tax revenue than it gets by relying on voluntary compliance. Tax enforcement is costly, so tax evasion—like tax avoidance—imposes a burden on the economy. A good tax system minimizes the scope for tax evasion in order to minimize the burden of enforcement.

When evaluating a tax system, one of the more difficult problems is measuring the amount of tax evasion that is going on. The term **underground economy** refers to the production of goods and services that is invisible to tax collectors, and to statisticians, because the transactions are clandestine. The **tax gap** is the amount of tax revenue that would have been collected had the economic transactions in the underground economy been subject to tax. One recent study by the IRS estimates the size of the tax gap for the personal income tax in 1992 between $93.2 billion and $95.3 billion, or around 17% of the revenue actually collected—a sizable sum.[15] However, some people believe, on the basis of Niskanen's theory of bureaucracy discussed in Chapter 5, that the IRS routinely overestimates the tax gap. Like other bureaucracies, the IRS has an incentive to maximize its budget. One way to do this is to convince Congress that vast amounts of additional revenue are waiting to be collected, if only the IRS had more staff.

Tax evasion takes two forms: failing to report income and taking false deductions. Businesses may fail to report income they receive "off the books," which is most likely to happen when they are paid in cash. Restaurant workers may not report tips they receive if they think the government has no way of finding out. False deductions are those taken for expenses that were not incurred, or that were incurred for a purpose other than earning income. For instance, a trip to Hawaii might be deducted as a business expense when in fact it was a pleasure trip.

The tax authorities use three main methods of enforcement: withholding, the paper trail, and the tax audit. Employers are required to withhold income taxes on wages they pay to their employees, and the withheld amount is submitted to the IRS. Also, wages paid to employees are reported to the IRS on a form (Form W2), and firms must send a notice to the IRS of royalties and interest they pay and to whom, even though they are not required to withhold taxes from such income. Similarly, securities dealers must inform the IRS of sales of stocks by their clients. The amounts in these reports can be cross-checked by IRS computers against the wages, interest, royalties, and capital gains that individual taxpayers report on their tax returns.

How much should the tax authorities crack down on tax evasion? Some people think the IRS is too diligent in its auditing and enforcement and terrorizes innocent taxpayers. Others think the IRS is not tough enough. The fact is that audits by the IRS are quite rare compared with audits in other countries. The IRS audited fewer than 1% of the 124 million individual returns filed in 1993, although audit rates are higher for firms and high-income individuals.

Still, left to their own incentives, the tax authorities may do too much auditing and too many other enforcement activities. If a government is concerned solely with the amount of revenue it collects, more enforcement is worthwhile as long as the additional revenue it brings in is greater than the additional costs of enforcement. The IRS has long claimed that increased enforcement "pays for itself" in higher revenues. By this logic, the optimal amount of enforcement is that which maximizes the net revenue to the government.

However, if economic efficiency is our criterion, an enforcement policy that maximizes net revenue implies a level of enforcement that is too high. We must remember that the tax revenue the government gains through greater enforcement is a loss to the taxpayer and represents only a transfer of money, not a gain to the economy.

---

[15]See "IRS Updates Estimates on Individual Tax Gap," *Tax Notes,* May 13, 1996, p. 857.

The enforcement cost, on the other hand, is a real resource cost to the economy. If we place positive weight on the well-being of the taxpayer, guilty or innocent of tax evasion, it is not efficient for the government to increase spending on enforcement simply because it gets more net revenue.

To find the efficient amount of tax enforcement, we must recognize that the social benefit of greater enforcement efforts is that it allows the government to collect a given level of revenue at lower tax rates. Tax evasion reduces the size of the tax base, making higher tax rates necessary on the activities where taxes are not evaded. This increases the excess burden from lost efficiency. If the reduction in the excess burden from greater enforcement is smaller than the cost, then it is not desirable to enforce more. The most efficient level of tax enforcement is less than the level that maximizes the net revenue of the government.

On the other hand, beliefs about equity also affect the optimal level of enforcement. Typically, tax cheats get a low distributional weight, perhaps even a negative one. If the tax cheat gets a distributional weight of zero, and enforcement costs and penalties affect only tax cheats—not innocent taxpayers—the optimal enforcement policy is that which maximizes the net revenue to the government. However, enforcement efforts snare innocent taxpayers along with the cheats, so it is likely that the optimal enforcement policy lies between one that maximizes revenue and one that maximizes efficiency.

CONCLUSION AND SUMMARY

Tax policy analysis is more of an art than a science. Many factors must be weighed and people disagree about the relative importance of the objectives we should try to achieve. But just as artists base their craft on certain abstract principles of form, color, and perspective, so do analysts of a tax policy base their judgments on efficiency, equity, and administrative costs. These concepts have been described in a framework that ignores much of the detail and complications of the actual tax system and its potential reforms, but we will make much use of them throughout the remainder of the book.

- Tax policy is analyzed to evaluate different tax systems in terms of their desirability to the economy. A tax system is judged according to three criteria: economic efficiency, distributional equity, and burden of administration and compliance.
- The excess burden of an excise tax is the loss in economic value from inefficiency caused by the tax. In the simplest case, the excess burden can be measured by the area of the deadweight loss triangle in a single market. The excess burden of a tax increases with the square of the tax rate, meaning that higher tax rates cause ever higher costs of lost economic efficiency.
- The marginal burden of a tax is the increase in the overall burden on the private economy when $1 of extra revenue is collected by increasing a tax rate. The marginal burden is greater than 1, indicating that $1 more revenue causes a burden of more than $1 on the private economy.

■ The optimal tax system collects a given amount of revenue at the least burden on the economy. To achieve an optimal system, tax rates should be set so that the marginal burdens of taxing each good are equal. If goods are independent, the optimal tax rate on a good is proportional to the inverse of its price elasticity.

■ The equity of a tax system is judged according to how it distributes the burden across taxpayers. Horizontal equity requires that taxpayers with equal ability to pay bear equal tax burdens. Vertical equity requires that taxpayers with greater ability to pay bear greater tax burdens.

■ The administrative and compliance burden of a tax system is another type of hidden burden. Although the direct administrative cost of running the federal tax system is a small fraction of the revenue collected, the indirect burden is much higher. The indirect burden includes the costs to the taxpayer of complying with the tax, as well as the deadweight losses caused by tax avoidance and evasion by taxpayers.

QUESTIONS FOR DISCUSSION AND REVIEW

1. The federal government currently levies an excise tax on fishing tackle of 11%. Suppose the market for fishing tackle is well-functioning in the absence of the tax. How does the excess burden of this tax depend on the slopes of the demand and supply curves for fishing tackle? If the government doubles the tax rate to 22%, would it double the amount of revenue it collects from the tax? Would it double the excess burden of the tax?

2. Rosie and Ted smoke the same number of cigars and drink the same amount of beer. But Rosie smokes more when she drinks more, whereas Ted smokes less when he drinks more, and vice versa. If the "sin" taxes are increased on both goods, who will suffer the largest increase in his (her) tax burden? (Assume that the taxes are fully passed on to the consumers.)

3. Some politicians advocate a substantial increase in the present federal excise tax on cigarettes, $10 per 1000. Assuming that only smokers themselves are harmed by cigarettes and that they are well informed (i.e., there are no externalities), under what conditions is it a good idea to tax cigarettes at a high rate as a matter of economic efficiency? Would it make sense to set the tax on cigarettes above the rate that maximizes the revenue from the tax?

4. If the marginal burden of taxing fishing tackle is 1.75 and the marginal burden of taxing cigarettes is 1.25, how should the tax rates on the goods be changed to improve economic efficiency? What is the efficiency gain when the government gets $1 more from taxing cigarettes and $1 less from taxing fishing tackle?

5. The federal government levies excise taxes on bows and arrows. The tax rate is 11% of the manufacturer's price on bows and 12.4% on arrows. Suppose the tax rate on bows is raised to 12.4%. What is likely to happen to the equilibrium quantity of bows and arrow if: (a) the quantity of bows falls and the quantity of arrows stays the same, (b) the quantity of both bows and arrows falls, or (c) the quantity of bows falls and the quantity of arrows rises?

6. Suppose the inverse demand curve for good X is given by the equation

$P_X^c = 6 - \dfrac{Q_X}{10}$ and the supply curve is perfectly elastic (horizontal) at $1. Good X is presently taxed at $2 per unit. Good Y (which is independent of good X) has

inverse demand curve $P_Y^c = 3 - \dfrac{Q_Y}{20}$ and

is also in perfectly elastic supply at $1. Good Y is untaxed.

a. How much tax revenue is collected and what is the excess burden of the $2 tax on X?

b. How much revenue is collected if the tax on good X is reduced to $1 per unit and good Y is taxed at $1 per unit?

c. What is the excess burden of taxing both goods at $1 per unit?

d. Compare the revenue and excess burden of taxing X alone versus taxing X and Y. Which tax system is preferable from the point of view of economic efficiency?

7. June Stephenson, a psychologist in California, advocates a "male" tax.[16] She argues that men commit the vast majority of crimes, which cost taxpayers over $60 billion each year for courts and prisons alone. In Stephenson's view, tax equity requires adding an extra $100 on the income tax return for each adult male. Would Stephenson's plan curtail crime? Discuss the equity of such a tax.

8. In 1993, the marginal tax rate (the tax paid on $1 additional income) for high-income taxpayers was raised from 31 to 36% or 39.6%. How would this affect tax avoidance by these taxpayers? Suppose that taxpayers whose marginal tax rate was increased to 39.6% avoid taxes on $20 billion more income as a result. What is the burden of this additional tax avoidance?

(Assume that the marginal cost of tax avoidance increases at a constant rate.)

9. Suppose the *marginal cost* of income tax avoidance is given by the linear function $.1 + .001 \cdot I$, where I is the amount of income sheltered from tax measured in billions of dollars (for example, $I = 5$ is $5 billion). Assume the income tax system is proportional.

a. How much income is sheltered if the income tax rate is 20%, and how much revenue does the government lose through tax avoidance?

b. What is the deadweight loss imposed on the economy by tax avoidance activities?

c. How would your answers change if the income tax rate were increased to 40%?

10. An economy has four people, two (named L1 and L2) with income of $1000 a month and two (H1 and H2) with income of $2000 a month. Under tax system A, people pay the following taxes: L1 = $50, L2 = $150, H1 = $150, and H2 = $250. Under tax system B, everyone pays $150 tax. Which system has greater vertical equity? Which system has greater horizontal equity? Overall, which system do you think is fairer? Why?

11. Internet Exercise. The IRS's tax education site at www.irs.ustreas.gov/prod/taxi/learninglab/whatisfair/index.html is interesting. The queen of an imaginary country visits a private detective and tells him she has a problem. "I need your help," she says. "The people are revolting. The country's going broke because of its tax problem, and I've got to find out the fairest way to tax our citizens. Travel to our three main cities, find out what's fair, and report back. Only you can help us!" Visit the three imaginary cities and draw some conclusions about their tax fairness. The last place—the Detective's Challenge—has a multiple-choice quiz. Take the quiz.

[16]June Stephenson, *Men Are Not Cost-Effective: Male Crime in America*, 1995

SELECTED REFERENCES

The concept and measurement of the excess
burden is developed in Harold Hotelling,
"The General Welfare in Relation to Problems
of Taxation ...," 1938; and Arnold C. Harberger, "Taxation, Resource Allocation and
Welfare," 1964.

The marginal burden is explained in
Edgar K. Browning, "The Marginal Cost of
Public Funds," 1984.

A discussion of optimal tax systems is
found in Joel Slemrod, "Optimal Taxes and
Optimal Tax Systems," 1990.

The costs of administering and complying
with the tax system are discussed in Joel Slemrod and Jon Bakija, *Taxing Ourselves*, 1996.

USEFUL INTERNET SITES

There are many sites on the Internet devoted
to analyzing tax policy. Three good places to
find studies in tax policy are the Office of Tax
Policy at the U.S. Treasury at www.treas.gov/
taxpolicy/, the Robert D. Burch Center for
Tax Policy and Public Finance at the University
of California, Berkeley, at elsa.berkeley.edu/
users/burch/, and the Office of Tax Policy
Research at the University of Michigan Business School at www.otpr.org/.

APPENDIX TO CHAPTER 12

Measuring the Loss in Consumers' Surplus

Throughout this chapter, we simplified the analysis by assuming that the quantities
demanded of taxed goods depend only on their prices, not on the amount of
income a consumer has to spend. Of course, few goods, if any, have this property.
In this appendix we analyze the loss in consumers' surplus and the resulting excess
burden when a taxed good is *normal*, meaning that the quantity demanded depends
positively on income. Perhaps the most important lesson from this complication is
that the excess burden of a tax depends on the *substitution effect* of the tax caused
by the rise in the price of the taxed good, not on the income effect of the tax.

In Figure A.12.1, a consumer with income M faces budget line B_0B_0 and buys
two goods X and Y. When neither good is taxed, the consumer maximizes utility
at point e and consumes Q_0 units of X. The maximum utility is U_0. Suppose a tax
on good X is fully passed on to the consumer, raising the price of X by the amount
of the tax. The consumer now faces the budget line B_0B_t and chooses point e_t and
consumes Q_t units of X. The maximum utility is reduced to U_t by the tax on X.
Measured in units of good Y, the revenue collected by the government is equal to
the vertical distance between B_0B_t and B_0B_0 at e_t, or distance e_tf.

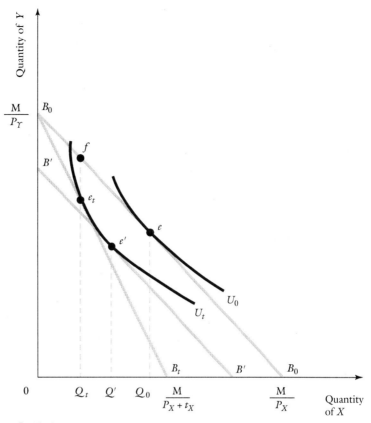

Figure A.12.1

Income and Substitution Effects of an Excise Tax

An excise tax on X shifts the budget line from B_0B_0 to B_0B_t, and the consumer purchases Q_t units of X rather than Q_0. With a lump-sum tax that causes an equivalent loss in utility, the consumer buys Q'. The reduction from Q_0 to Q' is the income effect of the excise tax, and the reduction from Q' to Q_t is the substitution effect. Because of the substitution effect, the equivalent lump-sum tax is larger than the revenue collected by the excise tax (distance $e_t f$)—the extra revenue is equal to the excess burden.

Suppose that instead of taxing X, the government levies a lump-sum tax on the consumer sufficient to reduce the maximum utility to U_t. Such a tax would shift the budget line to $B'B'$. This budget line has the same slope as B_0B_0, since the tax is lump sum, and the consumer maximizes utility at e' by consuming Q' units of X. Note that the vertical distance between B_0B_0 and $B'B'$ is greater than $e_t f$, meaning that the government gets more tax revenue from the lump-sum tax, even though it causes the same loss of utility to the consumer. The extra revenue is the excess burden of the tax on good X. The excess burden is caused by the substitution along indifference curve U_t when the price of X increases by the tax rate. If the consumer's indifference curves were right angles, there would be no excess burden.

The same information is shown in the demand curve diagram, Figure A.12.2. The demand curve labeled D is drawn assuming the consumer has the full amount

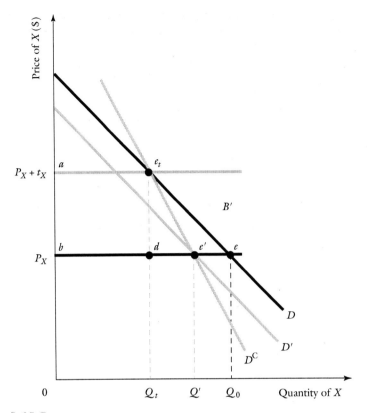

Measuring Excess Burden with the Compensated Demand Curve
The loss in consumers' surplus from a tax increase is measured exactly by the area of the trapezoid $ae_te'b$
using the compensated demand curve D^C. Along an ordinary demand curve like D, money income is held
constant, whereas along D^C, utility is held constant. To do this, compensating changes in lump-sum taxes
are assumed, which shift the ordinary demand curve as shown.

of income M to spend. The consumer buys Q_0 units of X when it is untaxed and
Q_t units when it is taxed. The demand curve labeled D' is the demand curve for X
when the consumer pays the lump-sum tax. Assuming that X is a normal good,
demand curve D' lies to the left of D because the consumer buys less X at each
price. In particular, when X is not taxed the consumer buys Q' units of X, rather
than Q_0. The points e, e_t, and e' correspond to the respective points in Figure
A.12.1. The loss in consumer's surplus is equal to the area of the trapezoid $ae_te'b$,
and the excess burden is the area of the triangle $e_te'd$. This is the amount by which
the loss in consumer's surplus exceeds the revenue collected by the tax on X (equal
to the area of the rectangle ae_tdb).

The demand curve drawn though the points e_te' is called the *compensated*
demand curve because the consumer is held to a particular indifference curve (U_t)
by a compensating change in his or her income (lump-sum tax). Consumer's sur-

plus is properly measured using the compensated demand curve rather than the market demand curve, but the error between the two measures is small if the income elasticity of the good is small.[17] That is why we assumed that the income elasticity of the taxed good(s) was zero to simplify the discussion in the chapter.

Reference for Appendix

Robert Willig, "Consumers' Surplus Without Apology," 1976.

---

[17]Although the difference between the simple consumer's surplus measure and the exact consumer's surplus measure is small relative to the exact measure, the error made in measuring the excess burden of the tax system using simple consumer's surplus can be quite large relative to the true excess burden.

The Federal

Tax System

The U.S. federal government is not just the largest tax collector in the country, it is the largest tax collector in the world. Moreover, nearly everyone in the United States pays federal taxes. For these reasons, Part Six concentrates on the describing and analyzing the federal tax system. The federal government collects most of its revenue from income taxes—92% of its revenue comes from income taxes if we include the payroll taxes that finance Social Security and Medicare. Although we focus on federal personal and corporation income taxes in Part Six, much of the analysis applies also to state and local personal and corporation income taxes. The specialized problems of state and local taxation are discussed in Chapter 19 in Part Seven.

In Chapter 13 we study the structure of the personal income tax system, the largest source of federal revenue. The personal income tax is very complicated, so we focus on the main features that determine the economic impacts of the tax. As we learn in this chapter, the federal income tax applies to most but not all income. Some forms of income are not taxed or taxed at lower rates depending on how the income is earned or how it is spent. These selective features of the income tax determine how the tax affects economic decisions, the allocation of resources, the distribution of the tax burden, and the excess burden collecting the tax. Chapter 14 examines the effects of the income tax on household behavior. We focus on three main effects: the effect of special features of the income tax that favor certain ways of earning or spending income; the effect of the income tax on the supply of labor; and the effect of the income tax on the level of household saving.

In addition to taxing personal income, the United States also taxes business income, mainly through the corporation income tax. In Chapter 15 we learn why the government taxes business income and how business income is defined for tax purposes. We also learn how business income tax system affects the organizational, operational, and financial decisions of business enterprises.

Federal surpluses and deficits are explained in Chapter 16. Federal surpluses and deficits are a topic in federal taxation because they are a choice about the timing of taxation. For example, the federal government presently has a surplus that it uses to pay down the national debt held by private individuals. This allows the government to lower taxes (for a given level of spending) in the future since it pays less in interest on the national debt. Similarly, when the government increases the national debt with deficit finance, future taxes are higher.

Finally, Chapter 17 describes the main federal tax reform proposals, and discusses their merits in terms of economic efficiency, fairness, and administrative costs.

13 Taxes on Personal Incomes

When asked what is the hardest thing in the world to understand, Albert Einstein allegedly answered, "the income tax." Indeed, the personal income is tax is complicated—only the corporation income tax, which we will cover in Chapter 15, is more so. Among the reasons people find the income tax so complicated are the arcane forms and worksheets that are necessary in order for a taxpayer to compute how much income tax he or she owes. Now, with tax preparation computer software, taxpayers are somewhat shielded from the computational difficulties of the income tax system. Nonetheless, as we will see in this chapter, understanding the income tax system is a difficult chore, although perhaps not the hardest in the world. However, because income taxes are so important as a source of government revenue, it is necessary for public finance economists to tackle this chore. If we include the FICA payroll tax discussed in Chapter 9 and the corporation income tax, taxes on incomes account for 92% of federal government revenue. Also, 46 states and many local governments levy taxes on personal and business incomes, which account for about 20% of their combined revenue.

THE PERSONAL INCOME TAX SYSTEM

In 1999 the personal income tax took over 11% of personal income of households and accounted for 48% of federal government receipts, making it the largest tax in the nation. As we see in Figure 13.1, the personal income tax has remained relatively constant in importance as a source of federal receipts, accounting for between 42% and 48% of federal revenue since 1950. It has also remained fairly constant as a fraction of personal income, taking between 8% and 11%. Despite this constancy, the revenue collected has grown dramatically as the economy has grown. Revenue collected by the personal income tax in 1950 was about $183 billion measured in dollars of 1999 purchasing power. By 1999 the tax had grown to $880 billion. In addition, the structure of the personal income tax has changed remarkably. For instance, in 1950 the personal income tax had 24 brackets, and income in the highest bracket was taxed at 94%. By 1999, the income tax had only five brackets, and income in the top bracket was taxed at just under 40%.

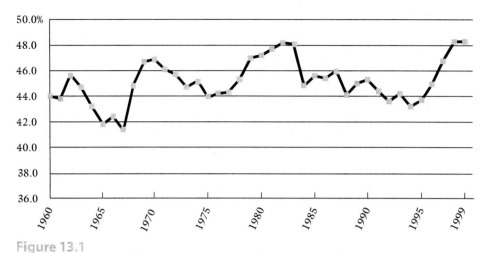

Figure 13.1

Personal Income Tax Revenue as a Percent of Federal Receipts

Personal income tax revenue has varied between 40% and 48% of federal receipts.
Source: Economic Report of the President, various years.

Some Terminology

One of the difficulties in understanding the structure of the income tax system is that many different terms are used. Adding to the confusion is the fact that the same term is often used for different things. We start by defining the terms as we will use them in this chapter to describe the income tax structure. First, we define an **exclusion** as any income that taxpayers need not report to the tax authority in determining the amount of tax they owe. For example, interest on bonds issued by state and local governments is not included in income for tax purposes, so this income is an exclusion.

Second, we define a **deduction** as any amount that is subtracted from reported income to determine the amount of income subject to tax. For instance, taxpayers who itemize their tax returns can subtract the amount of interest they pay on their home mortgage from their reported income when calculating the amount of income subject to tax. This is the mortgage interest deduction. Our use of the term *deduction* includes certain fixed amounts, called personal exemptions, that depend on the number of people in the taxpayer's family. Income that is not taxed, either because it is excluded or because it is deducted, is exempted, so in this chapter an **exemption** can be either an exclusion or a deduction.

Third, an amount that can be subtracted from the tax owed by the taxpayer is called a **tax credit.** For example, on the basis of their earned income, certain taxpayers could subtract up to $3816 from the amount of tax they owed in 1999. This is called the **earned income tax credit.** Note that a tax credit directly reduces the amount of tax owed, whereas an exemption (an exclusion or deduction) reduces the amount of income subject to tax. The tax saved from a credit is equal to the amount of the tax credit, whereas the tax saved from an exemption depends on the taxpayer's tax rate.

Another confusion concerns the term *tax rate*. The tax rate means the tax paid expressed as a percentage of the taxpayer's income. However, in the income tax system we must make a distinction between the taxpayer's **average tax rate (ATR)**, which is the tax paid divided by income, and the taxpayer's **marginal tax rate (MTR)**, which is the increase in tax resulting from a $1 increase in income subject to tax. Typically, the marginal tax rate is higher than the average tax rate. For instance, people in the 36% tax bracket often complain about their high tax rate, but 36% is their marginal tax rate, not their average tax rate. The average tax rate for someone in the 36% bracket can be as low as 25.5% of taxable income, and an even lower fraction of total income.

Elements of the Tax Structure

A full legal description of the income tax system takes up 4100 pages of the Internal Revenue Code (IRC), and as many more pages of the tax regulations that flesh out the skeleton outlined in the IRC. For our purposes, we don't need a detailed legal description. We need to know *who* is subject to tax, called the **tax unit;** *what* is subject to tax, called the **tax base;** and *how* the base is taxed, called the **tax rate schedule.** Even at this level of simplicity, we encounter many complications. Before dealing with the complications, let's briefly describe each of these elements.

THE TAX UNIT.   Everyone residing permanently in the United States and U.S. citizens wherever they reside must pay tax on his or her income, regardless of where in the world that income originates. People who are neither citizens nor residents are subject to tax only on income originating in the United States. Some types of income originating here, like interest income, are exempt from United States tax for foreigners. Thus the obligation to pay the American income tax depends on the taxpayer's residence, citizenship, source of income, and type of income. These are the general rules, and they may be modified according to the tax treaties the United States maintains with other countries.

Apart from identifying who must pay tax, the most important feature of the tax unit is that in the United States it is the *family* rather than the individual (although the income tax is sometimes called the individual income tax). In some other countries, the tax unit is the individual. Under the United States income tax, deductions and tax rate schedules depend on the taxpayer's marital status and the number of dependents. Taxpayers who are married must file as married and taxpayers who are single must file as single, or as head of household if they have dependents. Married taxpayers can file joint or separate tax returns; however, married taxpayers who file separately are not treated the same as single taxpayers. Married taxpayers filing a joint return pay taxes on their *combined* family income according to the tax schedule for married taxpayers. Married taxpayers who file separately keep their incomes separate, but they pay tax according to the married tax schedule. (This is explained further below.)

The fact that the tax unit is the family means that the amount of tax paid depends on the marital status of the taxpayer. In particular, the combined tax is usually increased when two taxpayers with similar incomes get married. This is popularly known as the

"And do you promise to love, honor, and cherish each other, and to pay the United States government more in taxes as a married couple than you would have paid if you had just continued living together?"

marriage tax or **marriage penalty.** In cases where two people marry and only one of them earns income, the amount of tax they pay may decrease instead.

The other way in which the tax unit takes account of family status is by making allowances for dependents supported by the taxpayer. These dependents are usually the taxpayer's children, but they may be other relatives such as grandchildren, parents, and grandparents, aunts, uncles, stepchildren, stepparents, and some in-laws. Specific tests determine whether a person living with and supported by the taxpayer is an eligible dependent. For each eligible dependent, the taxpayer can take a deduction called the **personal exemption.**

The reasons for choosing the family as the tax unit reflect both practicality and equity. The practical consideration is the fact that spouses typically commingle their funds, so that it would be artificial for them to separate their incomes and expenses for tax purposes. The equity consideration is that a taxpayer's ability to pay taxes depends on the size of his or her family. For instance, unmarried taxpayers have more difficulty sharing living expenses than married taxpayers. Couples with children have different abilities to pay from childless couples with the same family income.

DEFINING THE TAX BASE.   The income tax base is the amount of income that is taxed, specifically **taxable income.** Taxable income is defined according to two principles. First, it is measured on a *net* basis, meaning that expenses incurred to acquire income are subtracted from the gross receipts of the taxpayer. In practice, however, not all costs the taxpayer incurs by working can be subtracted. For instance, the cost of commuting to work cannot be subtracted, because the tax authorities view this as depending on the taxpayer's choice of where to live, and therefore as consumption, not as a cost of earning income. Second, taxable income is defined broadly. By this we mean that most of what we would normally construe as income is included in taxable income. As we will see, however, not everything that is income *in principle* is included in income for tax purposes.

Taxable income includes income earned as a consequence of employment, or **earned income;** income received as a consequence of owning property, or **capital income;** and some types of **transfer income.** Earned income includes all forms of employment compensation or earnings. Capital income includes receipts of interest, dividends, royalties, rental income, business profits, and *realized* net capital gains. A realized capital gain is the amount a taxpayer receives from selling property minus what was paid for it. Taxable income also includes some, but not all, transfers. A transfer is an amount received as a consequence neither of employment nor of the ownership of property, such as gifts and bequests from private individuals and benefits from government programs such as welfare and Social Security.

To give some idea of how broadly income is defined for tax purposes, Figure 13.2 compares taxable income as reported in the tax statistics with personal income as measured in the National Accounts. In 1997, taxable income amounted to $3.43 trillion, whereas personal income (according to the National Accounts) was $6.95 trillion. This means that 49.3% of personal income was taxed under the personal income tax system that year. Figure 13.2 shows how the fraction of taxable income to personal income has varied since 1950. In general it increased to a high of 56.5% in 1980, but it has declined since then.

THE GRADUATED TAX RATE SCHEDULE.   Unlike a sales tax, which is levied at the same rate on all taxpayers, the personal income tax rate varies according to the taxpayer's income. The tax rate varies because of the *graduated* tax rate schedule, which imposes different tax rates on income in different tax *brackets.* The tax brackets are defined by taxable income *thresholds.* For instance, in 1999 the threshold of the lowest tax bracket for a single taxpayer was taxable income of $25,750. Taxable income below this threshold is taxed at 15% for all taxpayers. Taxpayers with taxable income greater than this amount pay a higher tax rate, but only on income above the threshold. For instance, a taxpayer with taxable income of $35,750 is in the 28% tax bracket, but the 28% rate is a marginal tax rate. It applies only to the $10,000 of taxable income above the threshold of the first tax bracket. At present, the personal income tax system has five brackets. In the highest bracket, a tax rate of 39.6% applies to taxable income over the threshold of $283,150.

An income tax that has a single tax bracket is popularly known as a **flat tax.** A type of flat tax, championed by two Stanford economists—Robert Hall and Alvin Rabushka—was the centerpiece of Steven Forbes's campaign in the presidential primaries in 1996. Proponents of the flat tax argue that it is much simpler and would allow the average taxpayer to file a tax return the size of a postcard. Opponents of the flat tax argue that it is less equitable than the graduated tax rate schedule. We consider the flat tax in more detail in Chapter 17.

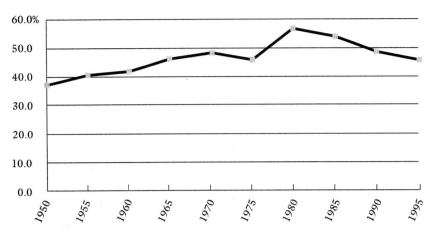

Figure 13.2

Taxable Income as a Percentage of Personal Income
Except for the early 1980s, taxable income has amounted to less than half of personal income. The rise in the percentage during the 1970s and early 1980s is usually attributed to the effect of inflation through "bracket creep," discussed later in this chapter.
Source: Statistical Abstract of the United States, various years.

Taxable Income by the Numbers

With this overview of the personal income tax structure in mind, we now look at some of the details of calculating taxable income. Basically, the taxable income (TI) of a taxpayer is determined according to the following equation:

$$TI = AGI - PE - \max(SD, ID),$$

where AGI is adjusted gross income, PE is personal exemptions, SD is the standard deduction, and ID is itemized deductions. Note that the taxpayer subtracts the maximum of either the standard deduction or itemized deductions. The calculation of taxable income is summarized in schematic form in Figure 13.3. We now describe these components in detail.

ADJUSTED GROSS INCOME (AGI).   The first step in calculating taxable in come is to find **adjusted gross income** (**AGI**). Although AGI is not the amount of income subject to tax, it plays an important role in the income tax system. For one thing, it is the main measure of a taxpayer's before-tax income and determines eligibility for tax deductions and for certain tax credits. AGI affects how much the taxpayer must pay in other ways as well.

A taxpayer's AGI is the sum of incomes received from all taxable sources minus adjustments. Incomes from taxable sources are wages and salaries, including self-employment income and tips, the value of fringe benefits unless explicitly exempted, income from barter, unemployment compensation, interest on bank accounts and bonds, dividends received from the ownership of stocks in companies, realized capital gains from the sale of property, rental incomes and royalties, unincorporated business

Adjusted Gross Income
(AGI)

EQUALS

Gross receipts from taxable sources

- Earned income including salaries, wages, tips, and fringe benefits not exempted from tax
- Income from property including interest, dividends, rents, royalties, and net *realized* capital gains
- Pensions and retirement allowances
- Some government transfers including unemployment compensation, part of Social Security benefits, and certain disability payments
- Prizes and awards, except "qualified" scholarships and fellowships
- Alimony (but not child support) received

MINUS

Adjustments

- Reimbursed employee expenses
- Contributions to Keogh retirement plans
- Part of health insurance expenses for the self-employed
- Alimony paid

Taxable income   *EQUALS*   AGI   *MINUS*

Personal exemptions

($2750 in 1999) for the taxpayer, spouse, and each eligible dependent

MINUS

Deductions

Standard deduction
($4300 if single and $7200 if married [filing jointly] in 1999)

OR

Itemized deductions
- Charitable donations (up to 50% of AGI)
- Interest payments on mortgage and home equity loans
- State and local income taxes
- State and local property taxes
- Uninsured medical expenses (in excess of 7.5% of AGI)
- Casualty losses (in excess of 10% of AGI)
- Miscellaneous deductions (in excess of 2% of AGI)

Figure 13.3

Personal Income Tax Base

This schematic indicates the main elements in calculating taxable income, the base of the personal income tax system.

profits, company pension and retirement benefits, distributions from special retirement savings plans like 401(k) plans and IRAs, up to 85% of Social Security benefits, certain disability payments, alimony (but not child support or divorce property settlements), and prizes, scholarships, and awards, except those qualified as exempt.

Adjustments are subtracted to get AGI and include trade and business expenses, business expenses by employees reimbursed by their employers and included in employees' gross income, alimony paid to a former spouse, and moving expenses. Self-employed taxpayers can subtract part of their health insurance expenditures, contributions to special retirement savings plans (called Keogh plans), and half the FICA (self-employment) tax they must pay on self-employment earnings.

Income must be included in AGI whether it takes the form of cash or goods and services received in kind, such as barter income earned when a dentist fixes a doctor's teeth in exchange for the doctor's treating the dentist's sick child. Barter income must be included as income to both parties, although much of this income probably goes unreported. In-kind income is converted into dollars at **fair market value,** which is the price taxpayers would have had to pay if they purchased the goods and services. Some forms of in-kind employee compensation are excluded. In particular, the value of health, dental, and group life insurance provided by the taxpayer's employer is excluded because it is explicitly exempted by law.

PERSONAL EXEMPTIONS (PE).   The taxpayer's family status affects the amount of tax paid because it affects the number and dollar amount of deductions. The personal exemption (PE) is a fixed amount ($2750 in 1999) that taxpayers deduct from AGI for themselves, for their spouse (if filing a joint return), and for each eligible dependent. Eligible dependents include children under age 19 (or 24 if attending an educational institution), and children or other relatives who pass certain tests. In particular, they must have Social Security numbers, live with the taxpayer for at least half the tax year, and depend on the taxpayer for support.

The total amount of personal exemptions is gradually reduced (*phased out*) for taxpayers with AGI above a certain level. These phaseouts increase the marginal tax rates of taxpayers with incomes in a certain range. The amount of personal exemptions is reduced by 2% for each $2500, or fraction thereof, of AGI above this threshold.

STANDARD DEDUCTIONS (SD) AND ITEMIZED DEDUCTIONS (ID).   Another fixed amount taxpayers can subtract from AGI is called the **standard deduction (SD).** Taxpayers can choose to subtract either a standard deduction or the total of their **itemized deductions (ID),** whichever is greater. The amount of the standard deduction depends on whether the taxpayer is single, a head of household, or married. In 1999, the standard deduction for single taxpayers was $4300, whereas that of married taxpayers filing jointly was $7200. Note that the standard deduction for married taxpayers is about 1⅔ that of single taxpayers, not twice as much. (Married taxpayers who file separately each get a standard deduction equal to half that of married taxpayers who file jointly.) This is one cause of the so-called marriage tax.

Instead of taking the standard deduction, taxpayers can itemize deductions for certain expenses. Most of these expenses are not incurred for the purpose of earning income, so the itemized deductions are not for the purpose of calculating *net* income. The amount that taxpayers can claim for itemized deductions is the sum of the following amounts: value of cash and property donated to qualified charitable organizations, income and property taxes (but not sales taxes) paid to state and local governments, interest payments paid to a lender on a mortgage or home equity loan, medical expenses and casualty losses that are not reimbursed by an insurer over a certain limit, and miscellaneous deductions over a certain limit.

Some itemized deductions are subject to limits. The deduction for charitable donations is limited to 50% of the taxpayer's AGI, or less in some cases. The deduction for mortgage interest is limited to mortgages and home equity loans of less than $1 million in total and on no more than two residences. Only unreimbursed medical expenses over 7.5% of AGI are deductible. Deductible casualty losses are losses on property due to a sudden, unexpected event like a storm or a fire, and only the excess over 10% of the taxpayer's AGI is deductible. Total miscellaneous deductions over 2% of AGI, such as unreimbursed job-related expenses by employees, can also be deducted.

The amount of itemized deductions is reduced for taxpayers with high levels of AGI. In 1999, the amount of itemized deductions was reduced by 3% of the amount by which the taxpayer's AGI exceeds $126,600. However, the total reduction from this provision cannot reduce the value of itemized deductions by more than 80%. The standard deduction is not reduced, even for high-income taxpayers, although few of them take the standard deduction.

Unlike the amount of the standard deduction, which depends on the marital status of the taxpayer, the amount of itemized deductions is a variable that depends on how taxpayers spend their income. Because taxable income is reduced by the total of itemized deductions for certain types of expenses, the government effectively *subsidizes* these expenses at the taxpayer's marginal tax rate. For instance, an itemizing taxpayer who increases charitable donations by $100 reduces taxable income by $100. If the taxpayer is in the 39.6% tax bracket, the income tax owed falls by $39.60, so the extra $100 donation costs the taxpayer only $60.40 ($100 minus $39.60).

Figure 13.4 shows the dollar amounts of AGI, personal exemptions, standard and itemized deductions, and taxable income for tax year 1997. It also shows the percentage of these totals received or claimed by taxpayers with AGI above and below $50,000. As we can see, although taxpayers with AGI above $50,000 account for less than a quarter of all taxpayers, they account for 64% of the total AGI of $4974 billion. The value of itemized deductions ($607 billion) is the largest amount subtracted from AGI, and 74% of this was claimed by taxpayers with AGI over $50,000. In contrast, 90% of the $443 billion in standard deductions were claimed by taxpayers with AGI less than $50,000. In total, $1541 billion in personal exemptions and standard and itemized deductions were subtracted from AGI to get taxable income, and taxpayers with AGI above $50,000 claimed 45% of this total. However, this is less than their share of AGI, so these taxpayers account for 72% of total taxable income in 1997.

Income Defined According to Principle

Up to this point, we have discussed the income tax base as defined by the letter of the IRC. This gives only a partial picture of what is included in taxable income and

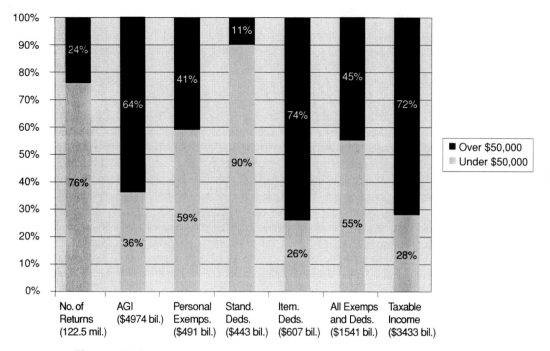

Figure 13.4

Income, Exemptions, and Deductions by Level of Adjusted Gross Income, 1997
Although taxpayers with AGI greater than $50,000 account for less than a quarter of all taxpayers, they account for a disproportionately greater share of income, itemized deductions, and personal exemptions
Source: Internal Revenue Service, *Statistics of Income Bulletin,* Fall 1999, available as file 97in03at.exe at http://www.irs.ustreas.gov/prod/tax_stats/soi/.

what is not. When the IRC is silent about a particular type of receipt, we don't know whether it is not included in AGI because it is not income or whether it is income but is excluded. In other words, we need a definition of *income in principle,* as well as the definition in the IRC, to get a complete picture. Knowing income in principle allows us to identify forms of income that are not subject to the income tax because they are ignored by the IRC.

THE HAIG-SIMONS DEFINITION.   The most widely accepted definition of income in principle was developed by Robert M. Haig and refined by Henry C. Simons nearly 70 years ago. Consequently, income in principle is commonly called **Haig-Simons income,** although it is also known as comprehensive income. Haig-Simons income is equal to the value of goods consumed plus the change in the net worth of the taxpayer over the course of the tax year. Net worth is the value of assets less liabilities. In other words, Haig-Simons income is the maximum consumption taxpayers can enjoy during the tax year without spending down their wealth. Consumption financed by spending down wealth is not income; it is a use of savings. Income in principle, then, is anything that provides consumption benefits or increases the taxpayer's net worth. It includes receipts from all sources, whether they are cash or in kind, whether they are spent or saved, and regardless of how they are spent.

EXCLUSIONS FROM HAIG-SIMONS INCOME. We use Haig-Simons income to obtain a better appreciation of the types and amounts of income excluded from the AGI of the taxpayer. These forms of income are excluded either because they are specifically exempt, such as the Section 106 exemption of certain employee fringe benefits, or because the IRC is silent about them, such as unrealized capital gains. Unrealized capital gains are increases in net worth due to the appreciation in the value of property held unsold by the taxpayer.

Forms of exempted income include medical and other insurance paid by the taxpayer's employer; an employer's contribution to a pension plan on behalf of the taxpayer; interest accruing on pension plans; 401(k) plans and Individual Retirement Accounts (IRAs); scholarships and fellowships to students working toward an academic degree that do not exceed tuition and course-related expenses; interest on bonds issued by state and local governments or nonprofit hospitals; and up to 50% of Social Security benefits. Also, $500,000 of capital gains realized from the sale of a residence by married taxpayers and $250,000 for single taxpayers is exempted. Income normally included in AGI is also exempted if taxpayers use the income in special ways. For instance, money deposited in special savings plans called 401(k) and 403(B) plans, named after the IRC sections that authorize them, is exempted if taxpayers sign salary-reduction agreements with their employers.

In each case, a form of consumption spending or an increase in net worth is excluded from taxpayers' AGI and therefore from taxable income, although such amounts are part of Haig-Simons income. For instance, employer-paid insurance is a form of consumption, just like automobile insurance purchased out of pocket. Similarly, contributions to pension and retirement saving plans are increases in net worth, just like money saved in a bank account.

Another type of income in principle excluded from taxation is some forms of transfer income. Actually, the IRC is quite inconsistent in its treatment of transfers. Private transfers like gifts and bequests are not taxed, although they may be subject to a separate estate and gift tax if they are large enough. Some government transfers are fully taxed, like unemployment benefits, while others are not taxed at all, like welfare benefits from the Temporary Assistance to Needy Families program, near-cash benefits like food stamps, and in-kind benefits from Medicaid and Medicare. Social Security benefits are partially taxed, depending on the economic circumstances of the taxpayer.

One problem in measuring Haig-Simons income is *valuation,* which means finding the equivalent cash value of in-kind income. The IRC requires in-kind income to be converted into dollars at its fair market value. For some types of Haig-Simons income, this is difficult because there are no market goods comparable to the in-kind income. For instance, unrealized capital gains may include the appreciation in value of a rare and unique painting hanging on the taxpayer's wall. However, exactly how much the painting has appreciated may be difficult to determine unless the taxpayer sells the painting and realizes the capital gain. Similarly, in-kind transfers like Medicare and Medicaid benefits are part of Haig-Simons income. The Haig-Simons definition requires that in-kind transfers be valued at their value to the recipient. The most readily obtained dollar value of in-kind transfers is their cost to the government, but as we saw in Chapter 8, the value of in-kind transfers to the recipient may be less than their cost.

UNREALIZED CAPITAL GAINS AND IMPUTED RENT.   Two forms of Haig-Simons income, in particular, are quite controversial. Many people argue that unrealized capital gains are not really income but are merely "paper" gains that cannot be consumed by taxpayers until realized. This argument is not correct, because taxpayers can borrow against unrealized capital gains and increase consumption. In less than 20 years, William Gates of Microsoft Corporation has become one of the richest individuals in the nation, if not the world, and no one could deny that Gates has an enormous power to consume. Yet most of his income has escaped income taxation because most of his acquired wealth took the form of unrealized capital gains and was not taxed.

Another argument is that taxes on unrealized capital gains are not avoided altogether; they are simply postponed until the gains are realized at a later date. However, postponing a tax is equivalent to reducing it. If a tax can be postponed, the benefit to the taxpayer is equivalent to getting an interest-free loan equal to the amount of the postponed tax. The equivalent value of postponing taxes for one year on $1 of capital gains is the taxpayer's tax rate times the annual interest rate. Since capital gains can be postponed many years or even indefinitely, this benefit of postponement is approximately equal to the outright exclusion of capital gains income from taxation.

In fact, it is not necessary to postpone realization forever. When taxpayers die and leave appreciated property to their heirs, the capital gain escapes income taxation altogether.[1] The reason is that the IRC permits the basis value of the transferred property (the cost on which the capital gain is calculated) to be "stepped up" to its market value at the time of a taxpayer's death. Only capital gains realized after a taxpayer's death are taxed as income to the heirs, should they sell the property.

The other disputed form of Haig-Simons income is imputed rent. A taxpayer who owns a home outright owns an asset worth, perhaps, hundreds of thousands of dollars. Unlike money in the bank, a home does not pay interest, but it provides consumption services in the form of shelter and comfort. The annual value of these services is equal to what it would cost to rent the house if the taxpayer didn't own it, and is called the *imputed* rent. Unlike interest on money in the bank, the income from the home is not taxed, but it is income according to the Haig-Simons principles.

Some people argue that the imputed rent on the taxpayer's home is not income, because it does not provide a cash inflow. However, other forms of noncash income, such as in-kind income from barter, are subject to income tax. Imputed rent is simply in-kind income attributable to the ownership of property.

Perhaps the main reason imputed rent is so disputed is the fact that taxpayers pay the in-kind income to themselves. We could argue that when taxpayers work for themselves—say, cleaning their own windows—we do not count the imputed wages as income. Then why count in-kind income from property, like imputed rent? Alternatively, we could argue that the imputed wages from washing one's own windows are part of Haig-Simons income, but most economists do not like to push the Haig-Simons definition this far because it requires imputing a value for leisure time.

---

[1]The capital gain may, however, be taxed under the separate estate and gift tax. See Chapter 17.

Whether these forms of income should be taxed need not detain us anyway. Our purpose is not to argue that Haig-Simons income is the "correct" measure of income for tax purposes, though some economists believe it is. The correct measure of income for tax purposes is determined by the efficiency, the equity, and the administrative costs of taxing it, as we discussed in Chapter 12. Our purpose in introducing Haig-Simons income is to understand the *selective* nature of the income tax base. The deductions and exclusions specified in the IRC, or those revealed by the Haig-Simons definition, all encourage taxpayers to earn or spend income in these preferred ways. It is these incentive effects that interest us most as economists, and we will consider them further in Chapter 14.

INFLATION AND CAPITAL INCOME.   The Haig-Simons definition of income reveals various forms of income that go untaxed. It also reveals a component of taxable income that is not really income in principle. Haig-Simons income is the value of consumption plus additions to *capacity to consume*. Capacity to consume is measured in dollars of constant purchasing power, but some assets held by taxpayers are fixed in dollar value, so inflation reduces their value measured in constant dollars. Under the current tax structure, the dollar income from such assets is taxed, but no adjustment is made for the reduction in asset value in constant dollars due to inflation.

For instance, suppose a taxpayer owns an asset with a fixed money value of $100 that pays $5 income during the year. If prices rise by 5%, the $5 just compensates the taxpayer for the reduction in the purchasing power value of the asset, so the taxpayer has constant capacity to consume. Nonetheless, the $5 is treated as income and taxed under the IRC.

To measure income from property correctly when prices rise, we should index the **cost basis** of the asset. This is done by subtracting from capital income the amount of money needed to keep the purchasing power value of the asset intact. We'll call the amount that must be subtracted the maintenance income, although it is not really income at all. If prices rise 5% over the tax year, the maintenance income of an asset worth $100 is $5. Hence if the money income from the property that year is $5, income in principle is zero.

The fact that capital income is mismeasured in the presence of inflation is often used as a reason for indexing capital gains income. If the price of stocks increases by no more than the inflation rate, the purchasing power of the taxpayer does not change, so why should the capital gain be taxed? Indexing capital gains can be accomplished by adjusting the cost basis of an asset to reflect the change in the price index over the period it is held. The capital gain is calculated as the excess of the sale price of the asset minus the indexed cost basis, rather than the dollar cost basis (as is done under the current system). This way the maintenance income is automatically subtracted from the measured capital gain.

Several objections can be made to an ad hoc attempt to index capital gains, however. The main objection is that not just capital gains need to be indexed. Interest income *and expenses* must be adjusted by subtracting the principal multiplied by the inflation rate to find the *real* interest income or expense. (This is explained further in Chapter 14.) If interest expenses are not indexed while capital gains are, taxpayers can borrow money to invest in assess that yield capital gains. Since indexed capital gains would be taxed while the unindexed interest expense could be deducted, the taxpayer would be allowed a form of tax arbitrage (see Chapter 12). Lawmakers believe that the problem of indexing all forms of capital income is just too complicated, so no proposal to index capital gains income has been enacted.

TAXES ON INCOME SAVED FOR RETIREMENT.   If taxes were levied on Haig-Simons income, income would be taxed in the year it is earned whether the taxpayers spend or save it. Income saved in conventional ways, like money in bank accounts or invested in stocks and mutual funds, is taxed this way. However, the tax system also allows taxpayers to earn certain types of deferred (saved) income, which is taxed when distributed to taxpayers—usually when they are retired—rather than when it is earned. A good example is earned benefits in a company pension plan. Such compensation is taxed not when employees earn it, but when they receive retirement benefits.

Since 1978, taxpayers have had another retirement savings option. They can designate that a portion of their pretax wages be deposited in a 401(k) plan set up by their employer. Employees of nontaxable organizations can do the same thing in a 403(b) plan. Such plans are also called **cash or deferred arrangements (CODAs)**. The income deposited in CODAs is excluded from the current AGI. In addition, employers can match deposits by employees dollar for dollar, and the matching contribution is also excluded from AGI. The money in these plans can be invested in various ways, and the income accruing on the principal (interest and dividends, etc.) accumulates tax-free. The annual contribution by an employee is limited to 15% of AGI, or $9240, whichever is smaller. In 1992, pension contributions and CODAs amounted to nearly $139 billion, or nearly half of annual personal saving. In 1996, over $1 trillion was invested in 401(k) plans, and the amount is growing rapidly.

The income deposited in a CODA is not exempt from tax for all time. When funds are withdrawn from the CODA, the amount is added to the taxpayer's AGI like ordinary income. If funds are withdrawn before the taxpayer is 59½ years old, an early withdrawal penalty of 10% is assessed. In some cases, taxpayers can borrow against the principal in their CODAs, but the loan must be repaid within a certain time or withdrawal penalties and taxes are levied. Interest paid on the loan is not deductible as an expense, even if the proceeds are invested in income-earning assets.

Regular Individual Retirement Accounts (IRAs) treat saved income in a similar way. Taxpayers (married, filing jointly) with AGI less than $50,000 can place up to $4000 each year in a "front-loaded" IRA; the limits are lower for single taxpayers. Front-loaded means that taxpayers contribute before-tax dollars because the IRA contribution is subtracted from gross income (as an adjustment to AGI) and excluded from taxation. Money withdrawn from the IRA is added to the taxpayer's AGI. Taxpayers with AGIs in excess of the above limit can make deposits to an IRA, but the contribution cannot be subtracted from AGI. However, interest earned on the amount invested is exempt from tax until it is withdrawn from the plan. In 1997 a new type of IRA, called the IRA Plus or Roth IRA, was introduced. The IRA Plus is "back-loaded," meaning that the contribution is not deductible, but withdrawals, including interest, are tax-free if the IRA is held for at least five years and the taxpayer is 59½ years old.

All these provisions effectively change the base of the United States tax system away from income in principle toward a consumption base, because consumption is equal to income less money saved. Taxpayers typically withdraw money from CODAs in retirement. In fact, if no limits were placed on the amounts that could be contributed to CODAs or when the funds could be withdrawn, the personal "income" tax would actually be a personal "consumption" tax. Some economists, such as Professor David Bradford of Princeton University, have argued that a personal consumption tax is superior to an income tax. In 1995, Senators Nunn of Georgia and Domenici of New Mexico proposed an Unlimited Savings Allowance (USA) tax of essentially this form. The choice between taxing income and taxing consumption is discussed further in Chapter 17.

Calculating the Amount of Tax Owed

Once taxable income is calculated, the amount of tax is found using the tax rate schedules. For many taxpayers, this means simply looking up the amount of tax owed on their taxable income in a table provided by the IRS. Calculating the amount of tax owed by the taxpayer is more complicated than simply multiplying taxable income by the tax rate, because the tax rate schedule is **graduated** into tax brackets. In 1999 (as noted above) the federal income tax system had five brackets. The income thresholds for the five tax brackets and the marginal tax rate applying to the income within each bracket are shown in Table 13.1 for single and married taxpayers filing jointly. The thresholds for joint filers apply to their combined incomes, and the same thresholds apply to the incomes of surviving spouses. The thresholds for married taxpayers who file separately are exactly half the respective thresholds for the joint filers, so they face the same tax schedule on their separate incomes.[2]

The amount of taxes paid by a single taxpayer with taxable income of $100,000 (assuming that none of it is capital gains) is calculated as follows. The first $25,750 of taxable income is taxed at 15% ($3863), the next $36,700 is taxed at 28% ($10,276), and the remaining $37,550 is taxed at 31% ($11,640). The total tax owed is $3863 + $10,276 + $11,640 = $25,779, so the taxpayer pays about 26% of taxable income in taxes. The taxpayer is in the 31% bracket, which means that an extra $1 of income is taxed at 31%.

When taxpayers with similar incomes get married, their combined income tax bill increases, a phenomenon known as the marriage tax. Table 13.1 reveals another cause of the marriage tax in addition to the smaller standard deduction mentioned earlier. In the first two brackets, the thresholds for married taxpayers filing jointly are 1⅔ times the respective thresholds for single taxpayers, rather than twice as great. In higher tax brackets, the ratios are even smaller. As a result, married taxpayers with similar incomes

---

[2]So why would a married couple file separately? Sometimes it is advantageous if one spouse can claim more of the itemized deductions. Also, miscellaneous expenses and medical expenses are deductible only to the extent they exceed 2% and 7.5% of AGI, respectively. This also provides an incentive to file separately to lower the AGI threshold above which the expenses can be deducted.

13.1   How Much Does Haig-Simons Income Exceed AGI?

While economists find Haig-Simons income (HSI) a useful benchmark, others believe that HSI exaggerates income. For example, when Donald Trump and Marla Maples were married in 1993, Harry Winston, a well-known jeweler, lent Ms. Maples a 105-carat, 325-diamond tiara valued at $2 million. Since Haig-Simons income includes gifts, the fair market rental value of the tiara was part of Maples' Haig-Simons income that year. Likewise, if a friend mows your lawn as a favor, your Haig-Simons income increases by what it would have cost you to hire someone to mow your lawn. (If you return the favor with an equal value of services, your friend's HSI is increased also. This is called barter income, and it is supposed to be included in AGI.)

Frequent-flyer points earned by employees flying on company business also raise the issue of Haig-Simons income. Since trips taken with points are consumption, the fair market value of the points is Haig-Simons income to the employee. In fact, the IRS thinks the value of the points should be included in the gross compensation paid to employees and counted in their AGI—a proposal strongly resisted by the airline companies. Because the fair market value of the points is often hard to determine, the IRS proposal is considered impractical.

Despite the difficulties in measuring Haig-Simons income, some attempts have been made. The IRS developed a hypothetical measure of income it calls *retrospective income,* which adds to AGI some of the Haig-Simons components currently excluded. These include excluded forms of income that must be reported to the tax author-

ities, such as interest on tax-exempt municipal bonds, tax-exempt capital gains on personal residences, nontaxable portions of pension and retirement saving distributions, and the accelerated part of depreciation deductions for unincorporated business. It does not, however, include some of the larger excluded items such as unrealized capital gains and imputed rent on owner-occupied dwellings. The table shows the AGI and retrospective income for the tax year 1997 for the top 20% of taxpayers and the remaining 80%.

According to these calculations, retrospective income is only about $135 billion greater than AGI, and the excluded income is distributed slightly more in favor of the top quintile than is AGI.

Critically analyze the following:

■ In 1997, AGI included nearly $350 billion of realized net capital gains, with over $315 billion of it going to taxpayers in the top quintile. Since in any given year people sell only part of the stocks they own, it would seem that HSI should be much higher than measured AGI because HSI includes unrealized capital gains. Suppose taxpayers hold stocks for five years on average and the stocks appreciate by the same dollar amount each year. How much does HSI exceed measured AGI because unrealized capital gains are excluded? (Hint: Under the stated assumptions, the $350 billion would be the five-year cumulative capital gain on one-fifth of the taxpayer's stocks.)

■ Does your answer to the above mean that taxing realized rather than accruing capital gains confers no advantage to taxpayers?

■ Would the addition to AGI of imputed rent on owner-occupied dwellings make a bigger difference to HSI? Why?

	Received by Lowest Four Quintiles	Received by Top Qunitile	Total ($ billion)
Adjusted gross income*	$2025 bil. (40.7%)	$2950 bil. (59.3%)	$4975
Retrospective income+	$2070 bil. (40.5%)	$3040 bil. (59.5%)	$5110

Sources: *Calculated by author from Internal Revenue Service, *Statistics of Income,* 1997. +"Tom Petska, Mike Strudles, and Ryan Petska, "Further Examination of the Distribution of Individual Income and Taxes Using a Consistent and Comprehensive Measure of Income," 1999.

Table 13.1   Federal Taxable Income Thresholds, 1999

Tax Bracket	Single Taxpayer	Married Taxpayers Filing Jointly
15%	$0–25,750	$0–43,050
28%	$25,751–62,450	$43,051–104,050
31%	$62,451–130,250	$104,051–158,550
36%	$130,251–283,150	$158,551–283,150
39.6%	$283,151–	$283,151–

Source: U.S. Master Tax Guide, 2000, Commerce Clearing House.

are pushed into a higher tax bracket at lower amounts of combined income than if they had remained single. The top tax bracket starts at $283,151 regardless of whether the taxpayer is single, married, or head of household.

To illustrate, suppose that a taxpayer with $100,000 of taxable income marries a taxpayer with the same taxable income. When the taxpayers are single, their combined tax is 2 × $25,779, or $51,558. Assuming that their combined taxable income remains $200,000 after they are married (actually, it is likely to rise if they both take the standard deduction), they now would pay tax of $55,354 on their combined income, which is obtained using the married taxpayer schedule. This represents a marriage tax of $3796 a year. The couple now pay over 27% of their combined taxable income in tax and are pushed into the 36% tax bracket, where any additional taxable income is taxed at 36%.

The thresholds shown in Table 13.1 are increased each year using the inflation rate of the previous year. Thus if prices rose 3% in 1999, all of the thresholds would be 3% higher in the 2000 tax year. The indexing of the thresholds, along with the personal exemptions and standard deduction, is to prevent **bracket creep.** Before 1985, the tax structure was not indexed, and inflation steadily pushed taxpayers into higher tax brackets, increasing the percentage of their income they paid as tax.

TAX CREDITS.   We have examined how to calculate the amount taxpayers theoretically owe, but this is not always the amount they must pay. To find the amount of tax they pay, taxpayers subtract the amounts of tax credits for which they are eligible. Some of these tax credits simply reflect taxes that have already been paid, such as the credit for taxes withheld and the foreign tax credit. The foreign tax credit is a tax credit given for income taxes paid to foreign governments. Three special tax credits not based on taxes already paid are part of the tax structure. They are the earned income tax credit, the household and dependent care tax credit popularly known as the child care tax credit, and the child tax credit.

The largest and most important tax credit is the earned income tax credit (EITC). The original purpose of the EITC was to offset the FICA payroll tax for low-income workers. The FICA tax has no standard deduction or personal exemptions, so it is the largest income tax that many low-income people pay. Since its introduction in 1975, the EITC has expanded beyond the purpose of offsetting the FICA tax and now provides actual cash assistance to low-income working families. For this reason, we discussed the EITC as part of the welfare system in Chapter 8.

The EITC provides a tax credit equal to a certain percentage of earned income up to a limit. Earned income includes wages, salaries, tips, and self-employment income, but not transfers such as welfare or property income such as interest and dividends. For taxpayers with no children, the tax credit rate is equal to 7.65%, which, not coincidentally, is the employee's share of the FICA tax. For taxpayers with one or more than one child, the tax credit rates are 34% and 40% respectively. This means, for example, that a taxpayer with two children gets a tax credit of 40 cents on every $1 of earned income up to the limit of $9540 in 1999.

Two features of the EITC are especially important. First, it is a **refundable** tax credit, which means that taxpayers get a tax refund for the credit even if they do not have to pay income tax. For example, in 1999 a married taxpayer with two children could earn up to $18,200 yet have no taxable income because of personal exemptions and the standard deduction. If the taxpayer is eligible for the EITC and has no taxable income, the government gives a tax refund for the credit nonetheless.

The second feature of the EITC is that it is phased out for taxpayers whose AGI exceeds a certain threshold. The EITC is intended for taxpayers with sufficiently low incomes. For taxpayers with two or more children, the phaseout rate is 21.06% of AGI above $12,400 in 1999. The EITC is completely phased out if the family's AGI exceeds $30,580 in this case. This phaseout feature raises the effective marginal tax rate facing low-income taxpayers, by 21 percentage points.

Another important tax credit is the child care credit. This provides a tax credit of between 20% and 30% of employment-related child and dependent care expenses incurred by taxpayers up to certain limits. To qualify, the taxpayer's children must be 13 years of age or younger or must pass a dependency test. Dependent adults may also qualify if they are physically or mentally incompetent. For taxpayers with AGI less than $10,000, the tax credit rate is 30%. For taxpayers with AGI above $10,000, the tax credit rate is reduced by one percentage point for each $2000 (or fraction thereof) of excess AGI. However, the child care tax credit is not reduced below 20%, so this rate is available for all tax-payers with AGI above $28,000. Like the phaseout of the EITC, the partial phaseout of the child care tax credit increases the effective marginal tax rate of low- and middle-income taxpayers.

Curiously, the income level above which the child care tax credit is reduced is the same for both married and single parents. This means that the child care tax credit is lower when the mother and father decide to get married and combine their taxable incomes. This causes a marriage tax on low-income families. Another curious feature is that, unlike the EITC, the child care tax credit is *not* refundable. This means that taxpayers benefit from the credit only if they pay income taxes. As a result, low-income taxpayers may benefit less from the child care tax credit even though they are given a higher rate of credit.

A third important tax credit is the child tax credit, which is $500 per child for up to two eligible children, with a smaller credit for additional children. This child tax credit should not be confused with the dependent exemption described earlier. A dependent exemption of $2750 is subtracted from income subject to tax for each child, whereas the child tax credit of $500 is subtracted from the amount of taxed owed. The full child tax credit is available for taxpayers whose AGI is less than a certain limit (in 1999, $110,000 if married filing jointly) and is phased out at 5% for taxpayers with income above the limit.

Other tax credits are available for qualified tuition and other expenses incurred for higher education. These tax credits are also phased out for high-income taxpayers.

A Medley of Marginal Tax Rates

Economists put special attention on a taxpayer's marginal tax rate (MTR), which is the increase in tax resulting from a small increase in income. The reason for this attention is that the MTR affects taxpayer decisions. For instance, suppose a worker could earn an extra $1000 in gross annual income by working overtime. Presumably, the worker will make the decision based on how much extra income he or she takes home after taxes are paid. The increase in take-home or disposable income is equal to the increase in gross income times one minus the taxpayer's MTR.

It would seem from the tax rate schedule in Table 13.1 that all taxpayers would fall into one of five different marginal tax rate brackets, ranging from 15% for low-income taxpayers to 39.6% for high-income taxpayers.[3] In fact, because of the phase-out of various tax credits, personal exemptions, and itemized deductions, marginal tax rates differ by much more than this. In addition to the nominal marginal tax rates, there are various "hidden" marginal tax rates. Consider, for example, a married taxpayer with two children and earned income of $20,000. Although this taxpayer is nominally in the 15% tax bracket, he or she probably receives the earned income tax credit (EITC). In this income range, an increase in income reduces the EITC by 21 cents for each extra dollar of AGI, which adds 21 percentage points to the nominal MTR. In addition, the taxpayer may receive the dependent care tax credit of up to $1200, which would be reduced by about $48 for each extra $2000 of AGI. This adds another 2.4 percentage points to the MTR. Adding these hidden marginal tax rates to the taxpayer's nominal MTR of 15% yields an *effective* MTR of over 38%. That is, the taxpayer's disposable income increases by less than $620 for each extra $1000 of gross earnings. At higher levels of AGI, where the tax credits are phased out, the taxpayer's MTR could be as low as 15%.

Middle- and high-income taxpayers also face hidden marginal tax rates. Married taxpayers whose AGI exceeds $110,000 (in tax year 1999) lose $50 of their child tax credit for every extra $1000 of AGI, which adds five percentage points to their nominal MTR. In addition, a taxpayer's itemized deductions are reduced by 3% of the amount by which the taxpayer's AGI exceeds $126,600 in tax year 1999. This means that the effective MTR for such taxpayers is 103% of their nominal MTR—for example, 40.8% rather than 39.6% for someone in the top income tax bracket. Even more complicated, taxpayers lose 2% of the value of their personal exemptions for each $2500 of AGI in excess of certain limits ($189,950 for married taxpayers

---

[3]Assuming they have positive taxable income. A taxpayer earning an amount less than the personal exemptions and deductions he or she can take has a nominal marginal tax rate of zero.

13.2   Taxing Family Values

Politicians like to talk about promoting family values. For this reason, nearly all of the candidates in the 2000 presidential race attacked the income tax for not being "family friendly" because of the marriage "tax" or penalty. Two-earner couples face a substantial tax increase when they marry because their combined standard deductions are reduced and the income thresholds that define the tax brackets are less generous. A marriage tax also faces some people who receive the earned income or the child and dependent care tax credits.

The income tax is quite family friendly in some regards. The income tax "subsidizes" children by giving more personal exemptions and tax credits to larger families. Also, couples with unequal incomes receive a marriage subsidy rather than paying a marriage tax. If one of the partners in a couple earns no income, his or her standard deduction is useless if the couple is not married. The combined tax of a couple is reduced when a partner with no income marries a partner with income. Once married, the couple gets the larger married standard deduction and can average (or split) their income by filing a joint return, often putting them in a lower tax bracket. However, the income tax system also subsidizes divorce by one-earner couples. Alimony paid is subtracted from the AGI of the earner and is taxed as income to the recipient. Thus divorced couples receive the benefit of income splitting and the benefit of the larger combined single standard deductions.

Professors Daniel Feenberg and Harvey Rosen of the National Bureau of Economic Research calculate that, in 1994, 52% of couples paid a marriage tax averaging $1244, whereas 38% received a marriage subsidy averaging $1399 ("There Is Still A Marriage Subsidy," *NBER Digest,* June 1994). Other economists have analyzed the impact of the income tax on marriage and fertility decisions. Professor James Alm of Georgia State University and Leslie Whittington of Georgetown University found that the mar-

riage tax reduces the probability of marriage by one-earner couples and increases the probability of divorce by married one-earner couples. Professors David Sjoquist and Mary Beth Walker of Georgia State University found that the marriage tax changes the timing of the marriage decision, retarding it for couples subject to the marriage tax and advancing it for couples who would receive a marriage subsidy. Other researchers have found that the subsidy for children provided by the income tax changes the timing of child birth. Because parents receive a dependent exemption for the whole calendar year regardless of when the baby is born, parents are more inclined to arrange for babies to be born later in the year, rather than earlier.

Analyze the following:

- Two of your friends don't know whether to get married in December this year or January next year. How would your advice to them depend on their income situation?

- Consider the following four features you might like in a tax system: (1) ability to pay is based on family income; (2) the tax rate structure is graduated; (3) no two taxpayers should pay more tax simply because they get married; and (4) no two taxpayers should pay less tax simply because they get married. Professor Harvey Rosen of Princeton University has pointed out that we can have any three of these features but not all four. Why? Which one would you prefer to give up?

- One of the presidential candidates has pledged to "abolish" the marriage tax, although he has not mentioned the marriage subsidy. In light of Rosen's observation above, how must the other features of the income tax system be changed in order to honor this pledge?

Sources: See James Alm and Leslie Whittington, "Marriage and the Marriage Tax," 1992; and David L. Sjoquist and Mary Beth Walker, "The Marriage Tax and the Rate and Timing of Taxation," 1995.

and $126,600 for single taxpayers in 1999). Using the 1999 value of $2750 per personal exemption, the effective MTR is equal to $(1 + .022 \cdot N)$ times the nominal MTR, where N is the number of personal exemptions for which the taxpayer is eligible. For example, a family of four persons in the top tax bracket faces an effective MTR of 43.1% rather than 39.6% once the phase-out of personal exemptions is factored in.[4]

The MTR may also vary according to the type of income. Although realized capital gains are added to AGI, they are not taxed at the nominal MTR unless the appreciating asset was held by the taxpayer for less than one year. For assets held more than one year, realized capital gains are taxed at 10% if the taxpayer is in the 15% tax bracket and at 20% if the taxpayer is in any other tax bracket. Thus, although a taxpayer in the top tax bracket has a MTR of 39.6% on ordinary income, the MTR on capital gains income is only 20%, provided the appreciating assets have been held for at least one year.

CONCLUSION AND SUMMARY

In this chapter we have surveyed the main tax levied by the federal government on the incomes of persons. Our purpose was to attain a good understanding of what forms of incomes are taxed and at what rates. In the process, we discovered just how complicated the income tax system really is. Some of the complications result from the fact that the income tax system is not just a system for raising revenue; it is a system for apportioning the burden of government across different households. Also, some of the complications are a result of provisions to encourage certain behavior—such as CODAs, which reduce taxes on retirement saving. Other complications, most of which we did not discuss, are for the purpose of limiting tax avoidance. Some complications exist for no good purpose at all—for example, the phaseouts of personal exemptions and itemized deductions. It would be straight forward to have additional tax brackets if that is their purpose. In Chapter 14, we study how this complicated income tax system affects taxpayers' behavior.

- The federal government obtains most of its revenue by taxing incomes, and income taxes are a significant source of revenue to state governments as well. The personal income tax is the largest tax in the economy and accounts for over 48% of federal receipts.

- The amount of income tax paid depends on a family's taxable income. Taxable income is gross income less adjustments, including the costs of acquiring income, minus personal exemptions and deductions. Gross income includes income from employment, income from property, and

---

[4]In fact, the MTR may increase by much more. The child tax credit is reduced by 5% for each excess increment of $1000 in AGI, and the value of personal exemptions reduced by 2% for each excess increment of $2500, *or part thereof*. The last clause means that an increment of a lesser amount counts the same as a full increment. This means that the effective MTR can be over 100% for small increases in AGI. A taxpayer who receives a small raise could end up with *less* take-home income after taxes!

some transfer income. Income from taxable sources must be included whether received in cash or in kind.

▨ The personal exemption is a fixed amount per family member. Taxpayers can elect to take the standard deduction, which is a fixed amount, or itemize their deductions. The most important itemized deductions are charitable gifts, interest on home mortgages, and state and local income and property taxes.

▨ Some forms of income are specifically excluded from gross income, such as employer-paid medical, dental, and group life insurance and contributions to company pensions and retirement savings plans. In addition, some forms of income are excluded because the income tax does not apply to everything that is income in principle.

▨ Income in principle is measured by a family's Haig-Simons income, which is the value of consumption plus the increase in net worth over the tax year. Haig-Simons income that is excluded from tax includes most transfers and unrealized capital gains. Some economists include imputed rent on the taxpayer's home as part of Haig-Simons income.

▨ Taxable income is taxed according to a graduated tax rate schedule that levies higher rates in higher income brackets. The tax rate in each bracket is a marginal tax rate that applies to increases or decreases in income within a tax bracket, as defined by income thresholds.

▨ The effective marginal tax rate of a taxpayer is raised by provisions that phase out personal exemptions, itemized deductions, and tax credits.

▨ Tax credits are amounts that are deducted from the taxes owed by the household. The most important is the earned income tax credit, which is a refundable tax credit that turns the United States income tax system into a form of negative income tax system.

QUESTIONS FOR DISCUSSION AND REVIEW

1. The 1894 income tax (2% of incomes above $4000) was ruled unconstitutional because it was not apportioned (i.e., did not collect revenue) among the states in accordance with their populations, as direct taxes (taxes on persons) were required to. Why isn't an income tax apportioned according to population? Is any direct tax apportioned according to population?

2. In Canada, the tax unit is the individual. Wherever possible, married taxpayers attempt to shift income to the spouse with the least taxable income. This type of tax avoidance is less common in the United States. Why?

3. A family earned $60,000 in wages in 1999 and put $4000 of this in a 401(k) plan under a CODA arrangement with its employer. The employer matched the taxpayer's 401(k) contribution and also paid the family's medical insurance, which has a market value of $4000 per year. In addition to the 401(k) plan, the taxpayer owns Internet stocks purchased at the beginning of 1999 for $2000, which were

worth $10,000 by the end of the year. The taxpayer sold half of the stocks at the end of the year. The taxpayer lives in a home they own free and clear. The taxpayer could rent out the home for $12,000 after depreciation and maintenance. What is the family's AGI and HSI? Assuming four persons in the family, what percentage of the family's HSI is taxable?

4. A property settlement (such as splitting bank accounts) received from a divorced spouse is not part of taxable income, but alimony is. The spouse who pays alimony can deduct it in calculating taxable income. Given this, would a couple planning an amicable divorce ever agree on alimony payments rather than a property settlement? If so, why?

5. Joey repairs Rachel's bike and sends her a bill for $50. Ross cleans Joey's windows and bills him $50. Ross owes Rachel $50, which he borrowed last week. Rachel tells Ross she will forget the money he owes her if he cancels his bill to Joey, and in return Joey tears up his bill to Rachel. Who, if anyone, must declare $50 in income?

6. Suppose the government wants to tax capital gains according to the Haig-Simons definition, and asks you how to do this. Which of the following would you recommend?

   a. Tax capital gains whether they are realized or not.

   b. Tax realized capital gains but index them for inflation.

   c. Tax indexed capital gains whether they are realized or not.

7. Suppose taxpayers who own their homes must add to taxable income an amount equal to the rent they could have received by renting the home out. According to the Haig-Simons criteria, do you think they should be allowed to deduct their mortgage interest payment on their homes? Why or why not?

8. How does the graduated tax rate schedule affect taxpayers whose incomes fluctuate from year to year? For instance, two taxpayers earn the same income (say, $150,000) over two years, but one of them earns it all in the first year and the other earns the same amount evenly over two years. Who pays more tax?

9. In 1999, a family with less than $110,000 income received a $500 tax credit as well as a $2750 dependent exemption for a child. Suppose the government decides to change the rules and the family can have the exemption or the credit, but not both. Would a family in the 15% tax bracket choose the exemption or the credit? What about a family in the 28% bracket?

10. Internet Exercise. Go to the IRS's tax statistics site for individual returns at http://www.irs.ustreas.gov/prod/tax_stats/soi/ind_gss.html. Download spreadsheet Table 1 (file 97INPREL.EXE), which summarizes information drawn from 1997 individual income tax returns by size of AGI. From this spreadsheet, calculate the percentage of total income from the following sources received by taxpayers whose AGI was less than $15,000 and by taxpayers whose AGI exceeded $200,000: salary and wages, tax exempt interest, realized capital gains, unemployment compensation. What percentage of all contributions to Individual Retirement Arrangements (IRAs) and to Keogh retirement plans were made by the same groups of taxpayers?

11. Internet Exercise. How do you think the percentage of taxpayers who pay a marriage penalty or receive a marriage subsidy (bonus) depends on the amount of income they have? Find out by reading "For Better or for Worse: Marriage and

the Federal Income Tax," an analysis by the Congressional Budget Office. It is available in the tax analysis section of their Studies and Reports site at www.cbo.gov/byclasscat.cfm?class=0&cat=33. See Chapter 3, Table 5 for details on how the marriage tax/penalty varies by taxpayers grouped by AGI. Give some possible explanations for the pattern you observe in this table.

SELECTED REFERENCES

Income in principle was defined in Robert Haig, *The Federal Income Tax,* 1921; and Henry C. Simons, *Personal Income Taxation,* 1938.

See James Alm and Leslie A. Whittington, "The Rise and Fall and Rise ... of the Marriage Tax," 1996, which documents changes in the marriage tax over time.

USEFUL INTERNET SITES

Information on the federal and state income tax systems is availale from numerous internet sites. Two good metasites with dozens of useful links are the Tax and Accounting Sites Directory at http://www.taxsites.com/ and the Essential Links tax page at http://www.el.com/elomks/taxes/.

14 Income Taxes and Household Behavior

In an effort to tax people according to their ability to pay, Parliament in seventeenth-century England levied a "house and window" tax. This was a type of a property tax for which the amount of tax depended on the number of windows in the taxpayer's house. The window tax made some sense. Bigger houses have more windows, and glass was expensive at the time, so the owner of a house with many windows must have a high ability to pay. It also led to some remarkable changes in the architecture of the period. Today, many tourists visiting England marvel at historic houses and wonder why they have so few windows. The windowless houses represent an early attempt by taxpayers to minimize the tax they pay.[1]

Although the modern United States income tax may not have had as big an impact on American architecture, it too alters people's behavior as they try to minimize the amount of tax they must pay. One reason the income tax affects household decisions is that the Internal Revenue Code (IRC) exempts income from certain sources or allows taxpayers to spend income on certain uses and deduct the spending from taxable income. Taxpayers are inclined to earn or use income in these tax-preferred ways. A second reason is that an income tax inherently affects some household decisions, even if taxable income were defined broadly enough to include all sources and uses. These household decisions include how much to work and how much to save.

EFFECTS OF TAX EXPENDITURES

Although the Internal Revenue Code (IRC) contains provisions, such as the personal exemptions, that exempt income in order to define the taxpayer's ability to pay, other provisions have the sole purpose of lowering the cost of certain activities

---

[1]By the eighteenth century, the window tax had been "graduated," like the modern income tax, so that it applied only to houses with more than seven windows. The window tax is discussed in William Kennedy, *English Taxation 1640–1799*, 1964.

to taxpayers. As such, they are equivalent using the tax system to subsidize an activity. The tax revenues lost because of these tax subsidies are called **tax expenditures.** This term—coined by the late Stanley Surrey, who was at one time an assistant secretary of the Treasury in President Johnson's administration—is used to describe revenue losses from tax provisions that are functionally equivalent to government spending programs. Surrey argued that the government "spends" funds simply by not collecting tax revenues normally due it. Using Surrey's logic, we find that the government "spends" enormous sums through the tax system. Total tax expenditures in 1999 amounted to about $472 billion for the federal government, or about 27% of its regular outlays.

A good example of a tax expenditure is the itemized deduction for charitable donations. Congress could authorize spending programs that subsidize charitable organizations by matching private donations with government funds. Instead, it indirectly spends money for the same purpose by authorizing taxpayers to deduct their charitable donations from taxable income. In effect, the government pays part of the private donations by giving up tax revenue. Unlike government spending, tax expenditures show up not as budget outlays, but as losses in government revenue.

Because tax expenditures represent revenue that could have been collected but wasn't, they are invisible in the government budget, which records only the funds spent. Surrey sought to make tax expenditures visible by advocating a **tax expenditure budget** that reports tax expenditures in the same way as outlays are reported in the regular budget. Since 1974, Congress has required that a list of tax expenditures be included in the budget published by the Office of Management and Budget. Table 14.1 lists the main tax expenditures in the United States' personal income tax system and the estimated revenue loss of each item in 1999. The various tax expenditures are grouped under the expenditure functions used to classify federal outlays. As we see from the table, the tax expenditures have a variety of purposes. Moreover, some of them cause substantial losses in revenue to the federal government and are equivalent to large spending programs.

The amount of a tax expenditure is measured by calculating the revenue lost because of the tax provision in question. The revenue loss is equal to the reduction in the taxable income of taxpayers multiplied by their respective marginal tax rates, summed over all taxpayers. For instance, if a taxpayer in the 28% tax bracket deducts from taxable income $1000 in charitable donations, the tax expenditure on this taxpayer is $280. This calculation presumes that the level of the activity is the same whether or not the tax expenditure is present. But because taxpayers are likely to change their behavior in response to the tax expenditure, the value of a tax expenditure is not necessarily the revenue that would be gained if the tax expenditure were eliminated.

The main reason we study tax expenditures is to understand how the income tax system affects the behavior of taxpayers, and the implications for tax policy. For this purpose, we take a closer look at three large tax expenditures in the personal income tax system: the deduction for charitable donations, the exclusion of employer-paid medical insurance, and a combination of tax expenditures for home ownership.

Table 14.1   Federal Revenue Loss for Tax Expenditures Affecting Individuals, 1999

Function	Millions of $
National defense and veterans affairs	
Exclusion of benefits and allowances of armed forces personnel	2,160
Exclusion of veterans disability compensation	3,210
Commerce and housing	
Exclusion of interest on life insurance	15,810
Exclusion of capital gains on residence	19,095
Deduction of mortgage interest	57,590
Deduction of real estate property tax	20,535
Step-up of capital gains at death	28,240
Education, training, and social services	
Charitable donations deduction (excluding health)	24,200
Child and dependent care tax credit	2,395
Health	
Exclusion of employer-paid medical insurance and workers' compensation premiums	87,850
Deduction for unreimbursed medical expenses	4,215
Charitable donations deduction (health)	2,860
Income and Social Security	
Exclusion of OASDI benefits	25,930
Exclusion of workers' compensation benefits	5,940
Exclusion of pensions, CODAs, and IRAs	86,670
Exclusion of employer-paid group life insurance premiums	2,170
Earned income and child tax credit	23,572
General-purpose fiscal assistance	
Exclusion of interest on general state and local debt	20,660
Deduction for state and local taxes (other than real estate)	39,235

Source: Statistical Abstract of the United States, 1999, Table 549.

The Deduction for Charitable Donations

The deduction for charitable donations was introduced in 1917, when the modern income tax was only three years old, to encourage philanthropy by the rich. At that time, the rich were the only people who had to pay income tax. As the income tax grew, so did the size of the charitable deductions tax expenditure. In 1999, over 32 million taxpayers deducted charitable donations from their taxable income, reducing government tax revenue by $26.5 billion.

Taxpayers can subtract from taxable income, as an itemized deduction, the amounts given to qualified charitable organizations, whether the donations are in cash, in kind, or in appreciated property. To qualify as a charity, an organization must be primarily religious, charitable, educational, scientific, or literary. Churches account for the largest fraction of tax-deductible donations made by taxpayers. Contributors must subtract the value of any goods or services received in return for their donations, and donations over $250 require a letter from the charity providing this information. Political contributions and donations to lobbying groups do not qualify for the deduction.

The economic analysis of the deduction for charitable donations begins by treating charitable donations as a consumption good. The fact that people make donations voluntarily reveals that they get satisfaction or utility from doing so; thus the amount spent on charity can be analyzed like spending on any other good. Following this logic, the amount of charitable donations by a taxpayer is measured on the horizontal axis and the price of giving to charity is measured on the vertical axis in Figure 14.1. Without a charitable donations deduction, the price of giving to the taxpayer is $1 per $1 of donations. That is, the taxpayer must give up $1 worth of other goods and services to purchase $1 worth of satisfaction by giving to charity. The demand curve for charity by a taxpayer is labeled D in Figure 14.1. Like the demand curve for any other good, the demand curve for charitable giving slopes

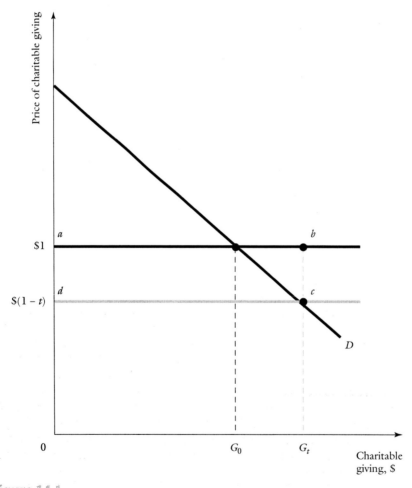

Figure 14.1

Effect of the Charitable Gifts Deduction on the Level of Private Donations
The amount of charitable giving depends on the "price" of giving to the donors. The charitable gifts deduction reduces the price of giving a dollar to charity from $1 to $1 minus the taxpayer's marginal tax rate t. Charitable gifts rise from G_0 to G_t accordingly.

downward. That is, if the price of giving is reduced, the taxpayer gives more to charity. How is the price of giving reduced? If taxpayers itemize their deductions, taxable income goes down by $1 for every $1 of charitable donations. In this case, the price of giving is not $1, but $1 minus the taxpayer's marginal tax rate, where the marginal tax rate is the tax saved by having $1 less taxable income. For instance, if the taxpayer is in the 28% tax bracket, the price of giving $1 to charity is 72 cents—the $1 given to charity minus the 28 cents in saved taxes.

Figure 14.1 shows the effect of the charitable donations deduction on the amount of donations by the taxpayer. Without a deduction, taxpayers face a price of giving equal to $1 and make G_0 dollars in donations. With a deduction, they face a price of giving equal to $(1 - t)$ dollars per $1 of donations, where t is the marginal tax rate.[2] At this lower price, taxpayers make G_t dollars of donations. The cost of the tax expenditure is measured as revenue lost, which is the area of rectangle *abcd*, which is the charitable donation G_t times the taxpayer's marginal tax rate t. It is also the outlay the government would have made had it encouraged charity with a spending program rather than a tax expenditure.

The amount by which charitable donations are increased depends on how much the deduction reduces the price of giving, and on the sensitivity of the quantity of giving to the price of giving. The reduction in the price of giving is equal to a taxpayer's marginal tax rate, and the sensitivity of donations to the price is measured by the price elasticity of the demand curve for charitable giving. Professor Charles Clotfelter of Duke University has studied how the price of giving affects the level of charitable donations by taxpayers. He finds that the price elasticity of charitable donations is around 1.27. This means that if the price of giving is lowered by 28% for taxpayers, the amount of donations would rise by over 35%.

As an approximation, a price elasticity also means that each $1 of government revenue lost because of the charitable donations deduction increases the amount of donations received by the charities by about $1.27. Therefore charities receive 27% more as a result of the charitable donations deduction than they would if the government were to eliminate the deduction and give the additional tax revenue directly to them.

One feature of using a tax expenditure to encourage charity is that the tax deduction reduces the price of giving more for high-income taxpayers than for low-income taxpayers. A taxpayer in the 15% tax bracket pays 85 cents per extra $1 of donations, whereas a taxpayer in the 39.6% tax bracket pays only 60.4 cents. A taxpayer who takes the standard deduction gets no subsidy at all and pays $1 for each $1 of donations.

This feature of a tax expenditure policy raises a serious question. Why should the charitable donations of high-income taxpayers be subsidized at higher rates than those of lower-income taxpayers? No one has a good answer. Some tax reformers advocate abolishing the charitable donations deduction, or replacing it with a tax credit at the

---

[2]The price of giving appreciated property is even lower because the taxpayer deducts the appreciated value of the property but doesn't pay tax on the capital gain. Suppose x% of the value of the property donated is appreciation. The price of $1 of giving is $1 minus the marginal tax rate minus x% of the marginal capital gains tax rate. For instance the price of giving appreciated property for someone in the 39.6% bracket is $\$(0.604 - x(0.28))$. For property that is mostly appreciation ($x = 1$), this is equal to about 32 cents per $1 of giving.

lowest tax rate (15%) for all taxpayers. With a tax credit, all taxpayers would get the same subsidy rate for their donations. Philanthropic organizations strongly oppose these changes because they believe that charitable donations would drop drastically if the deduction were abolished or reduced for high-income taxpayers.

The Exclusion of Employer-Paid Insurance Benefits

One of the largest tax expenditures is the exclusion from taxation of employee compensation paid in the form of medical care or insurance. This income is excluded from both the personal income tax and the FICA payroll tax. In 1999, the estimated revenue loss to the federal government was $83.1 billion. The exclusion for medical insurance was enacted during World War II, when wages were controlled and employees were scarce, in order to allow employers to attract workers.

The exclusion of employer-paid insurance benefits encourages taxpayers to demand (and employers to supply) more of this type of tax-free compensation. As explained in Chapter 9, governments in most countries play an important role in providing health care insurance. The United States government is different in that it makes extensive use of tax expenditures as a means of public finance for medical insurance. Most other advanced industrial countries have universal government medical insurance financed by government spending.

When the tax system is used to encourage medical coverage, insurance is subsidized at the taxpayer's marginal tax rate, so high-income taxpayers receive a higher rate of subsidy for their medical insurance than low-income taxpayers do. The analysis is complicated by the fact that FICA taxes are included. Taxpayers in the top tax bracket receive an implicit subsidy of 42.5% (the 39.6% marginal personal tax rate plus the 2.9% Medicare component of the FICA tax) on employer-paid insurance benefits, reducing the effective price of $1 of insurance to them to 57.5 cents. Taxpayers in the lowest tax bracket receive an implicit subsidy of 30.3% (the 15% marginal personal tax rate plus the full 15.3% FICA tax), reducing their price to just under 70 cents. In these calculations, we assume that the entire FICA tax is borne by employees.

Except for the FICA tax, the analysis of the tax expenditure for employer-paid medical insurance is similar to the analysis of the charitable donations deduction. The reduction in the price of medical insurance is calculated for taxpayers in the different tax brackets, and the effect on benefits demanded is estimated. We assume that employers respond to the increase in the demand for compensation in this form. Professors Stephen Woodbury and Wei-Jang Huang of the W. E. Upjohn Institute, a research organization dedicated to employment research, have studied the impact of this tax expenditure on the amounts of medical insurance provided. They estimate that the average taxpayer consumes 15% more medical insurance because of the exclusion of this form of income, and that high-income taxpayers consume as much as 25% more insurance.

Tax Expenditures for Home Ownership

Tax expenditures also encourage home ownership. The three main tax expenditures in this category are the deduction for mortgage interest, the deduction for real estate property taxes, and the exclusion of realized capital gains on the taxpayer's home. The revenue losses from these tax expenditures were $57.6 billion,

$20.5 billion, and $19.1 billion, respectively, in 1999. The interest on a home-owner's mortgage is not an expense of earning income, because the income on the home (the imputed rent) is not taxed. Instead, mortgage interest paid by the tax-payer is part of the cost of the consumption services provided by the home. In this respect it is no different from rent paid to a landlord, except that rent is not deductible from taxable income. Real estate property taxes are also part of the cost of home ownership because they finance the services provided to homeowners by local governments, such as streets, sidewalks, and public schools for their children.

Although it is not reported in the tax expenditure budget, most economists would count as a tax expenditure the revenue lost by excluding from tax the imputed rent on the taxpayer's home equity. The average homeowner has equity roughly equal to half the value of his or her home, so this tax expenditure is approx-imately equal to the revenue lost from the mortgage interest deduction.

The impact of these tax expenditures on the consumption of housing services is complicated by the fact that a home is an investment, and provides consumption services during the time the homeowner lives in it. Economists analyze the effect of home ownership tax expenditures using the theory of the investment user cost, a topic we study in Chapter 15. Briefly, the user cost is the annual cost of owning a home, and it is significantly reduced by the tax expenditures for home ownership, especially for taxpayers in the top tax bracket. The user cost of home ownership is reduced by less for low-income taxpayers, and renters receive no help at all, except indirectly through tax expenditures for the business income of landlords.

The tax expenditures for home ownership affect decisions about housing in two ways. First, because they are available only to homeowners—not to renters—they affect the decision whether to rent or own a home (known as the tenure decision). Second, by lowering the user cost of housing, they encourage homeowners to con-sume more housing. Homeowners consume more housing by owning larger and higher-quality homes. The subsidy for home ownership is biggest for high-income taxpayers, so their decisions are the most likely to be affected. Home ownership pat-terns are consistent with this view. Over 60% of consumers in the lowest income quintile (the 20% with the lowest incomes) are renters, whereas only about 16% of consumers in the top income quintile rent their homes.[3]

Empirically, the effect of the increased demand on the quantity of housing is difficult to determine. The increase in demand could increase housing prices rather than quantities, especially in the short run. It could also increase market interest rates as people assume larger mortgages. Some studies find that the elasticity of the demand for housing with respect to the user cost is approximately equal to 1. Assuming that the increase in demand is reflected in higher quantities rather than prices, this elasticity implies that taxpayers with incomes over $50,000 in 1990 con-sumed 23% more housing services as a result of the home ownership tax expendi-tures. Taxpayers with incomes of $30,000 consumed just 12% more housing.[4]

The effect of housing tax expenditures on economic efficiency is important. Many economists believe that the large tax expenditures for home ownership have

[3]See James M. Poterba, "Taxation and Housing Markets: Preliminary Evidence on the Effects of Recent Tax Reforms," 1990.
[4]James M. Poterba, "Taxation and Housing: Old Questions, New Answers," 1992.

diverted domestic savings away from productive business investment toward residential structures. In fact, nearly 30% of the capital stock in the United States is tied up in residential housing, a larger fraction than in most other countries. To the extent that American homeowners invest too much in housing, an excess burden is imposed because capital is not allocated where it is most valuable to the economy. Estimates of the excess burden from the tax expenditures for housing range from one half of 1% of GDP to over 3% of GDP.

The Incidence of Tax Expenditures

Who benefits most from these tax expenditures? To answer this question, we begin with the statutory incidence of tax expenditures, which tabulates the amount of tax saved by taxpayers in different income classes. We then consider the economic incidence of tax expenditures, which may differ from the statutory incidence because of shifting.

One highly criticized feature of many tax expenditures is their "upside-down" equity. By this we mean that high-income taxpayers enjoy the largest tax savings from the tax expenditures, while low- and middle-income taxpayers receive much less. Tax expenditures that take the form of variable deductions or exclusions from income are most likely to have upside-down equity. There are two reasons for this. First, high-income taxpayers typically have higher deductions or exclusions. Second, each dollar deducted or excluded yields larger tax savings to high-income taxpayers because they are in higher tax brackets. For example, consider a taxpayer in the 28% tax bracket with a $100,000 mortgage. He or she deducts about $8000 in mortgage interest each year, which reduces the amount of taxes owed by $2240 (28% of $8000). Compare this with a taxpayer in the 39.6% tax bracket. Such a taxpayer is likely to have a much larger home and a bigger mortgage. If this high-income taxpayer has a $1 million mortgage (the maximum allowed for the mortgage interest deduction), he or she pays about $80,000 a year in mortgage interest. In this case, the mortgage interest deduction yields a tax saving of $31,680 a year ($80,000 times 39.6%), which is 14 times the tax saving of the first taxpayer.[5]

Although the tax reductions from tax expenditures go disproportionately to high-income taxpayers, some of the benefits may be shifted to others because the tax expenditures change prices and factor rewards. That is, the economic incidence of tax expenditures may be different from their statutory incidence. Perhaps the best example of benefit shifting is the exclusion of interest income from municipal bonds, a tax expenditure of $20.7 billion. The tax-exempt bonds are held mainly by taxpayers in the highest income tax bracket, but these taxpayers do not reap the entire benefit. The interest rate paid on tax-exempt bonds is lower than the interest rate paid on taxable bonds, and this reduces the benefit to the holders of the tax-exempt bonds. For instance, suppose a taxpayer in the 39.6% bracket can earn 6% interest on taxable bonds and 3.6% on tax-exempt state and local bonds. In this case, the

---

[5]These calculations do not take into account the phaseout of itemized deductions for the high-income taxpayer or the fact that the low-income taxpayer could have taken the standard deduction, which his almost as much as his or her mortgage interest deduction.

taxpayer earns the same after-tax interest rate in either case. The lower interest on tax-exempt bonds represents an *implicit tax* on interest receipts.

If the taxpayer doesn't get the benefit, who does? Because municipalities borrow at a lower interest rate, state and local governments (and their taxpayers) benefit from this tax expenditure. As it happens, the interest rate on tax-exempt state and local debt does not fall enough to eliminate the entire advantage to the holders of the bonds, so the benefit of this tax expenditure is split between high-income taxpayers, especially those in the 39.6% bracket, and municipal governments.

EFFECTS OF THE INCOME TAX ON THE LABOR SUPPLY

The reason the government relies so heavily on the income tax is that many people consider it a fair tax because the amount of tax paid depends on ability to pay. We could argue, however, that the ability to pay the tax is best measured by the *ability to earn income,* not by actual income. For instance, a plastic surgeon who prefers to play golf six days a week has a greater ability to earn and to pay taxes than is indicated by his or her income. Unfortunately, the government cannot easily observe or measure ability to earn income, so it is more or less stuck with taxing income.

The income of taxpayers depends not just on their ability to earn income, but also on how much and how hard they work. By taxing income, the government affects the taxpayer's decision to work. Does an income tax cause taxpayers to work less in order to lower their taxable income, or does it cause them to work more in order to pay the tax? This is one of the most important questions about the effect of an income tax on household behavior.

A Theory of the Choice Between Labor and Leisure

We analyze the impact of the income tax on the taxpayer's incentive to work using the theory of the choice between labor and leisure. This theory assumes that taxpayers can freely choose how many hours a week they work. This view is highly simplified, of course, because not every worker has flexible hours. However, many workers can vary their hours of work by working overtime, moonlighting, or changing jobs. Also, if enough workers have a strong desire to work more or fewer hours, firms will want to accommodate them. Doing so makes the firms more desirable to work for, and they can then pay lower wages.

In Figure 14.2, a worker's leisure in hours per week is measured on the horizontal axis. By leisure we simply mean hours spent not working. Workers may use leisure time productively, as by cleaning house or looking after children, or for recreation and restoration. Each worker has 168 hours (7 days times 24 hours) a week to allocate between working and leisure. Consumption of market goods per week is measured (in dollars) on the vertical axis. We assume that workers earn a wage of W dollars per hour and have no income other than their earnings. A worker can take all 168 hours of the week as leisure, but in this case cannot consume any market goods. Alternatively, the worker could take no leisure and earn 168 times W dollars but then would have no time to enjoy the goods, let alone sleep. More

14.1   The Incidence of Tax Expenditures

The table below provides information on the amount of taxes saved by taxpayers in different income classes for three categories of tax expenditures. The home ownership and charitable gifts tax expenditures both have "upside-down" equity because the benefits accrue mainly to high-income taxpayers. The home ownership tax expenditures consist of the mortgage interest and property tax deductions taken by taxpayers who itemize. For example, a taxpayer with income over $200,000 saves $6202 in taxes on average from the home ownership tax expenditures and $4397 from the charitable gifts tax expenditure. Averaged over all taxpayers, the tax savings are $517 and $191, respectively. Taxpayers with incomes over $100,000 receive nearly 54% of combined tax expenditures for home ownership and charitable deductions even though they make up less than 8% of all taxpayers.

The family support tax expenditures are the earned income, child, and child care tax credits. As can be seen from the table, the benefits of these tax expenditures are distributed evenly over taxpayers with incomes less than $100,000. Low-income taxpayers benefit most from the earned income tax credit, and middle-income taxpayers benefit most from the child and child care tax credits.[1]

Critically analyze the following:

■ The home ownership and charitable tax expenditures are itemized deductions, whereas the family support tax expenditures are tax credits that are phased out or phased down for high-income taxpayers. Explain how this leads to the statutory incidence pattern observed in the table.

■ How might the homeownership tax expenditures be shifted? In answering this question, consider the following two cases: (1) the supply curve of housing is perfectly elastic (horizontal), (2) the supply of housing is perfectly inelastic (vertical).

■ Could the earned income tax credit be shifted? Consider the case in which the supply of labor curve of low-income taxpayers is perfectly elastic. How would the earned income tax credit affect this supply curve, and to whom is the benefit of the tax expenditure shifted?

---

[1] These calculations do not take into account the phase-out of itemized deductions for the high-income taxpayer or the fact that the low-income taxpayer could have taken the standard deduction, which is almost as much as his or her mortgage interest deduction.

Statutory Incidence of Selected Tax Expenditures (1999)

Income Class (in thousands)	Number of Returns in Class (in millions)	Home Ownership Tax Expenditures (Dollar Amounts)*		Charitable Gifts Tax Expenditure (Dollar Amounts)		Family Support Tax Expenditures (Dollar Amounts)+	
		Total ($ millions)	Per Return ($)	Total ($ millions)	Per Return ($)	Total ($ millions)	Per Return ($)
Below $20	48.7	$ 230	$ 5	$ 136	$ 3	$24,042	$494
$20 to $50	49.3	6,680	136	2,174	44	15,164	308
$50 to $75	19.8	12,511	632	3,910	197	5,555	281
$75 to $100	10.0	14,592	1,459	3,828	383	3,276	328
$100 to $200	8.5	22,253	2,618	5,453	642	1,664	196
Over $200	2.5	15,504	6,202	10,993	4,397	52	21
All	138.8	71,770	517	26,495	191	49,751	358

*Sum of mortgage interest and real estate tax deductions.
+Sum of earned income, child, and child care tax credits.
Source: Joint Committee on Taxation, Estimates of Federal Tax Expenditures for Fiscal Years 2000–2004, Tables 2 and 3, December 22, 1999. This document is available at http://www.house.gov/jct/pubs99.html.

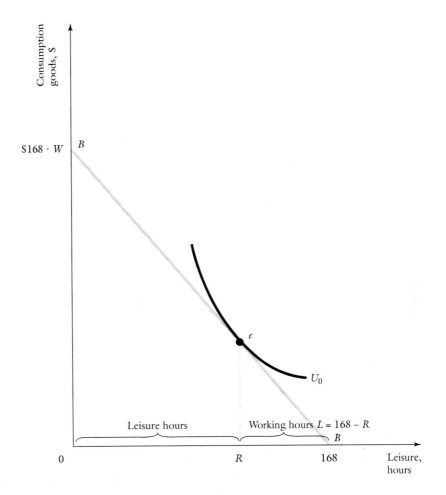

Figure 14.2

Labor Supply as a Labor-Leisure Choice

Budget line *BB* shows the worker's budget line between goods and leisure. The slope of the budget line is the wage rate *W*. A worker maximizes utility at point *e* where the slope of an indifference curve, which is the worker's MWTP for leisure, is equal to the wage rate. The worker takes *R* hours per week as leisure and works the remaining 168 minus *R* hours.

realistically, the worker chooses a point on the budget line *BB* between these two extremes.

We assume, as usual, that workers make the labor-leisure choice so as to maximize utility. The indifference curve map in Figure 14.2 shows the combinations of leisure and consumption that give the worker a constant level of utility. Indifference curves have the usual shape, and those farther from the origin represent higher levels of utility. The (absolute) slope of an indifference curve represents the worker's marginal willingness to pay (MWTP) for 1 hour of leisure. The fact that the indifference curves are convex toward the origin indicates that the MWTP for leisure declines as more leisure hours are taken.

A worker maximizes utility by choosing point e on the budget line. At this point, the MWTP for leisure is equal to the wage forgone by missing 1 hour's work. In other words, the price of one hour of leisure is the wage rate. The utility-maximizing choice between labor and leisure is to reserve R (for recreation) hours per week for leisure and work the remaining hours. The labor supply L of the worker is equal to $168 - R$ hours per week.

THE EFFECT OF A LUMP-SUM TAX.   To analyze the effect of an income tax on the labor supply, we'll first consider the effect of a lump-sum tax, in Figure 14.3. Recall that a lump-sum tax is a fixed amount, so the worker's tax bill cannot be changed by altering the number of hours worked. A lump-sum tax of T dollars shifts the budget line to $B_T B_T$, and a utility-maximizing worker chooses point e_T on the new budget line. Leisure is a normal good, so leisure falls from R to R_T hours as a result of the lump-sum tax. Since the number of hours in a week is fixed, hours worked rise from L to L_T. In other words, the taxpayer works more when the government levies a lump-sum tax. The reason is that the taxpayer works more in order to pay the tax.

THE EFFECT OF A PROPORTIONAL INCOME TAX.   With a proportional income tax, the government takes a constant fraction of a worker's earnings, so the after-tax (or take-home) wage falls to $W(1 - t)$, where t is the income tax rate. For instance, if the income tax rate is 25%, $t = 0.25$ and the take-home wage is three-quarters of the gross wage. The effect of a proportional income tax on the labor-leisure choice is shown in Figure 14.4. When an income tax is imposed, the worker faces budget line BB_t, which has an absolute slope equal to the after-tax wage $W(1 - t)$. Unlike the lump-sum tax, the income tax paid depends on the number of hours worked. The tax paid is equal to the vertical distance between budget line BB and BB_t at each point; the more hours worked, the more tax paid. The budget line BB_t is flatter than the no-tax budget line because the relative price of leisure—the after-tax wage—is reduced by the tax. For instance, if the gross wage rate is $10 an hour and the income tax rate is 25%, an hour of leisure costs the worker $7.50 (not $10) of forgone consumption.

Many people assume that a taxpayer would work fewer hours when an income tax is levied, because the lower reward for working would induce people to substitute leisure for consumption goods. However, in theory, the utility-maximizing point on budget line BB_t can lie to the right or left of point e, meaning that the worker may work fewer or more hours as a result of the tax. In Figure 14.4, we illustrate the case where the utility-maximizing point e_t on BB_t lies directly below e, so the worker works the same number of hours as before the tax was imposed.

The income tax can increase or decrease the hours worked because it has both an income and a substitution effect. The income effect of a tax was that highlighted by the lump-sum tax, which caused the worker to work more hours. Unlike the lump-sum tax, the income tax also lowers the price of leisure, which by itself causes the taxpayer to work fewer hours. The two effects work in opposite directions, so the combined effect is ambiguous.

In Figure 14.4, the amount of income tax paid at the utility-maximizing labor-leisure choice is the vertical distance ee_t. The substitution effect of the income tax

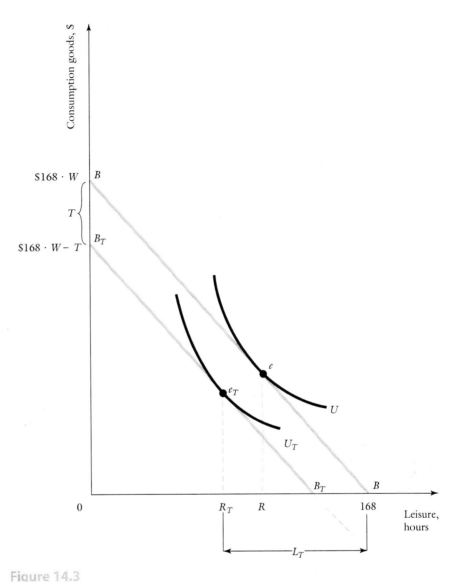

Figure 14.3
Effect of a Lump-Sum Tax on the Labor Supply
A lump-sum tax shifts the budget line from BB to $B_T B_T$ without altering the slope (the wage rate). The utility-maximizing choice changes from point e to point e_T. Since leisure is known to be a normal good, the demand for leisure falls from R to R_T and hours worked (the labor supply) rises to $L_T = 168 - R_T$ hours.

can be isolated by comparing the income tax with a lump-sum tax that collects the same revenue. If the income tax is removed and replaced with a lump-sum tax that collects the same revenue, the worker faces budget line $B'B'$, which also passes through point e_t. Facing this budget line, the worker maximizes utility at point e' and works $L' = 168 - R'$ hours, more hours than under the income tax. Although these two taxes yield the same revenue, the taxpayer works more hours under a

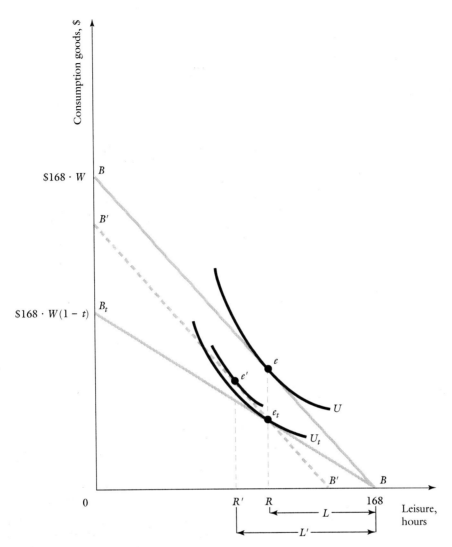

Figure 14.4

Comparing an Income Tax and a Lump-Sum Tax

An income tax shifts the goods-leisure budget line from BB to BB_t, which is flatter because the worker has a lower take-home wage. The worker may supply more or less labor with an income tax (this figure shows the case where the worker supplies the same amount of labor). With a lump-sum tax that collects the same revenue, the budget line $B'B'$ passes through point e_t but is parallel to BB. On $B'B'$ the worker takes less leisure and works more hours at point e'. The fall in the labor supply from L' to L is the substitution effect of the income tax.

lump-sum tax because (unlike an income tax) it does not lower the price of leisure and does not cause a substitution effect.

THE EXCESS BURDEN OF AN INCOME TAX. Because of the substitution effect, the income tax creates an excess burden by causing an inefficient labor-leisure

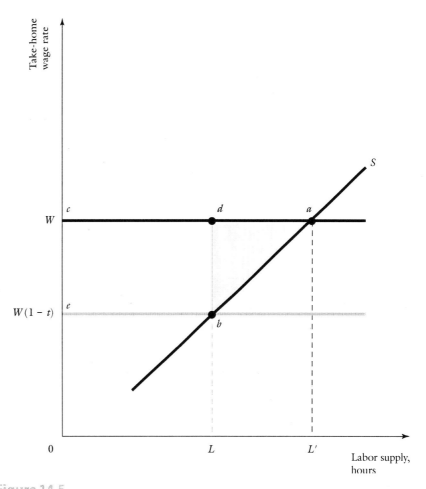

Figure 14.5
Excess Burden of an Income Tax
By lowering the take-home wage from *W* to *W*(1 − t), the income tax lowers the labor supply from *L'* to *L* relative to a lump-sum tax. The excess burden is the area of the shaded triangle *bad*, which represents the excess of the gross wage *W* over the value of leisure (height of the labor supply curve) for the lost labor hours.

choice. The excess burden of an income tax is shown in Figure 14.5, using the labor supply curve labeled *S*. This labor supply curve shows only the substitution effect of a change in the take-home wage on hours worked (for instance, the difference between *L* and *L'* in Figure 15.4). When the government levies an income tax, the after-tax wage is equal to *W*(1 − t) and the taxpayer works *L* hours per week. If the income tax is removed and the government levies a lump-sum tax to collect the revenue, the worker receives the full wage *W* for each hour worked and works *L'* hours. The total loss to the worker caused by the lower after-tax wage is the loss in producer's surplus, or the area of the trapezoid *cabe*. The government collects tax revenue equal to the area of the rectangle *cdbe*, so the net loss to the economy is the area of the triangle *bad*. The area of this triangle is the excess burden of the income tax.[6]

Using the formula for finding the area of a triangle, the excess burden (EB) of the income tax can be expressed as

$$EB = -\frac{1}{2} \cdot t \cdot W \cdot \Delta L,$$

where ΔL is the change in the labor supply caused by levying an income tax rather than a lump-sum tax. Using econometric estimates of the response by the labor supply to wages and income, economists have measured the excess burden of the income tax. Professor Jerry Hausman of MIT, whose empirical work on the effect of the income tax on the labor supply we discuss later, estimates the excess burden at 22% of the tax revenue collected. If this estimate is correct and was applicable in 1995, it means that the excess burden of the combined personal income tax is currently about $235 billion. Although this is a large amount, it may be the necessary cost of taxing people according to their ability to pay.

THE EFFECT OF FIXED EXEMPTIONS FROM TAXABLE INCOME.   Although the theory of labor-leisure choice does not predict whether the income tax increases or decreases the labor supply as compared with no tax at all, it is useful for analyzing the impact of changes in the tax rate schedule. Consider, for example, the effect of changing the level of the standard deduction or personal exemptions. Suppose that the economy has a proportional income tax to begin with, and in order to provide relief to low-income taxpayers, the government introduces an exemption of E dollars. What is the effect on the labor supply?

The introduction of the exemption is illustrated in Figure 14.6. Under a proportional income tax, a typical worker faces budget line BB_t and maximizes utility at point e. The exemption allows a taxpayer to earn E dollars without paying tax, so the budget line is now BEB_E.[7] We assume the taxpayer earns more than the exempted amount, so maximum utility is at point e_E. Because leisure is a normal good, the taxpayer takes more hours of leisure (R_E rather than R) and works fewer hours.

The effect of the exemption is the same as the effect of an increase in the taxpayer's nonwage income. Econometricians, who estimate the impact of the tax system on the labor supply, call the hypothetical income equivalent of an exemption its **virtual income.** The virtual income created by the exemption is equal to the amount of the exemption times the tax rate and is equal to the distance BV in Figure 14.6. Note that a taxpayer makes the same labor-leisure choice (point e_E) on budget line BEB_E or BVB_E. In either case, the taxpayer reduces the number of hours worked from $168 - R$ to $168 - R_E$.

---

[6]The excess burden is derived in the indifference curve diagram in the Appendix to this chapter.
[7]The worker earns the full wage W for first E/W hours worked and so moves along the budget line BB' initially until earnings exceed the exemption E.

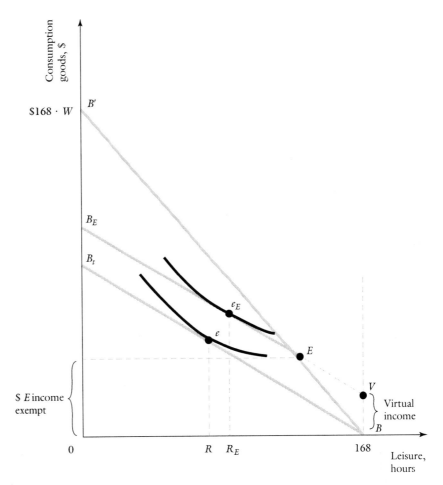

Figure 14.6

Effect of an Exemption on the Labor-Leisure Choice

If E dollars of income is exempt from tax, the worker faces budget line BEB_E. For a worker who earns more than the exempt income, the exemption is equivalent to a lump-sum increase in income by the amount of the saved tax (called virtual income V). Since leisure is a normal good, leisure hours rise from R to R_E and the labor supply falls.

Empirical Studies of the Effect
of Income Tax on the Labor Supply

Given the theoretical ambiguity about the impact of income taxes on the labor supply, it is not surprising that public finance economists are very interested in empirical studies of the labor supply. Econometricians estimate the effect of income taxes by analyzing data on variations in hours worked and the after-tax wage rate (measured in dollars of constant purchasing power) faced by workers. One source of such data is the income maintenance experiments of the 1960s and 1970s. In these experiments, a sample of families was placed under an alternative negative income tax system while a control sample was maintained under the existing income tax system. Other sources are aggregate time series data that report variations in hours and wages over time, and cross-sectional data that report variations in hours and wages across workers. The data preferred by econometricians are called longitudinal or **panel data.** These data report on a sample of families over several years, perhaps decades; they measure variations in hours and wages across workers and over time. One set of panel data, the Panel Study of Income Dynamics (PSID) collected by the University of Michigan, has been widely used to study the impact of the income tax system on the labor supply.

Nearly all studies find that the labor supply of married men between the ages of 25 and 50 years is insensitive, or inelastic, to the after-tax wage. In other words, the labor supply curve for married men is approximately vertical. A few studies find that the quantity of labor supplied by men might actually decrease as a result of an increase in the after-tax wage, which is a case of a "backward-bending" labor supply curve. Theoretically, the inelasticity of the male labor supply to the after-tax wage could mean one of two things. The first is that the income and substitution effects of changes in the after-tax wage cancel each other out, as in Figure 14.3. This leaves open the possibility that the separate substitution and income effects could be quite large. The second possibility is that the labor supply of married males is insensitive to both the after-tax wage and nonwage income, meaning that both the income and substitution effects are small or zero. Public finance economists would like to know which scenario is most likely because high (but canceling out) income and substitution effects would leave open the possibility that changes in the income tax can significantly affect the labor supply. Moreover, the excess burden of the income tax depends on the substitution effect, not the total effect, so a large excess burden is possible in this case even though the labor supply of men is inelastic.

The sensitivity of the labor supply of married women to the after-tax wage is subject to greater uncertainty. A number of studies find that the labor supply of married women is quite elastic to the after-tax wage. In the past, such sensitivity was attributed to the fact that many married women were "secondary" income earners in the family and had less labor force commitment than men. However, a few studies find that the labor supply curve of married women is inelastic, like that of men. The crucial difference between these studies is how the data from nonworking women were used in estimating the labor supply sensitivity. Much of the estimated sensitivity of the labor supply of married women comes from their decisions about whether or not to work (labor force exit and entry decisions) rather than how many hours to work. The wage rates that nonworking women could earn if they were employed are not directly observed and must be imputed—the so-called "missing wage problem." Researchers have found that the estimated sensitivity of the married women's labor supply depends critically on the methods used to impute these unobservable wages.

In an influential study, Professor Jerry Hausman of MIT used panel data to estimate the effect of income taxes on the labor supply using a method that incorporates both changes in the after-tax wage and the "virtual" income effects of the income tax system.[8] Hausman found that the substitution and income effects of after-

---

[8]Jerry A. Hausman, "Taxes and the Labor Supply," 1985.

tax wage changes are quite large for married men, even though the overall wage elasticity is low. The low overall wage elasticity is due to the fact that the substitution and income effects cancel each other out. Hausman also found that both the after-tax wage and income elasticities of the labor supply of married women are larger in magnitude than those of the men. Using his estimates, Hausman simulated the effect of the combined personal income and FICA taxes on hours worked and concluded that the income tax significantly decreases the labor supply. According to these simulations, the labor supply of married men is decreased as much as 8% and women as much as 18%. On the basis of these effects, Hausman calculates that the income tax causes a large excess burden, on the order of 22% of the revenue collected.

Hausman's work generated considerable controversy, as well as subsequent research using panel data. Some of this later work indicates that Hausman's results are sensitive to the specification of the estimated labor supply and the treatment of nonworking taxpayers. For example, Robert K. Triest, now of the Federal Reserve Bank of Boston, estimated labor supply functions using the same data as Hausman but found that the income tax system has little impact on the labor supply of married men under other alternative specifications. He also found that estimates for married women depend critically on the method used to estimate the labor supply function.[9] A controversial feature of Hausman's work was his assumption of a specific form for the worker's utility function between goods and leisure. Critics claim that this procedure forces the labor supply to appear more responsive to changes in the after-tax wage than is actually revealed by the data.[10] The debate, however, remains unresolved. Although many later studies using panel data find that the response of the labor supply to the income tax is small, a recent study finds that the income tax does affect the supply of labor, although the effect is not as great as Hausman estimated.[11]

A major problem with all empirical studies of the labor supply is the fact that taxpayers' marginal income tax rates depend on how much they work, a problem called endogeneity. Consider two types of taxpayers. The first is lazy and has a high demand for leisure and earns very little, while the second is a "workaholic" and earns much more. The marginal tax rate of the workaholic is higher than that of the lazy person simply because the latter has a preference for leisure. An econometric study might show that higher marginal tax rates (lower after-tax wages) actually increase hours worked, when in fact the relationship reflects the endogeneity of the tax rate.

One way econometricians seek to overcome the problem of endogeneity is to find a "natural experiment." To distinguish labor supply changes caused by changes in the tax system from those caused by other changes in the economic environment, we can use data spanning a time period over which the tax law changed. Two examples are the Tax Reform Act of 1986 (TRA86), which significantly lowered marginal tax rates for high-income taxpayers, and the Omnibus Budget Reconciliation Act of 1993 (OBRA93), which raised them again. In each case, we can isolate the effect of the tax system by observing how different groups are affected by the

[9]Robert K. Triest, "The Effect of Income Taxation on Labor Supply in the United States."

[10]Thomas MaCurdy et al., "Assessing Empirical Approaches for Analyzing Taxes and the Labor Supply," 1990.

[11]Thomas J. Kneiser and James P. Ziliak, *The Effects of Recent Tax Reforms on Labor Supply,* 1998.

change. Ideally, we would like a control group whose tax rates are not changed, and a "treatment" group whose tax rates are changed. Assuming both groups are affected in the same way by nontax events, the "difference in differences" technique estimates the change in the behavior of the treatment group before and after the tax change minus the change in the control group before and after the tax change. Professor Nada Eissa of the University of California, Berkeley, used this technique to compare the effect of TRA86 on women's labor supply using low-income and high-income women as the control and treatment groups, respectively.[12] She found, consistent with Hausman's earlier work, that changes in marginal tax rates have a significant impact on the labor supply of women.

EFFECTS OF THE INCOME TAX ON PERSONAL SAVING

The effect of the income tax on personal saving has been a major policy concern in recent years. The reason is not hard to understand—the fraction of income saved by Americans has fallen, and it can't get up. In 1999, net domestic saving in the United States was equal to only 2.4% of personal disposable income, one of the lowest rates in the industrialized world. Between 1970 and 1985, the saving rate averaged nearly 10% of personal income. In 1998, saving rates exceeded 10% of personal disposable income in France, Germany, Italy, and Japan. The low saving rate in the United States has been blamed on many causes, including the spendthrift ways of baby boomers, the soaring stock market, and the impact of the Social Security program. Whatever the cause, some economists and others argue that the income tax system in the United States discourages saving, and they promote tax reforms that would increase saving.

A Theory of Intertemporal Consumption Choice

The impact of the income tax on saving can be analyzed using the life-cycle theory of saving. The life-cycle theory explains how consumers decide to time their consumption over a lifetime. For simplicity, we assume that each consumer lives only two periods, the present and the future and has perfect foresight about the future (amounts of income, taxes, etc.). In the present, consumers work and receive a fixed amount of earnings; in the future they are retired and earn nothing. To consume in retirement, consumers must save some of their present earnings. We measure income and consumption in the present on the horizontal axis in Figure 14.7, and consumption in the future on the vertical axis.

A consumer faces an intertemporal budget line *BB* that intersects the horizontal axis at the consumer's present earnings *E*. At *E*, the consumer spends all earnings in the present, so nothing can be consumed in the future. The (absolute) slope of the intertemporal budget line is 1 plus the *real* interest rate on savings over the time interval. The real interest rate takes into account the change in the purchasing power of money between the present and the future. For simplicity, we assume

---

[12]Nada Eissa, "Taxation and Labor Supply of Married Women: The Tax Reform Act of 1986 as a Natural Experiment," 1995.

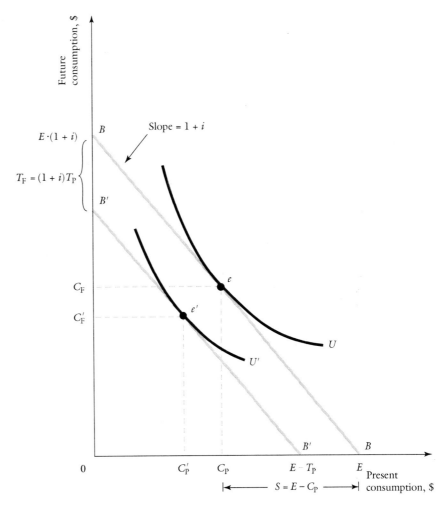

Figure 14.7
Saving and the Timing of Taxes
A household with earnings E in the present faces the budget line BB between present and future consumption, which has a slope of 1 plus the interest rate. The household maximizes lifetime utility at point e, where it saves E minus C_P of its current income. A lump-sum tax of T_P in the present reduces disposable income and decreases saving. An anticipated future lump-sum tax of T_F that has the same present value increases saving. In both cases, the consumer chooses the same levels of present and future consumption at point e'.

that the price level is steady, so the real interest rate is equal to the money interest, denoted i. Each \$1 saved in the present lets the consumer enjoy $1 + i$ dollars of consumption in the future, so if the consumer saved all earnings future consumption would equal $E(1 + i)$ dollars. The individual can consume in the present by saving less than this. Each \$1 of present consumption reduces future consumption by $1 + i$ dollars, so $1 + i$ is the relative price of present to future consumption.

How much does the consumer save? The main idea of the life-cycle theory is that consumers prefer to spread consumption evenly over a lifetime, rather than concentrating their consumption in one period. Analytically, this means that consumers have lifetime indifference curves of the usual shape, as shown in Figure 14.7. Lifetime utility is a measure of a consumer's satisfaction over his or her whole life, and not just in one period. Just as an ordinary indifference curve shows combinations of different goods that yield the same current utility, lifetime indifference curves show combinations of present and future consumption that yield the same lifetime utility. The (absolute) slope of a lifetime indifference curve is the marginal willingness to pay (MWTP) for present consumption.

The life-cycle theory proceeds by assuming that consumers save so as to maximize lifetime utility. To maximize lifetime utility, the consumer chooses point e where the intertemporal budget line BB is tangent to the highest possible lifetime indifference curve U. At point e, consumers' MWTP for present consumption is just equal to $1 + i$, the price of present consumption, and they consume C_P of their first-period earnings and save the rest. The amount saved, $S = E - C_P$, maximizes lifetime utility.

The Effects of Present and Future Taxes

The income tax affects the saving decision in two ways. The first depends on the timing of the tax payments made to the government, and the second depends on the change in the return on saving. The timing of tax payments matters because consumers want to spread the burden of taxes over a lifetime, just as they want to spread consumption over a lifetime. To see this, compare the effect of a lump-sum tax in the present and a lump-sum tax anticipated in the future. A present lump-sum tax of T_P dollars reduces the consumer's present take-home income to $E - T_P$ and shifts the intertemporal budget line to $B'B'$. The consumer reduces present and future consumption to C'_P and C'_F, respectively, and maximizes lifetime utility at point e'. Taxpayers spread the burden of present taxes over a lifetime by reducing saving.

Now consider a future lump-sum tax of T_F dollars. For simplicity, we assume that the future tax is equal to $T_P(1 + i)$, so the tax is equal in terms of *present value*. With an equal future tax, the intertemporal budget line is also $B'B'$ and the consumers maximize lifetime utility at e'. Because consumers reduce present consumption when the budget line shifts, they save more. Present earnings are unchanged at E dollars, and present consumption falls, so saving rises from $E - C_P$ to $E - C'_P$. The consumer saves more in the present in order to pay the future tax.

The Effect of Taxing the Return to Saving

An income tax also affects the level of saving by reducing the return on saving. The return on saving includes interest on saving in bank accounts or invested in bonds, and dividends and capital gains on saving invested in stocks. The effect of taxing this form of income is shown in Figure 14.8. The intertemporal budget line BB is drawn for an income tax that applies to earnings only, like the FICA tax. It intercepts the horizontal axis at the consumer's after-tax earnings, denoted E. With a tax on earnings, the consumer maximizes lifetime utility at point e, consumes C_P in the present, and saves $E - C_P$.

The budget line BB_t is drawn for an income tax that taxes the return on saving as well as earnings. The taxpayer now receives a lower after-tax interest rate $i(1 - t)$

on each \$1 saved, where t is the marginal tax rate on interest receipts.[13] The tax on the return to saving "tilts" the intertemporal budget line, making it flatter. This means that the price of present consumption relative to future consumption is reduced by the tax on interest. Because present consumption is made relatively cheaper, the taxpayer has an incentive to substitute present for future consumption.

Despite making present consumption relatively cheaper, taxing the return to saving can increase or decrease the level of saving. The consumer maximizes lifetime utility along intertemporal budget line BB_t at point e_t in Figure 14.8. Depending on the lifetime indifference curves, point e_t may lie to the right or the left of e, so present consumption after the tax may be higher or lower than C_P. In Figure 14.8 we draw the special case where e_t lies directly below e, so saving is not affected by the tax on the return to saving.

The reason the tax on interest can increase or decrease saving is that it has two offsetting effects. Most obviously, it discourages saving by lowering the after-tax interest rate. However, the tax on interest is paid in the future, when the interest is received. We saw earlier that a tax in the future causes the taxpayer to save more in the present. The timing of the interest tax increases saving and, in principle, could offset the decrease in saving due to the lower interest rate.

The intuitive reason for the ambiguity is clear if we assume that the taxpayer wants to save enough to acquire a given amount for a special purpose, say to make a down payment on a house. The amount the saver wants to acquire is called the *target wealth*. The tax on interest makes it harder to achieve the target wealth because the lower take-home interest rate accumulates less rapidly. To acquire the target wealth, the taxpayer must save more to offset the lower rate of interest accumulation. The total effect is ambiguous, because the tax raises the "price" of the down payment in terms of the amount of present consumption that must be given up. As a result, the taxpayer may reduce target wealth, perhaps by deciding to buy a less expensive home with a smaller down payment.

The After-Tax Return on CODAs and IRAs

Earlier we saw that the United States income tax contains special provisions allowing taxpayers to save for retirement in ways that are sheltered from the income tax. Specifically, income saved in "front-loaded" cash or deferred arrangements (CODAs) like 401(k) plans is not subject to tax when earned, but instead is taxed when the amount in the plan is distributed, usually after the taxpayer has retired. In addition, interest meanwhile accumulates tax-free on the value of plans.

What is the slope of the intertemporal budget line when saving is done in one of these plans? To find out, consider savers who put \$1 in a CODA-type plan in the first period and withdraw it in the second. A dollar of CODA saving reduces first-period consumption by $1 - t_1$ dollars, where t_1 is the marginal tax rate in the first period. A dollar of saving in a CODA reduces present consumption by less than \$1

---

[13]With inflation we need to find the marginal tax rate on the real interest rate $i - \pi$, where π is the inflation rate. Since nominal interest is taxed, the after-tax real interest rate to savers is $i(i - t) - \pi$. Hence the tax on the real interest rate is $\dfrac{i \cdot t}{i - \pi}$. Note that the tax rate is equal to t (the statutory rate) only in the case where π is equal to zero. If $\pi > 0$, the tax rate on real interest exceeds t.

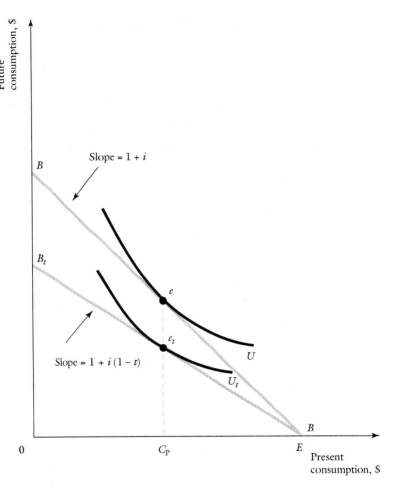

Figure 14.8

Effect of Taxing Interest Income

By taxing interest income, the price of present consumption is reduced, so the household faces the flatter budget line BB_t. The slope of BB_t is 1 plus the after-tax interest rate $i(1 - t)$. Although the after-tax interest rate is reduced, saving may rise or fall. In this figure, present consumption, and hence saving, is not affected by taxing interest.

because income tax would have to be paid on the income received as wages. When the $1 plus interest is withdrawn in the second period, future consumption is increased by $(1 + i)(1 - t_2)$ dollars, where t_2 is the taxpayer's marginal tax rate in the second period. The slope of the intertemporal budget line for income saved in a CODA is the increase in second-period consumption divided by the decrease in first-period consumption, or

$$\frac{(1+i)(1-t_2)}{(1-t_1)}.$$

If the marginal tax rates are the same for the two periods, this equals $1 + i$, which is the slope of the intertemporal budget line without taxes on interest. In other words, saving in a CODA plan eliminates the tax on interest for savers whose income tax rates are the same in the present and future. For this reason, CODA saving is called tax-sheltered.

In fact, for many taxpayers, the marginal tax rate is lower in the future than in the present because they are retired when they withdraw CODA funds. CODA saving allows taxpayers to average their income over a lifetime for tax purposes, as well as to defer taxes until retirement. No one would want to save in the ordinary way if people could save unlimited amounts in CODAs. However, the government puts limits on how much taxpayers can save each year in CODAs. Taxpayers who want to save more than the limit must use ordinary saving, on which they earn the after-tax interest rate.

Empirical Studies of Taxation and Saving

Like its impact on the labor supply, the impact of the income tax on saving has received much empirical study. Unfortunately, the empirical conclusions are, if anything, more uncertain than those about the labor supply. The main reason is that household decisions about saving are more complicated because they occur over time and depend on uncertain expectations about the future. Also, the taxation of savings income is more complicated because of the special treatment of retirement saving and pensions and the effect of inflation on interest rates. Empirical work has focused on two main issues: the effect of changes in the after-tax interest rate on the level of saving, and the effect of increased opportunities for tax-sheltered saving, like CODAs and IRAs.

Early studies of the determinants of aggregate consumption found that variations in the market interest rate have no significant statistical effect on the level of consumption, and hence no effect on saving. Rather, consumption depends mainly on the level of aggregate income. These studies implied that the ratio of saving to income is not affected by the interest rate, so the saving supply curve is vertical. From this early work, a "conventional" view emerged that saving is not appreciably affected by the income tax.

However, theory predicts that the saver's decision should depend on the *real* interest rate after income taxes, not the market interest rate. The after-tax real interest rate determines the increase in future consumption made possible by saving an extra $1. Unfortunately, it is difficult to measure this rate of return because it depends on the saver's marginal income tax rate and expectations about future inflation. In an influential study in 1978, Professor Michael Boskin of Stanford University found that an increase in the after-tax real interest rate significantly decreased consumption and increased saving. Boskin used the interest rate on municipal bonds minus the inflation rate to measure the after-tax rate of return on saving. He reasoned that the interest on municipal bonds is tax-free, so the interest rate on municipal bonds must adjust so as to give savers the same after-tax real return they get on interest from taxable sources.

The estimates in Boskin's study imply an elasticity of the savings supply with respect to the rate of return on saving of about 0.4, a much higher value than earlier researchers had found. Boskin's study was published at a time when policy makers were very concerned with the question whether Americans save enough. For

14.2   Do Tax-Sheltered Savings Plans Increase Saving?

Because of the econometric difficulties in estimating the interest elasticity of saving, some economists focus on whether tax-sheltered savings plans increase saving. Recall from Chapter 13 that money deposited in CODAs, like IRAs and 401(k) plans, is subtracted from gross income. Thus a deposit in a tax-sheltered saving plan reduces taxes currently paid by the depositer. Also, interest is not taxed until the funds are withdrawn. As we saw in Table 14.1, such plans cost the government $87 billion in tax revenue in 1999. For this reason alone, we would like to know whether the plans are effective at increasing saving.

At first glance, we would expect that the favorable tax treatment of IRAs and 401(k) plans should increase saving. In fact, the amount invested in these plans has grown dramatically. For example, assets in 401(k) plans grew by almost a trillion dollars from $92 billion in 1984 to $1061 billion in 1996.[1] However, while the favorable tax treatment provides an incentive for taxpayers to deposit funds in these accounts, the funds may not come from increased saving. For example, a taxpayer could withdraw money from a regular savings account and deposit it in an IRA to enjoy the tax advantage without any new saving. Money deposited in an IRA could come from three places—other non-IRA saving, taxes that would have been paid to the government, and new saving.

Several studies attempt to estimate how much of a dollar deposited in a tax-sheltered saving account comes from new saving. All estimate this fraction by comparing IRA saving with non-IRA saving for a sample of households when the limits on IRA saving are changed. Venti and Wise (1991) reason that if households substitute IRA saving for other saving, households with high IRA saving should have low non-IRA saving, and vice versa. According to their estimates, nearly two-thirds of IRA saving is new saving, with most of the rest

coming from reduced taxes. Gale and Sholz (1994) dispute this conclusion. They argue that some households are more inclined to save than others, so those with high IRA saving are also likely to have high non-IRA saving. A simple correlation would lead to the wrong conclusion that most IRA saving is new saving. Gale and Sholz compare saving by households that contribute the maximum amount to an IRA to those below the limit (and hence unaffected by changes in the limit) and conclude that less than 4% of IRA saving is new saving. Yet another study using different data (Joines and Manegold, 1995) finds an intermediate result that 19% to 26% of a dollar deposited in an IRA comes from new saving.

Critically analyze the following:

- If the estimates by Venti and Wise are correct and nearly two-thirds of IRA saving is new saving, what would happen to personal saving rates if the limits on IRA saving were removed? What if the estimates by Gale and Sholz are correct?

- Many companies match employee contributions to 401(k) plans and contribute a dollar for every dollar the employee contributes. If Gale and Sholz are correct that practically no tax-sheltered saving comes from new saving, how much would an employee in the 28% tax bracket reduce nonsheltered saving when he or she contributes a dollar to a 401(k) plan?

- Nearly all studies estimate that almost a third of IRA saving comes from the taxes saved by the taxpayer as a result of the deposit. If the government holds spending and other taxes constant, how would this affect the national (i.e., household plus government) saving rate?

---

[1]Pension and Welfare Benefits Administration, Department of Labor, *Private Pension Plan Bulletin*, Winter 1999–2000, Table E23.

this reason, his study ignited considerable interest in the question of whether the reliance on income taxes in the United States was partly responsible for the nation's low rates of saving. Boskin concluded that capital formation was significantly retarded by income taxes, and that an annual excess burden of $60 billion is imposed by taxing the return to saving. Subsequent studies seemed to confirm Boskin's high savings elasticity, and by the mid-1980s a new view was forming—that the income tax may be a significant reason for low levels of saving.

Unfortunately, as is often the case in empirical economics, later studies cast doubt on this view. For instance, Boskin's study used annual data from 1929 to 1969 including both the prewar and the postwar periods (excluding the years 1941 to 1946). When other time series data are used—for instance, quarterly data from the years 1952 to 1980, which exclude the depression years of the 1930s—the interest elasticity of saving is only about one-sixth that found by Boskin.[14] At present, economists are divided about the effect of the income tax on saving rates; however, the old conventional view—that the taxation of the return to saving does not significantly affect the level of saving—is very much alive.

CONCLUSION AND SUMMARY

The effect of income taxes on taxpayers' behavior is central to the subject of public finance and the policy debates that depend upon the knowledge of such effects. It is too bad that the conclusions from empirical studies on the most important of these effects are often uncertain. We hope for better in the future as "natural experiments" afford researchers better opportunities to isolate the impact of tax changes from the many other things affecting taxpayers' behavior. To a certain extent, the existence of tax expenditures is a sort of testament to the policy makers' belief that taxes affect behavior in significant ways. Why else allow sheltered retirement saving, unless policy makers believe that without such provisions retirement saving would be woefully inadequate? Most public finance economists approach their subject with the belief that it is best not to underestimate the effects of taxes on taxpayers' behavior regardless of the uncertainties in the evidence.

- The personal income tax affects household decisions in several ways. In general, taxing income affects the labor supply and decisions about saving. Lower tax rates for certain sources and uses of income encourage taxpayers to earn or spend income in those ways.

- Tax expenditures are losses in government revenue resulting from provisions in the tax system that are functionally equivalent to government spending. In 1999, the total amount of tax expenditures was over $470 billion.

- Three important tax expenditures affecting individuals are the charitable donations deduction, the exclusion of employer-paid medical insurance, and the mortgage interest deduction. These tax expenditures encourage taxpayers to make more charitable donations, receive more income in the form of insurance benefits, and consume more housing.

- Tax expenditures act like subsidies of the preferred activity, and the subsidy rate is equal to the taxpayer's marginal tax rate. As a result, high-income taxpayers receive a higher subsidy rate and derive more benefits from the tax expenditure than low-income taxpayers, a feature some-times called "upside-down" equity.

---

[14]I. Friend and J. Hasbrouk, "Savings and After-Tax Rates of Return," 1983.

▨ The income tax affects the labor supply through both an income effect, which increases hours worked, and a substitution effect, which decreases them. The total effect is ambiguous. The income effect occurs because taxpayers work harder in order to pay the tax. The substitution effect occurs because the income tax reduces the price of leisure or, equivalently, the reward of working.

▨ Empirical studies find that the income tax has little effect on hours worked by men of prime working age. In other words, their labor supply is insensitive to the after-tax wage. However, the income tax may significantly discourage the labor supply of married women, because the evidence indicates that their labor supply is more sensitive to the after-tax wage.

▨ Taxes affect the decision to save by changing the timing of tax payments and by reducing the return to saving. Present taxes reduce saving; anticipated future taxes increase it. The tax on the return to saving has an ambiguous effect because it reduces the price of present consumption relative to future consumption, but also makes it more difficult to accumulate a given target level of wealth.

▨ The empirical evidence on the effect of income taxes on saving is highly uncertain. Although some studies find saving significantly reduced by a lower after-tax return, other studies find smaller effects. Similarly, some studies find that the availability of CODAs significantly increases saving, whereas others find that it causes taxpayers to substitute CODAs for ordinary saving.

QUESTIONS FOR DISCUSSION AND REVIEW

1. What is the difference between taxing income and taxing the ability to earn? Do you think it is fair to tax people on their ability to earn income? Why or why not?

2. Suppose a household in the top income tax bracket receives employer-paid medical insurance. The medical insurance is worth $10,000 a year. What is the tax expenditure on this taxpayer? (Ignore the FICA tax in this question.)

3. A luxury good has a high income elasticity (greater than 1), whereas a necessity good has a low income elasticity. (Income elasticity is the percentage change in the consumption of the good divided by the percentage change in the consumer's income.) Holding the substitution effect constant, would the income tax be more or less likely to reduce the labor supply if leisure is a luxury rather than a necessity good? Why?

4. Suppose a taxpayer can earn $10 an hour before taxes and can work as many or as few hours as he or she pleases. The taxpayer's marginal willingness to pay per hour of leisure along an indifference curve is equal to $\dfrac{3 \cdot C}{R}$ where C is dollars spent on market goods per week and R is number of hours of leisure per week. A week has 168 hours, so this taxpayer's budget constraint is $C = 10 \cdot (168 - R) - T$, where T is the amount of tax that must be paid.

   a. How many hours a week will the taxpayer work if no income tax is levied?

   b. How many hours a week will he or she work if a proportional income tax of 40% is levied?

   c. How many hours will the taxpayer work if the 40% income tax exempts the first $100 of weekly earnings?

5. On the basis of empirical evidence about the labor supply elasticities of men and women, should income tax rates depend on the taxpayer's sex if the objective of the government is economic efficiency? (Hint: Apply the inverse elasticity rule discussed in Chapter 12.) Should the income tax rate be higher or lower for women? Discuss the equity aspects of taxing men and women differently.

6. To encourage people to work more, politicians from both political parties advocate letting them "keep more of what they earn." In 1997, Congress passed a tax bill that gives a $500 tax credit for each child. What is the difference between this child tax credit and the existing personal exemption for dependents? According to the theory of labor-leisure choice, how would such a credit affect the number of hours worked by a taxpayer?

7. In 1997, the government introduced a new type of IRA. These new IRAs are "back-loaded" in that contributions are not tax-deductible but interest is exempt from tax and no tax is imposed on withdrawals. Analyze the effects on the incentive to save of back-loaded IRAs as compared with the front-loaded type. Which, if either, is more likely to increase personal saving more in the current year? Why? Compare the effects of the two on current-year net national saving, assuming that the rest of the tax system and government spending remain the same.

8. Before 1987, taxpayers who itemized their returns could deduct interest payments on consumer loans, such as car loans and credit card debt. Since 1987, such deductions have not been possible. How does deductibility of interest on consumer debt affect a taxpayer's decision about saving? For simplicity, con-

sider the intertemporal choice of a taxpayer who has low income in the present and expects higher income in the future, using a diagram like Figure 14.8. Ignore limits on borrowing.

9. Internet Exercise. Although the Tax Reform Act of 1986 disallowed deductions for consumer interest payments, it left a loophole for taxpayers who own equity in their homes. Interest on home equity loans is deductible regardless of the purpose of the loan. Home equity loans come in two forms. The traditional form is a close-ended fixed payment like a regular mortgage, and the line of credit form is a revolving loan that permits borrowing from time to time at the homeowner's discretion. Tables 821 and 822 of the *1999 Statistical Abstract* (available at http://www.census.gov/statab/www/) document the growth in home equity loans and the uses for the borrowed funds. What evidence in these tables is consistent with the hypothesis that taxpayers are substituting home equity loans for consumer loans that do not have tax-deductible interest? What evidence appears contrary to this hypothesis?

10. Internet Exercise. The American Housing Survey conducted by the U.S. Census Bureau has information on housing by household and family income class. This information can be found at http://www.census.gov/hhes/www/housing/ahs/access.html, Table 2-12. Using information in this table, compare the tenure of occupied units (owner, renter) by income class with the benefits of the home ownership tax expenditures received by that income class as reported in Table 14.1. Can you conclude from this comparison that the greater tax benefit to higher-income households is responsible for the fact that a greater fraction of housing units is owned rather than rented by them? Why or why not?

SELECTED REFERENCES

The concept of tax expenditures was introduced in Stanley S. Surrey, *Pathways to Tax Reform*, 1973. This is still the best source for discussion of the concept because Surrey demolishes many of the arguments against viewing tax breaks as a hidden form of government spending.

For comprehensive study of charitable donations, see Charles T. Clotfelter, *Federal Tax Policy and Charitable Giving*, 1985. Stephen A. Woodbury and Wei-Jang Huang, in *The Tax Treatment of Fringe Benefits*, 1991, study the exclusion of employer-provided medical insurance.

Empirical studies of the effect of the tax system on the labor supply include Jerry A. Hausman, "Taxes and Labor Supply," 1985; and Robert K. Triest, "The Effect of Income Taxation on Labor Supply in the United States," 1990. Some new econometric methods for estimating the effects of taxes on economic behavior are found in Robert K. Triest, "Econometric Issues in Estimating the Behavioral Response to Taxation," 1998.

The effect of the rate of return on saving is estimated by Michael J. Boskin, "Taxation, Saving, and the Rate of Interest," 1978. The effects of tax-sheltered savings accounts on the level of saving are debated in the Symposium on Government Incentives for Saving in the *Journal of Economic Perspective*, Fall 1996.

A P P E N D I X   T O   C H A P T E R   1 4

The excess burden of an income tax can be illustrated in the diagram of the labor-leisure choice by comparing an income tax with a lump-sum tax that causes the same loss in utility to the worker. In Figure A.14.1, the budget line between goods and leisure without taxes is labeled BB and the budget line when an income tax is levied is labeled BB_t. The worker maximizes utility at e and e_t, respectively. To simplify, we assume that income and substitution effects are equal in magnitude, so the worker takes R hours of leisure and works L hours in both cases. The utility of the worker falls from U to U_t because of the income tax, and the revenue collected by the income tax is equal to the vertical distance ee_t.

Instead of an income tax, suppose the government levies a lump-sum tax T sufficient to cause the same loss in utility as the income tax. With lump-sum tax T, the worker faces budget line $B_T B_T$ and maximizes utility at point e_T, where he or she chooses R_T hours of leisure and works L_T hours. Although the level of utility is the same as with an income tax, the worker works more hours because the lump-sum tax does not reduce the price of leisure and cause a substitution of leisure for goods. The revenue collected by the lump-sum tax is equal to the vertical distance between BB and $B_T B_T$, which is the distance ee'. The distance between e_t and e' is the extra tax that could have been collected had the government not distorted the labor-leisure choice. This lost revenue is the excess burden of the income tax. Note in the

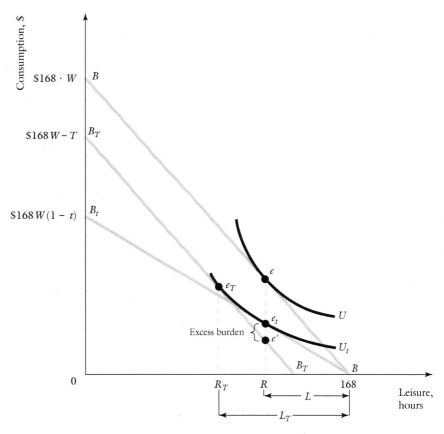

Excess Burden of an Income Tax

With an income tax, the worker faces budget line BB_t and maximizes utility at point e_t. Budget line B_TB_T is drawn for a lump-sum tax at which the worker gets the same level of utility U_t as with the income tax. The tax collected by the income tax is the vertical distance ee_t, whereas the revenue collected by the lump-sum tax is the vertical distance ee'. Since the consumer gets the same utility in either case, the lost revenue under the income tax is an excess burden.

example that the income tax causes an excess burden even though the total effect of the tax leaves the labor supply unaffected. This is because an excess burden is caused by the substitution effect of a tax.

15

Taxes on Business Income

Taxes on business, although poorly understood by most people, are often subject to as much controversy, if not more, than taxes on persons. The main tax on business, the corporation income tax, has substantially declined in importance as a source of government revenue. In 1999, the federal government collected just 10% of its total revenue from corporation income taxes. In 1952, it collected over 40%. Some people view this decline as a triumph for "corporate welfare." Others argue that all taxes are ultimately borne by people, and the decline reflects the fact that the government now has greater ability to tax people directly, as it should, rather than indirectly through businesses.

Despite the decline in the importance of the corporation income tax, taxes on businesses remain an important part of the tax structure in the United States, as in most other countries. Several types of taxes are levied on business. In the United States, governments levy taxes on payrolls, like the employers' share of the FICA tax (see Chapter 9), and on business income. Businesses also pay taxes to state and local governments on their personal and real property. Some states levy a tax on gross business receipts, which is a form of sales tax, and others levy a tax on the capital stock or share value of businesses, which is a form of property tax. In other countries, governments levy taxes on the *value added* by businesses.

In this chapter we focus on taxes on business income. (Other taxes levied on businesses, like the value-added tax, are discussed in Chapter 17.) We begin with the question of why taxes are levied on businesses rather than directly on people and then consider how business income is defined. We describe the corporation income tax, which is the most important tax on business income, and examine the effects of business income taxation on business decisions. We conclude with a discussion of the effects of business income taxes on the economy, including the incidence of business income taxes, and discuss some important business tax policy issues.

BUSINESS AND THE TAX SYSTEM

There are nearly 7 million business enterprises in the United States, coming in many different forms and sizes, and engaged in many different productive activities. Because of this diversity, analyzing and understanding how businesses are taxed and

448

the effects of taxation on their decisions is more difficult than for households. In this section we list the different forms of businesses, consider the question of why businesses are taxed, and present a simple example of a business that will facilitate our understanding of taxes on business income.

Business Organization and Taxation

In this chapter we limit our discussion to business enterprises engaged in producing goods and services for profit. That is, we exclude not-for-profit businesses, like many hospitals, and holding companies and funds that earn investment income only and do not produce goods or services. We also do not discuss financial institutions like banks, where peculiar tax issues arise. Even with these limitations, we must consider at least four different business forms and their tax treatment. Table 15.1 lists the different business forms and how the income of the business is allocated to owners and taxed. For unincorporated businesses, such as sole proprietorships and partnerships, business income is directly received by the owners and taxed as part of their personal income under the personal income tax. Business losses are similarly passed through and reduce the taxable income of the owners.

Corporations are business entities that are distinct from their owners, the shareholders. Typically the owner/shareholders have limited liability, which means that they are not responsible for the debts or obligations of the business, unlike in the case of proprietorships and general partnerships.[1] For corporations, business income is determined separately from the incomes of the owners. However, certain businesses of limited size can choose to be organized as S corporations. In this case, the

Table 15.1 **Classifications of Businesses for Tax Purposes**

Business Form	Business Income Allocation	Applicable Tax
Sole proprietorship	Personal income of owner	Personal income tax
Partnership	Income apportioned to partner' personal incomes according to partnership contract	Personal income tax
Subchapter S corporation	Income determined separately but passed through to shareholders according to number of shares owned	Personal income tax
Subchapter C corporation	Income determined and taxed separately from the income of owners/shareholders	Corporate income tax

[1] In some forms of partnership, called limited liability partnerships, the owners also have limited liability.

business income of the corporation, although determined separately from that of the shareholders, is not taxed at the level of the business. Rather business income (or loss) is passed through to the shareholders in proportion to their ownership of shares in the corporation and taxed as part of their personal income. Economists call such an arrangement an **integrated approach** to corporation income taxation.

Large corporations with shares that are traded on public stock exchanges are organized as C corporations. For C corporations, business income is both determined and taxed separately. Business income is taxed under the corporation income tax, which is different from the personal income tax and has its own rate schedule. Economists call this the **separate entity approach** to corporation income taxation. One of the implications of the separate entity approach is the so-called double taxation of equity income. Although the business income of a C corporation is separate from the income of the owner/shareholders, when the corporation distributes dividends to shareholders the income becomes personal income and is subject to personal income taxes. The personal tax on dividends received by shareholders is in addition to the corporation income tax previously levied on business income, hence the double taxation. For example, a dollar of corporate business income might be taxed at 35%, leaving 65 cents available for distribution. If distributed as a dividend to a shareholder in the 36% tax bracket, a further 23.4 cents (36% of 65 cents) is paid as personal income tax. The total tax levied on the dollar of business income is approximately 58 cents, or 58%. We consider the impact of the double taxation of corporate dividends on business decisions later in this chapter.

Why Tax Businesses at All?

Although businesses can pay taxes, all tax burdens are ultimately borne by people. Because a business is simply an organizational structure, not a natural person, it is largely meaningless to speak of "businesses bearing their fair share of the tax burden," as some politicians do when justifying taxes on businesses. The money that flows into a business comes from people, mainly the consumers who buy its products, and is eventually paid out to people in the form of wages and salaries to employees and management, bonuses to executives, interest to the firm's creditors, or dividends to shareholders.[2] Taxes paid by businesses simply divert part of the money flowing through the firm into the waiting hands of the tax collector. The burden of these taxes cannot be borne by the medium through which the income flows (the firms); it is shifted to people one way or another. If it were possible to remove the burden of taxes from human voters, popularly elected governments would have done so long ago.

So why tax businesses at all? Why not put the legal liability to pay all taxes on people, as either consumers, recipients of income, or owners of wealth? The answer has little to do with making business bear its fair share of the tax burden. The main reasons for taxing businesses are the following:

- ■ Businesses are convenient places where the government can collect taxes and enforce the tax rules. For this reason, businesses are sometimes described as

---

[2]This excludes the money used to buy materials and capital goods.

good "tax handles." The administrative convenience of taxing businesses is especially important because taxes levied on businesses may be economically equivalent to personal taxes that are more difficult to levy.

■ Taxes on businesses are sometimes needed to prevent tax avoidance. For instance, if income taxes were collected only when incomes are received by people, the taxes could be deferred indefinitely by saving income in a legally separate corporation where it would be untaxed. Preventing tax avoidance is a strong argument for having a separate corporation income tax.

■ Taxes on businesses are an important way in which the government can influence the production sector of the economy. For example, as discussed in Chapter 4, production activities may impose cost externalities, causing inefficient allocations of resources. Corrective taxes levied on firms are one way the government can improve economic efficiency when externalities are present.

■ Business taxes may be levied in exchange for benefits received by the firms from the legal and economic systems supported by the government. When the corporation income tax was first enacted in 1909, to avoid a constitutional challenge it was levied as an excise tax on the privilege of doing business in the corporate form. Some state corporate taxes, called franchise taxes, are levied on the privilege of doing business in the state.

Other arguments are made for taxing businesses, although some are political in nature rather than economic. The fact is that taxes on businesses do provide a political advantage for tax legislators. Because the burden of a business tax is shifted to people by the firms rather than levied directly on the people, the source of the burden is less transparent than if the tax had been levied directly. If politicians are lucky, the people who ultimately bear the tax burden may not blame the government at all. Perhaps the main reason government taxes businesses is that, like mountains, they are there. That is, if the government finds businesses a ready source of revenue, it will tax them whether doing so is a good idea or not.

An Illustrative Example of a Business

To better understand how business income is taxed, it is useful to have a simple model of a business in mind. Let's pretend we own a small business—say, a bagel bakery—which buys materials like flour and produces and sells bagels. Assume we lease the premises and own the equipment, such as kettles, ovens, and counters. We purchase the equipment and finance part of it with our own money (equity) and the rest with a loan from the bank (debt) at an interest rate of 10%. The firm's *balance sheet* reports the firm's assets and liabilities on a particular date (say, the beginning of the year) as shown in Table 15.2.

Over the year, the bakery receives revenue and incurs the costs of doing business. The *income statement* reports the receipts and outlays of the business for the year in a format similar to that of Table 15.3. We assume that in addition to buying materials and leasing the premises, the firm employs a baker, makes interest payments on its bank loan, submits payroll taxes on the wages it pays the baker, and pays property taxes on its equipment. We also assume the equipment incurs wear

Table 15.2   **Balance Sheet of a Bagel Bakery**

Assets		Liabilities and Equity	
Equipment	$60,000	Bank loan	$40,000
		Business equity	$20,000
Total assets	$60,000	Total liabilities and equity	$60,000

and tear and loses value over the year by an amount called **depreciation.** Finally, the owner also manages the business and draws a salary.[3]

In this income statement, we see that the net income of the business is equal to the gross receipts (revenue) received less the costs of doing business. These costs are categorized as the costs of the goods sold (materials plus wages paid to employees engaged in production), operating costs (overhead costs such as lease payments, management salaries, wages and salaries to employees not on the production line, depreciation, and deductible taxes on payrolls and property), and interest payments. Net income before income tax is the amount available to pay business income taxes, reinvest, or distribute as profit to the owner in some form. The business income tax is determined according to the rules set out in the Internal Revenue Code (IRC) described in the next section. Net income after taxes can be distributed to the owner as a dividend or reinvested in the firm—for example, to buy a new oven to increase the number of bagels produced.

DETERMINING BUSINESS INCOME

In the income statement above, business income is determined according to *Generally Accepted Accounting Principles* (GAAP). Taxable business income is determined by the rules set forth in the Internal Revenue Code, although many of these rules conform to GAAP. Before we describe the rules that determine taxable business income, it is useful to consider the more abstract question of how to define business income in principle.

Economic Business Income

In Chapter 13 we emphasized that the personal income of a household as measured in principle (called comprehensive or Haig-Simons income) differs in significant ways from taxable income as defined by the Internal Revenue Code. These differences are important in understanding the effect of income taxation on household decisions. The same is true for business income taxation. Business income as measured in principle, called **economic business income (EBI),** is equal to the maximum annual payment that could be paid to the owner(s) without reducing the value of the firm's assets. This corresponds to the definition of Haig-Simons income in Chapter 13, which is the maximum amount the household could spend in the year

---

[3]Typically, for larger businesses, the owners and managers are different people.

Table 15.3   Income Statement of a Bagel Bakery

Gross Receipts (Revenue)	$60,000
Cost of goods sold	$16,000
Materials	$6,000
Employee compensation	$10,000
Gross Income	$44,000
Operating costs	$20,000
Lease payments	$7,000
Manager's salary	$9,000
Depreciation	$2,000
Payroll and property tax paid	$2,000
Income Before Interest and	
Income Tax	$24,000
Interest paid	$4,000
Net Income Before Income Tax	$20,000
Income tax liability	$3,000
Net Income After Taxes	$17,000

without reducing its net worth. In both cases, note that income in principle is the amount that *could be* distributed to the owner (in the case of a business) or spent by the household, not the amount actually distributed or spent.

Economic business income is equal to the revenue received by the firm minus the opportunity cost of running the business excluding the implicit interest cost of owner equity. The latter is the interest the owner/shareholders could have earned on the money they invest in the firm. The opportunity cost of running the business includes current costs, such as materials and labor, and capital costs such as interest payments and depreciation. The most important differences between economic business income and accounting measures of business income involve interest expenses and the cost of depreciation.

Interest paid by the firm on money borrowed for business reasons is a cost of doing business. However, when inflation is present, the interest paid by a borrower does not reflect the real interest cost because the borrower can pay off the debt in dollars of reduced purchasing power. The real interest cost to a borrower is equal to the interest paid minus the amount borrowed multiplied by the inflation rate. The latter is equal to the decrease in the borrower's debt as measured in dollars of constant purchasing power. To simplify the discussion, we will assume no inflation except where necessary to understand the impact of the business tax system on firms' decisions.

Depreciation is the loss in value of a firm's tangible assets over the course of the year due to wear and tear, obsolescence, and a shorter useful life. **Economic depreciation** is the market value of the asset at the beginning of the year minus the market value of the asset at the end of the year. For example, the economic depreciation of an automobile purchased at the beginning of the year for $20,000 that could be sold for $15,000 at the end of the year is $5000. In many cases, the market value of a firm's assets cannot be readily determined, so the cost of depreciation is determined by schedules recognized as appropriate—under GAAP, for financial reports such as Table 15.3, or specified by the IRC—for determining taxable business income. For this reason, economic depreciation may be different from the schedular depreciation reported in financial statements (called book depreciation) and from that allowed by the tax authorities, called **Modified Accelerated Cost Recovery System, or MACRS**.

We can express economic business income (EBI) using the following equation:

$$\text{EBI} = R - W - T - r_B \times B - D.$$

In this equation, R is the gross revenue received by the firm; W is the sum of all current costs incurred by the firm including wages and salaries, materials, and lease and rental payments for rented capital; r_B is the real interest rate, equal to the nominal interest rate charged on firm debt less the inflation rate; B is the amount borrowed by the firm; and D is the economic depreciation on the firm's tangible assets. If there is no inflation and the depreciation cost reported in the income statement shown in Table 15.3 is economic depreciation, the economic business income of the bagel bakery is equal to its net income before income taxes ($20,000) reported in the income statement. However, if the inflation rate is 5% and the owner could sell the tangible assets at the end of the year for $59,000, EBI is higher than that reported in the income statement. In this case, economic depreciation is $1000 ($60,000 minus $59,000) and real interest payments are $2000 ($4000 minus 5% of $40,000), so economic business income is $23,000.

Taxable Business Income

Like net business income reported in the income statement, taxable business income is equal to gross revenue minus the costs of doing business. The IRC defines the cost of doing business as all outlays that are "ordinary and necessary" for carrying out a trade or business. To calculate taxable business income, most of the costs reported in the income statement are deducted from gross revenue, including materials, advertising, salaries and other benefits (such as health care and pensions) to employees and managers, bad debts, and payments for leased property. These items are called current costs and can be **expensed;** that is, they can be deducted in the year the costs are incurred. Interest payments to creditors are also deductible. For unincorporated businesses, where business and personal income are not separate, rules establish whether the interest paid is for business reasons (in which case it is deductible) or personal reasons (in which case it is not). All interest paid by corporations is deductible. Some taxes paid by the business are also deductible including payroll taxes, such as the employer's share of the FICA tax, and state and local taxes on business income and property. Federal business income taxes are not deductible.

DEDUCTIONS FOR DEPRECIATION.   The costs of durable assets like buildings and machines and some intangible assets, like patent rights, are not deducted in the year the firm acquires the asset. Instead, the firm receives deductions over the future useful life of the asset. The costs of intangible assets are amortized (spread out) over 15 years, and the costs of depreciable assets are determined according to MACRS schedules specified by the Internal Revenue Code.

A major difference between taxable business income and net business income reported in financial statements is the way in which the cost of depreciation is determined. For tax purposes, firms depreciate assets according to MACRS, which sets the maximum amount a firm can depreciate its tangible assets in a given year. Expenditures on most durable assets are depreciated (or, in the case of intangible assets, amortized) providing they have a finite useful life that can be determined with some degree of accuracy. Land does not have a finite life and therefore cannot be depreciated for tax purposes.

The purpose of depreciation is to spread the cost deductions for an asset over the period the asset earns income. Unlike current inputs, such as labor and materials, a durable input (capital) produces income for the firm over many years. For each type of depreciable asset, MACRS specifies a **recovery period,** which is the number of years over which the firm receives depreciation deductions, and a **recovery method,** which determines the dollar amount of depreciation allowed in each year of the recovery period. The length of the recovery period is roughly (in some cases, very roughly) related to the useful life of the asset. The recovery method determines the timing of the depreciation deductions over the recovery period.

MACRS actually contains two separate depreciation systems—the General Depreciation System (GDS) and the Alternative Depreciation System (ADS). The GDS schedules are more favorable to the firm, so they are most widely used and will be described here.[4] Buildings and structures are depreciated according to a **straight-line** recovery method. For the straight-line method, the MACRS deduction is equal to the initial cost of the asset divided by the length (in years) of the recovery period. For example, the recovery period for office buildings is 39 years. Hence, the annual MACRS depreciation deduction for an office building that cost the firm $780,000 is $20,000 a year for 39 years. With the straight-line method, the depreciation amount is the same for each year in the recovery period, so when the amount of the deduction is plotted against time, as in Figure 15.1(a), it is a straight (horizontal) line.

Firms can elect to depreciate assets other than real estate according to the **declining-balance** recovery method. With the declining-balance method, the depreciation deduction is a fixed percentage of the undepreciated cost basis of the asset. The percentage rate of depreciation depends on the recovery period of the asset. Assets other than real estate are classified into six recovery periods ranging from 3 years to 20 years, as shown in Table 15.4. For assets with recovery periods of 10 years or less, the percentage rate of depreciation is 200% divided by the number of years in the recovery period (this is called double declining balance). For instance, the recovery period for a truck is 5 years, so the percentage depreciation rate is 40% (200% ÷ 5). For assets with 15- or 20-year recovery periods, the percentage rate of depreciation is 150% divided by the number of years in the recovery period. Electricity generating equipment, which has a recovery period of 15 years, is depreciated at 10% (150% ÷ 15).

---

[4]Firms must use the ADS if they are subject to the Alternative Minimum Tax (AMT). The AMT is a separate tax system that sets a floor on the ability of firms to reduce taxable incomes using accelerated depreciation and other tax breaks.

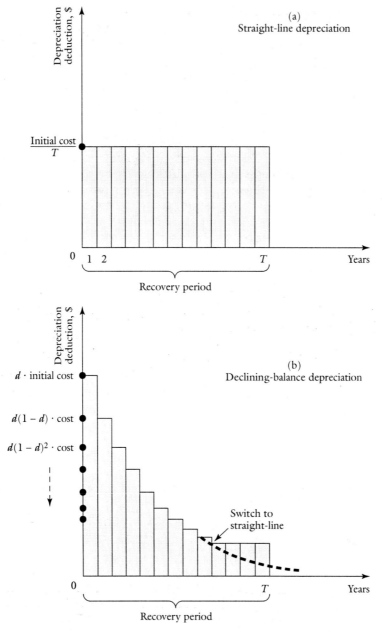

Figure 15.1

(a) Straight-Line Depreciation With the straight-line method, the firm gets a deduction for depreciation that is a fixed amount in dollars for each year of the recovery period. The amount is equal to the acquisition cost of the asset divided by the number of years in the recovery period.

(b) Declining-Balance Depreciation With the declining-balance method, the firm gets a deduction for depreciation that is a constant percentage of the undepreciated amount. The dollar amount of the deduction is greatest in the first year and declines over the recovery period. The percentage rate is determined by dividing either 200 or 150 by the number of years in the recovery period, as specified in the tax code.

Table 15.4   MACRS Depreciation Schedules

MACRS Recovery Period	Types of Items Included	Recovery Method
3-year property	Tractors, racehorses	Declining balance at 67%
5-year property	Automobiles, trucks, computers	Declining balance at 40%
7-year property	Office furniture, railroad locomotives, communication equipment	Declining balance at 28.6%
10-year property	Vessels, barges, agricultural structures	Declining balance at 20%
15-year property	Improvements to land, industrial electricity generating equipment	Declining balance at 10%
20-year property	Other farm buildings	Declining balance at 7.5%
27.5-year property	Residential rental property	Straight-line
39-year property	Nonresidential real estate	Straight-line

Source: Internal Revenue Service, *How to Depreciate Property,* Publication 946, http://www.irs.ustreas.gov/prod/forms_pubs/index.htm.

As the term *declining balance* implies, the amount allowed for depreciation declines over the recovery period. Figure 15.1(b) shows the depreciation deduction allowed by the declining-balance method. In the initial years of the asset's life, the declining-balance deduction is greater than the straight-line deduction, so firms would elect to use the former. After some years in use, the depreciation using the straight-line method is greater, and the firms can switch. In this case, the depreciation deduction is equal to the remaining undepreciated cost divided by the remaining years of life.

In Table 15.5, we calculate for different years the amount of depreciation allowed for an industrial electric generator (15-year recovery period, 150% declining balance) that has an initial cost of $50,000. We report the undepreciated balance

Table 15.5   Declining-Balance Depreciation Deduction with Switch to Straight-Line Method for a Generator

Years in Use	Undepreciated Cost	Declining-Balance Deduction	Straight-Line Deduction Over Remaining Life
1	$50,000	**$5,000**	$3,333.33
2	$45,000	**$4,500**	$3,214.28
3	$40,500	**$4,050**	$3,115.38
...	...	...	...
7	$26,572	$2,657	**$2,952**
...	...	...	...
10	$17,716	$1,772	**$2,952**
...	...	...	...
15	$2,952	$295	**$2,952**

in the second column and the amount that can be deducted under the declining-balance method in the third column. The fourth column shows the amount that can be deducted if the firm uses the straight-line method to depreciate the undepreciated cost over the remaining recovery period. In the example, the firm switches to the straight-line method starting in year 7.

THE ADVANTAGE OF ACCELERATED DEPRECIATION.   We have identified three different systems of depreciation: book depreciation as determined by GAAP; MACRS as determined by the IRC; and economic depreciation, which is the actual decrease in the value of a depreciable asset. In all cases, the firm writes off the full cost of a capital asset over a period of time corresponding to its useful life. Which system is most preferable to the firm?

The value to the firm of depreciation is equal to the present value (see Chapter 6) of the taxes saved as a result of the deduction. The sooner a firm can make depreciation deductions, the greater the present value of the taxes saved. A system whereby the firm receives depreciation deductions sooner rather than later is called **accelerated depreciation.** Accelerated depreciation describes a system in which the recovery period for tax purposes is shorter than the useful life of the asset, or where the firm can use declining-balance rather than straight-line depreciation. In fact, accountants often use the terms *accelerated depreciation* and *declining balance* interchangeably. Economists generally use accelerated depreciation to describe a situation where the firm takes depreciation tax deductions sooner than the asset loses economic value (economic depreciation).

To illustrate the advantage of accelerated depreciation, we will calculate the present value of the tax saving from depreciation deductions for the electricity generator in Table 15.5 using the straight-line and declining-balance methods. To calculate present value, the firm needs to discount tax savings occurring in future years. The present value of a dollar that is received in t years is equal to $\dfrac{1}{(1+i)^{t}}$, where i is the cost of capital to the firm. For simplicity, we assume that i is the rate of interest at which the firm can borrow and lend. Letting Z denote the present value of tax savings per dollar spent on the depreciable asset, we can write

$$Z = u \times \left[\frac{d_1}{1+i} + \frac{d_2}{(1+i)^2} + \cdots \frac{d_T}{(1+i)^T} \right].$$

In this equation, u is the rate of tax on business income, d_t is the depreciation deduction allowed in period t, and T is the number of years in the recovery period.

If the firm uses straight-line depreciation, we have $d_t = \dfrac{1}{T}$. The recovery period for a generator is 15 years, so $d_t = \$.067$. Assuming the firm can borrow and lend at 6% ($i = .06$) and business income is taxed at 35% ($u = .35$), we can use the formula to calculate $Z = .227$. That is, each dollar spent on the generator yields the firm a stream of future tax savings from depreciation deductions with a present value equal to 22.7 cents. Thus the value of the straight-line depreciation deductions on the $50,000 generator is $11,350.

The case of declining-balance depreciation is more complicated, particularly because the firm can switch to straight-line depreciation when it becomes advantageous to do so. In the case of declining-balance depreciation, $d_1 = d, d_2 = d(1 - d)$, $d_3 = d(1 - d)^2$, and so forth, where d is the rate of declining-balance depreciation (the generator has 150% declining balance, so $d = .1$). In Table 15.5, the firm switches to straight-line after six years so $d = 1/9$ (where 9 is the number of years remaining in the recovery period) from year 7 on. In this case we can calculate $Z = .236$, so by using the declining-balance (accelerated) depreciation schedule the firm receives a present value of tax savings equal to 23.6 cents for each dollar spent, or $11,800 on a $50,000 generator. (This is $450 more than under straight-line depreciation.)

In cases where depreciation is more accelerated, the advantage is that much greater. The advantage of accelerated (declining-balance) depreciation is greater the larger the percentage rate of depreciation (d) and the higher the interest rate (i). The advantage of accelerated depreciation is greater when interest rates are higher because depreciation tax deductions received in the future are discounted more and thus worth less.

THE CORPORATION INCOME TAX STRUCTURE

Now that we have learned how taxable business income is determined, we will discuss how it is taxed. For unincorporated businesses and for S corporations, business income is allocated to the owners of the business and taxed as personal income. The tax rate that applies to the business income depends on the total personal income of the owners. Most business income, however, is earned by C corporations, which are taxed according to the separate entity approach. That is, their business incomes are taxed under a separate corporation income tax system with its own schedule of tax rates. When the after-tax business income of the corporation is distributed to shareholders, it becomes the personal income of shareholders and is taxed again under the personal income tax. This is the double taxation of corporate income mentioned earlier.

Although C corporations account for less than 20% of businesses, they account for nearly 90% of gross business revenue and nearly two-thirds of all taxable business income. The corporation income tax is the third largest source of revenue for the federal government, and 45 states tax the income of corporations operating in their jurisdictions. In fiscal year 1998, the federal corporation income tax collected $189 billion, which is nearly 11% of total federal revenue. State corporation income taxes collected $36 billion, which is equal to nearly 4% of state and local tax revenue. To better understand the corporation income tax, it is useful to describe the tax unit, the tax base, and the tax rate schedule for the corporation income tax.

The Corporation Income Tax Unit

Unlike a proprietorship or partnership, the legal identity of a corporation is distinct from that of its owner/shareholders. Like natural persons, corporations can earn

A CASE IN POINT

15.1   Does a 300-Year-Old Viol Depreciate?

Successful concert musicians like the sound produced on seventeenth-century musical instruments such as Stradivari violins and Ruggeri viols. Like all businesses, musicians can deduct the costs they incur to earn income. Recently, a New York tax court addressed the question of whether musicians can deduct depreciation on their antique musical instruments. In principle, for a property to be depreciated for tax purposes, it must be subject to exhaustion, wear and tear, or obsolescence and have a determinable useful life. If the sound of a violin improves with age, can it be wearing out? If a viol is still going strong after 300 years, does it have a determinable useful life? The tax court decided that a professional musician could indeed depreciate a 300-year-old viol over five years under the provisions of MACRS, even though after five years the viol is likely to be worth more than the musician paid for it.

Similar concerns arise with other investments. Modern skyscrapers are depreciated over a 39-year useful life even though they will last much longer. The Empire State Building, constructed in the 1930s, is worth more today than it cost to build. Research and development investments, say to develop a new product, are expensed (that is, deducted in the year the expen-

diture is made) even though the products developed may earn income for a business over many years. In all such cases, MACRS allows the business to deduct investment costs over a far shorter time period than the useful life of the asset.

If assets are sold for more than their undepreciated cost basis, the seller must add the difference between the sale price and the undepreciated cost to business income. This is called **depreciation recapture.** The purchaser of the used asset depreciates the cost paid under the applicable schedule. The seller still benefits because the taxes paid on recapture are deferred until the time of sale.

Critically analyze the following:

- Suppose the musician purchased the above Ruggeri viol for $500,000 and depreciates it at double declining balance over five years. If he or she sells the instrument for $750,000 at the end of five years, how much must be added to business income at that time?

- Suppose a business sells a skyscraper that cost $78 million to build for $78 million 39 years later. What was the value to the taxpayer of deferring taxes if the interest rate is 6%?

- Would the value of deferring taxes be greater or less if the interest rate is 8%?

income, make contracts, sue and be sued, incur debt, hold assets, and declare bankruptcy. All corporations have limited liability, which means that the shareholders are not personally responsible for the debts and obligations of the business.[5] A corporation is created with a corporate charter granted by the state in which it is a resident. Many states charge a franchise tax for the privilege of granting the corporate charter. This franchise tax is a flat fee in some states and a tax on corporate assets in others. Once chartered, the corporation is a legal entity and subject to separate income taxation.

Since the corporation is an artificial person, many problems arise in defining the boundaries of the corporation. Problems arise in determining the residence of

---

[5] A hybrid form called a professional corporation is sometimes chartered for businesses providing professional services like health care and legal services. In a professional corporation, limited liability applies only to business transactions, and shareholders have unlimited liability for professional actions. For example, a doctor in a professional corporation could be sued for malpractice.

the corporation for tax purposes, from intercorporate ownership, and in controlling income flows between the corporation and its shareholders.

A corporation is a resident of the state and country in which it is chartered. However, many corporations have business operations in several states (interstate corporations) or several countries (multinational corporations). In this case, corporate business income may be subject to tax by several taxing authorities. For interstate corporations, income is apportioned to the states based on the volume of business activity within the state. Income of subsidiaries of U.S. corporations operating in foreign countries is not taxed until and unless the income is repatriated to the U.S. parent as interest, intercorporate dividends, or royalties.

A domestic corporation may conduct business operations through subsidiary corporations. Under the separate accounting approach, the income of subsidiary corporations is separate from that of the parent until the subsidiary pays dividends to the parent. Intercorporate dividends are discussed in the next section. In some cases, firms consolidate the incomes of wholly owned subsidiaries, so the incomes of the corporate parent and its subsidiaries are combined and the business is taxed as a single unit.

If a corporation distributes income or property to its shareholders, it must identify the distribution as a dividend, in which case the receipt is taxed as personal income of the shareholder, or a return of capital, in which case it is not taxed. To prevent shareholders from avoiding tax on distributions on shares, complicated rules govern corporate-shareholder distributions. For example, if a corporation were to distribute income by making indefinite interest-free loans to its shareholders, the amount distributed would be deemed a dividend for tax purposes.

The Corporation Income Tax Base

The taxable income of a corporation is equal to its business and investment income. As we have already learned, business income is equal to revenue from sales less the cost of doing business. Investment income is equal to interest, dividends, and realized capital gains received by the corporation. Unlike in the personal tax system, capital gains are taxed at the same rate as other forms of income under the corporation income tax.

In calculating business income, corporations receive, as a cost of doing business, many of the same deductions enjoyed by individuals under the personal income tax. These include deductions for state and local property and income taxes, mortgage interest payments, and charitable donations. Corporations do not receive personal deductions like the standard deduction. Two other important deductions received by corporations are the dividends received deduction and the net operating loss deduction.

The **dividends received deduction (DRD)** is equal to part or all of intercorporate dividends received by the corporation. If a parent corporation owns all of the shares in the subsidiary, the DRD is 100%, so dividends received by a parent corporation from a wholly owned subsidiary are not taxed as income to the parent. If a corporation owns only part of the shares in another corporation, the dividends received are considered portfolio income and the corporation receives a partial DRD (70% of dividends if it owns less than 20% of shares and 80% if it holds more than 20% of shares). The purpose of the

DRD is to prevent multiple levels of corporate taxation on dividends as they pass through the corporate ownership structure. Without the DRD, dividends from a subsidiary would be taxed at least three times: first as business income to the subsidiary, second as dividends received by the parent corporation, and finally as personal income when the dividends are ultimately distributed to the shareholders of the parent corporation. Dividends from subsidiaries operating in other countries do not receive a DRD; instead, the corporate parent receives a **foreign tax credit** for corporation income taxes paid by the subsidiary in the other country.

Corporations that have negative business net income (an operating loss) for the year also take the **net operating loss deduction**. If a corporation has a net operating loss, its taxable income is negative and it owes no corporation income tax. The corporation can deduct its net operating loss in the current business year from business income received in the three previous years and obtain a refund of corporation income taxes already paid. If the corporation does not have business income in the three previous years, it can carry the operating loss forward and deduct it from business income it receives during any of the next 15 years.

The Corporation Income Tax Rate Schedule

A corporation's income tax liability is found by applying the graduated corporate tax rate schedule to its taxable income. Tax rates applying to corporate income as of 1999 are given in Table 15.6. These rates apply to the income of a consolidated group of corporations as if it were a single company. As with the personal tax rate schedules, these are marginal tax rates and apply only to the amounts of income within the tax brackets. Unlike the personal income tax rate structure, where the graduation is for the purpose of vertical equity, the graduated corporate rate structure has no real justification.

This bizarre tax schedule is a product of history. The Tax Reform Act of 1986 set a *basic* corporation income tax rate of 34%, but as a concession to smaller businesses, lower rates were applied to the first $75,000 of corporate income. To remove the advantage of the lower tax rates from large corporations, an additional 5% tax was levied on corporate income between $100,000 and $335,000. In 1993, the basic corporation income tax rate was raised to 35%, but only on corporate incomes above $10 million. An additional 3% tax was introduced on corporate incomes between $10 million and $18⅓ million to remove the advantages of the 34% rate to larger firms. Whatever the reasons for this strange tax rate schedule, it is an excellent make-work policy for corporate tax accountants, who are charged with devising ways of minimizing the tax the corporation must pay.

Corporations also receive tax credits. Especially important for multinational corporations is the credit for corporation income taxes paid to foreign governments. Multinationals also get a credit for foreign taxes paid by their foreign subsidiaries. Businesses in general also receive a number of business incentive tax credits based on their investment outlays. For example, they can receive a tax credit of up to 70% of outlays they make to rehabilitate low-income housing. Recall that each $1 of tax credit is used to reduce the taxes paid by $1, so this tax credit means that the federal government picks up a large part of the cost of rehabilitating low-income hous-

Table 15.6 **Corporation Income Tax Brackets, 1999**

Taxable Income Thresholds ($ thousands)	Tax Rate (%)
0–50	15
50–75	25
75–100	34
100–335	39
335–10,000	34
10,000–15,000	35
15,000–18,333.3	38
18,333.3–	35

Source: U.S. Master Tax Guide, Commerce Clearing House, 1999.

ing. Tax credits are also given for the use of alternative fuels (such as grain alcohol as a substitute for petroleum-based gasoline), reforestation investments, investments in "economically depressed areas," and increases in expenditures for research and development. The government uses these tax credits to encourage firms to make "socially useful" expenditures.

Before 1987, business tax credits were more important because firms received a 10% tax credit for investment expenditures on equipment. A firm that spent $1 million on a machine could subtract $100,000 from its tax payment. The general investment tax credit was introduced in the 1960s to stimulate investment demand. It was abolished by the Tax Reform Act of 1986.

THE EFFECTS OF TAXES ON BUSINESS DECISIONS

Business income taxes affect many decisions made by firms. These include organizational decisions such as whether or not to operate as a corporation or as a proprietorship, production decisions such as how much output to produce and which inputs to use in production, and financial decisions such as whether to raise money for investments by issuing bonds or shares. These effects are caused by the way business income is defined for tax purposes and by the double taxation of shareholders' income under the corporation income tax. We begin by considering a business tax that would be neutral in its effects on business decisions.

The Neutrality of Taxes on Economic Profit

Economists assume that firms make decisions such as how much to produce, how many employees to hire, and whether to invest in new equipment so as to maximize **economic profit.** Economic profit (or "pure" profit) is equal to the revenue of the firm minus all costs of doing business, including the opportunity cost of owner equity. The opportunity cost of owner equity is equal to the real interest the owner/shareholders could have earned on the funds they have invested in the business. Economic profit, denoted π, can be expressed as $\pi = R - W - C$ where R is the gross revenue of the firm, W is current costs including wages and materials, and C is the **user cost of capital.** The user cost of capital is the annual cost to the firm of its invested capital. It can be expressed

$$C = r_A \times K + D$$

where D is economic depreciation, K is the amount of capital invested in the firm, and r_A is the weighted average cost of finance to the firm. Note that from the balance sheet, $K = B + E$ where B is the amount of funds borrowed and E is the amount of funds contributed by the owner/shareholders. Therefore, r_A is the equal to the fraction of the firm's capital stock financed by borrowing times the real interest rate on borrowing plus the fraction financed with the funds of the owner/shareholders times the real interest rate that could have been earned on those funds. That is,

$$r_A = \left(\frac{B}{K}\right) \times r_B + \left(\frac{E}{K}\right) \times r_E.$$

where r_B is the real interest rate on borrowed funds and r_E is the real interest rate that could have been earned on the owners' funds. For simplicity, we will assume that prices are steady, so the real interest rates are equal to market interest rates.

Note that economic profit is not the same as economic business income. Economic profit is the excess of business income over what the owners could have earned by investing their funds elsewhere. In fact, we can write EBI $= \pi + r_E \times E$. That is, economic business income is equal to economic profit plus the opportunity cost of owner equity.

The neutrality of taxing economic profit is illustrated in Figure 15.2, where the firm's output is measured on the horizontal axis and economic profit on the vertical axis. Economic profit initially rises as output rises, reaches a maximum, and then declines, as shown by the gross profit curve labeled π. The firm maximizes profit by producing output Q^*. If the government taxes economic profit at rate u, the economic profit kept by the firm after taxes is shown by the curve labeled $(1 - u)\pi$. The height of this curve is proportional to the height of the gross profit curve, so it too reaches a maximum at Q^*. Despite the tax on profit, the firm can do no better than Q^* after the tax is imposed, so the tax does not affect the output decision.

The tax on business income affects business decisions because it is *not* a tax on economic profit. Using the definition of taxable income described earlier and the definition of economic profit, we can express taxable business income (TBI) as

$$TBI = R - W - r_B \times B - MACRS$$
$$= \pi + r_E \times E + (D - MACRS)$$

where MACRS is the depreciation deduction allowed under MACRS and the other variables are as defined earlier. In other words, taxable business income is equal to economic profit plus the opportunity cost of owner's equity plus the difference between economic depreciation and MACRS. Since a tax on economic profit is neutral, the effect of taxes on business decisions depends on the last two terms.[6] In

---

[6]This is highly simplified. We assume no inflation, so market interest rates are equal to real interest rates. This assumption also allows us to ignore certain complications in accounting for the cost of goods sold out of inventory and the difference between the historic cost of capital (which is allowed under the IRC) and the cost of replacing depreciated capital.

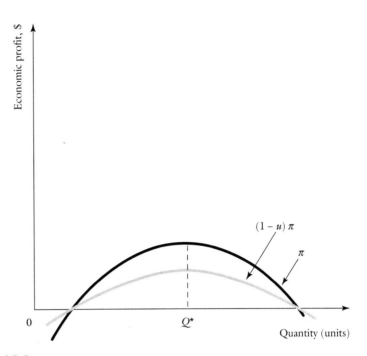

Figure 15.2
Neutrality of Taxing Economic Profit
A tax on economic profit does not affect business decisions, as is shown here for the decision of what output to produce. Economic profit π reaches a maximum at output Q^*, which would be the output of a profit-maximizing firm. If economic profit is taxed, the firm maximizes after-tax profit $(1 - u)\pi$, which also reaches a maximum at Q^*.

addition, the double taxation of investor income due to the separate entity approach to taxing C corporations also affects business decisions.

Business income taxes affect both the financial and investment decisions made by firms. First, the fact that interest costs are deducted only when funds are borrowed encourages the firm to finance investments with debt and discourages it from using equity finance. Second, the double taxation of dividends paid by C corporations encourages firms to retain income for reinvestment or use it to repurchase shares rather than distribute it to shareholders as dividends. Third, because part of the cost of an investment (the opportunity cost of equity funds) is not deducted from taxable income, the business income tax discourages investment. Fourth, investments that receive accelerated depreciation are encouraged (or discouraged less) than other investments. We will discuss each of these impacts in more detail.

The Effect of Business Taxes on Financial Decisions

Two major financial decisions made by firms are whether to raise funds by issuing debt or equity, and whether to distribute earnings as dividends or retain them for investment. Generally, the business tax system encourages the use of debt finance and the reinvestment of corporate earnings.

EFFECT ON THE CHOICE BETWEEN DEBT AND EQUITY.   Since interest payments are deductible from taxable income and dividends are not, the double taxation of corporate equity income provides an incentive for firms to raise funds for investment using debt rather than equity. Because interest payments are deducted from taxable income, income from investments financed by debt is subject only to the personal income tax when the interest is received by the creditors. Corporate income distributed as dividends is taxed under the corporation income tax as business income and under the personal income tax when the dividends are received by the shareholders.

The tax disadvantage of equity finance raises a question: Why don't corporations finance all their investments with debt? Why use equity and incur an extra level of taxation? In fact, most American corporations have a debt-to-equity ratio of 1 or less, so they raise at least as much through equity as they do through debt. Given the tax advantage of debt, this reliance on equity is sometimes called the **debt puzzle.**

One reason corporations raise funds with equity is that debt saddles them with a commitment to pay interest and eventually repay the principal, whereas equity does not. Sales receipts are typically uncertain, and if firms are unable to pay interest or repay debt when it is due, their creditors can force them into court and liquidate their assets. A failure to pay dividends has no such consequences—at worst, a company's shares take a drubbing in the stock market.

One theory about the choice between debt and equity is that corporations trade off the advantage of the tax deduction for interest against the increased risk of bankruptcy as their debt-to-equity ratio increases. According to this theory, a higher corporation income tax rate causes a firm to rely more on debt, but the increase in the risk of bankruptcy limits the degree to which the firm will use debt rather than equity.

Surprisingly, few studies have found a significant link between the ratio of debt to equity and the corporation income tax rate. For instance, large corporations face higher corporation income tax rates yet also have lower debt-equity ratios than smaller companies. The problem is that many things besides the corporation income tax rate affect a company's financing decision, and the debt-equity ratio measures the accumulated effects of past financing decisions as well as current ones. Professor Mackie-Mason of the University of Michigan attempted to disentangle these effects by examining how a company's *marginal* financing decision is affected by the corporation income tax rate. He found that a higher marginal corporation income tax rate significantly increased the probability that *new* investments would be financed with debt rather than equity.[7]

EFFECT ON THE DECISION TO DISTRIBUTE DIVIDENDS.   Although business income is taxed at the same rate whether it is distributed as dividends or reinvested within the company, the consequences for personal taxes are different. Corporate income that is distributed as dividends is taxed as ordinary income to shareholders at their personal marginal tax rates. Income that is reinvested or used to repurchase the company's shares increases the value of the shares held by the shareholders and is not subject to personal income taxes until they sell their shares and realize the

---

[7]See Jeffrey K. Mackie-Mason, "Do Taxes Affect Corporate Financing Decisions?" 1990.

capital gains. Even then, the personal tax rate on long-term capital gains is 20%,[8] so income from capital gains is taxed less than dividends if the shareholder is in a tax bracket greater than 20%.

For this reason, we would expect the combined corporate and personal tax systems to discourage companies from paying out dividends. A company's earnings are a convenient source of investable funds that do not require it to attract funds from outside the firm. Even if suitable investments are not available, a company can use its earnings to repurchase its own shares in the stock market.

In a typical year, however, corporations distribute about 65% of their earnings as dividends. Why do firms distribute earnings rather than reinvest them or repurchase shares, given that there is a tax disadvantage for shareholders in receiving dividends? Finance experts call this the **dividend puzzle.** Several theories try to explain the puzzle, but the explanation of special interest to students of the tax system is called the **trapped-equity theory.** According to the trapped-equity theory, in equilibrium the shareholders are actually indifferent between receiving dividends and having the income reinvested in the company. The reason is that the personal tax paid on dividends cannot be avoided by reinvesting the earnings; it can only be postponed. According to this theory, the dividends must be paid out eventually—if not in the present, then in the future. Therefore, the tax rate on dividends is irrelevant to the question of whether it is best to distribute the earnings now or reinvest them and distribute them in the future. The dividend tax must be paid in either case.

For example, suppose a company's shareholders are in the 36% personal tax bracket. If the company distributes $1 of earnings as dividends, the shareholders keep $.64 ($1 minus $.36 in personal taxes). Alternatively, suppose the company reinvests the earnings and distributes $1 + x$ dollars of dividends one year in the future (or any number of years in the future), where x is the annual return on capital invested in the company after corporate taxes are paid. Assuming that shareholders remain in the 36% bracket, they get $.64 \cdot (1 + x)$ in dividends one year hence.

In choosing between receiving dividends now or reinvesting the earnings in the company, the shareholders are interested only in the *relative* advantages of the alternatives. The relative advantage of reinvested earnings is measured by $.64 \cdot (1 + x)$ divided by $.64, or simply $1 + x$. The term .64 (1 minus the shareholder's marginal tax rate) cancels out. In other words, the shareholders are concerned only with the size of x, the rate of return on reinvested earnings within the company—not with the personal tax rate on dividends. The relative advantage of dividends and reinvested earnings is the same whatever the dividend tax rate, because the equity is trapped within the firm and cannot get out without the dividend tax being paid.

Several empirical studies have tried to answer the question of whether the business tax system actually discourages dividend distributions. These studies compared data on corporate dividend policies with the "traditional" view that dividend taxes discourage distributions and the trapped-equity view that dividend taxes do not matter. Although dividend-to-earnings ratios appear to be negatively related to higher tax rates on dividends, this could be explained by both theories. Those who

---

[8] A marginal tax rate of 28% is applied if the asset is held at least one year. For assets held 18 months or longer, the tax rate on capital gains is 20%.

take the traditional view believe their theory is vindicated by the fact that firms often repurchase shares without the tax authority treating the repurchase as a dividend distribution. Of course, the fact that dividends are distributed at all is inconsistent with the traditional view; hence the dividend puzzle lives on.

The Effect of Business Taxes on Investment Decisions

Perhaps the most important effect of business income taxation is on firms' investment decisions. The accumulated capital stock in American business enterprises amounted to over $11 trillion in 1994, and gross business investment (purchase of equipment and nonresidential structures) amounted to $667 billion. Economists believe that the tax system affects the amount of new investment, and therefore the accumulated stock over time, as well as the types of investment that are made (equipment, structures, inventory, innovations, and so on). The capital stock and the rate of investment are important determinants of the amount of wealth and the rate of growth of the economy.

A business will invest in a unit of capital if the marginal revenue from the investment each year is greater than or equal to the marginal user cost of capital—that is,

if $\frac{\Delta R}{\Delta K} \geq \frac{\Delta C}{\Delta K}$, where Δ denotes a small change in a variable. If economic profit were

taxed, both the marginal revenue from the investment and the marginal user cost of capital are reduced by one minus the business tax rate (that is, $1 - u$). Therefore any investment that is profitable in the absence of a tax on economic profit is profitable after the tax, so the investment decision of the firm is not affected by a tax on economic profit.

As we learned, however, the tax on business income is not a tax on economic profit. Most importantly, firms cannot deduct the opportunity cost of equity funds in determining net income. This raises the marginal user cost of capital relative to marginal revenue after taxes. Second, the deduction for depreciation under MACRS is usually different from economic depreciation. To the extent that MACRS gives the firm accelerated depreciation, this would lower the marginal user cost of capital relative to the marginal revenue after taxes. Typically, however, the advantage of accelerated depreciation is not enough to outweigh the nondeductibility of the cost of equity for tax purposes, so the user cost of capital is relatively higher after taxes.

This is illustrated in Figure 15.3 where the quantity of capital invested, say in terms of the dollar value of machines, is measured on the horizontal axis. The user cost per dollar of capital when there are no taxes is equal to the height of the horizontal line. The marginal revenue per unit of capital determines the demand curve for capital, labeled D_0, which is downward-sloping because the firm runs out of good investments as it invests more. In the absence of taxes, the firm maximizes profit by investing in K_0 machines, which is where the marginal revenue is equal to the marginal user cost.

The effect of the business income tax is to reduce the profit-maximizing level of investment to K_u machines. All revenue received by the firm is subject to income taxation, so after taxes the marginal revenue from investment is equal to the height of D_u, which is one minus the business tax rate times the height of D_0. The after-tax user

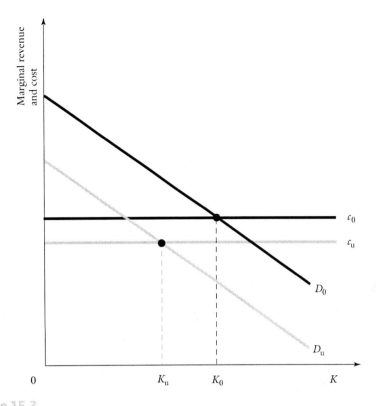

Figure 15.3.

The Effects of Business Income Tax on Investment

A tax on business income reduces the after-tax marginal revenue from capital and shifts the capital demand curve to D_u. Deductions for capital expenses also reduce the user cost of capital to c_u, but generally the reduction in c_u is less. Consequently, the capital stock desired by the firm falls.

cost of capital is equal to the height of the horizontal line labeled c_u. Because the full user cost of capital is not deducted from business taxable income, c_u is not reduced in the same proportion as D_u, so the profit-maximizing level of investment falls.

MARGINAL EFFECTIVE TAX RATES ON INVESTMENT.   The effect of business income taxes on the firm's investment decision varies from investment to investment, depending on how it is financed and on the degree to which depreciation is acclerated under MACRS. In Figure 15.3, the after-tax user cost of capital c_u is lower the greater the fraction of the investment financed with debt (because interest payments are deductible) and the more accelerated the depreciation schedule. For investments that are mostly financed with debt and receive greatly accelerated depreciation, the tax may reduce the user cost of capital more than the marginal revenue from the investment, and the firm will invest more because of the tax. To measure the varying impact of business income taxation on different investments, economists calculate the **marginal effective tax rate (METR)** on investment income.

The adjective *marginal* means that the tax rate applies to the increase in business income from additional investment by the firm, and *effective* means that the calculated tax rate includes all of the rules and provisions affecting the amount of tax paid, including the depreciation schedule.

If the statutory tax rate on business income as defined by the IRC is 35%, but the calculated METR is 25%—say because of generous depreciation deductions—it means that the effect of the business tax system is equal to a hypothetical tax of 25% on the economic business income (EBI) from the investment. In other words, the advantages of accelerated depreciation and other tax rules that define taxable income are translated into an equivalent reduction in the tax rate applying to EBI. The main difference between taxable business income and EBI is the deduction of MACRS rather than economic depreciation.

In Figure 15.3, the amount of tax paid per unit of capital (after adjusting for future depreciation deductions) is the vertical distance between the tax-adjusted user cost c_u and c_0. METR is usually expressed as a percentage of EBI before taxes, so the METR on investment when the capital stock is K_u is measured by $\dfrac{c_u - c_0}{\text{EBI}}$.

The numerator is the tax wedge, or the difference between what an investment earns and what the investor receives. This difference goes to the government as tax revenue. The denominator is EBI per unit of investment when the firm has capital stock K_u.

Table 15.7 reports METRs for different types of investments calculated by Jane G. Gravelle, an economist with the Congressional Research Service at the Library of Congress who is an expert on the taxation of capital income. Gravelle calculates the METRs for each type of investment undertaken by corporations and unincorporated businesses. These estimates reflect business tax rates only, and they do not include personal taxes on corporate dividends and capital gains. A more complicated calculation of the METRs would include the effects of personal taxes on capital incomes, but this would not affect the pattern of METRs across the different investments, because personal taxes do not depend on the type of investment. As the table indicates, METRs are higher for corporations than for unincorporated businesses.

Table 15.7 shows how the METRs on the income to equity owners from different investments changed from 1981 to 1992. Most of the changes in the METRs reflect the changes in business taxation enacted in 1986. These changes include reductions in business tax rates (the basic corporation income tax rate was reduced from 46% to 34% and marginal tax rates on personal income were reduced also), less accelerated depreciation schedules, and the elimination of the general investment tax

Table 15.7   Marginal Effective Tax Rates on Investments

Asset Type	Unincorporated (1981)	Unincorporated (1992)	Corporate (1981)	Corporate (1992)
Equipment	−45%	21%	−32%	30%
Inventories	38	30	54	41
Land	30	23	46	34
Structures	15	21	29	32
Apartments	18	20	31	30

Source: Jane Gravelle, *The Economic Effects of Taxing Capital Income*, 1994, Table 3.1.

credit of 10% for investment in equipment. Note that the combination very accelerated depreciation schedules and the general investment tax credit in 1981 resulted in a *negative* METR for equipment investment. In other words, in 1981 business investment in equipment was actually subsidized by the business tax system.[9]

Differences in the METRs across different investments affect how firms allocate their investment expenditures. In particular, firms spend more on investments with low METRs and less on investments with high METRs. This creates inefficiency and a deadweight loss, because firms invest for tax advantages rather than profitability. Suppose the marginal revenue before taxes on investments in structures is greater than the marginal revenue on equipment. Without taxes, firms would invest more in structures and less in equipment. However, if the METR on equipment is very low (or even negative, as it was in 1981), firms will invest in equipment for tax reasons. In fact, they will invest in equipment as long as the after-METR return on equipment is greater than the after-METR return on structures. This creates a deadweight loss from inefficiency because resources are not employed in uses that have the highest economic value.

The large variance in METRs across different investments shown in Table 15.7 for 1981 led to major reforms in business taxation designed to "level the playing field." Leveling the playing field means changing the business tax system so that the METRs on different investments are more equal. If the METRs are the same on different investments, the tax system does not favor one investment over another and firms allocate their investment spending more efficiently. As can be seen in Table 15.7, corporate tax reforms in 1986, mainly changing depreciation schedules and eliminating the investment tax credit for equipment, succeeded in leveling the playing field somewhat, although not completely. Unfortunately, some of the leveling of the playing field accomplished by the 1986 business tax reforms and shown in Table 15.7 has been undone by the introduction of other tax breaks for businesses in the 1990s.

EMPIRICAL EVIDENCE ON TAXES AND INVESTMENT.   The calculated METRs measure the size of investment incentives and disincentives caused by the tax system but do not tell us how firms respond to them. To determine the response of the firms, it is necessary to estimate the slope of the capital demand curve D_0 in Figure 15.3. If D_0 is quite steep, the quantity of capital demanded by the firm is not greatly affected by the level of the user cost, and therefore the tax on business income does not greatly distort the investment decision. If the demand curve is relatively flat, a tax will have a large effect on the firm's capital stock.

Rather than estimate the direct effect of the tax-adjusted user cost on the stock of capital, most empirical studies focus on the effect of the user cost on investment spending. A classic study by Professors Robert Hall and Dale Jorgenson examined the short-run effect of the investment tax credit on the level of aggregate investment spending using time series data. They concluded that investment spending was significantly affected by tax incentives, but later studies cast reasonable doubt on their

---

[9]Gravelle's calculated METRs do not include personal taxes on investment incomes, so the actual magnitude of the subsidy was smaller than Table 15.7 indicates.

conclusions.[10] Some studies allow for the user cost to affect investment spending with a time lag. Several studies find that investment spending, to the extent that it responds to tax incentives at all, responds with significant time lags, perhaps many years. One survey concludes that the preponderance of evidence from the studies of aggregate investment behavior suggests that taxes have little impact on the level of investment.[11]

In Table 15.7, we saw that the METRs on incomes from different types of investments were significantly affected by the reforms of 1986 that abolished the 10% investment tax credit for equipment, reduced depreciation rates, and lowered business tax rates. The main result of these changes was a large increase in the METR on investments in equipment relative to other forms of investment. As explained, this should improve economic efficiency as firms reduce investment in equipment and, perhaps, increase spending on other investments. It also provides a good "natural experiment" to determine the effects of the tax system on investment. On the basis of the neoclassical theory of the firm, we would expect a decline in equipment investment spending relative to other types of investments.

A preliminary study by Professors Alan Auerbach and Kevin Hassett, respectively of the University of Pennsylvania and Columbia University, found that investment spending on equipment was not significantly reduced by the changes of 1986, but these authors acknowledged that they had not controlled for all the variables that could affect investment spending. A later study using panel data at the firm level found that changes in the user cost from the tax reforms of 1986 and from earlier tax reforms significantly affected investment spending in the way predicted by the theory.[12]

THE INCIDENCE OF THE CORPORATION INCOME TAX

The corporation income tax is special in that its incidence is subject to more debate and uncertainty than the other major taxes in the federal revenue structure. In many studies of the distribution of the tax burden, the burden of a tax is presumed to be on the person with the legal liability to pay it—that is, the focus is on the statutory incidence. The assumption of statutory incidence is unsuited for the corporation income tax because a corporation is an artificial person and cannot bear the tax burden. We must consider the different ways in which the corporation income tax can be shifted and to whom it is shifted. The possibilities are numerous: the tax can be shifted to corporate shareholders, capital owners in general, managers and executives, consumers, corporate employees, or workers in general.

The simplest assumption we can make about the incidence of the corporation income tax is that it is borne by the shareholders in the corporation in proportion

---

[10]R. Hall and D. Jorgenson, "Tax Policy and Investment Behavior," 1967, estimated the effects on investment using a model in which firms have production functions of a specific form, called Cobb-Douglas. However, these types of production functions imply that the firms' capital demand curves have an elasticity of unity, by definition. Later researchers, including R. Eisner and M. Nadiri, "Investment Behavior and Neoclassical Theory: A Comment," 1970, used more general functional forms in order to let the data determine the elasticity.

[11]Robert Chirinko, "Business Fixed Investment Spending: A Critical Survey ...," 1993.

[12]See Alan Auerbach and Kevin Hassett, "Investment, Tax Policy, and the Tax Reform Act of 1986," 1990; and Jason Cummins, Kevin Hassett, and Glenn Hubbard, "Have Tax Reforms Affected Investment?" 1995.

to the income they receive on their shares. The Congressional Budget Office uses this assumption in its study of the incidence of federal tax liabilities across individuals and families. Taxpayers are classified into quintiles according to their Adjusted Family Income (AFI), which is determined by their family cash income divided by the Official Poverty Threshold for a family of the same size. The highest quintile represents the 20% of taxpayer/families having the highest AFI. According to the CBO, in 1999 the highest quintile bore 81% of corporation income taxes paid, as compared with 10% for the fourth quintile, 6% for the third, 3% for the second, and just 1% for the lowest quintile.[13] Under this assumption, the corporation income tax is one of the most progressive taxes in the federal tax system.

Economists doubt that the burden of the corporation income tax is borne by corporate shareholders alone. Rather, they believe that the burden is spread to owners of capital in general. Investors must earn the same after-tax return on corporate investments as they can earn elsewhere; otherwise, they will sell their corporate shares and purchase the other assets. Hence, the corporation inocme tax can push down the after-tax rate of return on corporate shares only if it pushes down the rate of return on alternative investments as well.

Alternatively, rather than pushing down the rate of return on all investments, the corporation income tax can be capitalized into the price of corporate shares. In Chapter 11 we explained that if market participants anticipate the future tax they must pay on an asset, its price declines by the present value of the future tax. In this case, the owners of the corporate shares suffer a capital loss equal to the future taxes even though the *rate* of return on corporate shares is not affected. The rate of return is equal to the ratio of the return and the price of a share, and it is not changed if the numerator and denominator of the ratio decline by the same percentage.

According to the capitalization hypothesis, the burden of the corporation income tax is borne not by *all* asset holders but only by those unlucky enough to own corporate shares at the time the corporation income tax is imposed or increased. By the same logic, if the corporation income tax were abolished tomorrow, we would expect current shareholders to enjoy a huge increase in the value of their shares because each share could pay higher dividends.

Some people believe that the corporation income tax might depress the wages and salaries paid to the company's management and employees. Again, economists caution that to the extent the tax can depress wages, it must do so economy-wide, not just in the corporate sector. If wages are reduced in the corporate sector only, corporate employees will look for employment in the higher-wage noncorporate sector, depressing wages there. Most economists doubt that the corporation income tax is borne by workers in the short run. If this were the case, the theory of tax equivalence would imply that the personal tax on dividends to shareholders is also borne by workers. According to the tax equivalence theorem, it should not matter whether a tax on a certain type of income is levied at the level of the individual or the firm.

As we saw in Chapter 11, Harberger's classic general equilibrium analysis of the corporation income tax treats the tax as a partial factor tax on the income of capital

---

[13]Congressional Budget Office, "Estimates of Federal Tax Liabilities for Individuals and Families by Income Category and Family Type for 1995 and 1999," May 1998, p. 38.

employed in the corporate sector of the economy.[14] According to this theory, capital and labor must shift between the corporate and noncorporate sectors of the economy so that each factor earns the same after-tax reward in the corporate sector as it earns in the noncorporate sector. Harberger found that although the corporation income tax could lower wages, because the labor-intensive manufacturing industries are in the corporate sector, the total effect of the corporation income tax is to depress the return on capital, so capital owners bear the burden. Although Harberger used a highly simplified model, more complicated computational general equilibrium models that incorporate more features of the economy have confirmed his result.

Some economists do believe that the burden of the corporation income tax could be shifted to labor in the long run. If the rate of return on capital is reduced by the corporation income tax, saving is reduced and less capital is accumulated over time. In the long run, the capital stock per worker is reduced by the corporation income tax, reducing the productivity of workers and, hence, wages. Through this mechanism, the corporation income income tax is shifted to labor in the long run. In fact, according to this argument, all taxes on capital income are borne by labor in the long run. Of course, the long run may be so far in the future that it has little relevance to current concerns about tax incidence.

A few economists believe that, like a sales tax, the corporation income tax is passed on to the consumers of corporate goods. This is probably the preferred theory in the corporate boardroom. Many corporate managers claim that they pass on the cost of corporation income taxes, just like any other cost increase, as higher prices. It is not surprising that managers of firms would hold this opinion, because they are likely to take a partial-equilibrium view of the impact of the tax. They assume that input prices are constant and ignore the possibility that factor rewards, like wages and interest rates, would decline because of the tax.

If, in fact, the corporation income tax is passed on to consumers, that would radically alter our conclusions about its incidence. Generally taxes borne by consumers, like sales taxes, are considered regressive, or proportional at best. So rather than being highly progressive, the corporation income tax would be regressive or proportional. Some studies of tax incidence hedge their bets by assuming that half the corporation income tax is borne by owners of capital and the other half is passed on either to consumers as higher prices or to labor as lower wages. This makes the corporation income tax neither regressive nor particularly progressive.

REFORMING BUSINESS INCOME TAXATION

Various ways of reforming business income taxation have been proposed. Unlike the case of personal income tax reform, where the distribution of the tax burden is so important, advocates of business income tax reform stress the need to simplify and rationalize the tax code. They argue that a simpler neutral tax system would enhance economic efficiency and reduce costs of compliance and enforcement. We briefly consider some of the major reforms proposed.

---

[14]A. C. Harberger, "The Incidence of the Corporation Income Tax," 1962.

Eliminating Business Tax Expenditures

Tax expenditures for business and investment are estimated to cost the government nearly $200 billion in fiscal year 2000.[15] Such tax breaks, along with an equal amount of direct business subsidies, have been described by Robert Reich, the former Secretary of Labor in the Clinton administration, as "Aid For Dependent Corporations" (AFDC, as in the pre-1996 federal welfare program for single parents) and by others as "Corporate Welfare." The most important of these tax expenditures include the special tax treatment of capital gains, accelerated depreciation, the special tax treatment of the insurance industry, tax breaks for multinational corporations, the deductibility of meals and entertainment expenditures by business, and the Research and Experimentation (R&E) tax credit. In addition, special tax breaks are often given to individual businesses.

Opponents of these tax breaks argue that they are both inefficient and inequitable. They are inefficient because they encourage businesses to allocate investment spending in order to take advantage of lower taxes rather than to maximize profitability. In other words, the tax breaks reduce the METR on some types of investments and raise it on others. They are inequitable because they give some businesses advantages over others and because the ultimate beneficiaries of these tax breaks are likely to be high-income taxpayers who own shares in the companies receiving the tax breaks. The latter, of course, depends on assumptions regarding the incidence of business taxes. Let's briefly describe a few of these tax breaks and proposals to reform them.

ACCELERATED DEPRECIATION.   As we have already learned, accelerated depreciation allows businesses to deduct from taxable income the cost of their machinery, equipment, and buildings faster than the assets actually wear out. This is a tax break because the firms get the deductions sooner than the income the assets generate, and firms prefer to receive deductions sooner rather than later. In addition, when the assets are financed with borrowed funds, the firms can deduct the interest payments they make. Together, greatly accelerated depreciation combined with interest deductions can make the METR on some investments negative—that is, the income from the investment is subsidized rather than taxed.

To completely eliminate the tax expenditure for accelerated depreciation, the tax code would need to be changed so that the amount deducted for tax purposes is equal to the economic depreciation of the asset—that is, the actual loss in the economic value of the asset over the year. Many tax experts believe that such a system would be impractical because it is difficult, and in some cases impossible, to measure economic depreciation for many business assets. Alternatively, the tax code could be changed to eliminate declining-balance depreciation and replace it with straight-line depreciation, and to lengthen the recovery period of long-lived assets like buildings.

TAX BREAKS FOR MULTINATIONAL CORPORATIONS.   U.S.- and foreign-owned multinational corporations are required to pay taxes on business income earned in the United States. Typically, however, foreign-owned corporations doing business

---

[15]Statement of Robert S. McIntyre, Director of Citizens for Tax Justice, before the House Committee on the Budget, June 30, 1999, p. 2.

in the United States pay lower taxes than U.S. companies with similar incomes. This is true because foreign-owned corporations can shift income out of the United States by setting "transfer prices." Transfer prices are prices the company uses internally for materials and parts purchased from the foreign parent and used by the U.S. subsidiary. For instance, a U.S. subsidiary of a Japanese automobile manufacturer may assemble cars in the United States using parts imported from its Japanese parent. By setting high transfer prices for the imported parts, the company reduces the net income of the U.S. subsidiary (because the costs of materials are deducted in calculating the taxable income of the U.S. subsidiary) and increases the net income of the Japanese parent.

U.S. multinational corporations can make similar use of income shifting. For instance, a U.S. computer manufacturer with subsidiary corporations abroad may deduct nearly all of its research and development (R&D) expenditures against U.S. income even though the products developed earn income for its foreign subsidiaries. A few years ago, Intel corporation won a case in tax court that allowed it to treat income from selling U.S.-made computer chips as Japanese income and therefore exempt from U.S. taxes. To make things worse, the same income was considered U.S. income in Japan and was exempted from Japanese taxes. Economists have termed such income "nowhere income."[16]

U.S. multinational corporations also receive the tax advantage of deferral. When the foreign subsidiary of the U.S. parent earns income abroad, the income is not considered as part of U.S. income until and unless the parent receives the income as interest, dividends, or royalties from the subsidiary. By reinvesting the income in the foreign subsidiary, the company can defer U.S. taxes on the income indefinitely.

Curbing multinational tax breaks would require an overhaul of the system that determines the source (country of origin) of business income. One idea for reform is to replace the current separate accounting method of taxing multinational corporations with a unitary approach similar to that used for interstate corporations in the United States. Under the unitary approach, the U.S. income of a multinational corporation would be based on its world income. The fraction of corporate world income apportioned to the United States would depend on the fraction of the company's world sales, assets, and payrolls within in the United States. (For more on the unitary approach, see Chapter 19.) However, business income taxation based on world income is generally opposed by foreign countries, who argue that the unitary approach extends the U.S. tax laws beyond its own borders (called extraterritoriality).

RESEARCH AND DEVELOPMENT TAX BREAKS.   A difficulty in eliminating business tax breaks is determining whether a tax deduction is justified economically. For instance, see the discussion of the deduction for business meals and entertainment expenses in A Case in Point 15.2. Tax expenditures for R&D spending by businesses present another example. R&D expenditures create

---

[16]Statement of Robert S. McIntyre, p. 9.

intangible assets for the firm, such as new products and production methods that earn income for the firm over many years. The business tax system treats R&D investments favorably in two ways. First, expenditures on R&D are expensed (that is, deducted in the year incurred), rather than amortized over the lives of the intangible assets created. Second, businesses receive the and Research and Experimentation (R&E) Tax Credit, equal to 20% of R&D spending in excess of a base amount, which is based on R&D spending relative to sales during the preceding four years.

R&D tax expenditures can be economically justified for some types of basic scientific research because developing new knowledge is a type of public good that benefits third parties. (Alternatively, we can view R&D as an activity that has benefit externalities.) As we learned in Chapters 3 and 4, commercial incentives are not adequate to induce firms to spend the efficient amount on such goods. However, in most cases, R&D expenditures are incurred for developing new products for which commercial incentives are ample. In this case, R&D tax breaks effectively subsidize profitable corporations like Microsoft and its shareholders.

Integration of Corporate Taxes

Another business tax reform, most recently recommended in a U.S. Treasury study, is the elimination of the double taxation of corporate equity income. Recall that corporate equity income is taxed twice under the separate entity approach to corporate taxation: once as corporate business income, and again as personal income when the company makes dividend distributions to shareholders. A lesser degree of double taxation also occurs when corporate earnings are retained, because shareholders must pay capital gains taxes when they sell their shares. The double taxation of corporate equity income distorts various business decisions including whether to incorporate, whether to finance corporate investments with debt or equity, and whether to distribute dividends. Double taxation also discourages investment by increasing the METR on corporate investment income.

Two methods of eliminating double taxation have been proposed. The first method, called **full integration,** would abolish the separate tax on corporation income. Instead, corporate income would be apportioned to the shareholders, as done presently for S corporations. Many tax experts believe this method is impractical for C corporations because their shares are publicly traded and may change hands many times during the tax year.

The second method, called the **imputation method,** provides dividend relief to corporate shareholders. This is the method recommended in the Treasury study and used in Canada and some European countries. The imputation method grants a tax credit to dividend recipients for part or all of the corporation income taxes previously paid on the dividends before distribution. The shareholder grosses up dividends received by the amount of the tax credit and adds the grossed up dividends to personal taxable income. This means that the shareholder's portion of the business income of the corporation is taxed at his or her prevailing marginal tax rate. The shareholder then subtracts the dividend tax credit from the amount of taxes owed. If the shareholder's marginal tax rate happened to be the same as the corporation income tax rate, he or she would owe no net taxes on the dividends received. If the shareholder's marginal tax rate is higher (lower) than the corporate rate, the shareholder pays taxes (receives a refund) on dividends received equal to the difference in the tax rates.

Although the economic case for integration is strong, Congress has not acted on the recommendation. Perhaps this is because the average voter views integration as primarily benefiting high-income taxpayers. For this reason, proponents of integration usually couple their proposal with a call to end the corporate tax breaks discussed above. If corporate tax breaks were eliminated as well as corporate taxes integrated, high-income taxpayers would not benefit as much or at all because the dollar value of revenue lost through corporate tax breaks is about equal to corporate tax revenue actually collected. The combination of integration and abolishing corporate tax breaks would substantially reduce the distortions in the business tax system and improve economic efficiency.

A Cash-Flow Business Tax

Perhaps the most fundamental reform proposed for the corporate tax is to change it to a cash-flow basis. A **cash-flow business tax is** part of the flat tax system proposed by numerous economists and politicians, which is discussed further in Chapter 17. The main advantage of a cash-flow tax is that it would considerably simplify business taxation. With a cash-flow tax, businesses would no longer receive deductions for depreciation (which causes considerable complexity in the tax system) or for interest paid. Rather, they would expense the costs of investments the same way they expense wages, materials costs, and some intangible investments. For instance, a business that spends a million dollars to buy a new machine would deduct its cost in the year it is purchased rather than taking depreciation deductions over a recovery period.

A cash-flow tax would change the base of the business tax from some measure of income to economic profit. Recall that economic profit is equal to business revenue minus all current costs (like wages and materials) and the user cost of capital. The cost of an investment is equal to the present value of the annual user cost of capital for the investment; therefore, expensing investment costs at the time of purchase is equivalent to deducting the user cost of capital for the investment up front.

Some people argue that a cash-flow tax would be a huge tax break for business because expensing is an extreme form of accelerated depreciation. However, unlike the case of accelerated depreciation, businesses would not receive deductions for interest payments under a cash-flow tax. For many businesses, the total deduction they make for accelerated depreciation and interest payments is greater than their investment spending, so they would pay more tax under a cash-flow tax than under the present system. In part this is because switching to a cash-flow tax would deprive businesses of tax deductions for investments they have already made. Switching to a cash-flow tax would therefore constitute a one-time levy on "old" capital, and business is likely to oppose the change on the grounds that it is inequitable.

A more fundamental objection to the cash-flow business tax concerns its relationship to the personal tax system. Because a cash-flow business tax is levied on eco-

15.2 Business Meals and Entertainment: Are They an Expense or a Tax Break?

In 1978, President Jimmy Carter described the U.S. income tax as a "disgrace to the human race." He was incensed by the fact that business executives could deduct their "three-martini lunches" as a business expense, while employees could not deduct the cost of their bologna sandwiches. He could have made an even stronger case. Businesses have taken deductions for yachts, jet airplanes for corporate travel, meals and alcohol in fine restaurants, hunting lodges, luxury skyboxes at sports events, swimming pools, golf tournaments, tennis lessons, and rock concerts. The management and employees no doubt have a great time at these events, but the taxpayers foot part of the bill. The money spent on meals and entertainment is deducted from business taxable income and reduces the taxes paid.

In 1987, deductions for meals and entertainment were limited to 80% of outlays, and in 1993 the fraction was reduced to 50%. Many economists question whether these expenditures should be deducted at all, because they are untaxed consumption for those who enjoy them. Business argues that such expenses are part of doing business, such as attracting clients or maintaining employee morale, and should be deducted. Who is right?

Critically analyze the following:

- It is reasonable that wining and dining clients will make them favorably inclined, and employees are surely happy to enjoy an exercise facility. You could also make clients favorably inclined with cash bribes ("kickbacks") and employees happy with cash bonuses. Such cash outlays are clearly deductible under the tax code providing they are legal. Why should it be any different with benefits provided in kind?

- Suppose these benefits to clients and employees could be valued and taxed as part of their income. Would it then be appropriate to allow business to deduct such costs?

- If these benefits cannot be taxed income to the clients and employees, is it possible to tax them equivalently by not allowing firms to deduct such costs from taxable business income? Explain using the tax equivalence theorem discussed in Chapter 10.

nomic profit, rather than business income, most experts believe it is more appropriate in a tax system based on consumption rather than income. In fact, the flat tax proponents who argue for a cash-flow business tax also propose changing the tax base of the federal tax system from income to consumption. If the government chooses to tax income at the personal level, it is necessary to tax income, not just economic profit, at the corporate level as well. Otherwise, people could avoid income taxes by arranging for personal income to be received and reinvested by personal corporations. The issue of taxing consumption versus income is discussed in Chapter 17.

CONCLUSION AND SUMMARY

The taxation of business income is one of the most complicated parts of the income tax system. For this reason, and because the effects on people are indirect, business income taxation is also one of the least understood parts. In this chapter we have described how business income is taxed and have analyzed how these taxes alter firms' decisions and, through these effects, how they affect the economy.

- The government levies several types of taxes on businesses, the most important being taxes on business income. Business income is taxed as personal income for unincorporated businesses and S corporations, but it is taxed separately under the corporation income tax for C corporations. C corporations include all large businesses whose shares are traded on public stock exchanges.

- Taxes are levied on business income because of administrative convenience (businesses are good "tax handles"), to prevent personal income tax avoidance, and to provide an instrument with which the government can affect the production decisions of firms.

- Business income is measured net of the costs of doing business. Economic business income is equal to gross business receipts less the economic (opportunity) cost of all business inputs except the implicit interest cost of equity capital. Economic depreciation is equal to the actual decrease in the value of business capital assets over the tax year.

- Net business income for tax purposes is equal to gross business receipts less the costs of doing business. The costs of doing business include the costs of labor and materials, operating costs such as advertising and lease payments, interest paid on business debt, all payroll taxes, state and local business income and property taxes, and depreciation of capital assets according to the MACRS schedules.

- A firm receives accelerated depreciation if it can take depreciation deductions for tax purposes sooner than the asset actually wears out. The value to the firm of depreciation tax deductions is greater the faster depreciation is accelerated.

- The business and financial incomes of C corporations are taxed separately under the corporation income tax system. Under this separate entity approach, equity income is double taxed because it is taxed as corporate income and again as personal income when the shareholders receive the income in the form of dividends or realized capital gains.

- Business income taxes affect decisions made by firms in several ways. In particular, firms are encouraged to use to debt to finance investments, to retain rather than distribute dividends, and to favor investments that receive accelerated depreciation. The incentive effect of business taxes on the firm's investment decisions can be measured using the Marginal Effective Tax Rate (METR).

- Taxes on business income are ultimately borne by people in the form of higher prices for goods and services or as lower factor rewards received. Most studies indicate that the incidence of the corporation income tax is on the owners of capital in general. Since capital ownership is concentrated in the hands of high-income taxpayers, the corporation income tax is considered a progressive tax.

- Current issues in business tax policy include eliminating business tax expenditures, integrating corporation and personal income taxes, and simplifying the business tax rules.

QUESTIONS FOR DISCUSSION AND REVIEW

1. Explain why it is more desirable to tax the following economic activities at the level of the business rather than the household.

   a. Profits used to purchase new equipment for the business.

   b. Goods and services exported to other countries.

   c. Electricity that creates air pollution when produced using coal-fueled generators.

2. What is the main difference between economic business income and business income as it is currently defined for tax purposes? Why would it be more difficult to administer a tax on economic business income than business income as it is currently defined?

3. Businesses can expense costs they incur for advertising. Do you think advertising is more like a current input (e.g., labor) or a capital input (e.g., equipment)? If advertising is a capital input, how does the business tax system affect a firm's decision to spend on advertising rather than purchase machinery?

4. Shortening the period of time over which the firm recovers the cost of a capital good accelerates depreciation for tax purposes. Do you think the advantage to the firm is greater or the same if the recovery period is shortened for an asset that is depreciated according to the straight-line method as compared with an asset that is depreciated according to the declining-balance method?

5. For investment expenditures other than buildings and structures, firms can choose between the straight-line or declining-balance method. We often observe firms starting with the declining-balance method and then switching to straight-line when the asset gets older, but not vice versa. Why?

6. Purchases of land cannot be depreciated, but improvements to land can. Suppose a business is choosing between two locations to construct a factory. The first location is level and the other is sloping and would have to be graded before building can commence. Once graded, the two parcels of land would have equal value. How would the business tax system affect the firm's choice (as compared with the case where there are no taxes)?

7. Suppose a C corporation has gross receipts of $800,000; pays wages and other employment costs of $500,000; spends $100,000 on new investment; distributes $177,750 in dividends; and gets an MACRS deduction of $200,000 on its existing capital. Assume that the firm has $2 million in existing capital, all financed with equity; that the economic depreciation of the capital is $50,000; and that shareholders could have earned an interest rate of 5% on the funds invested in the firm. What is the firm's taxable business income, its income in principle, and its economic profit?

8. Corporations engaged in related activities sometimes form partnerships (or syndicates) to undertake investments beneficial to both. To better align their incentives and prevent one firm from cheating on the other, they often swap some shares. Alternatively, one firm may acquire the other as a subsidiary. Which is most advantageous under the corporation income tax system? Why?

9. What is the difference between economic profit and economic business income? In this chapter we showed that a tax on economic profit is neutral—that is, it does not affect business decisions. What about a tax on economic business income?

10. Suppose the corporation income tax is abolished and the entire business income

of corporations is apportioned to shareholders and taxed as personal income (i.e., full integration). How would this affect the following.

a. The ratio of debt to equity chosen by corporations

b. The fraction of corporate earnings corporations distribute to shareholders.

11. Before 1986, firms received an investment tax credit of 10% for investment expenditures on equipment. For instance, a firm that spent a million dollars on new equipment would get a tax credit of $100,000. How would this affect the user cost of capital in equipment? How would it affect the marginal effective tax rate on business income from the equipment?

12. Internet Exercise. Download the 1996 Corporation Income Tax Statistics from the IRS site at http://ftp.fedworld.gov/pub/irs-soi/96coalcr.exe. This is a self-extracting file that provides corporation income tax statistics in both pdf (Acrobat) and Excel spreadsheet formats. In spreadsheet Table 3 (Table 2 in the text document), the data for corporations with positive net income show the total receipts, total deductions, net income, corporation income taxes paid, and other information for corporations classified by asset size. For all corporations, what percentage of gross receipts is deducted in calculating net income? What fraction of net income is paid in corporation income tax? How do these percentages vary between the smallest firms (those with no assets) and the largest (assets over $250 million)? What fraction of total deductions consists of depreciation? Interest paid? How does this differ between the smallest and largest corporations?

13. Internet Exercise. Opposition to "Corporate Welfare" (subsidies and tax breaks for corporations) is a topic that unites liberals, libertarian conservatives, and environmentalists. Three Internet sites that contain information, links, and political rhetoric on corporate welfare are taxpolicy.com (http://www.taxpolicy.com/cw/), porkwatch. com (http://www.porkwatch. com/), and the Corporate Welfare Information Center (http://www.corporations.org/welfare/index.html). Browse these sites and find information on the dollar values of some corporate tax breaks. What are the largest forms of corporate welfare in the tax system according to these sites? Corporate welfare in the form of direct subsidies seems to generate more outrage on these sites than tax breaks. Why do you think that is the case?

SELECTED REFERENCES

The double taxation of shareholders' equity income under the corporation income tax is explained in Charles E. McLure, Jr., *Must Income Be Taxed Twice?* 1979.

A discussion of how to measure the marginal effective tax rate (METR) is found in Don Fullerton, "Which Effective Tax Rate?" 1984. Recent estimates of METRs in the United States by Don Fullerton and Marios Karayannis are presented in Dale W. Jorgenson and Ralph Landau, eds., *Tax Reform and the Cost of Capital*, 1993, Chapter 10.

Recent work on the effect of taxes on business investment include Alan J. Auerbach and Kevin A. Hassett, "Tax Policy and Business Fixed Investment" 1992; and Jason G. Cummins, Kevin A. Hassett, and R. Glenn Hubbard, "Have Tax Reforms Affected Investment?" 1995.

A book that comprehensively describes how business taxes affect capital income is Jane G. Gravelle, *The Economic Effects of Taxing Capital Income*, 1994.

USEFUL INTERNET SITES

Numerous sites are devoted to the problem of corporate welfare. Links to these sites are available at the Corporate Welfare Information Center at http://www.corporations.org/welfare/.

Professor David Bradford of Princeton University provides a clear explanation of cash-flow taxation at http://www.tax.org/readings/Tn-21.htm.

16 Budget Surpluses and Deficits

A question circulating in Washington, D.C., these days is, "What is a bigger problem than a $100 billion deficit?" The answer is, "A $100 billion surplus." The point of the joke is that the current surplus on the federal budget and the projected surpluses, expected to amount to nearly $3000 billion over the next ten years, seem to have provoked as much political controversy as the persistent deficits that preceded. Rather than arguing about what to do *about* the deficit, politicians are now arguing about what to do *with* the surplus. Some believe that the surplus should be used to finance new spending programs or enhance existing ones, especially education and defense. Others argue that part of the surplus should be "given back to the taxpayers" as a tax cut. Nearly all argue that most of the surplus should be used to "save" Social Security, and Congress has overwhelmingly passed a bill to place the surpluses on the Social Security trust fund in a "lockbox" so they cannot be used to finance non–Social Security deficits. To make matters more confusing, some observers believe that, outside the Social Security trust fund, projected surpluses are hypothetical because they are based on planned cuts in existing programs that are unrealistic. Thus, arguing about what to do with the non–Social Security surplus is futile because it is not likely to materialize.

As this controversy shows, most people find issues concerning government budget surpluses and deficits bewildering. Ordinary taxpayers do not understand how the surplus or deficit affects them personally, anyway. In this chapter, we develop a framework that allows us to examine the economic implications of government policies regarding surpluses and deficits so that we can better evaluate the alternatives before us. The main idea that we will develop is that, given the path of government spending over time, policies concerning surpluses and deficits are policies about the *timing* of the taxes needed to finance the spending. A deficit is a way of delaying the current taxes, whereas a surplus is a way of lowering future taxes or forestalling higher taxes in the future.

SURPLUSES, DEFICITS, AND THE NATIONAL DEBT

We begin by reviewing terminology and facts. As we learned in Chapter 1, the budget balance (a surplus or deficit) is the difference between the government's annual revenue (which is mostly from taxes) and its annual outlays, which are equal to its program spending plus interest payments on the national debt. When revenue is equal to outlays, the budget balance is zero and the government has a **balanced budget**—a state of affairs that many people think is desirable. If outlays exceed revenue, the government has a **budget deficit** and must borrow an equal amount finance its outlays. If revenue exceeds outlays, the government has a **budget surplus** and can use the excess revenue to retire an equal amount of the outstanding national debt.

The **national debt** is the accumulated borrowing from all past deficits minus debt that has been retired with past surpluses. The national debt is a *stock* variable that is measured at a point of time, usually the end of the year, whereas the budget balance is a *flow* variable and is measured over an interval of time, conventionally a year. The budget balance is approximately equal to the change in the government debt over the year. Although this is simple enough, several subtle but important issues of measurement remain.

Measuring the Surplus or Deficit

The two most common measures of the budget balance are the **unified budget balance** reported in the U.S. federal budget and the **NIPA budget balance** reported by the Bureau of Economic Analysis in the National Income and Product Accounts (NIPA). These measures differ in the details of their calculation but are roughly equal in magnitude, at least in recent years. The unified balance is measured over the federal government's fiscal year (running from the beginning of October in the previous calendar year to the end of September in the current year). In contrast, the NIPA balance is measured over the calendar year. Another difference is that the unified budget balance is measured on a cash basis whereby revenues and outlays are recorded at the time the cash is received or disbursed. The NIPA balance, on the other hand, is measured on an accrual basis whereby revenues and outlays are recorded when they are earned or incurred whether or not cash changes hands at the time. Economists believe the accrual-based NIPA budget balance better measures the impact of the surplus or deficit on the economy.

The unified balance aggregates all budgetary receipts and outlays of the federal government, including the trust funds and federal government agencies. Revenue in the trust funds is earmarked for a specific purpose, like Social Security, and is technically separated from revenue in the general fund, which is used for the general purposes of the government. The unified surplus is approximately the amount by which the government can retire national debt held by private individuals (or the additional amount it must borrow from private individuals in the case of a unified budget deficit).[1] The unified balance is divided into the **on-budget balance** (sometimes called the non–Social Security balance), which excludes the trust funds and some government entities, like the post office, and the **off-budget balance,** which is all the rest. In the fiscal year 1999, the projected on-budget deficit for the federal

---

[1]The amount of debt retired also depends on changes in nonborrowed financing, mainly changes in cash reserves and direct loans to firms and individuals. For example, in fiscal year 1999, the unified surplus was about $80 billion but only $50 billion was used to retire the national debt. The remaining $30 billion was used to make government loans.

government is $4 billion, whereas the projected unified budget shows a surplus of $121 billion. The difference between the on-budget deficit and the unified budget surplus is the reason many people question whether the federal government really has a surplus to spend or use for tax cuts. The unified budget is in surplus because of a $121 billion surplus on the Social Security trust fund, which reflects an excess of Social Security tax revenue over outlays on Social Security benefits during fiscal year 1999. As explained in Chapter 9, the surplus on the Social Security trust fund is for the purpose of accumulating a reserve against the anticipated increase in Social Security outlays when the baby-boom generation retires. At present, the Social Security trust fund must be invested in Treasury bonds, so the off-budget surplus is used to purchase government bonds directly from the Treasury or from private investors.

Figure 16.1 shows the average unified, on-budget, and off-budget deficit (a negative value indicates a surplus) as a percentage of GDP (five-year averages) from 1960 to 1999. Several things should be noted. First, around 1970, the federal government began running significant deficits, reaching nearly 5% of GDP in the mid-1980s. Second, until the mid-1980s, the unified and on-budget balances were roughly equal, because the Social Security balance was small. Third, in the mid-1980s, as a result of Social Security reforms, the off-budget surplus began to rise, although the unified budget remained in deficit because of large on-budget deficits. In effect, the Treasury financed a large part of the unified deficit by selling bonds to the Social Security trust fund. Finally, in the mid-1990s, the on-budget deficit fell while the off-budget surplus continued to rise. As a result, the unified budget

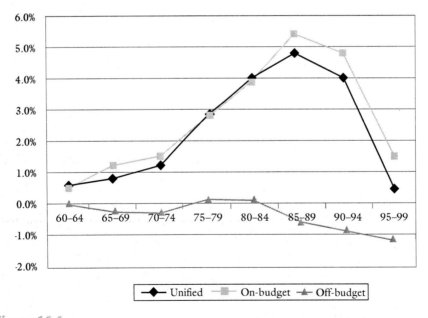

Figure 16.1

Federal Deficit as a Percentage of GDP (Five-Year Averages): 1960–1999

Between 1970 and 1990, the on-budget and unified federal deficits rose steadily as a percentage of GDP. After 1990, they fell sharply.

reached a surplus position by fiscal year 1998 for the first time in 28 years. When the unified budget is in surplus, the Social Security trust fund purchases bonds back from private investors, reducing the national debt, rather than purchasing new issues issued by the Treasury. Both the on-budget and off-budget surpluses are expected to continue for the next ten years, so by 2009 the CBO projects the unified budget surplus at over 3% of GDP. From 1999 to 2009, the total unified budget surplus is projected to equal $3000 billion, consisting of $2000 billion in off-budget (Social Security) surpluses and $1000 billion in on-budget surpluses.

Adjusting for Confounding Factors

The size of the surplus or deficit depends on the state of the economy, particularly the level of economic activity and the rate of inflation. Because the amount of taxes the government collects depends on income and consumption levels, revenue rises when the economy is buoyant and falls or grows more slowly when the economy is stagnant. Similarly, the amount the government must spend on some programs like welfare and unemployment insurance changes with the state of the economy, rising during recessions and falling during booms. In addition, inflation affects the amount of taxes the government collects, and the amount of many government transfer payments, like Social Security benefits, that are indexed to the rate of inflation. Inflation also increases interest rates, raising the interest cost of the national debt.

Economists sometimes adjust the measured budget balance to reflect these confounding factors. The first type of adjustment calculates the budget balance that would occur when the economy is operating at "full" employment. Because tax receipts are higher and outlays are lower when the economy is operating at or above full employment, the budget balance is increased and the government has a surplus or a smaller deficit. Similarly, during a recession, the deficit increases. To control for fluctuations in the budget balance over the business cycle, economists calculate the **standardized-employment budget balance** (or simply, the standardized budget balance). This is the hypothetical level of the budget balance that would occur when the economy is operating at its "potential" or full-employment capacity.

To adjust for the phase of the business cycle and determine potential GDP, analysts use the **nonaccelerating inflation rate of unemployment** (**NAIRU**). NAIRU is the level of unemployment at which inflationary pressures are kept in check. If the actual unemployment rate is consistently less than NAIRU, economists believe inflation rates must steadily rise. Government revenues and outlays are then calculated for potential GDP to obtain the standardized budget balance. When the actual unemployment rate is greater than NAIRU, the standardized deficit is less than the actual deficit (or the standardized surplus is greater than the actual surplus). For example, during a recession the actual budget is typically in deficit because tax revenue is lower, whereas the standardized budget could be balanced or in surplus.

The main uncertainty in calculating the standardized budget balance is finding NAIRU. At present, the federal government assumes that NAIRU is around 5.3%, although some economists believe it is lower than that. In 1999, the unemployment rate is about 4.3%, which is a full percentage point less than NAIRU. This means that the economy is operating above its normal level, so the actual surplus is greater than the standardized surplus. According to the Congressional Budget Office, the standardized budget surplus in 1999 is just $12 billion, whereas the projected actual unified budget surplus is $120 billion. In other words, most of the 1999 surplus is temporary and will disappear when the economy returns to a normal level of economic activity as defined by NAIRU.

Figure 16.2 shows the unified and standardized budget deficit as a percentage of GDP from 1960 to 1999. Note that the actual deficit fluctuates more than the standardized deficit because of the business cycle. When the economy enters a recession, as it did in 1975, 1981, and 1991, the actual deficit increases rapidly and is greater than the standardized deficit. In fact, the actual deficit remains greater than the standardized deficit after the recession is over, because the economy has to catch up to where it would have been had the recession not occurred. Later in this chapter, we will discuss how the cyclical behavior of the actual deficit performs as a built-in stabilizer for the economy.

The second type of adjustment takes into account the effect of inflation on the net interest paid on the national debt. Inflation increases interest rates, raising the cost of servicing the national debt. However, the inflation premium component of the interest rate is not really a cost to the government because inflation also reduces the size of the national debt measured in constant dollars. For example, if inflation

Figure 16.2

Actual and Standardized Federal Deficit (% of GPD) 1960–1999
The actual budget deficit fluctuates more over time than the standardized-employment budget deficit. The actual exceeds the standardized during recessions (such as 1982) and is less than the standardized during booms (such as the late 1990's).

were to increase by five percentage points, interest rates would rise by five percentage points to compensate lenders for the reduction in the purchasing power of the money they have lent. Borrowers, like the government, may pay a higher interest rate because of inflation, but are able to pay back their debt in dollars of reduced purchasing power. The inflation adjustment subtracts from the interest costs of the government an amount equal to the inflation rate times the outstanding government debt to reflect this fact. Alternatively, we can divide the nominal dollar amount of the national debt by a cost of living index to obtain the national debt measured in constant dollars. The annual change in the constant dollar value of the national debt is equal to the **real budget balance.** At the current low inflation rates, the real budget balance is only about $7 billion greater than the measured budget balance. When the budget balance is adjusted for both the level of economic activity and the inflation rate, we obtain the **structural budget balance.** The structural budget balance is an estimate of what the budget balance would be, given the existing programs and tax structure, if the economy operates at its normal (NAIRU) level of economic activity without inflation. The structural budget surplus is projected as about $20 billion in 1999.

The Causes of Past Deficits and Future Surpluses

People are often divided in their opinions about why the federal government had nearly three decades of budget deficits and about whether the current surplus can be expected to persist over the next 10 or 15 years, as projected by the Congressional Budget Office. Some argue that the cause of past deficits is excessive government spending, while others believe that the deficits were caused by massive (and, some say, irresponsible) tax cuts during the 1980s. Similarly, some people argue that the projected future surpluses are based on unrealistic assumptions about future government spending and revenue levels.

Figure 16.3 casts some light on this question by plotting federal government outlays, revenue, and their difference, which is equal to the deficit, from 1960 to 1999. All figures are five-year averages expressed as a percentage of GDP. As we see from the figure, the deficit rose from a small surplus in 1960–1964 to a deficit of around 4% of GDP by 1980–1984. This deficit persisted until after 1995, when it began its highly publicized fall. The figure shows that most of the change in the deficit before 1995 was the result of changes in the level of government outlays, not tax revenue. As a percentage of GDP, revenue actually rose from 18.5% in 1960–1964 to just over 20% in 1990–1994, but government outlays rose more from 18.8% of GDP to 23.3% over the same period. In other words, it was the increase in government spending, not reduced taxes, that accounts for the increase in the deficit. Similarly, we see that the decline in the deficit and the emergence of a budget surplus in the second half of the 1990s is mainly due to a sharp rise in federal revenue as a percentage of GDP, although government spending decreased somewhat as well. The large surpluses projected for the next decade by the CBO assume that government spending as a percentage of GDP will continue to fall, from 19.7% in 1998 to 17.1% by 2008, while tax revenues will remain constant at about 20.1% of GDP.[2]

---

[2]Congressional Budget Office, "The Economic Outlook and Budget Outlook: An Update," July 1999.

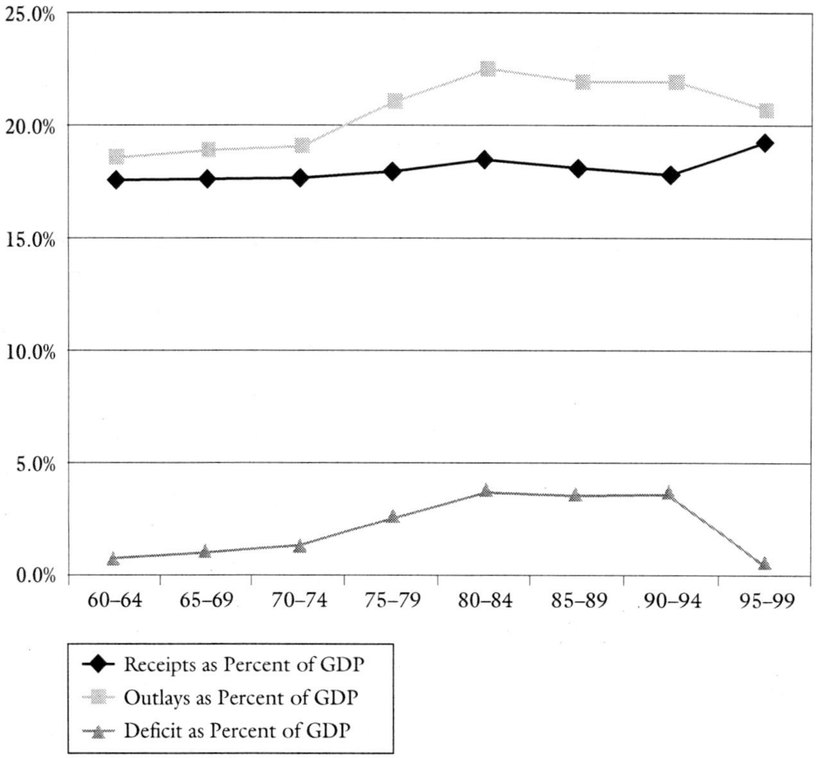

Figure 16.3

Contribution of Receipts and Outlays to the Federal Deficit: Five-Year Averages, 1960–1999

The increase in the deficit as a percentage of GDP was mainly due to a rise in outlays. The decrease in the deficit in the 1990s was due to a rise in tax receipts and a fall in outlays relative to GDP.

Receipts as Percent of GDP
Outlays as Percent of GDP
Deficit as Percent of GDP

Measuring the National Debt

Notwithstanding the much-touted surpluses, the federal government has a large national debt. Like the surplus, it can be measured in several ways. The *gross* national debt is the value of all outstanding government bonds of any maturity held by private investors or in government accounts. At the end of fiscal year 1999, the gross national debt amounts to $5615 billion dollars, or approximately $20,600 per person residing in the United States. Although many people find this figure alarming, several points help put this number in perspective. First of all, the federal government holds part of the gross national debt itself, mostly in the Social Security trust fund and in the holdings of the Federal Reserve System (FRS). The *net* national debt held by the public and state and local governments was $3670 billion at the end of fiscal year 1999, or $13,450 per person.[3] Second, although the dollar amount of national debt has grown rapidly over the past 25 years, we must remem-

---

[3]This figure includes the debt held by the Federal Reserve System, which held $458 billion of the national debt in 1998. The FRS holdings are included because, technically, the FRS is in the private sector. However, it could be argued that, as a practical matter, the FRS is part of the federal government and its holdings should be excluded from the net debt. However, the FRS issues cash and bank reserves against its holdings of government bonds, and these would then have to be included as a cash (non-interest-bearing) liability of the government.

ber that the purchasing power of the dollar has shrunk because of inflation. Hence, when comparing the national debt in 1970, for instance, with the national debt in 1999, we should adjust for changes in the cost of living and express the national debt in dollars of constant purchasing power. For example, although the net national debt in 1999 is 13 times as great as in 1970 in nominal dollar terms, it is 3.3 times greater when measured in dollars of constant purchasing power.

The third consideration that puts the size of the national debt in perspective is the size of the economy. Although the net national debt is much larger in 1999 than in 1970, the Gross Domestic Product (GDP) of the economy is also much larger. Just as a household with higher income can hold a larger debt without concern, so can a larger economy. A simple way of accounting for the changes in both the purchasing power of money and the size of the economy over time is to express the national debt as a percentage of GDP. Figure 16.4 shows how the net national debt as a percentage of GDP has changed since 1946. This figure shows why the problem of the national debt is not as bad as the dollar figure suggests, but also why some people are concerned about it nonetheless. In 1946, right after World War II, the ratio of the net national debt to GDP was at a historic high of over 100%. For the next three decades, the ratio declined steadily, reaching a low point of 25% in the middle of the 1970s. Beginning in the 1980s, the debt ratio began to rise, reaching 50.2% in 1993 and igniting new concern over the problem of the national debt. Recently, because of reduced levels of the unified budget deficit and, finally, a budget surplus, the ratio has leveled off and is now actually declining. Indeed, if the surplus projections of the CBO are correct, the net national debt will decline to just 6.4% of GDP, lower than any level recorded in the twentieth

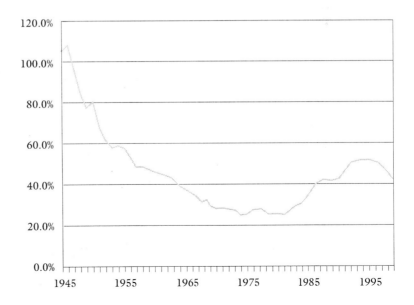

Figure 16.4

Federal Debt Privately Held as Percent of GDP: 1945–1999

As a percentage of GDP, the national debt declined steadily from World War II to 1975. After 1975, the ratio rose, but it began declining again in 1995.

century. In fact, longer-term projections by the Congressional Budget Office predict that the entire net national debt will be retired by the year 2012.

It should be noted that the ratio of the net national debt to GDP could decline even if the projected surpluses are not realized. For instance, if the unified budget is balanced rather than in surplus over the future, the debt ratio would decline nonetheless because GDP will grow while the national debt remains constant. Economists describe a situation in which the debt ratio declines because the national debt grows more slowly than the size of the economy as "growing out of the national debt."

Is the National Debt a Burden?

People don't know whether to be worried about the national debt or not because they hear conflicting different accounts about how serious a problem it is. The first account, an alarming view, claims that the national debt poses a serious burden and danger to the economic health of the nation. According to this view, a "day of reckoning" will arrive and the country will bear the cost of its past extravagance. A second view, far more sanguine, suggests that the national debt, at least at current levels, is not a burden at all, because "we owe it to ourselves."

VIEW 1: THE "DAY OF RECKONING." People who believe that the national debt poses a burden often draw an analogy between excessive government borrowing and a household that regularly spends more than it earns. A spendthrift household faces a bleak future of low consumption because it must work simply to repay its earlier debts plus interest. In the worst case, it is unable to pay its debts and is forced into bankruptcy.

Although the government is not a household, excessive government borrowing leads to a similarly painful future, according to the "day of reckoning" argument. If government debt is high relative to GDP, higher taxes are needed to service (pay interest on) the debt. Alternatively, government must cut spending on programs. In this way, the burden of current government spending may be shifted to future, as yet unborn, generations. Current generations enjoy current government programs without paying for their full cost, and future generations bear part of the burden by paying taxes on a larger government debt.

In addition, increased borrowing by the government raises market interest rates and makes private investments less profitable. As a result, the stock of government debt crowds out the ownership of productive capital in private wealth portfolios, like stocks and corporate bonds. With less capital, the economy is less productive. In a worst-case scenario, the government debt becomes so large that people would no longer voluntarily buy government bonds, because they are too risky. The government must then resort to printing money to finance its deficits, creating runaway inflation. Alternatively, the government must force people to buy government bonds, as in Stalinist Russia, when workers were paid with government bonds that could not be redeemed and were almost worthless, except as wallpaper.

VIEW 2: "WE OWE IT TO OURSELVES." A far more sanguine view is that government debt is not a burden, because the debt is owed by the population to itself. According to this view, the national debt cancels out for the economy as a whole. Although *we the people* as taxpayers are liable for the national debt, *we the people* as wealth holders own the bonds as an asset. Taking the economy as a whole, the national debt washes out because it is owed from one of our collective pockets to another. The taxes the government collects to pay interest on the debt are, in turn, received by the taxpayers as bondholders.

One problem with this view is that the national debt is not held entirely by American citizens, but is also held by foreigners. In fact, about 37% of the net national debt is held by foreigners. Thus, at the very least, this optimistic view should be modified to "we owe 63% of the national debt to ourselves."

Even then, we must be careful how we interpret the meaning of "we owe it to ourselves." Provided that we define *we* broadly enough, and ignore foreign-held debt, it is indeed true that government debt is both an asset and liability to the country as a whole. But the people who own the government bonds and receive the interest receipts are not necessarily the same people who pay the taxes. Perhaps the most important reason the *we* on the taxpayer side is different from the *we* on the bond-holder side is that the taxpayers include the future generations who must pay interest on the government debt long after the current generation of bondholders is gone. In the meantime, current generations are able to consume more and leave future generations with the bill. It is true, of course, that the future generations will also hold the bonds, but the difference is how they obtain them. If future generations purchase the bonds from the older generations who consume the proceeds, they buy the bonds but inherit the obligation to pay the interest on them. In this way, the burden of current government spending is passed on to future generations.

THE THEORY OF BUDGET SURPLUSES AND DEFICITS

Policy makers can do three things with the budget surpluses projected over the next ten years: increase government spending, reduce taxes, or use the surpluses to pay down the national debt. While taxpayers can easily see the benefits of enhanced government programs or reduced taxes, it less clear how they gain from a reduced national debt. Indeed, some people think it is immoral for the government to use the surplus to retire debt when so many can benefit from the other uses. For the same reasons, people oppose increases in taxes or reductions in government programs when the government has a budget deficit. To a large extent, however, this view is based on a fallacy. The fallacy is that the benefits of the surplus are somehow lost if it is used to pay down the debt. Similarly, it is thought that the pain of deficit reduction can be avoided by simply continuing to borrow.

In this section, we develop the idea that surpluses and deficits do not prevent people from enjoying benefits of a surplus or bearing the costs of reducing a deficit; they simply defer them to later years. Just as a household can consume more in the future by paying off its debts in the present, taxpayers can enjoy reduced taxes or avoid higher taxes in the future by using the surplus to retire the national debt in the present. In other words, given the levels of government spending, surpluses and deficits simply change the *timing* of tax payments. To understand this, we need to consider the government's budget constraint.

16.1   Do We Need a Balanced Budget Amendment?

Many states are required to balance their budgets according to their constitutions. Some politicians believe that the federal government should also be required to balance its budget, and they have proposed amendments to the U.S. Constitution to that effect. In the last decade, two such proposals were passed by the House of Representatives but failed narrowly in the Senate, where they require a 60% majority. (Even if passed by the Congress, a Constitutional amendment would require two-thirds of the states to ratify it.) Proponents have vowed to try again, although the impetus for such an amendment has been reduced by the fact that the federal government now has a surplus.

The main argument for a balanced budget amendment is to protect future generations from burdens imposed by selfish current generations that demand more government spending than they are willing to finance with current taxes. According to this view, the political process is responsive mainly to the wishes of current voters and ignores the interests of future generations, who get short shrift from such budget policy. Most economists find little merit in a balanced budget amendment. They argue that it would unduly hamstring the government during a recession, when a deficit can act as a built-in stabilizer. However, the nearly three decades of sizable fed-

eral deficits from 1970 to 1998 convinced some people that the government is not just using deficits as a temporary stabilizing tool, but as a way of avoiding the need to adjust spending or tax rates. This view is supported by generational accounting estimates that show the average tax rate on future generations will be significantly higher than that on current generations.

Critically analyze the merits of a balanced budget amendment by answering the following:

- The deficit is measured over an interval of time, conventionally a year, but it could be measured over a shorter interval like a quarter, or a longer interval like a biennium (two years). If the budget is to be balanced, do you think it should be balanced every year or over a shorter or longer interval? Why?

- We saw that there are many measures of the budget balance. Which measure do you think should be used—the on-budget balance, the unified balance, or some other measure? Why?

- If a balanced budget amendment restricted the government to a unified balanced budget, what would happen to the net debt to GDP ratio over the future? What if the amendment required the on-budget measure to balance?

The Government's Intertemporal Budget Constraint

People do not always realize that the government must obey budget constraints over time, just like a household. Suffice it to say that the government's budget constraints are considerably less binding than those of any household because the government has an enormous capacity to borrow. However, as we will see below, that capacity does have limits.

The first constraint is more of an accounting identity than a budget constraint, although it is usually called the government's *annual budget constraint*. Let G_t denote government spending on programs in year t, T_t government tax revenue collected in year t, B_t the stock of government debt held by private investors at the beginning of year t, and i the interest rate on government debt. For simplicity, we assume that the interest rate on government debt is the same from year to year, so i does not have a time subscript. The government's annual budget constraint for the current year (assume that $t = 0$ denotes the current year) is equal to

$$B_1 - B_0 \equiv G_0 + i \cdot B_0 - T_0.$$

This equation states that outstanding stock of government debt at the beginning of next year (B_1) minus the stock of debt at the beginning of the current year (B_0) is equal to government program spending in the current year (G_0), plus the interest the government must pay on its debt (iB_0), minus the taxes it collects during the year (T_0). If $B_1 - B_0$ is negative, the government has a surplus; that is, it collects more in taxes than it spends.

This is an annual budget constraint, and each year the government satisfies a similar constraint. For instance, next year ($t = 1$) the government must satisfy $B_2 - B_1 \equiv G_1 + i \cdot B_1 - T_1$, and so on for every year indefinitely. We can solve the annual budget constraint in year 0 for B_1 and substitute it in the budget constraint for year 1 and continue this for all years in the indefinite future. When we are finished, we can rearrange our terms to obtain the government's intertemporal budget constraint. In particular,

$$T_0 + \frac{T_1}{(1+i)} + \frac{T_2}{(1+i)^2} + \frac{T_3}{(1+i)^3} + \dots$$

$$= B_0 + G_0 + \frac{G_1}{(1+i)} + \frac{G_2}{(1+i)^2} + \frac{G_3}{(1+i)^3} +$$

The three dots indicate that the sums go on in similar progression forever. The left-hand side of this equation is equal to current taxes collected by the government plus the present value of all the taxes the government will ever collect in the future. The right-hand side is current government debt and current program spending plus the present value of government program spending (not spending on interest payments) in all future years.

The government's intertemporal budget constraint is similar to the intertemporal budget constraint faced by the individual household. A household must earn enough in the present and the future to pay for its present and future consumption spending as well as repay with interest any loans it takes out. That is, its current after-tax income plus the discounted after-tax incomes it receives in the future must be enough to repay its current debt and cover the sum of its current spending and the discounted value of future spending. The difference between the government's intertemporal budget constraint and that of a household is simply that the government is perpetual and lives forever, so the sums have an infinite number of terms. The household is mortal and its future is limited in duration. Also, of course, the government may borrow on different terms (lower interest rates, no borrowing constraints, etc.) from most households.

To see the implications of the government's budget constraint, assume that program spending is fixed in every year and that the government balances its budget every year after the current one. That is, $T_t = \bar{G}_t + i \cdot B_t$ for $t = 1,2,3,\dots$. A bar over a variable indicates that it is fixed in value. Suppose now that the government collects more tax revenue in the present than it needs to finance its current outlays and uses the excess to reduce the national debt. That is, $T_0 > \bar{G}_0 + i \cdot B_0$, so by the government's annual budget constraint, $B_1 - B_0 < 0$. In this case, the government begins its next fiscal year with a smaller debt, so the amount of interest it must pay to service the debt is smaller. Given its program spending, the government can reduce taxes next year and every year thereafter. If the government also runs a surplus next year, instead of reducing taxes, the level of debt and the amount of interest that must be paid are reduced still further in subsequent years.

Similarly, if the government has a deficit and finances part of its outlays by borrowing, rather than taxes, the national debt increases. In future years, the government must make higher interest payments to service the larger national debt, which, given program spending, requires higher future taxes. Thus, surplus and deficit policy is really a choice about tax policy. Just as the government can choose to tax some goods more heavily than others, it can choose to tax less in the present but more in the future, or vice versa. As economists, we are interested in learning the economic effects of this change in the timing of taxation, and in understanding the circumstances under which it is desirable for the government to have a surplus or deficit rather than balance its budget in every year.

We can now return briefly to the question of using the budget surplus to save Social Security. As we learned in Chapter 9, current Social Security taxes are used to finance benefits to current retirees. As the number of future retirees increases because of demographic factors, future Social Security taxes will have to rise or benefits per retiree will have to be reduced. Using the surplus to retire the national debt will reduce the government's future interest burden and free up funds that can be used to pay future Social Security benefits. This reduces the need to raise Social Security taxes (or cut benefits) in the future. If, instead, the government uses the surplus to increase current spending or reduce current taxes, the national debt and the required interest payments will not be reduced and taxes must rise in the future to maintain the current level of Social Security benefits to retiring baby boomers.

The Timing of Taxes and the Individual

If surplus and deficit policy simply changes the timing of tax payments, how does this affect taxpayers' behavior? Should it matter *when* the government taxes them or just *how much*? David Ricardo, a famous nineteenth-century British economist, proposed that farsighted, rational taxpayers would be indifferent to the timing of taxes. That is, they would treat deficits as equivalent to higher future taxes and surpluses as equivalent to lower future taxes. We call this idea **Ricardian equivalence.** Because Ricardian equivalence is usually proposed in the context of a deficit rather than a surplus, we will assume the government has a deficit in the following discussion. The same reasoning applies, in reverse, when the government has a surplus.

RICARDIAN EQUIVALENCE: WHY THE BUDGET BALANCE MAY NOT MATTER. We illustrate the Ricardian equivalence proposition in Figure 16.5. A taxpayer lives for two periods and has earned income of M dollars in each. We that assume the government collects T dollars in taxes in each period, so the taxpayer's disposable income is $M - T$ dollars in each period. The taxpayer faces an intertemporal budget

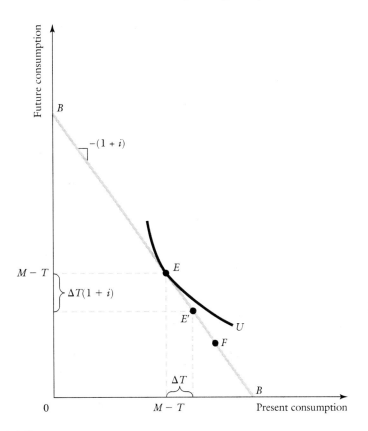

Figure 16.5
Effect of a Change in the Timing of Taxes
The consumer faces the intertemporal budget line *BB* and maximizes lifetime utility at the endowment point *E*, with saving of zero. A reduction in present taxes matched by an increase in future taxes of equal present value does not shift the budget line, provided that the consumer borrows and lends at the same rate of interest as the government. However, the change in timing shifts the endowment point to E′. To maintain maximum utility, the consumer saves the tax decrease.

line *BB* passing through the endowment point *E*. We assume that the taxpayer can borrow and lend as much as he or she wants at interest rate i, so the (absolute) slope of the intertemporal budget line is $1 + i$. In Figure 16.5, the highest indifference curve along *BB* is drawn tangent to the budget line at the endowment point, so the level of saving that maximizes the lifetime utility of the taxpayer is zero. Likewise, we assume that the government balances its budget and does not issue bonds in the first period.

What happens if the government, through fiscal policy, changes the first-period tax on the taxpayer by $\Delta T < 0$ (a reduction in first-period taxes) but maintains spending in all periods? Because spending is unchanged, the government must borrow the first-period revenue lost by cutting taxes. The intertemporal budget constraint requires it to increase future tax revenue by an equal amount in present value. For simplicity, we assume that the taxes are increased in the second period enough to pay interest and redeem the bonds issued in the first period. (That is, the government satisfies its intertemporal budget constraint over two periods.) If the government borrows and lends at the same interest rate as the taxpayer, the second-period tax increase is $-\Delta T \cdot (1 + i) > 0$. We also assume that the taxpayer fully recognizes the increase in future taxes implied by the increase in the government deficit.

What is the effect of these tax changes on the taxpayer's intertemporal budget constraint? In the current period, disposable income rises to $M - (T + \Delta T)$, but future disposable income falls to $M - (T - \Delta T \cdot [1 + i])$ dollars. The combined effect is to shift the "disposable income endowment point" from E to E' along the same intertemporal budget constraint without changing the position of the intertemporal budget line. The fiscal policy changes the timing of taxes but does not change the amount taxpayers can consume over a lifetime.

Because the intertemporal budget line is not changed by the fiscal policy, the taxpayer continues to maximize lifetime utility at point E. To stay at point E after the policy changes, the taxpayer must save the current tax reduction and use the proceeds, including the interest on the savings, to pay the second-period taxes. In other words, by purchasing the government bonds issued to finance the first-period deficit, the taxpayer enjoys the same maximum lifetime utility as when the government balanced its budget. According to this Ricardian equivalence proposition, a policy that simply changes the timing of taxes does not affect the taxpayer's consumption decision. The taxpayer saves the reduction in current taxes, so national saving—the sum of private and government saving—is not affected by the policy.

WHY THE BUDGET BALANCE MAY MATTER AFTER ALL.   We can identify several reasons that Ricardian equivalence may fail in practice, just as Ricardo himself did when proposing it. Whether Ricardian equivalence is an economic fact or a theoretical curiosity, the reasons it may fail to hold are useful for understanding how and why the budget balance might affect the economy.

■ One reason the budget balance may matter is that some taxpayers borrow at a higher interest rate than the government. A decrease in current taxes will not simply move the endowment point along the same intertemporal budget line; it will shift the budget line as well. The reduction in current taxes is equivalent to a loan obtained at more favorable terms than taxpayers can arrange for themselves.

■ A related point is that some taxpayers are *liquidity-constrained* and desire to borrow to increase present consumption spending, but no one will lend to them. For example, suppose the utility-maximizing point on *BB* in Figure 16.5 lies at a point like F rather than E (we would need to redraw the indifference curves), but taxpayers must choose point E because no one will lend to them. If the government cuts current taxes, shifting the disposable income endowment point toward F, taxpayers will spend, not save, the increase in disposable income even if they fully anticipate higher future taxes. In effect, by cutting current taxes the government lends to taxpayers when no one else will.

- Taxpayers may be "myopic" and not anticipate that higher future taxes are implied by a deficit. In this case, the taxpayer may spend part of the decrease in current taxes in the mistaken belief that disposable lifetime income has increased, when it hasn't. In this case, deficits "trick" people into making mistakes about how to allocate their resources over a lifetime.

- Another reason the budget balance may matter is that the taxes that must be paid in the future by individual taxpayers may be uncertain, even if the total future tax is known from the government's budget constraint. Individuals may not know what share of future taxes they will be asked to pay. In this case, Ricardian equivalence depends on how the household treats an uncertain increase in future taxes relative to the certain decrease in current taxes.

- Finally, taxpayers may expect that some of the future taxes will be levied after they are dead. In this case, a taxpayer's disposable lifetime income is indeed increased by a deficit. In the next section, we will see that how taxpayers respond to taxes in the far future depends on whether they are selfish or care about their descendants.

The Timing of Taxes and Overlapping Generations

In the above example, the timing of taxes is changed within the lifetime of an individual taxpayer. However, a big difference between people and the government is that people are mortal and must balance their income and outlays over a finite time interval. The government is immortal and has, effectively, all of time over which to balance its budget. Consequently, the taxes needed to balance the government's intertemporal budget constraint may be levied long after the people who are now alive are dead.

If people are selfish and care only about their own consumption, they will ignore taxes levied after their death. In this case, lower current taxes made possible by deficit finance will increase the lifetime disposable incomes of current generations and lower those of future generations. As a result, total spending in the economy rises because the current generations spend more; and future generations, whose lifetime incomes are decreased, are not around to affect the level of current spending.

But what if people are not selfish? What if, as seems most likely, people care about other members of their families as well as themselves? Professor Robert Barro, currently of Harvard University, pointed out that Ricardian equivalence will hold for mortal taxpayers who care about the consumption of their children enough to make gifts and bequests to them. As a matter of fact, the amount of bequests from parents to their children is very large. However, Barro's argument requires not just bequests, but a specific form of bequest behavior based on *altruism,* where the utility of the parents (old generation) depends not only on their own consumption but also on the consumption of the children (young generation). When altruistic parents choose bequests that maximize their utilities, a deficit will be offset by larger bequests (and therefore larger private saving).

This argument is illustrated in Figure 16.6. For simplicity, we assume that the sum of the lifetime incomes of the parent and the child is fixed, and the amount is

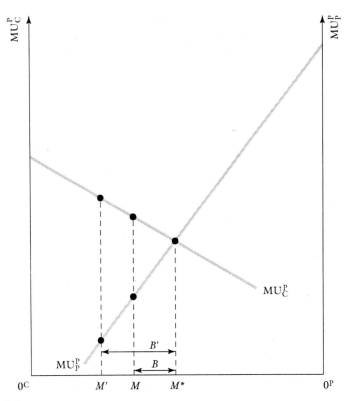

Figure 16.6

Ricardian Equivalence and Intergenerational Transfers

The marginal utility of an altruistic parent from the child's consumption is shown by the schedule MU_C^P, and the marginal utility from the parent's own consumption is shown by the schedule MU_P^P. The base of the diagram is combined family income, and the initial distribution between parent and child is at M. The distribution that maximizes the parent's utility is M^*, so the parent leaves bequest B. If a deficit reduces the child's income and raises the parent's to M', the parent compensates by leaving a larger bequest B'.

shown by the horizontal distance $0^C 0^P$. Consumption by the child is measured to the right of the origin 0^C and consumption by the parent to the left of the origin 0^P. The schedule labeled MU_C^P shows the marginal utility that the altruistic parent derives from consumption by the child, and the schedule MU_P^P shows the marginal utility the parent derives from his or her own consumption. Marginal utility decreases with consumption, so MU_C^P declines to the right and MU_P^P declines to the left. The total utility of the parent is the area under the combined curves, so utility is maximized at the point where the two schedules intersect.

The point labeled M is the distribution of income ($0^C M$ for the child and $0^P M$ for the parent) when no bequest is made. The parent does not maximize utility at this point, because the parent's marginal utility from the child's consumption is greater than the parent's marginal utility from his or her own consumption. The parent maximizes utility by making a bequest B to increase the child's consumption to $M^* = M + B$. If a deficit raises the parent's income and decreases the child's (say, to point M'), the parent compensates with a larger bequest B' in order to maintain the utility-maximizing distribution of consumption. The intuitive argument is quite easy. The parents want their own decisions, not the government's, to determine the allocation of consumption between themselves and their children. They do this by saving their tax reduction and increasing their bequest enough so that the children can pay the future taxes.

If the future taxes are levied far in the future, the children will leave larger bequests to their own children, and so on. By linking the taxes on future generations, no matter how distant, to the bequests of current generations, Barro shows that mortal, altruistic taxpayers act like immortal taxpayers and treat changes in the budget balance as simply a change in the timing of the family's tax payments.

THE ECONOMIC EFFECTS OF THE BUDGET BALANCE

Many economists doubt that households treat deficits as equivalent to future taxes, as assumed under the Ricardian equivalence hypothesis. In this case, budget surpluses and deficits affect the behavior of the households and, consequently, the economy. Without Ricardian equivalence, households would treat a reduction in taxes matched by a deficit as an increase in their disposable incomes, and an increase in taxes matched by a surplus as a decrease in their disposable incomes. Put differently, the households holding the government bonds would treat the national debt as net wealth, so when it rises they feel wealthier and spend more, and when it declines they feel less wealthy and spend less. In this section, we analyze the impact of the budget balance on the levels of the interest rate, the level of saving, and the level of investment when households do not act in accordance with the assumptions of the Ricardian equivalence hypothesis.

The Effects on Interest Rates, Saving, and Investment

When the assumptions of Ricardian equivalence do not hold, surpluses and deficits are not automatically offset by equal and opposite changes in the level of private saving. Instead, a surplus or deficit causes the market interest rate to change and affects the level of private investment. This is shown in Figure 16.7, where the level of saving and investment is measured on the horizontal axis and the interest rate is measured on the vertical axis. The curve labeled S represents the amount of saving done by private individuals and businesses in the economy net of their borrowing. As interest rates rise, households and firms typically save more, so the curve is upward-sloping. The downward-sloping curve labeled D is the demand for loanable funds by businesses that demand them to finance their investment spending. When the government balances its budget it contributes nothing to national saving, so the market equilibrium interest rate r_0 and is determined by the intersection of the private saving supply and investment demand curves.[4] At this interest rate, the equilibrium level of private investment is I_0 is equal to private saving S_0.

When the government has a budget deficit, it is doing negative saving. The curve labeled S^D shows the level of national savings when the government has a

---

[4]This analysis ignores investment and saving abroad.

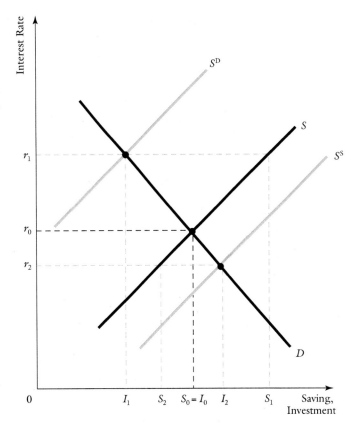

Figure 16.7

**Crowding Out
and Crowding In**

A budget deficit reduces the national supply of saving from S to S^D raising interest rates and crowding out rpivate investments from I_0 to I_1. A budget surplus does the opposite.

deficit. The horizontal distance between S and S^D is the amount of the deficit. The market equilibrium interest rate must now adjust to equate the level of national saving to the amount of loanable funds demanded by investing firms. Because the government absorbs part of private saving to finance its deficit, the interest rate must rise to r_1 to clear the capital market. At the higher interest rate, private saving rises to S_1 and private investment falls to I_1. Economists describe the process that reduces investment in this way as **crowding out.** Note that the amount of investment crowded out by the deficit is less than the amount of the deficit, because the rise in interest rates encourages additional private saving.

When the government has a budget surplus, the government saving is added to private saving to get national saving. In the case of a surplus, the national savings is given by the curve S^S which lies to the right of curve S by the amount of the surplus. The equilibrium interest rate is pushed down in this case to r_2 and investment rises to I_2, while private saving falls somewhat to S_2. In this case, private investment is **crowded in.** Note, however, that investment does not rise by the amount of the surplus, because households save less at the lower interest rate, partly offsetting the effect of the surplus on national saving.

How would this analysis change if households behaved as assumed by the Ricardian equivalence hypothesis? In this case, a deficit would cause the private saving curve to shift to the right by the amount of the deficit as households increase their saving to pay for the expected future taxes. Similarly, a surplus causes the private saving curve to shift to the left because households expect lower taxes in the future (as compared with the case of a balanced budget) and consume more today. In both cases, the national saving curve is not affected by the budget balance, so the equilibrium interest rate and level of investment are unchanged. If Ricardian equivalence holds, the budget balance neither crowds in nor crowds out investment spending.

Evidence on Ricardian Equivalence

Given the clear predictions of the Ricardian equivalence hypothesis, it is perhaps surprising that the empirical evidence is inconclusive and ambiguous. Some researchers argue that the hypothesis cannot be rejected on the basis of statistical evidence, and therefore it may be a good approximation of how deficits affect (or, in this case, do *not* affect) the economy. In fact, Professor John Seater of North Carolina State University surveyed the research on the Ricardian equivalence hypothesis and concluded that "Ricardian equivalence is strongly supported by the data."[5] This conclusion may be a minority opinion within the profession of economics. Some economists claim that the evidence is clearly inconsistent with the Ricardian equivalence hypothesis.

The research that Professor Seater summarizes examines how changes in government spending, taxes, and deficits affect consumption and real interest rates. Ricardian equivalence is the *null* hypothesis, or the hypothesis to be rejected. For example, the Ricardian equivalence hypothesis implies that neither household consumption nor market interest rates are affected by whether government finances its spending with borrowing or taxes. Cuts in current taxes will be saved to pay the future taxes implied by the higher national debt. If the evidence does not show that a change in the national debt affects consumption, the null hypothesis (Ricardian equivalence) cannot be rejected. The evidence that the national debt does not affect consumption spending seems strong, but the evidence on interest rates is less so.

Professor Seater also summarizes the weaknesses of the studies he surveys. For one thing, the ability of the statistical tests to reject the null hypothesis, called the power of the tests, may not be very high. For this reason we may mistakenly accept the null hypothesis of Ricardian equivalence when in fact it is false, a mistake statisticians call a type II error. Also, researchers disagree with how trends in the variables should be dealt with. Taxes, consumption, and the national debt all increase in a similar trend over time, making it difficult to specify a good statistical test.

Without delving into the complications of econometric research, Figure 16.8 shows why many economists reject the Ricardian equivalence hypothesis. This figure shows gross saving as a percentage of GDP for the private sector, the government sector (which includes both the federal level and subfederal levels), and the nation (the sum of private and government saving) over five-year periods from 1960 to 1998. By averaging over five-year intervals, we abstract from year-to-year fluctuations. Gross saving includes capital consumption, so it does not represent the increase in the wealth of the economy. Instead it includes saving that is done to replace and maintain the capital stock.

---

[5]John J. Seater, "Ricardian Equivalence," 1993.

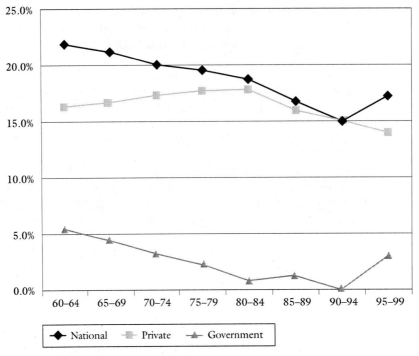

Figure 16.8
National, Private, and Government Gross Saving Rates as a % of GDP
The national saving rate is the sum of the private and government saving rates. The national saving rate
declined from 1960–64 to 1990–94 and rose thereafter, mirroring the same pattern in the government sav-
ing rate. This is contrary to the hypothesis of Ricardian equivalence.
Source: Statistical Abstract of the United States, various years.

Figure 16.8 shows that gross national saving fell steadily over the 35-year period
from 21.8 percent of GDP during the period 1960–1964 to 15.1 percent in the
1990–1994 period. This drop of 6.7 percentage points was mainly due to the
decline of gross government saving from 5.4 percent of GDP to 0 percent over the
same time period. Contrary to the Ricardian equivalence hypothesis, the gross private saving rate did not rise to compensate for the drop in the gross government
saving rate. In fact, it fell 1.3 percentage points over the period. Similarly we see
that gross government saving rose in the last half of the 1990s, and gross national
saving also rose, contrary to the Ricardian hypothesis.

Of course, the fact that the change in private saving did not offset the change
in government saving is not proof that Ricardian equivalence is invalid. Other things
might have affected private saving. For instance, private saving does not include
unrealized capital gains in real estate and the stock market, both of which have been
large since 1985.

THE BUDGET BALANCE AND FISCAL POLICY

What determines whether it is a good idea for the government to have a surplus or
a deficit? Given that surplus and deficit policies are essentially policies about the tim-

ing of taxes, we can evaluate this question using many of the same criteria we used to evaluate tax policy. In particular, the desirability of a surplus or deficit depends on its effects on stabilization, economic efficiency, and equity.

The Budget Balance as a Built-In Stabilizer

We saw in Figure 16.2 that the size of the budget surplus varies over the business cycle, falling during recessions and rising in booms. Economists believe that this is a desirable feature because it smooths out the fluctuations in economic activity. That is, the amplitude of the business cycle would be much greater without the stabilizing effect of budget surpluses and deficits.

Fluctuations in the level of economic activity may have supply-side causes, such as fluctuations in productivity, or demand-side causes, such as fluctuations in consumer or business investment demand. Although most economists believe the economy is self-correcting, and recessions and booms eventually end from natural causes, a type of viscous cycle may prolong and exaggerate the cycle. For example, if businesses reduce their demand for investment goods, and no other component of demand increases, the economy slows down. In addition, workers may be laid off in the capital goods industries. Since these workers have less income to spend, consumer demand decreases, which reduces demand further.

Business cycle fluctuations impose economic costs, such as adjustment costs when economic resources must seek employment in other industries, and efficiency costs when resources are left idle. To the extent that the budget balance can smooth out these fluctuations, these costs are reduced. This is the reason most economists believe that the cyclical fluctuations in the budget balance perform a useful economic function.

To see why deficits and surpluses are stabilizing, consider what would happen if the government were forced to balance its budget every year. If the economy enters a recession during the year, government tax revenue would fall and some expenditure, like welfare and unemployment insurance, would rise, pushing the budget balance into deficit. To balance its budget during a recession, the government would either have to cut spending or raise tax rates. Either policy would reinforce the recession. If the government reduced its spending, government demand for goods and services would fall, adding to the decline in demand by consumers and firms. If, instead, the government balanced its budget by raising tax rates, consumers would have less to spend, reducing private demand for goods and services further. By temporarily financing government spending with a deficit during a recession, the government avoids the negative effects of these policies. Some economists argue that the government should do more than rely on this "built-in" stabilization. The government should actually increase spending or cut tax rates during a recession. Similarly, the government should cut spending and raise tax rates during a boom to prevent the economy from "overheating." The latter idea, of course, is not as popular as the former.

The Budget Balance and the Excess Burden of Taxes

So far, we have assumed that the taxes levied each year are lump-sum taxes that do not distort the economic decisions made by households and firms. More realistically, taxes are levied on economic activities and are likely to be distortionary. Distortionary taxes cause excess burdens each year as well as collecting revenue. The budget balance, by changing the timing of the taxes, also changes the size of the excess burdens levied in different years. For example, an increase in the deficit allows the government to lower present tax rates, reducing the current excess burden, but it raises future excess burdens. In this way, however, the deficit can alter the overall size of the excess burden of the tax system.

For simplicity, let's assume that the government raises revenue each year by taxing the labor income, and the excess burden is caused by distorting the labor-leisure choice. The total excess burden of the tax system is the present value of the annual excess burdens over the indefinite future, or the excess burden in the current year plus the discounted excess burdens in future years. The optimal fiscal policy (or tax timing policy) is to minimize the present value of the excess burdens caused by present and future taxes subject to the government's intertemporal budget constraint. In other words, optimal fiscal policy is just an example of the optimal tax problem described in Chapter 12.

Under reasonable conditions, the optimal policy is one for which the government *smoothes tax rates over time*. That is, deficits and surpluses should be used to avoid the need to levy excessively high or low tax rates in any given year, and the tax rate should be maintained more or less constant over time. The time-invariant tax rate must be high enough to raise the needed tax revenue.

The reason tax smoothing makes possible a lower total excess burden can be explained using the *square rule* discussed in Chapter 12. Recall that according to the square rule, the size of the excess burden rises with the square of the tax rate. If the tax rate is lower in the present than in the future, a surplus can reduce the total excess burden. The reduction in future tax rates made possible by the surplus reduces the future excess burden by a large amount. Of course, the lost revenue has to be made up with higher tax rates in the present, but according to the square rule, the increase in the present excess burden is less than the decrease in the future excess burden.

The implications of tax smoothing for fiscal policy are quite clear. A deficit reduces the excess burden of the tax system if the government runs deficits in years when outlays are abnormally high, such as during a war or national emergency, or when its tax base is abnormally low, such as during recessions. Similarly, if the government anticipates higher spending in the future, it can avoid the need to levy inefficiently high tax rates in the future by accumulating a surplus in the present.

The Budget Balance and Generational Equity

The issue of generational equity arises when Ricardian equivalence does not hold. With Ricardian equivalence, changes in the size of the national debt do not change the burdens on future generations, because they receive larger or smaller bequests as well as a larger or smaller national debt. However, if parents are not altruistic, as required by Ricardian equivalence, changes in the national debt can alter the distribution of tax burden among generations and raise issues of intergenerational equity. Later, we will see that other government policies, such as Social Security, can also redistribute wealth between generations, even if they do not change the national debt.

The main mechanism by which the national debt shifts tax burdens to future generations was described earlier. A deficit allows current generations to enjoy government consumption and lower taxes. If these generations subsequently sell their government bonds to a younger generation, they enjoy an increase in their lifetime disposable incomes. Younger generations are made worse off because they bought the government bonds but inherited the obligation to pay the taxes needed to pay interest on them. The bonds they purchased are collectively worthless because they are simultaneously an asset and a liability.

Given that the national debt can shift tax burdens to future generations, what are the equity (or fairness) issues involved? As we saw in Chapter 7, we can evaluate the fairness of a policy in terms of two criteria of equity: the *benefit principle* and the *ability-to-pay-principle*. The benefit principle is quite clear in its implications. An increase in the national debt is unfair to future generations if they do not receive benefits from government spending comparable to the increased burden they bear. When current generations receive all the benefits from the deficit-financed government consumption and future generations pay part of the cost, the policy is unfair in the same way that it is unfair to enjoy a meal in a restaurant and expect someone else to pay the bill.

If government bonds are used to finance government investments, rather than consumption, the conclusion is quite different. If future generations inherit a larger stock of public capital—for instance, a national highway system that benefits them—it is reasonable that they should bear part of the tax burden, according to the benefit principle of equity. Thus, deficits that finance government investment spending do not raise the same questions of generational equity as deficits that finance government consumption spending.

When the ability-to-pay principle of equity is used to evaluate the fairness of fiscal policy, things are less clear. According to the vertical equity principle, the government should distribute the burden of taxes according to ability to pay. If future generations have greater ability to pay than current generations, it may be equitable to shift a larger burden to them, regardless of whether they get more benefit from government spending. Vertical equity explains why some people believe that the national debt is not a problem as long as it does not grow faster than the economy. An economy is larger because it has more, and richer, people with greater ability to pay the taxes needed to service the larger national debt. Shifting tax burdens to more numerous and richer future generations does not seem unfair.

Generational Accounting and the Hidden National Debt

Ironically, no matter how economists refine and adjust the measured budget balance, any measure has limited meaning at best. Some economists go so far as to assert that the budget balance is virtually a meaningless number. The reason is that the budget balance is a very narrow measure of the change in government liabilities, and an equivalent policy can be implemented that does not show up as a surplus or deficit. In other words, just as the government can make hidden spending that does not show up in the budget, it can also have "hidden" deficits. For this reason, some economists advocate a wholly different approach to measuring how much the government shifts the tax burden among generations.

We have emphasized that an increase in the national debt can transfer the tax burden from the old to the young, and from current to future generations. However, intergenerational transfers can occur even if the government balances its budget every year. In other words, the change in the national debt is a partial and incomplete measure of deferred tax burdens, at best. For this reason, Professor Kotlikoff of Boston University and his associates have devised a new way of monitoring the generational impact of government tax and transfer policies. They call the method **generational accounting.**

To understand the need for generational accounting, we consider a phenomenon that Kotlikoff calls the arbitrary nature of fiscal labels. Sometimes monetary flows between the public and the government are labeled taxes and transfers. At other times they are labeled loans and repayments. According to Kotlikoff, the actuality of intergenerational transfers does not depend on these labels, any more than the actuality of a dog depends on whether it is called *chien* in France or *gou* in China. However, the size of the budget balance and the national debt depends on the labels we use. A change in the labels changes the size of the budget balance and the national debt.

To see this, compare how we label transactions under the Social Security program with similar transactions stemming from fiscal policy. As we saw in Chapter 9, the Social Security program levies *taxes* on current younger, working generations and uses the revenue to make *transfers* to older, retired generations. If the amount of tax revenue is enough to cover the transfers, the program budget is balanced and no deficit is measured. However, when the current cohorts of workers retire in the future, they too will be eligible to receive a transfer from the government as a result of having paid Social Security taxes. What if the Social Security taxes collected from workers are labeled "loans to the government" and the transfers they receive when they are retired are labeled "loan repayments plus interest"? With this change in labels, we see that the Social Security system is little different from Treasury bonds sold to the taxpayers and redeemed when they retire. The only difference is that when the transaction takes place with Treasury bonds, it is recorded as a deficit. In the Social Security program, the transactions are labeled taxes and transfers. By relabeling the transactions, we can turn the revenue collected by the Social Security tax ($444 billion in 1999 from Old Age Survivors and Disability Taxes) into a deficit because it obligates the government to make future payments, even though under the existing labeling system the Social Security program shows a surplus.

By relabeling, we can also make a deficit disappear. Just label all the money the government receives from borrowing as "voluntary taxes" and future government payments needed to retire the bonds in the future as "transfers in gratitude" for the voluntary taxes paid earlier. *Presto,* no deficit! Kotlikoff and his associates devised generational accounting precisely to avoid this "tyranny of labels." How can we tell what intergenerational transfers are actually going on when the national debt can be turned into almost any number by an arbitrary choice of labels?

The central plan for constructing the generational accounts is to project the net payments by taxpayers grouped according to their age and sex over the remainder of their lives. The payments include all federal, state, and local taxes. From these gross payments we subtract cash and in-kind transfers received over the taxpayer's lifetime, including Social Security benefits, government health insurance, unemployment insurance, and welfare. We assume that all existing persons, including the newborn, pay taxes and receive transfers over their remaining lives under the policies that exist at the time the accounts are reported. Projections are based on specific assumptions about growth rates, and the present value of these net payments is determined by assuming a realistic discount rate.

The government's intertemporal budget constraint requires that the present value of net taxes (taxes less transfers) levied on living and all future generations equal the present value of government current and future spending. Assuming that existing spending programs are maintained, we can calculate the rate of net tax that must be levied on the lifetime incomes of future generations to satisfy this intertemporal budget constraint.

Jagadeesh Gokhale of the Federal Reserve Bank of Cleveland has estimated that the present value of the government's spending obligations is $31.5 trillion.[6] Assuming that generations currently living are taxed throughout their lives at current tax rates, the present value of net taxes on living generations is $22.1 trillion, which leaves a $9.4 trillion fiscal burden on all generations unborn (as of 1995). Gokhale estimated that a net tax rate of 49.2% will have to be levied on the lifetime incomes of future generations to maintain the existing government spending plan.[7] By comparison, if persons born in 1995 are taxed at existing rates, their lifetime net tax rate is 28.6%. These figures suggest a considerable generational inequity. Gokhale further estimated that in order to lower the tax on future generations so that they are taxed at the same rate as the living, the lifetime tax rates on current generations would have to rise in 1998 to 32.3%.

Surpluses, Deficits, and "Saving" Social Security

Perhaps nothing is more confusing to people than the relationship between Social Security and budget surpluses or deficits. In 1999, the House of Representatives proposed and overwhelmingly passed a bill that puts the surplus on the Social Security trust fund in a "lockbox," so that it can be used only to pay for Social Security benefits. The idea of putting every penny of the Social Security surplus in a lockbox has taken hold because many people think that the Social Security trust fund surplus is a sham. They point out that the Social Security surplus has been used to fund non–Social Security government spending, and they fear it will continue to do so. A newspaper cartoon in the mid-1990s showed a retired baby boomer opening a huge lockbox in the year 2025, only to find a piece of paper from the government saying "IOU." The cartoon was commenting on the fact that the Social Security trust fund is invested in government bonds, which are simply IOUs of the government issued to finance current spending.

How does government budget policy affect the future solvency of the Social Security program? What do politicians mean when they accuse their opponents of

---

[6]See Jagadeesh Gokhale, "Generational Equity and Sustainability in U.S. Fiscal Policy," 1998.
[7]Gokhale's estimate did not take into account planned spending changes in the Balanced Budget Act of 1997. It is these changes that account for much of the projected on-budget surpluses over the next 15 years.

"raiding" Social Security to fund new government spending or enact large tax cuts? How does legislation establishing a Social Security lockbox prevent such raids from occurring? To answer these questions, recall from Chapter 9 that the Social Security program is mainly a pay-as-you-go program that finances current benefits to retirees with current payroll tax revenue. The problem of future solvency is simply that the number of retirees will grow rapidly relative to the number of workers when the baby-boom generation begins retiring. Payroll tax rates would then have to rise to unacceptable levels to maintain the program on a pay-as-you-go basis, or benefits would have to be cut. Such policies would increase the excess burden of taxation and shift tax burdens to future generations. To prevent this, government has to save more now, by running a surplus. Although the assets of the Social Security trust fund have been growing since the mid-1980s because of off-budget surpluses, the unified budget, which measures total government saving, remained in deficit until 1998. In other words, the overall government has actually begun to save only recently. The current policy debate swirls around the issue of preventing this projected government saving from being dissipated by new spending programs or tax cuts.

As mentioned earlier, the Congressional Budget Office (CBO) projects a $3000 billion surplus for the federal government over the next decade, consisting of a $1000 billion on-budget surplus and a $2000 billion Social Security surplus. If realized, this projected surplus could be used to pay down the national debt, almost eliminating it by the year 2009. If the national debt were eliminated, the interest costs of the government would be reduced by over $200 billion, and the money could be used to "save" Social Security. Rather than devoting "every penny" of this $3000 billion surplus to saving Social Security, however, the administration proposes increases in spending and some modest tax cuts that would dissipate much of the $1000 billion on-budget surplus. While the Republican majority in Congress opposes the spending increases, it would like to enact tax cuts that would similarly dissipate the on-budget surplus.

Although no one has proposed using the Social Security surplus to increase spending or decrease taxes, many economists and others fear it could happen if the projected on-budget surplus fails to materialize. In this case, a decision to increase spending or cut taxes may cause an on-budget deficit, which would absorb some or all the Social Security surplus. Good reasons support this fear. First of all, as we saw earlier, the projected on-budget surplus is based on the assumption that government spending will fall relative to GDP. By law, the CBO must base its budget projections on the assumption that spending on discretionary government programs, like national defense, will not exceed the strict limits that Congress imposed under the Balanced Budget Act of 1997. If, in fact, discretionary government spending keeps pace with inflation and growth in the economy, the on-budget surplus will not materialize. Second, the limits on discretionary spending exclude special emergency appropriations, such as the money spent on the United States contribution to NATO's military operations in Kosovo. Future emergency appropriations depend on unforeseen events and could be large enough to substantially reduce the on-budget surplus. Third, most economists believe the economy is presently operating above its normal level and that growth will slow down in the future. If the current unemployment rate is less than NAIRU, which many economists believe, the

A CASE IN POINT

16.2 Using the Surplus to Save Social Security—
Double-Counting or Creative Accounting?

In his 1998 State of the Union Address, President Clinton proposed that "we devote every penny of every future surplus" to save Social Security. In 1999, Clinton revealed a budget that projects unified surpluses summing to $4900 billion between 1999 and 2014, $2800 billion of which are on the Social Security trust fund and $2100 billion on-budget. The president also proposed additional on-budget spending initiatives for defense, Medicare, and Universal Savings Accounts that sum to $2100 billion, completely dissipating the projected on-budget surplus. All of the Social Security surplus will be used to pay down the net debt, so the trust fund will increase by $2800 billion while the net debt will decline by $2800 billion.

Perhaps to redeem his promise to use "every penny" for Social Security, President Clinton included an innovative plan to augment the Social Security trust fund. The Treasury will create $2800 billion in special new bonds and *give* them to the Social Security trust fund. The president's critics cried foul, claiming that he was double-counting. He already proposed spending the $2100 billion on-budget surplus, so how could it be used again to augment the trust fund? The president's defenders claim there is no double-counting.

More on this can be found in "Saving Social Security: Is the Surplus the Answer?" by David Altig and Jagadeesh Gokhale. which can be found on the Federal Reserve Bank of Cleveland's web site at www.clev.frb.org.

Critically analyze this issue by answering the following:

- Although the gift of the bonds will be treated as a receipt by the trust fund, it is not clear at this time how the transaction will be treated for on-budget purposes. Let's assume it will be treated as an outlay. If so, what would be the projected 15-year value for the on-budget surplus, the trust fund surplus, and the unified surplus if the president's plan were adopted?

- How much will the *gross* national debt increase by 2014 if the plan is adopted? What about the *net* national debt?

- After the trust fund surplus is used to buy back government bonds from private investors, the Treasury will pay the interest on the national debt to the trust fund, rather than to the private investors. This provides the trust fund with receipts that can be used to pay Social Security benefits. If the Treasury gives bonds to the trust fund, as proposed, additional receipts will accrue to the fund as well, since the bonds bear interest. Explain how the transaction of giving bonds to the trust fund can be interpreted as a promise to use general revenue to pay future Social Security benefits.

standardized surplus, which measures the surplus at the economy's "normal" level of economic activity, is less than the actual surplus. In this case, the surplus will be smaller or nonexistent when the economy returns to its normal level of activity.

For these reasons, the projected on-budget surplus is tenuous at best, and proposals to increase spending or cut taxes could end up being financed with the Social Security surplus. The Social Security lockbox bill, introduced by Representatives Herger and Shaw of California and Florida, respectively, is designed to prevent this from happening. The bill blocks consideration of any budget resolution containing an on-budget deficit unless a majority of the House and three-fifths of the Senate approve. In effect, it requires the government to balance its on-budget outlays and receipts each year, so that the Social Security surplus can be used to pay down the national debt. This legislation poses some danger, however. If the economy goes into a recession, a budget deficit will arise because of the fall in income tax revenue. Unless enough representatives and senators decide otherwise, the Herger-Shaw bill would prevent the government from considering a budget resolution that stabilizes the economy with an on-budget deficit.

CONCLUSION AND SUMMARY

We began this chapter by claiming that people do not really know what to make of budget surpluses and deficits. Such confusion is understandable, given the different ways in which the budget balance can be measured. Furthermore, as advocates of generational accounting point out, the budget balance is an imperfect way of measuring the net burden shifted to future generations because it depends on how government transactions are labeled. Nonetheless, current policies concerning the budget balance are of great importance for the future health of the U.S. economy. For a given set of labels, the budget balance is a measure of government saving. Because the evidence suggests that the level of government saving affects the level of national saving, contrary to the Ricardian hypothesis, the projected surpluses over the next 15 years offer the government an opportunity to address the future insolvency of the Social Security program.

- The federal surplus is the excess of government receipts over outlays during the year, and it represents the amount by which the government can pay down the national debt. Although the federal budget has been in deficit for the past 28 years, large surpluses are projected over the next 15 years.

- The unified budget balance includes the surplus on the Social Security trust fund, while the on-budget balance excludes trust fund transactions. The standardized budget balance is adjusted for the state of the economy and measures the budget balance when the economy operates at its normal level of activity.

- The national debt is the accumulated deficits over the past less debt retired with surpluses. Although the dollar amount of the national debt is often emphasized, the size of the debt relative to GDP is a better measure.

- Policies about the budget balance are policies about the timing of taxes. According to the government's intertemporal budget constraint, the present value of taxes collected in all years must equal the present value of spending in all years. Thus if spending is fixed, a budget surplus allows the government to lower taxes (or avoid raising them) in the future.

- Many people view the national debt as a burden on future generations. Whether it is in fact a burden depends on how the budget balance affects private saving decisions. According to the Ricardian equivalence hypothesis, people anticipate the future tax consequences of the budget balance on themselves and their heirs, and change their personal saving levels accordingly. In this case, the budget balance and the national debt do not affect the economy.

- The desirability of a surplus or deficit depends on its impact on economic stability, efficiency, and generational equity. Surplus policies that smooth tax rates over time and counter fluctuations in the business cycle are desirable. Policies that shift large burdens to future generations in order to avoid the unpleasant alternatives of raising current taxes or cutting spending are not desirable.

■ The government can use the projected budget surpluses to "save" Social Security from future insolvency by using them to pay down the government debt. Although politicians have agreed to use Social Security trust fund surpluses to retire the national debt, some want to use the on-budget surpluses to increase government spending or cut current taxes. Economists fear that such policies may eat into the Social Security surpluses if the on-budget surpluses fail to materialize.

QUESTIONS FOR DISCUSSION AND REVIEW

1. Suppose budgetary federal spending and revenue are $1700 billion and $1825 billion while outlays and gross receipts of federal agencies and trust funds are $320 billion and $445 billion, respectively. What is the unified budget balance? What is the on-budget balance?

2. Suppose the growth rate of GDP increased and the budget balance stayed the same. How would this affect the ratio of the national debt to GDP in the future?

3. It is sometimes claimed that the national debt cannot be a burden on future generations, because the amount borrowed never has to be paid back. As the government bonds mature, they can be replaced with new issues. Suppose an increase in the national debt is never retired; explain why this means larger tax burdens in the future nonetheless.

4. Suppose you can earn interest on your bank account or borrow money at 5% per year. If the government increases your tax this year by $500 and announces that you will certainly pay $525 less in tax one year hence, how much less would you spend this year? How much less will you save? Assume that you will not die or leave the country in the meantime. If you think that you would spend less, explain why you would spend

more if the government doesn't reduce your taxes. Remember that you can borrow.

5. It is often pointed out that, except for the amount owed to foreigners, we collectively owe the national debt to ourselves. Does this mean that an increase in the national debt cannot shift burdens to future generations? Why or why not? Suppose that all of an increase in the national debt is owed to foreigners. How would this affect the burden on future generations if current generations are selfish? What if members of the current generation are altruistic to their descendants in the way described by Barro?

6. Economists have long argued that if the government were required to balance its budget, it should balance its budget over the business cycle rather than annually. Explain how such a policy could be implemented using the standardized budget balance. Assuming the government balances its budget by varying tax rates, would a permanent decrease in NAIRU require the government to raise or lower its taxes in a particular year?

7. The Treasury has recently begun to issue Treasury Indexed Bonds (TIBs) as well as conventional Treasury Bonds (TBs) to finance the national debt. The principal of

a TIB is increased each year by the rate of inflation. Thus, when the bonds are redeemed on maturity, the lender receives a principle that is equal in purchasing power to the amount lent when the bonds were issued. Because the lender is protected against inflation, the interest rate on TIBs is about presently about three percentage points less than the interest rate on TBs. Suppose the entire national debt were funded with TIBs rather than TBs. How would this affect the level of the current budget balance? How would it affect the size of the budget balance in the future when the TIBs are redeemed?

8. How does the generational equity or inequity of budget policy depend on the way in which the government spends the proceeds? Which is more likely to create generational equity in your opinion: an increase in the national debt to spend more on education or to spend more on Medicare for retirees?

9. According to the generational accounts created by Auerbach and Kotlikoff, future generations are likely to face substantially higher tax rates than current generations. What does this finding, assuming that it is true, imply about the effect on excess burden of the tax system of an increase in current taxes holding government spending in all periods constant?

10. What would be the effect of the following on the unified deficit and on the burden on future generations according to generational accounts?

   a. The government raises Medicare payroll taxes and uses the proceeds to enhance benefits to current retirees.

   b. The government abolishes or privatizes the Social Security program (see Chapter 9 on privatizing Social Security)

from this day on, and gives Treasury bonds to people who have paid Social Security taxes in the past equal to the benefits owed them by the program.

11. Internet Exercise. Each year the government faces many spending and taxing options that affect the budget balance. The effect on the budget balance includes all such effects. For example, a policy to increase the salaries of federal workers would also increase income tax revenue. The National Budget Simulator maintained by the Center for Community Economic Resources at the University of California, Berkeley, allows the user to alter different federal government spending levels and calculates the effect on the budget balance. Access the simulator at www.garnet.berkeley.edu:3333/budget/budget.html and choose some alternatives that you think would be desirable. Justify why you would choose these alternatives, and report the impact of your policy decision on the budget balance using the simulator.

12. Internet Exercise. We mentioned in this chapter that the growth in the national debt between 1970 and 1993 is less dramatic when the debt is expressed in dollars of constant purchasing power (the "real" national debt). Use a spreadsheet like Excel™ to calculate and chart the real national debt from 1970 to 1993 in dollars of 1982–1984 purchasing power. You can obtain the needed data in spreadsheet form in the *Economic Report of the President, 1999,* at www.access.gpo.gov/usbudget/fy2000/erp.html. The national debt numbers are found in Table B-81, and the Consumer Price Index numbers are found in Table B-60.

SELECTED REFERENCES

The argument that fiscal irresponsibility during the Reagan administration has saddled future generations with huge tax burdens is made in Benjamin Friedman, *Day of Reckoning*, 1988.

The modern Ricardian equivalence argument is explained clearly by Robert J. Barro, "The Ricardian Approach to Budget Deficits," 1989. Econometric evidence on the validity of the Ricardian equivalence proposition is surveyed in John J. Seater, "Ricardian Equivalence," 1993.

Some of the various ways in which the budget balance is (mis)measured are described in Robert Eisner, *How Real is the Federal Deficit?* 1986; and in Laurence J. Kotlikoff, *Generational Accounting*, 1992.

David Altig and Jagadeesh Gokhale, "Saving Social Security: Is the Surplus the Answer?" *Economic Commentary*, Federal Reserve Bank of Cleveland, April 1, 1999.

William Gale and Alan Auerbach, "Does the Budget Surplus Justify Big Tax Cuts?" *Tax Notes*, March 22, 1999, and "Does the Budget Surplus Justify Big Tax Cuts: Updates and Extensions," *Tax Notes*, October 18, 1999.

USEFUL INTERNET SITES

Historical information on federal budget surpluses and deficits can be found on the Congressional Budget Office homepage at http://www.cbo.gov/.

Projections of federal budget surpluses are found in Congressional Budget Office, "The Economic and Budget Outlook," July 1999, which can be found on the CBO's web site.

Numerous articles analyzing the surplus and the policy options it presents can be found in the Issues: Budget Analysis section at www.policy.com.

17

Reforming the Federal Tax System

Many people are surprised to learn that Congress abolished the income tax in 1998. It was largely a symbolic act, however. The income tax will continue to operate until the end of 2002, and beyond that unless Congress passes a substitute for the income tax before then. However, the fact that Congress passed this measure indicates how dissatisfied many people are with the existing tax system. The income tax is considered too complex by nearly everybody, and taxpayers resent the heavy burden of complying with its arcane and often incomprehensible provisions. Others believe the tax system is unfair because some people are better able to take advantage of its many "tax breaks" than are others. Economists, in particular, believe it is inefficient and imposes a larger deadweight burden on the economy than is necessary. For all of these reasons, tax reform is a perennial policy issue.

"Tax reform" describes a significant change in the tax system designed to make it more efficient, more fair or equitable, and less complex. Typically, tax reform is revenue neutral—that is, the overall level of tax revenue collected is neither increased nor decreased. Only the method of collection is changed. *Incremental* tax reform attempts to accomplish these goals by making targeted changes in the existing tax system while leaving its overall structure in place. *Fundamental* tax reform completely overhauls the existing system or replaces it with an entirely different tax system. Congress hopes to instigate fundamental tax reform by prospectively abolishing the income tax.

In this chapter, we seek to understand the main issues at stake in tax reform, particularly fundamental tax reform. Specifically, we identify the arguments for and against replacing the existing income tax with an entirely different tax. To do this we need to understand how any new tax system would differ from the existing income tax system. As we learned in Chapter 13, a tax system can be described in terms of the tax *unit* (who is taxed), the tax *base* (what is taxed), and the tax rate *structure* (how the base is taxed). Fundamental tax reform would change any or all of these. Incremental tax reforms would leave the tax unit, tax base, and tax rate structure more or less the same, and change the details of the tax system. For example, to eliminate the marriage tax, the government might add an extra deduction or tax credit for two-earner families. Similarly, to achieve a different distribution of the tax burden, it could raise or lower the tax rates in the different tax brackets.

"This year, tax reform has radically changed the federal tables and methods for calculating witholding taxes."

Source: © The New Yorker Collection 1987 George Booth from cartoonbank.com. all rights reserved.

Most of the proposed fundamental tax reforms would change the tax unit, tax base, and tax rate structure. Perhaps the most far-reaching aspect of a fundamental tax reform is a change in the tax base. As we learned earlier, the federal government derives most of its revenue from taxing income. Instead of taxing income, it could tax consumption or wealth. Under the existing tax system, federal revenue from taxes on consumption and wealth is relatively insignificant. Consumption and wealth are more important as tax bases for state and local governments. In addition to excise taxes, most states levy a retail sales tax (RST), while the real estate property tax, a tax levied on the value of land and structures, is the main source of revenue for local governments. Under most proposals for fundamental tax reform, the base for the federal tax system would be changed from income to consumption. For that reason, we focus on the implications of taxing consumption in this chapter. Before turning to that topic, we will introduce some of the main tax reforms that have been proposed.

ALTERNATIVES TO THE EXISTING INCOME TAX

Given that the federal income tax system raises vast sums of revenue—about $1200 billion in 1999—the feasible alternatives to the income tax all take the form of broad-based taxes. It is doubtful, for example, that the government could rely on environmental taxes alone for the needed revenue, as advanced by proponents of the "green tax shift." Several alternative tax systems seem capable of raising the vast sums of money required. We describe each of them briefly.

The Flat Tax

For some time, a leading contender to replace the existing income tax system has been the "flat" tax designed by Professors Hall and Rabushka of Stanford University and presently championed by Representative Richard Armey (R-TX). The term *flat tax* is somewhat of a misnomer—the tax would be better described as a flat *rate* tax. Under this tax, income above a certain level, around $35,000 for a family of four, would be taxed at the same tax rate, rather than according to a graduated tax rate schedule as is presently done.

Actually, the Hall-Rabushka flat tax is a far more radical change in the tax system than the elimination of the tax brackets. For one thing, many of the tax expenditures in the existing tax system, such as the mortgage interest and charitable donations deductions and the exemption of employer-paid fringe benefits like medical insurance, would be eliminated. Also, the flat tax applies only to wages, salaries, and pension income, and leaves income from savings, such as interest, dividends, and capital gains, untaxed. Perhaps most important, the flat tax significantly changes the way business income is taxed. Most business tax expenditures are eliminated, and the investment spending is deducted as a cost of doing business in the year the expenditures are made. Deductions for depreciation and interest paid on business debt are eliminated. The redefined business income is taxed at the same rate applying to households. There is no double taxation of investment income, as there is presently under the combined personal and corporate tax systems (see Chapter 15).

Although the flat tax, for all its changes, seems to remain a tax on income, the proposal actually changes the tax base from income to consumption. We shall see why later in this chapter.

The National Sales Tax

Proposals for a National Retail Sales Tax (NRST) have received a fair amount of attention recently. Representatives Dan Schaefer (R-CO) and Billy Tauzin (R-LA) have proposed an NRST to replace the income tax system. Under the Schaefer-Tauzin proposal, the federal personal and corporation income tax, the estate and gift tax, and most excise taxes would be abolished, along with the Internal Revenue Service. The federal government would collect its revenue from a retail sales tax modeled on those levied by state governments. An NRST is levied on the gross revenue businesses receive from selling goods and services to households and exempts business to business sales. To lighten the sales tax burden on low-income families, each family would receive a rebate equal to the tax rate times the official poverty level of income for a family of the same size. For example, the official poverty level for a family of four persons (two adults and two children under age 18) was $16,895 in 1999. If a NRST were levied at 17%, all such families would receive an annual rebate of $2872.

An alternative to an NRST is a value-added tax (VAT). The central governments of most industrial countries except the United States obtain a substantial share of their revenue from a VAT. Some people believe the U.S. federal government should copy the experience of these other countries and levy a national VAT, either as a replacement for the income tax or to raise additional revenue. Others propose a VAT as a replacement for the payroll taxes currently used to finance the social insurance programs. A federal VAT would tax the value added to goods and services by businesses, where value added is the gross revenue of a business minus costs incurred for materials and investments. Unlike the NRST, the VAT would be levied on all sales transactions, whether business to households or business to business.

The Consumed Income Tax

Also in the running is the Unlimited Savings Account (USA) tax proposed by Senators Peter Domenici (R-NM) and Sam Nunn (D-GA). The USA tax would be similar to the existing personal income tax except that households can make unlimited contributions to tax-deferred savings plans, such as IRAs and 401(k) plans. As a result, all income saved by the taxpayer is not taxed when it is received, but withdrawals from saving are taxed as ordinary income. Since income minus saving is equal to household consumption, the USA tax is sometimes described as a personal consumption tax.

Unlike a sales tax, the USA tax is levied on persons rather than transactions, so it can have personal exemptions or deductions and a graduated rate structure similar to existing personal income tax. In fact, the Domenici-Nunn proposal retains the standard deduction and itemized deductions for mortgage interest and charitable donations. Consumed income (less deductions) is taxed according to a rate structure with three tax brackets ranging from 8% to 40%. The Domenici-Nunn plan also replaces the corporation income tax with an 11% VAT. The VAT would apply to all business revenue minus the costs of materials and investment.

In addition to the above fundamental tax reforms, a variety of incremental tax reforms have been proposed. These proposals would make piecemeal reforms in the existing tax system to make it more efficient, fair, and simple. To make the tax system more efficient and fair, many tax expenditures, such as deductions for mortgage interest, charitable donations, and state and local taxes, could be eliminated and the extra revenue used to reduce tax rates. Alternatively, the main tax expenditures could be converted from deductions (which favor high-income taxpayers) to credits. This makes the tax system fairer in the eyes of those proposing the reforms. Eliminating or reducing tax expenditures that favor high-income taxpayers makes it possible to simplify the tax system in several ways. For instance, the tax system would be simplified significantly if the phaseout provisions in the existing system and the alternative minimum tax were eliminated. The sole purpose of these complicated provisions is to limit the use of tax expenditures by high-income taxpayers.

CONSUMPTION AS A TAX BASE

Most of the federal tax reforms under debate would change the tax base from income to consumption, so it is important to understand the implications of a major federal tax on consumption rather than income. We can best understand consumption as a tax base by comparing consumption with income as measured in the national income and product accounts (NIPA) compiled by the Bureau of Economic Analysis. Table 17.1 shows the sources and uses of personal disposable income in the NIPA accounts for 1999. As we can see from this table, personal consumption expenditures in 1999

Table 17.1 Sources and Uses of Income (NIPA, 1999)

Sources of Income	Dollars (in billions)	Uses of Income	Dollars (in billions)
Wages, salaries, and other labor compensation	$5008.1	Personal consumption expenditures	$6257.3
Proprietor income	658.5	Interest payments and transfers to the rest of the world	226
Rents, interest, and dividends	1441.5	Personal saving	156.3
Transfer payments	1018.2		
Personal income	8126.6		
Less personal taxes and social insurance contributions	1486.7		
Personal disposable income	6639.9	Personal outlays and saving	6639.9

Source: Bureau of Economic Analysis, Table 2.1 Personal Income and Its Disposition, http://www.bea.doc.gov/bea/nipatbls/NIP2-1.HTM.

amounted to $6257.3 billion, which was 93% of the $6639.7 billion of personal disposable income received by households in 1999. The difference between personal consumption and personal income is equal to saving, interest paid by households, and personal taxes and social insurance contributions.

Of course, not all of the items under sources of personal income are taxed under the personal income tax. Labor compensation includes nonwage compensation such as employer-paid fringe benefits that go untaxed under the personal income tax. Similarly, not all of personal consumption expenditures would be taxed, even under the broadest possible tax. For example, the personal consumption expenditures in Table 17.1 include the imputed space rent for owner housing, which is no easier to tax as consumption than it is as income.

Methods of Taxing Consumption

The fact that consumption is equal to income minus saving means that the government can tax consumption in different ways. One way is to impose a tax on all sales or purchases of goods and services. This is called an **indirect consumption tax** because the tax is imposed on transactions of goods and services rather than on people. Existing indirect taxes on consumption include state and local retail sales taxes and federal, state, and local excise taxes. Another way to tax consumption is to measure personal income as is done presently, but subtract the net amount that households save. This would require taxpayers to report income as they do now, but they would be allowed to subtract the amount they save each year from their income in determining the amount of tax they must pay. Conversely, they would be required to add the amount they borrow or withdraw from their savings to their income. Economists call such a tax a consumed-income tax, or more simply, a **personal consumption tax.** Note that a personal consumption tax would require that the tax authorities monitor the amount the taxpayer deposits or withdraws from his or her savings each year, just as is currently done for 401(k) plans and IRAs. The difference would be that taxpayers could deposit unlimited amounts to such savings plans and could withdraw amounts at any age without penalty. The current system, with its limits on the amount taxpayers can deposit into tax-deferred savings plans and penalties for early withdrawals, is sometimes called a *hybrid* tax. This is because it is neither a pure income tax nor a pure consumption tax; rather, it mixes the features of both income and consumption taxes.

Still another way to tax consumption is to tax the wage and transfer receipts of the household. If levied over a person's lifetime, a tax on consumption is equivalent to a tax on wages, salaries, other forms of labor compensation, plus transfers and gifts received by the household. To see this, suppose a taxpayer earns $100 in wages this year and spends it next year. In the meantime, he or she saves the income in a savings account earning 10% interest. With a consumption tax, say of 20%, the government collects $22 next year when the taxpayer spends the amount saved plus the interest earned over the year. This leaves the household with $110 − $22 = $88 worth of goods and services. With a wage tax, the government would collect $20 this year on $100 wages, leaving the household $80 to save. This would give the household $88 including interest to spend next year. Although the government gets only $20 in revenue this year, the government can have $22 next year by saving the tax revenue and earning 10% interest. Generalizing this example, over a person's lifetime the present value of consumption spending must equal the present value of labor income, hence a tax on consumption and a tax on wage receipts are equivalent. Only the timing of the payments by the taxpayer and the revenue receipts by the government are different under the two taxes. Since both the households and the government can borrow and lend at the going interest rate, they are indifferent about the timing.

Note that the tax on household receipts must apply only to wages and transfers and not to interest and dividends; otherwise the return on saving is taxed twice   once when it is earned and again when it is spent. Also, the equivalence between taxing wage receipts and consumption outlays holds only if the two taxes apply over the entire lifetime of the household. For example, if the government switched from a wage tax to a consumption tax halfway through a person's lifetime, he or she would pay a heavier tax burden. Wages saved before that time would be taxed twice—first when they were earned and again when they are spent.

The equivalence of these three ways of taxing consumption are important for understanding many of the tax reform proposals under debate. The USA tax is a personal consumption tax on consumed income, whereas the NRST is an indirect tax on household consumption spending. The Hall-Rabushka flat tax is a tax on wage income that excludes all forms of capital income. All of them have in common the fact that they would shift the base of the federal tax system from income to consumption.

Technical Issues in Taxing Consumption

One complaint about taxing income is that it is inordinately difficult to tax some forms of income, especially business and capital income; therefore, the income tax has to be complicated. One of the big issues in the debate about tax reform is whether taxing consumption would involve more or less complexity than taxing income. Proponents of taxing consumption often point to the state RSTs as proof that taxing consumption this way would be easier than taxing income. States collect RST revenue from vendors at relatively low administrative and compliance costs, and compliance is very high—over 98% by some estimates. Moreover, the RST does not put households under the financial scrutiny of the government, as they are now by the Internal Revenue Service. For this reason, the Schaefer-Tauzin NRST proposes to abolish the IRS and let the U.S. Treasury or the existing state sales tax revenue authorities collect the NRST revenue.

Despite the apparent simplicity of the state retail sales tax systems, taxing consumption properly has its own set of difficulties. We consider a few of them in this section.

THE TAX TREATMENT OF CONSUMER DURABLES.   When a family rents a house, such spending is obviously consumption. But what if it buys a house instead? The purchase of a house is actually the purchase of future housing consumption from owning the house. A house is consumed not when the family buys it but rather when the family lives in it over the years. The housing consumption is equal to the hypothetical rent the family would pay each year to live in the house, called the *imputed rent* on owner-occupied housing. To tax annual consumption by homeowners, the tax authorities would need to impute the value of housing services received in kind by the homeowners. Fortunately, a simpler method is available.

Although it is difficult to measure and tax the annual services provided by a durable good like housing, an equivalent policy is to tax spending on consumer durables. This is done with an indirect consumption tax by levying a sales tax on home purchases. With a personal consumption tax, housing consumption is taxed if all housing payments, such as a down payment and mortgage payments, are taxed. This is accomplished automatically, provided that outlays cannot be deducted from income under the personal consumption tax system (as interest payments are currently under the existing income tax system).

A consumption tax that is levied on all consumption spending, including spending on consumer durables, is called an **expenditure tax.** Taxing spending on consumer durables is equivalent to taxing in advance the consumption services the durable goods provide in the future, so economists describe the taxes on consumption services from durables as *prepaid* under an expenditure tax. The price of a house capitalizes the value of housing consumption, just as the price of a share of stock capitalizes the dividends the stockholder expects to receive. Since the price of a house is equal to the present value of its future housing services, taxing the purchase of a house is equivalent to taxing the future services. Taxing all cash payments on a durable, such as the down payment and mortgage payments on a house, is also equivalent to taxing its annual consumption services.

Because the consumption services of a durable good are taxed in advance, double taxation occurs if the durable good is taxed when it is resold by the owner. To avoid taxing consumption every time the durable good changes hands, it is necessary to refund the taxes paid by the seller or exempt used durable goods from further taxation.

FINANCIAL AND OTHER SERVICES.   Measurement problems also occur if the value of financial services is taxed. Instead of paying interest on certain deposits, banks and other financial intermediaries provide services to the depositor in the form of security and check-writing privileges. These services are household consumption, but there is no corresponding cash transaction. For this reason, unlike in the case of a consumer durable, it is not possible to tax financial services using the prepayment method. Instead, the value of the financial services would have to be imputed (as the foregone interest that could have been earned on an interest-bearing account) and somehow taxed as consumption of the household. Alternatively, the costs of providing these services to the firm could be taxed at the level of the firm. This is possible under a value-added tax (VAT), which we discuss later, but not under an RST.

Government goods and services pose another problem. People enjoy consumption of government goods and services paid for with taxes rather than purchases. To tax such consumption, it would be necessary to levy taxes on taxes paid by households, which is neither difficult nor unusual. For example, the value of many goods and services subject to the retail sales taxes levied by the states includes federal and state excise taxes paid at the manufacturers' level. Alternatively, government goods and services could be taxed by taxing the cost of producing them. In this case, the sales tax is levied on government purchases of goods and services and wages paid to government employees.

Taxing government goods and services raises another problem, however. Under a consumption tax, investment goods are not taxed, only consumption goods. Governments provide households with a mixture of consumption goods (like garbage pickup) and investment goods (like education). If government goods and services are taxed, some means would be needed to ensure that only government consumption goods are taxed.

GOODS AND SERVICES USED IN FURTHER STAGES OF PRODUCTION.   To tax consumption, government should tax only *final* goods or services purchased by households, not intermediate goods purchased by businesses. The value of intermediate goods, such as raw materials and semiprocessed goods, is included in the final goods produced with them, so taxing intermediate goods would cause double taxation.

Investment goods such as plant and equipment purchased by businesses are also intermediate goods, although they are counted as final goods in the national income and product accounts. They are final goods because they are not physically embodied in other goods, but they are not final *consumption* goods. Although capital goods are not embodied in other goods, their services are used to produce other goods and the value of the services is included in the value of the final goods. For instance, welding robots purchased by a car manufacturer are not physically embodied in cars produced, but the value of their welding services is included in the value of the cars.

To tax consumption and only consumption, it is necessary to avoid imposing sales taxes on goods and services used in further stages of production. The difficulty is that it is not always apparent when an output is final consumption, because the output may be used for consumption or for further production. For example, heating oil purchased by a family to heat its home is a final consumption good, but the same heating oil purchased by a business to heat its factory is a production input. It is the use of the good, not its physical nature, that determines whether it is or is not final consumption.

Why does it matter whether production inputs are taxed as consumption? The main reason the government should avoid taxing production inputs is **tax cascading,** also called **tax pyramiding.** Sales taxes on intermediate goods raise costs to the firms that produce the final goods, so the taxes are included in the prices of the final goods. If the final outputs are also taxed, double taxation occurs. Tax cascading describes the phenomenon of accumulating and compounding taxes when intermediate goods are taxed as they pass through the different stages of production, processing, and distribution.

Tax cascading not only increases the effective tax rates on final consumption goods, it also causes the effective sales tax rates to vary from one good to another. Final goods and services produced with many taxed production inputs have higher effective tax rates than those produced with few taxed inputs. Variations in tax rates on different final goods and services caused by tax cascading make the sales tax system less efficient and less equitable. Also, tax cascading encourages firms to vertically integrate (combine many stages of production within one firm) for tax purposes, whether or not it makes economic sense to do so. Tax cascading is illustrated with a numerical example later in this chapter.

Indirect Taxes on Consumption

Although it is called an indirect tax, a sales tax on consumption goods and services is the most direct (i.e., straightforward) way of taxing consumption. A national sales tax could be designed in two ways. The National Retail Sales Tax (NRST) applies to all transactions in goods and services between businesses and households. Because it applies only to retail sales (i.e., sales from businesses to households), the NRST is a **single-stage sales tax.** The value-added tax (VAT), which taxes all transactions, including business to business and business to household transactions, is a **multistage sales tax.**

For either type of tax, the main problem is to ensure that all forms of final consumption are taxed and that investment and intermediate goods and services (goods and services used to produce other goods and services) are not taxed. Consumption goods and services are typically produced in several stages, usually by different businesses. For instance, bagels sold to consumers are the final (retail) stage of a chain of production and distribution. The earlier stages include the farm businesses that grow the wheat, the milling businesses that grind the wheat into flour, and the manufacturing businesses (bakeries) that make the bagels from the raw ingredients. After manufacture, the bagels may pass through wholesale businesses that make the bagels available to local retail sellers before finally being sold by the retailers to the ultimate consumer. Sometimes, several stages of production may be combined in one business, such as when a bakery makes its own bagels and sells them directly to the consumers. When several stages of production are combined in one firm, the firm is said to be vertically integrated.

To prevent tax cascading (or pyramiding), a single-stage sales tax like the NRST must exempt goods and services purchased by businesses for the purpose of resale or further processing. Thus, for example, a restaurant that buys bagels would be exempted from paying the NRST on the purchase because the bagels are resold to restaurant customers and the tax is paid at that time. Under most state retail sales taxes, businesses are granted a license or identification number that exempts them from tax. A similar method is proposed for the NRST. A problem with this method is that a "business" can use its exemption to purchase goods and services for consumption by the owner rather than resale. Some means is needed to prevent households from avoiding the NRST by the means of setting up proprietorships to receive a business tax exemption.

This type of tax avoidance can be reduced if the sales tax is levied on all transactions, including business to business transactions. A multistage sales tax is levied on all transactions at every stage of production as the good or service is sold and resold in the production and distribution chain. One type of a multistage sales tax called a **gross receipts tax (GRT)** is levied on all business receipts whether they are from selling goods and services to final consumers or other businesses. The GRT is considered a poor tax because it causes significant tax cascading. To prevent such tax cascading, multistage taxes can be levied on the value added of businesses rather than their gross receipts.

THE VALUE-ADDED TAX (VAT).   The most common multistage sales tax in the industrial world is called the **value-added tax (VAT)**. In fact, every industrial country in the world, except Australia and the United States, levies a national VAT. The VAT is different from the turnover tax because only the value added by a business, not its gross receipts, is taxed. The value added by a firm is the gross receipts of the firm minus the value of taxed goods and services used as inputs. These inputs may include both intermediate goods and capital goods. Unlike the turnover tax, a properly designed VAT does not cause tax cascading.

In Tables 17.2 and 17.3, we compare a gross receipts turnover tax (GRT) and a VAT of 10% for a good (bagels) produced in different stages by different firms. For simplicity, we ignore capital inputs and assume that the output of each stage is produced using intermediate goods from previous stages (materials) and labor. In this case, the value added by each firm is simply equal to its labor cost. To simplify further, we assume that materials are not used in the initial farming stage. Of course,

Table 17.2   Cascading of a Gross Receipts (Turnover) Tax on Bagels

Stage	Output	Materials	Cost of Materials	Labor Cost	Gross Receipts	10% GRT
Farmer	Wheat	None	0 cents	10 cents	10 cents	1 cent
Miller	Flour	Wheat	11 cents	20 cents	31 cents	3 cents
Baker	Bagel (wholesale)	Flour	34 cents	30 cents	64 cents	6 cents
Retailer	Bagel (retail)	Bagel (wholesale)	70 cents	40 cents	$1.10	11 cents
Household	None	Bagel (retail)	$1.21		Accumulated tax 21¢	

Table 17.3   Equivalence of a VAT and a Tax on the Retail Value of Bagels

Stage	Output	Materials	Cost of Materials	Labor Cost (Value Added)	Gross Receipts	10% VAT
Farmer	Wheat	None	0 cents	10 cents	10 cents	1 cent
Miller	Flour	Wheat	11 cents	20 cents	31 cents	2 cents
Baker	Bagel (wholesale)	Flour	33 cents	30 cents	63 cents	3 cents
Retailer	Bagel (retail)	Bagel (wholesale)	66 cents	40 cents	$1.06	4 cents
Household	None	Bagel (retail)	$1.10			Accumulated tax 10¢

in reality production chains are not linear like this example, and farmers do purchase materials. In each stage of our example, the cost of materials used is equal to the gross receipts of the previous stage plus the gross receipts tax.

Examining Table 17.2, we see that the GRT imposed on the earlier stages of production is built into the costs of the materials in later stages, causing tax cascading. For instance, the cost of the wheat to the miller includes the GRT paid by the farmer. In the final consumption stage, the price of a bagel to the consumer includes the taxes levied at all stages. The total accumulated tax on a bagel is 21 cents, rather than 10 cents (10% of the dollar cost of the bagel). This shows how tax cascading can dramatically increase the sales tax rate as a percentage of the price of the final good.

In Table 17.3 we illustrate a VAT, which is also a multistage sales tax but is levied only on the value added by each firm, not on gross receipts. In this case, the tax does not cause cascading. The total tax on a bagel is 10 cents, which is 10% of the cost of the bagel. Note that the price of a bagel without a sales tax is just the sum of the values added at each stage of the production process. Thus, the 10% multistage VAT is no different from a 10% single-stage tax on the final good (retail bagels) sold to consumers.

MEASURING VALUE ADDED.   How do the tax authorities measure the value added by a firm? Several methods can be used, although only one is encountered in practice. The simplest to understand is the *subtraction method,* which measures taxable value added by subtracting the cost of taxed materials from the gross receipts of the firm. For example, in Table 17.2 the miller in the second stage would subtract the 11-cent cost of the wheat from the 31-cent gross receipts from selling the flour to get 20 cents value added. A subtraction-method VAT, also called a **business transfer tax,** was proposed for the United States by Senator William Roth of Delaware in 1986 and is an important part of the recent proposal for a flat tax, as we discuss later.

The method used in all countries that levy a VAT is called the **invoice credit method.** With this method, every business pays the VAT on its gross receipts after receiving a credit for the amount of tax paid on purchased materials. The amount of tax credited is that shown on the invoice for the materials. In the example, at the second stage of bagel production, the miller pays 11 cents for wheat but receives a tax credit for the 1 cent of tax included in the price; hence the net cost of the wheat to the miller is just 10 cents. The miller sells the flour for 30 cents (the net cost of materials plus value added) and pays 3 cents tax on gross receipts. After subtracting the 1-cent tax credit on the purchase of wheat, the net tax paid by the miller is 2 cents, which is 10% of the miller's value added. The same thing happens at each stage, so by the end of the production process a total of 10 cents in value-added tax is levied.

One advantage of the invoice method is that it facilitates audits of taxpayers. Another advantage of the invoice method is that the government can impose different tax rates on different goods. For instance, most countries with VATs levy lower sales tax rates on certain goods and services, such as food, books, and legal services. To keep track of how much VAT has been paid on purchased inputs when businesses pay different rates of tax, it is necessary to use the invoice method. Multiple tax rates would not be possible under the subtraction-method VAT (the business transfer tax).

DIFFERENT BASES FOR VATs.   Although all the VATs in the world are levied on consumption, they could be levied on other bases. In fact, a VAT could be levied on GDP, income, or consumption, depending on how the capital costs of the firm are treated. To see this, we must complicate our bagel production line and allow capital costs at each stage. To grow wheat, the farmer needs a tractor; and to make flour, the miller needs a mill. Likewise, the baker needs an oven and the retailer needs a storefront, so each stage of production uses the services of capital. The value of capital's services at each stage is measured by the user cost of capital (see Chapter 15), which is equal to the interest cost plus the economic depreciation of the capital used by the firm.

With a GDP-type VAT, none of the user cost of capital is deducted, so the user cost of capital is included in the value added of the firm and is taxed by the VAT. Only intermediate goods and services purchased from other businesses are deducted in determining value added. If this type of VAT were levied on all goods and services, the base of the VAT would equal the value of all final goods and services produced in the economy, whether they are consumption goods or capital goods. The value of all such "final" goods and services is equal to the gross domestic product (GDP) of the economy; hence the name GDP-type VAT. This is the broadest possible base for a tax, so it is capable of raising large amounts of revenue at low tax rates.

An income-type VAT allows deductions for economic depreciation in measuring value added, but not for purchases of capital goods. In this case, the interest part of the user cost of capital, but not depreciation, is taxed by the VAT. If this type of VAT were applied to all goods and services produced in the economy, the tax base would be net national product, or national income. Such a VAT is equivalent to a proportional income tax, but income is taxed as it is generated in firms rather than as it is received by households.

Although GDP-type and income-type VATs do not cause tax cascading from the accumulation of taxes on materials, they do cause tax cascading because of taxes on the services of capital goods. Firms producing capital goods pay the VAT on their value added, and this tax is passed on to businesses buying the capital goods. Because under a GDP-type VAT the buyers do not get a tax credit for their purchases of capital goods, the tax paid on capital goods is incorporated into the price of the final goods. With this type of tax cascading, a GDP-type or income-type VAT discourages the use of capital goods in production. This provides a different perspective on why income taxes discourage investment, as we discussed in Chapter 15.

Although a VAT could be levied on GDP or income, most existing VATs are levied on consumption. In other words, the costs of both materials and capital goods are subtracted from gross receipts to calculate value added. A credit is given for taxes paid on the purchases of capital goods, because measuring the user cost of capital is too difficult. By excluding capital goods from the tax base, the VAT applies to final consumption goods and services only. Under a consumption-type VAT, tax cascading does not occur to any significant degree.

FLAT TAX OR VAT?   Most people think the flat tax is merely a reform of the existing personal income tax system that replaces the existing five tax brackets with a single tax bracket. In fact, the flat tax, at least the one proposed by Robert Hall and Alvin Rabushka of Stanford University, is much more than this. The Hall-Rabushka flat tax would replace the income tax system with a special form of VAT. The relationship between the flat tax and the VAT is an instructive application of the principle of tax equivalence, so we describe it in some detail here.

The centerpiece of the Hall-Rabushka flat tax is not just a single tax bracket but an integration of the business and personal tax systems in the form of a consumption tax. The business side of the flat tax is a subtraction-method consumption VAT that allows the usual deductions for materials and investment expenditures from gross business receipts. Since investment expenditures are deducted, the Hall-Rabushka flat tax is a consumption tax, not an income tax. Unlike the VAT levied in other countries, the flat tax would also allow firms to deduct employee compensation from gross business receipts. Wages and salaries are taxed as personal income to the recipients rather than as value added by firms; according to the tax equivalence theorem, this does not affect the economic impact of the tax. The purpose of the innovation is to allow the tax authorities to exempt a certain amount of wage income (as much as $35,000 per family in some proposals) so as to make the tax progressive. The exemption redresses one of the more serious objections to the VAT—that it imposes undue burdens on low-income families with limited ability to pay.

Although the flat tax would lower the marginal tax rate for those in the top tax bracket, high-income earners would lose many tax breaks that they have under the existing system, including the exclusion of in-kind fringe benefits. In-kind employee compensation would not be taxed as personal income under the flat tax, but it would be taxed by the VAT part of the tax because in-kind compensation would not be deductible from business gross receipts. In addition, on the personal side, the flat tax would eliminate the mortgage interest deduction, which disproportionately benefits high-income taxpayers by exempting their consumption of housing services.

Perhaps the most radical feature of the Hall-Rabushka proposal is the fact that it is levied on consumption. However, the tax could also be levied on income without changing the main features of the proposal. We saw earlier that a VAT can be levied on income by limiting deductions for capital expenses to depreciation rather than allowing deductions for investment expenditures. If an income VAT rather than a consumption VAT was used for the business side, the flat tax would appear less radical, and perhaps more politically palatable.

POLICY ISSUES IN TAXING CONSUMPTION

Up to now we have focused mainly on the mechanics of levying taxes on consumption. This informs us *how* we can tax consumption, but not *whether* we should tax consumption. Whether we should tax consumption depends on the economic as well as the administrative merits of doing so. We evaluate these merits using the methods described in Chapter 12; that is, by examining the economic efficiency, fairness (or equity), and administrative/compliance costs of taxing consumption.

Are Consumption Taxes More Efficient?

It is sometimes argued that consumption taxes are more efficient than income taxes. The reason is that consumption taxes, unlike income taxes, do not distort the choice between present and future consumption. According to this argument, under an income tax saving is too low for economic efficiency because the income tax lowers the after-tax return to saving. An income tax causes an "intertemporal distortion" and leaves the economy with less investable funds, a lower capital stock per worker, and a lower growth rate than it would have with a consumption tax.

Inefficiency is caused because an income tax changes the relative price of present and future consumption. The relative price of present and future consumption can be measured by the amount of future consumption given up to consume one more unit of consumption in the present. Without an income tax, a household must give up $1 + r$ units of consumption one year hence in order to consume $1 more (save $1 less) in the present, where r is the annual rate of return on saving measured in units of constant purchasing power (the *real* rate of interest). If r is 5%, a household gives up 1.05 units of goods one year in the future to consume 1 unit in the present. When the household saves for more than 1 year, we must take into account the compounding of interest. For example, a household gives up $(1 + r)^{10}$ units of consumption in 10 years by consuming 1 unit today, so if r is 5 percent, 1.63 units of consumption is given up in 10 years.

When an income tax is levied at rate t, the relative price of present consumption falls to $1 + r(1 - t)$ units of consumption next year. If t is 40% and r is not affected by the tax, the taxpayer gives up $1 + 0.05(0.6) = 1.03$ units of consumption next year to consume 1 more unit in the present. The relative price of present consumption is reduced by about 2% (1 minus 1.03 divided by 1.05). The effect on the relative price of present consumption is greater the longer the household saves. If we compound over 10 years, a household gives up $(1.03)^{10} = 1.34$ units of consumption 10 years hence to consume 1 unit now when the income tax rate is 40%. In this case, the relative price of present consumption is reduced by 18% The reason the relative price is affected more is that the income tax is compounded along with the interest rate. This is another form of tax cascading.

A CASE IN POINT

17.1   How High Would a National Sales Tax Rate Be?

One of the advertised advantages of a broad national sales tax is a relatively low rate; advocates of the NRST argue that a rate as low as 15% could be imposed. In fact, the sales tax rate could be as high as 45%, depending on how the rate is defined, how broad a measure of consumption is taxed, and how much revenue the government needs to collect with the tax. The latter depends on whether the sales tax replaces the personal income, corporate income, and excise taxes alone or whether it also replaces the payroll tax. It also depends on whether federal purchases of goods and services are subject to the tax and whether a universal rebate is given.

The sales tax rate can be defined on a tax-exclusive basis, which is how existing state retail sales tax rates are defined, or on a tax-inclusive basis, which is how income tax rates are defined. To compare the NRST rate with existing sales tax rates, the former is most appropriate, whereas to compare the NRST with existing income tax rates, the latter is most appropriate. For example, suppose a consumer spends $100, including $20 in sales tax. On a tax-exclusive basis, the sales tax rate is 25% ($20 divided by $80), whereas on a tax-inclusive basis the tax rate is 20% ($20 divided by $100).

The potential consumption tax bases are shown in the table. A broad definition of consumption that excludes only rent and imputed rent on residences and the imputed value of banking services would amount to $4655 billion in 1994. A narrower base that excludes food consumed at home, all financial services, medical care, new residential housing, local transit, and nonprofits would amount to only $2823 billion. The table also shows the amounts of revenue collected in 1994 by the existing federal taxes. Revenue from the personal income, corporation income, and excise taxes amounted to $797 billion. Including $462 billion collected from the social insurance payroll taxes, the total revenue need of the government was $1259 billion in 1994. The last columns of the table indicate the sales tax rates on both the tax-inclusive and tax-exclusive bases to collect the needed revenue.

Critically analyze the following:

- In comparing a national sales tax with the existing income tax rates, which sales tax rate (tax-inclusive or tax-exclusive) should be used? In comparing rates with existing state retail taxes, which rate should be used?

- Both of the consumption tax bases listed in the table include $516 billion in federal government purchases. Given that the federal government would have to pay tax on its purchases, how would this affect the amount of revenue it needs? How would this affect the required sales tax rate?

- The calculated tax rates in the table assume that no universal rebate is given. Suppose the universal rebate averages $1500 per family for 80 million families. What would be the sales tax rate required to replace the income and excise taxes if the broad measure of consumption is the tax base?

National Sales Tax Rates Using Alternative Assumptions

Consumption Tax Base	Billions of Dollars (1994)	Federal Taxes Replaced	Billions of Dollars (1994)	Sales Tax Rate Needed	
				Inclusive Base (%)	Exclusive Base (%)
Broad (excludes rent, imputed rent, and banking services)	$4655	Income and excise	$797	14.6	17.1
		Income, excise, and payroll	$1259	21.3	27
Narrow (excludes also food, medical care, financial services, new housing, nonprofits)	$2823	Income and excise	$797	22	28.2
		Income, excise, and payroll	$1259	30.8	44.6

Source: The consumption tax bases are from Congressional Budget Office, *Comparing Income and Consumption Tax Bases,* Table 8, July 1997.

By reducing the relative price of present consumption, an income tax encourages consumers to substitute present for future consumption as a means of getting lifetime utility. This is an inefficient decision by consumers because present consumption is not really cheaper; it only appears cheaper because of the income tax. For the economy as a whole, 1.05 units of future consumption are given up to consume an extra $1 today even if the consumer gives up just 1.03 units after tax. The government bears part of the cost as lost tax revenue that it would have collected on the interest. Of course, the consumer ignores this "social cost" of consuming now and saves too little from the point of view of overall economic efficiency.

A tax on consumption at the same rate in the present and the future leaves the relative price of present and future consumption to households unchanged. Unlike an income tax, a consumption tax is neutral with respect to the timing of consumption. Letting s denote the tax rate on consumption, the price of 1 unit of present consumption is $1 + s$ dollars including the tax. If the dollar is saved and used to purchase $1 + r$ units of consumption next year, the consumer pays $(1 + r)$ times $(1 + s)$ next year. The relative price of present to future consumption remains $1 + r$ after the consumption tax [equal to $(1 + r)(1 + s)$ divided by $(1 + s)$]. Because the relative price of present and future consumption is not affected by the tax, households are not inclined to substitute present for future consumption under the consumption tax as they are under an income tax.

The argument that consumption taxes are more efficient than income taxes is less convincing once we recognize that income and consumption taxes both distort the choice between labor and leisure. Once one distortion is present, the theory of the "second-best" tells us we cannot conclude that a consumption tax is more efficient simply because it does not distort the timing of consumption. Recall from Chapter 2 that, in the theory of the second-best, two "wrongs" can make a right.

First, we should make it clear why a consumption tax affects the choice between labor and leisure. Income taxes affect this choice by lowering the after-tax (take-home) wage a worker earns from an hour of employment. This lowers the price of leisure because an hour of leisure costs taxpayers their take-home wage. Although consumption taxes do not lower the take-home wage, they affect the labor-leisure choice because leisure is not taxed. Consumption taxes increase the price the consumer must pay for the market goods, so the taxpayer's *real* wage—measured in units of purchasing power—is reduced, although the take-home wage in dollars is not affected.

This is illustrated in Figure 17.1 which shows the choice between consumption and leisure for a household consumer that spends all of its earnings. Hours of leisure consumed are measured on the horizontal axis, and units of goods consumed are measured on the vertical axis. The household has 168 hours a week to allocate to leisure or to working at a money wage of W dollars. We assume that the price of a unit of consumption is $1. Without taxes, the budget line between goods and leisure is BB, which intersects the vertical axis at W times 168 units of consumption. If the government taxes consumption, the budget line is shifted to BB'. Although the take-home wage remains W dollars, the household must pay $1 + s$ for a unit of consumption, where s is the consumption tax rate. The budget line now intersects the vertical axis at $\dfrac{W \cdot 168}{1 + s}$ units of consumption and has an absolute

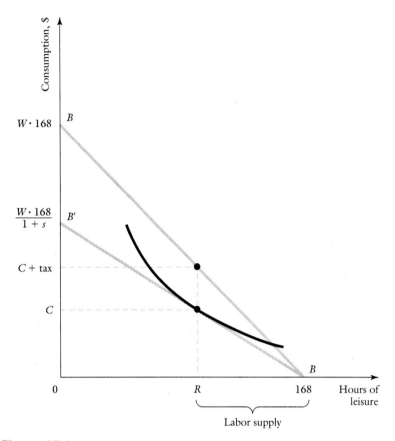

Figure 17.1

Effect of a Consumption Tax on the Labor-Leisure Choice

Without taxes, the consumer faces the budget line *BB* between leisure hours (horizontal axis) and spending on consumption (vertical axis). The slope of *BB* is the wage rate *W*. If consumption is taxed at rate *s*, the budget line is the flatter one, *BB'*, so the relative price of leisure is reduced. The change in the labor supply is ambiguous because a consumption tax, like an income tax, has both income and substitution effects.

slope of $W/(1 + s)$. The relative price of leisure is reduced by a consumption tax just as with an income tax. Because a wage tax is levied on a base that includes the tax, whereas a consumption tax is levied on a base that excludes the tax, a consumption tax of $s = t/(1 - t)$ has the same effect on the slope of the budget line as an income tax at rate t. For example, a 25% sales tax reduces the price of leisure by the same amount as a 20% income tax.

Given that a consumption tax distorts the labor-leisure choice, it may be less efficient than an income tax. Consumption is typically less than income, so if the government needs to raise the same amount of revenue, it must levy the consumption tax at a higher rate than an income tax. This causes a bigger distortion of the labor-leisure choice and a greater excess burden.

Fairness and Consumption Taxes

Whatever the efficiency gains from a consumption tax, such a reform is not likely if enough people believe that taxing consumption is less fair than taxing income. As we have already learned, there are many different concepts of fairness, so, not surprisingly, people hold different opinions on the matter. Proponents of a sales tax believe it is fairer than the income tax because everybody pays the same tax rate. In fact, one group promoting a national sales tax calls itself Americans for Fair Taxation. Opponents of a consumption tax, particularly of the sales variety, argue that it is very unfair because it places higher tax burdens on low-income families and lighter burdens on the rich. They believe that a consumption tax is regressive, so it is unfair in terms of vertical equity.

Political philosophers have long debated the merits of taxing consumption versus income. Early arguments emphasized the benefit principle of taxation. Recall that the benefit principle assumes that tax burdens should somehow be related to the benefits people receive. The seventeenth-century British philosopher Thomas Hobbes argued that consumption taxes are fairer than income taxes because people pay tax on how much of society's output they consume (i.e., how much they benefit), rather than on how much they produce. In Hobbes's view, a hard-working miser who earns a high income and consumes little is a benefactor for society. Such a miser consumes little of what he or she produces, so others must be able to consume more. In Hobbes's view, it is fairer that misers pay tax on their low consumption rather than their high incomes.

Modern discussions of fairness concentrate on vertical equity measured in terms of ability to pay. For this reason, the debate centers on how the burden of a consumption tax is borne across different income groups. The incidence of a consumption tax would depend on whether it is an indirect (sales-type) consumption tax or a personal tax on consumed income. A sales tax is levied on transactions, so the rate of tax must be the same for everyone. A personal consumption tax is levied on the individual, so it can have a graduated rate structure like that of the existing income tax.

Although the rate of tax under an NRST is the same for everyone, it is clear that the burden of a sales tax as a percentage of income would decline as income rises, making the NRST regressive. The reason is that families with higher income tend to consume a smaller fraction of their income, hence the amount of sales tax paid as a percentage on income declines as income rises. Professor Gilbert Metcalf of Tufts University has calculated the income incidence of the NRST under alternative assumptions. He considers an NRST of 17% (the tax-inclusive rate proponents claim would be revenue neutral) on a broad measure of consumption. The change in annual tax paid as a percentage of annual income for families in the different income deciles is shown in the second column of Table 17.4. The average tax rate for families in the lowest decile would increase over 64% if an NRST replaced the existing income tax, whereas the average tax rate for families in the highest decile would decrease 7%. The switch to the NRST is uniformly regressive across income groups, as shown in the table.

Some argue that this type of annual incidence measurement exaggerates the regressivity of the NRST. For one thing, saved income does not escape tax altogether under a consumption tax; the saved income is taxed in the future when it

Table 17.4   **The Income Incidence of a National Sales Tax**

Income Decile	Percentage Change in Annual Average Tax Rate	Percentage Change in Lifetime Average Tax Rate	Percentage Change in Lifetime Average Tax Rate with Universal Rebate
1	64.3%	5.7%	2.2%
2	2.4	4.0	1.5
3	17.4	1.0	−.9
4	11.5	1.0	.2
5	7.3	1.2	.8
6	2.3	.4	.04
7	3.9	.4	.1
8	−.6	−2.0	−2.0
9	−.9	−1.3	−.3
10	−7.0	−2.0	.1

Source: Gilbert E. Metcalf, "The National Sales Tax: Who Bears the Burden?" Cato Policy Analysis No. 289, December 8, 1997, available at http://www.cato.org/pubs/pas/pa289.html.

is consumed. Annual incidence ignores these future taxes. Also, most people are not locked into a particular income decile all of their lives. We learned in Chapter 7 that many people move from decile to decile over the course of their lives. For this reason, many economists believe that the lifetime incidence of the different taxes is better for comparing the vertical equity of consumption and income taxes. Recall from Chapter 11 that a lifetime incidence study measures a taxpayer's lifetime tax burden (the present value of taxes paid over a lifetime) as a percentage of his or her lifetime income. Metcalf also estimates the percent increase in the lifetime tax rate for families in different income groups resulting from a switch to the NRST from the income tax. The results are shown in the third column of Table 17.4. As can be seen, the NRST remains more regressive than the income tax even when lifetime incidence is measured, although less regressive than the annual incidence estimates indicate.

To mitigate the regressivity of the NRST, advocates propose that the tax be coupled with a Universal Rebate. The Universal Rebate is a lump-sum transfer (sometimes called a demogrant) given to every family that is equal to the NRST tax rate times the official poverty income level for a family of given size. In theory, this would remove the burden of the NRST from families with incomes lower than the poverty level. The Universal Rebate does reduce the regressivity of the NRST. The change in the lifetime tax rate of each decile resulting from a switch to an NRST coupled with a Universal Rebate is shown in the last column of Table 17.4. Although the lifetime tax rates for families in the lowest income deciles are still increased, the overall distribution of the tax burden is not appreciably changed.

The Universal Rebate does come with a cost, however. The touted advantages of the NRST are a lower tax rate and administrative simplicity. The Universal Rebate reduces both of those advantages. To finance the rebate, the tax rate would have to be much higher because the Universal Rebate would cost the government hundreds of billions of dollars each year. Furthermore, the administration of the Universal Rebate would require some of the complexity we find in the existing income tax system. Each family would have to apply for the rebate and provide truthful information about the number of family members. To prevent people from misrepresenting the size of their families in order to receive a larger Universal Rebate, an agency similar to the IRS would need to monitor rebate applications.

Fundamental tax reform raises another difficult horizontal equity issue called **transitional equity.** Transitional equity describes the extent to which a change in the tax system would differentially affect taxpayers who are similar in ability to pay but different in other respects. A major change in the tax system will inevitably create winners and losers among similar households. For example, many tax reform proposals would eliminate the current subsidy to home ownership given through the mortgage interest deduction. People who assumed large mortgages to purchase homes would be adversely affected relative to people who have paid off their mortgages or rent their homes.

Switching from an income tax to a consumption tax would create a major transitional equity problem for people of different ages. People at the end of their working careers would be affected adversely relative to people starting out or in the middle of their careers. For example, people nearing retirement who worked their entire lives paying taxes on their earnings would now face paying taxes again as they consume their retirement savings. One could not blame them for feeling that they are treated unfairly by a change to a consumption tax. There is no simple answer to the problem of transitional equity. It is possible to "grandparent" people who spent their working lives under the income tax system, but this would significantly add to the administrative and compliance costs of the system. If older people are exempted from the consumption tax, what would prevent them from purchasing goods and services for their children and friends?

The equity issues are less serious for a personal consumption tax such as the USA tax proposed by Senators Domenici and Nunn. With a personal consumption tax that exempts saved income, the tax rate applying to a taxpayer can depend on the level of the taxpayer's consumption, just as the income tax rate depends on the level of the taxpayer's income. A personal consumption tax system can have a graduated tax rate structure so that rich families with high consumption levels pay a higher tax rate than do low-consumption families. In fact, in principle, the tax rate structure could be chosen to achieve the same incidence as the existing income tax. Transitional equity problems would be less severe under the USA tax as well.

Administrative and Compliance Costs

The high administrative and compliance cost of the existing income tax system is one of the major motives for fundamental tax reform. Advocates of such reforms point to the high costs of the income tax system and claim that their preferred tax would drastically reduce these costs. In some cases, these claims are exaggerated. A case in point is the NRST. Advocates of the NRST believe that their plan would eliminate most of the administrative and compliance costs of the federal revenue system because individuals would no longer need to file tax returns and the IRS could be abolished. In fact, costs would be incurred by businesses who must remit the tax. NRST advocates acknowledge this but argue that the state experience with retail sales taxes suggest that these costs would be low.

Economists doubt that the low costs of administering the state RSTs will transfer easily to the NRST. One reason is the tax rate. Rates for state RSTs average around 6% on a tax-exclusive basis. An NRST applied to the broadest conceivable consumption base and assuming no avoidance or evasion could require a tax-exclusive rate of about 20% to collect the same revenue as is currently collected by the income tax system. This implies a combined federal and state sales tax rate of at least 25%. At such high rates, sales tax avoidance and evasion would be a much bigger problem than is presently the case for the typical state sales tax. Rules would become more complex and enforcement more intrusive, just as with the current income tax. Indeed, nearly all countries that have tried single-stage sales tax rates over 10% have experienced serious avoidance and evasion problems. That is why countries that rely on sales taxes adopt the invoice method multistage VAT, which has self-enforcement features. Moreover, a Universal Rebate to relieve tax burdens on low-income families would significantly add to the administrative and compliance costs of the NRST.

In general, there are reasons to believe that consumption can be taxed with lower administrative and compliance costs than income. The major reasons for the high administrative and compliance cost of the income tax system lie in the taxation of various forms of capital income and the taxation of corporate income. Under a properly designed consumption tax, such as a VAT or a USA tax, there is no need to tax capital income, and the business tax system can be drastically simplified. Although businesses would need to comply with the increased demands of a VAT, they would no longer need to comply with the far more complicated corporation income tax system.

OTHER TAX BASE SHIFTS

We have focused on the possibility of shifting the federal tax system from income to consumption in this chapter because that is the thrust of most suggested fundamental tax reforms. Some groups suggest shifts in the tax base that are more radical. Many environmental groups, for example, suggest shifting the tax base away from income toward environmentally damaging activities and compounds, a reform sometimes called the **green tax shift.** Other reformers advocate shifting the tax base from income to wealth, mainly for equity purposes.

The Green Tax Shift

The idea of coupling tax reform with environmental policy has received much attention recently. Environmental tax reformers argue that the United States could achieve a more efficient tax system by reducing taxes on income and consumption and raising taxes on pollution. They argue that it makes sense to tax activities that should be discouraged, like pollution, rather than activities that should be encouraged, like work. Although environmental taxes would probably not raise sufficient revenue to replace the income tax, revenue from these taxes could be used to reduce income tax rates. Also, personal and corporate tax expenditures that are harmful to the environment would be eliminated, raising more revenue. Environmental tax

17.2   Tax Reform—Rhetoric and Reality

Efficiency, fairness, and, especially simplicity are frequently cited as the main reasons for changing or reforming the tax system. However, it is not clear that the tax "reforms" enacted achieve these objectives, at least for long. The Tax Reform Act of 1986 (TRA86) was the last time the federal government undertook major tax reform. The main purpose of TRA86 was to simplify the tax system, and to a certain degree it achieved these objectives. It collapsed the 14 tax brackets into 3, lowered the tax rate in the top bracket from 50% to 28%, and removed millions of taxpayers from the tax rolls by substantially increasing the standard deduction and personal exemptions. It also eliminated a number of tax expenditures, including deductions for interest on consumer loans and state and local sales taxes. It abolished the lower tax rate for capital gains, and all income was taxed at the same rate. In other respects, however, TRA86 added to the complications in the tax system. It introduced a 33% tax bracket called the "bubble" for middle-income taxpayers designed to retract the advantage of the lower tax brackets and the personal exemptions from higher-income taxpayers. It added complicated provisions restricting the use of passive loss shelters, many of which had been introduced by earlier tax legislation designed to "simplify" the tax system, called the Economic and Tax Reform Act of 1981. The net effect of TRA86 was to add several hundred pages to the tax code and scores of new tax forms.

Many of the provisions of TRA86 were undone or weakened by subsequent changes in the tax law. The Omnibus Budget Reconciliation Act of 1990 (OBRA90) rescinded the bubble but introduced a new 31% tax bracket along with complicated "hidden" tax brackets taking the form of phaseouts of personal exemptions and itemized deductions. OBRA90 also reintroduced differential taxation of capital gains because they were not subject to the new 31% bracket. OBRA93 added two new tax brackets, 36% and 39.6%, again exempting capital gains from the higher rates. It vastly expanded the Earned Income Tax Credit for low-income families, and the perceived potential for abuse of this credit subsequently led to complicated qualifying provisions. It also increased the fraction of Social Security benefits subject to tax.

The Tax Relief Act of 1997 completed the job of dismantling the TRA86 reforms. Tax rates on capital gains were reduced further, with reductions depending on how long the assets are held by taxpayers. This introduces a host of new complications. New types of IRAs (the Roth and nonworking-spouse IRAs) were introduced, along with complicated provisions governing the ability of taxpayers to roll over one type into another. Large new tax expenditures in the form of the child tax credit and tax credits for higher education were introduced. Most analysts agree that as the United States entered the twenty-first century, its tax system is more complicated and arbitrary than ever.

Critically analyze the following:

- Some people perceive a tax reform/deform cycle. Political pressures lead to the proliferation of special tax breaks, especially when times are good and revenue is plentiful. This narrows the tax base, necessitating higher tax rates in the future. Eventually, a point is reached at which it becomes politically attractive to broaden the tax base by cleaning up the tax breaks in exchange for lower rates. This sets the stage for another cycle. If this is true, in what stage of the cycle is the United States now (year 2000) and what is the prognosis for the future?

- In Chapter 5, we learned that majority voting can lead to cycles, called the voting paradox. Explain how cyclical majorities could lead to a tax reform/deform cycle.

- One argument for fundamental tax reform, as opposed to incremental measures like TRA86, is to break the tax reform/deform cycle. Of the fundamental reforms considered in this chapter, which one do you think is most likely to break the reform/deform cycle? Why?

reformers believe that Americans would enjoy a double dividend from such reforms in the form of a cleaner environment and a more efficient tax system.

A good example of an environmental tax shift is a current proposal to enact a carbon tax. Carbon dioxide released by burning fossil fuel is believed to be a major contributor to global warming, which will increase the average world temperature by several degrees over the next century. Such an increase would cause considerable economic and environmental damage. To arrest global warming, environmentalists propose a tax on the carbon content of fossil fuels. Representative Stark (D-CA) has proposed a bill that would phase in a carbon tax of $30 per ton over five years. When fully phased in, Stark's carbon tax would raise about $36 billion in revenue. Many countries in the world already have carbon taxes. For example, Denmark has a carbon tax of $52 a ton. Other countries tax carbon through excise taxes on fossil fuels. In 1988, the United States had the lowest implied tax on carbon (through gasoline taxes, etc.) of any developed country, at $28 a ton. France, Italy, and Sweden are the highest, with implied carbon tax rates of $229, $223, and $214, respectively.[1]

Many economists, although granting the possible merits of the green tax shift, doubt that it can form the basis for comprehensive tax reform. For one thing, environmental taxes are not sufficiently broad-based to raise enough revenue to replace the income tax. Second, environmental taxes are likely to be regressive and therefore unsuitable as the main source of government revenue. For example, Professor James Poterba of MIT estimates that a carbon tax imposes a tax burden that is more than six times as high relative to income for taxpayers in the lowest-income decile as for those in the highest income decile.[2]

Perhaps for these reasons, many environmental tax reformers couple their call for environmental taxes with a shift to taxes on site value. This resurrects an idea proposed over a hundred years ago by the political economist and reformer Henry George, who campaigned for president on the platform of abolishing all taxes except for a single tax on land. Since land is a form of wealth, we discuss this type of tax reform later in this chapter.

Taxes on Wealth

Although wealth is often confused with income, they are different measures of ability to pay. A person can have high income and little wealth, or vice versa, although the two are usually positively correlated (wealthy people usually have high incomes). The broadest measure of personal wealth is *net worth*, which is the value of a family's assets minus its liabilities. For instance, to find net worth, we sum up the value of a family's home, possessions such as furniture and cars, money in bank accounts, and the value of stocks and bonds, and subtract the amounts of debts such as mortgages, car loans, and unpaid bills. Note that wealth is measured at a point in time, so economists call it a *stock variable*. In contrast, income is a *flow variable* because it is measured over an interval of time. If we are told that someone's income is

---

[1]P. Hoeller and M. Wallin, "Energy Prices, Taxes and Carbon Dioxide Emissions," *Economics and Statistics Department Working Paper #106,* Organization for Economic Cooperation and Development, 1991.
[2]J. M. Poterba, "Tax Policy to Combat Global Warming," *National Bureau of Economic Research Working Paper #3649,* 1991.

$10,000, we'd need to know whether it is measured over a week, a month, or a year to know whether it was high or low.

Although some people become wealthy in an instant—for example, by inheriting a fortune or winning a lottery—more often a person's net worth is the result of decisions and events occurring over longer periods of time. For instance, a person's net worth is increased by saving (consuming less than one's income) and decreased by dissaving (consuming more than one's income) over time. At an instant of time, a person's net worth is more or less fixed. Economists describe wealth as *predetermined* by the past accumulation decisions of the taxpayer.

Would-be tax reformers, contemplating the unequal distribution of wealth in the United States, sometimes lament the absence of wealth taxes and advocate some form of personal wealth tax. Some European countries levy taxes on personal wealth above a certain amount. However, such taxes have proved difficult to administer, and they are not a major source of government revenue in the countries that levy them.

It is easy to understand why governments may be tempted to tax wealth, particularly if they could tax it "once and for always." Since the stock of wealth is predetermined by past decisions and is fixed at a point in time, a one-time tax on wealth is a lump-sum tax that does not distort economic decisions. A wealth tax (unlike an income tax) would not discourage the labor supply or discourage saving. In fact, it could make people work and save more in the future, at least in theory. Also, a wealthy person has a high ability to pay the tax, so the government need not worry about putting an undue burden on the poor, as it would with a head tax that is the same for everybody. In other words, a one-time wealth tax seems both efficient and equitable.

More realistically, it is doubtful that general wealth taxes are efficient or fair. People would not believe that a wealth tax is a one-time event, so they would anticipate a recurrence and alter their behavior. Anticipation of future wealth taxes would discourage the taxpayer's labor supply, and saving in particular. We can also question the fairness of taxing wealth. If people are wealthy because they scrimped and saved after paying taxes on their incomes, taxing their wealth seems a punitive form of *ex post facto* double taxation. It is also horizontally inequitable because people who had the same income and opportunity to accumulate wealth, but chose to spend their income as they earned it, pay less tax over a lifetime.

For these reasons, many economists think that if income is properly taxed, there is no need to tax wealth. Wealth taxes are desirable only when wealth is accumulated from untaxed income, such as unrealized capital gains. Governments in the United States make little attempt to tax the wealth held by individuals, except real estate. Rather, they tax wealth only when it is transferred from one person to another as a bequest or gift. We discuss these forms of wealth taxes below.

Taxes on Transfers of Wealth

It is said that nothing is certain except death and taxes. These two great human fears are combined in another way: a taxpayer's death can trigger certain taxes, in particular the estate tax levied by the federal government and the estate and inheritance taxes levied by the states. An estate tax is levied on the net worth of a decedent, whereas an inheritance tax is levied on the amount received from an estate by an heir. These two taxes are commonly lumped together and called **death taxes.**

Most states levy a "pickup" death tax. This tax simply takes advantage of the tax credit allowed under the federal estate tax for a certain amount of state death taxes. Thus the state tax is levied simply to "pick up" revenue that would otherwise go to the federal government. The taxpayer pays no more tax as a result of the state death tax—the tax simply determines whether the federal or state government receives the revenue. For this reason, we concentrate on the federal tax.

The federal estate tax is levied on the amount of the **taxable estate** according to a graduated tax rate schedule. The taxable estate is equal to the value of the assets held by the taxpayer at the time of death, less bequests to a spouse, debts, contributions to charities, funeral expenses, and the costs of administering the estate. An estate left to a surviving spouse is not subject to the tax. The estate tax rate schedule has 17 brackets, each with its own marginal tax rate, starting at 18% on the first $1 and rising to a top bracket rate of 55%. The top marginal estate tax rate applies to estates in excess of $3 million.[3] Although every dollar of the taxable estate is subject to tax, the federal government allows a nonrefundable **unified tax credit** against the tax liability levied on the estate. Given the tax rate schedule, this means that no tax is paid on the first $675,000 of the taxable estate (as of 2000). Only taxable estates over $675,000 are taxed, but given the graduated rate schedule, the marginal tax rate begins at 37% on the first $1 of taxable estate. The Taxpayer Relief Act gradually increases the unified tax credit until 2006. In that year, only estates in excess of $1 million will be taxed.

An obvious incentive provided by a tax on transfers of wealth at death is for taxpayers to arrange to transfer wealth before dying by making gifts to their heirs. Such transfers are called *inter vivos* transfers. In fact, the incentive to make inter vivos transfers is so obvious that the federal government also levies a gift tax precisely to prevent such tax avoidance. Taxes on gifts are calculated according to the estate tax rate schedule, so the federal tax is often called the *unified* estate and gift tax. Gifts are taxed according to the cumulative lifetime transfers and final estate left by the donor according to a complicated procedure. However, the donor can make gifts of $10,000 ($20,000 for married couples) per recipient each year without tax consequences, and unlimited gifts in the form of tuition and medical expenses.

For all its complexity and its high rates, the federal estate and gift tax actually raises a relatively small fraction of federal revenue. In 1999, total revenue from this tax amounted to $26 billion, or just 1.4% of federal tax revenue. Given the size of annual bequests in the United States, this is a surprisingly small amount. We have already mentioned some explanations, such as the fact that bequests to spouses and charities are not taxed and the existence of the unified credit and credit for state death taxes. Another reason is the fact that much of the estate tax can be avoided with careful estate planning. In fact, estate planning is big business for tax accountants and lawyers.

Reform of federal wealth taxes in the United States does not seem high on the agenda. While many reformers, concerned about the unequal distribution of wealth,

---

[3]The benefits of the unified tax credit and the lower tax rates in the graduated schedule are phased out for estates over $10 million, making the marginal tax rate 60% on such large estates.

advocate higher wealth taxes, the current direction of reform is toward reducing and perhaps abolishing the estate and gift tax, the only form of federal wealth taxation. Those who promote abolishing the estate and gift tax argue that the tax is too complex and costly to enforce to justify the amount of revenue it collects. Occasionally, arguments for higher taxes on wealth are heard, such as the proposal for a net worth tax by real estate billionaire Donald Trump during his brief flirtation with a presidential candidacy for the Reform party in 1999. For whatever reasons, taxes on wealth have never been a popular idea in the United States, except for the land tax.

Taxes on Land and Site Value

Taxes on real estate property are the main form of wealth taxation in the United States at the present time. Most property tax revenue, amounting to $235 billion in 1999, is collected by local governments, such as cities, towns, and school districts. These property taxes, which are levied on the value of land and structures owned by households and businesses, are discussed at length in Chapter 19. In this section, we discuss the merits of shifting the local property tax and other sources of government revenue as well, to a single tax on land or site value.

The desirability of collecting government revenue by taxing land goes back to Adam Smith's *Wealth of Nations* in 1776. The idea of a single tax on land was revived by one-time presidential candidate and political reformer Henry George in his 1879 book *Progress and Poverty*. George observed that land booms are often accompanied by decreased wages, which he attributed to land speculators withholding vacant land from production in anticipation of capital gains. To end the speculative holding of vacant land and make it available for production, George advocated that the government abolish all taxes except for taxes on land. The tax would apply to all land, whether developed or not, and only to land, not to structures and improvements. Because raw land is immobile and fixed in supply, a tax on land does not impair economic efficiency, nor can it be shifted from the landowners to others. Landowners as a group are typically more wealthy, so George argued that a tax on land is more equitable. By removing all other taxes, which fall on production and consumption, the land tax would unleash economic activity and raise living standards, a sort of double dividend.

George's argument is shown in Figure 17.2, where the amount of land is measured on the horizontal axis and the price of land is measured on the vertical axis. It is generally believed that the supply of land is fixed—as the humorist Will Rogers once said, "Buy land; they aren't making any more of it"—so the supply of land is shown by the vertical supply curve in Figure 17.2. The fixed quantity of land available in the community is denoted $\bar{L}$. The demand for land is shown by the downward-sloping demand curve D. The intersection of the demand curve with the fixed supply curve determines the equilibrium value V_0 of land.

When a landowner must pay property tax on the value of land owned, the price a potential buyer is willing to pay is reduced by the amount of the tax. In principle, the price a buyer will offer is reduced by the present value of the property taxes that the buyer must pay on the land. Subtracting the property tax from the demand curve, we obtain the after-tax demand curve D_t. As a result of the property tax, the equilibrium value of the land falls to V_t. The difference V_0 minus V_t is the present

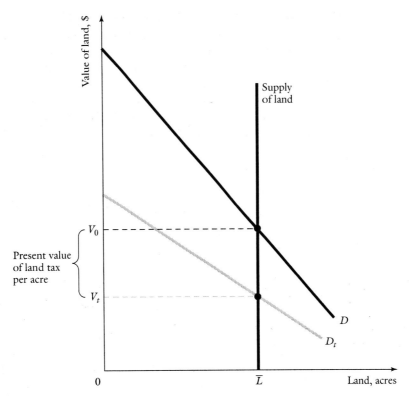

FIGURE 17.2

Effect of a Tax on Land

Land is in fixed supply at $\bar{L}$, so a tax on land reduces its value by the present value of the future taxes that must be paid. The tax on land shifts the demand curve from D to D_t, which reduces the value of an acre of land from V_0 to V_t because the supply curve is vertical. In this case, the incidence of the tax on land is borne entirely by the owners.

value of the future property taxes that must be paid on an acre of land. Since the supply of land is fixed, no change in quantity occurs. The imposition of the property tax is like a lump-sum tax on the people who own the land at the time the tax is levied. This is an example of *tax capitalization,* explained in Chapter 11.

The problem with George's land tax, as with any property or wealth tax, is that it requires an assessment process. The value of a piece of land depends, among other things, on its location and amenities. To tax the value of land holdings, the government would need to determine the market value of each piece of land in every tax year. Unless the land is sold, the market value of the land must be imputed by assessors. Even if the land is sold, it may be difficult to separate the value of the land from the value of the structures and improvements on the land without imputation. Moreover, it does not seem possible to impose a land tax (or, for that matter, a property tax) on a nationwide or even on a regional basis. This would require an army of federal land assessors, which would lead to greater intrusions on privacy than results from the current practices of the IRS. Except at the local level, a single land tax does not seem any more likely today than it was in Henry George's time.

gists, believe that such a tax would benefit society by reducing urban sprawl and revitalizing inner cities. By taxing land, households would be less inclined to demand large parcels of property with their homes, reducing the flight to the suburbs. Residential density would be increased, reducing road congestion, pollution, and the need for extensive infrastructure investments by local governments in sewers and transportation. Because improvements would not increase an owner's property tax bill, incentives would be greater for rehabilitating existing properties within the cities.

CONCLUSION AND SUMMARY

Public finance economists are fascinated by the topic of tax reform. The shortcomings of the existing system seem clear, and the benefits of an improved tax system in terms of greater efficiency and reduced compliance costs could amount to hundreds of billions of dollars. What is puzzling is the apparent inability of the political process to deliver this bonanza to the American people. The reason lies partly in the conflicts between efficiency, equity, and simplicity inherent in any tax system. However, some tax reforms, such as reducing personal and corporate tax expenditures, could increase efficiency and equity while reducing complexity. Ultimately, the problem lies in the fact that any type of tax reform, whether incremental or fundamental, creates modest gains for the many and larger losses for the few. Proposals to reform the tax system bring out lobbyists in droves to protect cherished tax breaks. The intense lobbying preceding the Tax Reform Act of 1986 was described by Jeffrey Birnbaum and Alan Murray in *Showdown at Gucci Gulch.*

- Tax reform is a program of changes in the tax system to make it more efficient, fairer, and simpler for taxpayers to understand and obey. Fundamental tax reform would replace the existing tax system with a new one, whereas incremental tax reform would modify the existing tax system in significant ways.

- Fundamental tax reforms under consideration include a flat tax, a national retail sales tax, a value-added tax, and a consumed income tax. Incremental tax reforms would broaden and clean the income tax base while reducing marginal tax rates.

- The above fundamental tax reforms all change the tax base from income to consumption. Consumption is equal to income minus saving, so all the reforms would eliminate taxes on income from savings.

- Sales taxes are levied on transactions in goods and services, whereas direct consumption taxes, like the consumed income tax, are levied on persons. One advantage of the consumed income tax is that it can be tailored to the individual taxpayer's ability to pay.

- A retail sales tax is a single-stage sales tax on sales from businesses to households and exempts business to business sales. A value-added tax is a multistage sales tax levied on all sales, but businesses deduct the costs of materials and investment goods already taxed. This prevents tax cascading.

- The broadest measure of consumption is about 93% of personal income. However, many components of consumption, such as housing, financial services, and medical care, may be difficult to tax for technical or political reasons.

■ Unlike the income tax, a consumption tax does not distort the choice between present and future consumption and is more efficient for that reason. Like the income tax, a consumption tax distorts the choice between goods and leisure. To the extent that tax rates are higher because consumption is a narrower base than income, a consumption tax can be less efficient than an income tax.

■ Opinion is divided on whether a consumption tax is more or less fair than an income tax. Sales-type consumption taxes significantly increase annual tax burdens on low-income families and lower annual burdens on high-income families because the former consume a larger fraction of their income. Also, it is difficult to exempt low-income families from sales taxes, or levy higher sales tax rates on high-income families.

■ Some economists believe that consumption taxes are simpler to administer than income taxes because they do not require complicated provisions for taxing capital and business income. States are able to levy retail sales taxes at low cost, and other countries raise vast amounts of revenue from the value-added tax at relatively low cost.

■ Some environmental groups advocate dropping taxes on desirable activities like work and consumption and shifting them to activities and compounds that cause environmental damage. An important element of such a "green tax shift" is a carbon tax, which is levied on the carbon content of fossil fuels.

■ Wealth taxes have never been important in the United States, except for property taxes. Currently the federal government taxes wealth only through estate and gift taxes. Local governments tax wealth in the form of real estate. Followers of Henry George and their modern counterparts advocate shifting the property tax and other taxes to land. In their view, land is an ideal tax base because land is in fixed supply, so land taxes do not distort economic decisions and cannot be shifted from the landowners.

QUESTIONS FOR DISCUSSION AND REVIEW

1. A revenue-neutral tax reform collects the same revenue before and after the tax system is changed. What are the different ways a taxpayer might benefit from a revenue-neutral tax reform even though he or she pays the same amount of tax?

2. Given that personal saving is such a small fraction of income, why does it make a difference whether income or consumption is used as the tax base?

3. How would the annual tax burdens of the following people be affected if the government were to switch this year from taxing income to taxing consumption? How would their lifetime burdens be affected?

   a. Mr. Grasshopper consumes all of his income this year and more. In fact, he borrowed to buy a car.

   b. Ms. Ant saves much of her income for a rainy day. This year she saved 25%.

   c. Grandmother and Grandfather have just retired and are planning to enjoy their retirement with the money they saved while working.

4. Explain the sense in which levying a sales tax on the purchase of a new house is equivalent to levying a sales tax on the amount it would rent for each year. How does the timing of the tax payments differ? Should the sales tax apply to homes that are resold? If so, which ones?

5. Both a retail sales tax and a value-added tax avoid the problem of tax cascading, but they do it differently. How does each type of sales tax avoid tax cascading? Which method is more likely to lead to tax evasion?

6. Evaluate the following assertion: "Consumption taxes are less efficient than income taxes because taxpayers can avoid the tax by saving."

7. Two taxpayers, X and Y, earn $100,000 this year and nothing next year. Consumption goods cost $1 each, and the bank pays 10% interest on savings. X saves half of his income and spends it next year, whereas Y saves only 10% of her income to spend next year. Would X and Y pay the same present value of taxes over the two years if a 50% consumption tax is levied? What if a 50% income tax is levied? What does this example imply about the horizontal equity of consumption versus income taxes?

8. A worker earns $10 an hour and buys goods at $1 per unit. What is the relative price between goods and leisure if the government levies a 20% income tax? Show that the relative price of goods and leisure is the same if the government levies a 25% tax on the price of the goods instead of taxing income. How is it possible that the relative price is the same, given that the tax rates are different?

9. One often hears that a good tax system provides a "level playing field" by taxing all activities equally, thereby favoring and

disadvantaging none. Fellow textbook author Professor Jeffrey Perloff of the University of California, Berkeley, says that there should be a tax on everyone who talks about "leveling the playing field." Do advocates of environmental tax reform think that a level playing field is a good tax policy? Use the theory externalities and corrective taxes to explain why a level playing field is not necessarily a good policy.

10. At one time, city lots in Charleston, Virginia, were taxed according to the number of feet of road frontage. Visitors to Charleston are surprised to see that many of the city's antebellum mansions are built on long, narrow lots with the narrow end of the mansion facing the street.[4] How would the architecture of Charleston have been different if the city had levied a Henry George land tax?

11. Internet Exercise. Tax reform groups go to great lengths to promote their favorite tax system or to knock the alternatives. And they find no better place to make their case than the Internet. Since they are trying to affect political action, they must make their preferred tax appealing to the average voter. These psychological or "gut level" appeals are not captured in the academic arguments found in this textbook. Check out two such sites, the Flat Tax site at http://www.flattax.gov/ and the Americans for Fair Taxation site at http://www.fairtax.org/. Identify ways in which each site attempts to make its favored tax system appealing to the average voter. How does each site attempt to downplay features the average voter may not like?

12. Internet Exercise. Although the United States does not tax personal net wealth, some countries, like Holland, do. Details on the Dutch net worth tax are found at http://www.intax.nl/wealth.htm. Use this

---

[4]Pam Neary, "OutLANDish TAXes?" 1999.

site to answer the following questions. What is the base of the Dutch net worth tax? What is the rate of tax? What are the main exemptions? (Note: The NLG is the Dutch guilder, worth about 42 cents in June 2000.)

13. Internet Exercise. The Virtual Economy Homepage, maintained by the Institute for Fiscal Studies in the United Kingdom, allows the user to change the fiscal system of the U.K. economy by changing income tax rates, sales (VAT) tax rates, and other fiscal variables. The model calculates the impact of the fiscal changes on important economic variables, such as the growth rate (from capital accumulation), the unemployment rate, and the distribution of the tax burden. The model is available at http://ve.ifs.org.uk/Hard.shtml. Use the model to determine the effect of decreasing income tax rates and increasing sales tax rates on the U.K. economy. For example, reduce the base income tax rate by five percentage points, and increase the VAT by five percentage points. Try to explain the reported impacts using what you have learned in this textbook.

SELECTED REFERENCES

The consumption and income tax bases are compared in Congressional Budget Office, "Comparing the Income and Consumption Tax Bases," CBO paper, July 1997.

The original and best source on the flat tax is Robert E. Hall and Alvin Rabushka, *The Flat Tax*, 2nd ed., Hoover Institution Press, 1995.

Part III of Joel Slemrod and Jon Bakija's book, *Taxing Ourselves*, MIT Press, 1996, contains an extensive discussion of the main issues of tax reform.

The potential effects of fundamental tax reform on the economy are analyzed by some of the country's leading public finance economists in Henry J. Aaron and William G. Gale, *Economic Effects of Fundamental Tax Reform*, The Brookings Institution, 1996.

USEFUL INTERNET SITES

Sites promoting one form of tax reform or another are too numerous to list. Taxreform.com at http://www.taxreform.com/ lists the advantages and disadvantages of the different options and lets you cast a vote for your favorite.

Links to many tax-reform groups and organizations are found at http://www.taxsites.com/policy.html#reform-oversight. The National Tax Association also has links to tax-reform topics and groups at http://www.ntanet.org/.

PART SEVEN

State

and Local

Public Finance

Despite the overwhelming size of the federal government, we should not lose sight of the fact that the United States is a federal system. The U.S. Constitution divides powers between the federal and state governments, and indeed, people often have more contact with the governments of their state and their locality than they do with the federal government. The activities of state and local governments constitute a significant fraction of the economy, with state and local spending amounting to over 40% of all government spending, and about 12% of GDP.

Chapter 18 describes the main functions of state and local governments and describes the special problems they face in implementing policies, given their limited jurisdictions and the free mobility of households and firms between jurisdictions. We develop the idea of local public goods, which are nonrival and nonexcludable goods available only to people living within a defined geographic area. We then address the question of whether choice of community (voting with one's feet) leads to an efficient allocation of such goods. We also discuss the concept of fiscal federalism, which is the study of which level of government is best suited to carry out a certain governmental function.

State and local governments, with their limited and overlapping jurisdictions, face special constraints not faced by the federal authorities in collecting their taxes. In Chapter 19, we examine the diverse landscape of differing state and local tax systems, and the problems state and local governments face in taxing economic activity within their jurisdictions. These problems include increased opportunities for tax avoidance, as firms and households engage in economic activity outside the jurisdiction, and the possibility of multiple taxation, as several taxing jurisdictions lay claim to the right to tax the same economic activities.

18

Spending by State and Local Governments

Politicians talk a lot about "devolution" or "the new federalism." They are referring to the passing or transferring of fiscal responsibilities and authority from one level of government to another, usually from the federal government, with its national authority, to the many states and local governments, which have authority only in their own jurisdictions. In August 1996, Congress approved legislation ending the 60-year-old federal cash welfare program by turning the program over to the state governments. The federal government's main role from now on will be to send a fixed sum of money, known as a block grant, to the states to let them run their own welfare programs. Medicaid, a major federal program that provides health insurance to the poor, may get the same treatment in the future.

The current emphasis on devolution stems from a recurrent political and economic question in the United States: What is the appropriate and rational division of fiscal responsibilities and political power among the nation's various levels of government? For example, is it desirable that state and local governments have their own programs to provide welfare to poor residents, rather than having a national program? What are the main spending policies of state and local governments? How do state and local governments differ from the federal government? In this chapter we study the spending policies of state and local governments with these types of questions in mind.

THE FUNCTIONS OF STATE AND LOCAL GOVERNMENT

State and local governments operate under constraints and conditions that are different from those on the federal government. One reason is the division of powers in the Constitution of the United States. The Constitution does not enumerate powers for the states as it does for the federal government, but it does expressly prohibit them from doing certain things. Most important, the states cannot pass laws that impede the movement of people or goods among them, such as placing taxes on goods imported from other states. This prohibition can also constrain the states' policies on spending. The state of California, which gives relatively high welfare benefits to poor residents, would like to give smaller benefits to new residents to discourage them from moving into California from less generous states. But this policy has been challenged on the grounds that it limits interstate migration and is therefore unconstitutional.

A second difference is the sheer number of subnational governments. In 1997, in addition to the 50 states, there were nearly 87,500 overlapping local government entities. These included nearly 39,000 general administrative units, such as counties, municipalities, and townships, as well as units administering specific spending functions, such as school and fire districts. This multiplicity of state and local governments allows for considerable variation in spending policies from place to place. By contrast, most federal government programs are uniform across the nation.

A third difference is the fact that people can move from the jurisdiction of one local government to that of another. Tax and spending programs of state and local governments apply only to their own residents, and only residents can vote in local elections. But people and firms move freely among the state and local jurisdictions. In fact, according to the Census, the average citizen of the United States moves nearly 12 times during a lifetime. Between March 1997 and March 1998, nearly 43 million people, about 16% of the population, changed their residence. Although most of these remained within the same county, nearly 8 million settled in a new county within the same state, and more than 6 million migrated to a new state.

State and local fiscal and spending policies may affect migration among jurisdictions. For instance, a person may move to a different community because it offers more desirable schools, or out of a state because its taxes are too high. The effect of in- and out-migration is likely to influence the fiscal decisions made by local governments. In contrast, the federal government is not greatly concerned about people moving in or out of the country in response to its policies, except, perhaps, for illegal immigration. These examples illustrate the fact that state and local governments make their spending and tax decisions under conditions different from those the national government faces. In this chapter we analyze state and local spending policies in light of their special circumstances.

State and Local Government Spending

The combined spending by state and local governments (measured on the basis of National Income and Product Accounts, NIPA) amounted to $1089 billion in calendar year 1999, or 41% of total government spending that year. This number nets out grants from state governments to local governments, but it includes the $224 billion of federal grants-in-aid given to the states to spend on specified programs. That is, grants-in-aid are counted as part of state and local rather than federal spending. If the grants-in-aid are counted as federal spending, state and local government spending amounts to 33% of the total. By either measure, the relative size of state and local spending has grown slightly over the past 30 years. In 1970, state and local spending including grants-in-aid amounted to 38% of total government spending, or 30% if federal grants are excluded.

State and local government spending is concentrated on different functions from federal spending, which is concentrated mainly on national defense, Social Security, and Medicare. The largest share of state and local spending is for education, which accounts for 29%. Other important state spending programs are highways and health and hospitals. At the local level, environment (which includes sanitation), housing, police, and firefighting are important, as well as education. The composition of state and local spending by function for fiscal year 1996 is shown in Table 18.1.

Levels and composition of spending by state and local governments vary from state to state. For instance, in fiscal year 1996 per capita general expenditures by state and local governments averaged $4485 over all 50 states but ranged from $10,395 in Alaska to $3465 in Arkansas.

Demand for State and Local Public Goods

Why do the level and type of spending vary from one state or locality to another? Economists believe that differences in state and local spending reflect differences in the demands for government spending by the residents. People can express their demand for local government goods and services through voting or by moving to jurisdictions that provide more of the public goods they want. People in different localities may have different demands for government spending because they have different tastes or, more likely, because they have different incomes or face different costs for the government goods. Economists study the demand for local government spending by matching variations in government spending on different goods across localities to variations in residents' incomes and the costs of government goods to residents.

A difficulty with estimating the demand for local government spending is deciding whose income and costs matter. Government goods are not like private goods: Individuals cannot directly choose the quantities of government goods that are best for them, nor do they face a market price. Instead, everyone in the jurisdiction pays

Table 18.1   **Direct Expenditures of State and Local Spending by Function (Fiscal Year 1996), Percent**

Function	Local	State	State and Local Combined
Education	37.2%	17.5%	28.6%
Public welfare	2.2	3.8	2.9
Health and hospitals	7.6	8.5	8.0
Highways	4.0	7.8	5.7
Police, fire, and corrections	8.8	5.3	7.2
Natural resources, waste, and environment	7.0	3.1	4.0
Housing and development	2.6	.4	3.0
Government administration	4.0	3.8	3.9
Gross interest	4.2	4.2	4.2
Utilities and liquor stores	10.8	1.7	6.8
Insurance trust	1.9	15.4	7.8
Other	9.7	28.5	17.9
Total, dollars	786 billion	608 billion	1394 billion

Source: U.S. Bureau of the Census, *Statistical Abstract of the United States, 1999*, Table 512

taxes and enjoys the same level of government goods. Do differences in per capita spending on government goods across jurisdictions reflect differences in average incomes, or something else?

One theory, based on a hypothesis about voting that we studied in Chapter 5, is that demand for government goods is determined by the **median voter,** a hypothetical person whose vote is decisive in a majority election. For example, a voter who desires a certain quantity of a local government good (say, school services) such that half the remaining voters prefer the same quantity or more and the other half prefer the same quantity or less is the median voter on this issue. If the median voter model is correct, we can treat local public goods as if they were determined by the demand of the median voter.

Economists study the demand for state and local government spending using the **median voter model** by postulating that the quantity demanded of a government good depends on the income and the cost of the good to the median voter. Under certain conditions, the income of the median voter can be measured by the median income in the jurisdiction. The median income is the level of personal income for which half the voters have more and half have less. (This is one measure of the *average* income in the community.) The cost of the government good to the median voter is measured by his or her **tax price,** which is the median voter's share of an increase in the community's taxes needed to finance an extra unit of the government good. This measures the price to the median voter in lost private consumption. The tax price to the median voter depends on how the local government taxes its residents, but usually it is assumed to be the tax share of the voter with the median income.[1]

After the demand for state and local government spending has been estimated as a function of income, tax prices, and demographic variables, we can measure the price and income elasticities of local government goods. The **price elasticity** of a good measures the sensitivity of the quantity demanded of a good to its price, and it is defined as the percentage change in the quantity demanded divided by the percentage change in the price to the decision maker (who is the median voter in this case). The **income elasticity** measures the sensitivity of the quantity demanded to the income of the decision maker and is defined as the percentage change in the quantity demanded divided by the percentage change in income (the median income in the community in this case). Everything else affecting the demand for the government good is held constant, and the changes in price and income are assumed to be small.

Several studies have analyzed the demand for local government goods and services. Most find that the price elasticities of the government goods are negative (the demand curves for government goods slope down, like those for private goods) and that the income elasticities are positive, meaning that government goods are normal goods. In most cases, however, the magnitudes of the elasticities are small, indicating that the demands for government goods are *inelastic* with respect to price

---

[1]An alternative to the median voter model is the *dominant party model,* which assumes that the decision is made by a policy maker who cares about the "average" person in the community. This policy maker wants to maximize the community's social welfare. In the dominant party model, the per capita income of the community and the per capita tax burden determine the demand for government goods.

and income. Generally, goods with low magnitudes for price and income elasticities are called *necessities*.

For instance, one study finds that the price elasticity for education (local public schools) lies between minus 0.37 and minus 0.51. A price elasticity of minus 0.51 implies that a 10% increase in the tax price of education would cause the quantity of education demanded to fall by about 5%. The same study finds that the income elasticity for education lies between 0.6 and 0.75. An income elasticity of 0.75 implies that a 10% increase in personal income would increase the quantity of education demanded by about 7.5%. Most local government goods have demands that are inelastic to price and income, except parks and recreation, which have an income elasticity greater than 1 in some studies. This would make them "luxuries" according to the standard classification. Also, public assistance (welfare) is elastic with respect to both price and income in some studies.[2]

THE THEORY OF LOCAL PUBLIC GOODS

A **local public good** is a good that is nonrival in a limited geographic area. In other words, all consumers residing within that area can consume the local public good, and extra consumers do not increase the cost of providing it. Many local public goods are nonexcludable as well, meaning that people living in the geographic area cannot be prevented from consuming these goods if they do not pay. For this reason, local public goods must be financed with taxes rather than prices. Roads, parks, and the quality of the local environment are other examples of local public goods.

Providers of local public goods must deal with special problems that result from the fact that the good can be consumed only within a limited geographic area. We will consider the most important of these problems.

Jurisdictional Spillovers

Since local public goods benefit only the consumers residing within a limited geographic area, and not the nation at large, many such goods are provided by local governments. Spending by local governments is financed with taxes on the residents in their jurisdictions. Often, however, the geographic area of a local public good extends beyond the boundaries of the political jurisdiction that provides it. This causes a **jurisdictional spillover** from local government spending. Jurisdictional spillovers can be viewed as a type of externality imposed by one local jurisdiction on the residents of another. These spillovers may be benefit externalities, if the local public goods benefit the residents in other jurisdictions; or they may be cost externalities, if the local public good imposes costs on the residents of other jurisdictions.

For instance, if the city of Chicago takes measures to reduce the dumping of wastes into Lake Michigan by its residents, the benefits of this public good are enjoyed by the residents of other towns and cities on Lake Michigan as well as by

---

[2]The price and income elasticities for local education are reported by R. Inman, "The Fiscal Performance of Local Governments: An Interpretative Review," 1979 (Table 9.1), who also reports and compares the results of other studies.

Chicagoans. However, the cost of this public good is paid for by the residents of Chicago. The benefit to residents of other cities is a benefit externality as far as the city of Chicago is concerned. On the other hand, if the police in a residential suburb chase criminals out of their jurisdiction to make the local residents safer, the local public good imposes a cost externality on the residents of neighboring jurisdictions who get the criminals.

Local Public Goods and Community Size

It seems a strange question to ask, but why do we have so many towns and cities? If local public goods benefit a large population at the same cost as a small population (because they are nonrival), wouldn't it be better if we had just one huge city? That way, we could spread the cost of local public goods over the largest population and have lower local taxes. The answer, of course, is that other things matter for the optimal number and size of communities besides spreading the cost of local public goods.

For one thing, some local public goods may be congestible, so that the larger population causes congestion costs. For instance, local roads become congested as the number of drivers increases, so they are described as congestible rather than fully nonrival local public goods. (This will not surprise commuters on local expressways in American cities.) The fact that some local public goods are congestible means that larger quantities of these goods are needed for larger populations, so the extra people may just as well live in another city. A second advantage of having many localities is the presence of a fixed factor, like land. Only a given amount of land is available within the geographic area served by the local public good, so the more people who live in a city to consume the public good, the more crowded and expensive land becomes. The third advantage of many communities is diversity in the tastes of residents. This reason is important enough to discuss at some length.

Accommodating Different Tastes for Public Goods

For a public good like national defense, the same quantity must be consumed by all individuals in the country, whether they like it a lot or not at all. However, a local public good is consumed only by the residents of the geographic area in which it is available. People can choose to consume a local public good simply by moving in or out of the area where it is available. Diversity in consumption of public goods is possible by having many communities. This can increase economic efficiency.

To make things simple, suppose there are two types of people, in equal numbers. The first type (O) loves the outdoors and has a high marginal willingness to pay (MWTP) for public parks. The second type (A) suffers from hay fever and agoraphobia (fear of open spaces) and prefers pavement to parks. Suppose both types live in a single community. To keep things simple, we also assume that the parks in the community do not get crowded and that the agoraphobics cannot relieve their suffering by distancing themselves from the parks. Given that the outdoor types and the agoraphobics must live together, what is the efficient quantity of parks to have in this community? We assume that the marginal cost (MC) of parkland is the value of the land for private uses—say, for buildings.

As we saw in Chapter 3, the efficient quantity of a public good requires that the community's MWTP, which is the sum of the MWTPs of all consumers, be equal to the marginal cost of the good. When types O and A must live together in one community, the positive marginal willingness to pay summed over the O's (MWTP^O) is added to the marginal willingness to pay summed over the A's (MWTP^A) to find the community's MWTP for parks. The MWTP of the agoraphobics is negative because they suffer from having parks. Alternatively, we can treat the negative of the MWTP of the agoraphobics as an additional marginal cost of having parks, or the marginal cost of suffering to agoraphobics (MC^A = −MWTP^A). Thus the efficient quantity of parks in this single community requires that MWTP^O equal the marginal cost of parkland, MC, plus the marginal cost of suffering by agoraphobics, MC^A.

The efficient quantity of this local public good (parks) in a community that consists of both types (O and A) is shown in Figure 18.1. The downward-sloping MWTP (demand) curve for parks by outdoors people is labeled MWTP^O. The marginal cost of the parkland is given by the horizontal schedule, MC. To get the total marginal cost of parks, we must add to MC the marginal cost imposed on agoraphobics (which is the negative of their MWTP). The total marginal cost of parks is shown by the upward-sloping schedule MC + MC^A. The efficient quantity of parks in the single community is Q^{ALL}.

If forming a new community has no costs, both the outdoors people and the agoraphobics are better off (a Pareto improvement) by separating and living apart. The O's can live in a community with lots of parks, and the A's can live in a community with as little open space and flora as possible. The efficiency gain from this arrangement is equal to the areas of the two shaded triangles in Figure 18.1. The left-hand triangle represents the gain to agoraphobics from not having to suffer from the unwanted (by them) quantity of parks Q^{ALL}. By living apart, the agoraphobics also save the taxes they had to pay for the unwanted parks, but this is a transfer from the A's to the O's, so it is not part of the net gain. The right-hand triangle is the gain to the outdoors people, who can now have more parks by living separately. In the combined community, the efficient quantity of parks had to take into account the marginal cost of suffering by the agoraphobics. If the community consists only of outdoors people, the efficient quantity of parks is that at which MWTP^O is equal to the marginal cost of the parkland, MC. The efficient quantity of parks for the community of O's is Q^O, which is greater than Q^{ALL}. The area of the right-hand triangle is the excess of MWTP over MC by the O's for the additional parks.

This example illustrates that having different communities for people with different tastes for local public goods can improve economic efficiency. It is not necessary for differences in taste to be as extreme as the one in this example. Even if a local public good is enjoyed by everyone but some people like it more than others, the quantities provided by different communities can be tailored to the tastes of their residents. In this case, however, it is also necessary to consider the higher costs of providing nonrival goods to numerous communities with smaller populations. The optimal size and number of communities must balance the efficiency gains from satisfying diverse tastes against the costs of serving smaller populations. This general idea forms the basis of the **Tiebout hypothesis** first proposed in 1956 by Professor Charles Tiebout of the University of Washington.

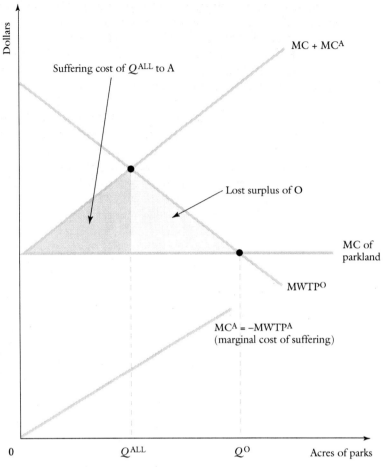

Figure 18.1

The Benefit from Increased Community Choice

The marginal cost of parks is the MC of parkland plus the negative MWTP for parks by agoraphobics. If agoraphobics and outdoors lovers must live in the same community, the efficient quantity of parks is Q^{ALL}, where the MWTP for parks by outdoors lovers is equal to the marginal cost of parks. If the two types live in different communities, the agoraphobics have no parks and the outdoors lovers have Q^O. The gain to separation is equal to the area of the two shaded triangles. The left-hand triangle is the cost of suffering to agoraphobics, and the right-hand triangle is the lost surplus to outdoors lovers from having a compromise quantity of parks in a united community.

The Tiebout Hypothesis: "Voting with One's Feet"

We've emphasized that one difference between public and private goods is the individual consumer's ability to choose the quantities consumed. People choose the types, amounts, and qualities of private goods they want to consume. However, the same type, quantity, and quality of a public good must be consumed by everyone, and consumers can exercise only collective choices, as through voting. Tiebout recognized that this restriction is valid only when people cannot move between communities. When it is possible to choose among communities with different types and quantities of local public goods, people can choose local public goods by choosing among different communities. In the example discussed above, outdoors people can choose communities offering lots of parks, and agoraphobics can choose communities offering lots of buildings. Choosing among communities by migrating is called "voting with one's feet."

Tiebout argued that, under certain conditions, efficient quantities of local public goods are provided by local governments if people can "vote with their feet." One way of interpreting Tiebout's hypothesis is that it is a generalization of the fundamental theorem of welfare economics described in Chapter 2. According to this theorem, under certain conditions, consumers' choices among market goods lead to the production of efficient quantities. Tiebout's hypothesis states that voting with one's feet substitutes for market forces in attaining efficient quantities of local public goods.

ASSUMPTIONS NEEDED FOR THE TIEBOUT HYPOTHESIS.   Like the fundamental theorem about the efficiency of markets, Tiebout's hypothesis about the efficiency of voting with one's feet requires special, restrictive assumptions. The most important are these:

- Individuals can move easily (at no cost) among communities and are not tied to a particular community for nonfiscal reasons, such as occupational opportunities. In other words, individuals can choose the community they like best on the basis of the local public goods and services available.

- The optimal-sized community is finite. That is, the fact that nonrival goods are available to large populations at the same cost as for small populations does not require the entire population to congregate in a single large community. Further, the community managers who supply local public goods do so to attract the population needed for an optimal-sized community.

- The total population of the country is large enough to allow numerous communities of optimal size for people to choose among. In particular, there are enough communities offering different "packages" of local public goods to satisfy the diversity in tastes for public goods within the population.

- Local public goods are financed by a per capita levy (an equal tax on every resident) or by a benefit tax. A benefit tax is a tax that is equal to the value of the benefits an individual receives from the public goods provided by the community.

- Individuals are fully informed about the tax levels and the quantities and qualities of local public goods and services available in every community.

- There are no jurisdictional spillovers. That is, the local public goods provided and the taxes levied by a community affect its residents only, not residents of other communities.

These assumptions guarantee that the choice of community is merely a choice of a "package" of local public goods and the community's tax is the "price" of consuming the package. In effect, Tiebout's assumptions make the choice of a package of local public goods like the choice of a package of private goods.

This equivalence can be explained with an analogy. Consumers shop for private goods at the supermarket, choosing the goods they want at the prices listed on the shelf and putting them into a shopping basket. The total cost of the goods in the shopping basket is rung up at the checkout counter. We know from the fundamental theorem of welfare economics that, without market failure, this "consumer choice" process is efficient because consumers buy each good only if their MWTP for it is at least as high as its price.

Suppose that instead of letting consumers fill their own baskets, a supermarket manager fills numerous baskets with different bundles of goods. The number of baskets filled is large enough that every possible combination of goods can be found in some basket. The total value of the goods in the basket is summed to obtain a "basket price" that is posted on the basket. Rather than shopping from the shelves, the consumers choose among baskets and buy the one that pleases them most by paying the posted basket price. The goods in unsold baskets are taken out and recombined to make more of the baskets that are in demand. Since every consumer can find a basket with the bundle of goods he or she would have chosen, the "basket choice" equilibrium is the same as the "consumer choice" equilibrium even though the process is different. (People vote with their feet in the former, and with their hands in the latter.) Since the consumer choice equilibrium is efficient, so is the "basket choice" equilibrium.

Tiebout's hypothesis is easily understood by substituting "community choice" for "basket choice." Of course the goods in the community baskets are nonrival (at least some of them are), but all the people choosing them have the same preferences and pay the same price, so no conflict of interests occurs among them. Exclusion is possible because a consumer must live in the community and pay the community's tax in order to enjoy the community's public goods. If they do not pay their local taxes, they do not get the local public goods.

LIMITS OF THE TIEBOUT HYPOTHESIS.   Using this analogy, we can understand the necessity of Tiebout's conditions and how "market failure" in the provision of local public goods occurs when these conditions are not satisfied. For instance, if some bundles of goods come only in "blue" baskets, but a particular consumer, for some reason, will buy only a "red" basket, that person's choice of goods is constrained. Similarly, individuals may live in a community despite a more desirable (for them) combination of local public goods elsewhere, perhaps because their jobs are there. Also, if the goods in one basket cause "basket spillovers" into other baskets, the choice of baskets will not be efficient. For example, if the aroma of a strong cheese in one basket permeates the air around adjoining baskets, a fussy consumer may avoid them even if they contain the bundle of goods he or she wants. Alternatively, the sight of fresh flowers in one basket (which can be consumed free) may attract consumers to adjoining baskets. With basket spillovers, choosing among baskets is not equivalent to choosing among individual goods, and inefficiency can occur.

Perhaps the must important of Tiebout's conditions is the assumption about the form of local government finance. Tiebout's assumption about local taxes is needed to prevent free rides. Imagine that a community provides nice parks and finances them with a tax on earnings. This community will attract free riders, perhaps retirees who are past their earning years and are living on their savings. In a community that taxes earnings, the retirees can enjoy the parks "free." The assumption that the community levies a per capita tax or a benefit tax prevents such free riding.

The biggest local tax residents pay is a proportional levy (a fixed percentage) on the value of the real estate property they own in the community, mainly the value of their land and homes. Can free riding occur when communities rely on the property tax? The answer is yes, because people can free ride by minimizing the value of property they own in the community. For instance, suppose a community of high-income people with expensive homes provides high-quality schools for their children. If people can enjoy the benefits of these fine schools by entering the community and buying small, inexpensive homes, they will do so. Effectively, the residents owning little property in the community are subsidized by those who own more. A homeless family could enjoy the benefits without paying any property taxes at all.

Tiebout's hypothesis can be rescued, at least partially, if communities can enforce zoning laws.[3] For instance, expensive communities often require building lots to be of a certain minimum size and new houses to be of a certain minimum value. Many communities prohibit manufactured homes, mobile homes, and multi-family units. Such zoning laws prevent people from moving into communities with expensive local public goods and enjoying the package at a cut rate by holding a minimum value of taxable property.

Another problem is the assumption that communities can maintain their populations at the optimal size. People freely migrate and choose where to live on the basis of the benefits and costs to themselves. They ignore the external benefits or costs they impose on the residents of the communities they enter or leave. For this reason, individuals may not make efficient decisions about migration. People may flock to a desirable location—say, to enjoy a warm climate—and the costs they impose on the existing residents by overcrowding and congesting the region are ignored. Nor can the existing residents of the region exclude the newcomers, except through imperfect means such as zoning. Similarly, people who leave an area make it less desirable for those remaining because the per capita cost of public goods increases for a smaller population.

Despite its limitations, Tiebout's hypothesis can serve as a useful organizing principle. It can help explain how and why a community forms, the effects of local fiscal policy on migration, and certain aspects of intergovernmental relations.

THE ECONOMIC THEORY OF FEDERALISM

The economic theory of federalism, also called **fiscal federalism,** describes how the different economic functions of government are matched with the level of government best equipped to carry them out efficiently. For instance, we would expect that state governments would not produce the efficient quantity of national

[3]Bruce W. Hamilton, "Zoning and Property Taxation in a System of Local Governments," 1975.

18.1   Charles Tiebout Meets Ronald Coase

Interjurisdictional spillovers are a type of externality. Communities produce too little of public goods that confer external benefits on their neighbors and too much of public goods that impose external costs. The reasoning is that described in Chapter 4. In making local government decisions, the community managers disregard the effects on residents of neighboring jurisdictions because those residents do not vote or pay taxes in decision-making jurisdiction. Back in the days when cities and towns were geographically distant, this may have been less of a problem. Today, a multiplex of separate communities exists side by side within an urban area, with jurisdictions separated by no more than a street. With more jurisdictions to choose from, people have greater opportunity to vote with their feet. According to Tiebout's hypothesis, this should result in a more efficient allocation of local public goods. However, the same proximity increases the likelihood of interjurisdictional spillovers and the inefficiency of externalities. Did Tiebout get it wrong?

Not according to Ronald Coase. Coase argued that when one party undertakes activities that confer benefits or costs on others, the opportunity exists for bribes and side payments (Coasian bargaining) that would bring about a more efficient allocation. For example, a commercial campground might pay a neighboring pig farmer to keep the odor down. Similarly, if community A enjoys an external benefit from local public goods provided by neighboring community B, community A should be willing to pay B to increase the quantity to the efficient level.

A good example of the Coase theorem in action is the Loan-a-Cop program between three neighboring communities in California.[1] East Palo Alto had a rather serious crime problem, with 42 homicides among its 25,000 residents in 1992. However, East Palo Alto crime is not a problem for its own residents alone; it also affects the residents of the nearby affluent communities of Palo Alto and Menlo Park. Recently, the mayors of the three communities engaged in a little Coasian bargaining. East Palo Alto, a relatively poor community, could not afford to increase its police force in order to reduce crime. As a result, Palo Alto and Menlo Park decided to "lend" some police officers to their less fortunate neighbor. East Palo Alto received an additional 34 police officers on loan. In 1993, after the program was implemented, the homicide rate fell 86% in East Palo Alto, no doubt also benefiting the residents of Palo Alto and Menlo Park.

Critically discuss the following:

- When a community is adversely affected by the actions of a neighbor, it can seek redress by appealing to a higher authority—the state government. The state may then instruct the offending community to stop what it is doing unless it compensates the harmed community. How would this affect the efficiency of community decisions according to the Coase theorem?

- Suppose in one case, a community's local public good benefits just one other community, and in the second case, a community's local public good benefits a large number of other communities. In which case is Coasian bargaining more likely to bring about the efficient quantity of the public good? Why?

- Police can reduce crime in a community by catching criminals or by deterring them through greater vigilance. The second strategy may encourage criminals to try their luck elsewhere. With this in mind, explain why Palo Alto and Menlo Park might choose to lend police officers rather than to give East Palo Alto money to hire more of its own police officers.

---

[1]Susan Rossi, "Three Towns Find a Way to Contain Crime: Loan-a-Cop," 1994, pp. 15–16.

defense—they would produce too little, and local governments would produce even less. National defense is a national public good, but state and local governments are responsible and responsive only to their own voters. Much of the benefit from national defense spending would go to nonresidents, while all the cost was borne by the residents. Local voters would pressure their governments to free ride on providing national defense. Unless the local governments make a cooperative treaty, state and local spending on national defense would be too little to provide the efficient quantity of defense for the nation.

Of course, state and local governments could negotiate a defense treaty that stipulated the amount of defense spending by each. Separate nations enter into defense treaties like NATO that have exactly such stipulations. But any treaty would involve bickering about how the cost of national defense should be shared. It would also require a method of ensuring that the signatories fulfilled their obligations. If a treaty member cheated and underspent on national defense, who would punish it, and how? Defense problems of this sort plagued the original 13 states under the Articles of Confederation, and in 1787 prompted them to "form a more perfect union" that would "provide for the common defense."

For these reasons it is clear that a national government, responsive and responsible to everyone in the country, is best suited for functions that involve the *national interest*. These national interests include the functions enumerated for the federal government in Article 1, Section 8, of the Constitution, such as national defense, maintaining a monetary system, conducting international diplomacy, setting rules for immigration, and performing other functions where the national interest is clear.

On the other hand, the national government would be a cumbersome instrument to provide a local public good like fire protection.[4] Effective fire protection is limited by the time it takes to respond to a call, so only people within a confined area benefit. Also, how much fire protection is needed depends on local characteristics such as the dryness of the climate, the construction materials used for local structures (e.g., wood in Seattle, adobe in Santa Fe), and the density of the population. Although a national government could, in principle, run local fire stations, its performance would be inefficient and unresponsive to local preferences. Local decisions, such as whether to buy a new fire truck and whether it should be yellow or red, would require approval by bureaucrats who were distant in geography and interests from the decision. Spending policies would be determined by politicians elected by the voters of the nation at large rather than the locality. Local conditions and preferences would not count for much in determining those spending decisions. For these reasons, it is clear that local governments can best perform the function of fire protection.

Benefits of Decentralization

The main advantage of decentralized government lies in "diversity." Different local governments can accommodate diverse tastes and can act as fiscal "experiments" that may lead to efficient innovations adoptable by all local governments. Also, the cost of errors in policy is limited to the jurisdiction, and others can learn from an error. We discuss the main benefits of decentralized government in turn below.

---

[4]Although, of course, the federal government does provide fire protection for national assets, such as the national forests.

GREATER VOICE.   There is a long-standing belief that state and local governments are "closer to the people" than the national government. The reason is clear enough. A local government is elected by and responsive to a group of voters sharing common interests due to their geographic proximity to each other, whereas the national government is elected by and responsive to voters in the nation at large. Although members of the House and Senate may be elected for individual districts and states, these legislators must work, and compromise, with their counterparts from other parts of the country. Demands for government functions that affect only or mainly the residents of a local jurisdiction and not the residents of other jurisdictions are best voiced through a decentralized political system that does not commingle local concerns with national interests.

Another feature that makes local government more responsive to the wishes of the people is the possibility of direct voting initiatives. *Direct voting* (as the term implies) means that the voters can vote directly on a spending or tax program, such as a school bond issue, rather than voting for representatives who decide the issue on their behalf. As a practical matter, it is not possible to vote directly on federal programs, so all federal decisions are made by representatives. However, direct voting at the local and state levels is quite common.

GREATER CHOICE.   The United States is a pluralistic society, meaning that the desires of people with varying tastes and disparate religious, ethnic, and economic backgrounds must be accommodated in public decision making. In many cases, conflicting interests among the disparate groups over the quantities of government goods can be accommodated by giving people a choice among many decentralized governments. This, of course, is the essence of the Tiebout hypothesis.

The federal government usually has, and in some cases must have, uniform policies across the nation so that no choice is offered except by changes in the national program. Whatever program is chosen, it is the same for everybody in the country, despite differences in their preferences. Such uniformity is not always the best solution, even when the policy is directed at a desirable goal. For instance, the federal Clean Air Act sets uniform national standards for air quality. Because it is a cost externality, we know that market forces lead to too much air pollution. But is it desirable to have a uniform policy across the nation? With a uniform policy, communities with poor air quality must clean it up to federal standards, while those with good air quality are not affected. What could be wrong with this?

The reason a uniform federal regulation may be undesirable is that it might forbid variations that allow choices to communities of people with different tastes. Air quality is often costly in communities with heavy industry, and forcing firms to reduce pollution may result in lower wages. Industry might move to communities with laxer standards and pay higher wages to attract workers to a community with polluted air. With local variations in air quality standards, people who want to "purchase" higher air quality could do so by moving to communities with cleaner air and lower wages. People who are not strongly averse to air pollution could enjoy higher wages and proximity to their jobs by living in communities with more air pollution.

Local pollution standards would be an efficient outcome, provided that air quality is a local public good and does not affect other communities. If there are spillovers of air pollution onto other communities, the air quality standards chosen by local governments are likely to be too lax. If such spillovers are serious enough, they could justify federal standards. For instance, governors from states in the Northeast promote tighter federal air quality standards because pollution from the Midwest adds to unhealthy air pollution in their states.

COMPETITION AND INNOVATION.   We generally think of market competition as a good thing that benefits consumers. If a business produces a good with better (or the same) quality at the same (or lower) cost than its competitors, it will profit and the consumers will benefit. The same argument can hold for local government. Towns that provide better-quality government at lower cost will attract residents, while communities with inefficient governments will lose them. The inefficient governments must change their policies or risk becoming ghost towns. Competition among local governments for residents will benefit the consumers by forcing community managers to squeeze out wasteful government spending and provide more valuable government services for each tax dollar.

Another argument for decentralized government is that a multiplicity of governments provides many "laboratories" for experimentation, innovation, and comparisons of performance. A national program—say, getting people off welfare and into gainful employment—is the same across the entire country. If it does not work well and improvements are sought, its performance can be judged only against programs in other countries. Changing a national program may bring a risk of mistakes that will harm everyone in the country. Such policies carried out at the state level can provide as many as 50 different programs pursuing the same objective. This allows for ample opportunity to compare performance. Moreover, mistakes affect only the residents in the adopting state, and successful programs in one state can be imitated in the others to the benefit of all. This is the advantage of *parallel innovation*, which is utilized by private businesses in research and development. Business firms often set up competing teams of researchers to develop a new product or process, with the teams copying each other's successes while avoiding each other's mistakes.

THE BENEFIT PRINCIPLE OF EQUITY.   All of the above benefits from decentralization result from increased economic efficiency. As is stressed throughout this book, concerns about equity are important as well. One notion of equity is the benefit principle. Many people derive satisfaction from the knowledge that the people who benefit from a public good or service are those who pay for it. The benefit principle of equity is satisfied automatically for market goods. It is also satisfied when local public goods are provided by local governments. Typically, local taxes are higher in communities that provide more and better-quality local public goods. Because these goods are paid for and consumed by the residents of the community providing them, and not by others, the benefit principle is satisfied. The benefit principle may not be satisfied if local public goods are provided at the national level, because the federal government collects taxes from everyone in the country. This is a common complaint when the federal government funds projects for local public goods. For instance, a federally funded museum would benefit only the residents of the city in which it is built, but everyone in the country pays for it.

Benefits of Centralization

The advantages of centralization are easier to understand than its disadvantages. For this reason, we should be careful to avoid thinking that bigger is always better. Nonetheless, sometimes there are clear advantages to having a higher level of government, which serves a larger population, perform a certain function.

INTERNALIZING JURISDICTIONAL SPILLOVERS.   As in the example of air pollution from one region affecting another, the presence of jurisdictional spillovers can lead to inefficient policy decisions by local governments because external benefits and costs to nonresidents are ignored. In Chapter 4 we saw how inefficiencies from externalities among firms can be eliminated if the firms merge, thus "internalizing" the externalities. In the same way, when a government function that has jurisdictional spillovers is performed by a higher level of government, the externalities are internalized because the higher level of government is responsive to the interests of all citizens. This eliminates inefficiencies caused by interjurisdictional spillovers.

When programs have jurisdictional spillovers on neighboring communities only, an alternative to state or federal provision is to expand the boundaries of local government. As once-separate cities and towns have grown and spread out so that they now are adjoining, the potential for jurisdictional spillovers increases. This has led to the growth of regional governments and metropolitan areas as a means of internalizing them.

AVOIDING BEGGAR-THY-NEIGHBOR POLICIES.   Another example of a jurisdictional spillover is a beggar-thy-neighbor policy. A community development program may appear attractive to an individual community because it generates increased commercial activity and tax revenue. However, this may simply divert commercial activity from other jurisdictions, so that the first community gains what the others lose. If the community development policy is expensive, the cost of attracting the activity to the first jurisdiction outweighs the benefits to all jurisdictions combined.

A good example is the current civic preoccupation with building stadiums at taxpayers' expense to attract or keep major league sports teams. Suppose city A builds a stadium to attract a sports team, and the tax revenue the team generates. This is done if the benefits from a larger tax base for A outweigh the cost of the stadium. Suppose city B has a usable but older and less attractive stadium. Because of the new stadium in A, B loses its team and the tax revenue that team generated. Building the new stadium in A may increase the combined tax revenue of the two cities by very little, so the resources used to build the new stadium are wasted simply to attract tax revenue from one community to another. The same sort of thing happens when local governments engage in *tax competition* to attract businesses from other states by offering tax breaks. In the process, all local governments may lose tax revenue. Tax competition is explained further in Chapter 19.

Decisions made by a higher level of government are not likely to be influenced by beggar-thy-neighbor gains. In the example of the stadium, a higher level of government including both cities would weigh the gain in tax revenue to A against the cost of the stadium *plus* the loss in tax revenue to B. The new stadium would be built at the taxpayers' expense only if the net benefits to residents of both communities justified the cost.

ECONOMIES OF SCALE.   Just as large firms may produce goods at lower unit costs because of economies of scale, so may larger governments provide public goods at lower unit costs than smaller local governments. One reason a higher level of government may have such economies of scale is that the duplicative administrative costs of having several smaller lower-level governments are avoided. Alexander Hamilton, one of the authors of the *Federalist Papers*, made this argument for a new federal government during the debate about the ratification of the Constitution. In Number 13, Hamilton argued that three defense confederacies, which the 13 states would probably have formed without the Constitution, would be more costly to maintain than the union. In other cases, lower unit costs are possible because better production methods are possible at higher levels of output. That is, the public goods are produced with economies of scale.

One government function that is likely to have economies of scale is collecting taxes. Higher levels of government are usually able to collect taxes at lower administrative costs. The lower costs reflect the elimination of duplicative tax administration facilities and the fact that higher levels of government have lower enforcement costs because taxpayers cannot escape taxes by moving to another jurisdiction.

Economies of scale in producing public goods can be exploited by smaller local governments if they "contract out." In this case, the production of a public good is separated from the provision of that good. With contracting out, some local governments exploit economies of scale by producing more of a public good than they need for themselves, and other governments purchase the excess for their residents. For example, rather than running its own schools a small jurisdiction may pay to send its children to schools in a larger jurisdiction nearby. Some towns contract out for everything from garbage collection to police patrols. In fact, contracting out even occurs at the state level. Oklahoma, which has crowded prisons, pays Texas, which has excess prison space, to confine prisoners who cannot be housed in its own penitentiaries.

HORIZONTAL AND VERTICAL EQUITY.   As mentioned, one advantage of local government financing of public goods is that it satisfies the benefit principle of equity. However, to many people the ability-to-pay principle of equity is more compelling. The ability-to-pay principle has two parts: horizontal equity, which requires that people with equal ability to pay bear equal burdens in supporting government; and vertical equity, which requires that people with greater ability to pay bear larger burdens. Indeed, vertical equity may require redistribution of income from those with high ability to pay (the "haves") to those with low ability to pay (the "have-nots"). In general, higher levels of government are better equipped to attain horizontal and vertical equity than the lower levels of government.

To begin with, ability to pay varies widely across jurisdictions. For instance, in 1998 per capita personal income in Mississippi was only $18,958, whereas in Connecticut it was almost twice as high: $37,598. It is not possible, of course, for state governments to redistribute income from states with high ability to those with low ability to pay in accordance with the principle of vertical equity. Voluntary transfers from a high-income state to a low-income state are possible, but they are not likely to occur because of the free-rider problem.

The principle of horizontal equity is also difficult to achieve with decentralized government. Suppose two people with equal ability to pay live in different jurisdictions. If the jurisdictions have different fiscal policies, people with equal ability to pay may receive different benefits from government or bear different tax burdens, depending on where they live. For example, a poor person may receive greater assistance in one jurisdiction than in another. Of course, if mobility is easy, people can move between jurisdictions in response to such differences in taxes and benefits.

This last point illustrates that not only may local governments achieve the benefit principle of equity; because of free migration of residents, they may be constrained by it. That is, any significant departure from benefit taxation by local governments causes adverse migration. Suppose jurisdiction A decides to redistribute income from its "haves" to its "have-nots," while a nearby jurisdiction, B, levies taxes according to the benefit principle. The "haves" in A will have an incentive to move to B, where they receive benefits equal to the taxes they pay, while the "have-nots" will stay put in A. Indeed, the "have-nots" in B may move into A. In other words, jurisdiction A becomes a magnet attracting the "have-nots" and repelling the "haves," a circumstance all local governments would like to avoid.

INTERGOVERNMENTAL GRANTS

An important characteristic of the American system of multilevel government is the large number and amounts of **intergovernmental grants.** An intergovernmental grant, or transfer, is money transferred from one government to another, usually to aid particular types of program spending. For example, many state governments make grants to school districts to finance the cost of running schools, and the federal government makes grants to the state governments for various functions ranging from highways to health care. Unlike the recipient of a **direct expenditure,** the recipient of an intergovernmental grant is another government, not someone in the private sector. Of course, the ultimate recipient could be the same in either case. For example, a teacher's salary could be paid by a school district that receives grants from the state government, or by the state government directly, as in the state of Hawaii, which has no school districts.

Instead of being performed by a higher level of government, a government function can be performed by a lower level of government and financed wholly or in part by grants from a higher level of government. Most intergovernmental grants are paid by higher levels of government to lower levels, though a few go the other way. For instance, federal grants to state and local governments, commonly, called **grants-in-aid,** were $262 billion in the calendar year 1999. This is 32.4% of state and local government expenditures from their own sources.

Federal grants-in-aid must be spent for particular purposes, and the purposes may be broadly or narrowly specified. Purposes of federal grants-in-aid according to spending functions are shown in Table 18.2 for fiscal years (FY) 1965 and 1999.

Table 18.2   Federal Grants to State and Local Governments by Function

	Percent of Total Federal Grants	
Function	FY 1965	FY 1999
Health	5.7%	43.8%
Income security	32.2	22.5
Education, job training	9.6	14.8
Transportation	37.6	11.1
Community development	5.9	3.3
Natural resources, agriculture, environment	6.4	1.6
General government, justice	2.1	2.2
Other	.5	.7

Source: U.S. Bureau of the Census, *Statistical Abstract of the United States, 1999,* Table 508.

As we see, the purpose of federal intergovernmental grants has changed over the years. In 1965 the largest fraction of these grants was for transportation, mainly highways. By 1999, nearly 44% of the federal grants were for health, reflecting federal aid to state-administered Medicaid programs.

The composition of state to local intergovernmental grants is shown in Table 18.3 for fiscal years 1965 and 1993. State to local grants are predominantly for education.

Effects of Different Types of Grants

Government policy makers and economists are interested in the effects of intergovernmental grants on the spending decisions of the recipient government. To analyze these effects, intergovernmental grants are classified into various types. The classification is based on how the amount of the grant depends on the spending policies of the recipient government.

NONCATEGORICAL GRANTS.   A **noncategorical grant** is a lump-sum amount that can be spent by the recipient government as it sees fit. Such grants are called **revenue sharing** because the government making the grant effectively shares its general tax revenue with the recipient government. At present in the United States,

Table 18.3   State Grants to Local Governments by Function

	Percent of Total State Grants	
Function	FY 1965	FY 1993
Education	58.9%	62.4%
Highways	11.5	4.4
Public welfare	17.2	13.2
Other specific functions	4.6	11.6
General support	7.9	8.4

Source: Tax Foundation, *Facts and Figures on Government Finance,* 30th ed., 1995, Table E.8.

small amounts of noncategorical grants are made by state governments to local governments and by the federal government to Puerto Rico and the District of Columbia. The federal government made noncategorical grants to all state and local governments before 1986.

Since the recipient government can spend a noncategorical grant any way it wants, such grants are called "no strings" federal money. The recipient can spend more on existing programs, establish new programs, or use the grant to reduce local government taxes (that is, provide tax relief). The impact of a noncategorical grant on spending versus its impact on tax relief by the recipient government is illustrated in Figure 18.2. Spending by the recipient government on, say, local public goods is measured on the horizontal axis, and private consumption spending by its residents is measured on the vertical axis. The budget line between government and private goods in the recipient jurisdiction without grants is shown by BB'. The vertical intercept of BB' is the total income in the community. A dollar of local government spending requires a dollar of local taxes, so private consumption spending

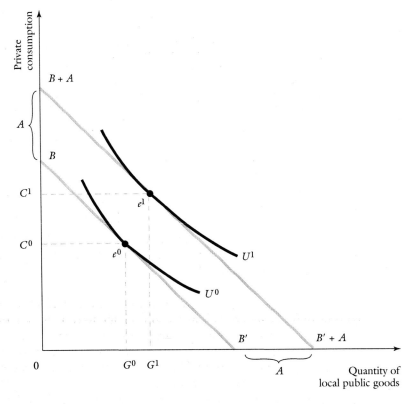

Figure 18.2

Effect of a Noncategorical Intergovernmental Grant
A noncategorical grant shifts the local jurisdiction's budget line between private and local public goods to the right without changing the marginal cost of the public good to the jurisdiction. Typically this increases the quantity of public and private goods consumed, because part of the grant is used to reduce local taxes.

is reduced by a dollar of government spending. This means that the absolute value of the slope of BB' is 1.[5]

We assume that the local government maximizes the utility of its residents, whose preferences between local public and private goods are represented by the indifference curve map shown in Figure 18.2. Alternatively, these indifference curves represent the preferences of the median voter or the social welfare function of the local government. The local government maximizes the community's utility at point e^0 when it spends G^0 on local public goods, leaving residents with disposable income C^0 to spend on private goods.

Suppose that the local government receives a noncategorical grant of A (for "aid") dollars. Such a grant shifts its budget constraint to the right without changing the slope. The new budget line is $(B + A)(B' + A)$ in Figure 18.2 Because the grant is noncategorical, all of it could be used to reduce local taxes (and increase private consumption) by A dollars, or it could be used to increase local government spending by A dollars. The noncategorical grant is equivalent to an increase in local income, so its effect is described by the *income effect* of the grant. With the grant, the utility-maximizing equilibrium is e^1, and local government spending increases to G^1, assuming that local public goods are normal goods. If private consumption is a normal good, as seems likely, some of the noncategorical grant is used to provide tax relief to local residents, and private consumption rises to C^1.

The quantitative effect of a noncategorical grant on local government spending depends on the income elasticity of such spending. If the income elasticity is equal to 1, for example, the local government allocates the grant to public and private spending in the same proportions that the community's total income is used for these two purposes. Thus if the local government spends 15% of the community's income, 15% of a noncategorical grant is spent on local public goods and the remaining 85% is used for tax relief. Earlier, we saw that the income elasticity for local government spending is less than 1, for instance in the range of 0.6 to 0.8. This suggests that a noncategorical grant that increases local income by 1% causes local government spending to rise by only 0.6% to 0.8%. A smaller fraction of the grant is used for local government spending than the fraction of total local income spent by the local government. According to theory, most of a noncategorical grant is used to lower local taxes (or to avoid local tax increases that would have been necessary without the grant).

CATEGORICAL GRANTS.   **Categorical grants** are given for a specific spending purpose or program. For example, grants for highways must be spent on highways, and grants for schools must be spent on schools. In addition, a categorical grant may be subject to numerous other restrictions or mandates. For example, recently the federal government required states to impose a .08% blood alcohol limit for determining driving while intoxicated, or they would lose part of their federal highway grants. Categorical grants often require much bureaucratic "red tape."

---

[5]If local taxes are deductible from income taxes by a higher level of government, such as state and local income and property taxes, the slope will be less than 1, depending on the marginal tax rate of the state residents.

Recipient governments must document how the grant is spent, and the granting government audits recipient governments to ensure that they spent the grant in the manner prescribed and have complied with all restrictions and mandates. State and local governments that wish to innovate their programs must apply for federal permission, and this is often a time-consuming process.

A categorical grant can be a block grant or a matching grant. A **block grant,** also called a nonmatching grant, is a fixed amount of money that must be spent on the specified purpose only. The size of the block grant is the same regardless of the level of spending on the purpose by the recipient government. A **matching grant** is a variable amount that increases as the recipient government spends more on the specified purpose.

A block grant of A dollars for purpose i—say Temporary Assistance to Needy Families—is shown in Figure 18.3. We see that this grant affects the budget line in the local jurisdiction in a way similar to the noncategorical grant in Figure 18.3.

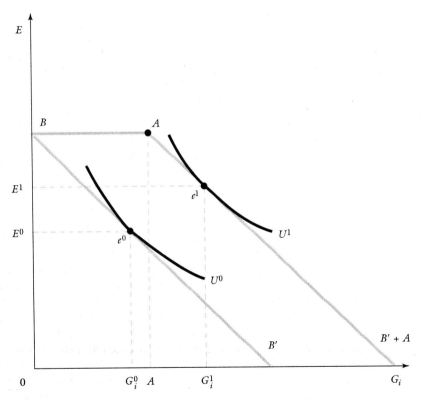

Figure 18.3

Effect of a Block Grant

A block grant of A dollars must be used for a specified purpose. The quantity of the specified public good i is measured on the horizontal axis, and spending on all other goods on the vertical axis. If the recipient jurisdiction spends more on the specified public good than the amount of the block grant, as shown, the block grant has the same impact as a noncategorical grant. Combinations northwest of point A cannot be purchased with the block grant, but the local jurisdiction doesn't want them anyway.

Spending by the recipient government on the specified purpose, local public good *i*, is measured on the horizontal axis; and local spending on all things, including other local government spending and tax relief (private consumption), is measured on the vertical axis. The block grant shifts the budget line to the right in a parallel fashion, but the budget line is truncated above *A*. That is, no more than 0*B* can be spent on purposes other than *i* with or without the block grant, because the grant cannot be used to finance other spending programs or provide tax relief. However, the block grant affects local spending in exactly the same way as does a noncategorical grant, provided that the local government spends more on the specified purpose than the value of the block grant. Economists say that this is because money is *fungible* (i.e., interchangeable). If the recipient government reduces its own spending on purpose *i* by the full amount of the grant, the recipient has that much to spend on other things.

With a matching categorical grant, the granting government and the recipient government each pay a fraction of the total spending on the specified purpose. The increase in the grant per dollar of spending by the recipient government from its own resources is called the **match rate.** For instance, if the granting government gives $1 of grant for every $2 the local government spends from its own revenues on purpose *i*, the match rate is equal to one-half. The effect of the match rate is to lower the cost of public good *i* to the recipient government. For instance, if the match rate is one-half, the recipient government can increase total spending by $3 on purpose *i* at a cost of $2 of its own funds. Thus the tax price of $1 of public good *i* to local residents in local taxes is 67 cents, rather than $1. More generally, if the match rate is *m*, the tax price to local residents of government spending on the specified purpose is $1/(1 + m)$ per dollar.

The effect of a matching categorical grant is shown in Figure 18.4. Without the grant, the budget line for the local government is *BB′*, which has an absolute slope of 1. As in Figure 18.3, spending on the specified purpose is measured on the horizontal axis and spending on everything else, including other government spending and private spending, is measured on the vertical axis. The budget line with a matching grant is shown as *BM*. If the match rate is *m*, the slope of *BM* is equal to $1/(1 + m)$. Note that with a matching grant, the local budget line is flatter. The higher the match rate, the flatter the budget line. In effect, the granting government subsidizes spending on the specified purpose by local residents.

A matching categorical grant stimulates more spending on the specified purpose than a block grant does, because the matching grant lowers the price of the specified public good to the recipient jurisdiction. Like all economizing decision makers, local governments spend more on public goods and services if the price is lower. This is not to say that none of a matching grant is used for tax relief. Figure 18.4 shows a case where the recipient increases spending on other things, perhaps including tax relief, when it receives a matching grant.

The matching grant described above is called an **open-ended** matching grant because the granting government matches spending by the recipient government no matter how large the total grant that must be made. Most matching grants are **closed-ended,** or capped. This means that the granting government matches spending by the recipient government up to a maximum value, the cap. Once the cap has

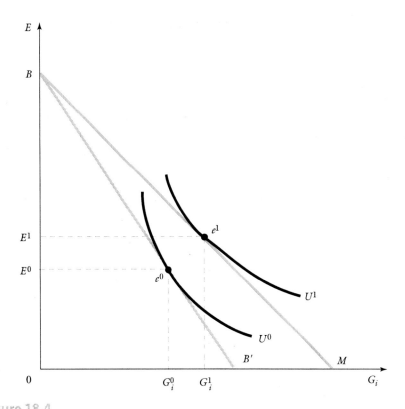

Figure 18.4

Effect of a Matching Intergovernmental Grant

A matching grant lowers the marginal cost of the specified local public good i to the jurisdiction, so the budget line is flatter. Specifically, the jurisdiction's budget line is BB' without the grant and BM with the grant. Although, relative to a nonmatching grant, a matching grant increases spending on the specified public good, it can also increase spending on other goods from E^0 to E^1 as shown.

been reached, the amount of the grant is not increased by more spending by the recipient government. If the recipient government spends less than the cap, a closed-ended grant has the same effects as an open-ended grant. If the recipient government spends more than the cap, the matching grant has the same effect as a nonmatching grant.

THE FLYPAPER EFFECT.   A puzzling feature of intergovernmental grants is the **flypaper effect.** The term describes the fact that nonmatching categorical grants seem to increase spending by the recipient governments by more than they should, according to the theory explained above. The grants seem to "stick" to the purpose for which they were intended, and are not used for other forms of spending and tax relief.

As explained earlier, a nonmatching categorical grant should affect the recipient just like a noncategorical grant because money is fungible. A noncategorical grant is like an increase in jurisdictional income, so we'd expect most of it to be used for tax relief and not for government spending. Given the income elasticity of local government spending, we'd expect, at most, an increase in local government spending by 10 to 15 cents per $1 of grant. But studies indicate that recipient governments increase spending by as much as 40 to 65 cents per extra $1 of nonmatching grant.[6]

It is difficult to understand why the flypaper effect occurs. One reason consistent with the theory is that the recipient government wants to spend less on the specified purpose than the amount of the grant, a possibility shown in Figure 18.5. Given a noncategorical grant, the recipient government would choose point e^1 and spend G_i^1 on the local public good. Note that a noncategorical grant allows the recipient to choose allocations in the segment $A(B + A)$ of the budget line. With a nonmatching categorical grant, the recipient must spend the full grant (A dollars) on the specified

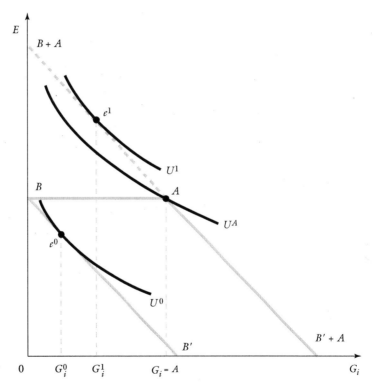

Figure 18.5

An Explanation for the Flypaper Effect

A block grant of A for local public good i increases spending on it by a larger amount if the recipient government would like to spend less than the grant allows. With a noncategorical grant, the jurisdiction's budget line is $(B + A)(B' + A')$ and the recipient spends G_i^1 on local public good i. With a block grant, the jurisdiction's budget line $BA(B' + A)$ is kinked at A. The jurisdiction maximizes local welfare by spending all of the block grant on the specified purpose. This is one explanation for the flypaper effect—the observed tendency for intergovernmental grants to "stick" where they are intended.

---

[6]Steven Craig and Robert P. Inman, "Education, Welfare and 'New Federalism,'" 1985.

purpose or lose $1 of grant for each $1 less of spending. That is, the recipient government must use it or lose it. In this case, its best policy is to spend the entire grant, so it chooses point A and spends the grant on the specified public good.

Unfortunately, this theory does not fully explain the flypaper effect. In most cases, the recipient government spends some of its own revenue on the specified purpose, so it is not "corner-constrained," as the above example assumes. Another explanation of the flypaper effect is based on the perceptions of the local voters. Voters may resist local tax increases, but they are accustomed to the existing level of taxes. If so, the recipient government is more likely to use grant money for government spending than to provide tax relief. If the granting government were to reduce the grant in the future, the local government would face the painful prospect of raising local taxes.

Some economists argue that the flypaper effect might be a statistical illusion. Although the grants are nonmatching in principle, in practice they may be matching. The granting government may make "nonmatching" grants only for purposes where it is likely that the funds will be spent rather than used to provide tax relief. Or it may give the grants to recipient governments that are more likely to spend the funds. For instance, a recipient government that contributes little of its own funds to the specified purpose so as to keep local taxes low may find itself "shortchanged" on future grants. In this case, it may treat nonmatching grants as disguised matching grants.[7] This type of statistical bias can explain some of the observed correlation between nonmatching grants and spending by recipient government.

EQUALIZING GRANTS FOR EDUCATION   One reason for intergovernmental grants is to equalize access to public goods across local jurisdictions that have different fiscal capacities. The **fiscal capacity** of a jurisdiction is a measure of its power to raise revenue for public purposes, or its tax base. Since most taxes are based on income, consumption, or wealth, affluent jurisdictions have larger tax bases and can spend more on local public goods than poorer jurisdictions. One way in which intergovernmental grants can equalize access to local public goods is by using variable match rates. Higher match rates are given to jurisdictions that have low fiscal capacity.

State government grants to local school districts for education use equalizing formulas that go beyond the variable match rates. State supreme court decisions require some states to finance public schools so that spending per pupil is the same in all school districts regardless of the district's tax base. Education grant formulas are designed for this purpose. The simplest form of equalizing education grant is **foundation aid**, a lump-sum grant paid to a school district that is equal to the minimum expenditure per pupil required of the district. The amount of the grant may be adjusted to reflect higher or lower education costs in the district, or to offset a higher or lower district tax base. In particular, the value of the grant may be reduced by an amount equal to a basic property tax rate (specified in the formula) times the property tax base (the assessed value of taxable property) of the district.

---

[7]This argument was made by Howard Chernick, "An Econometric Model of the Distribution of Project Grants," 1979.

This means that the higher the tax base of the district, the lower the foundation aid per pupil it receives.

Some states use a formula that adds to the foundation grant a component called the **guaranteed tax base.** This component is equal to the education property tax rate set by the district times the difference between a guaranteed tax base and the tax base in the district. The combination of a foundation grant and a guaranteed tax base received by a school district can be expressed as

$$\text{Total grant} = F + t \cdot (B_{G} - B),$$

where F is the foundation grant per student, t is the property tax rate in the district, B_{G} is the guaranteed tax base, and B is the tax base per student in the district.

For instance, if a district levies an education property tax rate of $20 per $1000 of assessed property value ($t = 0.02$) and its property tax base per student is $50,000 less than the guaranteed tax base ($B_{G} - B = 50,000$), the district receives a grant component for the guaranteed tax base of $1000 per pupil in addition to its foundation grant.

A guaranteed tax base component in the grant formula provides an incentive for the recipient district to increase its property tax rate. If the district in the above example increases its levy rate to $30 per $1000, its education grant increases by $500 per pupil. Thus the guaranteed tax base lowers the price of education to the recipient jurisdiction in the same way as a matching grant. However, the guaranteed tax base component of the grant can be manipulated by the recipient district. If a district simultaneously raises its levy rate and lowers its assessed property values (or does not increase assessed values as market values rise), the education grant is increased while the residents pay the same local school taxes.

Intergovernmental Grant Policy

So far we have analyzed the different types of grants and their effects. In this section, we discuss the functions that these grants are meant to serve. Is one type of grant better than another for a certain function? For that matter, why make grants at all? Why not let the local level of government raise its own revenue?

We begin with unconditional grants. Although unconditional federal grants are no longer made to state and local governments, we saw that block grants may be equivalent if the recipient spends its own revenue on the specified purpose as well. Why should the federal government make unconditional grants? One reason is economics of scale in collecting taxes. If the federal government can collect taxes at a lower cost than state and local governments can, it is efficient for it to collect taxes from the residents of all jurisdictions and distribute the funds as unconditional grants to be spent on local public goods.

A second reason is vertical equity. Residents in poor jurisdictions are unable to afford the same level of government goods as residents in affluent jurisdictions because incomes, property values, and other economic activities that determine the local tax bases are smaller. That is, a poor jurisdiction has a low fiscal capacity. Unconditional grants equalize fiscal capacities by increasing the revenue available to local governments in poor jurisdictions. Such grants also provide the residents with more private goods, because they can be used to lower local tax rates.

One problem with this "revenue sharing" purpose for intergovernmental grants is that the recipient governments may treat the revenue as costless. When a local government raises taxes for public goods, it takes care that the benefits outweigh the burden of the taxes on local residents; otherwise, the residents may punish the politicians in local elections. With intergovernmental grants, the burden of the tax is blamed on the taxing government while the spending government receives credit for the program. In these circumstances, the recipient government will spend money on programs that it would not implement if it had to raise its own taxes.

Unconditional grants leave the use of the funds entirely to the discretion of the recipient government. If the recipient government knows best how to use the funds, this seems desirable. Now let's consider why the granting government might prefer to give the grants on a matching basis. The granting government uses a matching grant when the local government spends "too little" on a purpose, from the perspective of the whole economy. We saw earlier that local governments would spend too little (less than the efficient quantity) on local public goods that provide benefit spillovers to nonresidents. A matching grant causes a larger increase than an unconditional grant in government spending on a specified purpose. By subsidizing local public goods with benefit spillovers, matching grants function like the corrective subsidies for activities that have benefit externalities.

The justification for nonmatching categorical grants is less clear. As compared with an unconditional grant, in theory a nonmatching grant increases spending on a specified purpose only if it is more than the recipient government wants to spend. If this is true, why attach strings to the grants in the first place, incurring the administrative costs of audits and compliance? A possible answer is the puzzling "flypaper effect," which suggests that the grant "sticks" with its specified purpose. Another answer is that categorical grants allow the granting government to maintain control over the details of the programs it funds. One form of control is intergovernmental mandates, which are obligations placed by the higher level of government on a lower level, requiring the latter to provide certain programs or services.

A mandate without a grant of funds, called an **unfunded mandate,** imposes requirements and costs on the lower government without providing any funds. The granting government can qualify categorical grants with mandates. If a recipient government does not comply with the mandate, the granting government can withhold part of the categorical grant. State governments can apply for waivers exempting them from mandates and restrictions, but the federal government may or may not grant the waiver, depending on its own policy objectives.

STATE AND LOCAL GOVERNMENT SPENDING ON EDUCATION

Spending on education is the largest component of state and local government expenditures. In fiscal year 1995, state and local governments spent nearly $400 billion on education, about 29% of all direct spending by state and local government. About 75% of this is for instruction; the rest is for construction and interest on school bonds. The distribution of this spending between state governments and local governments and between K–12 education and higher education is shown in Table 18.4.

As we see from the table, 70% of education spending is on K–12 education and most of this is by local governments. Although the local governments (school districts) account for nearly all of K–12 spending, some of it is financed through intergovernmental transfers from the state governments. In 1996–1997, 45% of school finance was by local governments, 48% was state governments, and the rest was federal finance. Higher and other (adult education and technical colleges) education spending accounts for the other 30% of direct spending on education, most of which is financed by the state governments.

The Rationale for Government Education Spending

In 1950, only a third of the population had a high school diploma and only 6% had a college degree. By 1998, 83% of the population had a high school diploma, and 24% had a college degree. Today nearly all children between the ages of 5 and 17 attend school, and 67% of high school graduates enroll in a postsecondary educational institution. Ninety percent of K–12 students are enrolled in public schools, and nearly 80% of college students are in public colleges. What are the economic reasons for the extensive involvement of government in providing education?

EDUCATION AND MARKET FAILURE.   We learned in the first chapters of this book that government provision of a good or service may be in response to market failure. What type of market failure explains state and local government involvement in education? One possibility is that education may be a local public good of the type we discussed earlier in this chapter. However, it seems doubtful that education is a nonrival good, because educating more students requires more education spending.

Table 18.4   Spending on Education by Level of Government, Fiscal Year 1995–6

	Direct Spending by State Governments (billions of $)	Direct Spending by Local Governments (billions of $)	Spending by State and Local Governments (billions of $)	Percent of Total
K–12 education	$3	$277	$279	70%
Higher education and other	$104	$15	$120	30%
Total education spending	$107	$292	$399	100%
Percent of total	27%	73%	100%	

Source: U.S. Census, United States State and Local Government Finances by Level of Government: 1995–6, http://www.census.gov/govs/estimate/96stlus.txt.

In fact, one of the most heated debates in education policy is that some children are short-changed and receive lower-quality education than do others. Rivalry seems to be a fact about education. Education is also an excludable good, as private schools can and do charge tuition. For these reasons, public good theory is of limited use in explaining government involvement in education. Instead, government involvement is best explained in terms of benefit externalities and, especially, equity.

Education adds to children's human capital, making them more productive. Much of this education could be provided by parents at their own expense. Is there any reason to believe that, left to their own resources, parents would not provide enough education (i.e., the efficient level) for their children? If parents care about their children, they will provide education as long as the marginal benefit to the child exceeds the marginal cost to the family. In this case, education is provided as long as it is "profitable" to the family. The family's marginal benefit from more education (say, one additional year of school) is the increased earning power of the children when they enter the labor force as adults, plus the value of the day care services the school provides to the parents. The family's marginal cost is the out-of-pocket expense of a year of school plus the opportunity cost (or forgone value) of the child's time. The latter is not very important for young children, but it is an important cost of education to adults in the form of lost earnings.

The external benefits of education are those that accrue to society at large rather than to the student or the family. The existence of external benefits from education is not in doubt. It is difficult to imagine how an advanced industrial economy could function if the population were illiterate and ignorant of, for instance, science and civics. However, the question of whether parents provide sufficient education for their children depends on whether external benefits are present *at the margin*. Quite possibly, most of the external benefits from education are inframarginal (or side effects) of the type explained in Chapter 4. Such external benefits are not a cause of inefficiently low levels of education, and the government need not increase education to make the economy more efficient.

What if some parents are selfish and do not care enough about their children to educate them sufficiently? Left to their own resources, selfish parents provide too little education for their children because the benefits of education (higher future earnings) accrue to the child while the parents pay the cost. In this case, the main benefit from education is external to the family member who makes the decisions about education. Not only are the benefits of education to the child lost, but external benefits for society are lost as well. While these external benefits are inframarginal when the parents are caring and give their children sufficient education, they are cause for societal concern in the case of selfish or negligent parents. For instance, selfish or negligent parents may not educate their children enough to make them employable as adults. The child's lack of education incurs costs on taxpayers, such as crime, illiteracy, and welfare dependency. The external benefits of providing public education for street urchins like the fictional Oliver Twist are easy to understand.

Perhaps it is the concern about selfish or negligent parents that explains why the government not only makes schooling available for all children but makes it *compulsory*. All states require that children receive schooling (or an equivalent education in the home) until they reach age 16, and some states require children to stay in school until they are 18.

Another market failure that provides a reason for government involvement is the fact that people cannot easily borrow against the value of their human capital. As mentioned, education confers benefits in the future, but its cost must be paid in the present. Since human capital can be owned only by the person in whom it is embodied, it cannot be used as collateral for a loan. Lenders are reluctant to lend money for people to invest in human capital because the human capital cannot be repossessed, so families without financial assets may be unable to obtain funds to pay for their children's education, even if the future benefits outweigh the costs. In particular, capital market constraints make it difficult for young adults from poor families to attend college. Although the higher future earnings from a college education may be worth the cost, a financially strapped, low-income family cannot afford the lost earnings and tuition of working-age children who attend college.

If students or their families are unable to borrow for education, the return on investment will be higher than the rate of return on other investments. Some evidence for this is found. The high returns to education can justify government programs that guarantee loans to college students, particularly those whose families lack sufficient financial assets.

EDUCATION AND EQUITY.   Most people believe that children should not be denied an education because their families cannot afford it. Although this could explain why the government provides free schooling for children, it is not a complete explanation, because it does not explain why the free schooling is not means-tested. For instance, most people believe that children should not be denied medical care because their families can't afford it, yet only children from poor families receive Medicaid at public expense. If this type of equity is the concern, why shouldn't free education be available only for poor children rather than for all children?

It seems that the equity concerns about education go beyond the desire to ensure access for the needy. Although public schooling is universal, families who want to send their children to private schools pay private school tuition in addition to their school taxes. In other words, they must pay twice to educate their children at private schools—once for school taxes and again for tuition. The effect is to equalize the quality of education received by children from different backgrounds by making it very costly for higher-income families to send their children to higher-quality private schools. This effect is called "leveling down" because it equalizes educational opportunities by making it harder for high-income families to provide more education for their children, rather than making it easier for low-income families to provide more education for theirs.

Why would a society want to make educational attainment more equal by leveling down? One possibility is that education magnifies natural inequalities in abilities by making more able people even more productive. Providing more education to less able people may not be as effective at equalizing incomes as limiting educational opportunities for more able people. If this is the reason for leveling down, it may not be a good policy. It is more efficient to let more able people become more productive, and give help to less able people through the tax and transfer system.

Savage Inequalities

In the United States we have always professed the ideal of equality in public education. Even the Supreme Court's infamous *Plessy* v. *Ferguson* decision of 1896, which upheld policies of racial segregation—including segregated public schools— gave lip service to the ideal of equality, with its doctrine of "separate but *equal*" facilities. Despite the ideal of equality in public education, the reality has been quite different. Jonathon Kozol's book *Savage Inequalities* (1991) documents the more egregious cases of inequalities in public schools by contrasting the nation's best public schools with its worst. Kozol argues that these educational inequalities are particularly savage because inadequate education of poor children perpetuates the cycle of poverty from generation to generation.

The main cause of inequality in public schools is the means by which they are financed. Traditionally, public schools have been provided by local governments and financed with local property taxes. Since wealthier people live in districts where property values are high, ample funds are available for high-quality public schools. In contrast, children in poor districts, where property values are low, do not get the same high quality of schools, because school tax revenue is insufficient. Simply put, wealth determines where people live and the quality of the public schools children attend. Poor people cannot afford to live in expensive school districts, so their children do not get the benefit of better public schools.

National attention was focused on the inequality in local public school financing by a landmark court case in California, *Serrano* v. *Priest* (1976). In 1967, John Serrano of Los Angeles complained to the principal of his son's school about the poor quality of instruction. He was told that his district could not afford better instruction and that he should move to a nearby wealthier district to get better instruction for his son. In a case that reached the California supreme court, Serrano's lawyers successfully argued that the availability of high-quality education should not depend on a district's wealth. The court eventually found that any scheme for financing public education that relates expenditure per pupil in public schools to a district's property tax base violated the "equal protection" clause of the state constitution. This obligated the government of California to adopt a school financing system that not only equalizes the availability of school funds among the districts, but also prevents the wealthier districts from collecting additional taxes to spend on local schools—that is, requires leveling down. This is done through the structure of the educational grants made by the state government to the school districts.

The *Serrano* case had an impact outside California. Similar court cases have been tried or are under consideration in other states, and in some *Serrano* provided a precedent for similar rulings. As a result, public schools in these states have become less reliant on local property taxes and more reliant on grants from the state government as a source of finance. These grants are structured to equalize spending per pupil across school districts within a state. Although this has reduced disparities in school expenditures per pupil within states, large disparities remain across the states. For instance, in 1998 public school spending per pupil ranged from a high of $10,650 in Alaska to a low of $3900 in Utah. Some of this reflects differences in costs, since teachers' salaries are higher in Alaska than in Utah, but even after adjusting for cost differences, substantial state-to-state differences in per pupil spending remain.

Disparities in spending per pupil across the states could be eliminated if the federal government were to assume a larger role in equalizing grants for education. However, a decision by the U.S. Supreme Court (*San Antonio Independent School District* v. *Rodriguez,* 1973) overturned a ruling by a federal district court in Texas that per pupil spending disparities violated the equal protection clause of the federal Constitution. Thus the federal government has no constitutional mandate to equalize educational spending across the states.

Instead, the federal government relies on programs like Head Start to equalize the benefits of education to children from poor families. Head Start provides preschooling and other services, including medical and nutritional benefits, to children from low-income families. The purpose is to overcome the inadequate learning skills of children from poor families so that they start school on equal terms with other children. In 1997, 794,000 children were enrolled in the Head Start program and $4 billion was spent on the program. Evidence on the effectiveness of Head Start is mixed. Children previously enrolled in Head Start perform better in school than children from similar backgrounds who were not enrolled; however, the difference narrows or vanishes after several years of schooling.

Savage Inefficiencies?

Most people are very concerned about the quality of the schooling their children receive and are willing to pay more for better schools. Surprisingly, not a lot of evidence supports the view that more spending improves educational quality. For example, public school spending per K–12 student measured in dollars of constant purchasing power rose 93% between 1970 and 1995, but the average student performance on standardized tests, like the Scholastic Aptitude Test (SAT), declined 4%. A possible explanation for this curious fact is that the relative price of education has risen, along with most other services. However, this cannot be the whole story. The number of teachers per student also rose between 1970 and 1995, from one teacher for every 22 students to one teacher for every 17 students. Also, the experience and level of educational attainment of the teachers rose over the same period, so presumably the teachers are of higher quality in 1995 than in 1970. It seems that student achievement has been dropping, even though school resources per student have been rising.

Some people argue that the decline in SAT scores is not indicative of declining achievement because the composition of the test takers has changed. In particular, the proportion of students completing high school and intending to go on to college (and therefore taking the SAT) has increased. The SAT is now taken by students who 25 years ago would not have aspired to college and may have even dropped out of high school. There is some support for this argument. Scores on other standardized tests, such as the Proficiency Test Score, which is a test administered to a

18.2   School Vouchers: The Milwaukee Parental Choice Program[1]

In 1990, the Milwaukee School District in Wisconsin began the nation's first experimental voucher plan, known as the Milwaukee Parental Choice Program (MPCP). The MPCP provides vouchers (worth about $4400) to families with incomes less than 175% of the national poverty threshold, allowing them to send their children to private, nonsectarian schools (called choice schools). Choice schools cannot discriminate among applicants and must select applicants by lottery if they do not have enough space for all who apply. Researchers are now assessing the results, and the process has ignited a fierce debate between voucher advocates and opponents.

Voucher advocates believe that the MPCP confirms their view that school choice improves education. They cite improved reading and math scores on standardized tests, increased parental satisfaction, and lower dropout rates as proof. Voucher opponents argue that the observed improvement is spurious and results from other factors. Both sides have resorted to sophisticated econometric methods to make their point.

Studies of the MPCP program compare the performance of students in the "treatment" group (students who attended choice schools on vouchers) with a control group (students who did not). To make any inferences from such experiments, the treatment and control groups should be similar in all respects except treatment. In an official study of the MPCP, Professor John Witte of the University of Wisconsin compared the test scores of voucher students at choice schools with a random sample of students in pubic schools. He controlled statistically for other factors that might affect student performance, such as parental income and ethnicity. He concluded that, once the other factors are controlled, the test scores of the voucher students are not statistically different from the test scores of students in the control group. Voucher opponents have seized on Witte's results as proof that vouchers do not work.

Professor Paul E. Peterson of Harvard University and his colleagues have contested Witte's results. They argue that a random sample of students from the public school system is not a good control group because of *selection bias*. Families who choose to send their children to choice schools are not the same as families who do not. They use students who applied for the voucher program but were rejected in the lottery as a more similar and hence a better control group. Comparing these groups, Peterson et al. found that both reading and test scores were higher for the treatment group, although it took several years for the improvement to occur. Voucher advocates have seized on Peterson's results as proof that vouchers do work.

Critics argue that Peterson's results are subject to *attrition bias*, because almost half of the voucher students drop the program. Therefore, improved scores may reflect the fact that voucher students who do well in the choice schools remain there rather than the fact that choice schools improve test scores. To resolve this debate, Professor Cecilia Rouse of Princeton University analyzed the data using an econometric technique called the fixed effects method. The fixed effects attempts to control for all individual characteristics that affect performance. She found that voucher students do better at mathematics but not at reading. Both advocates and opponents of vouchers claim that her work supports their position.

Critically analyze the following:

▪ The studies described above all attempt to test the hypothesis that a child selected at random would, on average, learn better in a choice school than in a public school. Even if this question could be answered to the satisfaction of all, would it determine whether vouchers are a good idea? That is, even if the students in the Milwaukee experiment do no better in the choice schools, might vouchers on a nonexperimental basis improve the quality of education?

(continued)

A Case in Point (continued)

In medical experiments, researchers control for the "placebo effect." Research has shown that people who receive treatment may do better simply because they are being treated, not because the treatment itself is effective. For this reason, members of the control group in a medical experiment may receive a sugar pill so that they think they are being treated. Could the placebo effect affect the results of voucher experiments? Would the results alter the case for or against vouchers?

Some people argue that there is a simple experiment that resolves the debate. Give

vouchers to everyone and let the parents (who have the greatest interest in the welfare of their children), not the researchers, decide whether school choice improves learning. What are the pros and cons of letting parents decide?

[1]A review with references of the different MPCP studies by the American Federation of Teachers (who are opposed to vouchers) is Edward Muir and F. Howard Nelson, "Social Science Examinations of the Milwaukee Voucher Experiment," August 1998. It is available at http://www.aft.org/research/vouchers/mil/rouse/rouse.htm.

---

representative sample of students at a given age, show no overall tendency to decline. In fact, mathematics and science scores increased on these tests.

Nonetheless, some economists, who have looked at differences in spending per pupil in different schools, have found no evidence that more resources improve students' performance. One proponent of this view is Professor Eric A. Hanushek of the University of Rochester, who surveyed 187 empirical studies examining the relationship between resources per student and performance. He concludes that there is "no systematic relationship between school expenditure and student performance."[8] People who are convinced by this evidence believe that public schools may already have ample resources, and what is needed are policies to ensure that the schools use the available resources more efficiently.

REFORMING PUBLIC SCHOOLS: A MATTER OF CHOICE.   Many people are united in the belief that something is seriously wrong with the American public school system. They are divided, however, about exactly how to fix it. Some people blame inadequate funding, others blame inequitable funding, and still others blame the teachers' unions. Economists have long argued that at least part of the problem is the monopoly power exercised by public schools. Within a school district, parents who are dissatisfied with their public school have few alternatives other than to move to another district or send their children to private schools, doubling the cost of education. As a result, schools have little incentive to respond to "dissatisfied customers."

It is not surprising, then, that the rallying cry of some school reformers is "choice." The hope is that by increasing the ability of parents to choose the school their children attend, parental choice will screen out the badly run schools and the poor teachers. One of the earliest proponents of such choice is the Nobel laureate Milton Friedman, who proposed a system of **school vouchers**—coupons exchangeable for school tuition. Suppose that the combined state and local spending per pupil is $6000 a year. Under

---

[8]"Can Equity Be Separated from Efficiency in School Finance Debates?" in Emily Hoffman (ed.), *Essays on the Economics of Education,* 1993.

Friedman's proposal, the government gives each parent a school voucher worth $6000 per school-age child rather than sending the money directly to the schools. This voucher can be "spent" on tuition at any school, public or private, and the parents can augment it with their own funds if they wish. Parents would use the vouchers to shop for good schools for their children, and schools would compete for students (and vouchers) by offering better instruction and better facilities.

Advocates of vouchers argue that they would improve learning by forcing schools to compete for students by offering better education. Advocates also argue that low-income and minority families stand to gain the most from vouchers. Well-to-do families can already afford to send their children to private schools or move to expensive communities that provide high-quality public schools. Opponents of vouchers argue that vouchers would undermine the public school system because public funds would be diverted to private schools. Opponents also argue that vouchers would increase disparities in education. Choice schools would compete for the best students, leaving the less able students in the public schools, which would decline in quality because of decreased funding. Opponents also argue that there is no evidence that students do better in private schools than in public schools (see A Case in Point 18.2). Finally, opponents argue (and have successfully challenged in court) that voucher programs are unconstitutional because they allow public money to finance the education in private religious schools, which violates the Constitutional separation of church and state.

Given that vouchers are considered too radical or unconstitutional, proponents of choice have suggested more limited ways of expanding choice. One possibility is vouchers that can be used for public schools only. Although this would limit competition from private schools, it would foster competition among public schools. This could be combined with **charter schools,** which have been tried in some districts. The charter school plan allows groups of teachers and parents to propose new and more efficient ways of providing education by forming their own school within the district. Parents can choose to send their children to the new charter schools. Charter schools are free from state rules and regulations but are held accountable for raising students' achievement.

A more limited option is the **magnet school.** In this case, schools within a district are allowed to specialize in some field of education—such as the arts, science, or mathematics—to develop a reputation for excellence in that field. Parents can apply to send their children to magnet schools rather than the school to which they are assigned. All these limited reforms can be viewed as attempts to introduce some of the competitive powers of the marketplace into the public school system while limiting the extent to which selective forces can lead to increased educational disparities.

CONCLUSION AND SUMMARY

In a way, state and local public finance is more complicated than that of the federal government. Not only is there much variety across the country, but the interdependence of state and local programs with federal programs is also complex. Despite the complication, we must remember that state and local governments play a very important role. In our everyday lives, we probably come into contact with the government of our city or state more often than we do with the federal government.

In this chapter we have concentrated on describing and analyzing the spending functions of these governments. In the next chapter, we discuss the special problems faced by these governments in collecting taxes.

- State and local governments function differently from the federal government because of constitutional constraints, limited geographic jurisdictions, and the effect of migration in and out of their jurisdictions.

- State and local government spending is concentrated mainly on education, public assistance, roads, civilian safety, resources, and sanitation. Empirical studies of demands for local government goods and services find that they have low income and price elasticities, suggesting that they are "necessities."

- A local public good is a nonrival good that can be consumed only by people living within a limited geographic area. If the area includes several political jurisdictions, the local public good causes jurisdictional spillovers.

- People can express choices for local public goods by moving to jurisdictions offering their most desired package of such goods. In some cases, this "voting with one's feet" leads to the provision of efficient quantities of local public goods by the local authorities, a result known as the Tiebout hypothesis.

- Many conditions may lead to the provision of inefficient quantities of local public goods, including jurisdictional spillovers. However, jurisdictional spillovers need not result in inefficiency if communities engage in "Coasian bargaining."

- The appropriate assignment of governmental functions to the level of government best suited to carry them out is called economic or fiscal federalism. Decentralized government allows people to express different choices for local public goods, either by voting or by moving. Local government also allows for more competition and innovation in providing local public goods.

- Centralized government can internalize jurisdictional spillovers and exploit economies of scale in producing public goods and in collecting taxes. It is also better suited for attaining government objectives on the basis of ability-to-pay principle of equity.

- Intergovernmental grants are a common feature of federalism in the United States. Most of these grants are categorical, meaning that they must be spent on a specified purpose. Some of the grants are given on a matching basis, which means that the amount of the grant is greater if the recipient government spends more on the specified program. A block grant is a fixed amount of money given to a recipient government to be spent for a specified purpose.

- Education is the largest component of state and local spending. Nine out of ten K–12 students attend public schools, and eight out of ten college students attend a state-funded college.

- Equity is a major reason education is provided by the government, yet inequalities in school funding remain because of the way public schools are financed.

- Advocates of school choice argue that vouchers would improve both equity and efficiency. Opponents argue that vouchers would lead to a two-tier education system with greater inequity.

QUESTIONS FOR DISCUSSION AND REVIEW

1. The estimated demand for public school education is inelastic with respect to its price (about minus 0.5 or less). Suppose the price of education rises because teachers' wages rise. Will government spending on public school education rise or fall?

2. Explain whether you think the following government goods and services are best provided by the government that provides them, or whether it would be better if they were provided by a higher or lower level of government.

   a. Prisons are provided by the state governments.

   b. HOV (carpooling) lanes on urban stretches of the interstate highway system are mainly paid for by the federal government.

   c. National parks are provided by the federal government.

   d. Sewage disposal is provided by city governments.

3. According to Tiebout's mechanism of "voting with one's feet," locational choice leads to efficient levels of local government goods and services. Perhaps the most important local government good that people consider in choosing a location is the quality of the schools. How do equalizing grants from state to local governments affect the working of the Tiebout mechanism with respect to public schools? Is this a conflict between efficiency and equity?

4. We often hear that an advantage of devolution is that the many state and local governments can serve as "laboratories" for experimentation and innovation in government. Would such an advantage be a local or a national public good? What does your answer imply about the appropriate attitude of the federal government toward experimentation by state and local governments? Should it encourage experimentation or remain neutral?

5. Explain carefully why the "flypaper effect" is a puzzle to economists. Suppose voters' sentiment against an increase in local taxes is stronger than sentiment in favor of a tax decrease. Can this explain the flypaper effect?

6. Cities compete with each other to host conventions by building convention centers and paying for attendant services, such as traffic control. Is such competition likely to improve economic efficiency? Explain.

7. Under the federal cash welfare program as it existed before August 1996 (Aid to Families with Dependent Children), the federal government gave a higher match rate to states with low incomes than to those with high incomes. Yet typically, these states had smaller benefits and stricter eligibility rules than their better-off counter-parts. Does this contradict the theory that higher match rates should stimulate more spending by the recipient government? Why or why not?

8. How does the method by which public schools are financed in most states contribute to inequality in public school spending per student? Suppose that a state uses a financing scheme that maintains average spending per student statewide but equalizes spending per student in all school districts (such as by financing schools with a state sales tax). How might this affect parents' willingness to send their children to public schools in wealthier school districts? In poorer districts? How would it affect voting on school spending?

9. Suppose that a voucher system for higher education is instituted. In this program,

all families with college-eligible children would receive a voucher equal in value to current state spending per college student. The voucher can be used at any university, private or public, within the state. Do you think this would affect the relative emphasis that universities place on teaching versus research by faculty? If so, how? Is your answer consistent with revealed preferences between research universities and community colleges under the existing public financing system?

10. Internet Exercise. Everybody is familiar with magazine articles that attempt to rate the best cities in which to live. Howard J. Wall, a senior economist at the Federal Reserve Bank of St. Louis, analyzed the rankings of cities in the different surveys and found that there is little agreement among them. The reason is that different surveys use different criteria for livability. He constructed a "rational index" of livability based on "voting with your feet." Wall's list ranks cities according to in- and out-migration, with the most livable being those with the highest rates of in-migration and the least livable those with out-migration or the lowest rates of in-migration. Wall's list is available at http://www.stls.frb.org/publications/re/1999/b/re/1999b14.

html. Do you think Wall's method of ranking the livability of cities is better than ranking them according to fixed criteria? Is it likely that a city can be considered more desirable (less desirable) to live in by a majority of the population yet rank low (high) on Wall's list? Why or why not?

11. Internet Exercise. Economists Anne Case, James Hines, and Harvey Rosen find evidence that states "copycat" the fiscal policies of neighboring states.[9] That is, states are more similar in government spending patterns and tax systems to neighboring states than states that are farther away. The U.S. Census Bureau reports state spending and revenue structures at http://blue.census.gov/govs/state/98stus.txt. Access this site and find the percentage of state spending on different functions (education, public welfare, etc.) for your state. How do these percentages compare with those of a neighboring state? With a state in another part of the country? Is your single observation in agreement with the hypothesis of Case et al.? What are some reasons states are more likely to adopt copycat spending patterns of nearby states than distant states?

SELECTED REFERENCES

The famous Tiebout hypothesis is proposed by Charles M. Tiebout in "The Pure Theory of Local Expenditures," 1956. The theory of fiscal federalism is described at length in Wallace Oates, *Fiscal Federalism*, 1972. A textbook specializing in public finance at the state and local level is Ronald C. Fisher, *State and Local Public Finance*, 2nd ed., 1996.

The case for school vouchers is outlined in John Chubb and Terrence Moe, *Politics, Markets and America's Schools*, 1990. Valerie Lee and Anthony Bryk question Chubb and Moe's evidence in "Science or Policy Argument: A Review of the Quantitative Evidence in Chubb and Moe's *Politics, Markets and America's Schools*, 1993.

---

[9]A. C. Case, J. R. Hines, and H. S. Rosen, "Copycatting: Fiscal Policies of States and Their Neighbors," *Journal of Public Economics*, October 1993.

USEFUL INTERNET SITES

Numerous sites provide information on state and local government spending or pointers to information on individual states. These include The U.S. Census Bureau at http://www.census.gov/govs/www/index.html, FinanceNet at http://www.financenet.gov/ and StateNews at http://www.statenews.org/.

Good links are also found at the National Association of Budget Officers site at http://www.nasbo.org/ and Stateline at http://www.stateline.org/.

19

State
and Local
Taxes

In 1996, the Congress passed legislation prohibiting a state from taxing the pension benefits of former residents who had left the state. Typically, these taxpayers were retirees who had worked and earned income in the state in the past, and some of their income was deferred and given to them as pension benefits. Retired emigrants may also own Individual Retirement Accounts (IRAs) and Cash or Deferred Arrangements (CODAs) on which no tax was paid when the income was earned. If a retiree earns the income in a state that allows deferral and then moves to a state—such as Florida—that does not levy an income tax, state income taxes are never paid. Opponents of the legislation, mainly the states trying to tax the pensions, were disappointed. In their view, the income was earned in the state, and the taxpayers were given a privilege by being allowed to defer state taxes. Not only did the state have a right to tax the income because the source was in the state, but also retirees who moved to states without an income tax received a special advantage over the taxpayers who remained. Proponents of the legislation saw things differently. They viewed the legislation as a victory that prevents states from "taxing without representation." People who do not live in a state do not receive state government services or vote in state elections—so why should they pay taxes there?

The problem of "source taxation," as this attempt to tax pension benefits is called, illustrates an important difference between the taxing ability of state governments and the federal government. States cannot tax people and businesses living and operating outside their borders, whereas the federal government can tax everyone in the nation. The federal government can allow taxpayers to defer taxes on income without worrying about losing the ability to tax the income if the taxpayer moves after the income is earned but before it is spent (as long as the taxpayer does not leave the country and renounce his or her citizenship). A state government must worry about people who leave its jurisdiction, especially if another state offers a more attractive tax environment.

In this chapter, we focus on the special problems state and local tax authorities face because of their limited tax jurisdictions. Also, although there is only one federal government, there are many state and local governments. Thanks to multiple jurisdictions, taxpayers, especially businesses, may be subject to taxes in more than one jurisdiction on the same income or sales. As a result, some means is needed for establishing who has taxing authority, as well as determining the tax base within the jurisdiction. Similar problems arise when businesses, such as multinational corporations, operate in several countries.

PROBLEMS FACED BY MULTIPLE TAX AUTHORITIES

Where there are many taxing authorities, complications in tax policy arise that do not face a national taxing authority like the federal government. Such complications arise within a country when the tax policies of different states and local governments overlap, and internationally when multinational corporations maintain operations in several countries. These problems include determining the ability and right to tax, multiple taxation, the allocation of the tax base among the competing authorities, tax exporting, and tax competition. We discuss each of these in more detail below.

Establishing the Right to Tax

State and local tax authorities, with their limited tax jurisdictions, face more constraints on their ability to tax than does the federal government, with its national taxing authority. The three most important reasons are as follows:

- *Constitutional constraints on discriminatory taxes by states.* Various provisions in the Constitution of the United States have been interpreted by the courts as preventing states from levying taxes that interfere with the movements of goods, services, businesses, and people across state borders. This is called the *interstate commerce clause.* In addition, the Fourteenth Amendment requires states to offer all citizens within their borders "equal protection of the law," which effectively prevents the states from levying taxes that overtly discriminate against out-of-state persons and businesses.

- *Mobility of taxpayers and goods and services.* As we saw in the case of the sunbelt-bound retirees, taxpayers can move out of a state and, therefore, out of the reach of its taxing authority. This is especially important for businesses that can locate outside a state but can easily sell their products to state residents because the interstate commerce clause prevents policies that burden commerce among the states. For example, out-of-state mail-order firms can easily sell products in a state but cannot be forced to collect sales taxes on purchases by residents unless the firms have substantial presence in a state.

- *Limited and overlapping tax jurisdictions.* Not only is it difficult for a local jurisdiction to tax people or firms outside its borders, but taxpayers may carry out economic functions in many states, exposing themselves to potential "double" taxation. For instance, a manufacturer might make parts in one state, assemble them in a second state, and sell the final product in a third state. All states where the firm operates may want to tax part or all of its economic activity.

Two alternative bases can be used for taxing income and goods in a multijurisdictional economy. The first is called the **residence basis** in the context of income taxation or the **destination basis** in the context of sales taxation. In this case, a jurisdiction taxes income received by persons residing within its borders regardless of whether the income comes from a source within the jurisdiction or outside. Similarly, the jurisdiction taxes goods consumed within its borders (i.e., the destination of the goods is within the jurisdiction) regardless of whether the goods are produced by local firms or imported from firms outside the jurisdiction.

The second basis is called the **source basis** in the context of the income tax or the **origin basis** in the context of sales taxes. A jurisdiction may tax income that is generated (has a source) within its borders regardless of whether or not the recipient of the income lives in the jurisdiction. Similarly, it may tax goods that are produced (have their origin) within its borders, regardless of whether they are consumed in the locality or exported.[1]

Generally, personal income taxes have a residence basis, so residents pay taxes on their income to the government of the jurisdiction regardless of the income's source. However, taxes on business incomes are usually levied according to their source. Most state sales taxes are levied on an origin basis, meaning that the tax is imposed on goods sold within the state regardless of where they are consumed. Some states, however, use the destination principle and do not tax goods that are delivered to consumers out of state or those purchased by nonresidents. Also, states attempt to impose use taxes to tax goods purchased out of state but consumed within, although they have limited ability to do this.

To tax a person or firm, the state must establish that it has the legal authority to levy the tax. Under the residence principle, the authority is based on a formal test of residency, such as the number of days in the year that a taxpayer resides in a state or country, or whether a firm is incorporated in the state. (Under tax law, a person or business can be resident in several tax jurisdictions at the same time.) As a practical matter, the ability of a jurisdiction to tax also depends on whether the taxpayer holds property within the jurisdiction that can be seized in the event of nonpayment.

Most states rely on retail sales taxes (RSTs) for a substantial fraction of their revenue. The RST is collected from the vendor on sales made to its customers. When can a state force a vendor to register under its sales tax system and collect taxes on goods sold to persons in the state? This question was taken up by the United States Supreme Court in *National Bellas Hess* v. *State of Illinois* in 1967. Bellas Hess was a mail-order firm located in Missouri that regularly solicited business in Illinois by sending catalogues to that state's residents. The state of Illinois attempted to force Bellas Hess to register and remit Illinois sales tax on sales to Illinois residents because the firm carried out business in the state. On the basis of the interstate commerce clause, the Supreme Court ruled that the mere solicitation of business in a state does not constitute **nexus,** the legal term for a substantial presence that would allow a state to require a business to comply with its tax laws. For nexus, the court ruled, a firm must have a physical presence in the state, such as an outlet or employees. Because of the *Bellas Hess* decision, states have been unable to collect sales taxes on mail-order firms unless the firms have outlets in the state.

---

[1]However, it cannot tax goods exported from the state more than goods consumed in the state. This would constitute a tax on exports, which is proscribed by the interstate commerce clause.

In 1992, the Supreme Court revisited the mail-order problem in *Quill* v. *North Dakota*. In this case, the Court reaffirmed the inability of a state to force mail-order firms to collect sales taxes for states in which they do not have nexus but left the door open for Congress to pass a law enabling states to tax mail-order firms. To date, Congress has not passed such a law.

Allocating the Tax Base

Although a firm may have its headquarters in the state where it is incorporated, it typically produces and sells its products in many states. For instance, a company might have a plant producing parts in one state and a plant assembling the parts into the final product in another. It may have sales outlets in all states. Not surprisingly, any state where an interstate corporation has a substantial business presence, or nexus, may attempt to tax the income of the company. To avoid double taxing the same business income, it is necessary to have a method of allocating the tax base among competing tax jurisdictions. If every state in which the interstate corporation has a nexus attempts to tax its whole income, the problem of double or multiple taxation arises. Also, an impediment to interstate commerce is created because firms will avoid operating in many states.

One method, known as **separate accounting,** treats the firm's operations in different states as if they were different businesses. With the separate accounting method, businesses calculate their revenues and costs for each jurisdiction in which they operate.

The federal government uses the separate accounting method when taxing the income of multinational corporations. A typical multinational corporation has a parent corporation in one country, such as the United States, and operates subsidiary corporations in other countries. The U.S. government taxes the income of the parent corporation, and the governments in the countries where the subsidiaries are located have the right to tax the incomes of the subsidiaries. Under the separate accounting method, the income of the subsidiary corporations in foreign countries is separate from that of the parent until the income is repatriated to the parent in the form of interest, intercorporate dividends, royalties, and other payments. When the U.S. parent corporation receives income from its foreign subsidiaries, it becomes taxable in the United States.[2]

To prevent the double taxation of foreign income, U.S. taxpayers receive a **foreign tax credit** for income taxes paid to foreign governments. Alternatively, taxpayers can deduct foreign taxes in determining their U.S. taxable income, although most taxpayers take the credit because it is more favorable. The foreign tax credit is limited to the amount of income taxes paid to the foreign government or the amount of tax owed on the income in the United States, whichever is less.

---

[2]To prevent tax avoidance by corporations that set up "paper" corporations in countries with low corporate tax rates, the subpart F provision of corporate tax law subjects nonoperating income of foreign subsidiaries in tax havens to U.S. taxation.

Separate accounting is impractical within the nation because the operations of a business in one state contribute to and depend on its operations in other states. For instance, the parts of a car might be produced and assembled in different states. How is the total value of the car apportioned when nearly every part is essential to its overall value? How are overhead costs, such as the costs of management at the head office, apportioned to the operations of the business in different states? Any method of separate accounting involves arbitrary assignments of revenues and costs and can be manipulated by the corporation to avoid taxes.

Because of the impracticality of separate accounting, states use **formula apportionment** to determine the income of an interstate corporation operating within their jurisdiction. Formula apportionment calculates the fraction of the nationwide business income of an interstate corporation to be apportioned to a state using fractions of measurable activities taking place in the state, such as payrolls, property ownership, and sales. The most common formula for apportioning business income is specified in the *Uniform Division of Income for Tax Purposes Act* and is called the UDITPA formula.

The **UDITPA formula** apportions a fraction of an interstate corporation's national income to a state using the simple average of the percentage of the corporation's property (A), sales (R) and payroll (W) taking place in the state. Symbolically, the corporation's income in state S (or Υ^S) is

$$\Upsilon^S = \frac{f_A^S + f_R^S + f_W^S}{3} \cdot \Upsilon$$

where Υ is the corporation's national business income, f_A^S is the percentage of the value of property (at historic cost) owned by the corporation located in state S, f_R^S is the fraction of the corporation's sales that take place in the state, and f_W^S is the fraction of the corporation's payroll that is paid in the state. For example, according to the formula, the state income of a corporation whose property, sales, and payroll are completely within the state $(f_A^S = f_R^S = f_W^S = 1)$ is equal to its national income. On the other hand, for a corporation that holds all its property and pays all its payroll in state S but sells none of its product there, state income is two-thirds of its national income.[3]

One desirable feature of formula apportionment, besides its administrative practicality, is that double or multiple taxation of company income is avoided if all states use the same formula. Since the fractions of property, payrolls, and sales must add up to 1 when summed over all states, 100% of the corporation's national income, and no more, is apportioned to the states. If, however, some states use different formulas, as is the case, some degree of double taxation is possible, although in practice it is probably small.

---

[3]In interpreting this formula, we should keep in mind the issue of nexus. Conceivably, a company could sell 100% of its output in a state yet not have nexus if it has no employees or property in the state. Even though the formula apportions one-third of the company's income to the state on the basis of sales, the state has no legal authority to tax the company.

What is the tax base when a state levies a tax on business incomes using formula apportionment? Using the theory of tax equivalence, we can show that a state tax on apportioned business income is equivalent to a combination of taxes. In particular, a tax on business income apportioned according to the UDITPA formula is equivalent to the state's levying a particular set of taxes on the property, sales, and payrolls of the firm within the state. This equivalence is useful because it can be used to analyze the economic incentives of a tax on apportioned business income; the economic effects are a combination of the economic effects of property, sales, and payroll taxes.

A more complicated multijurisdictional problem occurs when a corporation operates subsidiary corporations in other states. A subsidiary corporation is a second corporation owned by the first corporation. Under the separate entity principle of corporate taxation, a parent corporation and its subsidiary are separate entities. However, most states find it impractical to treat related corporations set up outside the state as separate firms, because this would allow firms to shift income into or out of the state at will.

One method firms use to shift income out of a state (or out of the country) is **transfer pricing**, which is the setting of artificial prices for goods and services sold by one corporation to a related corporation. For example, suppose a parent corporation delivers parts to a subsidiary at transfer prices far below the market value of the parts. This would effectively shift business income or profit from the parent corporation to its subsidiary. If corporations are treated as separate entities, they could use transfer pricing to shift income to low-tax states.

As a result, most states practice what is called the unitary method. The **unitary tax method** treats a group of corporations as a single firm for tax purposes. The national income of a group of corporations is calculated and apportioned among the states using formula apportionment. Most states use the *water's-edge* unitary method, which consolidates related corporations within the United States but does not include related foreign corporations.

The Efficiency of Multijurisdictional Taxes

A good tax system interferes as little as possible with the efficient use of the economy's resources. Recall that economic resources are used efficiently when they are employed where they have highest value. Generally, if resources are employed inefficiently, a Pareto improvement (an increase in one group's utility without decreasing anyone else's) is possible if the resources are reallocated to the higher-valued uses.[4] The criterion of economic efficiency is more problematic for state and local taxes. The question is whether a government should be concerned with efficiency on an economy-wide scale (national efficiency) or with efficiency within its own jurisdiction (jurisdictional efficiency).

---

[4]Obtaining an actual Pareto improvement may require redistribution of income from the gainers to the losers.

To achieve national economic efficiency, economic resources should be employed any place in the nation where they have the highest pre-tax value. This is also called **locational efficiency.** Since capital is highly mobile, most discussions of locational efficiency concern the locational incentives facing investors. If capital can earn a higher pre-tax return in state A than in state B, it should be invested in state A for national efficiency. At the nationally efficient allocation, capital should earn the same pre-tax return wherever it is located.

State tax systems can easily conflict with national efficiency. For example, if states tax capital income on a source basis (that is, they tax the income of capital located within the state whether owned by a resident or not), differences in state tax rates will influence the location decisions of investors. Capital may be invested in a state because that state has a lower tax rate, not because capital is more productive there. If some states tax on a residence basis while others tax on a source basis, inefficiency is caused even if all states levy the same tax rate. A mix of residence- and source-based taxes by different states is called *tax disharmony.* With tax disharmony, capital income is subject to double taxation—once where it is located and again where the owner of the capital lives—causing investors to locate their capital to avoid double taxation rather than on the basis of the highest productivity.

If all states tax income from capital on a residence basis, national efficiency is achieved. Capital owners pay the same local rate of tax on their income whether their capital is located within or outside the jurisdiction where they live. Since capital is taxed according to the residence of the investor, no one has an incentive to employ capital elsewhere because of a different tax rate.[5] This feature of residence-based taxation is called **capital export neutrality,** because it does not affect whether capital stays or leaves the taxing jurisdiction.

Although national efficiency is best for the whole economy, it may not be the objective of state or local governments. This fact can be explained in terms of the Pareto criterion that underlies the desirability of economic efficiency. A nationally efficient policy increases benefits to the residents of a state without making nonresidents worse off. However, any policy that improves the welfare of state residents would be viewed as good by the state government, even if nonresidents are made worse off. Costs imposed on nonresidents are not likely to matter to state legislators, who are elected by residents only.

To the extent that state and local governments care about efficiency at all, they are more likely to care about jurisdictional efficiency. Jurisdictional efficiency requires that economic resources be employed where they have highest value to the jurisdiction. For this to occur, capital should be invested outside the state when the return *after taxes paid to other states* is at least as great as the return in the state. At the most efficient allocation, the after-tax return in the other states should be equal to the before-tax return within the state. The local government ignores taxes paid to other states, since they do not benefit its residents.

Jurisdictional efficiency is obtained if a state levies its income tax on a residence basis and gives a tax deduction for taxes paid to states in which the capital was

---

[5]However, investors may have an incentive to move to low-tax states.

located. In this case, only the after-tax return on capital invested out of state is subject to residence tax. To the extent that another state levies income taxes at source, double taxation occurs and national efficiency is not obtained. However, this would not bother a state concerned with jurisdictional efficiency, so it has no reason to worry about tax disharmony. Problems of tax disharmony must be solved with tax treaties among states, or with a solution imposed by the national government.

Tax Exporting

Ideally, politicians would like to levy taxes that burden people who cannot vote in elections. That way, the government gets revenue to spend on programs that benefit residents while the nasty part—the tax—is borne by people outside the jurisdiction who cannot object at election time. Although states and local governments have no authority to tax people outside their jurisdictions, we saw in Chapter 11 that the burden of taxes can be shifted. When the burden of a tax is shifted to someone outside the jurisdiction, we call it **tax exporting.**

One way that state and local governments export tax burdens is through the *federal offset,* which is made possible because taxpayers who itemize their federal income taxes can deduct state and local income and property taxes (see Chapter 13). If, for example, a New York family in the 28% federal tax bracket pays $5000 in deductible state and local taxes, it saves $1400 in federal personal income taxes by taking the deduction, which reduces its taxable income by $5000. In effect, the federal government pays part of the family's state and local taxes. Of course, to get sufficient revenue for its own programs, the federal government must levy a higher federal tax rate, so the cost of the $1400 tax saving to the New York family is exported to the taxpayers of the country at large.

Tax exporting also occurs if state and local taxes themselves are borne by nonresidents through the usual mechanisms of tax shifting, as described in Chapter 11. Because constitutional restrictions prevent overt tax discrimination between residents and nonresidents, state and local governments usually engage in tax exporting by taxing particular goods and services likely to be purchased by out-of-state consumers or by visitors to the state.

A case of successful tax exporting is shown in Figure 19.1, where a state levies an excise tax on a good produced by businesses inside the state and purchased by consumers from outside the state. The attempt to export the tax is successful because the supply curve of the taxed good is horizontal, so the entire excise tax is shifted in the form of a higher price to the (nonresident) consumers. The state obtains revenue equal to the cross-hatched rectangle, and the nonresident consumers bear a tax burden equal to the loss in consumers' surplus shown as the shaded trapezoid. The nonresident consumers bear both the revenue and the excess burden of the exported tax. This example of tax exporting requires that producers in the state, as a group, have market power in the sense that the national price of the good is determined within the exporting state. If consumers can easily buy the product from producers in other states, the tax cannot be exported.

To successfully export a tax, it is not enough that the taxed good be purchased by out-of-state residents. As we learned in Chapter 11 it is possible for a tax to be

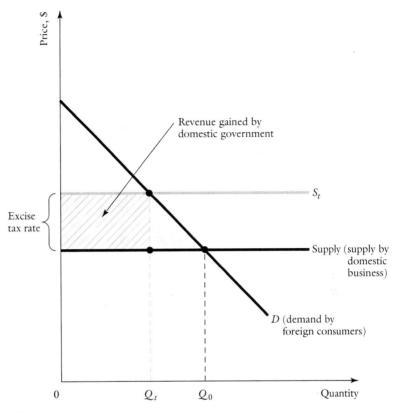

FIGURE 19.1

Exporting an Excise Tax to Nonresident Consumers
If the supply curve of domestic producers is horizontal and the good is demanded only by nonresident consumers, the tax is "exported." The price of the good rises by the full amount of the excise tax, and non-resident consumers lose consumers' surplus equal to the shaded trapezoid. The domestic government gains revenue equal to the cross-hatched rectangle.

borne by the producers rather than the consumers. This would be the case if the supply curve in Figure 19.1 were vertical rather than horizontal. In this case, the producers' price of the taxed good would fall by the amount of the tax, and the domestic producers, rather than the nonresident consumers, would bear the burden of the tax.

In general, a tax on production is exported when the consumers are predominantly nonresident and resident producers have an *elastic* supply curve. The elastic supply curve means that the tax shows up as a higher price to the consumers. A less common form of tax exporting occurs when domestic consumers are the main buyers of a good from nonresident producers who have an *inelastic* supply curve. In this case, a local excise tax reduces the price to the nonresident producers rather than raising the price to resident consumers. For this type of tax exporting, the consumers in the state, as a group, must have market power in buying the good from nonresident sellers.

Tax Competition

Another phenomenon in setting state and local taxes is tax competition. **Tax competition** occurs when a local government sets its tax rate marginally below the tax rates prevailing in other localities in order to attract the tax base—say, business and personal income—into its jurisdiction. By "stealing" another locality's tax base, a low-tax jurisdiction can collect more revenue despite its lower tax rates.

For instance, suppose states A and B both have income generated within their borders of $100 billion and each has a state income tax rate of 20% and collects $20 billion in tax revenue. Suppose when A lowers its tax rate to 18%, some businesses leave B and move into A, raising its tax base to $120 billion while lowering B's to $80 billion. As a result, state A now collects $21.6 billion while B's revenues decline to $16 billion. Collectively, the two states lose tax revenue, but state A, which lowered its tax rate, gets more revenue.

Of course, this is not the end of the process. When state B begins to lose businesses to state A, it will retaliate by lowering its state tax rate. In fact, it might lower its rate to 17%, not only to keep its own businesses but to attract businesses from A. Like two firms engaged in a price war, each state undercuts the tax rate of the other to attract a larger tax base, but in the end both states lose revenue. Although some taxpayers gain from tax competition, the states must raise revenues in other ways where tax competition is not possible. These alternative taxes may be less efficient or less equitable, so tax competition can force states to adopt less desirable tax structures.

In the extreme case, tax competition may limit local taxing jurisdictions to benefit taxes. A *benefit tax* exists when taxpayers receive a benefit from local government programs equal in value to the local taxes they pay. In this case, lower tax rates in other states do not cause taxpayers to change locations, because they would lose a benefit equal to the tax they save. For instance, if a community levies high property taxes to provide fine public schools, lower property taxes elsewhere will not attract residents if they value the schools by as much as they pay in higher taxes.

STATE AND LOCAL TAX STRUCTURE

State and local taxes do not loom as large as federal taxes in the budgets of most households, but they are significant nonetheless. In 1999, state and local taxes from their own sources amounted to $904 billion, or 11.6% of personal income. Unlike the federal government, which relies mainly on income taxes, state and local governments rely to a significant degree on sales and property taxes as well as income taxes. Some states also collect severance taxes, which are taxes on firms that remove resources, such as lumber, fish, and minerals, from state land and waters.

The percentages of state, local, and combined state and local tax revenue from different sources are shown in Table 19.1. This table lists the percentage of own-source revenue by type of tax for state, local, and combined state and local governments. The figures represent averages for the 50 states and the District of Columbia. As shown, the largest fraction of state and local tax revenue is derived from general sales taxes, but income taxes, excise taxes, and property taxes also contribute significant fractions.

19.1   Welcome, Taxpaying Traveler

One of the main ways that state and local governments attempt tax exporting is by levying high "tourism" taxes on goods and services purchased by visitors. These goods and services include lodging, restaurant meals, amusement parks, and rental cars. Tourist taxes are prevalent in states and localities that are popular destinations for tourists, such as Hawaii and New York City. As we learned earlier, tax exporting is successful only if the taxed goods and services are bought primarily by visitors rather than locals. Also, the tourism tax must raise prices to the visiting buyers rather than lower prices to local sellers. This will be the case if the demand curve for the tourist goods and services is inelastic and the supply curve is elastic. For Hawaii, this seems to be the case. Professor Carl Bonham and his associates at the University of Hawaii studied the impact of changes in the Hawaii hotel tax on hotel receipts.[1] They found no evidence that hotel receipts are reduced by increases in the tax or increased by reductions. This suggests that the conditions for tax exporting are satisfied in Hawaii.

As tempting as tourism taxes are, they are not always the bonanza that the states and localities think they are. Even if hotel room taxes are fully shifted to consumers, the number of visitors may decline. In this case, governments intent on tax exporting must worry about reduced tourism if tax rates are too high. In addition to room taxes, tourists pay state sales taxes on other purchases they make during their visit, so if high hotel room taxes discourage tourism, the local government could end up with less revenue overall.

In 1990, New York City had the highest hotel room tax in the nation at 21.25% for a $100 room. This included a flat $2 per room charge, a 6% city tax, and a 5% state tax. To top it off, the state general sales tax of 8.25% was applied to the hotel guest's bill. The impact on tourists was heightened by the fact that the taxes were itemized on four separate lines of a hotel guest's bill, making them very visible. Before long, conventions and organized tours were unofficially boycotting New York City, and the hotel industry was complaining that tourism and hotel room receipts were down significantly. It seems that the high New York tax intended for visitors was hurting New Yorkers. In 1994, New York reduced the combined hotel room tax to 16.7%. After the reduction in the tax rate, revenue from the hotel taxes actually increased, along with room occupancy. It appeared that at the high 1990 tax rate, New York had reached the downward-sloping part of the revenue curve described in Chapter 10.

An econometric analysis by the New York City Independent Budge Office found this was not the case. Once other factors influencing the demand for hotel rooms in New York were considered, the decrease in the tax rate lowered net revenue. However, the increase in hotel occupancy rates plus increased spending by tourists on other taxable goods offset more than half the loss in revenue from the lower rate. This suggests that the price elasticity of demand for hotel rooms in New York is high enough that tax exporting is incomplete. The IBO study is available at http://www.ibo.nyc.ny.us/pubtax1.html.

Critically analyze the following:

- What are the differences between Hawaii and New York City that could account for why the former might have better ability to export taxes?

- Bonham et al. found that the gross receipts of hotel businesses did not decline with increases in the hotel room tax. What does the demand curve for hotel rooms have to look like if this result is accurate?

- In some cases, localities use hotel room taxes to finance programs that promote tourism, such as convention centers, stadiums, events, and other tourist-related activities. Can a locality export taxes this way?

---

[1] Carl Bonham et al., "The Impact of the Hotel Room Tax: An Interrupted Time Series Approach." 1992.

Table 19.1   **State and Local Tax Structures (Fiscal Year 1996)**

Type of Tax	State Government (% of own-source revenue)	Local Government (% of own-source revenue)	State and Local (% of combined revenue)
General sales	33.3%	11.0%	24.5%
Selective sales	16.0	4.8	11.6
Personal income	31.9	4.9	21.3
Corporate income	7.0	1.0	4.6
Property	2.4	73.7	30.4
Licenses	3.3	.4	2.1
Death and gift	1.3	n.a.	.8
Severance and other	4.8	4.6	4.7
Total own-source tax	$418 billion	$271 billion	$689 billion

Source: Statistical Abstract of the United States, 1999, Table 504.

A Diverse Tax Landscape

Not only do state and local tax structures differ from the federal tax structure, but tax structures differ markedly from state to state. Most states levy income and sales taxes, but some states levy sales taxes but not income taxes, or vice versa. Reliance on selective sales taxes also varies.

Table 19.2 reports tax structures of selected states in terms of percentage of tax revenue collected from each source. This table reveals large variations in tax structures—from Alaska, which gets most of its revenue from corporate income and severance taxes on businesses, to Washington, which relies on sales and property taxes. Also noteworthy is the importance of revenue collected from license taxes in Delaware, the selective sales taxes in New Hampshire, and personal income taxes in Oregon.

Table 19.2   **State Tax Structures in Selected States (Fiscal Year 1996)**

State	Personal Income Tax Revenue	Corporate Income Tax Revenue	General Sales Tax Revenue	Selective Sales Tax Revenue	Revenue from License Taxes	Property Tax Revenue	Death and Gift Tax Revenue	Severance Tax and Other Revenue
All	32.1%	7.0%	33.3%	15.8%	6.4%	2.4%	1.3%	1.7%
Alaska	0	21.5	0	6.5	5.2	3.7	.1	63.0
California	36.0	10.1	32.9	8.9	5.3	5.8	1.1	.1
Delaware	37.4	9.8	0	15.0	31.6	0	1.3	4.9
Illinois	33.5	9.4	29.3	19.8	5.5	1.2	1.1	.2
Massachusetts	53.9	9.9	21.0	10.3	3.2	0	1.5	.4
N. Hampshire	6.2	21.5	0	51.2	12.9	.1	4.5	3.6
Oregon	63.9	6.8	0	13.4	13.2	0	.9	1.8
Washington	0	0	58.4	15.9	4.7	17.0	.6	3.4

Source: Statistical Abstract of the United States, 1999, Table 522.

Table 19.3 **Differences in Tax Rates Across the 50 States (2000)**

	Maximum MTR on Personal Income	Maximum MTR on Corporate Income	General Sales Tax Rate	Gasoline Excise Tax Rate	Cigarette Excise Tax Rate
Highest (levy states)	12% (N. Dak.)	9.99% (Penn.)	7.0% (Miss. and R.I.)	32¢ a gal. (Conn.)	$1.00 a pack (Hawaii)
Lowest (levy states)	2.8% (Penn.)	4.0% (Kansas)	3.0% (Col.)	7.5¢ a gal. (Ga.)	2.5¢ a pack (Va.)
No-tax states	Alaska, Fla. Nev., S. Dak., Tex., Wash., Wyo.	Nev., S. Dak., Tex., Wash., Wyo.	Alaska, Del. Mont., N.H., Ore.	None	None

Source: Federation of Tax Administrators, *State Tax Rates and Structure,* http://www.taxadmin.org/fta/rate/tax_stru.html.

The diversity of the tax landscape across the 50 states in 2000 is also shown in Table 19.3. This table shows the highest and lowest maximum personal and corporation income tax rates, general sales tax rates, and selected excise tax rates. As shown, seven states do not levy personal income taxes and five of these do not levy corporate income taxes either. The maximum (top-bracket) marginal tax rate on personal and corporate incomes levied by the states is between 10% and 12%, and the lowest marginal tax rate on income is around 3%. General sales taxes vary less from state to state. Although five states do not levy a general sales tax, the highest rate is 7% and the lowest rate is 3% among those states that do levy a sales tax. We should keep in mind that these are the state tax rates; local governments also levy sales taxes in most of these states, so the combined rate is higher in most communities.

Excise tax rates vary widely from state to state. For example, in 2000 the state excise tax on gasoline varies from a low of 7.5 cents per gallon to a high of 32 cents. Cigarette excise tax rates vary even more, from a low of 2.5 cents per pack to a high of $1.

Although interstate differences in excise tax rates are fairly informative, differences in income and sales tax rates do not give a complete picture, because the tax bases may differ as well. For instance, one state may tax income narrowly defined at a high rate while another may tax income broadly defined at a low rate. To fully appreciate the extent of interstate income and sales tax differences, we must study how the tax base can vary from state to state.

State Income Taxes

In Chapter 13, we saw that federal taxable income is equal to adjusted gross income (AGI) minus personal exemptions and the taxpayer's choice of itemized deductions or the standard deduction. Federal taxes payable are found by applying the tax rate schedule to taxable income and subtracting federal tax credits from the calculated amount. In general, states that levy income taxes follow the federal model to some extent. In fact, in some cases the states literally copy the federal income tax structure.[6]

The simplest way for a state to copy the federal tax structure is to use federal income tax paid by a resident taxpayer as the base for the state tax. This kind of arrangement, called *piggybacking,* determines the state income tax as a percentage of the federal income tax owed by a state resident. In 1999, only North Dakota, Rhode Island, and Vermont used the piggyback method. For instance, the state income tax liability of a Rhode Island resident is 27.5% of federal income tax liability; thus a taxpayer who pays $10,000 in federal taxes must pay $2750 in income taxes to the state of Rhode Island. Piggybacking means that the state effectively adopts both the federal tax base and the federal tax rate structure.

The next easiest way to copy the federal tax is to adopt the federal definition of taxable income, or a modified version that does not allow a deduction for state taxes. This method, adopted by several states, allows states to have their own rate schedules but follows the federal model in the definition of AGI and the deductions and exemptions allowed. The state tax schedule can have more or fewer tax brackets than the federal schedule. Some states (such as Colorado) levy a flat rate (single bracket) of 5% on federal taxable income; other states (such as Idaho) have eight tax brackets as compared with the five federal brackets.

Under the Federal-State Tax Collection Agreement, the federal government can agree to collect income taxes on behalf of states that piggyback on the federal tax or use federal taxable income (or a slightly modified version thereof). Although the federal government would collect the taxes at no cost to the state, no state has availed itself of the opportunity. In contrast to the autonomous state income tax systems in the United States, nine out of ten Canadian provinces use the piggyback method and have the Canadian federal government collect their taxes through a tax collection agreement.

Further from the federal system, a state can adopt the federal definition of AGI but assign its own deductions and exemptions so that state taxable income is different from federal taxable income. Most states use this method.

Finally, a state can ignore the federal tax system altogether and define gross income in its own way and have its own exemptions, deductions, and rate schedule. For example, the state of Pennsylvania defines gross income more broadly than the federal tax does. Four states besides Pennsylvania have income tax systems that are unrelated to the federal model. States that define taxable income differently from the federal government and use different tax rate structures increase the cost of tax compliance to their residents, since people have two sets of tax rules to comprehend and obey.

State and Local Sales Taxes

The state retail sales tax was introduced in the 1930s, when revenue from other state tax sources declined sharply with the onset of the Depression. The first state to introduce a retail sales tax was Mississippi, in 1930, and by 1939, 23 states had levied retail sales taxes. During the postwar period, the general sales tax became the

---

[6]Most of the information about states in this section and the next is drawn from Advisory Commission on Intergovernmental Relations, *Significant Features of Fiscal Federalism,* vol. 1, 1995.

most important single source of revenue for the states combined. In 1999, 45 states and the District of Columbia had retail sales taxes of some form, with only Alaska, Delaware, Montana, New Hampshire, and Oregon not levying a general sales tax. In states levying the retail sales tax, it accounts for about 33% of state revenue on average. The rate of sales tax levied by state governments ranges from 3% in Colorado to 7% in Mississippi and Rhode Island. The state of Washington is the most reliant on the retail sales tax as a source of state revenue; it collects over 58% of its own-source tax revenue this way. Local governments also levy retail sales taxes. As of 1997, the highest combined state and local sales tax rate was 9% in Alabama (Mobile), Louisiana (New Orleans), and New York (Yonkers).

Although retail sales taxes are called general sales taxes, they are not levied on all goods and services. Some goods, such as groceries, are exempted to mitigate the alleged regressive incidence of sales taxes. Of the 45 states with retail sales taxes, 28 exempt groceries and 10 exempt prescription drugs in total or in part.

Some goods and services are exempted from the retail sales tax for reasons that make little, if any, economic sense. In fact, the criteria determining whether a retail transaction is or is not taxable are among the more arbitrary features of sales taxation. Originally, sales taxes were levied on sales of *personal tangible property* only. As a result, many services, especially personal services like haircuts and lawyers' services, are not subject to the retail sales tax in most states. But some services are taxed, particularly if they are rendered in conjunction with a tangible property such as the repair of a taxable good.

The distinction between tangible and intangible property leads to some rather strange outcomes. For instance, the RST of nearly every state includes the rental of a movie or a videotape as a taxable item, but in many of the states watching the same movie on pay-per-view cable television is a service and is not taxed. Similarly, renting a carpet-cleaning machine is taxable, but hiring a carpet-cleaning service is not. Although the same service is rendered in both cases, it is the presence of the tangible item—the videotape or the carpet-cleaning machine—that determines whether the transaction is taxable.

The fact that many services are exempt has created a serious problem for states that are heavily reliant on the sales tax as a source of revenue. Services are the most rapidly growing form of consumption spending, and have been for some time. For instance, in 1959 spending on services amounted to about 40% of personal consumption expenditures, but by 1999 they accounted for 57% of total personal consumption spending. This means that if a sales tax exempts most services, the tax base (the amount taxed) grows less rapidly than the economy as a whole and becomes progressively narrower (covering less and less of total spending). Because the more rapidly growing services are exempt, sales tax revenue grows less rapidly than the economy of the state.

State and Local Property Taxes

Real estate is the main form of wealth that is subject to tax in the United States. In 1999, the revenue from taxes on real estate property amounted to $237 billion, all of it collected by state and local governments. Most, about 95%, was collected by local governments. The property tax is the mainstay of local governments, accounting for

19.2   Taxation in Cyberspace

Perhaps the hottest topic in state and local public finance right now is the issue of taxing Internet commerce. In 1998, the U.S. Congress passed the Internet Tax Freedom Act (ITFA) barring all new taxes on Internet commerce for three years. In 2000, the House voted to extend the moratorium for another five years. Proponents of the ITFA argue that it is needed to protect the fledgling industry. Internet merchants could face attempts by more than 50,000 localities with 7000 different sales tax systems to tax Internet access, remote (internet) sales, or even the flow of information on the Internet. Opponents argue that the IFTA favors Internet commerce over "brick and mortar" merchants and threatens to erode revenues from state sales taxes, the main source of state revenue.

The central legal and practical issue in Internet taxation is nexus. Recall that the Supreme Court ruled that a state cannot force a vendor to collect the state's sales tax on a transaction unless the vendor has a physical presence in the state. Determining nexus for Internet commerce presents the tax authorities and the courts with new and unresolved issues. The point of sale for an Internet transaction is indeterminate. Is it the location of the seller (e-tailers), the Web host where the seller advertises, the Internet service provider (ISP) that maintains physical routing equipment to serve its subscribers, or nowhere? Some e-tailers have considered establishing a Web host aboard a satellite so that no state (or country) could claim jurisdiction.

Even if the legal nexus issue could be resolved, collecting sales taxes on Internet commerce would be complicated. The seller would have to determine which jurisdiction levies the tax, whether the good is taxable in that jurisdiction, and at what rate. If an Internet purchase is a physical good delivered to the customer, the customer's residence would determine the taxing authority according to the destination principle of sales taxation. Unfortunately, ZIP codes do not always correspond to the tax jurisdiction. Moreover, goods such as music and software may be delivered online and the seller has no way of knowing where the buyer is located. Privacy is another issue. For sellers to collect taxes on Internet sales, buyers would have to provide personal information to the seller. This is not normally required when sales taxes are levied on ordinary transactions.

Exempting Internet commerce has its own problems. If Internet commerce grows as predicted, the state sales tax base may be seriously eroded (the state sales tax has been described as "roadkill on the information superhighway"). Sales tax rates will have to increase if states are to collect the same revenue, increasing the tax advantage of Internet sellers. Exempting Internet commerce also favors Internet merchants over brick-and-mortar merchants, creating inefficiency and inequity. The so-called "digital divide" also causes inequity because higher-income families have greater access to the Internet than lower-income families. State sales taxes that exempt Internet commerce will be more regressive because low-income families shop less on the Internet and more at brick-and-mortar locations.

Critically analyze the following:

- Some people have proposed a federal sales tax on Internet commerce, with the revenue distributed to the states. What advantage does the federal government have over state governments in levying sales taxes on Internet commerce? What are the problems in distributing the revenue to the states?

- Some states have proposed cooperative agreements. The state in which the Internet seller is located can keep 50% of the tax revenue it collects from the seller on sales to customers in another state. Given the theory of tax competition, are such cooperative agreements likely to work? Why or why not?

- In many cases, shipping and handling charges on Internet purchases offset the tax saving from Internet shopping. Explain how this creates a deadweight loss on the economy.

75% of own-source tax revenue. Cities and townships, counties, school districts, and other special-use districts all levy property taxes. School districts are particularly important because property taxes are the main source of school finance.

THE MECHANICS OF LEVYING PROPERTY TAXES.   One problem occurs in levying property taxes that does not occur in the administration of the other major taxes. The value of taxed properties must be determined whether or not they are subject to market transactions. In fact, many of the properties may not have been subject to a market transaction for years. As a result, the value of the properties to be taxed—the property tax base—must be established through an assessment process.

In 1991, the total assessed value of property in the United States was $6.9 trillion. Over half of this was residential real estate and land, but commercial property is also part of the tax base. Since the property tax is levied mainly by local governments, the assessment process is decentralized, and each tax jurisdiction hires its own assessors to determine the fair market values of taxable properties within the jurisdiction. The assessed value of property, which is the base of the property tax, is determined from the estimated market values.

Property values can be estimated in several ways. The comparison method estimates the value of a property by using the market values of comparable properties that have been bought and sold recently. The cost method can be used to estimate the value of structures by determining their replacement costs. A third method, useful for valuing leased commercial property, is the income method, which estimates the property value from the income earned for the owner over the life of the property. Once an assessed value has been determined, it may be adjusted periodically to reflect changes in neighborhood property values as revealed by the prices of comparable properties bought and sold.

When the value of a property is determined, the amount of tax is found by multiplying the **assessed value** of the property by the **levy rate.** The levy rate is usually expressed as dollars of tax per $1000 of assessed value, but it is sometimes expressed as a decimal fraction called the **mill rate.** The levy rate may differ according to the use of the property; for instance, the levy rate on land used for agriculture is usually less than that on land used for residential purposes.

Given the total assessed property value in the taxing jurisdiction, the levy rate can be set so as to collect the revenue needed by the local government. In some states, upper limits are set on the permissible levy rate, or increases in the levy rate must be approved by referendum. Often, however, a homeowner's property tax bill rises even though the levy rate is fixed. During times of rising property prices, homeowners find their property taxes rising because the assessed value of their homes rises. For this reason, some states, such as California, have placed limits on how much assessed property values can rise from year to year.

Levy rates in different jurisdictions cannot be easily compared, because some jurisdictions have a high levy rate but low assessed values, or vice versa. In some jurisdictions, the assessed value is equal to the market value of the property, whereas others use fractional assessments that value property at less than market value.[7] To

---

[7]Fractional assessment is sometimes used to tax residential and commercial property at different effective tax rates.

compare property tax rates in different jurisdictions, we must consider differences in the **assessment ratio,** which is the assessed value of property divided by the market value. The **effective levy rate** is equal to the statutory levy rate multiplied by the assessment ratio.

Table 19.4 shows the nominal and effective levy rates in selected cities in the United States in 1998. Two things can be observed from this table. First, the effective levy rate on property varies greatly from city to city. Second, variations in the effective levy rate may come about from differences in the nominal levy rate or differences in the assessment ratio from city to city.

THE ECONOMIC EFFECTS OF THE PROPERTY TAX.   How does the property tax affect decisions made by taxpayers, and what are the economic consequences of these effects? An old idea is that a property tax on land has no economic effects and is equivalent to a lump-sum or neutral tax on landowners. As we discussed in Chapter 17, it is generally believed that the supply of land is fixed. A landowner must pay property tax on the value of land owned, so the price a potential buyer is willing to pay is reduced by the amount of the tax. In principle, the price a buyer will offer is reduced by the present value of the property taxes that the buyer must pay on the land. Since the supply of land is fixed, the price of land must fall by the amount of taxed levied on land. In effect, the property tax on land is a lump-sum tax on the people who own the land at the time the tax is levied. This is an example of *tax capitalization,* explained in Chapter 11.

This simple story is incomplete, so in fact the property tax can have economic effects. Even if the supply of land is fixed, the levy rate may differ according to the use of the land, so the property tax affects how land is used. For instance, a higher effective levy rate may apply if the land is used for residential purposes than if it is used for agricultural purposes. In this case, the property tax discourages the use of land for residential purposes. Similarly, vacant unimproved land has a lower value than improved land (cleared land with utilities and road access). If landowners plan to hold land for some length of time, the existence of the property tax encourages them to hold it in unimproved form.

Perhaps the most important effect of the property tax is on the quantity of structures. Although the quantity of structures is fixed at a point in time, it can vary

Table 19.4   Residential Property Tax Rates in Selected Cities (1998)

City	Nominal Levy Rate ($ per thousand)	Assessment Ratio	Effective Levy Rate ($ per thousand)
Milwaukee, Wis.	30.30	.991	30.00
Detroit, Mich.	57.60	.407	23.40
Fargo, N. Dak.	479.90	.042	20.20
Columbia, S.C.	362.50	.04	14.50
Chicago, Ill.	88.40	.16	14.10
Washington, D.C.	9.60	.97	9.30

Source: Government of the District of Columbia, *Tax Rate and Tax Burdens: A Nationwide Comparison, 1998,* Table 4, p.19.

over time because of new construction and the depreciation of existing structures. Since the value of the structures is taxed by the property tax, the property tax acts to reduce the quantity of structures.

This is shown in Figure 19.2. A simple assumption is that the long-run supply of structures is horizontal, as shown, so we assume that structures are available at a constant $\bar{V}$ dollars per square foot. The price that buyers are willing to pay for the structures, disregarding the property tax, is given by the downward-sloping demand curve D. The intersection of the demand and horizontal supply curves determines the equilibrium quantity of structures Q_0.

The property tax reduces the price that buyers are willing to pay for structures by the present value of the property taxes that must be paid. This is shown by the after-tax demand curve D_t, which intersects the horizontal supply curve at the

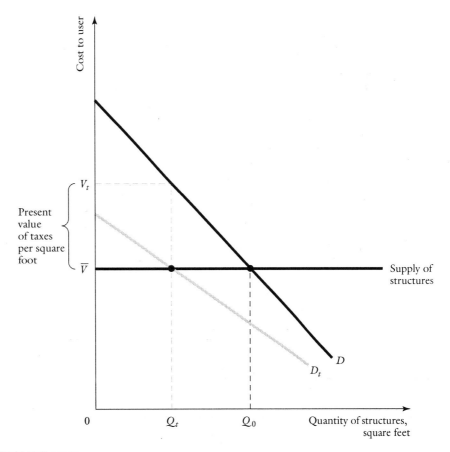

FIGURE 19.2

Effect of a Property Tax on Structures

Unlike land, the supply of structures is in variable supply. Here structures can be built at a constant supply price of $\bar{V}$ and a property tax reduces the quantity of structures from Q_0 to Q_t. As a result of a smaller stock of structures, the cost to consumers rises by the present value of the property taxes from $\bar{V}$ to V_t. In this case, the incidence of the property tax on structures is entirely on the users.

quantity Q_t. With a horizontal supply curve, it is the equilibrium quantity of structures that falls as a result of the property tax, not property values. At quantity Q_t, buyers are willing to pay $\bar{V}$ per square foot of structures plus the present value of the property taxes that must be paid. This is equal to V_t, which represents the total cost of the structures to the buyers.

Of course, the assumption of a long-run horizontal supply curve for structures is a simplification. If the supply curve of structures is upward-sloping, the price of structures is also affected by the property tax. In this case, the property tax reduces not only the equilibrium quantity of structures but also the value of structures.

Considerable attention has been paid to the effects of differences in the effective property tax rates across different jurisdictions. If all jurisdictions levy the same effective property tax rate, no tax incentive is provided to shift construction of structures from one place to another. When some jurisdictions levy higher taxes on property than neighboring jurisdictions, new homeowners may be encouraged to locate and build in the lower-tax jurisdictions. This view has been challenged by the argument that the property tax is a benefit tax.

A benefit tax is one viewed as coming with an attached benefit of equal value. In choosing a jurisdiction, a homeowner will look at both the benefit and the property tax rates. For instance, if a community has higher property taxes but offers better schools, the higher taxes may be viewed as simply the price of better services. If the property tax is viewed as a benefit tax by most homeowners, it does not distort economic decisions in the way a tax usually does.

WHO BEARS THE PROPERTY TAX?   An unsettled debate about the property tax concerns its incidence. Two different views define the debate on this question. The first is that the property tax is regressive because it is an excise tax on the consumption of housing and, at least for families with less than average incomes, housing is a necessity. The second is that the property tax is progressive (or at least proportional) because it is a tax on wealth and is borne by owners of property. Both views are correct, under the right assumptions.

The view that the property tax is regressive focuses on the fact that residential property is the main component of the property tax base. Because housing expenditures are a larger fraction of the budgets of low-income people than of high-income people, the property tax is regressive if it increases the cost of housing. The idea that the property tax is equivalent to an excise tax and raises the cost of housing depends on the assumption that the supply curve of property is horizontal, as it is for structures in Figure 19.2. In this case, the quantity of structures is reduced by the property tax and the cost of housing rises by the present value of property tax payments to V_t.

What causes the demand price to rise? It is the fact that structures are in shorter supply because of the property tax and can command higher rents. As we see in Figure 19.2, the cost of housing rises by the full amount of the property tax, so that rents must rise enough to compensate the owners for their higher costs. In other words, the property tax is fully passed on to the users of property, just as if the government levied an excise tax on rents.

The opposing view, that the property tax is a wealth tax on the property owners, is sometimes called the "new view," although in fact it is very old. Taxed property is in fixed supply, so the value of the property is depressed by the amount of the tax. The property tax is not passed on as higher rents to the users, since the owners' costs do not rise. Because the ownership of property is more concentrated in the hands of the rich, from this argument we would conclude that the property tax is progressive.

Clearly, these two views of the incidence of the property tax hinge on the slope of the supply curve of property. For this reason, both views can be partially right. If land is in fixed supply, the property tax on land is shifted to the owners and is a progressive wealth tax. At the same time, if structures are in completely elastic supply, the part of the property tax that falls on structures is shifted to the users and is a regressive tax on the consumption of housing.

The difference in the incidence of the property tax according to the two views is shown in Table 19.5, based on work by the late Joseph Pechman of the Brookings Institute. Pechman calculated the property tax as a percentage of income (the effective property tax rate) for taxpayers in each decile of family income under the two different views. A decile is 10% of the population, so the first decile is the 10% with the lowest family incomes and the tenth decile is the 10% with the highest family incomes. The first column shows the property tax burden as a percentage of income across the income deciles, assuming that the entire property tax is borne by the property owners. The second shows the distribution of the property tax burden, assuming that the tax on structures is fully shifted to the users of the property—say, in the form of higher rents—so that it is an excise tax on housing consumption. As expected, the property tax as a percentage of income rises as we move up the income scale when it is assumed that the whole property tax is borne by property owners. As a tax on wealth, it is progressive. However, when we assume that the property tax on structures is shifted to the consumers, its burden is a higher percentage of income for the lowest income deciles and falls as we move up the

Table 19.5 Annual Incidence of the Property Tax Under Alternative Assumptions

Deciles Based on Adjusted Family Income (thousands)	Property Tax Burden as Percentage of Income *(Whole property tax is borne by owners of property)*	Property Tax Burden as Percentage of Income *(Property tax on improvements is borne by consumers of shelter)*
1	0.7%	3.5%
2	0.7	2.6
3	0.9	2.2
4	0.9	2.1
5	1.0	2.1
6	1.2	2.1
7	1.2	2.1
8	1.3	2.2
9	1.7	2.2
10	3.5	2.2
Top 1% of the population	4.7	2.2

Source: Joseph Pechman, *Who Paid the Taxes, 1966–1985?* 1985, Table 4-10.

income scale. Since a large part of the property tax is a tax on housing consumption under this assumption, the property tax is regressive.

PROPERTY TAX RELIEF MEASURES. Whatever the incidence of the property tax, governments worry that it imposes an undue tax burden on people with a low ability to pay. As a result, many states and localities adopt measures that provide property tax relief to certain groups of taxpayers, particularly those with low incomes, the elderly, and the infirm. The three main types of property tax relief are homestead exemptions, homestead credits, and circuit-breaker programs.

A **homestead exemption** is a fixed amount subtracted from the assessed value of the homeowner's property to obtain the taxable assessed value. When the homestead exemption is available to all taxpayers, it is analogous to the standard deduction or personal exemption under the personal income tax. A **homestead credit** is a fixed amount that is subtracted from the amount of property tax owed. Since the levy rate is the same for all taxpayers, a homestead exemption and a homestead credit are equivalent policies. Most states give homestead exemptions or credits in some form and amount, but many limit them to certain groups of people such as the elderly, the disabled, and veterans. Some give relief only if hardship is proved.

A **circuit-breaker program** is a special type of property tax relief that is activated when the property tax paid by a household exceeds a certain fraction of its income. The same relief is given to renters if the rent they pay exceeds a certain fraction of their income. The programs are called circuit breakers because they operate like the safety device that breaks the current in an overloaded electrical circuit. Similarly, if a household's budget is overloaded by the property tax, relief in the form of a rebate is triggered.

Incidence of All State and Local Taxes

In 1996, Citizens for Tax Justice, a group concerned with the distributional impact of the tax system, released its study of the incidence of state and local taxes. The study concluded that most states have regressive tax systems, which place larger relative tax burdens on poor and middle-income families than on well-off families. Averaging over the 50 states and including the federal offset for state and local taxes, the study found that the 20% of nonelderly families with the lowest incomes paid 12.4% of their incomes in state and local taxes, while the 20% with the highest incomes paid just 8.6%.[8]

The findings of this study can be attributed mainly to the fact that state and local governments rely to a significant degree on sales and property taxes, and the assumptions and methodology used in the study ensured that these taxes would appear highly regressive.[9] In fact, the study found that in states where governments

---

[8]Citizens for Tax Justice, *Who Pays? A Distributional Analysis of the Tax Systems in All 50 States,* June 1996, appendix I, p. 52.

[9]For instance, the study assumed that sales taxes are shifted to consumers as higher prices and not back to factor owners; it used income rather than spending to measure a family's ability to pay; and it used annual rather than lifetime incidence. It also neglected the effect of higher sales taxes on the amount of transfer income received by low-income families through indexing.

rely mainly on sales and property taxes, the tax systems were "very regressive." Whatever the validity of its conclusions, however, the study does address an important issue. How does the incidence of state and local taxes differ from that of federal taxes and why? To answer this question, we must consider not only the different types of taxes levied by state and local governments, but the different ways in which state and local taxes are shifted.

The mobility of goods and factors plays a major role in determining the incidence of state and local taxes. Because of geographic mobility of goods and factors, the state and local tax base is likely to be more sensitive to the state and local tax rate (more elastic) than the federal tax base is to the federal tax rate. A state or locality that levies a tax rate much higher than its neighbors' may discover a much reduced tax base.

How does this affect the incidence of state and local taxes? The general rule of tax incidence—taxes are disproportionately borne by those individuals least able to change their economic plans in response to them (see Chapter 11)—implies that mobility between jurisdictions is an important determinant of who bears local taxes. In particular, taxpayers who are geographically immobile and cannot easily arrange to earn incomes or buy goods and services outside the jurisdiction will bear a larger share of local taxes than taxpayers who are mobile. Likewise, owners of land are likely to bear a disproportionate share of the state tax burden, because land is immobile.

To see this, suppose a state attempts to tax capital located within its borders at a high rate. In a closed economy, a capital tax reduces the return on capital to owners, and it is progressive because capital ownership is concentrated in high-income groups. However, if capital is mobile and easily moved out of the jurisdiction to other, nontaxing jurisdictions, the incidence of the tax on capital must be shifted to owners of nonmobile factors, perhaps workers who cannot find jobs outside the state, or to consumers. If capital is easily moved, it must earn the same return after taxes within the state that it can get in other states, so the before-tax rate of return must rise by the state tax rate. A higher before-tax rate of return means that other factors in the state must receive lower rewards, or consumers must pay more for the goods and services produced in the state.

This line of reasoning suggests that the incidence of a tax in a state depends on the tax rates prevailing in the other states. We assumed above that other states do not tax capital, so capital owners can avoid the tax by moving capital out of state. In this case, the before-tax return on capital in the taxing state must rise enough to compensate for the local tax. However, if all states tax capital at the same rate, capital owners cannot escape the tax by moving capital among states, so the return on capital is not affected. A tax on a mobile factor is shifted to immobile factors only if the local tax rate is significantly different from rates in other states. The incidence of a tax on capital levied at the same rate in all states is the same as the incidence of a national tax, whereas a differentially high rate of tax is shifted to immobile factors or to the consumers.

For example, suppose all 50 states tax capital income at 25% and capital earns a rate of return of 8% before taxes. Investors take home 6% after taxes no matter where they invest their capital. Now suppose that one state—say, Rhode Island—taxes capital at 50%. If capital earned the same rate of return before taxes in Rhode

Island as in the other states, the after-tax return would fall to 4% and investors would shift their capital elsewhere to earn 6%. Since Rhode Island is small, it cannot affect the return on capital in the nation, but as capital gets scarce in Rhode Island the before-tax rate of return must rise. In equilibrium, the rate of return must rise to 12%, so the after-tax return is equal to that available elsewhere. The increase in the before-tax return to capital must reduce rewards to other, immobile factors or raise prices to consumers. All told, half the 50% Rhode Island tax is borne by capital and half is shifted to immobile factors.

CONCLUSION AND SUMMARY

The analysis of multiple tax jurisdictions is complicated, and perhaps a little esoteric, but it addresses problems that are significant and will become even more significant in the future. Two reasons explain this. First, at the national level, state and local spending and taxes may grow in importance if politicians make good on their promise to devolve more federal powers to the states. Second, the international mobility of goods, services, and factors has grown rapidly in the past few decades, and this trend is likely to accelerate in the future, especially as globalization and the growth of regional free-trade areas continues. Both of these developments will increase the likelihood that tax authorities will face greater problems of limited and overlapping jurisdictions.

- State and local tax authorities face constraints different from those on the federal government because the Constitution forbids restrictions on the mobility of persons and firms, and because of the limited and overlapping nature of their tax jurisdictions.

- In an open jurisdiction, such as a state or nation, an income tax can be levied on a residence basis, meaning that the place where the recipient lives has the right to tax; or on a source basis, meaning that the place where the income is earned has the right to tax. Similarly, a sales tax can be levied on a destination or an origin basis.

- States cannot force businesses to pay taxes unless they have a substantive presence, or nexus, within its borders. The Supreme Court has ruled that the mere solicitation of business does not constitute nexus, so states cannot force mail-order firms to collect retail sales taxes on sales to residents.

- Because businesses typically operate in many states, business income must be apportioned among the states for tax purposes. This is done with formula apportionment, which assigns a fraction of a firm's national business income to a state on the basis of percentage of the firm's property, payroll, and sales located there.

- Tax exporting occurs when a local tax is shifted to persons living outside the taxing jurisdiction. Tax competition is a beggar-thy-neighbor policy by a state or local tax authority that lowers the local tax rate in order to attract the tax base of a neighboring jurisdiction.

- The tax structures of state and local governments differ from that of the federal government and from each other. On average, state and local governments are less reliant on income taxes and more reliant on sales and property taxes than the federal government.

▪ Forty-three states levy taxes on personal income. Most of them pattern their income taxes on the federal model, although they may have their own deductions, exemptions, and tax rate structures.

▪ Forty-five states levy retail sales taxes. Most of these sales taxes are similar in structure, although they may differ in the goods and services that are exempted. Most states exempt intermediate goods, groceries, and personal services.

▪ The property tax is the main source of revenue for most local governments. To the extent that it falls on land, the property tax is a lump-sum tax on landowners and cannot be shifted. The property tax on structures may be shifted forward to consumers of housing services.

▪ The incidence of state and local taxes across income classes is less progressive than the federal tax system, and by some measures it is quite regressive. The different incidence of state and local taxes is a function not only of their different tax structures but also of the mobility of taxpayers and tax bases across jurisdictional boundaries.

QUESTIONS FOR DISCUSSION AND REVIEW

1. Many states levy a "use tax" on big-ticket items consumers buy out of state, like boats or furniture. The use tax rate is equal to the state sales tax rate. Is a state sales plus use tax an origin-based tax or a residence-based tax?

2. Barnes and Noble, a bookstore chain with stores in most states, recently spun off its Internet commerce site, BarnesandNoble.com, as a separate company. Explain why it would do this using the principle of nexus for state sales taxes.

3. Which of the following state taxes are most likely to be exported, and why?

    a. Tax on ski accommodations in Colorado.

    b. Tax on wheat in Kansas.

    c. Tax on subway fares in New York City.

4. As mentioned, many localities levy taxes on tourism by taxing goods and services most likely to be purchased by temporary visitors. In some cases, the revenue from these taxes is used to improve tourist facilities, such as convention centers and riverside walks. Would it make a difference for the incidence of a tourist tax whether the revenue is used this way or to benefit residents? Why?

5. In Chapter 15, we showed that a tax on the economic profit of a firm is neutral and does not affect its decisions. Would this be true for a state or local tax on economic profit? Why or why not?

6. Citizens for Tax Justice is dismayed that state and local tax systems are not as progressive as the federal tax system, and indeed may be regressive. Is it likely that a state could unilaterally adopt a very progressive tax system? Why or why not?

7. In Chapter 11 we saw that an excise tax may be shifted to consumers as a higher gross price or to producers as a lower net price. Compare the incidence of federal and state excise taxes on gasoline. Is a state gas tax likely to be borne by consumers and producers in the same way as the federal tax? Why or why not? Does it matter whether the state taxes gasoline at the same rate as other states or at a much higher rate?

8. In Chapter 10, we saw that an increase in a tax rate on a good can decrease the amount of revenue collected. Is this more or less likely to happen if the tax is a state tax rather than a federal tax? Why? Is it possible that a cut in the state excise tax rate could raise state revenue and reduce (national) economic efficiency at the same time? Explain.

9. Which method of apportioning the income of a business among the states in which it operates is more likely to cause tax competition: separate accounting or formula apportionment? Why?

10. Professional athletes have an inordinate interest in state tax systems. They pay income tax on their salaries to the state in which their team is located. For example, in major league baseball, Los Angeles Dodger star Gary Sheffield was traded from the Florida Marlins in 1998. Since Sheffield had a no-trade clause in his contract, he agreed to be traded only if the Dodgers compensated him for the state income taxes he would pay by moving from Florida to California. Florida does not have a state income tax. Who

bears the California state income tax on Sheffield's salary?

11. Internet Exercise. People are always interested in how tax burdens differ from state to state. Rankings of states by tax burdens are readily available. States can be ranked according to state tax burdens per capita or by state tax burdens as a percentage of income. Consult the Federation of Tax Administrators site at http://www.taxadmin.org/fta/rate/tax_stru.html where both rankings can be found. Compare your state's ranking in terms of both criteria. Is it ranked higher (larger burdens) in per capita or percentage terms? What accounts for the difference, if any, in your state's ranking on the two lists?

12. Internet Exercise. The web site State-line.org makes it easy to compare the tax systems of different states at http://www.stateline.org/taxesandbudget/. It provides a program that allows you to select different states, with the program reporting the percentage of state tax revenue from personal income, corporate income, general sales, selective sales, property, and other taxes for the states you selected. Use this site to compare the tax structure of your state with that of another state of similar size and income. In which state would you prefer to earn income? In which state would you prefer to spend your income?

SELECTED REFERENCES

The problems of limited jurisdiction in levying sales taxes are discussed in John F. Due and John L. Mikesell, *Sales Taxation: State and Local Structure and Administration*, 1994, Chapter 10; and many issues about taxing interstate corporations are covered in Charles E. McLure, Jr., ed., *The State Corporation Income Tax*, 1984.

USEFUL INTERNET SITES

Accounting Site at http://www.taxsites.com/index.htm has a large number of links to information on state and local tax systems. See also the state tax links on Taxweb at http://www.taxweb.com/state/index.html and the Census Bureau's survey of state and local finance at http://www.census.gov/govs/www/index.html. Sponsors of the ITFA have an Internet Tax Freedom Homepage extolling the virtues of keeping the Internet free from taxes at http://cox.house.gov/nettax/. The E-fairness site at http://www.e-fairness.org/ promotes equal tax treatment of Internet and brick-and-mortar commerce. More information on taxing Internet commerce can be found at the National Tax Association site at http://www.ntanet.org.

MAIN APPENDIX
Some Tools of the Trade

Microeconomic theory seeks to explain how economic agents (households and firms) make decisions and how their independent decisions are brought into agreement through market forces. The basic concepts of microeconomic theory are important tools that help us understand how government spending and tax policies affect decisions by households and firms, and the impact of these policies on market prices and quantities. In this Appendix, we briefly review two important elements of microeconomic theory used in the text that may be unfamiliar to some readers: indifference curve analysis of consumer demand and output decisions by profit-maximizing firms. We also review the simple supply and demand model familiar from courses on economic principles, and we briefly explain regression analysis—the main statistical tool used in empirical economics.

CONSUMPTION CHOICES BY UTILITY-MAXIMIZING HOUSEHOLDS

Households (families and individuals) make decisions about what quantities of goods and services to consume and what quantities of factors to supply to firms. (Henceforth, we shall understand the term *goods* to include both goods and services.) In making these choices, we assume that households are motivated by self-interest and maximize their satisfaction or utility. Households are assumed to be **price-takers,** meaning that they ignore any small effects their decisions might have on market prices.

We explain the theory of utility maximization for household consumption choices only, ignoring utility-maximizing decisions about the supply of factors. To do this, we assume that households have a fixed amount of money to spend on consumption goods and buy the goods at given market prices. (Actually, the amount of money a household has to spend depends on how many hours it chooses to work.) The consumption choice of the household depends on its budget and on its preferences.

The Household's Budget Line

Households can buy only those consumption bundles they can afford. A household that has money income M (say, $100) to spend over a given time period and faces

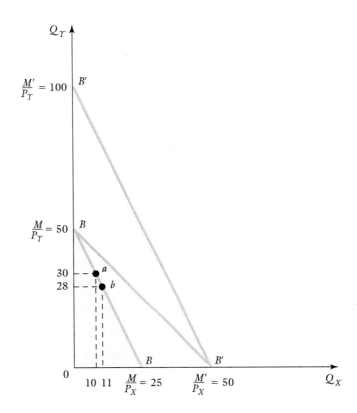

Figure A.1

Effects of Changes in Income and Prices on the Budget Line

An increase in income shifts the budget line outward from the origin, from *BB* to *B'B'*, without changing its slope. A decrease in the price of good *X* shifts the budget line out to *BB'*, making it flatter.

money prices P_X and P_Y (say, $4 and $2) can afford any combination of two goods X and Y lying in its budget set. The budget set is shown by the shaded triangle in Figure A.1. The boundary of the budget set, labeled *BB*, is the household's **budget constraint** or *budget line,* which shows all of the consumption bundles that exhaust the household's money income. That is, the quantities of the goods in the bundle multiplied by their respective prices sum to the household's income. Consumption bundles lying above or to the right of the budget line cannot be purchased by the household. The household would like them, but it can't afford them. The absolute slope of the budget line (that is, ignoring the minus sign) is the ratio of the price of good X (on the horizontal axis) to the price of good Y, or

the **relative price** $\dfrac{P_X}{Q_Y}$

From the budget line, we see that the relative price of good X expresses the number of units of good Y that a household must give up to get an extra unit of good Y. If the money price of X is $4 and the money price of Y is $2, the relative price of X is 2, indicating that the household has to give up 2 units of Y to consume 1 more unit of X. For example, if the household consumes 10 units of X and 30 units of Y at point a, it can consume 11 units of X by giving up 2 units of Y and consuming 28 at point b.

The household's budget line is shifted by a change in its money income or by a change in money prices in the market place. An increase in money income, ceteris

Figure A.2
An Indifference Curve Map
This map shows the bundles of consumption goods that give the consumer the same level of utility. Indifference curves curve toward the origin, so the absolute slope of the indifference curve (called the marginal rate of substitution or marginal willingness to pay) gets flatter as more of good X is consumed.

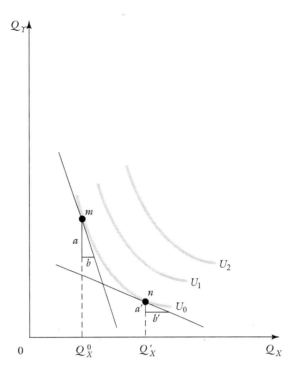

paribus, shifts the budget line away from the origin without changing its slope. For example, if we double the household's money income to M', the household faces budget line $B'B'$, which is twice as far from the origin as BB. Because money prices have not been changed, the slope of $B'B'$ is the same as the slope of BB.

A decrease in the price of good X also shifts the budget line away from the origin, but it does so by pivoting the budget line around its vertical intercept. For example, if the price of good X is cut in half, the household faces budget line BB', which has half the slope of budget line BB. When the price of X falls to $2, the relative price of X falls to 1, which is the slope of budget line BB'.

Household Indifference Curves

What a household buys depends on its preferences (or tastes) as well as its budget. Preferences determine how much satisfaction, or **utility**, households get from a bundle of goods. We assume that a household's preferences can be expressed as a utility function $U = f(Q_X, Q_Y)$ where U is the level of the household's utility, Q_X is the number of units of good X consumed, and Q_Y is the number of units of good Y consumed. We assume that both X and Y are desirable to the household, so its utility increases as consumption of either good increases.

We can express the household's utility function with the **indifference curve map** shown in Figure A.2. The term *map* is descriptive because indifference curves are analogous to the contour lines on topographic maps that connect points having the same elevation. Similarly, indifference curves connect consumption bundles that give the household a given level of utility. Since the household gets the same level of utility from all consumption bundles lying on the same indifference curve, the household is indifferent among them.

Although the exact preferences of different households may be different, preferences have certain common features that can be expressed as properties of indifference curves. First, indifference curves are negatively sloped because if more of one good is consumed, less of the other must be consumed in order for the household to be indifferent between the bundles. Second, assuming that the goods are fully divisible and preferences are continuous (they exhibit no jumps), we can draw as many indifference curves in the map as we like (even though we show only a few in Figure A.2). However, different indifference curves cannot intersect each other. Third, indifference curves that are farther from the origin correspond to higher levels of utility. Thus, indifference curve U_2 in Figure A.2 corresponds to a higher level of utility than curve U_1, which in turn corresponds to a higher utility level than curve U_0, and so on.

A fourth property of an indifference curve concerns its curvature. The indifference curves in Figure A.2 are not linear; rather, they all curve toward (are convex to) the origin. This means that as we move down an indifference curve (as the household consumes more X and less Y), it gets flatter. The flatness of an indifference curve is measured by its slope at a given point, which for a nonlinear curve is the slope of a line drawn tangent to it at the point in question. For example, at point m the absolute slope of the indifference curve U_0 is the rise a of the tangent line divided by the run b.

The absolute slope of an indifference curve has an important meaning. It represents the maximum number of units of good Y the household is willing to give up to consume one more unit of X, so it is the **marginal willingness to pay** (**MWTP**) for good X (also called the **marginal rate of substitution** in many microeconomics textbooks). The term *marginal* indicates that the slope represents the willingness to pay for an *extra* unit of X, not for all of the units consumed. The fact that indifference curves are convex to the origin means that the preferences of the household exhibit **diminishing marginal willingness to pay** for good X as more of it is consumed. For example, at point n on indifference curve U_0, where more of X and less of Y is consumed than at point m, the indifference curve is flatter, indicating that the amount (of Y) the household is willing to pay in order to consume another unit of X is less.

In Figure A.3 we plot the quantity of X on the horizontal axis and the household's MWTP for X on the vertical axis. The MWTP curve labeled D^C plots the absolute slope of the indifference curve U_0 at each quantity of X. If the household faces a given price for good X (say, P_X^0 in the figure) and has sufficient income to attain utility level U_0, the D^C curve tells us what quantity of good X the household will demand (Q_X^0 in the figure) at that price. For this reason, the curve is a special type of demand curve called a **compensated demand curve.** It is compensated because at different prices the household gets different incomes, so that it can always reach indifference curve U_0.

The compensated demand curve is special because it can be used to measure consumer's surplus. **Consumer's surplus** is the area under D^C above P_X^0, and is equal to the amount of income the household would be willing to pay (in addition

Figure A.3
Consumer's Surplus
The compensated demand curve D^C shows the marginal willingness to pay for good X as a function of the quantity of X consumed. The area under D^C above the price paid by the consumer is consumer's surplus. A decrease in the price from P_X^0 to P_X^1 increases consumer's surplus by the area of the lightly shaded trapezoid $P_X^0 mnP_X^1$.

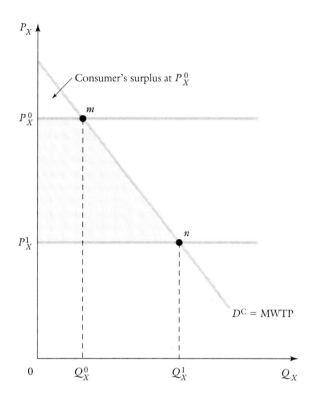

to what it actually does pay, P_X^0 times Q_X^0) to consume quantity Q_X^0 rather than go without the good altogether. Since the household would be willing to pay this amount but doesn't have to, it is called surplus. Utility-maximizing households can also be thought of as maximizing their consumer's surplus, or "getting the most value for their money."

Consumer's surplus can be used to find the change in income that has the same effect on household utility as a change in the price. For example, suppose the price the consumer must pay for each unit of good X falls to P_X^1. We all know that a fall in price makes us better off, but along D^C the household is always compensated with enough income to achieve utility level U_0. How much income must be taken away? The answer is the area of the shaded trapezoid in the figure. In other words, a fall in the price of good X has an effect on the consumer equivalent to an increase in income equal to the area of this trapezoid. This fact is useful in analyzing the effect of price changes on the utility of the household.

The Utility-Maximizing Choice of Consumption

We now put the household's budget constraint and its preferences together to determine what consumption bundle the household chooses when it has a given income and faces certain prices. In Figure A.4, the utility-maximizing consumption bundle is denoted e where the household consumes Q_X^0 units of good X and Q_Y^0 units of good Y and gets the highest possible utility level U_0 it can afford, given its budget.

Figure A.4

Figure A.4

Utility Maximization

The household maximizes utility along its budget line *BB* by choosing the consumption bundle where the budget line is tangent to the highest indifference curve.

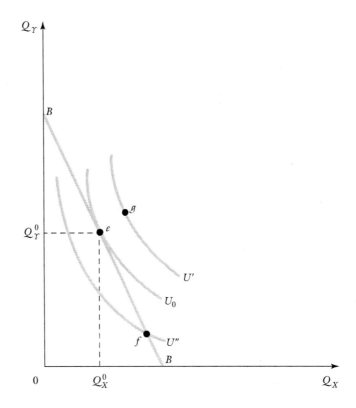

At point e, the budget line is tangent to the highest possible indifference curve. This requires that two conditions are satisfied. First, the household is on its budget line, so it is consuming a bundle it can afford. Second, the indifference curve has the same slope as the budget line, meaning that the household's MWTP for a unit of good X is equal to what it has to pay for a unit of good X (both in terms of good Y) at market prices. Note that at bundle g the household's MWTP is equal to the relative price of good X, but the household cannot afford to buy bundle g. On the other hand, the household can afford to buy bundle f, but this bundle does not give as much utility as e because the household's MWTP for X is less than the relative price of X.

Effects of Changes in Income and Prices

The specific consumption bundle on the budget line chosen by the household depends on the peculiarities of its preferences, such as the exact position and shape of its indifference curves. The main purpose of consumer theory is not to explain the precise bundle chosen but to explain how households change their consumption when they experience changes in income or prices.

As mentioned, a change in income shifts the budget line away from the origin to $B'B'$ without changing its slope. Generally, the household responds by consuming more of all goods, as shown in Figure A.5. In response to an increase in income,

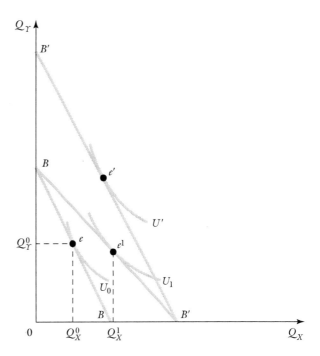

Figure A.5

Effects of Changes in Income and Prices on the Consumption Bundle

An increase in income changes the utility-maximizing bundle from e to e', and consumption of both goods increases if both are normal. A decrease in the price of good X increases consumption of good X from Q_X^0 to Q_X^1.

the utility-maximizing bundle changes from point e to point e' and consumption of both X and Y increases. Any good for which consumption increases when household income increases is called a **normal** good. Although unusual, it is theoretically possible for a household to reduce its consumption of a good when its income increases. Such a good is called **inferior**.

The impact of a decrease in the price of good X is shown in Figure A.5. A decrease in the price of X from P_X^0 to $P_X^{'}$ pivots the budget line away from the origin as shown (even though the money income of the household is not changed). The household maximizes utility at point e^1 along the flatter budget line BB', and the household gets a higher utility level U_1. Provided that good X is normal, the decrease in price must cause the household to increase its consumption of the good. This increase reflects two effects. First, because the budget line is farther from the origin, the decrease in the price of X acts like an increase in the income of the household, so the household wants to consume more because X is a normal good. This is called the **income effect** of the price change. Second, because the relative price of good X is lower, the household substitutes good X for good Y as a means of getting utility. This is called the **substitution effect** of the price change. The increase from Q_X^0 to Q_X^1 reflects both the income and the substitution effects of the decreased price.

The effects of changes in income and prices on consumption of good X can be shown by the more familiar demand curve in Figure A.6, where we measure the quantity of good X consumed on the horizontal axis and the price of good X on the vertical axis. A decrease in the price of good X from P_X^0 to P_X^1 causes the household to move along the demand curve from point a to point b and increase

Ordinary and Compensated Demand Curves
As the price of good X falls from P_X^0 to $P_{X'}^1$ consumption of good X rises along the ordinary demand curve D. The compensated demand curve D^C indicates the substitution effect of the price change. The remaining increase from Q_X^C to Q_X^1 is the income effect of the price decrease.

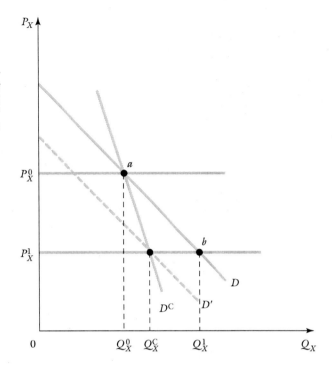

consumption from Q_X^0 to Q_X^1. The demand curve labeled D is the **ordinary demand curve** along which the consumer has constant money income.

If good X is normal, the ordinary demand curve is flatter than the compensated demand curve D^C, along which income is adjusted so that the consumer remains on a given indifference curve (here U_0). When the price of X falls, the household would suffer a loss in money income along the compensated demand curve. This reduction in money income would shift the ordinary demand curve to the left to D' because X is a normal good and consumption declines at each price when the household has less income to spend. Consequently, at P_X^1 the household would consume Q_X^C rather than Q_X^1 along the compensated demand curve. The increase in consumption from Q_X^C to Q_X^1 is the income effect of the price decrease, and the increase from Q_X^0 to Q_X^C is the substitution effect. To simplify explanations in the text, we often assume a small income effect, so that the difference between Q_X^C and Q_X^1 and between demand curves D and D^C are small enough to ignore.

OUTPUT DECISIONS BY COMPETITIVE FIRMS

In a market economy, most decisions about what goods to produce and how to produce them are made by private businesses. These firms are motivated to maximize the economic profit of their owners. Profit is the surplus of sales revenue over and above the costs of producing goods. **Economic profit** differs from accounting profit in that all costs are subtracted whether or not cash outlays are made. Most important, in order to calculate economic profit we subtract the

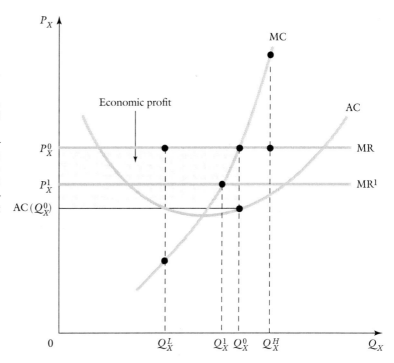

Figure A.7

Profit-Maximizing Output of a Firm

Facing a fixed price P_X^0, the firm maximizes profit by producing Q_X^0 where marginal cost equals marginal revenue. Profit is the area of the shaded rectangle, which is equal to multiplying the difference between price and average cost by the profit-maximizing output. A decrease in price to P_X^1 causes the firm to reduce output to Q_X^1, so the marginal cost curve MC is the firm's supply curve.

opportunity cost of factors supplied by the owners, including their capital and labor. The opportunity cost is the value the owner's factors could have earned in alternative employment.

The Cost Structure of the Typical Firm

An important constraining factor on a firm's decisions is its **cost structure**, the relationship between cost of production and output. As in the case of preferences, we ignore the idiosyncratic elements of firms' cost structures and concentrate on the general properties of the cost structure for a typical firm.

The usual cost structure of a firm producing good X is shown in Figure A.7, where the output of good X is measured on the horizontal axis. A firm's costs consist of two components: **fixed costs**, which are the same no matter what level of output the firm produces; and **variable costs**, which increase with output. The sum of fixed and variable costs is the firm's **total cost**. Typically, variable costs increase at an increasing rate because of diminishing returns in production. On the vertical axis of Figure A.7, we measure the **marginal cost (MC)** of the firm, which is the increase in total cost incurred when the firm produces one more unit of output. For most firms, marginal cost increases with output, as shown by the curve labeled MC. Although MC is a cost per unit of output, it should not be confused with **average cost (AC)** which is total cost divided by output. Because fixed costs are spread over a larger output, average cost initially declines as output rises. Because of rising marginal cost, at some output level AC reaches a minimum and rises thereafter, as shown by the U-shaped curve labeled AC in Figure A.7. The rising MC curve intersects the U-shaped AC curve at its minimum point.

Profit Maximization by a Competitive Firm

We assume the firm produces X so that the total cost is minimized at each level of output. This allows us to focus on the level of output chosen by the firm. We restrict our analysis to competitive firms—that is, firms that take market prices as given and unaffected by their output decisions.

The level of output chosen by a competitive, profit-maximizing firm is determined by its marginal cost schedule and the price it receives for its output. Because the price the firm receives per unit of output is fixed, it is equal to the increase in the firm's sales revenue made possible by producing an extra unit of output, or its **marginal revenue**. The marginal revenue curve of a price-taking firm is a horizontal line equal to the market price of the good it produces, and is labeled MR in Figure A.7. In order to maximize profit, a firm produces the level of output at which marginal cost is equal to marginal revenue (market price for a price-taking firm). In Figure A.7, the profit-maximizing output when the firm sells output at P_X^0 is Q_X^0. At any output less than Q_X^0, say Q_X^L, price is greater than marginal cost, so an increase in output adds more to the firm's sales revenue than to its total costs. Since profit is the difference between sales revenue and total cost, an increase in output increases profit at Q_X^L. On the other hand, at output Q_X^H marginal cost is greater than price, so the firm increases profit by reducing output. Each unit less output reduces the firm's total cost by MC and reduces the firm's revenue by the price, which is less than MC. By this reasoning, we see that the firm's profit is maximized (or its loss is minimized) at Q_X^0.

We can now show that the supply curve of the competitive firm is its marginal cost curve. The supply curve plots the output chosen by a firm at each level of the market price. At a lower price, say P_X^1 in Figure A.7, the firm produces the smaller output Q_X^1 as given by the MC curve. In other words, at each market price the output chosen by the firm is determined by the MC curve at that price.

The economic profit of the firm can be expressed two ways. The first is to multiply the difference between price and average cost by the output of the firm. Since price times output is the firm's sales receipts and average cost times output is the firm's total cost, this yields the economic profit. In Figure A.7, the maximized profit when the firm faces price P_X^0 is the shaded rectangle. The second way to show the profit in the figure is the area above the MC curve below the price received by the firm. This is shown by the shaded area in Figure A.8 (we have not drawn the AC curve in this figure in order to simplify it). Actually, the shaded area shown is equal to profit plus the fixed cost of the firm, which is known as producer's surplus. **Producer's surplus** is the value of the firm's sales receipts in excess of variable costs. Profit-maximizing firms also maximize their producer's surplus. In fact, producer's surplus is the same as economic profit when fixed costs are zero.

COORDINATING DECISIONS THROUGH MARKETS

An important feature of a market economy is the absence of a centralized planner who ensures that firms produce the outputs that households want or hires the factors the households seek to rent out. Instead, the coordinating is done by imper-

Figure A.8

Producer's Surplus

Producer's surplus is the excess of the firm's revenue P_X^0 times Q_X^0 minus total variable cost, which is the area under the marginal cost curve. It is shown by the shaded area.

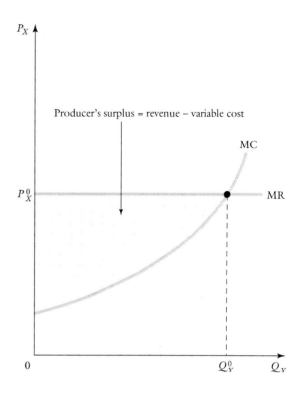

Producer's surplus = revenue − variable cost

MC

P_X^0 MR

0   Q_X^0 Q_X

sonal market forces. Firms that produce outputs no one wants (or can be made to want) will lose money and end up either changing their plans or going out of business. Firms that anticipate the outputs people want and produce them at lowest cost will earn economic profit and thrive.

The Supply and Demand Model

The simple supply and demand model explains how independent decisions by households and firms are brought into agreement through market forces. The demand curves for good X by individual households are summed horizontally (that is, at each price the quantities demanded by all households are summed to find the total quantity demanded at that price) to get the **market demand curve** for good X labeled D^{MARKET} in Figure A.9. Like household demand curves, the market demand curve slopes down. The supply (marginal cost) curves of the individual firms are summed horizontally to get the **market supply curve** labeled S^{MARKET}. Like the supply curves of individual firms, the market supply curve slopes up. Total outputs supplied and demanded in the market are measured on the horizontal axis, and the market price is measured on the vertical axis.

The market equilibrium output is Q_X^0 where the quantity produced by firms is just equal to the quantity demanded by the households. This quantity is willingly produced by competitive firms and willingly purchased by households when the market price is P_X^0. For this reason, P_X^0 is called the **market-clearing price**. It is reasonable that over time the market price and the market-clearing price must converge. For example, if the market price is higher than the market-clearing

Figure A.9
Supply and Demand Model

The intersection of the market demand and supply curves shows the market equilibrium at which the quantity supplied by firms is equal to the quantity demanded by households. This equilibrium is brought about by adjustment of the market price to the market-clearing level.

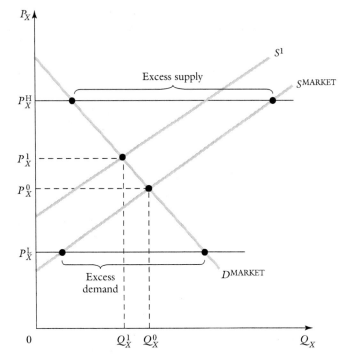

price—say, P_X^H in Figure A.9—firms produce more units of X than can be sold, so competitive pressures push the price down. If the market price is lower than the market-clearing price, say P_X^L in Figure A.9, firms produce less units of X than households want to buy, so the market price is bid up.

The supply and demand model is useful for understanding how various economic events affect the market. For example, suppose good X is caffe lattes. A severe winter frost in Brazil would raise the price of coffee beans and raise the marginal cost of producing lattes. This would cause an upward shift in the supply curve of lattes to S^1 as shown in Figure A.9. As a result, the market-clearing price increases from P_X^0 to P_X^1 and the market equilibrium quantity falls from Q_X^0 to Q_X^1. The market-clearing price can also be increased by an upward shift in the market demand curve for lattes, perhaps because of a change in preferences or an increase in household income that would shift the individual demand curves.[1]

Price Elasticities of Demand and Supply

The impact of events on market prices and quantities depends on the shape of the demand and supply curves. Perhaps most important is the sensitivity of quantity demanded or supplied to a change in the market price. Economists measure this sensitivity in terms of price elasticity. The price elasticity of quantity demanded is usually denoted by the Greek letter η (eta). The

price elasticity of good X is $\eta_X = -\dfrac{\Delta Q_X^D}{\Delta P_X} \cdot \dfrac{P_X}{Q_X^D}$,   where Δ denotes a small

---

[1]The market demand curve for lattes would also shift up if income is redistributed to coffee lovers from people who do not like coffee.

change in a variable, Q_X^D is the quantity demanded of X, and P_X is its market price. The negative sign is used express the elasticity as a positive number. Similarly, the price elasticity of supply, denoted by the Greek letter ε (epsilon), is

$$\varepsilon_X = \frac{\Delta Q_X^S}{\Delta P_X} \cdot \frac{P_X}{Q_X^S}$$ where Q_X^S is the quantity of X supplied. Since the supply curve

is upward-sloping, it is not necessary to convert this into a positive number.

When the price elasticity of demand is high (η is greater than 1), the demand curve is called *elastic*. Typically, this is represented in a diagram by a rather flat demand curve. Similarly, when the supply curve is elastic (ε is greater than 1), the supply curve is drawn flat. The impact of economic events, such as a frost in areas that grow coffee beans, on the market price of the good in question (lattes), depends on the price elasticities of demand and supply. In particular, the more price-elastic demand or supply (the flatter the curves), ceteris paribus, the greater the impact of the event on the quantity and the less the impact on price.

THE MEASUREMENT OF ECONOMIC RELATIONSHIPS: REGRESSION ANALYSIS

As scientists, economists must measure relationships between economic variables—say, the relationship between price and quantity for our demand curve. Unfortunately, economists do not have the same scope for controlled experiments that most physical sciences have, so they are forced to rely on natural experiments thrown up by economic events. Typically, economic variables are subject to random changes as well, so statistical methods must be used to establish whether the observed relationships are real or statistical accidents. The combination of economic theory and statistical methods used by economists is called **econometrics**.

A major tool of econometrics is **regression analysis**. Simple linear regression analysis estimates a linear relationship between two variables—an independent variable, e.g., market price; and a dependent variable, e.g., quantity demanded, that depends on the independent variable. To do this, economists must gather data that show variation in the two variables. Such variation may occur over time in **time-series data**, over households in **cross-sectional data,** or over both time and households in **panel data**. We will assume that we have time series data consisting of observations of the quantity demanded and the market price of good X over time.[2] Suppose the observations are as given in the Table A.1.

We plot these data as points in the **scatter diagram** of Figure A.10. Typically, the dependent variable is plotted on the vertical axis, so Figure A.10 is drawn with quantity on the vertical axis, rather than on the horizontal axis as is usually done in a demand curve diagram (such as in Figure A.6). The object of linear regression analysis is to fit the best straight line, called a regression line, through these data

---

[2]However, economists do not usually get to observe quantity demanded; they observe just the equilibrium quantity in a market, which depends on both demand and supply relationships. To insure that we are observing variations in quantity demanded, econometricians require that certain *identifying conditions* be satisfied. For example, if good X is lattes and we know that the variation in our sample of observations is the result of changes in coffee bean prices that shifted the supply curve over time, we would know that we have identified the relationship between quantity demanded and market price, not quantity supplied.

TABLE A.1   **Time Series Observations of Quantity Demanded and Market Price**

Period	Quantity Demanded	Market Price, $
1	100	$2.00
2	60	2.50
3	150	1.50
4	130	1.00
5	50	3.00
6	120	2.00

points. The slope and intercept of the fitted line are the estimated parameters of the relationship.

A method of fitting a regression line called ordinary least squares estimation gives estimated parameters that have desirable properties under some conditions. Basically, the least squares estimate minimizes the sum of the squared deviations of the dependent variable from the values predicted by the regression line. The least squares regression line is shown in Figure A.10. For the data points in our example, it is $Q^D = 201.7 - 50P$, where Q^D is the quantity demanded and P is the market price. This equation states that the predicted quantity demanded is equal to

Figure A.10
Fitting a Regression Line to Observations
The scatter diagram shows observations of quantity demanded and market price over time. A demand curve can be fitted to these points by least squares regression, which positions the line so as to minimize the sum of the squared deviations of the dependent variable (quantity demanded) from the values predicted by the regression line.

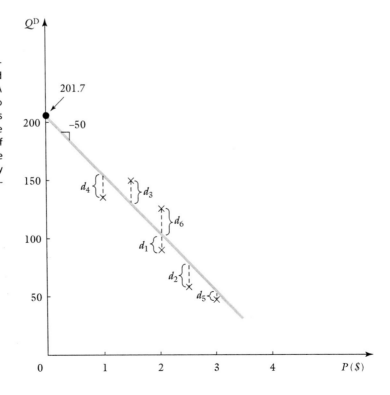

201.7 units minus 50 times the price. The least squares estimate of the vertical inter-cept of the demand curve is 201.7 and the least squares estimate of the increase in quantity demanded resulting from $1 decrease in price is 50. For instance, if the price is $2, the predicted quantity demanded is 101.7 units. The deviations of the six observed values of Q from their predicted values are shown by the braced dis-tances d_1, d_2, etc.

The least squares technique will fit a regression line to any scatter of points. But how much information do the estimated parameters provide? This depends on how dispersed or concentrated the data points are around the fitted line. The amount of dispersion is measured by a statistic called the **standard error of estimate** (**SEE**), which is found by taking the square root of the sum of the squared deviations divided by the number of observations minus 2 (the number of degrees of freedom to fit a straight line in the two-variable case). In our example, the SEE is quite low, indicating that the regression line fits the observations well. If the SEE is high, it means that the regression line fits the observations quite loosely.

Typically, a dependent variable depends on several independent variables. For instance, we know that quantity demanded depends on household income as well as market price. Linear regression analysis can be easily extended to include several independent variables. Using **multiple linear regression**, we can isolate the statis-tical effect of changes in each independent variable on the dependent variable. Sta-tistical methods substitute for controlled experiments as a way of holding constant other variables that affect the dependent variable.

GLOSSARY

Ability-to-pay principle of fairness The idea that fairness requires tax burdens commensurate with the taxpayer's ability to pay.

Absolute tax incidence The distribution of the burden of a tax as compared with no tax at all.

Accelerated depreciation A depreciation schedule that allows firms to depreciate assets faster than they actually decline in value (i.e., faster than **economic depreciation**).

Adjusted gross income (AGI) Taxpayer's income before **personal exemptions** and **deductions** are subtracted.

Adverse selection The phenomenon that insurance is more attractive to people who have a higher probability of suffering a loss than to those who have a low probability.

Agenda manipulation Manipulating the agenda of proposals on which the electorate votes in order to achieve a more favorable outcome for the agenda-setter.

Annualize Convert an accumulated **present value** into an equivalent annual flow.

Arrow's possibilities theorem A logical result showing that a limited and reasonable set of requirements precludes the possibility of aggregating individual preferences into a **social welfare function.**

Assessed value The value of property for the purpose of a property tax.

Assessment ratio The ratio of the **assessed value** of a property to its market value.

Average cost A firm's total costs divided by its output.

Average indexed monthly earnings (AIME) The monthly wages of a Social Security beneficiary, measured in dollars of constant purchasing power and averaged over the period of covered employment.

Average tax rate Taxes paid divided by the income of the taxpayer.

Balanced budget. A budget in which revenue/receipts are equal to expenditures/outlays.

Base broadening Increasing the number of goods subject to a sales tax or the amount of income subject to an income tax in order to lower the tax rate.

Benefit-cost analysis A set of techniques that measures the economic benefits and costs of government programs and projects.

Benefit-cost ratio The ratio of the present value of benefits to the present value of costs.

Benefit principle of fairness The fairness principle that taxes paid by a taxpayer should depend on the benefits he or she receives from the programs financed by the taxes.

Benefit reduction rate The reduction in a **means-tested transfer** payment received per additional dollar of **countable income.**

Benefit tax A tax that entitles the taxpayer to a certain benefit; e.g., the Social Security payroll tax.

Benefit-to-tax ratio The ratio of benefits received from a government program, like Social Security, to taxes paid into the program.

Bequest effect The effect of a government policy on saving through its effect on the size of the bequest parents wish to leave to their children.

Block grant A lump-sum **intergovernmental grant** that can be used for a block of programs.

Borda voting rule A voting system in which voters rank outcomes and points are assigned according to the ranking. The outcome with the most points wins.

Bracket creep An increase in the real taxes people pay because inflation bumps people into higher tax brackets when the brackets are not indexed to the cost of living.

Breakeven income The level of income at which a taxpayer neither pays taxes nor receives a **refundable tax credit** under a **negative income tax.**

Budget constraint (line) The set of consumption bundles that exhaust a household's income at market prices.

Budget deficit The excess of budgeted government spending over government revenues from taxes, user fees, and other charges.

Budget share The amount spent on a good by a household divided by its total spending.

Budget surplus The excess of budget receipts over budget outlays

Burden sharing The distribution of the cost of a public good across the people who jointly enjoy it.

Bureaucracy The government agencies that implement programs chosen by the political decision makers.

Business transfer tax A type of **value-added tax** that determines a firm's value added by subtracting the value of purchases of taxed inputs from the firm's gross receipts.

Capital export neutrality A property of a tax system that taxes **capital income** at the same rate whether capital is located within the taxing jurisdiction or outside it.

Capital income Income such as dividends, interest, and capital gains that is derived from the ownership of property.

Capitation tax A tax of a fixed amount per person.

Cash or deferred arrangement (CODA) A compensation arrangement that allows employees to choose cash or a deferred contribution to a retirement plan.

Categorical grant An **intergovernmental grant** that the recipient government must spend on a purpose specified by the granting government.

Certainty equivalent value The certain amount of income an individual is willing to give up for the right to an uncertain income.

Charter schools Schools independently chartered outside of school district control.

Circuit-breaker program A program giving property tax relief (perhaps as a grant) based on the difference between the property tax liability and a specified fraction of the taxpayer's income.

Closed-ended grant A **matching grant** that has a cap or maximum value.

Club good A **congestible public good** for which it is possible to practice **price exclusion,** making it a good candidate for provision by a club (private membership organization).

Coinsurance The part of an insured expenditure that is paid by the insured person, not the insurance company.

Command and control An environmental policy that requires polluters to meet quantitative standards at their own expense.

Common property resource A **rival good** or resource for which it is not possible to practice **price exclusion,** so all users have free access.

Compensated demand curve The demand curve for a good when the consumer is compensated with income for any change in utility caused by changes in the price of the good.

Compensation principle The principle that a **Pareto improvement** in welfare occurs if the people who gain from a change in the allocation of resources can make a cash payment sufficient to compensate those who lose.

Computational general equilibrium model A general equilibrium model that uses a numerical solution algorithm to find allocations satisfying general equilibrium.

Condorcet winner An alternative that cannot be defeated by a majority of voters.

Congestible public good A public good for which the benefits per user are decreased as more people use the good at the same time.

Consumer sovereignity The principle that the consumer is the best judge of his or her own satisfaction.

Consumers' surplus The amount consumers are willing to pay to consume a certain quantity of good in excess of what they do pay.

Consumption rate of interest The rate of interest that savers earn by deferring consumption to the future.

Contingent valuation method A method that attempts to value a population's willingness to pay for a public good by surveying a sample of respondents.

Contract curve The set of all Pareto optimal allocations in an **Edgeworth box diagram.**

Cooperative equilibrium A market equilibrium in which individuals coordinate their decisions rather than making decisions independently.

Copayment A **coinsurance** arrangement in which the insured person pays a fixed dollar amount per unit of the insured good or service consumed.

Corrective tax subsidy A tax subsidy levied to correct a market failure due to an externality.

Cost basis The cost of an asset at the time of its sale.

Cost structure The relationship between a firm's cost and its output.

Countable income A household's gross income minus disregarded income, used to determine the amount of a means-tested transfer for which the household is eligible.

Cross-sectional data Data consisting of observations of economic variables for different households.

Crowding in Opposite of **crowding out**.

Crowding out A situation in which borrowing by the government raises interest rates and reduces business borrowing for investment.

Cyclical majorities A situation in which a majority of voters prefers alternative A to B, B to C but also prefers C to A.

Deadweight loss The burden of a tax that is not recouped by the government as tax revenue.

Declining-balance depreciation A depreciation schedule whereby the amount of depreciation in each year is a given fraction of the undepreciated cost of the asset.

Deductible The amount of an insured expenditure that must be paid by the insured before the insurance company pays any benefits.

Deduction Certain amounts or expenditures that taxpayers can subtract from their **adjusted gross income** in calculating their **taxable income.**

Deficit The excess of government spending over revenues in a year.

Delayed retirement credit An increase in one's Social Security benefit as a result of delaying retirement.

Demogrant A lump-sum transfer to everyone in a community.

Depreciation The loss in the value of an asset due to wear, tear, and obsolesence.

Depreciation recapture An amount equal to the sale price of a used asset minus its undepreciated value.

Destination-based tax A tax based on the location of the final user of a good or service.

Differential tax incidence The change in the distribution of the tax burden when one tax is replaced with another.

Diminishing marginal willingness to pay The observation that the amount a household is willing to pay for an extra unit of a good decreases as the quantity of the good consumed rises.

Direct expenditure A government expenditure financed with taxes levied by the same government rather than an intergovernmental transfer.

Direct tax A tax levied on persons.

Direct voting A political system in which public decisions are voted directly by the people rather than through representative bodies.

Discount factor A factor (less than 1) used to convert future benefits and costs into **present values,** usually equal to [1/1 + interest rate] raised to a power equal to the number of years in the future that the benefit or cost occurs.

Discounting The process of multiplying future costs and benefits by the appropriate **discount factors** to take into account the fact that future benefits and costs are worth less than present benefits and costs.

Distributional equity A belief that certain distributions of income are inherently more fair than others.

Distributional weight A weight applied to a dollar benefit or cost to an individual to reflect the individual's ability to pay.

Earmarked tax A tax for which the revenues collected are used for a certain purpose and only that purpose.

Earned income Income earned by "sweat of the brow," including wages and self-employment income, but not income from property such as dividends, interest, and capital gains.

Earned income tax credit A **refundable tax credit** for low-income households based on their **earned income.**

Econometrics The statistical techniques used to measure the relationship between economic variables.

Economic business income Business income as measured according to Haig-Simons principles.

Economic depreciation The decrease in the economic value of an asset over an interval of time due to wear and tear, obsolescence, and a shorter remaining lifetime.

Economic efficiency An allocation of resources in which each resource is employed where it has highest economic value.

Economic incidence The distribution of the tax burden, taking into account **tax shifting.**

Economic profit The revenue of a firm minus the costs of production, including the opportunity cost of factors owned by the owners of the firm.

Economies of scale A situation where the average cost of production declines as output rises.

Edgeworth box diagram A diagram used to analyze the allocation of two goods or factors to two different uses.

Efficiency cost The cost of not using an economy's resources most efficiently (see also **Dead weight loss**)

Effective levy rate The **levy rate** that applies to the **assessed value** of property multiplied by the **assessment ratio.**

Effluent charge (effluent fee) A charge for the right to discharge wastes into the environment.

Entitlement A benefit to which an individual has a right by virtue of meeting the eligibility requirements.

Equity-efficiency trade-off The possibility that increased government redistribution to achieve equity leads to a corresponding decline in economic efficiency.

Equality line The **Lorenz curve** in a hypothetical society in which income is equally distributed.

Equivalence scale A means of comparing household incomes when households have different characteristics, such as size.

Excess burden A burden on a taxpayer over and above the dollar value of taxes paid.

Excise tax A tax levied on the purchase or sale of a particular good or service.

Exemption An amount of income not subject to personal income tax.

Existence value The willingness to pay for a natural asset that depends on its mere existence and not on its value in use.

Expenditure tax A **personal consumption tax** which taxes income less saving.

Expensed cost Deduction current costs incurred within the tax year, as opposed to depreciation or amortization, as is done for capital costs.

Experience rating Insurance rates set according to past experience of the insured.

Externality A benefit or cost resulting from a market transaction that affects persons who are not parties to the transaction.

Factor substitution effect The effect of a **partial factor tax** on factor rewards caused when employers change their use of factors in response to the higher cost of the taxed factor.

Fair market value The price at which a thing would be sold by a willing seller to a willing buyer.

First-best An optimum constrained only by limits on resources.

Fiscal capacity The ability of a state or locality to finance government services.

Fiscal federalism The assignment of economic functions to different governments according to which level is best suited for carrying out the function.

Fixed cost Business costs that do not depend on the level of output.

Flat tax A tax that applies at the same tax rate to all taxable income.

Flypaper effect The observation that a larger fraction of an intergovernmental grant is spent by the recipient government (rather than being used to give local tax relief) than is spent out of the community's own resources.

Foreign tax credit A **tax credit** given for income taxes paid to a foreign government.

Formula apportionment The dividing of the income of an interstate corporation among competing tax jurisdictions according to a formula based on the fractions of sales, employment, and assets taking place in the jurisdiction.

Foundation aid An **intergovernmental grant** that provides a floor level of expenditure on a specified program (usually education) by the recipient government.

Free-rider problem The problem of financing a public good when people can enjoy it without contributing to its cost.

Functional incidence The distribution of the tax burden according to factor ownership.

Fundamental theorem of welfare economics A logical result showing that the allocation of resources brought about by a **perfectly competitive** market system is **Pareto optimal.**

Funded social security program A social security program for which current contributions are saved in order to pay out future benefits.

Full loss offset A tax system that allows losses to be fully deducted from taxable income.

General equilibrium A set of prices that clear all markets simultaneously.

Generalized net present value criterion A benefit-cost criterion requiring that projects be chosen so as to maximize the total net present value.

Generational accounting A method for determining the **generational incidence** of changes in government tax and transfer policies.

Generational incidence The distribution of tax and transfers across persons born in different years.

Gini ratio (coefficient of income concentration) A number between zero and one that is a summary measure of concentration in the income distribution across households.

Government failure A situation in which political incentives cause governments to choose policies that reduce **economic efficiency,** or to fail to implement policies that would improve economic efficiency.

Government-pays policy A policy for which the costs of correcting for an externality are borne by the government (taxpayers).

Graduated rate structure A tax structure that applies successively higher tax rates to incomes in successively higher tax brackets.

Grants-in-aid Transfers from the federal government to state and local governments to help them finance established programs.

Green tax shift A proposal to use taxes on polluting goods to raise government revenue in lieu of income taxes.

Gross receipts tax A tax on the gross sales receipts of businesses.

Guaranteed income The amount received under a negative income tax system by a taxpayer with no income.

Guaranteed tax base A type of **intergovernmental grant** to school districts that is structured to ensure that districts using the same **levy rate** will get the same amount of revenue.

Haig-Simons income Income as it is defined in principle and equal to the consumption of the taxpayer plus the increase in his or her net worth.

Harberger's general equilibrium model A two-sector model useful for analyzing the incidence of a **partial factor tax.**

Health Maintenance Organization (HMO) A health care provider that agrees to care for a patient in exchange for a fixed payment.

Hedonic method A method of constructing the **shadow price** of a **nonmarket good** from values of the attributes of the good as revealed in the market prices of other goods.

Homestead exemption (credit) A fixed reduction from the **assessed value** of the taxpayer's principle residence (or credit against property taxes owed) in order to provide property-tax relief to taxpayers.

Horizontal equity The belief that equity requires that people with equal abilities be subject to equal amounts of tax.

Imputed rent The net rent that a homeowner would have pay to live in a house identical to the one he or she owns.

Income effect The effect of an increase in price on quantity demanded that is equivalent to a reduction in the household's income.

Income elasticity A measure of the sensitivity of the consumption of a good to the level of consumer income.

Income incidence The distribution of the tax burden across taxpayers with different incomes.

Income-to-poverty ratio The ratio of a household's income to the poverty level of income for a household of the same characteristics.

Indifference curve map A representation of a consumer's preferences by mapping the bundles of goods that give the consumer the same level of utility.

Indirect tax A tax levied on transactions in goods and services.

Individual transferable quota A marketable quota that allows the bearer to catch a certain fraction of fish in the fishery.

Inequality aversion A property of the **social welfare function** indicating that more equal distribution of utilities gives higher social welfare.

Inferior good A good for which consumption declines as income rises.

Inframarginal externality An external benefit or cost that is not affected by small changes in output around the market equilibrium level.

Insured earnings Earnings on which social insurance taxes have been paid by the employee, the employer, or both.

Integrated approach to corporate taxation A corporate income tax that is coordinated with the personal income tax so income earned by corporations and paid to shareholders as dividends is taxed only once.

Intensive factor A factor of production used intensively in a taxed good.

Intergovernmental grant A transfer from one level of government to another.

Internal rate of return The hypothetical discount rate at which the net present value of a project is equal to zero.

Intertemporal budget line A line showing the combinations of present and future consumption available to a household, given its income and the rate of interest at which it borrows and lends.

Inverse elasticity rule A result in optimal tax theory stating that the **second-best** efficient tax rate on a good is inversely related to the price elasticity of the good.

Investment rate of interest The rate of return that can be earned on private investments.

Invoice credit method A type of **value-added tax** in which firms are given a tax credit for value-added taxes paid on inputs as reported on invoices.

Itemized deductions Deductions allowed for specified expenses including charitable gifts, mortgage interest, and state and local income and property taxes.

Jurisdictional spillovers Benefits and costs from the policies and programs of one local jurisdiction affecting residents of other jurisdictions.

Levy rate The rate of property tax applying to the **assessed value** of property.

Life-cycle theory of saving The theory that personal saving is undertaken to smooth the stream of consumption over a person's lifetime.

Lifetime tax burden The **present value** of taxes paid over a taxpayer's lifetime.

Lifetime utility A measure of the overall level of satisfaction consumers derive from consuming goods over a lifetime.

Lindahl equilibrium An allocation whereby individuals choose the quantity of **public good** they prefer at **Lindahl prices.**

Lindahl tax prices Individualized **tax prices** that are set equal to each consumer's **marginal willingness to pay** for a **public good.**

Local public good A **public good** that benefits only those consumers living within the local region.

Locational efficiency A situation in which factors of production are located in regions where they have highest productivity.

Logrolling Voting for programs that do not directly benefit the voter in order to secure the votes of others for programs that are strongly desired.

Lorenz curve A curve the provides a visual representation of the degree of income inequality in an economy.

Lump-sum tax A tax of a fixed amount that must be paid regardless of the consumption, income, or wealth of the taxpayer.

Magnet schools Schools that attempt to attract good students with excellent education.

Marginal abatement cost The incremental cost to a firm of reducing its emissions of pollution.

Marginal burden (marginal cost of public funds) The increase in the tax burden caused when the government collects one more dollar of tax revenue.

Marginal cost The increase in a firm's costs when it produces one more unit of output.

Marginal effective tax rate The tax rate applying to an extra dollar of investment income, taking into account deductions for financing and depreciating the asset generating the income.

Marginal rate of substitution The absolute slope of an indifference curve.

Marginal revenue The increase in a firm's revenue from producing an extra unit of output.

Marginal tax rate The tax rate applying to an additional dollar of **taxable income.**

Marginal willingness to pay (**MWTP**) The amount a consumer is willing pay in order to consume an extra unit of output. Another name for the slope of an indifference curve.

Market-clearing price The market price at which the quantity demanded of the good is equal to the quantity supplied.

Market demand curve The horizontal sum of the demand curves of all individuals buying in a market.

Market failure A circumstance that causes markets to bring forth outputs at levels that are not economically efficient.

Market supply curve The horizontal sum of the supply curves of all firms selling in a market.

Marriage tax (penalty) The increase in the combined income taxes paid when individuals get married and must file the married tax rate schedule rather than the single schedule.

Match rate The increase in a **matching grant** when the recipient government spends a dollar more of its own funds on the program.

Matching grant Intergovernmental grants for which the paying government increases the amount of the grant if the receiving government spends more on the prescribed program.

Means-tested transfer A transfer that is available to people only if their income and wealth fall below certain levels.

Median voter The voter or voters whose most desired quantity of a government good lies at the midpoint of voters' opinion, with half the remaining voters wanting more and the other half wanting less.

Merit good A good for which the quantity demanded for social reasons is greater than the quantity demanded by individuals for private reasons.

Mill rate Another name for the **levy rate.**

Mixed economy An economy in which the allocation of resources is decided by both government and private markets.

Modified Accelerated Cost Revovery System (**MACRS**) The system that governs the depreciation rates firms can use for tax purposes.

Moral hazard The fact that people take less care to avoid loss when they are insured.

Multistage sales tax A sales tax that applies to all firms whether they sell to consumers or to other firms.

Multiple linear regression A statistical means of establishing the relationship between a dependent variable and several independent variables.

National debt The outstanding stock of bonds issued by the federal government measured at a point in time, usually year-end.

Natural monopoly A market in which costs dictate the existence of no more than one firm.

Need standard The maximum income a family can have and still be eligible for welfare.

Negative income tax A tax that makes transfers (negative taxes) to taxpayers with taxable income below a certain level.

Net operating loss deduction A deduction taken by businesses for operating losses that resulted in other tax years.

Net present value The **present value** of benefits minus the present value of costs.

Network externality A situation in which the benefits or costs to an individual of taking an action depend on the number of other individuals taking the same action.

Neutrality A government tax policy that neither favors nor hinders some activities over others.

NIPA budget balance The **budget balance** as measured using the National Income and Product Account methodology.

Nexus The legal requirement of attachment that must be met in order for a subnational government to tax an entity.

Nonaccelerating inflation rate of unemployment (NAIRU) The hypothetical level of unemployment below which inflation would increase.

Nonappropriable benefit A benefit for which it is not possible for the provider to charge a price or fee to the beneficiary.

Noncategorical grant (revenue sharing) A lump-sum **intergovernmental transfer** that can be used for any purpose by the recipient, with "no strings attached."

Noncooperative equilibrium (Nash equilibrium) An equilibrium in that all individuals make decisions independently without coordination.

Nonexcludable good A good for which it is prohibitively costly to prevent someone from consuming it without paying.

Nonmarket goods (services) Goods and services that people value which are not provided through markets.

Nonrival good The property of a **public good** that allows it to be consumed by more consumers without the need to produce more of it.

Normal good A good for which consumption rises as income rises.

Normative economics Economic methods for determining whether economic outcomes are socially desirable. See also **welfare economics.**

Numeraire good A good whose physical units are used as the unit of account.

Off-budget balance The **unified budget balance** minus the **on-budget balance.**

Official poverty threshold (OPT) The level of income below which a family of given size is considered in poverty for the purpose of federal programs.

On-budget balance The difference between budget revenue and budget outlays.

Open-ended grant A **matching grant** that has no upper limit.

Ordinary demand curve The demand curve showing quantity demanded at each level of price, holding constant the money income of the consumer.

Origin-based tax A tax that applies to goods only if they are produced within the taxing jurisdiction.

Orphan drug problem A case in which markets do not provide a good even though the total willingness to pay for it exceeds total cost, because **consumers' surplus** is a **nonappropriable benefit.**

Output substitution effect The effect of a **partial factor tax** on factor rewards caused when consumers change their consumption of goods as a result of the tax.

Overlapping generations model A model that includes the demographic feature of coexisting younger and older generations coexisting.

Panel data Observations of economic variables for a sample of households over several years.

Parentalism (paternalism) The belief that government officials know what is better for recipients than the recipients themselves.

Pareto improvement An outcome that makes possible an increase in the utility of some households without others being made worse off.

Pareto optimal The description of an allocation for which it is not possible to make a **Pareto improvement.**

Partial equilibrium A condition in which one market clears without consideration of effects in other markets.

Partial factor tax A tax that applies to the income of a particular factor when it is employed in a particular use.

Pay-as-you-go social security A social security program that finances benefits to current retirees with taxes on current workers.

Pay-off matrix A table of the pay-offs to the different players in a simple form game.

Payment standard The amount of income below which a family's **countable income** must fall in order to be eligible for welfare.

Pecuniary externality. A situation where a market decision by one agent affects the price paid or received by another.

Perfectly competitive A market in which all market participants are **price-takers,** and markets are not subject to **market failure.**

Personal consumption tax A tax on consumption that is levied directly on persons on the basis of their annual consumption expenditures (income less saving).

Personal exemption A deduction from taxable income of a fixed amount for the taxpayer, the taxpayer's spouse, and the taxpayer's dependents.

Point voting A system in which the voter has a budget of votes that can be allocated across different public choices.

Political action committees Groups organized for the purpose of influencing politicians and political outcomes.

Polluter-pays policy A policy for which the costs of correcting an externality are borne by the polluter.

Positive economics Analysis that predicts how an economy functions.

Potential Pareto improvement A **Pareto improvement** requiring lump-sum redistribution in order to be realized.

Poverty gap (income deficit) The total amount of income needed to bring every family who is below the **Official Poverty Threshold** up to the threshold.

Poverty line The **Official Poverty Threshold.**

Poverty rate The percentage of families who have incomes below the **Official Poverty Threshold.**

Preference revelation mechanism A scheme for getting households to reveal their true **marginal willingness to pay** schedules.

Present value The value of a future receipt or payment multiplied by the appropriate **discount factor.**

Price elasticity A measure of the sensitivity of quantity demanded or supplied to the market price.

Price-taking behavior Behavior by individuals and firms who assume that their decisions do not affect market prices.

Primary insurance amount The Social Security benefit for a worker retiring at age 65.

Prisoner's dilemma A situation in which independent and noncooperative actions lead to outcomes that are inferior to the cooperative outcome for all parties.

Process principle of fairness A fairness principle based on the idea that the same rules should apply to everyone.

Producers' surplus The excess of sales revenue over and above the total variable cost of the seller.

Progressive tax incidence A term that describes **tax incidence** when the ratio of the tax burden to income (or some other measure of the taxpayer's ability to pay) is higher for households with higher income.

Property-value method A method of valuing an environmental quality variable by observing different values of properties located in areas with different levels of environmental quality.

Proportional tax incidence A situation in which tax burdens of different taxpayers are the same fraction of their incomes.

Prospective payment system The system of compensating hospitals for services to Medicare patients by giving them fixed payments that depend on the illness treated, not on the costs incurred.

Public choice The theory of how decisions are made in government.

Public finance (public economics) A field of economics that studies the role of government in the economy and the impact of its spending and tax policies.

Pure public good A good which is **nonrival** and **nonexcludable.**

Pure private good A good that is both rival and excludable.

Quintile share The fraction of all income received by 20 percent of the population stratified according to income.

Ramsey rule A result in optimal tax theory stating that the **second-best** efficient tax system causes consumers to reduce their consumption of taxed goods in the same proportion.

Rational voter apathy The argument that a rational person will not vote because the benefits do not justify the costs.

Rationally ignorant The argument that a rational person will not become informed about public issues because the benefits do not justify the cost.

Real budget balance The budget balance adjusted to reflect the effect of inflation on the interest rate on government debt.

Real interest rate The market interest rate minus the rate of inflation.

Recovery method The method for determining an asset's depreciation in each year of its **recovery period.**

Recovery period The interval of time over which a firm depreciates a unit of capital for tax purposes.

Refundable tax credit A **tax credit** for which the government refunds to the taxpayer the excess of the tax credit over the amount of tax owed.

Regional incidence The distribution of the tax burden across people living in different parts of the country.

Regression analysis A statistical method of fitting a line or curve to points (observations) in a **scatter diagram.**

Regressive tax incidence A term that describes **tax incidence** when the ratio of the tax burden to income is lower for households with higher incomes.

Relative price The ratio of money prices of two goods.

Rent-seeking behavior Actions taken by **political action committees** that attempt to increase their incomes at the expense of the rest of the population.

Replacement rate The percentage of a household's lost earnings replaced by a government social insurance program.

Residence-based tax A tax based on whether the taxpayer lives in the taxing jurisdiction.

Retirement effect The possibility that Social Security increases personal saving by inducing beneficiaries to retire earlier.

Retirement hazard rate The number of people of a given age who retire in a year as a percentage of people who were a year younger and working in the previous year.

Revenue curve (Laffer curve) The relationship between tax revenue and the tax rate, which is increasing at low tax rates and decreasing at sufficiently high tax rates.

Revenue sharing A program whereby the Federal government shares its revenue with the States by making **noncategorical intergovernmental transfers**

Ricardian equivalence hypothesis The proposition that households perceive government borrowing as equivalent to future taxes and therefore increase their saving by the amount borrowed.

Rival good A good having the property that benefits to one household cannot be enjoyed by others.

Samuelson's condition The condition for the efficient quantity of a **public good** requiring that the sum of the **marginal willingness to pay** by all households in the economy equals the **marginal cost** of producing the good.

Scatter diagram A diagram that plots observations of an independent variable, measured on the horizontal axis, against those of a dependent variable, measured on the vertical axis.

School vouchers A grant to a household that can be used to pay tuition at a school.

Second-best An optimum in a situation where not all the conditions for a **first-best** optimum can be satisfied.

Selective tax A tax that applies to some but not all economic activities.

Sensitivity analysis A method of determining how much the **net present value** of a project is changed by a change in assumptions.

Separate-entity approach to corporate taxation A corporate tax system that applies to the income of corporations in addition to personal taxes levied when the income is distributed to shareholders.

Severance tax A tax levied on firms when they remove resources from the natural environment.

Shadow price The **marginal willingness to pay** for an output and the **marginal cost** of an input in a government project.

Single-payer system A universal government health care system in which the government is the only purchaser of medical insurance.

Single-peak preferences Preferences for a **public good** having the property that utility falls continually as the output rises above or declines below the voter's most preferred quantity.

Single-stage sales tax A tax levied only on firms at a particular stage in the production and distribution process (for example, retailers).

Size distribution of income Household incomes distributed according to the size of income.

Social discount rate The interest rate at which society is willing to trade future for present consumption.

Social insurance program Government transfers that provide pensions, disability payments, health insurance, and unemployment compensation to eligible persons.

Social security trust fund An off-budget account into which Social Security taxes are contributed and out of which social security benefits are paid.

Social Security wealth The **present value** of a person's future Social Security benefits.

Social welfare function A function that defines the welfare of society as a function of the utilities of the individual members.

Source-based tax A tax on income according to where it is earned rather than where the taxpayer lives.

Specific egalitarianism An equity principle holding that equality in consumption of some goods, such as education and health care, is more desirable than equality in consumption in general.

Specific factor A factor of production used only in producing a taxed good.

Square rule The fact that the **excess burden** of a tax increases in proportion to the square of the tax rate.

Standard deduction. A tax deduction of fixed value available to all taxpayers.

Standard error of estimate A measure of how well a **regression line** fits the points in a **scatter diagram.**

Standardized-employment budget balance The budget balance that would prevail if the economy were operating at a given benchmark rate of employment.

Start-up bonus The advantage of a **pay-as-you-go social security** system that allows pensions to be paid to retirees who have made insufficient contributions at the start of the program.

Statistical life A life that is lost by a group of people at risk according to a statistical probability.

Statutory incidence The distribution of the tax burden according to taxes paid.

Straight-line depreciation A depreciation schedule for which the amount of the depreciation deduction is the same in every year of the **recovery period.**

Strategic voting Voting contrary to one's interests on an issue in order to win a preferred alternative on later rounds of voting.

Structural budget balance The **standardized-employment budget balance** adjusted for the inflation premium in interest rates.

Substitution effect The effect on the consumption of a good caused by a change in its **relative price,** holding utility constant.

Supermajority voting rule A voting rule that requires more than a majority of votes in order for an alternative to pass.

Target efficiency The extent to which benefits of a government program reach the people intended.

Tax arbitrage Taking advantage of different tax rates on income and expenses in order to reduce taxes paid.

Tax base The economic variable subject to tax.

Tax capitalization The reduction in the market value of an asset that reflects the **present value** of taxes paid on future incomes earned by the asset.

Tax cascading (pyramiding) The accumulation of a **multistage sales tax** on a good as it passes through different stages of production.

Tax competition Competitive reductions in tax rates by jurisdictions in an attempt to increase their **tax bases** at the expense of other jurisdictions.

Tax credit An amount that is subtracted from taxes owed.

Tax equivalence A situation in which two different taxes collect the same amount of revenue and have the same economic effects.

Tax expenditure The amount of revenue lost from a tax preference where the same objective could have been obtained by a budgetary expenditure.

Tax expenditure budget A document that records the amounts of the different **tax expenditures** according to the same functional categories used in the regular budget document.

Tax exporting Collecting revenue from a tax that is borne by people living outside the jurisdiction levying the tax.

Tax gap The amount of tax that could be collected if economic activity in the **underground economy** were taxed.

Tax incidence The distribution of the tax burden across households grouped according to some relevant characteristic, such as income.

Tax price The increase in a voter's taxes when an extra unit of a government good or service is produced.

Tax rate schedule The relationship between taxes owed and the amount of **taxable income.**

Tax shifting The shifting of a tax burden as a result of changes in prices and factor rewards caused by the imposition of the tax.

Tax structure A description of the amounts of government revenue received from different types of taxes.

Tax unit The entity subject to tax.

Tax-exclusive rate Taxes paid as a percentage of a **tax base** that excludes taxes paid.

Tax-inclusive rate Taxes paid as a percentage of a **tax base** that includes taxes paid.

Taxable estate The amount of an estate subject to estate taxes.

Taxable income Income subject to tax or **adjusted gross income** minus **personal exemptions** and **deductions.**

Temporary Assistance for Needy Families (TANF) The system of cash welfare programs established by welfare reform in 1996.

Tiebout hypothesis The proposition that local governments are efficient because people can "vote with their feet".

Time series data Observations of an economic variable over different time periods.

Total cost The sum of the **fixed costs** and **variable costs** of a firm.

Total willingness to pay The amount a consumer is willing to pay to consume a certain quantity of a good rather than none at all.

Transfer income Income received as neither a consequence of work effort nor ownership of property.

Transfer in-kind. A government transfer of a good or service, such as health care.

Transfer programs Government spending programs that give grants of money or goods and services to households and firms.

Travel-cost method A method of determining a population's willingness to pay for a public good based on its observed willingness to bear travel costs to enjoy the good.

Turnover tax A **multistage sales tax** levied on the sales revenue of businesses at every stage of the production process.

UDITPA formula A convention for apportioning the income of interstate corporations among the states in which they operate, on the basis of a simple average of the fractions of national sales, assets, and payrolls that take place within the state.

Underground economy Economic activities that are unrecorded and cannot be easily monitored by the tax authorities.

Unfunded mandate An obligation to provide a good or service, placed on a lower level of government by a higher level of government without the funds needed to finance it.

Unfunded social security program A **pay-as-you-go social security** program.

Unified budget The federal budget that consolidates transactions on federal trust funds and the budgets of federal government agencies as well the regular budget.

Unified budget balance The balance on the unified budget.

Unified tax credit A tax credit ($192,800 in 1996) against the taxpayer's liability under the unified estate and gift tax.

Uniform tax rates A tax that applies to all goods at the same percentage rate.

Unitary method The treatment of a group of related corporations as a single entity for tax purposes.

User fee A price paid by users of a government good or service.

Utilitarianism A doctrine that defines the good of society as the sum of the utilities of the people living in it.

Utilities possibilities curve A curve showing the feasible distributions of utilities in an economy.

Utility The satisfaction derived from consuming goods and services.

Value-added tax (VAT) A tax levied on the sales receipts of a business minus its purchases of taxed materials.

Variable cost The part of a firm's costs that depends on its output.

Vertical equity A principle of equity governing how tax burdens should be distributed across taxpayers with different abilities to pay.

Virtual income The lump-sum amount of income equivalent in value to a tax deduction or lower tax rate.

Vote competition hypothesis The hypothesis that politicians behave in a way that maximizes their probability of being elected.

Voting paradox The fact that majority voting by voters with **transitive** preferences can lead to intransitive (inconsistent) public choices.

Voting rule A rule that determines which alternative wins an election.

Wealth substitution effect A reduction in personal saving because households substitute **Social Security wealth** for private wealth.

Welfare dependency A situation in which welfare recipients become dependent on welfare as a source of income for extended periods of time.

Welfare economics Economic methods used to evaluate the desirability of alternative economic allocations.

Workfare A system of welfare that requires able-bodied recipients to engage in community service or other work-related activities.

REFERENCES

Aaron, Henry J. Who Pays the Property Tax? A New View, Brookings Institution, Washington, DC, *1975.*

Aaron, Henry J. *The Economic Effects of Social Security,* Brookings Institution, Washington, DC, 1982.

Aaron, Henry J. and William G. Gale (eds.). *Economic Effects of Fundamental Tax Reform,* Brookings Institution, Washington, DC, 1996.

Advisory Commission on Intergovernmental Relations, *Significant Features of Fiscal Federalism,* Vol. 2, 1994.

Advisory Commission on Intergovernmental Relations. *Significant Features of Fiscal Federalism,* Vol. 1, 1995.

Alm, James, and Leslie A. Whittington. "Marriage and the Marriage Tax," in Proceedings of the Eighty-fifth Annual Conference on Taxation—1992, National Tax Association, 200–205.

Alm, James, and Leslie A. Whittington. "The Rise and Fall and Rise … of the Marriage Tax," *National Tax Journal* 44, #4 (December 1996), 571–589.

Angrist, Joshua, and Alan Krueger. "Does Compulsory School Attendance Affect Schooling and Earnings?" *Quarterly Journal of Economics* 106, #4 (November 1991), 979–1014.

Arrow, Kenneth. "An Extension of the Basic Theorems of Welfare Economics," *Proceedings of the Second Berkeley Symposium,* University of California Press, Berkeley, 1951.

Arrow, Kenneth. *Social Choice and Individual Values,* Wiley, New York, 1951.

Arroyo, Luis Larrain. "Privatizing Social Security in Latin America," *National Center for Policy Analysis Report #221,* January 1999.

Atkinson, A. B. *The Economics of Inequality,* 2nd ed., Clarendon Press, Oxford, 1983.

Auerbach, Alan J., Jagadeesh Gokhale, and Laurence J. Kotlikoff. "Generational Accounting: A Meaningful Way to Evaluate Fiscal Policy," *Journal of Economic Perspectives* 8, #1 (Winter 1994), 73–94.

Auerbach, Alan J., and Kevin A. Hassett. "Tax Policy and Business Fixed Investment in the United States," *Journal of Public Economics* 47, #2, (March 1992), 141–170.

Auerbach, Alan J., and Kevin A. Hassett. "Investment, Tax Policy, and the Tax Reform Act of 1986," in *Do Taxes Matter?* Joel Slemrod (ed.), MIT Press, Cambridge, MA, 1990, 11–47.

Ault, Hugh J., and David F. Bradford. "Taxing International Income: An Analysis of the U.S. System and Its Economic Premises," in Assaf Razin and Joel Slemrod (eds.), *Taxation in the Global Economy,* University of Chicago Press, Chicago, 1990, 1–46.

Ballard, Charles L. "The Marginal Efficiency Cost of Redistribution," *American Economic Review* 78, #5 (December 1988), 1019–1033.

Ballard, C. L., John B. Shoven, and John Whalley. "General Equilibrium Computations of the Marginal Welfare Costs of Taxes in the United States," *American Economic Review* 75, #1 (March 1985), 128–138.

Ballard, C. L., John B. Shoven, and John Whalley. "The Total Welfare Cost of the United States Tax System: A General Equilibrium Approach," *National Tax Journal* 38, #2 (June 1985), 125–140.

Barro, Robert J. "The Ricardian Approach to Budget Deficits," *Journal of Economic Perspectives* 3, #2 (Spring 1989), 37–54.

Beach, Carol M. "Taxing the Internet," *Microsoft Slate* (March 29, 1997).

Becker, Gary, Michael Grossman, and Kevin Murphy. "An Empirical Analysis of Cigarette Addiction," *American Economic Review* 84, #3 (June 1994), 396–418.

Bentham, Jeremy. *Principles of Morals and Legislation* (1791), reprinted by Prometheus, Buffalo, NY, 1988.

Bergson, A. "A Reformulation of Certain Aspects of Welfare Economics," *Quarterly Journal of Economics* 52 (February 1938), 310–334.

Bickley, James M. "How Much Revenue Could a U.S. VAT Yield?" *Tax Notes* (August 30, 1993), 1273–1278.

Billings, R. Bruce. "Demand-Based Benefit-Cost Model of Participation in a Water Project," *Journal of Water Resources Planning and Management* 116, #5 (1990), 593–609.

Bipartisan Commission on Entitlement and Tax Reform. *Final Report to the President*, Superintendent of Documents, Washington, DC, January 1995.

Birnbaum, Jeffrey H., and Alan S. Murray. *Showdown at Gucci Gulch: Lawmakers, Lobbyists and the Unlikely Triumph of Tax Reform*, Vintage Books, New York, 1988.

Bishop, Richard C., and Thomas A. Heberlein. "Measuring Values of Extra Market Goods: Are Indirect Measures Biased?" *American Journal of Agricultural Economics* 61, #5 (1979), 926–930.

Black, D. "On the Rationale of Group Decision Making," *Journal of Political Economy* 56, #1 (February 1948), 23–34.

Boadway, Robin W., and Neil Bruce. *Welfare Economics*, Basil Blackwell, Oxford, 1984.

Boardman, Anthony E., David H. Greenberg, Aidan R. Vining and David L. Weimer. *Cost-Benefit Analysis: Concepts and Practice*, Prentice Hall, 1996.

Bonham, Carl, Edwin Fujii, Eric Im, and James Mak. "The Impact of the Hotel Room Tax: An Interrupted Times Series Approach," *National Tax Journal* 45, #4 (December 1992), 433–441.

Boskin, Michael J. "Taxation, Saving, and the Rate of Interest," *Journal of Political Economy* 86, #2, Part 2 (April 1978), S3–S27.

Bradford, David F. *Untangling the Income Tax*, Harvard University Press, Cambridge, MA, 1986.

Brook, Robert H., et al. *The Effects of Coinsurance on the Health of Adults: Results from the Rand Health Experiment*, Rand, Santa Monica, CA, 1984.

Browning, Edgar K. "The Marginal Cost of Public Funds," *Journal of Political Economy* 84, #2 (April 1976), 283–298.

Browning, Edgar K., and William R. Johnson. *The Distribution of the Tax Burden*, American Enterprise Institute, Washington, DC, 1979.

Browning, Edgar K. and William R. Johnson. "The Trade-off Between Equality and Efficiency," *Journal of Political Economy* 92, #2 (April 1984), 175–203.

Buchanan, James M., and Gordon Tullock. *The Calculus of Consent*, University of Michigan Press, Ann Arbor, 1962.

Burkhauser, Richard V., Douglas Holtz-Eakin and Stephen E. Rhody. "Labor Mobility and Inequality in the United States and Germany During the Growth Years of the 1980s," *International Economic Review* 38, #4 (November 1997), 775–794.

Burtraw, Dallas. "Trading Emission to Clean the Air: Exchanges Few but Benefits Many," Resources for the Future, Washington, DC, Winter 1996.

Carlson, Curtis, Dallas Burtraw, Maureen Cropper and Karen Palmer, "Sulfur Dioxide Control by Electric Utilities: What are the Gains from Trade?" Discussion Paper 98–44, Resources for the Future, Washington, DC, July 1998.

Casperson, Eric, and Gilbert Metcalf. "Is a Value Added Tax Regressive? Annual Versus Lifetime Incidence Measures," *National Tax Journal* 47, #4 (December 1994), 731–746.

Chernick, Howard A. "An Economic Model of the Distribution of Project Grants," in *Fiscal Federalism and Grants-in-Aid,* Peter M. Mieszkowski and W. H. Oakland (eds.), Urban Institute, Washington, DC, 1979.

Chirinko, Robert. "Business Fixed Investment Spending: A Critical Survey of Modeling Strategies, Empirical Results, and Policy Implications," *Journal of Economic Literature* 31, #4 (December 1993), 1875–1911.

Chubb, John and Terrence Moe. *Politics, Markets and America's Schools,* Brookings Institution, Washington, DC, 1990.

Citizens for Tax Justice. *The Hidden Entitlements,* Washington, DC, 1996.

Citizens for Tax Justice. *Who Pays? A Distributional Analysis of the Tax Systems in All 50 States,* Washington, DC, 1996.

Citro, Constance F., and Robert T. Michael (eds.). *Measuring Poverty: A New Approach,* National Academy Press, Washington, DC, 1995.

Clawson, Marion. *Methods of Measuring the Demand for and Value of Outdoor Recreation,* Resources for the Future, Washington, DC, 1959.

Clotfelter, Charles T. *Federal Tax Policy and Charitable Giving,* University of Chicago Press, Chicago, 1985.

Coase, Ronald H. "The Problem of Social Cost," *Journal of Law and Economics* 3 (October 1960), 1–44.

Cohen, Barbara, and Nathan Young. *Evaluation of the Washington State Food Stamp Cashout Demonstration,* Urban Institute, Washington, DC, 1992.

Collender, Stanley E. *Guide to the Federal Budget: Fiscal 2001,* Urban Institute, Washington, DC, 2000.

Commerce Clearing House. *1999 U.S. Master Tax Guide,* Chicago, 1998.

Congress of the United States, Congressional Budget Office. *Effects of Adopting a Value-Added Tax,* Washington, DC, 1992.

Congress of the United States, Congressional Budget Office. *Assessing Future Trends in the Defense Burdens of Western Nations,* Washington, DC, 1993.

Congress of the United States, Congressional Budget Office. "Comparing Income and Consumption Tax Bases," Washington, DC, July 1997.

Congress of the United States, Congressional Budget Office. "Long-Term Budgetary Pressures and Policy Options," Washington, DC, May 1998.

Congress of the United States, Congressional Budget Office. "Estimates of Federal Tax Liabilities for Individuals and Families by Income Category and Family Type for 1995 and 1999," Washington, DC, May 1998.

Congress of the United States, Congressional Budget Office. "The Economic Outlook and Budget Outlook: An Update," Washington, DC, July 1999.

Congress of the United States, Congressional Budget Office. *Budget of the United States Government, 2000: Analytic Perspectives,* Washington, DC, 2000.

Congress of the United States, Committee on Ways and Means. *Estimates of Federal Tax Expenditures for Fiscal Years 1995–1999,* Washington, DC, November 1994.

Congress of the United States, Committee on Ways and Means. *1994 Green Book,* Washington, DC, July 1994.

Congress of the United States, Committee on Ways and Means. *1998 Green Book,* Washington, DC, November 1998.

Cornes, Richard, and Todd Sandler. *The Theory of Externalities, Public Goods, and Club Goods,* 2nd ed., Cambridge University Press, New York, 1996.

Craig, Steven, and Robert P. Inman. "Education, Welfare and 'New Federalism,'" in Harvey S. Rosen (ed.), *Studies in State and Local Public Finances,* University of Chicago Press, Chicago, 1986.

Crews, Clyde. *Ten Thousand Commandments: An Annual Policymaker's Snapshot of the Federal Regulatory State,* Competitive Enterprise Institute, 1999.

Cummins, Jason G., Kevin A. Hassett, and R. Glenn Hubbard. "Have Tax Reforms Affected Investment?" in James M. Poterba (ed.), *Tax Policy and the Economy,* Vol. 9, MIT Press, Cambridge, MA, 1995.

Danziger, Sheldon, Robert Haveman, and Robert Plotnick. "How Income Transfers Affect Work, Savings, and the Income Distribution," *Journal of Economic Literature* 29, #3 (September 1981), 975–1028.

Danzon, Patricia M. "Hidden Overhead Cost: Is Canada's System Really Less Expensive?" *Health Affairs,* (Spring, 1992).

Dawson, J. E., and Peter J. E. Stan. *Public Expenditures in the United States: 1952–1993,* RAND Corporation, Santa Monica, CA, 1995.

Downs, A. *An Economic Theory of Democracy,* Harper and Row, New York, 1957.

Due, John F., and John L Mikesell. *Sales Taxation: State and Local Structure and Administration,* 2nd ed., Urban Institute, Washington, DC, 1994.

Dupuit, Jules. "De la Mesure de l'Utilité des Travaux Publics," *Annals des Ponts et Chaussées,* 2nd series, 8 (1844).

Economic Report of the President, 1981. U.S. Government Printing Office, Washington, DC, 1981.

Economic Report of the President, 1992. U.S. Government Printing Office, Washington, DC, 1992.

Economic Report of the President, 1994. U.S. Government Printing Office, Washington, DC, 1994.

Economic Report of the President, 1997. U.S. Government Printing Office, Washington, DC, 1997.

Economic Report of the President, 2000. U.S. Government Printing Office, Washington DC, 2000.

Eisner, Robert. *How Real Is the Federal Deficit?* Free Press, New York, 1986.

Eisner, Robert, and M. Nadiri. "Investment Behavior and Neoclassical Theory: A Comment," *Review of Economics and Statistics* 52, #2 (May 1970), 216–222.

Eissa, Nada. "Taxation and Labor Supply of Married Women: The Tax Reform Act of 1986 as a Natural Experiment," National Bureau of Economic Research Working Paper 5023, February 1995.

Farrell, Joseph. "Information and the Coase Theorem," *Journal of Economic Perspectives* 1, #2 (Fall 1987), 113–129.

Federal Reserve Bank of Kansas City, *Income Inequality: Issues and Policy Options,* 1998.

Feldstein, Martin S. "Social Security, Induced Retirement, and Aggregate Capital Accumulation," *Journal of Political Economy* 82, #5 (September–October 1974), 905–926.

Feldstein, Martin S. "On the Theory of Tax Reform," *Journal of Public Economics* 6, #1–2 (July–August 1976), 77–104.

Feldstein, Martin S., and Daniel Feenberg. "The Effect of Increased Tax Rates on Taxable Income and Economic Efficiency: A Preliminary Analysis of the 1993 Tax Rate Increases," National Bureau of Economic Research Working Paper 5370, November 1995.

Feldstein, Martin S. "The Missing Piece in Policy Analysis: Social Security Reform," *American Economic Review* 86, #2 (May 1996), 1–14.

Fisher, Ronald C. *State and Local Public Finance,* 2nd ed., Richard D. Irwin, Burr Ridge, IL, 1996.

Friedman, Benjamin. *Day of Reckoning*, Random House, New York, 1988.

Friend, Irwin, and Joel Hasbrouck. "Saving and After-Tax Rates of Return," *Review of Economics and Statistics* 65, #4 (November 1983), 537–548.

Fullerton, Don. "Which Effective Tax Rate?" *National Tax Journal* 37, #1 (March 1984), 23–41.

Fullerton, Don, and Marios Karayannis. "Chapter 10 United States," in Dale W. Jorgenson and Ralph Landau (eds.), *Tax Reform and the Cost of Capital*, Brookings Institution, Washington, DC, 1993.

Fullerton, Don, and Diane Lim Rogers. *Who Bears the Lifetime Tax Burden?* Brookings Institution, Washington, DC, 1993.

Gale, William G., and John Karl Scholz. "IRAs and Household Saving," *American Economic Review* 84, #5 (December 1994), 1233–1260.

Gelles, Gregory M. "Costs and Benefits of HIV-1 Antibody Testing of Donated Blood," *Journal of Policy Analysis and Management* 12, #3 (Summer 1993), 512–531.

George, Henry. *Progress and Poverty*, Hogarth, London, 1966.

Gokhale, Jagadeesh. "Should Social Security be Privatized?" *Economic Commentary*, Federal Reserve Bank of Cleveland (September 15, 1995).

Gokhale, Jagadeesh. "Generational Equity and Sustainability in U.S. Fiscal Policy," *Economic Commentary*, Federal Reserve Bank of Cleveland, April 15, 1998

Gokhale, Jagadeesh, Benjamin R. Page, and John R. Sturrock. "Generational Accounts for the United States: An Update," *Federal Reserve Bank of Cleveland Economic Review* 33, #4 (Fall 1997).

Goodall, Edward. *The Noble Philosopher*, Prometheus, Buffalo, NY, 1994.

Gordon, H. Scott. "The Economic Theory of a Common Property Resource: The Fishery," *Journal of Political Economy* 62, #2 (April 1954), 124–142.

Gottschalk, Peter, and Timothy N. Smeeding. "Cross-National Comparisons of Earnings and Income Inequality," *Journal of Economic Literature* 35, #2 (June 1997), 633–687.

Gottschalk, Peter, and Timothy N. Smeeding. "Empirical Evidence on Income Inequality in Industrial Countries," Luxembourg Income Study Working Paper #154, February 1999.

Gramlich, Edward M. *A Guide to Benefit-Cost Analysis*, 2nd ed., Prentice Hall, Englewood Cliffs, NJ, 1990.

Gravelle, Jane G. *The Economic Effects of Taxing Capital Income*, MIT Press, Cambridge, MA, 1994.

Gravelle, Jane G., and Dennis Zimmerman. "Cigarette Taxes to Fund Health Care Reform," *National Tax Journal* 47, #3 (September 1994), 575–590.

Guttman, George. "IRS Updates Estimates on Individual Tax Gap," *Tax Notes* (May 13 1996), 857–858.

Hahn, Robert W. "Government Analysis of the Benefits and Costs of Regulation," *Journal of Economic Perspectives* 12, #4 (Fall 1998), 201–210.

Haig, Robert Murray. *The Federal Income Tax*, Columbia University Press, New York, 1921.

Hall, Robert E., and Dale W. Jorgenson. "Tax Policy and Investment Behavior," *American Economic Review* 57, #3 (June 1967), 391–414.

Hall, Robert E., and Alvin Rabushka, *The Flat Tax*, 2nd ed., Hoover Institution, Stanford, CA, 1995.

Hamilton, Bruce W. "Zoning and Property Taxation in a System of Local Governments," *Urban Studies* 12, #2 (June 1975), 205–211.

Hanushek, Eric A. "Can Equity Be Separated from Efficiency in School Finance Debates" in Emily P. Hoffman (ed.), *Essays on the Economics of Education*, Upjohn Institute, Kalamazoo, MI, 1993, 35–68.

Harberger, Arnold C. "The Incidence of the Corporation Income Tax," *Journal of Political Economy* 70, #3 (June 1962), 215–240.

Harberger, Arnold C. "Taxation, Resource Allocation and Welfare," in *The Role of Direct and Indirect Taxes in the Federal Revenue System,* Princeton University Press, Princeton, 1964, 25–75.

Harberger, Arnold C. *Taxation and Welfare,* Little, Brown, Boston, 1971.

Harrison, David, Jr., and Daniel L. Rubinfeld. "Hedonic Housing Prices and the Demand for Clean Air," *Journal of Environmental Economics and Management* 5, #2 (1978), 81–102.

Hausman, Jerry A. "Taxes and Labor Supply," in Alan J. Auerbach and Martin Feldstein (eds.), *Handbook of Public Economics,* Vol. 1, North Holland, Amsterdam, 1985, 213–263.

Haveman, Robert. "Should Generational Accounts Replace Public Budgets and Deficits?" *Journal of Economic Perspectives* 8, #1 (Winter 1994), 95–111.

Hicks, John. "The Valuation of Social Income," *Economica,* New Series 7 (May 1940), 105–124.

Hoeller, P., and M. Wallin. "Energy Prices, Taxes and Carbon Dioxide Emissions," Economics and Statistics Department Working Paper #106, Organization for Economic Cooperation and Development, Paris, 1991.

Hotelling, Harold. "The General Welfare in Relation to Problems of Taxation," *Econometrica* 6, #3 (July 1938), 242–269.

Hotelling, Harold. "Stability in Competition," *Economic Journal* 39 (March 1929), 41–57.

Hubbard, R. Glenn, and Jonathan S. Skinner. "Assessing the Effectiveness of Savings Incentives," *Journal of Economic Perspectives* 10, #4 (Fall 1996), 73–90

Hurd, Michael D. "Research on the Elderly: Economic Status, Retirement, Consumption and Saving," *Journal of Economic Literature* 28, #2 (June 1990), 565–637.

Inman, Robert P. "The Fiscal Performance of Local Governments: An Interpretative Review," in Peter M. Mieszkowski and Mahlon Straszheim (eds.), *Current Issues in Urban Economics,* Johns Hopkins University Press, Baltimore, 1979, 270–321.

Internal Revenue Service, Statistics of Income Division. *Individual Income Tax Returns 1997,* Washington, DC, 1999.

Ippolito, Dennis S. *Hidden Spending,* University of North Carolina Press, Chapel Hill, 1984.

Jenkin, Fleeming. "On the Principles That Regulate the Incidence of Taxes," *Papers Literary, Scientific,* 1887, 107–121.

Kaldor, Nicholas. "Welfare Propositions in Economics and Interpersonal Comparisons of Utility," *Economic Journal* 49 (September 1939), 549–552.

Karoly, Lynn A. "The Trend in Inequalities Among Families, Individuals, and Workers in the United States," in Sheldon Danziger and Peter Gottschalk (eds.), *Uneven Tides: Rising Inequality in America,* Russell Sage Foundation, New York, 1993.

Katz, Michael L., et al. "Symposia: Network Externalities," *Journal of Economic Perspectives* 8, #2 (Spring 1994).

Kennedy, William. *English Taxation, 1640–1799,* Bell, London, 1913.

Kingson, Eric, and James Schulz (eds.). *Social Security in the 21st Century,* Oxford University Press, Oxford, 1997.

Kneisner, Thomas J., and James P. Ziliak, *The Effects of Recent Tax Reforms on Labor Supply,* American Enterprise Institute, Washington D. C., 1998.

Kotlikoff, Laurence J. "Testing the Theory of Social Security and Life Cycle Accumulation," *American Economic Review* 69, #3 (June 1979), 396–410.

Kotlikoff, Laurence J. *Generational Accounting,* Free Press, New York, 1992.

Kotlikoff, Laurence J., and Jeffrey Sachs. "It Is High Time to Privatize Social Security," *The Brookings Review* 15, #3 (Summer 1997), 16–23.

Kozol, Jonathan. *Savage Inequalities: Children in America's Schools,* Harper Perennial, New York, 1992.

Krutilla, John V., and Otto Eckstein. *Multiple Purpose River Development: Studies in Applied Economic Analysis,* Johns Hopkins Press, Baltimore, 1958.

Laffer, Arthur B. "Statement Prepared for the Joint Economic Committee," reprinted in A. B. Laffer and J. P. Seymour (eds.), *The Economics of the Tax Revolt: A Reader,* Harcourt Brace Jovanovich, New York, 1979, 75–79.

Lee, Valerie E., and Anthony S. Bryk. "Science of Policy Argument? A Review of the Quantitative Evidence in Chubb and Moe's *Politics, Markets, and America's Schools,*" in Rasell, Edith and Richard Rothstein (Eds.) *School Choice: Examining the Evidence,* Economic Policy Institute Washington, DC, 1993, 185–208.

Leimer, Dean R., and Selig D. Lesnoy. "Social Security and Private Saving: New Time Series Evidence," *Journal of Political Economy* 90, #3 (June 1982), 606–629.

Leonard, Herman B. *Checks Unbalanced,* Basic Books, New York, 1986.

Levin, Jonathan, et al. "Symposium: The Economics of Voting," *Journal of Economic Perspectives* 9, #1 (Winter 1995), 3–98.

Levitt, Steven D., and James M. Synder, Jr. "The Impact of Federal Spending on House Election Outcomes," *Journal of Political Economy* 105, #1 (February 1997), 30–53.

Levy, Frank, and Richard J. Murnane. "U.S. Earnings Levels and Earnings Inequality," *Journal of Economic Literature* 30, #3 (September 1992), 1333–1381.

Lipsey, Richard G., and Kelvin J. Lancaster. "The General Theory of Second Best," *Review of Economic Studies* 24, #2 (1956), 11–32.

MacKie-Mason, Jeffrey K. "Do Taxes Affect Corporate Financing Decisions?" *Journal of Finance* 45, #5 (December 1990), 1471–1493.

MaCurdy, Thomas, David Green, and Harry J. Paarsch. "Assessing Empirical Approaches for Analyzing Taxes and Labor Supply," *Journal of Human Resources* 25, #3 (Summer 1990), 415–90.

McIntyre, Robert S. "Statement Before the House Committee on the Budget," Washington, DC, June 30 1999.

McLure, Charles E., Jr. "The Elusive Incidence of the Corporation Income Tax: The State Case," *Public Finance Quarterly* 9, #4 (October 1981), 395–413.

McLure, Charles E., Jr. *Must Income Be Taxed Twice?* Brookings Institution, Washington, DC, 1979.

McLure, Charles E., Jr. (ed.). *The State Corporation Income Tax,* Hoover Institute Press, Stanford, 1984.

McLure, Charles E., Jr. *The Value Added Tax: Key to Deficit Reduction?* American Enterprise Institute, Washington, DC, 1987.

Meade, James E. *Trade and Welfare,* Oxford University Press, London, 1955.

Metcalf, Gilbert E. "The National Sales Tax: Who Bears the Burden?" *Cato Policy Analysis No. 289,* Cato Institute, Washington, DC, December 1997.

Mitchell, Olivia S., James M. Poterba, and Mark Warshawsky. "New Evidence on the Money's Worth of Individual Annuities," *American Economic Review* 89, #5 (December 1999), 1299–1318.

Moffitt, Robert. "The Incentive Effects of the U.S. Welfare System: A Review," *Journal of Economic Literature* 30, #1 (March 1992), 1–61.

Moon, Marilyn. *Medicare Now and in the Future,* 2nd ed., Urban Institute, Washington, DC, 1996.

Moon, Marilyn. "Growth in Medicare Spending: What Will Beneficiaries Pay?" Urban Institute, Washington, DC, May 1999.

Moon, Marilyn, Barbara Gage and Alison Evans. "An Examination of Key Medicare Provisions in the Balanced Budget Act of 1997," Urban Institute, September 1997.

Mueller, Dennis C. *Public Choice II,* Cambridge University Press, New York, 1989.

Neary, Pam. "Outlandish Taxes," *New Rules Journal* (Summer 1999), 12–15.

NBER Digest. "There Is Still a Marriage Tax" (June 1994).

New York Times. "Suburban Taxes are Higher for Blacks, Analysis Shows" (August 17, 1994).

New York Times. "30 Are Charged in Trafficking of Food Stamps" (September 13, 1994).

New York Times. "Justices Back State Tax on Interstate Fares" (April 4, 1995).

New York Times. "Cost of 'Quiet on the Set' is Escalating" (July 27, 1995).

Newhouse, Joseph P. "Symposium of Health Care Reform," *The Journal of Economic Perspectives* 8, #3 (Summer 1994).

Niskanen, William A. Jr. *Bureaucracy and Public Economics,* Aldine Press, Chicago, 1971; reprinted by Elgar, Brookfield, VT, 1994.

Oates, Wallace E. *Fiscal Federalism,* Harcourt Brace Jovanovich, New York, 1972.

Office of Management and Budget. "Draft Report on the Costs and Benefits of Federal Regulations," Washington, DC, January 2000.

Ohls, James C., and Harold Beebout. *The Food Stamp Program: Design Tradeoffs, Policy, and Impacts,* Urban Institute, Washington, DC, 1993.

Okun, Arthur M. *Equality and Efficiency, The Big Tradeoff,* Brookings Institution, Washington, DC, 1975.

Olson, Mancur. *The Logic of Collective Action,* Harvard University Press, Cambridge, MA, 1965.

Organization for Economic Cooperation and Development. *OECD in Figures,* Paris, 1996.

Organization for Economic Cooperation and Development. *Economic Outlook* #65, Paris, June 1998.

Passell, Peter. "Economic Scene," *New York Times* (May 11, 1995).

Passell, Peter. "Economic Scene," *New York Times* (December 14, 1995).

Passell, Peter. "How Chile Farms Out Nest Eggs," *New York Times,* (March 24, 1997).

Pechman, Joseph A. *Who Paid the Taxes, 1966–85,* Brookings Institution, Washington, DC, 1985.

Perloff, Jeffrey. *Microeconomics,* 2e, Addison Wesley Longman, Boston, 2001.

Petska, Tom, Mike Strudler, and Ryan Petska. "Further Examination of the Distribution of Individual Income and Taxes Using a Consistent and Comprehensive Measure of Income," Statistics of Income Research Paper 213534, Internal Revenue Service, March 2000.

Phelps, Charles E. *Health Economics,* HarperCollins, New York, 1992.

Pigou, A. C. *The Economics of Welfare,* Macmillan, London, 1920.

Poterba, James M. "Lifetime Incidence and the Distributional Burden of Excise Taxes," *American Economic Review Papers and Proceedings* 79, #2 (May 1989), 325–330.

Poterba, James. "Tax Policy to Combat Global Warming: On Designing a Carbon Tax," in Dornbusch, R. and J. M. Poterba (eds.), *Global Warming: Economic Policy Responses,* MIT Press, Cambridge MA, 1991, 71–108.

Poterba, James M. "Taxation and Housing: Old Questions, New Answers," *American Economic Review* 82, #2 (May 1992), 237–242.

Poterba, James M. "Taxation and Housing Markets: Preliminary Evidence on the Effects of Recent Tax Reforms," in Joel Slemrod (ed.), *Do Taxes Matter?* MIT Press, Cambridge, MA, 1990, 141–160.

Poterba, James M. "Is the Gasoline Tax Regressive?" in David Bradford (ed.), *Tax Policy and the Economy,* Vol. 5, MIT Press, Cambridge, MA, 1991, 145–164.

Powers, Elizabeth T. "Welfare Reform and the Cyclicality of Welfare Programs," *Economic Commentary,* Federal Reserve Bank of Cleveland (June 1996).

Ridker, Ronald. *Economic Costs of Air Pollution: Studies in Measurement,* Praeger, New York, 1967.

Romer, Thomas, and Howard Rosenthal. "Bureaucrats Versus Voters: On the Political Economy of Resource Allocation by Direct Democracy," *Quarterly Journal of Economics* 93, #4 (November 1979), 563–587.

Rossi, Susan. "Three Towns Find a Way to Contain Crime: Loan-a-Cop," *Governing* 7, #7 (April 1994), 15–16.

Rothschild, Michael and Joseph E. Stiglitz. "Equilibrium in Competitive Insurance Markets: An Essay in the Economics of Incomplete Information," *Quarterly Journal of Economics* 90, #4 (November 1976), 630–649.

Samuelson, Paul A. "A Diagrammatic Exposition of a Theory of Public Expenditure," *Review of Economics and Statistics* 37 (1955), 350–356.

Sandler, Todd, and Keith Hartley. *The Economics of Defense,* Cambridge University Press, Cambridge, 1995.

Sawhill, Isabel V., and Mark Condon. "Is U.S. Income Inequality Really Growing?" *Policy Bites* (June 1992).

Sawhill, Isabel V., and Daniel P. McMurrer. "How Much Do Americans Move Up and Down the Economic Ladder?" Urban Institute, Washington, DC, December 1996.

Schwartz, Stephen I. (ed.). *Atomic Audit: The Costs and Consequences of U.S. Nuclear Weapons Since 1940,* Brookings Institution, Washington, DC, 1998.

Seater, John J. "Ricardian Equivalence," *Journal of Economic Literature* 31, #1 (March 1993), 142–190.

Sen, Amartya. *On Economic Inequality,* Clarendon, Oxford, 1973.

Sheppard, Lee A. "Collecting the Tax on Frequent Flyer Benefits," *Tax Notes* (May 31, 1993), 1140–1142.

Sheppard, Lee A. "The Musicians' Tax Shelter," *Tax Notes* (September 5, 1994), 1259–1264.

Shepsle, Kenneth A., and Mark S. Bonchek. *Analyzing Politics: Rationality, Behavior and Institutions,* Norton Webbook at http://www.wwnorton.com/college/polisci/analyzing/webbook/home.html.

Short, Kathleen, John Ireland and Thesia Garner. "Experimental Poverty Measures: 1998," U.S. Census Bureau, Washington D. C., September 1999.

Simons, Henry C. *Personal Income Taxation,* University of Chicago Press, Chicago, 1938.

Sjoquist, David L., and Mary Beth Walker, "The Marriage Tax and the Rate and Timing of Marriage," *National Tax Journal* 48, #4 (December 1995), 547–57.

Slemrod, Joel. "Optimal Taxes and Optimal Tax Systems," *Journal of Economic Perspectives* 4, #1 (Winter 1990), 157–178.

Slemrod, Joel. (ed.). *Tax Progressivity and Income Inequality,* Cambridge University Press, Cambridge, MA, 1994.

Slemrod, Joel, and Jon Bakija. *Taxing Ourselves,* MIT Press, Cambridge, MA, 1996.

Small, Kenneth A., Clifford Winston, and Carol A. Evans. *Road Work: A New Highway Pricing and Investment Policy,* Brookings Institution, Washington, DC, 1989.

Smith, Adam. *The Wealth of Nations,* 1776; reprinted by Random House, New York, 1937.

Social Security Administration. *Fast Facts and Figures About Social Security,* Washington, DC, 1999.

Solnick, Sara J., and David Hemenway, "The Deadweight Loss of Christmas: Comment," *American Economic Review* 86, #5 (December 1996), 1299–1305.

Squire, Lyn, and Herman G. van der Tak. *Economic Analysis of Projects,* Johns Hopkins University Press, Baltimore, 1975.

St. Clair, David J. *The Motorization of American Cities,* Praeger, New York, 1986.

Stephenson, June. *Men Are Not Cost-Effective: Male Crime in America,* Harper Perennial, New York, 1995.

Steurle, C. Eugene, and Jon M. Bakija. *Retooling Social Security for the Twenty-First Century,* Urban Institute, Washington, DC, 1994.

Surrey, Stanley S. *Pathways to Tax Reform,* Harvard University Press, Cambridge, MA, 1973.

Tax Foundation. *Facts and Figures on Government Finance,* 30th ed., Washington, DC, 1995.

Tiebout, Charles M. "The Pure Theory of Local Expenditures," *Journal of Political Economy* 64, #5 (October 1956), 416–424.

Triest, Robert K. "The Effect of Income Taxation on Labor Supply in the United States," *Journal of Human Resources* 25, #3 (Summer 1990), 491–516.

Triest, Robert K. "Econometric Issues in Estimating the Behavioral Response to Taxation," *National Tax Journal* 51, #4 (December 1998), 761–772.

U.S. Department of Commerce, Bureau of the Census. "A Brief Look at Postwar U.S. Income Inequality," *Current Population Reports* (June 1996).

U.S. Department of Commerce, Bureau of the Census. *Money Income of Households, Families, and Persons in the United States: 1992,* Washington, DC, 1993.

U.S. Department of Commerce, Bureau of the Census. "Poverty in the United States, 1998," Washington, DC, September 1999.

U.S. Department of Commerce, Bureau of the Census. *Statistical Abstract of the United States, 1995,* 115th ed., Washington, DC, 1995.

U.S. Department of Commerce, Bureau of the Census. *Statistical Abstract of the United States, 1996,* 116th ed., Washington, DC, 1996.

U.S. Department of Commerce, Bureau of the Census. *Statistical Abstract of the United States, 1998,* 118th ed., Washington D. C., 1998.

U.S. Department of Commerce, Bureau of the Census. *Statistical Abstract of the United States, 1999,* 119th ed., Washington D. C., 1999.

U.S. Department of Commerce, Bureau of Economic Analysis. *Survey of Current Business,* Washington, DC, October 1997.

U.S. Department of Labor, Bureau of Labor Statistics. *Consumer Expenditure Survey, 1990–91,* Washington, DC, 1993.

U.S. Department of Labor, Pension and Welfare Benefits Administration. *Private Pension Plan Bulletin,* Washington, DC, Winter 1999–2000.

U.S. Department of the Treasury, Office of Tax Analysis. "Household Income Changes Over Time: Some Basic Questions and Facts," July 1992.

U.S. Environmental Protection Agency. "Environmental Protection: Is It Bad for the Economy?" Washington, DC, July 1998.

Venti, Steven F., and David A. Wise. "Government Policy and Personal Retirement Saving," in James M. Poterba (ed.), *Tax Policy and the Economy,* Vol. 6, 1992, 1–41.

Waldfogel, Joel. "The Deadweight Loss of Christmas," *American Economic Review 83,* #5 (December 1993), 1328–1336.

Willig, Robert. "Consumer's Surplus Without Apology," *American Economic Review* 66, #4 (September 1976), 589–597.

Wolff, Edward N. "Recent Trends in the Size Distribution of Household Wealth," *Journal of Economic Perspectives* 12, #3 (Summer 1998), 131–150.

Woodbury, Stephen A., and Wei-Jang Huang. *The Tax Treatment of Fringe Benefits,* Upjohn Institute, Kalamazoo, MI, 1991.

Zeckhauser, Richard J. "Optimal Mechanisms for Income Transfer," *American Economic Review* 61, #3, Part I (June 1971), 324–334.

INDEX

Page numbers followed by t, f *and* n *refer to tables, figures, and notes respectively.*

Off-budget deficit, 485-487, 486t
Office of Management and Budget
    (OMB)
    on cost of government
        regulation, 22
    and federal balance sheets, 23
    website, 26
Office of Tax Policy (U.S.
    Treasury), website, 386
Office of Tax Policy Research (U.
    Michigan), website, 386
Official poverty threshold (OPT),
    201, 216, 226, 227-228
*Oklahoma Tax Commission v.
    Jefferson Lines, Inc.,* 312
Okun, Arthur, 219
Old Age, Survivors, Disability, and
    Health Insurance (OASDHI)
    programs, 255
Omnibus Budget Reconciliation Act
    (1993), effects of, 435-436, 537
On-budget balance, 485
On-budget deficit, 485-487, 486t
OPT. *See* Official poverty threshold
Optimal distribution of wealth
    (Edgeworth), 217-219, 217f
Oregon, tax structure, 600t
Organization for Economic
    Cooperation and Development
    (OECD)
    typical tax structure, 14-16, 15f
    website, 26
Origin basis, in state and local
    taxation, 591
Orshansky, Mollie, 225
Output externalities, 89
Output substitution effect, 347
Overlapping generations model,
    263, 263f, 264f

P

Panel data, 434
Panel Study of Income Dynamics
    (PSID), 201
Parentalism in government
    programs, 247
Pareto improvement
    definition of, 31-32
    in Edgeworth box diagram, 53-
        55, 54f
    in pollution abatement, 107
Pareto optimal, definition of, 31
Pareto's criterion, 31-32
Pareto's rule, 195
Pareto, Vilfredo, 31, 195
Partial equilibrium analysis, 344-345
Partial factor tax, 299, 345
Patents, and public good, 80-82
Paternalism in government
    programs, 247
Pay-as-you-go system (PAYGO),
    18, 256

and baby boom retirement, 271-
    272, 272f
vs. funded systems, 262-265,
    263f, 264f
Payment standard, in transfer
    payments, 231
Payoff matrix, 63-64, 63t
PCCM. *See* Primary care case
    management
PE. *See* Personal exemptions
Peace dividend, 10
Pecuniary externalities, 95-96
Perfectly competitive market, 40
Permits, variable and tradable, in
    pollution control, 105-108, 106f
Personal consumption tax, 520-521
Personal exemptions (PE)
    characteristics of, 396, 400
    effect on labor force, 432, 433f
Personal Responsibility and Work
    Opportunity Reconciliation Act
    of 1996 (PRWORA), 224, 231
    and food stamp eligibility, 237
    problems addressed by, 244
Personal Security System (PSS)
    accounts, 276
Peterson, Paul E., 582
PIA (Primary insurance amount), in
    Social Security, 258
Plessy v. Ferguson (1896), 580
Pocketbook, voting one's, 123-128,
    124f
Point voting, 144
Political action committees (PACs)
    definition of, 145
    nature and purpose of, 148-150
Political economy. *See* Public choice
Political process, voters' lack of
    confidence in, 121
Politicians
    and bureaucracy, 153, 154
    reasons for office-seeking, 150
    as vote seekers, 145-148, 146f
Politics
    buying votes, 149
    dynamics of, in democracy, 145-
        148, 146f
    pork-barrel, 149
Polluter-pays policy, 1078
Pollution. *See also* Green tax shift
    as externality, 100-103, 102f
    federal government control of,
        103-108
        corrective taxes and
            subsidies, 110-112, 111f
        effluent charges and fees,
            108, 110f
        variable and tradable permits,
            105-108, 106f, 109
    marginal abatement cost in,
        105-108, 106f
    websites on, 117
Pork-barrel politics, 149

Positive economics, 30
Possibilities theorem (Arrow),
    137-138
Poterba, James, 341
Poverty
    definition of, 225-226, 227-229
    government spending on, 224
    means-tested transfer
        programs, 229-230, 230t
        cash transfers, 230-234
        impact of cash *vs.* in-kind
            transfers, 244-247,
            245f, 246f
        impact on family structure,
            242-244
        in-kind transfers, 234-237
        and recipient's willingness
            to work, 237-241,
            238f, 240f, 242f
    incidence of, 224, 225-227, 227f
    and means-tested transfer
        programs
        in-kind transfers
            reasons for, 247-249
    measurement of, 225-229
    official threshold of, 225-226
    and ownership of household
        goods, 229t
    and Social Security, 270-271
    websites on, 252
Poverty gap, 226
Poverty line, 226
Poverty rate, 226, 227f
PPO (Preferred Provider
    Organization), Medicare and,
    283
PPS (Prospective payment system),
    284
Preference revelation mechanisms,
    140-141, 142f
Preferred Provider Organization
    (PPO), Medicare and, 283
Present value
    and discounting, 177-179
    in valuation of benefits and
        costs, 161
Present value of benefits (PVB), 179
Present value of costs (PVC), 179
Price elasticity
    of government good, 552-553
    in taxed goods, 305
Price-setting behavior, impact of
    excise taxes on, 315-317, 316f
Primary care case management
    (PCCM), Medicaid and, 235
Prisoner's dilemma, 62-64, 63t
Private good
    efficiency in, 59-62, 60f
    pure, 57
Privatization, 113-114
Process principle of equity, 212
Producer's surplus, and excess tax
    burden, 355-356